Microsoft®
PUBLISHER 2013
COMPLETE

Joy L. Starks

Indiana University Purdue University Indianapolis

CENGAGE
Learning®

Australia • Brazil • Japan • Korea • Mexico • Singapore • Spain • United Kingdom • United States

D1119768

SHELLY
CASHMAN
SERIES®

CENGAGE
Learning·

Microsoft® Publisher 2013: Complete
Joy L. Starks

Executive Editor: Kathleen McMahon

Product Manager: Caitlin Womersley

Associate Product Manager: Crystal Parenteau

Editorial Assistant: Sarah Ryan

Print Buyer: Julio Esperas

Director of Production: Patty Stephan

Content Project Manager: Divya Divakaran,
PreMediaGlobal

Development Editor: Ashlee Welz Smith

Senior Brand Manager: Elinor Gregory

Market Development Manager: Kristie Clark

Market Development Manager:
Gretchen Swann

Marketing Coordinator: Amy McGregor

QA Manuscript Reviewers: Jeffrey Schwartz,
John Freitas, Serge Palladino, Susan Pedicini,
Danielle Shaw, Susan Whalen

Art Director: GEX Publishing Services, Inc.

Text Design: Joel Sadagursky

Cover Design: Lisa Kuhn, Curio Press, LLC

Cover Photo: Tom Kates Photography

Product Management, Indexer, Proofreader,
Photo Researcher, and Composition:
PreMediaGlobal

Microsoft and the Office logo are either registered trademarks or trademarks of Microsoft Corporation in the United States and/or other countries. Cengage Learning is an independent entity from the Microsoft Corporation, and not affiliated with Microsoft in any manner.

Library of Congress Control Number: 2013940548

ISBN-13: 978-1-285-16732-9
ISBN-10: 1-285-16732-5

Cengage Learning
20 Channel Center Street
Boston, MA 02210
USA

Cengage Learning is a leading provider of customized learning solutions with office locations around the globe, including Singapore, the United Kingdom, Australia, Mexico, Brazil, and Japan. Locate your local office at:
international.cengage.com/region

Cengage Learning products are represented in Canada by Nelson Education, Ltd.

To learn more about Cengage Learning, visit **www.cengage.com**

Purchase any of our products at your local college bookstore or at our preferred online store at **www.cengagebrain.com**

Printed in the United States of America
2 3 4 5 6 7 17 16 15 14

Microsoft® PUBLISHER 2013
COMPLETE

Contents

Microsoft **Publisher 2013**

CHAPTER ONE
Creating a Flyer

CHAPTER TWO
Publishing a Trifold Brochure

Preface

The Shelly Cashman Series® offers the finest textbooks in computer education. We are proud that, since Microsoft® Office 4.3, our series of Microsoft® Office textbooks has been the most widely used in education. With each new edition of our Office books, we make significant improvements based on the software and comments made by instructors and students. For this Microsoft® Publisher 2013 text, the Shelly Cashman Series development team carefully reviewed our pedagogy and analyzed its effectiveness in teaching today's Office student. Students today read less but need to retain more. They need not only to be able to perform skills, but also to retain those skills and know how to apply them to different settings. Today's students need to be continually engaged and challenged to retain what they're learning.

With this Microsoft® Publisher 2013 text, we continue our commitment to focusing on the users and how they learn best.

Objectives of This Textbook

Microsoft® Publisher 2013: Complete is intended for a six- to nine-week period in a course that teaches Publisher 2013 in conjunction with another application or computer concepts. No experience with a computer is assumed, and no mathematics beyond the high school freshman level is required. The objectives of this book are:

- To offer an in-depth presentation of Microsoft® Publisher 2013

- To expose students to practical examples of the computer as a useful tool

- To acquaint students with the proper procedures to create publications suitable for coursework, professional purposes, and personal use

- To help students discover the underlying functionality of Publisher 2013 so they can become more productive

- To develop an exercise-oriented approach that allows learning by doing

The Shelly Cashman Approach

A Proven Pedagogy with an Emphasis on Project Planning

Each chapter presents a practical problem to be solved within a project planning framework. The project orientation is strengthened by the use of the Roadmap, which provides a visual framework for the project. Step-by-step instructions with supporting screens guide students through the steps. Instructional steps are supported by the Q&A, Experimental Step, and BTW features.

A Visually Engaging Book That Maintains Student Interest

The step-by-step tasks, with supporting figures, provide a rich visual experience for the student. Callouts on the screens that present both explanatory and navigational information provide students with information they need when they need to know it.

Supporting Reference Materials (Quick Reference)

With the Quick Reference, students can quickly look up information about a single task, such as keyboard shortcuts, and find page references to where in the book the task is illustrated.

Integration of the World Wide Web

The World Wide Web is integrated into the Publisher 2013 learning experience with (1) BTW annotations; (2) BTW, Q&A, and Quick Reference Summary webpages; and (3) the Learn Online resources for each chapter.

End-of-Chapter Student Activities

Extensive end-of-chapter activities provide a variety of reinforcement opportunities for students to apply and expand their skills through individual and group work. To complete some of these assignments, you will be required to use the Data Files for Students. Visit www.cengage.com/ct/studentdownload for detailed access instructions, or contact your instructor for information about accessing the required files.

New to this Edition

Enhanced Coverage of Critical Thinking Skills

A new Consider This element poses thought-provoking questions throughout each chapter, providing an increased emphasis on critical thinking and problem-solving skills. Also, every task in the project now includes a reason *why* the students are performing the task and *why* the task is necessary.

Enhanced Retention and Transference

A new Roadmap element provides a visual framework for each project, showing students where they are in the process of creating each project, and reinforcing the context of smaller tasks by showing how they fit into the larger project.

Integration of Office with Cloud and Web Technologies

A new Lab focuses entirely on integrating cloud and web technologies with Publisher 2013, using technologies like blogs, social networks, and SkyDrive.

More Personalization

Each chapter project includes an optional instruction for the student to personalize his or her solution, if required by an instructor, making each student's solution unique.

More Collaboration

A new Research and Collaboration project has been added to the Consider This: Your Turn assignment at the end of each chapter.

Instructor Resources

The Instructor Resources include both teaching and testing aids, and are available for download by logging in at login.cengage.com. The Instructor Resources include:

INSTRUCTOR'S MANUAL Includes lecture notes summarizing the chapter sections, figures, and boxed elements found in every chapter; teacher tips; classroom activities; lab activities; and quick quizzes in Microsoft® Word files.

SYLLABUS Easily customizable sample syllabi, which cover policies, assignments, exams, and other course information.

FIGURE FILES Illustrations for every figure in the textbook in electronic form.

POWERPOINT PRESENTATIONS A multimedia lecture presentation system that provides slides for each chapter. Presentations are based on chapter objectives.

SOLUTIONS TO EXERCISES Includes solutions for all end-of-chapter and chapter reinforcement exercises.

TEST BANK Test banks include 112 questions for every chapter, featuring objective-based and critical thinking question types, including page number references and figure references, when appropriate.

DATA FILES FOR STUDENTS Include all the files that are required by students to complete the exercises.

ADDITIONAL ACTIVITIES FOR STUDENTS Consist of Chapter Reinforcement Exercises, which are true/false, multiple-choice, and short answer questions that help students gain confidence in the material learned.

Learn Online

CengageBrain.com is the premier destination for purchasing or renting Cengage Learning textbooks, eBooks, eChapters, and study tools at a significant discount (eBooks up to 50% off Print). In addition, CengageBrain.com provides direct access to all digital products, including eBooks, eChapters, and digital solutions, such as CourseMate and SAM, regardless of where purchased. The following are some examples of what is available for this product on www.cengagebrain.com.

Student Companion Site The Student Companion Site reinforces chapter terms and concepts using true/false questions, multiple-choice questions, short answer questions, flash cards, practice tests, and learning games, all available for no additional cost at www.cengagebrain.com.

SAM: Skills Assessment Manager Get your students workplace-ready with SAM, the market-leading proficiency-based assessment and training solution for Microsoft® Office! SAM's active, hands-on environment helps students master Microsoft® Office skills and computer concepts that are essential to academic and career success, delivering the most comprehensive online learning solution for your course! Through skill-based assessments, interactive trainings, business-centric projects, and comprehensive remediation, SAM engages students in mastering the latest Microsoft® Office programs on their own, giving instructors more time to focus on teaching. Computer concepts labs supplement instruction of important technology-related topics and issues through engaging simulations and interactive, auto-graded assessments. With enhancements including streamlined course setup, more robust grading and reporting features, and the integration of fully interactive MindTap Readers containing Cengage Learning's premier textbook content, SAM provides the best teaching and learning solution for your course.

MindLinks MindLinks is a new Cengage Learning Service designed to provide the best possible user experience and facilitate the highest levels of learning retention and outcomes, enabled through a deep integration of Cengage Learning's digital suite into an instructor's Learning Management System (LMS). MindLinks works on any LMS that supports the IMS Basic LTI open standard. Advanced features, including gradebook exchange, are the result of active, enhanced LTI collaborations with industry-leading LMS partners to drive the evolving technology standards forward.

course|notes™
quick reference guide

CourseNotes

Cengage Learning's CourseNotes are six-panel quick reference cards that reinforce the most important and widely used features of a software application in a visual and user-friendly format. CourseNotes serve as a great reference tool during and after the course. CourseNotes are available for software applications, such as Microsoft® Office 2013. There are also topic-based CourseNotes available for Best Practices in Social Networking, Hot Topics in Technology, and Web 2.0. Visit www.cengagebrain.com to learn more!

About Our Covers

The Shelly Cashman Series is continually updating our approach and content to reflect the way today's students learn and experience new technology. This focus on student success is reflected on our covers, which feature real students from The University of Rhode Island using the Shelly Cashman Series in their courses, and reflect the varied ages and backgrounds of the students learning with our books. When you use the Shelly Cashman Series, you can be assured that you are learning computer skills using the most effective courseware available.

Textbook Walk-Through

The Shelly Cashman Series Pedagogy: Project-Based — Step-by-Step — Variety of Assessments

Roadmaps provide a visual framework for each project, showing the students where they are in the process of creating each project.

Step-by-step instructions provide a context beyond the point-and-click. Each step provides information on why students are performing each task and what will occur as a result.

Roadmap

In this chapter, you will learn how to create the flyer shown in Figure 1–1 on the previous page. The following roadmap identifies general activities you will perform as you progress through this chapter:

1. CUSTOMIZE the TEMPLATE options such as choice, color scheme, and font scheme.
2. NAVIGATE the interface and SELECT objects.
3. REPLACE placeholder TEXT.
4. DELETE OBJECTS you do not plan to use in the publication, if any.
5. FORMAT the TEXT in the flyer.
6. INSERT GRAPHICS in placeholders and in other locations, as necessary.
7. FORMAT PICTURES by adding borders and styles.
8. ENHANCE the PAGE by repositioning and aligning objects.
9. PRINT and EXIT the publication.
10. OPEN and REVISE the publication.

At the beginning of step instructions throughout the chapter, you will see an abbreviated form of this roadmap. The abbreviated roadmap uses colors to indicate chapter progress: gray means the chapter is beyond that activity, blue means the task being shown is covered in that activity, and black means that activity is yet to be covered. For example, the following abbreviated roadmap indicates the chapter would be showing a task in the Format Text activity.

1 CUSTOMIZE TEMPLATES | 2 NAVIGATE & SELECT | 3 REPLACE TEXT | 4 DELETE OBJECTS | 5 FORMAT TEXT
6 INSERT GRAPHICS | 7 FORMAT PICTURE | 8 ENHANCE PAGE | 9 PRINT & EXIT | 10 OPEN & REVISE

Use the abbreviated roadmap as a progress guide while you read or step through the instructions in this chapter.

To Run Publisher

...re using a computer to step through the project in this chapter and you
...ens to match the figures in this book, you should change your screen's
...366 × 768. For information about how to change a computer's resolution,
...ffice and Windows chapter at the beginning of this book.
...lowing steps, which assume Windows 8 is running, use the Start screen
...box to run Publisher based on a typical installation. You may need to ask
...r how to run Publisher on your computer. For a detailed example of the
... summarized below, refer to the Office and Windows chapter.

...Start screen and search for a Publisher 2013 tile. If your Start screen contains
...r 2013 tile, tap or click it to run Publisher and then proceed to Step 5. If
...screen does not contain the Publisher 2013 tile, proceed to the next step to
...the Publisher app.

...rom the right edge of the screen or point to the upper-right corner of the
...display the Charms bar and then tap or click the Search charm on the Charms
...splay the Search menu.

...blisher as the search text in the Search box and watch the search results
...the Apps list.

...k Publisher 2013 in the search results to run Publisher.

...lisher window is not maximized, tap or click the Maximize button on its title
...ximize the window (Figure 1–2).

To Select a Template

1 CUSTOMIZE TEMPLATES | 2 NAVIGATE & SELECT | 3 REPLACE TEXT | 4 DELETE OBJECTS | 5 FORMAT TEXT
6 INSERT GRAPHICS | 7 FORMAT PICTURE | 8 ENHANCE PAGE | 9 PRINT & EXIT | 10 OPEN & REVISE

Templates are displayed as **thumbnails**, or small images of the template, in the template gallery. The thumbnails are organized by publication type (for example, Flyers); within publication type, they are organized by purpose or category (for example, Marketing) and then alphabetically by design type. Publisher groups additional templates into folders. The following steps select an event flyer template. *Why? An event flyer template contains many of the objects needed to create the desired concert flyer.*

1
- In the Publisher start screen, tap or click BUILT-IN to display the built-in templates.
- Scroll down to display the desired publication type (in this case, Flyers) (Figure 1–3).

Q&A Why does my list look different? It may be that someone has downloaded additional folders of templates on your system. Or, the resolution on your screen may be different. Thus, the size and number of displayed folders may vary.

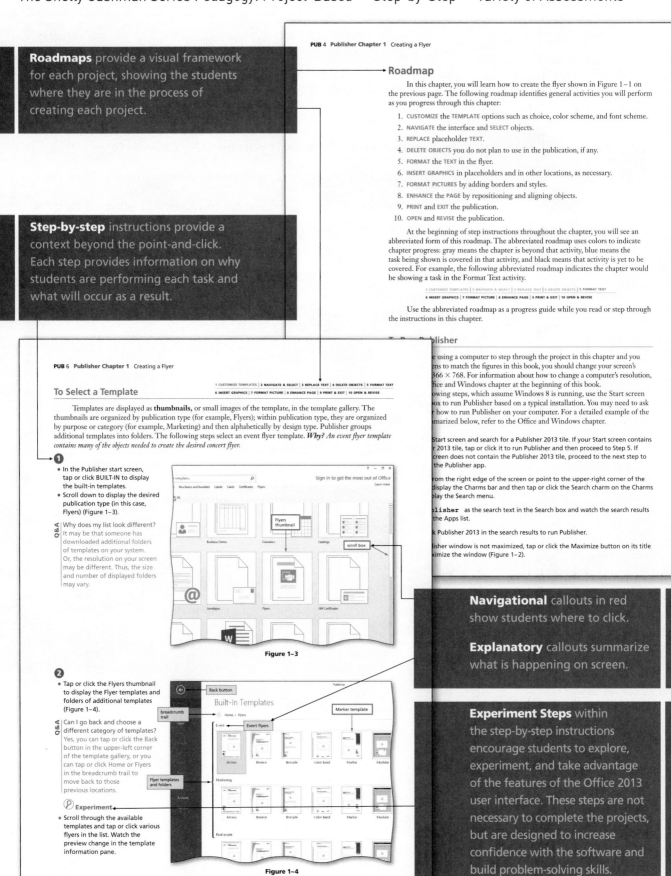

Figure 1–3

2
- Tap or click the Flyers thumbnail to display the Flyer templates and folders of additional templates (Figure 1–4).

Q&A Can I go back and choose a different category of templates? Yes, you can tap or click the Back button in the upper-left corner of the template gallery, or you can tap or click Home or Flyers in the breadcrumb trail to move back to those previous locations.

Experiment
- Scroll through the available templates and tap or click various flyers in the list. Watch the preview change in the template information pane.

Figure 1–4

Navigational callouts in red show students where to click.

Explanatory callouts summarize what is happening on screen.

Experiment Steps within the step-by-step instructions encourage students to explore, experiment, and take advantage of the features of the Office 2013 user interface. These steps are not necessary to complete the projects, but are designed to increase confidence with the software and build problem-solving skills.

Q&A boxes anticipate questions students may have when working through the steps and provide additional information about what they are doing right where they need it.

❸

- Tap or click the Marker thumbnail in the Event category (Figure 1–5).

Q&A Could I use a different template? You could, but it does not have the same features as the template used in this chapter.

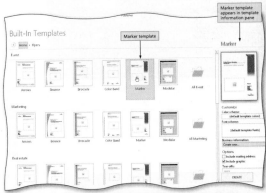

Figure 1–5

Does it make any difference which color scheme and font scheme you use?
Yes. The choice of an appropriate template, font, and color scheme is determined by the flyer's purpose and intended audience. For example, in this concert flyer about a blues band, the Navy color scheme helps connect the audience with the name of the band. The Flow font scheme uses a Calibri rounded font for the heading. Calibri is a sans serif font, meaning it has no flourishes on individual letters, and is suitable for print publications.

Customizing Templates

Once you choose a template, you should make choices about the color scheme, font scheme, and other components of the publication. A **color scheme** is a defined set of colors that complement each other when used in the same publication. Each Publisher color scheme provides four complementary colors. A **font scheme** is a defined set of fonts associated with a publication. A **font**, or typeface, defines the appearance and shape of the letters, numbers, and special characters. A font scheme contains one font for headings and another font for body text and captions. Font schemes make it easy to change all the fonts in a publication to give it a new look. Other customization options allow you to choose to include business information, a mailing address, a graphic, or tear-offs.

BTW
Font Schemes
Choose a font scheme that gives your flyer a consistent, professional appearance and characterizes your subject. Make intentional decisions about the font style and type. Avoid common reading fonts such as Arial, Times New Roman, and Helvetica that are used in other kinds of print publications. Flyers are more effective with stronger or unusual font schemes.

Consider This boxes pose thought-provoking questions with answers throughout each chapter, promoting critical thought along with immediate feedback.

Chapter Summary

In this chapter, you learned to choose a publication template, se
publication, delete objects in a publication, insert a picture with
a print publication as a web publication. The items listed below
learned in this chapter, with the tasks grouped by activity.

Enter and Format Text
Autofit Text (PUB 28)
Bold Text (PUB 27)
Change Text Direction (PUB 32)
Check Spelling as You Type (PUB 21)
Enter Tear-Off Text (PUB 23)
Increase the Font Size (PUB 31)
Italicize Text (PUB 28)
Replace Other Text (PUB 19)
Replace Placeholder Text (PUB 17)
Underline Text (PUB 31)

Graphics
Apply a Picture Style (PUB 36)
Change the Border Color (PUB 38)
Insert a Picture from a Storage Device (PUB 39)
Set the Weight of a Border (PUB 37)
Use the Picture Placeholder (PUB 34)

Prepare a Web Publication
Change Document Properties (PUB 43)
Change the Background (PUB 50)
Insert a Hyperlink (PUB 48)

Pre

Sav

Print
Pri

Select
Ali
Co

Delete an Object (PUB 24)
Deselect an Object (PUB 18)
Hide the Page Navigation Pane (PUB 13)
Move an Object (PUB 41)
Resize an Object (PUB 42)
Select an Object (PUB 14)
View Whole Page (PUB 15)
Zoom (PUB 15)

Templates
Choose Publication Options (PUB 8)
Select a Template (PUB 6)

Consider This: Plan Ahead box presents a single master planning guide that students can use as they create documents on their own.

What decisions will you need to make when creating your next publication?
Use these guidelines as you complete the assignments in this chapter and create your own publications outside of this class.

1. Select template options.
   a) Select a template that matches your need.
   b) Choose font and color schemes determined by the flyer's purpose and audience.
2. Choose words for the text.
   a) Replace all placeholder and default text.
   b) Add other text boxes as necessary; delete unused items.
3. Identify how to format various objects in the flyer.
   a) Use bold, underline, and italics for emphasis.
   b) Autofit the text to make the flyer easy to read.
4. Find the appropriate graphic(s).
5. Determine whether the flyer will be more effective as a print publication, web publication, or both.
   a) Insert any necessary hyperlinks.
   b) Consider creating a background for web publication.

CONSIDER THIS

Textbook Walk-Through

Chapter Summary A listing of the tasks completed within the chapter, grouped into major task categories in an outline format.

Apply Your Knowledge This exercise usually requires students to open and manipulate a file that parallels the activities learned in the chapter.

Chapter Summary

In this chapter, you learned to choose a publication template, set font and color schemes, enter text in a publication, delete objects in a publication, insert a picture with a style and border, print a publication, and save a print publication as a web publication. The items listed below include all the new Publisher skills you have learned in this chapter, with the tasks grouped by activity.

Enter and Format Text
Autofit Text (PUB 28)
Bold Text (PUB 27)
Change Text Direction (PUB 32)
Check Spelling as You Type (PUB 21)
Enter Tear-Off Text (PUB 23)
Increase the Font Size (PUB 31)
Italicize Text (PUB 28)
Replace Other Text (PUB 19)
Replace Placeholder Text (PUB 17)
Underline Text (PUB 31)

Graphics
Apply a Picture Style (PUB 36)
Change the Border Color (PUB 38)
Insert a Picture from a Storage Device (PUB 39)
Set the Weight of a Border (PUB 37)
Use the Picture Placeholder (PUB 34)

Prepare a Web Publication
Change Document Properties (PUB 43)
Change the Background (PUB 50)
Insert a Hyperlink (PUB 48)

Preview the Web Publication in a Browser (PUB 53)
Save a Print Publication as a Web Publication (PUB 51)

Print
Print a Publication (PUB 44)

Select, Zoom, and Manipulate Objects
Align an Object (PUB 42)
Collapse and Expand the Page Navigation Pane (PUB 14)
Delete an Object (PUB 24)
Deselect an Object (PUB 18)
Hide the Page Navigation Pane (PUB 13)
Move an Object (PUB 41)
Resize an Object (PUB 42)
Select an Object (PUB 14)
View Whole Page (PUB 15)
Zoom (PUB 15)

Templates
Choose Publication Options (PUB 8)
Select a Template (PUB 6)

What decisions will you need to make when creating your next publication?

 ...apter and create your own publications outside of this class.

...flyer's purpose and audience.

...ems.

...rint publication, web publication, or both.

...n.

How should you submit solutions to questions in the assignments identified with a symbol?

Every assignment in this book contains one or more questions identified with a symbol. These questions require you to think beyond the assigned publication. Present your solutions to the questions in the format required by your instructor. Possible formats may include one or more of these options: write the answer; create a document that contains the answer; present your answer to the class; discuss your answer in a group; record the answer as audio or video using a webcam, smartphone, or portable media player; or post answers on a blog, wiki, or website.

Apply Your Knowledge

Reinforce the skills and apply the concepts you learned in this chapter.

Editing a Flyer with Text, Graphic, and Tear-Offs

Note: To complete this assignment, you will be required to use the Data Files for Students. Visit www.cengage.com/ct/studentdownload for detailed instructions or contact your instructor for information about accessing the required files.

Instructions: Your brother is in charge of advertising his 10-year class reunion. He has asked you to help him with editing the text, graphic, and tear-offs. You produce the flyer shown in Figure 1–76.

Perform the following tasks:

1. Run Publisher and open the file Apply 1-1 Class Reunion Flyer from the Data Files for Students.

2. Tap or click the Major Heading default text and drag to select it. Type **10-Year Reunion Gym Party!** to replace the text.

3. Tap or click the Subheading default text box and then drag the text to select it. Type **05/21/15** to replace the text.

4. Tap or click the default bulleted text and then press CTRL+A to select all of the text. Type the following text, pressing the ENTER key at the end of each line.
   Wear your letter jacket!
   Show your school spirit!
   High School Gym!
   7:00 p.m.!
   RSVP to Jesse by 05/07/15!

5. Tap or click one of the tear-offs, type **Jesse** and then press the ENTER key. Type **402-555-1306** to finish entering the text. Tap or click outside the tear-offs to synchronize them. If requested by your instructor, use your name in the tear-offs.

6. Select the text in the attention getter sunburst shape and replace it with the text shown in Figure 1–76.

7. Select the attention getter and change the border weight to 6 point, using the Shape Outline button (DRAWING TOOLS FORMAT tab | ShapeStyles group).

8. At the top of the flyer, select the picture placeholder. Tap or click the picture placeholder icon to display the Insert Pictures dialog box. Use Office.com Clip Art to search for a picture related to academics, similar to the one shown in Figure 1–76.

Extend Your Knowledge

Extend the skills you learned in this chapter and experiment with new skills. You may need to use Help to complete the assignment.

Creating a Flyer from Scratch

Instructions: You have been asked to create a flyer to remind students to vote. You decide to start from scratch to create the flyer shown in Figure 1–77.

Perform the following tasks:

1. Run Publisher and select the Blank 8.5 × 11" template.
2. Tap or click the More button (PAGE DESIGN tab | Schemes group) and then select the Bluebird color scheme.
3. Tap or click the Scheme Fonts button (PAGE DESIGN tab | Schemes group) and then select the Office Classic 1 font scheme.
4. Tap or click the Pictures button (INSERT tab | Illustrations group) and then navigate to the Data Files for Students. Insert the graphic named, Extend 1-1 Decorative Rectangle. Move it as necessary to approximately the center of the page.

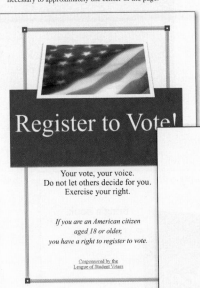

5. Insert a second picture from the Data Files for Students named, Extend 1-1 Blue Rectangle. Move it to the upper-center as shown in Figure 1–77.
6. Tap or click the Online Pictures button (INSERT tab | Illustrations group) and then search Office.com Clip Art for a graphic of an American flag. Move the graphic to the upper-

Figure 1–77

b. Before typing the text, click the Font Color arrow (HOME tab | Font group) and then choose a white color. Type the text, `Register to Vote!` and then autofit it.

c. Draw another text box below the first one. Tap or click the Font Color arrow (HOME tab | Font group) and then choose a black color. Tap or click the Bold button (HOME tab | Font group). Tap or click the Center button (HOME tab | Paragraph group) and then type the text shown in Figure 1–77.

d. Repeat Step 7c for the next text box and format the text italic.

e. Repeat Step 7c for the last text box and format the text underlined.

f. If requested to do so by your instructor, add the name of your voting location to the flyer.

8. Save the file with the file name, Extend 1-1 Vote Flyer Complete.
9. Submit the file in the format specified by your instructor.
10. When would you use a template instead of creating a flyer from scratch that contains only the fields you need? Was formatting the font before you typed easier than selecting text and formatting it afterward?

Analyze, Correct, Improve

Analyze a publication, correct all errors, and improve the design.

Making Changes to a Web Flyer

Note: To complete this assignment, you will be required to use the Data Files for Students. Visit www.cengage.com/ct/studentdownload for detailed instructions or contact your instructor for information about accessing the required files.

Instructions: Your community is trying to promote its community garden. A former gardener created the website shown in Figure 1–78 using Publisher, but it has several issues. You decide to improve the flyer. Run Publisher and open the file, Analyze 1-1 Community Garden Web Flyer.

Figure 1–78

Continued >

Sidebar annotations:

Extend Your Knowledge projects at the end of each chapter allow students to extend and expand on the skills learned within the chapter. Students use critical thinking to experiment with new skills to complete each project.

Analyze, Correct, Improve projects call on the students to analyze a file, discover errors in it, fix the errors, and then improve upon the file using the skills they learned in the chapter.

Textbook Walk-Through

Analyze, Correct, Improve *continued*

1. Correct Correct the date on the flyer. This year's event is March 25. The flyer still has default text in the lower-left corner. If requested to do so by your instructor, insert your community and your phone number. The website listed in the lower-right corner should be a hyperlink. Resize any text boxes whose text wraps awkwardly.

2. Improve Each of the text boxes seems to be a different font size. Choose a large size for the main heading. Change the description text to best fit and then increase or decrease the fonts in the lower text boxes so that they all match. Choose to make them all bold. Align objects horizontally with each other and with the margins. Correct the misspelled word. Change the color scheme to an all green color scheme such as Green or Floral. Experiment with different font schemes. Save the document using the file name, Analyze 1-1 Community Garden Flyer Complete. Submit the revised document in the format specified by your instructor.

3. ⊛ What errors existed in the starting file? How did creating consistency in font sizes enhance the publication? Did changing the color scheme improve the effectiveness of the flyer? What other improvements would you make?

In the Labs

Design, create, modify, and/or use a publication following the guidelines, concepts, and skills presented in this chapter. Labs 1 and 2, which increase in difficulty, require you to create solutions based on what you learned in the chapter; Lab 3 requires you to create a solution, which uses cloud and web technologies, by learning and investigating on your own from general guidance.

Lab 1: Creating a Sign-Up Sheet

Problem: The Self-Defense Club on campus would like you to create a sign-up sheet for students who want to take classes in the Fall semester. You decide to look through Publisher's templates for an appropriate flyer to use as a starting point. You create the flyer shown in Figure 1–79.

Perform the following tasks:
1. Run Publisher. In the template gallery, click BU...
2. In the Event group, click the All Event folder to ...
   the end of the list and select the Company Sign ...
3. Customize the template with the Alpine color sc...
   publication.
4. Tap or click the Event Title placeholder text to s...
   the ENTER key. Type `Classes` to finish replac...
5. Tap or click the description placeholder text to s...
   ENTER key at the end of each line. The last line ...
   `Learn the techniques you need to pr...`
   `Prepare now, for the event you hope...`
   `Classes will be held on Thursdays th...`
   `Easy to learn. Gain confidfence. Be...`
6. Press and hold or right-click the misspelled wor...
7. Press and hold or right-click the text box and th...
8. Change the Date text, Date: 00/00/00, to `Fall...`
9. Change the Time text, Time: 00:00, to `7:00-8...`

Bring a book.
Take a book.

Date: Nov. 4th

Book Swap

• *Bring the books you are willing to part with*
• *Pick up books you need or just want to read*
• *Get a head start on your spring reading*
• *Mingle with other book lovers*

Located in the Library Courtyard

Time: 10:00 a.m.

State University

918.555.8642
mrs.jones@mrsj.edu

Figure 1–81

Instructions:
1. Open the file named, Lab 1-3 Book Swap Flyer, from the Data Files for Students.
2. Insert a picture and format it as shown in Figure 1–81.
3. If requested to do so by your instructor, change the email address to your email address.
4. Save the presentation on SkyDrive in the Publisher folder using the file name, Lab 1–3 Book Swap Flyer Complete.
5. Submit the assignment in the format specified by your instructor.
6. ⊛ When would you save one of your files for school or your job on SkyDrive? Do you think using SkyDrive enhances collaboration efforts? Why?

⊛ Consider This: Your Turn

Apply your creative thinking and problem solving skills to design and implement a solution.

1: Creating an Advertisement
Personal/Academic

Part 1: You attend a college that is famous for its Department of Dance. Students who major in dance are required to complete internships as dance instructors. Because you are a computer

Continued >

In the Lab Three in-depth assignments in each chapter that require students to apply the chapter concepts and techniques to solve problems. One Lab is devoted entirely to Cloud and Web 2.0 integration.

Consider This: Your Turn exercises call on students to apply creative thinking and problem solving skills to design and implement a solution.

Office 2013 and Windows 8: Essential Concepts and Skills

Microsoft product screen shots used with permission from Microsoft Corporation.

Objectives

You will have mastered the material in this chapter when you can:

- Use a touch screen
- Perform basic mouse operations
- Start Windows and sign in to an account
- Identify the objects in the Windows 8 desktop
- Identify the apps in and versions of Microsoft Office 2013
- Run an app
- Identify the components of the Microsoft Office ribbon

- Create folders
- Save files
- Change screen resolution
- Perform basic tasks in Microsoft Office apps
- Manage files
- Use Microsoft Office Help and Windows Help

Office 2013 and Windows 8: Essential Concepts and Skills

This introductory chapter uses Publisher 2013 to cover features and functions common to Office 2013 apps, as well as the basics of Windows 8.

Roadmap

In this chapter, you will learn how to perform basic tasks in Windows and Publisher. The following roadmap identifies general activities you will perform as you progress through this chapter:

1. SIGN IN to an account
2. USE WINDOWS
3. USE features in Publisher that are common across Office APPS
4. FILE and folder MANAGEMENT
5. SWITCH between APPS
6. SAVE and manage FILES
7. CHANGE SCREEN RESOLUTION
8. EXIT APPS
9. USE ADDITIONAL Office APP FEATURES
10. USE Office and Windows HELP

At the beginning of the step instructions throughout the chapter, you will see an abbreviated form of this roadmap. The abbreviated roadmap uses colors to indicate chapter progress: gray means the chapter is beyond that activity, blue means the task being shown is covered in that activity, and black means that activity is yet to be covered. For example, the following abbreviated roadmap indicates the chapter would be showing a task in the Use Apps activity.

1 SIGN IN | 2 USE WINDOWS | 3 USE APPS | 4 FILE MANAGEMENT | 5 SWITCH APPS | 6 SAVE FILES
7 CHANGE SCREEN RESOLUTION | 8 EXIT APPS | 9 USE ADDITIONAL APP FEATURES | 10 USE HELP

Use the abbreviated roadmap as a progress guide while you read or step through the instructions in this chapter.

Introduction to the Windows 8 Operating System

Windows 8 is the newest version of Microsoft Windows, which is a popular and widely used operating system. An **operating system** is a computer program (set of computer instructions) that coordinates all the activities of computer hardware, such as memory, storage devices, and printers, and provides the capability for you to communicate with the computer.

The Windows operating system simplifies the process of working with publications and apps by organizing the manner in which you interact with the computer. Windows is used to run apps. An **app** (short for application) consists of programs designed to make users more productive and/or assist them with personal tasks, such as desktop publishing or browsing the web.

The Windows 8 interface begins with the **Start screen**, which shows tiles (Figure 1). A **tile** is a shortcut to an app or other content. The tiles on the Start screen include installed apps that you use regularly. From the Start screen, you can choose which apps to run using a touch screen, mouse, or other input device.

Figure 1

Using a Touch Screen and a Mouse

Windows users who have computers or devices with touch screen capability can interact with the screen using gestures. A **gesture** is a motion you make on a touch screen with the tip of one or more fingers or your hand. Touch screens are convenient because they do not require a separate device for input. Table 1 on the next page presents common ways to interact with a touch screen.

If you are using your finger on a touch screen and are having difficulty completing the steps in this chapter, consider using a stylus. Many people find it easier to be precise with a stylus than with a finger. In addition, with a stylus you see the pointer. If you still are having trouble completing the steps with a stylus, try using a mouse.

Table 1 Touch Screen Gestures		
Motion	**Description**	**Common Uses**
Tap	Quickly touch and release one finger one time.	Activate a link (built-in connection) Press a button Run a program or an app
Double-tap	Quickly touch and release one finger two times.	Run a program or an app Zoom in (show a smaller area on the screen, so that contents appear larger) at the location of the double-tap
Press and hold	Press and hold one finger to cause an action to occur, or until an action occurs.	Display a shortcut menu (immediate access to allowable actions) Activate a mode enabling you to move an item with one finger to a new location
Drag, or slide	Press and hold one finger on an object and then move the finger to the new location.	Move an item around the screen Scroll
Swipe	Press and hold one finger and then move the finger horizontally or vertically on the screen.	Select an object Swipe from edge to display a bar such as the Charms bar, Apps bar, and Navigation bar (all discussed later)
Stretch	Move two fingers apart.	Zoom in (show a smaller area on the screen, so that contents appear larger)
Pinch	Move two fingers together.	Zoom out (show a larger area on the screen, so that contents appear smaller)

© 2014 Cengage Learning

CONSIDER THIS

Will your screen look different if you are using a touch screen?

The Windows and Microsoft Office interface varies slightly if you are using a touch screen. For this reason, you might notice that your Windows or Publisher screens look slightly different from the screens in this book.

Windows users who do not have touch screen capabilities typically work with a mouse that has at least two buttons. For a right-handed user, the left button usually is the primary mouse button, and the right mouse button is the secondary mouse button. Left-handed people, however, can reverse the function of these buttons.

Table 2 explains how to perform a variety of mouse operations. Some apps also use keys in combination with the mouse to perform certain actions. For example, when you hold down the CTRL key while rolling the mouse wheel, text on the screen may become larger or smaller based on the direction you roll the wheel. The function of the mouse buttons and the wheel varies depending on the app.

Table 2 Mouse Operations

Operation	Mouse Action	Example*
Point	Move the mouse until the pointer on the desktop is positioned on the item of choice.	Position the pointer on the screen.
Click	Press and release the primary mouse button, which usually is the left mouse button.	Select or deselect items on the screen or run an app or app feature.
Right-click	Press and release the secondary mouse button, which usually is the right mouse button.	Display a shortcut menu.
Double-click	Quickly press and release the primary mouse button twice without moving the mouse.	Run an app or app feature.
Triple-click	Quickly press and release the primary mouse button three times without moving the mouse.	Select a paragraph.
Drag	Point to an item, hold down the primary mouse button, move the item to the desired location on the screen, and then release the mouse button.	Move an object from one location to another or draw pictures.
Right-drag	Point to an item, hold down the right mouse button, move the item to the desired location on the screen, and then release the right mouse button.	Display a shortcut menu after moving an object from one location to another.
Rotate wheel	Roll the wheel forward or backward.	Scroll vertically (up and down).
Free-spin wheel	Whirl the wheel forward or backward so that it spins freely on its own.	Scroll through many pages in seconds.
Press wheel	Press the wheel button while moving the mouse.	Scroll continuously.
Tilt wheel	Press the wheel toward the right or left.	Scroll horizontally (left and right).
Press thumb button	Press the button on the side of the mouse with your thumb.	Move forward or backward through webpages and/or control media, games, etc.

*Note: The examples presented in this column are discussed as they are demonstrated in this chapter.

© 2014 Cengage Learning

Scrolling

A **scroll bar** is a horizontal or vertical bar that appears when the contents of an area may not be visible completely on the screen (Figure 2). A scroll bar contains **scroll arrows** and a **scroll box** that enable you to view areas that currently cannot be seen on the screen. Tapping or clicking the up and down scroll arrows moves the screen content up or down one line. You also can tap or click above or below the scroll box to move up or down a section, or drag the scroll box up or down to move to a specific location.

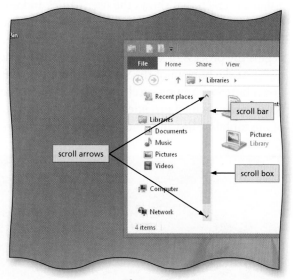

Figure 2

BTW

Pointer
If you are using a touch screen, the pointer may not appear on the screen as you perform touch gestures. The pointer will reappear when you begin using the mouse.

BTW

Minimize Wrist Injury
Computer users frequently switch between the keyboard and the mouse while using Publisher; such switching strains the wrist. To help prevent wrist injury, minimize switching. For instance, if your fingers already are on the keyboard, use keyboard keys to scroll. If your hand already is on the mouse, use the mouse to scroll. If your hand is on the touch screen, use touch gestures to scroll.

What should you do if you are running Windows 7 instead of Windows 8?
Although Windows 8 includes several user interface and feature enhancements, many of the steps in this book work in both Windows 7 and Windows 8. If you have any questions about differences between the two operating systems or how to perform tasks in an earlier version of Windows, contact your instructor.

CONSIDER THIS

Keyboard Shortcuts

In many cases, you can use the keyboard instead of the mouse to accomplish a task. To perform tasks using the keyboard, you press one or more keyboard keys, sometimes identified as a **keyboard shortcut**. Some keyboard shortcuts consist of a single key, such as the F1 key. For example, to obtain help in many apps, you can press the F1 key. Other keyboard shortcuts consist of multiple keys, in which case a plus sign separates the key names, such as CTRL+ESC. This notation means to press and hold down the first key listed, press one or more additional keys, and then release all keys. For example, to display the Start screen, press CTRL+ESC, that is, hold down the CTRL key, press the ESC key, and then release both keys.

Starting Windows

It is not unusual for multiple people to use the same computer in a work, educational, recreational, or home setting. Windows enables each user to establish a **user account**, which identifies to Windows the resources, such as apps and storage locations, a user can access when working with the computer.

Each user account has a user name and may have a password and an icon, as well. A **user name** is a unique combination of letters or numbers that identifies a specific user to Windows. A **password** is a private combination of letters, numbers, and special characters associated with the user name that allows access to a user's account resources. An icon is a small image that represents an object, thus a **user icon** is a picture associated with a user name.

When you turn on a computer, Windows starts and displays a **lock screen** consisting of the time and date (Figure 3a). To unlock the screen, swipe up or click the lock screen. Depending on your computer's settings, Windows may or may not display a sign-in screen that shows the user names and user icons for users who have accounts on the computer (Figure 3b). This **sign-in screen** enables you to sign in to your user account and makes the computer available for use. Tapping or clicking the user icon begins the process of signing in, also called logging on, to your user account.

At the bottom of the sign-in screen is the 'Ease of access' button and a Shut down button. Tapping or clicking the 'Ease of access' button displays the Ease of access menu, which provides tools to optimize a computer to accommodate the needs of the mobility, hearing, and vision impaired users. Tapping or clicking the Shut down

Figure 3a

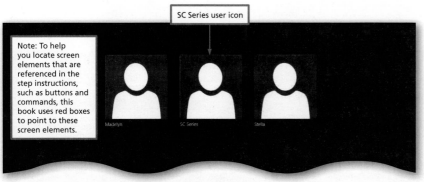

Note: To help you locate screen elements that are referenced in the step instructions, such as buttons and commands, this book uses red boxes to point to these screen elements.

SC Series user icon

Madelyn   SC Series   Stella

Figure 3b

BTW
Q&As
For a complete list of the Q&As found in many of the step-by-step sequences in this book, visit the Q&A resource on the Student Companion Site located on www.cengagebrain.com. For detailed instructions about accessing available resources, visit www.cengage.com/ct/studentdownload or contact your instructor for information about accessing the required files.

button displays a menu containing commands related to restarting the computer, putting it in a low-power state, and shutting it down. The commands available on your computer may differ.

- The Sleep command saves your work, turns off the computer fans and hard disk, and places the computer in a lower-power state. To wake the computer from sleep mode, press the power button or lift a laptop's cover, and sign in to your account.

- The Shut down command exits running apps, shuts down Windows, and then turns off the computer.

- The Restart command exits running apps, shuts down Windows, and then restarts Windows.

To Sign In to an Account

1 SIGN IN | 2 USE WINDOWS | 3 USE APPS | 4 FILE MANAGEMENT | 5 SWITCH APPS | 6 SAVE FILES
7 CHANGE SCREEN RESOLUTION | 8 EXIT APPS | 9 USE ADDITIONAL APP FEATURES | 10 USE HELP

The following steps, which use SC Series as the user name, sign in to an account based on a typical Windows installation. *Why? After starting Windows, you might be required to sign in to an account to access the computer's resources.* You may need to ask your instructor how to sign in to your account. If you are using Windows 7, skip these steps and instead perform the steps in the yellow box that immediately follows these Windows 8 steps.

1

- Swipe up or click the lock screen (shown in Figure 3a) to display a sign-in screen (shown in Figure 3b).

- Tap or click the user icon (for SC Series, in this case) on the sign-in screen, which depending on settings, either will display a second sign-in screen that contains a Password text box (Figure 4) or will display the Windows Start screen (shown in Figure 5 on the next page).

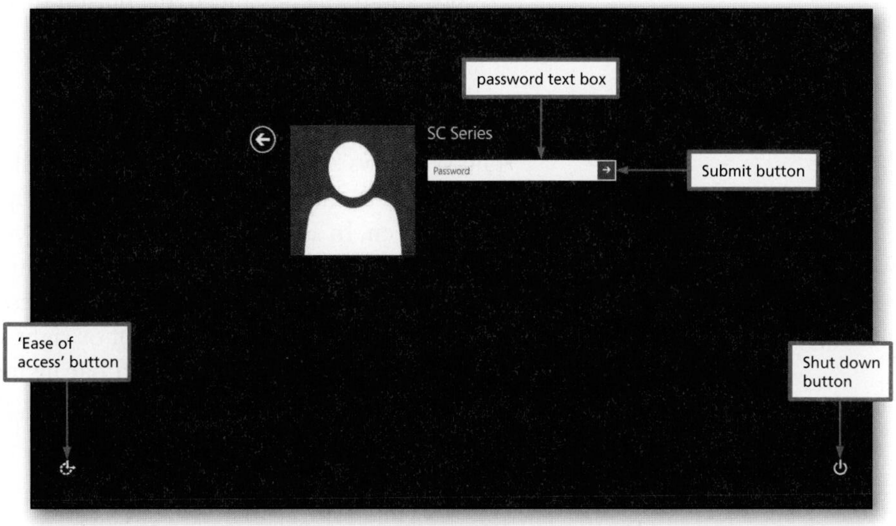

Q&A

Why do I not see a user icon?
Your computer may require you to type a user name instead of tapping or clicking an icon.

What is a text box?
A text box is a rectangular box in which you type text.

Why does my screen not show a password text box?
Your account does not require a password.

SC Series

password text box

Password

Submit button

'Ease of access' button

Shut down button

Figure 4

- If Windows displays a sign-in screen with a password text box, type your password in the text box.

2

- Tap or click the Submit button (shown in Figure 4 on the previous page) to sign in to your account and display the Windows Start screen (Figure 5).

Q&A

Why does my Start screen look different from the one in Figure 5?
The Windows Start screen is customizable, and your school or employer may have modified the screen to meet its needs. Also, your screen resolution, which affects the size of the elements on the screen, may differ from the screen resolution used in this book. Later in this chapter, you learn how to change screen resolution.

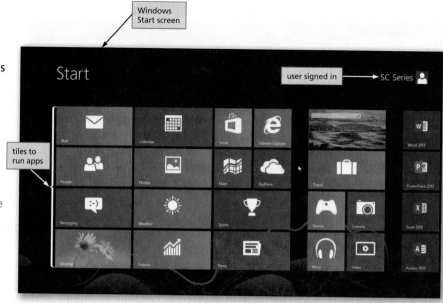

Figure 5

How do I type if my tablet has no keyboard?
You can use your fingers to press keys on a keyboard that appears on the screen, called an on-screen keyboard, or you can purchase a separate physical keyboard that attaches to or wirelessly communicates with the tablet.

To Sign In to an Account Using Windows 7

If you are using Windows 7, perform these steps to sign in to an account instead of the previous steps that use Windows 8.

1. Click the user icon on the Welcome screen; depending on settings, this either will display a password text box or will sign in to the account and display the Windows 7 desktop.

2. If Windows 7 displays a password text box, type your password in the text box and then click the arrow button to sign in to the account and display the Windows 7 desktop.

The Windows Start Screen

BTW
Modern UI
The new Windows 8 user interface also is referred to as the Modern UI (user interface).

The Windows Start screen provides a scrollable space for you to access apps that have been pinned to the Start screen (shown in Figure 5). Pinned apps appear as tiles on the Start screen. In addition to running apps, you can perform tasks such as pinning apps (placing tiles) on the Start screen, moving the tiles around the Start screen, and unpinning apps (removing tiles) from the Start screen.

If you swipe up from the bottom of or right-click an open space on the Start screen, the App bar will appear. The **App bar** includes a button that enables you to display all of your apps. When working with tiles, the App bar also provides options for manipulating the tiles, such as resizing them.

CONSIDER THIS

How do you pin apps, move tiles, and unpin apps?

- To pin an app, swipe up from the bottom of the Start screen or right-click an open space on the Start screen to display the App bar, tap or click the All apps button on the App bar to display the Apps list, swipe down on or right-click the app you want to pin, and then tap or click the 'Pin to Start' button on the App bar. One way to return to the Start screen is to swipe up from the bottom or right-click an open space in the Apps list and then tap or click the All apps button again.

- To move a tile, drag the tile to the desired location.

- To unpin an app, swipe down on or right-click the app to display the App bar and then tap or click the 'Unpin from Start' button on the App bar.

Introduction to Microsoft Office 2013

Microsoft Office 2013 is the newest version of Microsoft Office, offering features that provide users with better functionality and easier ways to work with the various files they create. These features include enhanced design tools, such as improved picture formatting tools and new themes, shared notebooks for working in groups, mobile versions of Office apps, broadcast presentations for the web, and a digital notebook for managing and sharing multimedia information.

Microsoft Office 2013 Apps

Microsoft Office 2013 includes a wide variety of apps such as Word, PowerPoint, Excel, Access, Outlook, Publisher, OneNote, InfoPath, SharePoint Workspace, and Lync:

- **Microsoft Word 2013**, or Word, is a full-featured word processing app that allows you to create professional-looking documents and revise them easily.

- **Microsoft PowerPoint 2013**, or PowerPoint, is a complete presentation app that enables you to produce professional-looking presentations and then deliver them to an audience.

- **Microsoft Excel 2013**, or Excel, is a powerful spreadsheet app that allows you to organize data, complete calculations, make decisions, graph data, develop professional-looking reports, publish organized data to the web, and access real-time data from websites.

- **Microsoft Access 2013**, or Access, is a database management system that enables you to create a database; add, change, and delete data in the database; ask questions concerning the data in the database; and create forms and reports using the data in the database.

- **Microsoft Outlook 2013**, or Outlook, is a communications and scheduling app that allows you to manage email accounts, calendars, contacts, and access to other Internet content.

- **Microsoft Publisher 2013**, or Publisher, is a desktop publishing app that helps you create professional-quality publications and marketing materials that can be shared easily.

- **Microsoft OneNote 2013**, or OneNote, is a note taking app that allows you to store and share information in notebooks with other people.

- **Microsoft InfoPath Designer 2013**, or InfoPath, is a form development app that helps you create forms for use on the web and gather data from these forms.

- **Microsoft SharePoint Workspace 2013**, or SharePoint, is a collaboration app that allows you to access and revise files stored on your computer from other locations.

- **Microsoft Lync 2013** is a communications app that allows you to use various modes of communications such as instant messaging, videoconferencing, and sharing files and apps.

Microsoft Office 2013 Suites

A **suite** is a collection of individual apps available together as a unit. Microsoft offers a variety of Office suites, including a stand-alone desktop app (boxed software), Microsoft Office 365, and Microsoft Office Web Apps. **Microsoft Office 365**, or Office 365, provides plans that allow organizations to use Office in a mobile setting while also being able to communicate and share files, depending upon the type of plan selected by the organization. **Microsoft Office Web Apps**, or Web Apps, are apps that allow you to edit and share files on the web using the familiar Office interface. Table 3 on the next page outlines the differences among these Office suites.

Apps/ Licenses	Office 365 Home Premium	Office 365 Small Business Premium	Office Home & Student	Office Home & Business	Office Professional
Word	✓	✓	✓	✓	✓
PowerPoint	✓	✓	✓	✓	✓
Excel	✓	✓	✓	✓	✓
Access	✓	✓			✓
Outlook	✓	✓		✓	✓
Publisher	✓	✓			✓
Lync		✓			
OneNote			✓	✓	✓
InfoPath		✓			
Licenses	5	5	1	1	1

Table 3 Office Suites

© 2014 Cengage Learning

During the Office 365 installation, you select a plan, and depending on your plan, you receive different apps and services. Office Web Apps do not require a local installation and are accessed through SkyDrive and your browser. **SkyDrive** is a cloud storage service that provides storage and other services, such as Office Web Apps, to computer users.

CONSIDER THIS

How do you sign up for a SkyDrive account?

• Use your browser to navigate to skydrive.live.com.

• Create a Microsoft account by tapping or clicking the 'Sign up now' link (or a similar link) and then entering your information to create the account.

• Sign in to SkyDrive using your new account or use it in Publisher to save your files on SkyDrive.

Apps in a suite, such as Microsoft Office, typically use a similar interface and share features. Once you are comfortable working with the elements and the interface and performing tasks in one app, the similarity can help you apply the knowledge and skills you have learned to another app(s) in the suite. For example, the process for saving a file in Publisher is the same in PowerPoint, Excel, and the other Office apps. While briefly showing how to use Publisher, this chapter illustrates some of the common functions across the Office apps and Office identifies the characteristics unique to Publisher.

Running and Using an App

To use an app, such as Publisher, you must instruct the operating system to run the app. Windows provides many different ways to run an app, one of which is presented in this section (other ways to run an app are presented throughout this chapter). After an app is running, you can use it to perform a variety of tasks. The following pages use Publisher to discuss some elements of the Office interface and to perform tasks that are common to other Office apps.

Publisher

Publisher is a powerful desktop publishing (DTP) app that assists you in designing and producing professional-quality publications such as newsletters, brochures, flyers, logos, signs, catalogs, cards, and business forms. Using Publisher, you easily can change the shape, size, and color of text and graphics. You can include many kinds of graphical objects, including mastheads, borders, tables, images, pictures, charts, and web objects in publications, as well as integrate spreadsheets and databases.

To Run an App from the Start Screen

The Start screen contains tiles that allow you to run apps, some of which may be stored on your computer. *Why? When you install an app, for example, tiles are added to the Start screen for the various Office apps included in the suite.*

The following steps, which assume Windows is running, use the Start screen to run Publisher based on a typical installation. You may need to ask your instructor how to run Publisher on your computer. Although the steps illustrate running the Publisher app, the steps to run any Office app are similar. If you are using Windows 7, skip these steps and instead perform the steps in the yellow box that immediately follows these Windows 8 steps.

1

- If necessary, scroll to display the Publisher tile on the Start screen (Figure 6).

Q&A
Why does my Start screen look different?
It may look different because of your computer's configuration. The Start screen may be customized for several reasons, such as usage requirements or security restrictions.

What if the app I want to run is not on the Start screen?
You can display all installed apps by swiping up from the bottom of the Start screen or right-clicking an open space on the Start screen and then tapping or clicking the All apps button on the App bar.

How do I scroll on a touch screen?
Use the slide gesture; that is, press and hold your finger on the screen and then move your finger in the direction you wish to scroll.

Figure 6

2

- Tap or click the Publisher 2013 tile to run the Publisher app and display the Publisher start screen (Figure 7).

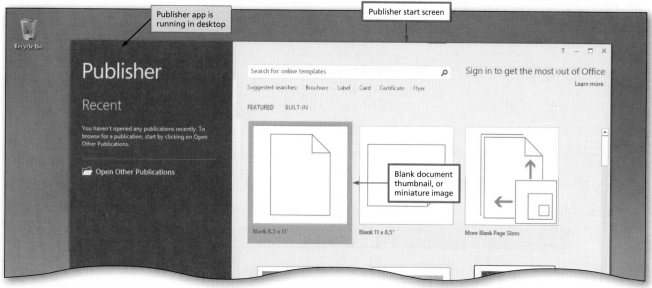

Figure 7

● Tap or click the Blank 8.5 × 11" thumbnail on the Publisher start screen to create a blank Publisher publication in the Publisher window (Figure 8).

Q&A

What happens when you run an app?

Some apps provide a means for you to create a blank publication, as shown in Figure 7 on the previous page; others immediately display a blank publication in an app window, such as the Publisher window shown in Figure 8. A **window** is a rectangular area that displays data and information. The top of a window has a **title bar**, which is a horizontal space that contains the window's name.

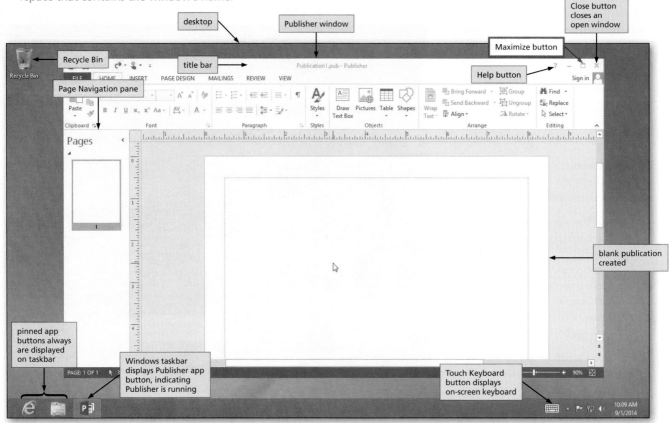

Figure 8

Other Ways

1. Tap or click Search charm on Charms bar, type app name in search box, tap or click app name in results list

2. Double-tap or double-click file created in app you want to run

---

To Run an App Using the Start Menu Using Windows 7

BTW

Touch Keyboard
To display the on-screen touch keyboard, tap the Touch Keyboard button on the Windows taskbar. When finished using the touch keyboard, tap the X button on the touch keyboard to close the keyboard.

If you are using Windows 7, perform these steps to run Publisher using the Start menu instead of the previous steps that use Windows 8.

1. Click the Start button on the Windows 7 taskbar to display the Start menu.

2. Click All Programs at the bottom of the left pane on the Start menu to display the All Programs list.

3. If the Publisher app is located in a folder, click, or scroll to and then click, the folder in the All Programs list to display a list of the folder's contents.

4. Click, or scroll to and then click, the app name (Publisher, in this case) in the list to run the selected app.

Windows Desktop

When you run an app in Windows, it may appear in an on-screen work area app, called the **desktop** (shown in Figure 8). You can perform tasks such as placing objects in the desktop, moving the objects around the desktop, and removing items from the desktop.

Some icons also may be displayed in the desktop. For instance, the icon for the **Recycle Bin**, the location of files that have been deleted, appears in the desktop by default. A **file** is a named unit of storage. Files can contain text, images, audio, and video. You can customize your desktop so that icons representing apps and files you use often appear in the desktop.

To Switch between an App and the Start Screen

1 SIGN IN | 2 USE WINDOWS | 3 USE APPS | 4 FILE MANAGEMENT | 5 SWITCH APPS | 6 SAVE FILES
7 CHANGE SCREEN RESOLUTION | 8 EXIT APPS | 9 USE ADDITIONAL APP FEATURES | 10 USE HELP

While working with an app, such as Publisher, or in the desktop, you easily can return to the Start screen. The following steps switch from the Publisher app to the Start screen. *Why? Returning to the Start screen allows you to run any of your other apps.* If you are using Windows 7, read these steps without performing them because Windows 7 does not have a Start screen.

- Swipe in from the left edge of the screen, and then back to the left, or point to the lower-left corner of the desktop to display a thumbnail of the Start screen (Figure 9).

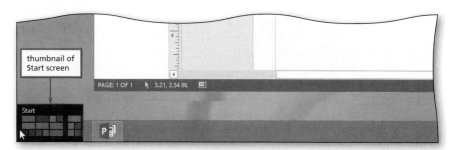
Figure 9

- Tap or click the thumbnail of the Start screen to display the Start screen (Figure 10).

- Tap or click the Desktop tile to redisplay the Publisher app in the desktop (shown in Figure 8).

Figure 10

Other Ways

1. Press WINDOWS key to display Start screen	2. Swipe in from right edge, tap or click Start charm

To Maximize a Window

Sometimes content is not visible completely in a window. One method of displaying the entire contents of a window is to **maximize** it, or enlarge the window so that it fills the entire screen. The following step maximizes the Publisher window; however, any Office app's window can be maximized using this step. *Why? A maximized window provides the most space available for using the app.*

1

- If the Publisher window is not maximized already, tap or click the Maximize button (shown in Figure 8 on page OFF 12) next to the Close button on the window's title bar to maximize the window (Figure 11).

Q&A

What happened to the Maximize button?
It changed to a Restore Down button, which you can use to return a window to its size and location before you maximized it.

How do I know whether a window is maximized?
A window is maximized if it fills the entire display area and the Restore Down button is displayed on the title bar.

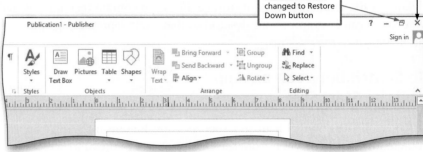

Figure 11

Other Ways

1. Double-tap or double-click title bar	2. Drag title bar to top of screen

Publisher Window, Ribbon, and Elements Common to Office Apps

The Publisher window consists of a variety of components to make your work more efficient and publications more professional. These include the workspace, page layout, scratch area, Page Navigation pane, ribbon, mini toolbar, shortcut menus, Quick Access Toolbar, and Microsoft Account area. Most of these components are common to other Microsoft Office apps; others are unique to Publisher.

The **page layout** contains a view of the publication page, all the objects contained therein, plus the guides and boundaries for the page and its objects (Figure 12). The default (preset) view is **Single Page view**, which shows the publication on a mock sheet of paper in the Publisher workspace.

Scroll Bars You use a scroll bar to display different portions of a publication in the publication workspace. At the right edge of the workspace is a vertical scroll bar. A horizontal scroll bar appears at the bottom. On a scroll bar, the position of the scroll box reflects the location of the portion of the publication that is displayed in the workspace.

Status Bar The **status bar**, located at the bottom of the publication window above the Windows taskbar, presents information about the publication, the progress of current tasks, and the status of certain commands and keys; it also provides controls for viewing the publication. As you type text or perform certain tasks, various indicators may appear on the status bar.

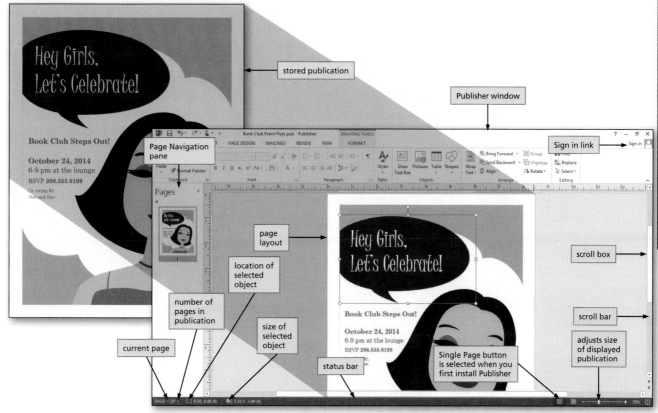

Figure 12

The left side of the status bar in Figure 12 shows the current page followed by the total number of pages in the publication, the location of the selected object, and the size of the selected object. The right side of the status bar includes buttons and controls you can use to change the view of a publication and adjust the size of the displayed publication.

Ribbon   The ribbon, located near the top of the window below the title bar, is the control center in Publisher and other Office apps (Figure 13). The ribbon provides easy, central access to the tasks you perform while creating a publication. The ribbon consists of tabs, groups, and commands. Each **tab** contains a collection of groups, and each **group** contains related commands. When you run an Office app, such as Publisher, it initially displays several main tabs, also called default or top-level tabs. All Office apps have a HOME tab, which contains the more frequently used commands.

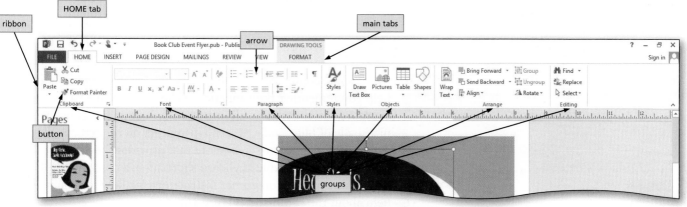

Figure 13

In addition to the main tabs, the Office apps display **tool tabs**, also called contextual tabs (Figure 14), when you perform certain tasks or work with objects such as pictures or tables. If you insert a picture in a Publisher publication, for example, the PICTURE TOOLS tab and its related subordinate FORMAT tab appear, collectively referred to as the PICTURE TOOLS FORMAT tab. When you are finished working with the picture, the PICTURE TOOLS FORMAT tab disappears from the ribbon. Publisher and other Office apps determine when tool tabs should appear and disappear based on tasks you perform. Some tool tabs, such as the TABLE TOOLS tab, have more than one related subordinate tab.

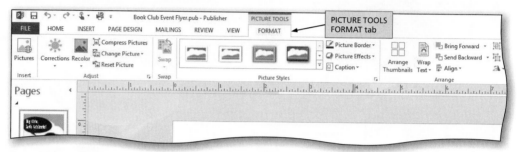

Figure 14

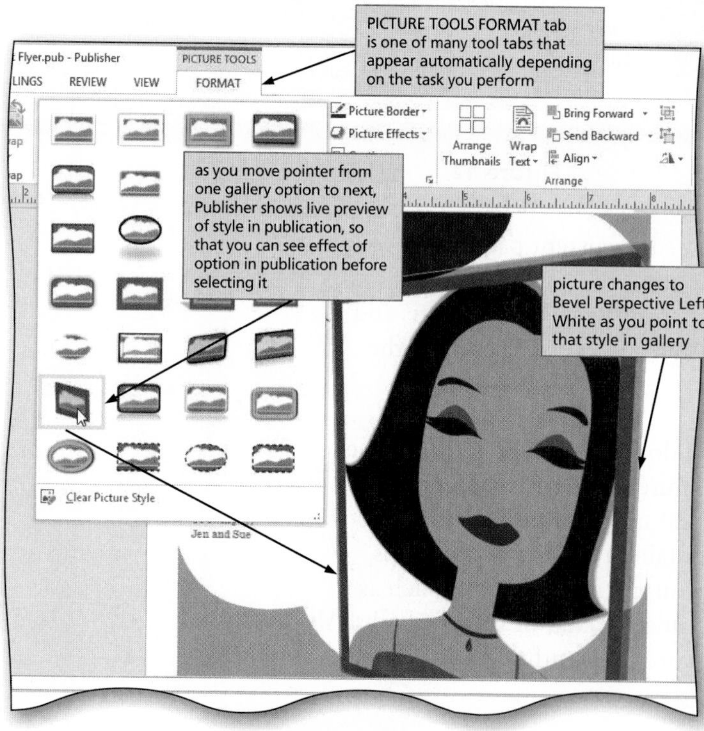

Items on the ribbon include buttons, boxes, and galleries (shown in Figure 13 on the previous page). A **gallery** is a set of choices, often graphical, arranged in a grid or in a list. You can scroll through choices in an in-ribbon gallery by tapping or clicking the gallery's scroll arrows. Or, you can tap or click a gallery's More button to view more gallery options on the screen at a time.

Some buttons and boxes have arrows that, when tapped or clicked, also display a gallery; others always cause a gallery to be displayed when tapped or clicked. Most galleries support **live preview**, which is a feature that allows you to point to a gallery choice and see its effect in the publication — without actually selecting the choice (Figure 15). Live preview works only if you are using a mouse; if you are using a touch screen, you will not be able to view live previews.

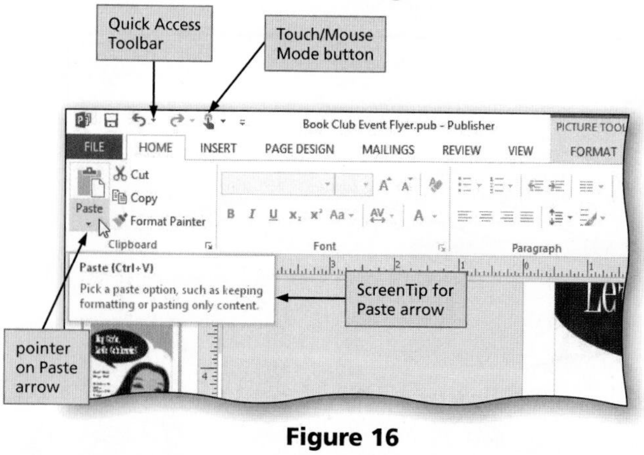

Figure 15

Some commands on the ribbon display an image to help you remember their function. When you point to a command on the ribbon, all or part of the command glows in a shade of blue, and a ScreenTip appears on the screen. A **ScreenTip** is an on-screen note that provides the name of the command, available keyboard shortcut(s), a description of the command, and sometimes instructions for how to obtain help about the command (Figure 16).

Figure 16

Some groups on the ribbon have a small arrow in the lower-right corner, called a **Dialog Box Launcher**, that when tapped or clicked, displays a dialog box or a task pane with additional options for the group (Figure 17). When presented with a dialog box, you make selections and must close the dialog box before returning to the publication. A **task pane**, in contrast to a dialog box, is a window that can remain open and visible while you work in the publication.

BTW
Touch Mode
The Office and Windows interfaces may vary if you are using Touch mode. For this reason, you might notice that the function or appearance of your touch screen in Publisher differs slightly from this book's presentation.

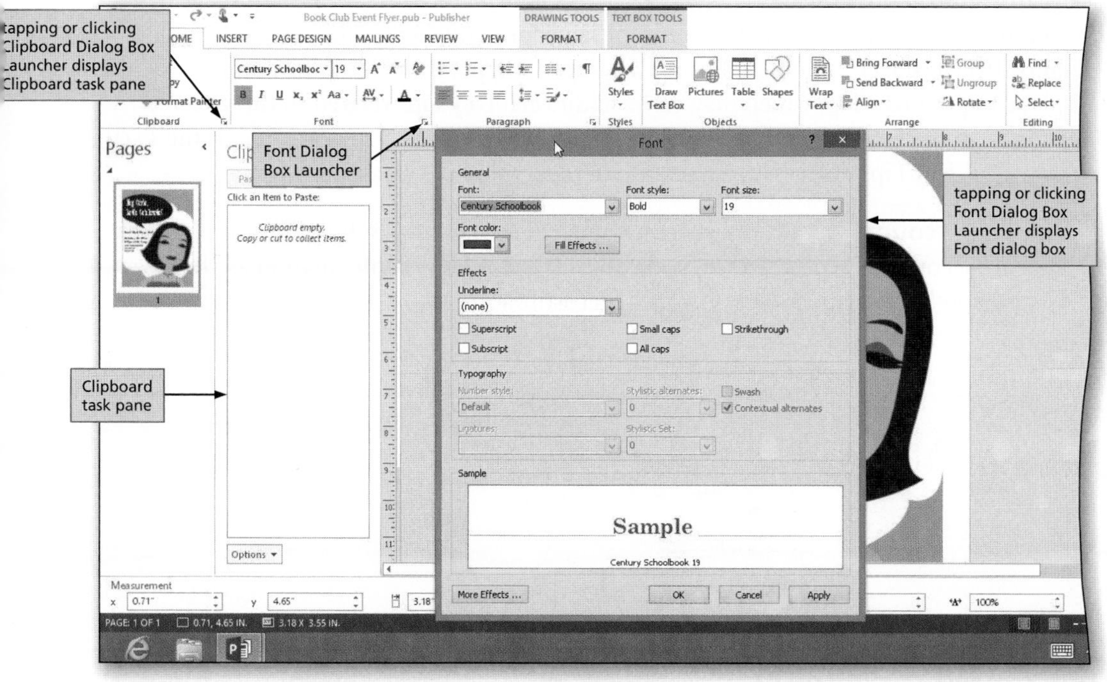

Figure 17

Mini Toolbar The **mini toolbar**, which appears automatically based on tasks you perform, contains commands related to changing the appearance of text in a publication (Figure 18). If you do not use the mini toolbar, it disappears from the screen. The buttons, arrows, and boxes on the mini toolbar vary, depending on whether you are using Touch mode versus Mouse mode. If you press and hold or right-click an item in the publication window, Publisher displays both the mini toolbar and a shortcut menu, which is discussed in a later section in this chapter.

All commands on the mini toolbar also exist on the ribbon. The purpose of the mini toolbar is to minimize hand or mouse movement.

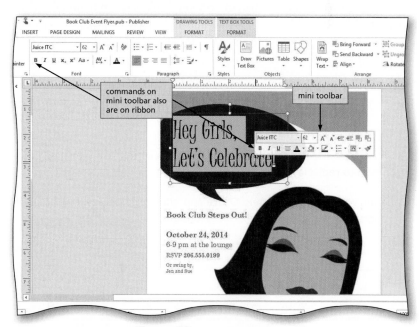

Figure 18

Quick Access Toolbar The **Quick Access Toolbar**, located initially (by default) above the ribbon at the left edge of the title bar, provides convenient, one-tap or one-click access to frequently used commands (shown in Figure 16). The commands on the Quick Access Toolbar always are available, regardless of the task you are performing. The Touch/Mouse Mode button on the Quick Access Toolbar allows you to switch between Touch mode and Mouse mode. If you primarily are using touch gestures, Touch mode will add more

BTW
Turning Off the Mini Toolbar
If you do not want the mini toolbar to appear, tap or click FILE on the ribbon to open the Backstage view, tap or click Options in the Backstage view, tap or click General (Publisher Options dialog box), remove the check mark from the 'Show Mini Toolbar on selection' check box, and then tap or click the OK button.

space between commands on menus and on the ribbon so that they are easier to tap. While touch gestures are convenient ways to interact with Office apps, not all features are supported when you are using Touch mode. If you are using a mouse, Mouse mode will not add the extra space between buttons and commands. The Quick Access Toolbar is discussed in more depth later in the chapter.

KeyTips If you prefer using the keyboard instead of the mouse, you can press the ALT key on the keyboard to display **KeyTips**, or keyboard code icons, for certain commands (Figure 19). To select a command using the keyboard, press the letter or number displayed in the KeyTip, which may cause additional KeyTips related to the selected command to appear. To remove KeyTips from the screen, press the ALT key or the ESC key until all KeyTips disappear, or tap or click anywhere in the app window.

Microsoft Account Area In this area, you can use the Sign in link to sign in to your Microsoft account. Once signed in, you will see your account information as well as a picture if you have included one in your Microsoft account.

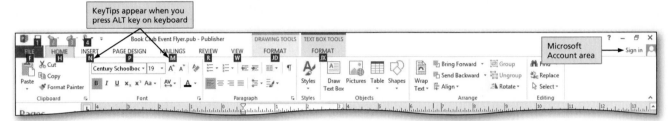

Figure 19

To Display a Different Tab on the Ribbon

1 SIGN IN | 2 USE WINDOWS | 3 USE APPS | 4 FILE MANAGEMENT | 5 SWITCH APPS | 6 SAVE FILES
7 CHANGE SCREEN RESOLUTION | 8 EXIT APPS | 9 USE ADDITIONAL APP FEATURES | 10 USE HELP

When you run Publisher, the ribbon displays seven main tabs: FILE, HOME, INSERT, PAGE DESIGN, MAILINGS, REVIEW, and VIEW. The tab currently displayed is called the **active tab**.

The following step displays the INSERT tab, that is, makes it the active tab. *Why? When working with an Office app, you may need to switch tabs to access other options for working with a publication.*

• Tap or click INSERT on the ribbon to display the INSERT tab (Figure 20).

 **Experiment**

• Tap or click the other tabs on the ribbon to view their contents. When you are finished, tap or click INSERT on the ribbon to redisplay the INSERT tab.

Q&A | If I am working in a different Office app, such as PowerPoint or Access, how do I display a different tab on the ribbon?
Follow this same procedure; that is, tap or click the desired tab on the ribbon.

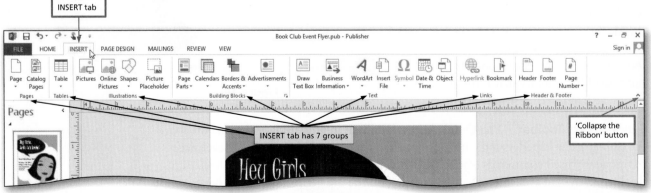

Figure 20

To Collapse and Expand the Ribbon and Use Full Screen Mode

To display more of a publication or other item in the window of an Office app, some users prefer to collapse the ribbon, which hides the groups on the ribbon and displays only the main tabs, or to use **Full Screen mode**, which hides all the commands and just displays the publication. Each time you run an Office app, such as Publisher, the ribbon appears the same way it did the last time you used that Office app. The chapters in this book, however, begin with the ribbon appearing as it did at the initial installation of Office or Publisher.

The following steps collapse, expand, and restore the ribbon in Publisher and then switch to Full Screen mode. *Why? If you need more space on the screen to work with your publication, you may consider collapsing the ribbon or switching to Full Screen mode to gain additional workspace.*

1

- Tap or click the 'Collapse the Ribbon' button on the ribbon (shown in Figure 20) to collapse the ribbon (Figure 21).

Q&A What happened to the groups on the ribbon?
When you collapse the ribbon, the groups disappear so that the ribbon does not take up as much space on the screen.

What happened to the 'Collapse the Ribbon' button?
The 'Pin the ribbon' button replaces the 'Collapse the Ribbon' button when the ribbon is collapsed. You will see the 'Pin the ribbon' button only when you expand a ribbon by tapping or clicking a tab.

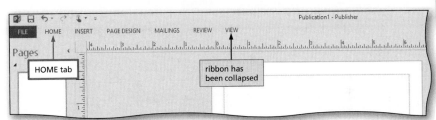

Figure 21

2

- Tap or click HOME on the ribbon to expand the HOME tab (Figure 22).

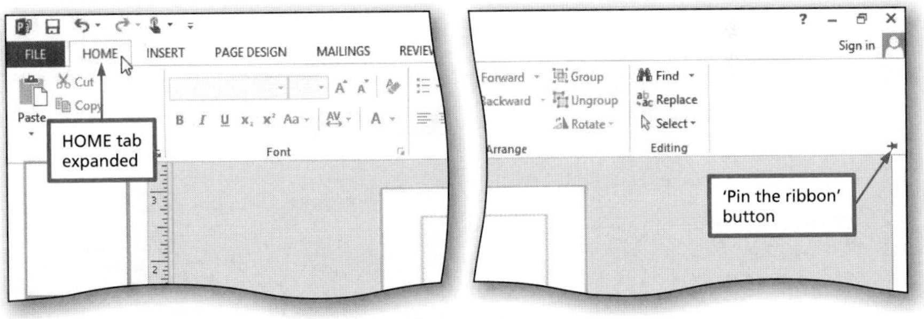

Q&A Why would I click the HOME tab?
If you want to use a command on a collapsed ribbon, tap or click the main tab to display the groups for that tab. After you select a command on the ribbon, the groups will be collapsed once again.
If you decide not to use a command on the ribbon, you can collapse the groups by tapping or clicking the same main tab or tapping or clicking in the app window.

Figure 22

Experiment

- Tap or click HOME on the ribbon to collapse the groups again. Tap or click HOME on the ribbon to expand the HOME tab.

3

- Tap or click the 'Pin the ribbon' button on the expanded HOME tab to restore the ribbon.

Other Ways
1. Double-tap or double-click a main tab on the ribbon   2. Press CTRL+F1

To Use a Shortcut Menu to Relocate the Quick Access Toolbar

When you press and hold or right-click certain areas of the Publisher and other Office app windows, a shortcut menu will appear. A **shortcut menu** is a list of frequently used commands that relate to an object. ***Why? You can use shortcut menus to access common commands quickly.*** When you press and hold or right-click the status bar, for example, a shortcut menu appears with commands related to the status bar. When you press and hold or right-click the Quick Access Toolbar, a shortcut menu appears with commands related to the Quick Access Toolbar. The following steps use a shortcut menu to move the Quick Access Toolbar, which by default is located on the title bar.

1

- Press and hold or right-click the Quick Access Toolbar to display a shortcut menu that presents a list of commands related to the Quick Access Toolbar (Figure 23).

Q&A What if I cannot make the shortcut menu appear using the touch instruction?

When you use the press and hold technique, be sure to release your finger when the square appears on the screen to display the shortcut menu. If the technique still does not work, you might need to add more space around objects on the screen, making it easier for you to press or tap them. Click the 'Customize Quick Access Toolbar' button and then click Touch/Mouse Mode on the menu. Another option is to use the stylus.

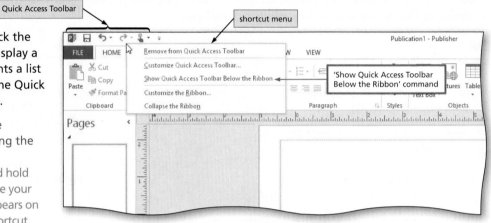

Figure 23

2

- Tap or click 'Show Quick Access Toolbar Below the Ribbon' on the shortcut menu to display the Quick Access Toolbar below the ribbon (Figure 24).

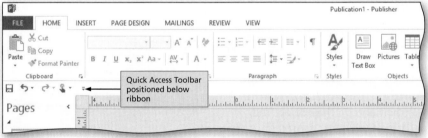

Figure 24

3

- Press and hold or right-click the Quick Access Toolbar to display a shortcut menu (Figure 25).

4

- Tap or click 'Show Quick Access Toolbar Above the Ribbon' on the shortcut menu to return the Quick Access Toolbar to its original position (shown in Figure 23).

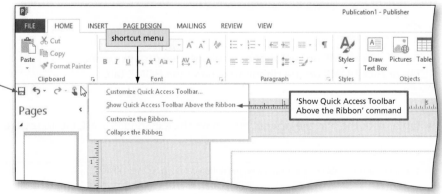

Figure 25

Other Ways

1. Tap or click 'Customize Quick Access Toolbar' button on Quick Access Toolbar, tap or click 'Show Below the Ribbon' or 'Show Above the Ribbon'

To Customize the Quick Access Toolbar

The Quick Access Toolbar provides easy access to some of the more frequently used commands in the Office apps. By default, the Quick Access Toolbar contains buttons for the Save, Undo, and Redo commands. You can customize the Quick Access Toolbar by changing its location in the window, as shown in the previous steps, and by adding more buttons to reflect commands you would like to access easily. The following steps add the Quick Print button to the Quick Access Toolbar in the Publisher window. *Why? Adding the Quick Print button to the Quick Access Toolbar speeds up the process of printing.*

1

- Tap or click the 'Customize Quick Access Toolbar' button to display the Customize Quick Access Toolbar menu (Figure 26).

Q&A Which commands are listed on the Customize Quick Access Toolbar menu?

It lists commands that commonly are added to the Quick Access Toolbar.

What do the check marks next to some commands signify?

Check marks appear next to commands that already are on the Quick Access Toolbar. When you add a button to the Quick Access Toolbar, a check mark will be displayed next to its command name.

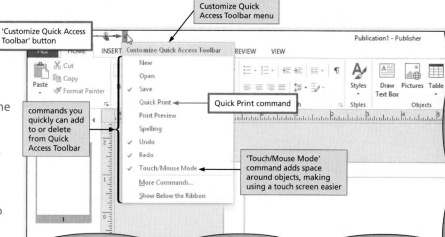

Figure 26

2

- Tap or click Quick Print on the Customize Quick Access Toolbar menu to add the Quick Print button to the Quick Access Toolbar (Figure 27).

Q&A How would I remove a button from the Quick Access Toolbar?

You would press and hold or right-click the button you wish to remove and then tap or click 'Remove from Quick Access Toolbar' on the shortcut menu or tap or click the 'Customize Quick Access Toolbar' button on the Quick Access Toolbar and then click the button name in the Customize Quick Access Toolbar menu to remove the check mark.

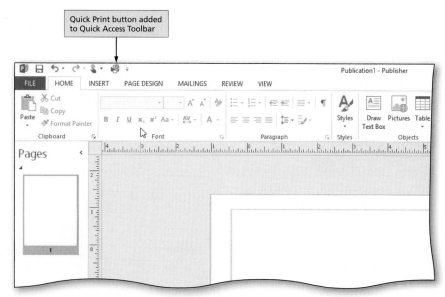

Figure 27

Other Ways

1. Tap or click File on ribbon, tap or click Options button, tap or click 'Quick Access Toolbar' button (Publisher Options dialog box), choose settings, tap or click OK button

To Enter Text in a Publication

A typical task to do in Publisher is to enter text by typing on the keyboard. The following steps create a text box and enter text. *Why? In Publisher, you must enter text into a text box on the page layout.*

1

- Tap or click the Draw a Text Box button (HOME tab | Objects group), and then drag a small text box at the top of the page layout.

- Type `Book Club Steps Out` as the text (Figure 28).

Q&A What is the blinking vertical bar to the right of the text?
The blinking bar is the insertion point, which indicates where text, graphics, and other items will be inserted in the publication. As you type, the insertion point moves to the right, and when you reach the end of a line, it moves down to the beginning of the next line.

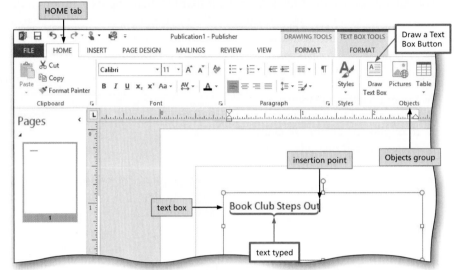

Figure 28

What if I make an error while typing?
You can press the BACKSPACE key until you have deleted the text in error and then retype the text correctly.

Why does a circle appear below the insertion point?
If you are using a touch screen, a selection handle (small circle) appears below the text so that you can format the text easily.

2

- Press the ENTER key to move the insertion point to the beginning of the next line (Figure 29).

Q&A Why did blank space appear between the entered text and the insertion point?
Each time you press the ENTER key, Publisher creates a new paragraph and inserts blank space between the two paragraphs. Depending on your settings, Publisher may or may not insert a blank space between the two paragraphs.

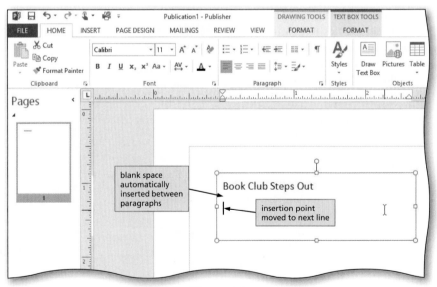

Figure 29

Saving and Organizing Files

While you are creating a publication, the computer stores it in memory. When you save a publication, the computer places it on a storage medium such as a hard disk, solid state drive (SSD), USB flash drive, or optical disc. The storage medium can be permanent in your computer, may be portable where you remove it from your computer, or may be on a web server you access through a network or the Internet.

A saved publication is referred to as a file. A **file name** is the name assigned to a file when it is saved. When saving files, you should organize them so that you easily can find them later. Windows provides tools to help you organize files.

BTW
File Type
Depending on your Windows settings, the file type .pub may be displayed immediately to the right of the file name after you save the file. The file type .pub is a Publisher 2013 publication.

CONSIDER THIS

How often should you save a publication?

It is important to save a publication frequently for the following reasons:

• The publication in memory might be lost if the computer is turned off or you lose electrical power while an app is running.

• If you run out of time before completing a project, you may finish it at a future time without starting over.

Organizing Files and Folders

A file contains data. This data can range from a research paper to an accounting spreadsheet to an electronic math quiz. You should organize and store files in folders to avoid misplacing a file and to help you find a file quickly.

If you are taking an introductory computer class (CIS 101, for example), you may want to design a series of folders for the different subjects covered in the class. To accomplish this, you can arrange the folders in a hierarchy for the class, as shown in Figure 30.

The hierarchy contains three levels. The first level contains the storage medium, such as a hard disk. The second level contains the class folder (CIS 101, in this case), and the third level contains seven folders, one each for a different Office app that will be covered in the class (Word, PowerPoint, Excel, Access, Outlook, Publisher, and OneNote).

When the hierarchy in Figure 30 is created, the storage medium is said to contain the CIS 101 folder, and the CIS 101 folder is said to contain the separate Office folders (i.e., Word, PowerPoint, Excel, etc.). In addition, this hierarchy easily can be expanded to include folders from other classes taken during additional semesters.

The vertical and horizontal lines in Figure 30 form a pathway that allows you to navigate to a drive or folder on a computer or network. A **path** consists of a drive letter (preceded by a drive name when necessary) and colon, to identify the storage device, and one or more folder names. A hard disk typically has a drive letter of C. Each drive or folder in the hierarchy has a corresponding path.

By default, Windows saves publications in the Documents library, music in the Music library, pictures in the Pictures library, and videos in the Videos library.

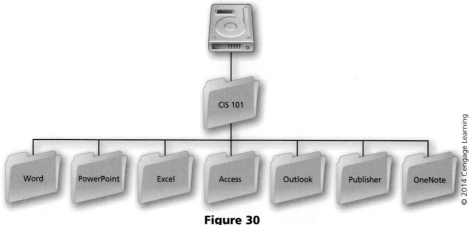

Figure 30

A **library** helps you manage multiple folders stored in various locations on a computer and devices. It does not store the folder contents; rather, it keeps track of their locations so that you can access the folders and their contents quickly. For example, you can save pictures from a digital camera in any folder on any storage location on a computer. Normally, this would make organizing the different folders difficult. If you add the folders to a library, however, you can access all the pictures from one location regardless of where they are stored.

The following pages illustrate the steps to organize the folders for this class and save a file in a folder:

1. Create the folder identifying your class.
2. Create the Publisher folder in the folder identifying your class.
3. Save a file in the Publisher folder.
4. Verify the location of the saved file.

To Create a Folder

1 SIGN IN | 2 USE WINDOWS | 3 USE APPS | 4 FILE MANAGEMENT | 5 SWITCH APPS | 6 SAVE FILES
7 CHANGE SCREEN RESOLUTION | 8 EXIT APPS | 9 USE ADDITIONAL APP FEATURES | 10 USE HELP

When you create a folder, such as the CIS 101 folder shown in Figure 30 on the previous page, you must name the folder. A folder name should describe the folder and its contents. A folder name can contain spaces and any uppercase or lowercase characters, except a backslash (\), slash (/), colon (:), asterisk (*), question mark (?), quotation marks ("), less than symbol (<), greater than symbol (>), or vertical bar (|). Folder names cannot be CON, AUX, COM1, COM2, COM3, COM4, LPT1, LPT2, LPT3, PRN, or NUL. The same rules for naming folders also apply to naming files.

The following steps create a class folder (CIS 101, in this case) in the Documents library. *Why? When storing files, you should organize the files so that it will be easier to find them later.* If you are using Windows 7, skip these steps and instead perform the steps in the yellow box that immediately follows these Windows 8 steps.

- Tap or click the File Explorer app button on the taskbar to run the File Explorer app (Figure 31).

Q&A | Why does the title bar say Libraries?
File Explorer, by default, displays the name of the selected library or folder on the title bar.

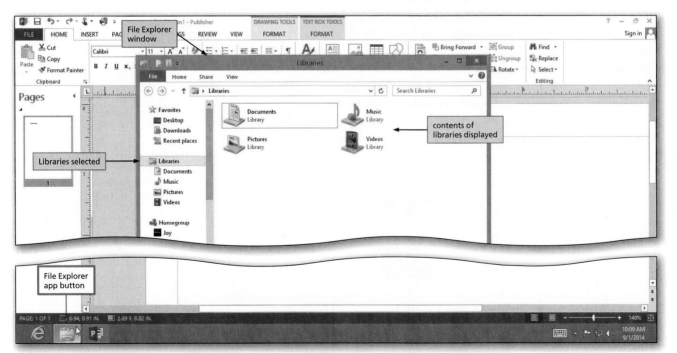

Figure 31

2

- Tap or click the Documents library in the navigation pane to display the contents of the Documents library in the file list (Figure 32).

Q&A What if my screen does not show the Documents, Music, Pictures, and Videos libraries?
Double-tap or double-click Libraries in the navigation pane to expand the list.

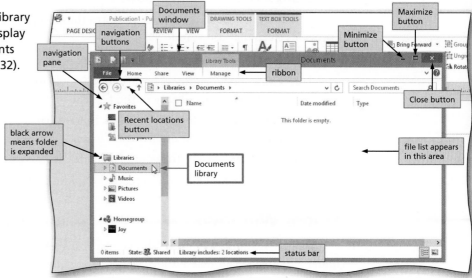

Figure 32

3

- Tap or click the New folder button on the Quick Access Toolbar to create a new folder with the name, New folder, selected in a text box (Figure 33).

Q&A Why is the folder icon displayed differently on my computer?
Windows might be configured to display contents differently on your computer.

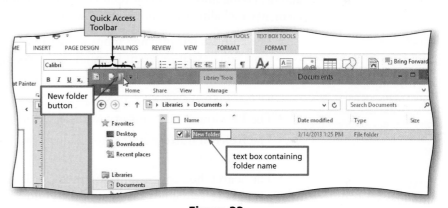

Figure 33

4

- Type **CIS 101** (or your class code) in the text box as the new folder name.
If requested by your instructor, add your last name to the end of the folder name.

- Press the ENTER key to change the folder name from New folder to a folder name identifying your class (Figure 34).

Q&A What happens when I press the ENTER key?
The class folder (CIS 101, in this case) is displayed in the file list, which contains the folder name, date modified, type, and size.

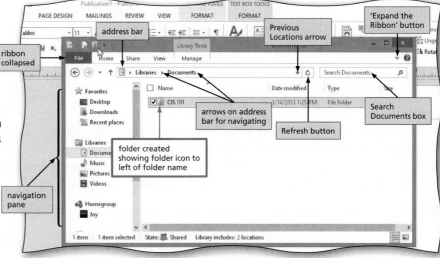

Figure 34

Other Ways

1. Press CTRL+SHIFT+N   2. Tap or click the New folder button (Home tab | New group)

To Create a Folder Using Windows 7

If you are using Windows 7, perform these steps to create a folder instead of the previous steps that use Windows 8.

1. Click the Windows Explorer button on the taskbar to run Windows Explorer.
2. Click the Documents library in the navigation pane to display the contents of the Documents library in the file list.
3. Click the New folder button on the toolbar to display a new folder icon with the name, New folder, selected in a text box.
4. Type `CIS 101` (or your class code) in the text box to name the folder.
5. Press the ENTER key to create the folder.

Folder Windows

The Documents window (shown in Figure 34 on the previous page) is called a folder window. Recall that a folder is a specific named location on a storage medium that contains related files. Most users rely on **folder windows** for finding, viewing, and managing information on their computers. Folder windows have common design elements, including the following (shown in Figure 34).

BTW

The Favorites Area
In the navigation pane, the **Favorites area** shows your favorite locations. By default, this list contains only links to your Desktop, Downloads, and Recent places.

BTW

The Libraries Area
In the navigation pane, the **Libraries area** shows all of the folders included in the library.

- The **address bar** provides quick navigation options. The arrows on the address bar allow you to visit different locations on the computer.
- The buttons to the left of the address bar allow you to navigate the contents of the navigation pane and view recent pages.
- The **Previous Locations arrow** displays the locations you have visited.
- The **Refresh button** on the right side of the address bar refreshes the contents of the folder list.
- The **search box** contains the dimmed words, Search Documents. You can type a term in the search box for a list of files, folders, shortcuts, and elements containing that term within the location you are searching. A **shortcut** is an icon on the desktop that provides a user with immediate access to an app or file.
- The **ribbon** contains five tabs used to accomplish various tasks on the computer related to organizing and managing the contents of the open window. This ribbon works similarly to the ribbon in the Office apps.
- The **navigation pane** on the left contains the Favorites area, Libraries area, Homegroup area, Computer area, and Network area.

To Create a Folder within a Folder

1 SIGN IN | 2 USE WINDOWS | 3 USE APPS | 4 FILE MANAGEMENT | 5 SWITCH APPS | 6 SAVE FILES
7 CHANGE SCREEN RESOLUTION | 8 EXIT APPS | 9 USE ADDITIONAL APP FEATURES | 10 USE HELP

With the class folder created, you can create folders that will store the files you create using Publisher. The following steps create a Publisher folder within the CIS 101 folder (or the folder identifying your class). *Why? To be able to organize your files, you should create a folder structure.* If you are using Windows 7, skip these steps and instead perform the steps in the yellow box that immediately follows these Windows 8 steps.

- Double-tap or double-click the icon or folder name for the CIS 101 folder (or the folder identifying your class) in the file list to open the folder (Figure 35).

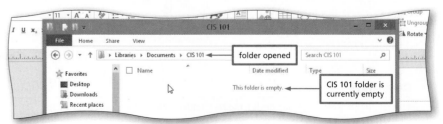

Figure 35

- Tap or click the New folder button on the Quick Access Toolbar to create a new folder within the current folder.

- Type **Publisher** in the text box as the new folder name.

- Press the ENTER key to rename the folder (Figure 36).

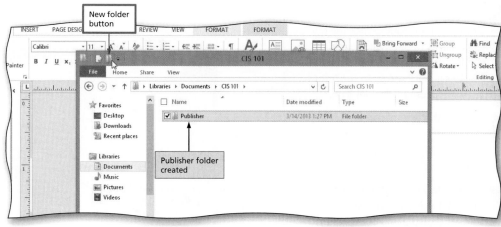

Figure 36

Other Ways	
1. Press CTRL+SHIFT+N	2. Tap or click the New folder button (Home tab | New group)

TO CREATE A FOLDER WITHIN A FOLDER USING WINDOWS 7

If you are using Windows 7, perform these steps to create a folder within a folder instead of the previous steps that use Windows 8.

1. Double-click the icon or folder name for the CIS 101 folder (or the folder identifying your class) in the file list to open the folder.

2. Click the New folder button on the toolbar to display a new folder icon and text box for the folder.

3. Type **Publisher** in the text box to name the folder.

4. Press the ENTER key to create the folder.

To Expand a Folder, Scroll through Folder Contents, and Collapse a Folder

1 SIGN IN | 2 USE WINDOWS | 3 USE APPS | 4 FILE MANAGEMENT | 5 SWITCH APPS | 6 SAVE FILES
7 CHANGE SCREEN RESOLUTION | 8 EXIT APPS | 9 USE ADDITIONAL APP FEATURES | 10 USE HELP

Folder windows display the hierarchy of items and the contents of drives and folders in the file list. You might want to expand a library or folder in the navigation pane to view its contents, slide or scroll through its contents, and collapse it when you are finished viewing its contents. **Why?** *When a folder is expanded, you can see all the folders it contains. By contrast, a collapsed folder hides the folders it contains.* The following steps expand, slide or scroll through, and then collapse the folder identifying your class (CIS 101, in this case).

- Double-tap or double-click the Documents library in the navigation pane, which expands the library to display its contents and displays a black arrow to the left of the Documents library icon (Figure 37).

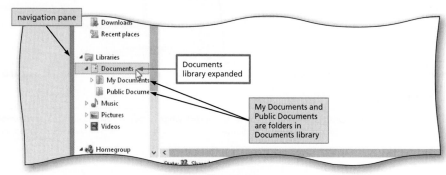

Figure 37

2

- Double-tap or double-click the My Documents folder, which expands the folder to display its contents and displays a black arrow to the left of the My Documents folder icon.

 What is the My Documents folder? When you save files on your hard disk, the My Documents folder is the default save location.

- Double-tap or double-click the CIS 101 folder, which expands the folder to display its contents and displays a black arrow to the left of the folder icon (Figure 38).

Experiment

- Slide the scroll bar down or click the down scroll arrow on the vertical scroll bar to display additional folders at the bottom of the navigation pane. Slide the scroll bar up or click the scroll bar above the scroll box to move the scroll box to the top of the navigation pane. Drag the scroll box down the scroll bar until the scroll box is halfway down the scroll bar.

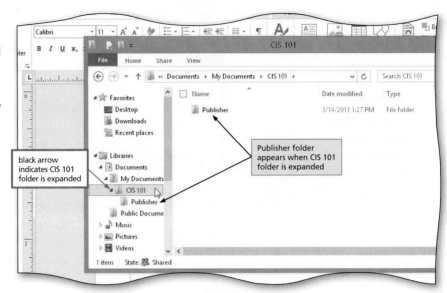

Figure 38

3

- Double-tap or double-click the folder identifying your class (CIS 101, in this case) to collapse the folder (Figure 39).

 Why are some folders indented below others? A folder contains the indented folders below it.

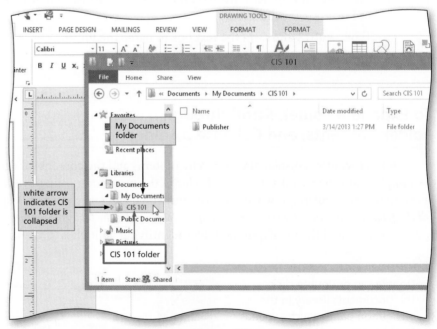

Figure 39

Other Ways

1. Point to display arrows in navigation pane, tap or click white arrow to expand or tap or click black arrow to collapse

2. Select folder to expand or collapse using arrow keys, press RIGHT ARROW to expand; press LEFT ARROW to collapse.

To Switch from One App to Another

You want to save the Publisher file containing the text you typed earlier. Publisher, however, currently is not the active window. You can use the app button on the taskbar and live preview to switch to Publisher.

Why? By clicking the appropriate app button on the taskbar, you can switch to the open app you want to use. The steps below switch to the Publisher window; however, the steps are the same for any active Office app currently displayed as an app button on the taskbar.

1

- If you are using a mouse, point to the Publisher app button on the taskbar to see a live preview of the open publication(s) or to see the window title(s) of the open publication(s), depending on your computer's configuration (Figure 40).

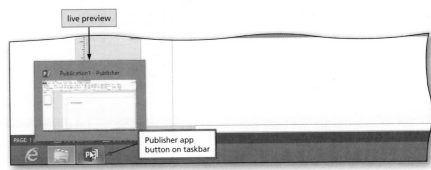

Figure 40

2

- Tap or click the Publisher app button or the live preview to make the app associated with the app button the active window (Figure 41).

Q&A What if multiple documents are open in an app?
Tap or click the desired live preview to switch to the window you want to use.

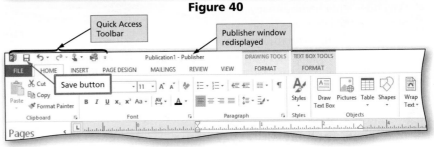

Figure 41

To Save a File in a Folder

The following steps save a file in the Publisher folder contained in your class folder (CIS 101, in this case) using the file name, Book Club Event Flyer. *Why? Without saving a file, you may lose all the work you have completed and will be unable to reuse or share it with others later.*

1

- Tap or click the Save button (shown in Figure 41) on the Quick Access Toolbar, which depending on settings, will display either the Save As gallery in the Backstage view (Figure 42) or the Save As dialog box (Figure 43 on the next page).

Q&A What is the Backstage view?
The **Backstage view** contains a set of commands that enable you to manage documents and data about the documents.

What if the Save As gallery is not displayed in the Backstage view?
Tap or click the Save As tab to display the Save As gallery.

How do I close the Backstage view?
Tap or click the Back button in the upper-left corner of the Backstage view to return to the Publisher window.

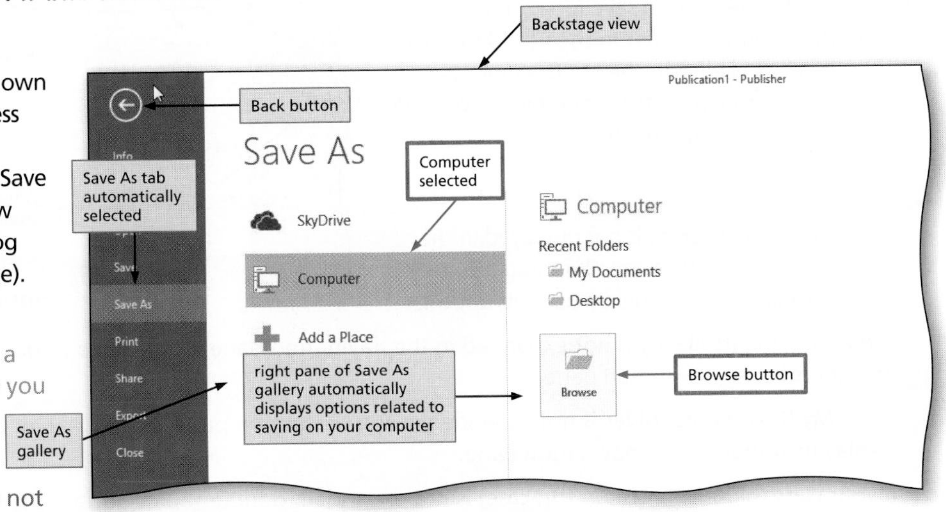

Figure 42

2

- If your screen displays the Backstage view, tap or click Computer, if necessary, to display options in the right pane related to saving on your computer; if your screen already displays the Save As dialog box, proceed to Step 3.

 What if I wanted to save on SkyDrive instead?
You would tap or click SkyDrive. Saving on SkyDrive is discussed in a later section in this chapter.

- Tap or click the Browse button in the right pane to display the Save As dialog box (Figure 43).

 Why does a file name already appear in the File name box?
Publisher automatically suggests a file name the first time you save a publication. The file name normally consists of the word, Publisher, followed by a number. Because the suggested file name is selected, you do not need to delete it; as soon as you begin typing, the new file name replaces the selected text.

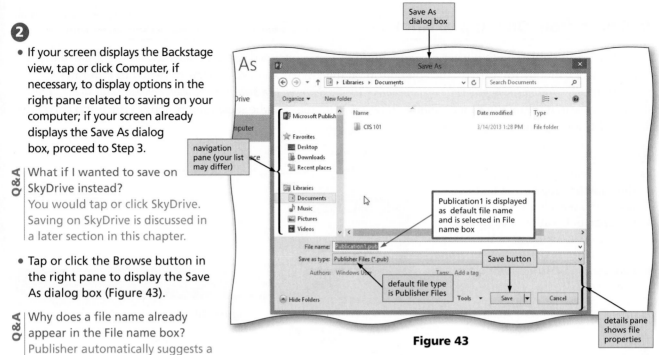

Figure 43

3

- Type **Book Club Event Flyer** in the File name box (Save As dialog box) to change the file name. Do not press the ENTER key after typing the file name because you do not want to close the dialog box at this time (Figure 44).

Figure 44

 What characters can I use in a file name?
The only invalid characters are the backslash (\), slash (/), colon (:), asterisk (*), question mark (?), quotation mark ("), less than symbol (<), greater than symbol (>), and vertical bar (|).

4

- Navigate to the desired save location (in this case, the Publisher folder in the CIS 101 folder [or your class folder] in the My Documents folder in the Documents library) by performing the tasks in Steps 4a and 4b.

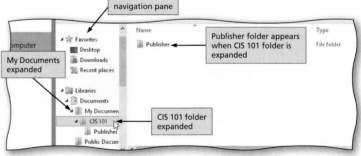

Figure 45

4a

- If the Documents library is not displayed in the navigation pane, slide to scroll or drag the scroll bar in the navigation pane until Documents appears.

- If the Documents library is not expanded in the navigation pane, double-tap or double-click Documents to display its folders in the navigation pane.

- If the My Documents folder is not expanded in the navigation pane, double-tap or double-click My Documents to display its folders in the navigation pane.

- If your class folder (CIS 101, in this case) is not expanded, double-tap or double-click the CIS 101 folder to select the folder and display its contents in the navigation pane (Figure 45).

 What if I do not want to save in a folder?
Although storing files in folders is an effective technique for organizing files, some users prefer not to store files in folders. If you prefer not to save this file in a folder, select the storage device on which you wish to save the file and then proceed to Step 5.

4b

- Tap or click the Publisher folder in the navigation pane to select it as the new save location and display its contents in the file list (Figure 46).

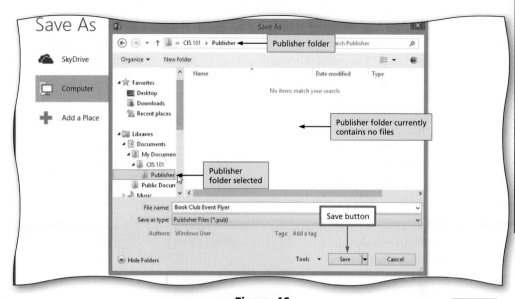

Figure 46

5

- Tap or click the Save button (Save As dialog box) to save the publication in the selected folder in the selected location with the entered file name (Figure 47).

Q&A How do I know that the file is saved?

While an Office app such as Publisher is saving a file, it briefly displays a message on the status bar indicating the amount of the file saved. In addition, the file name appears on the title bar.

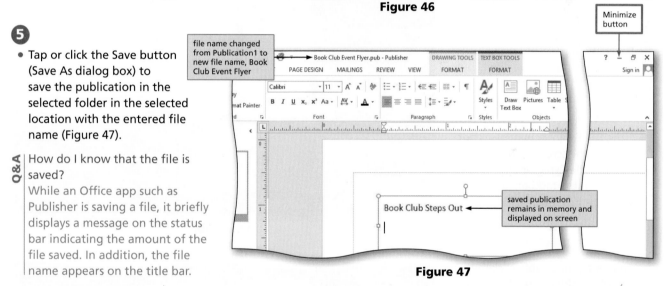

Figure 47

Other Ways

1. Tap or click FILE on ribbon, tap or click Save As in Backstage view, tap or click Computer, tap or click Browse button, type file name (Save As dialog box), navigate to desired save location, tap or click Save button

2. Press F12, type file name (Save As dialog box), navigate to desired save location, tap or click Save button

Navigating in Dialog Boxes

Navigating is the process of finding a location on a storage device. While saving the Book Club Event Flyer file, for example, Steps 4a and 4b in the previous set of steps navigated to the Publisher folder located in the CIS 101 folder in the My Documents folder in the Documents library. When performing certain functions in Windows apps, such as saving a file, opening a file, or inserting a picture in an existing document, you most likely will have to navigate to the location where you want to save the file or to the folder containing the file you want to open or insert. Most dialog boxes in Windows apps requiring navigation follow a similar procedure; that is, the way you navigate to a folder in one dialog box, such as the Save As dialog box, is similar to how you might navigate in another dialog box, such as the Open dialog box. If you chose to navigate to a specific location in a dialog box, you would follow the instructions in Steps 4a and 4b.

To Minimize and Restore a Window

Before continuing, you can verify that the Publisher file was saved properly. To do this, you will minimize the Publisher window and then open the CIS 101 window so that you can verify the file is stored in the CIS 101 folder on the hard disk. A **minimized window** is an open window that is hidden from view but can be displayed quickly by clicking the window's app button on the taskbar.

In the following example, Publisher is used to illustrate minimizing and restoring windows; however, you would follow the same steps regardless of the Office app you are using. *Why? Before closing an app, you should make sure your file saved correctly so that you can find it later.*

The following steps minimize the Publisher window, verify that the file is saved, and then restore the minimized window. If you are using Windows 7, skip these steps and instead perform the steps in the yellow box that immediately follows these Windows 8 steps.

1

- Tap or click the Minimize button on the Publisher window title bar (shown in Figure 47 on the previous page) to minimize the window (Figure 48).

Q&A Is the minimized window still available?
The minimized window, Publisher in this case, remains available but no longer is the active window. It is minimized as an app button on the taskbar.

- If the File Explorer window is not open on the screen, tap or click the File Explorer app button on the taskbar to make the File folder window the active window.

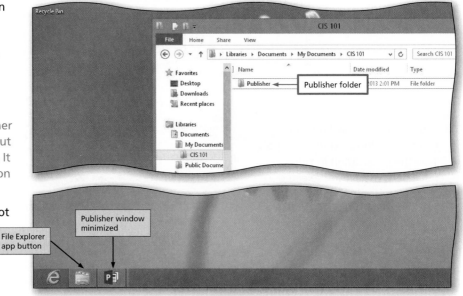

Figure 48

2

- Double-tap or double-click the Publisher folder in the file list to select the folder and display its contents (Figure 49).

Q&A Why does the File Explorer app button on the taskbar change?
A selected app button indicates that the app is active on the screen. When the button is not selected, the app is running but not active.

3

- After viewing the contents of the selected folder, tap or click the Publisher app button on the taskbar to restore the minimized window.

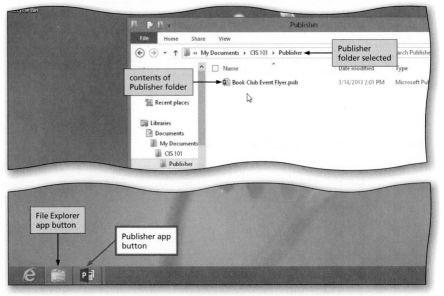

Figure 49

Other Ways

1. Press and hold or right-click title bar, tap or click Minimize on shortcut menu, tap or click taskbar button in taskbar button area

2. Press WINDOWS+M, press WINDOWS+SHIFT+M

TO MINIMIZE AND RESTORE A WINDOW USING WINDOWS 7

If you are using Windows 7, perform these steps to minimize and restore a window instead of the previous steps that use Windows 8.

1. Click the Minimize button on the app's title bar to minimize the window.
2. If the Windows Explorer window is not open on the screen, click the Windows Explorer button on the taskbar to make the Windows Explorer window the active window.
3. Double-click the Publisher folder in the file list to select the folder and display its contents.
4. After viewing the contents of the selected folder, click the Publisher button on the taskbar to restore the minimized window.

To Save a File on SkyDrive

1 SIGN IN | 2 USE WINDOWS | 3 USE APPS | 4 FILE MANAGEMENT | 5 SWITCH APPS | 6 SAVE FILES
7 CHANGE SCREEN RESOLUTION | 8 EXIT APPS | 9 USE ADDITIONAL APP FEATURES | 10 USE HELP

One of the features of Office is the capability to save files on SkyDrive so that you can use the files on multiple computers without having to use external storage devices such as a USB flash drive. Storing files on SkyDrive also enables you to share files more efficiently with others, such as when using Office Web Apps and Office 365.

In the following example, Publisher is used to save a file to SkyDrive. *Why? Storing files on SkyDrive provides more portability options than are available from storing files in the Documents library.*

You can save files directly to SkyDrive from within Word, PowerPoint, Publisher, and Excel. The following steps save the current Publisher file to the SkyDrive. These steps require you have a Microsoft account and an Internet connection.

1

- With the Publisher window active, tap or click FILE on the ribbon to open the Backstage view (Figure 50).

Q&A | What is the purpose of the FILE tab?
The FILE tab opens the Backstage view for each Office app, including Publisher.

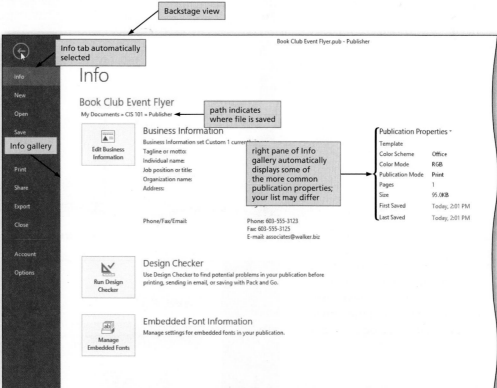

Figure 50

2

- Tap or click the Save As tab in the Backstage view to display the Save As gallery.

- Tap or click SkyDrive to display SkyDrive saving options or a Sign in button, if you are not signed in already to your Microsoft account (Figure 51).

Q&A What if my Save As gallery does not display SkyDrive as a save location?
Tap or click 'Add a Place' and proceed to Step 3.

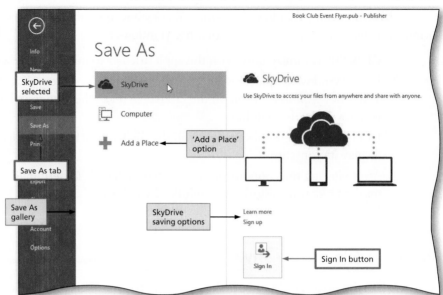

Figure 51

3

- If your screen displays a Next button, enter your email address and then click the Next button.

- If your screen displays a Sign in button, tap or click it to display the Sign in dialog box (Figure 52).

Q&A What if the Sign in button does not appear?
If you already are signed into your Microsoft account, the Sign in button will not be displayed. In this case, proceed to Step 5.

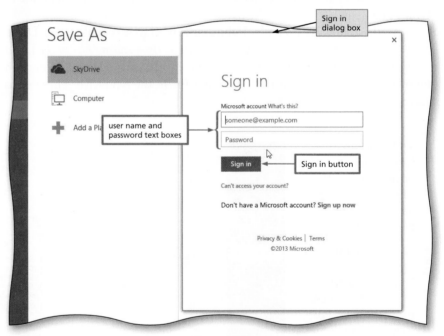

Figure 52

4

- Type your Microsoft account email address (or user name and password) in the text boxes and then tap or click the Sign in button (Sign in dialog box) to sign in to SkyDrive.

5

- Tap or click your SkyDrive to select your SkyDrive as the storage location (Figure 53).

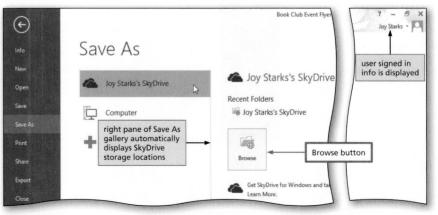

Figure 53

6

- Tap or click the Browse button to contact the SkyDrive server (which may take some time, depending on the speed of your Internet connection). The Save As dialog box will display (Figure 54).

Q&A Why does the path in the address bar contain various letters and numbers?
The letters and numbers in the address bar uniquely identify the location of your SkyDrive files and folders.

7

- Tap or click the Save button (Save As dialog box) to save the file on SkyDrive.

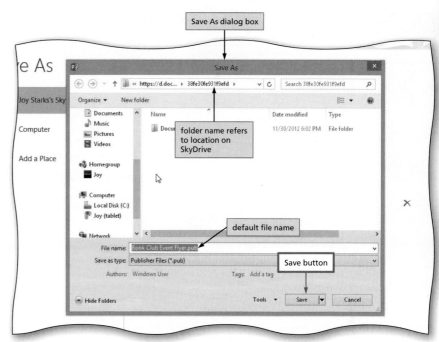

Figure 54

To Sign Out of a Microsoft Account

If you are using a public computer or otherwise wish to sign out of your Microsoft account, you should sign out of the account from the Accounts gallery in the Backstage view. Signing out of the account is the safest way to make sure that nobody else can access online files or settings stored in your Microsoft account. *Why? For security reasons, you should sign out of your Microsoft account when you are finished using a public or shared computer. Staying signed in to your Microsoft account might enable others to access your files.*

The following steps sign out of a Microsoft account from Publisher. You would use the same steps in any Office app. If you do not wish to sign out of your Microsoft account, read these steps without performing them.

1 Tap or click FILE on the ribbon to open the Backstage view.

2 Tap or click the Account tab to display the Account gallery (Figure 55).

3 Tap or click the Sign out link, which displays the Remove Account dialog box. If a Can't remove Windows accounts dialog box appears instead of the Remove Account dialog box, click the OK button and skip the remaining steps.

Q&A Why does a Can't remove Windows accounts dialog box appear?
If you signed in to Windows using your Microsoft account, then you also must sign out from Windows, rather than signing out from within Publisher. When you are finished using Windows, be sure to sign out at that time.

4 Tap or click the Yes button (Remove Account dialog box) to sign out of your Microsoft account on this computer.

Q&A Should I sign out of Windows after removing my Microsoft account?
When you are finished using the computer, you should sign out of Windows for maximum security.

5 Tap or click the Back button in the upper-left corner of the Backstage view to return to the publication.

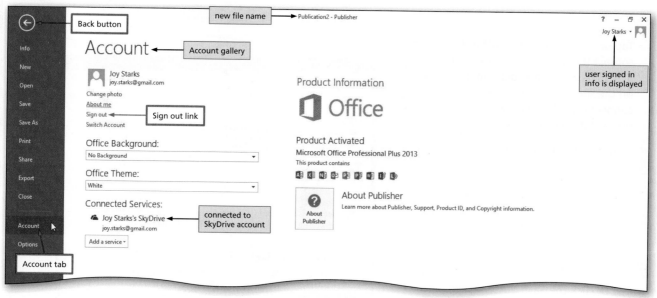

Figure 55

Screen Resolution

Screen resolution indicates the number of pixels (dots) that the computer uses to display the letters, numbers, graphics, and background you see on the screen. When you increase the screen resolution, Windows displays more information on the screen, but the information decreases in size. The reverse also is true: as you decrease the screen resolution, Windows displays less information on the screen, but the information increases in size.

Screen resolution usually is stated as the product of two numbers, such as 1366 × 768 (pronounced "thirteen sixty-six by seven sixty-eight"). A 1366 × 768 screen resolution results in a display of 1366 distinct pixels on each of 768 lines, or about 1,050,624 pixels. Changing the screen resolution affects how the ribbon appears in Office apps and some Windows dialog boxes. Figure 56, for example, shows the Publisher ribbon at screen resolutions of 1366 × 768 and 1024 × 768. All of the same commands are available regardless of screen resolution. The app (Publisher, in this case), however, makes changes to the groups and the buttons within the groups to accommodate the various screen resolutions. The result is that certain commands may need to be accessed differently depending on the resolution chosen. A command that is visible on the ribbon and available by tapping or clicking a button at one resolution may not be visible and may need to be accessed using its Dialog Box Launcher at a different resolution.

Comparing the two ribbons in Figure 56, notice the changes in content and layout of the groups and galleries. In some cases, the content of a group is the same in each resolution, but the layout of the group differs. For example, the same gallery and buttons appear in the Styles groups in the two resolutions, but the layouts differ. In other cases, the content and layout are the same across the resolution, but the level of detail differs with the resolution.

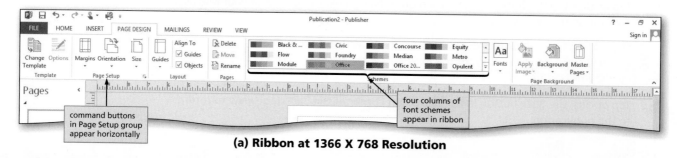

(a) Ribbon at 1366 X 768 Resolution

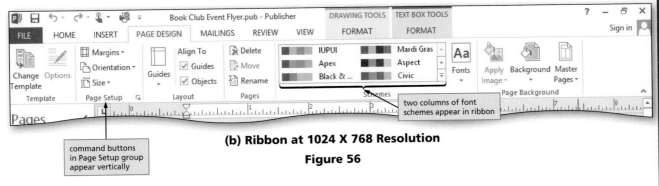

(b) Ribbon at 1024 X 768 Resolution

Figure 56

To Change the Screen Resolution

1 SIGN IN | 2 USE WINDOWS | 3 USE APPS | 4 FILE MANAGEMENT | 5 SWITCH APPS | 6 SAVE FILES
7 CHANGE SCREEN RESOLUTION | 8 EXIT APPS | 9 USE ADDITIONAL APP FEATURES | 10 USE HELP

If you are using a computer to step through the chapters in this book and you want your screen to match the figures, you may need to change your screen's resolution. *Why? The figures in this book use a screen resolution of 1366 × 768.* The following steps change the screen resolution to 1366 × 768. Your computer already may be set to 1366 × 768. Keep in mind that many computer labs prevent users from changing the screen resolution; in that case, read the following steps for illustration purposes.

1

- Tap or click the Show desktop button, which is located at the far-right edge of the taskbar, to display the Windows desktop.

Q&A I cannot see the Show desktop button. Why not?
When you point to the far-right edge of the taskbar, a small outline appears to mark the Show desktop button.

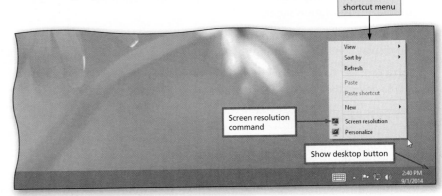

Figure 57

- Press and hold or right-click an empty area on the Windows desktop to display a shortcut menu that contains a list of commands related to the desktop (Figure 57).

Q&A Why does my shortcut menu display different commands?
Depending on your computer's hardware and configuration, different commands might appear on the shortcut menu.

2

- Tap or click Screen resolution on the shortcut menu to open the Screen Resolution window (Figure 58).

3

- Tap or click the Resolution button in the Screen Resolution window to display the resolution slider.

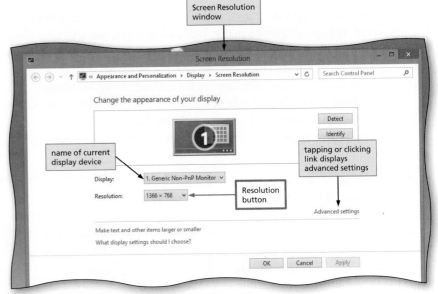

Figure 58

- If necessary, drag the resolution slider until the desired screen resolution (in this case, 1366 × 768) is selected (Figure 59).

Q&A

What if my computer does not support the 1366 × 768 resolution?

Some computers do not support the 1366 ×768 resolution. In this case, select a resolution that is close to the 1366 × 768 resolution.

What is a slider?

A **slider** is an object that allows users to choose from multiple predetermined options. In most cases, these options represent some type of numeric value. In most cases, one end of the slider (usually the left or bottom) represents the lowest of available values, and the opposite end (usually the right or top) represents the highest available value.

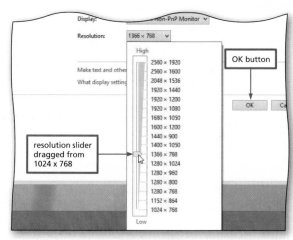

Figure 59

- Tap or click an empty area of the Screen Resolution window to close the resolution slider.

- Tap or click the OK button to change the screen resolution and display the Display Settings dialog box (Figure 60).

- Tap or click the Keep changes button (Display Settings dialog box) to accept the new screen resolution.

Q&A

Why does a message display stating that the image quality can be improved?

Some computer monitors or screens are designed to display contents better at a certain screen resolution, sometimes referred to as an optimal resolution.

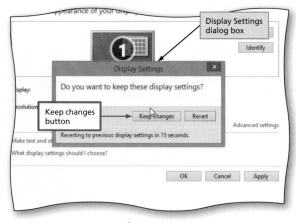

Figure 60

To Exit an App with One Document Open

1 SIGN IN | 2 USE WINDOWS | 3 USE APPS | 4 FILE MANAGEMENT | 5 SWITCH APPS | 6 SAVE FILES
7 CHANGE SCREEN RESOLUTION | 8 EXIT APPS | 9 USE ADDITIONAL APP FEATURES | 10 USE HELP

When you exit an Office app, such as Publisher, if you have made changes to a file since the last time the file was saved, the app displays a dialog box asking if you want to save the changes you made to the file before it closes the app window. *Why? The dialog box contains three buttons with these resulting actions: the Save button saves the changes and then exits the Office app, the Don't Save button exits the Office app without saving changes, and the Cancel button closes the dialog box and redisplays the file without saving the changes.*

If no changes have been made to an open publication since the last time the file was saved, the Office app will close the window without displaying a dialog box.

The following steps exit Publisher. You would follow similar steps in other Office apps.

- If necessary, tap or click the Publisher app button on the taskbar to display the Publisher window on the desktop.

- If you are using a mouse, point to the Close button on the right side of the Publisher window title bar (Figure 61).

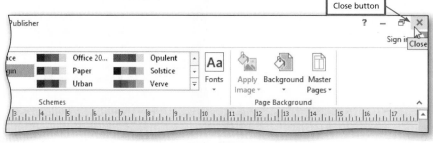

Figure 61

2

- Tap or click the Close button to close the publication and exit Publisher.

Q&A | What if I have more than one publication open in Publisher?
You could click the Close button for each open publication. When you click the last open publication Close button, you also exit Publisher. As an alternative that is more efficient, you could press and hold or right-click the Publisher app button on the taskbar and then tap or click 'Close all windows' on the shortcut menu to close all open publications and exit Publisher.

3

- If a Microsoft Publisher dialog box appears, tap or click the Save button to save any changes made to the publication since the last save.

Other Ways

1. Press and hold or right-click the Publisher app button on Windows taskbar, click 'Close all windows' on shortcut menu   2. Press ALT+F4

To Copy a Folder to a USB Flash Drive

1 SIGN IN | 2 USE WINDOWS | 3 USE APPS | **4 FILE MANAGEMENT** | 5 SWITCH APPS | 6 SAVE FILES
7 CHANGE SCREEN RESOLUTION | 8 EXIT APPS | **9 USE ADDITIONAL APP FEATURES** | 10 USE HELP

To store files and folders on a USB flash drive, you must connect the USB flash drive to an available USB port on a computer. The following steps copy your CIS 101 folder to a USB flash drive. *Why? It often is good practice to have a backup of your files. Besides SkyDrive, you can save files to a portable storage device, such as a USB flash drive.* If you are using Windows 7, skip these steps and instead perform the steps in the yellow box that immediately follows these Windows 8 steps.

1

- Insert a USB flash drive in an available USB port on the computer to connect the USB flash drive.

Q&A | How can I ensure the USB flash drive is connected?
In File Explorer, you can use the navigation bar to find the USB flash drive. If it is not showing, then it is not connected properly.

2

- Tap or click the File Explorer app button on the taskbar to make the folder window the active window.

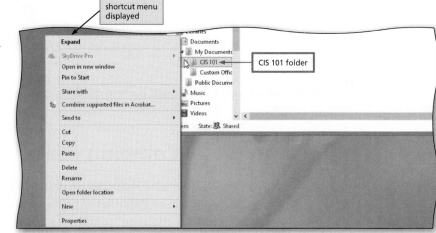

Figure 62

- If necessary, navigate to the CIS 101 folder in the File Explorer window (see Step 4a on page OFF 30 for instructions about navigating to a folder location).

- Press and hold or right-click the CIS 101 folder to display a shortcut menu (Figure 62).

3

- Tap or click Send to, which causes a submenu to appear (Figure 63).

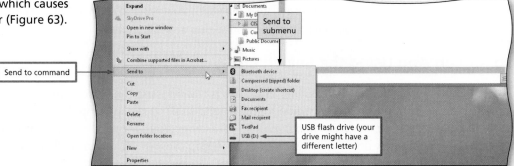

Figure 63

- Tap or click the USB flash drive to copy the folder to the USB flash drive (Figure 64).

Q&A Why does the drive letter of my USB flash drive differ?
Windows assigns the next available drive letter to your USB flash drive when you connect it. The next available drive letter may vary by computer, depending on the number of storage devices that currently are connected.

Figure 64

To Copy a Folder to a USB Flash Drive Using Windows 7

If you are using Windows 7, perform these steps to copy a folder to a USB flash drive instead of the previous steps that use Windows 8.

1. Insert a USB flash drive in an available USB port on the computer to open the AutoPlay window.
2. Click the 'Open folder to view files' link in the AutoPlay window to open the Windows Explorer window.
3. Navigate to the Documents library.
4. Right-click the CIS 101 folder to display a shortcut menu.
5. Point to Send to, which causes a submenu to appear.
6. Click the USB flash drive to copy the folder to the USB flash drive.

Break Point: If you wish to take a break, this is a good place to do so. To resume at a later time, continue to follow the steps from this location forward.

BTW
The Charms Bar
When you swipe in from the right edge of the screen or point to the upper-right edge of your screen, Windows displays the **Charms bar** with commands to help you use and manage the operating system. The Charms bar contains five buttons: Search, Share, Start, Devices, and Settings.

Additional Common Features of Office Apps

The previous section used Publisher to illustrate common features of Office and some basic elements unique to Publisher. The following sections continue to use Publisher to present additional common features of Office.

In the following pages, you will learn how to do the following:

1. Use the Charms bar.
2. Run Publisher using the search box.
3. Open a publication in Publisher.
4. Close the publication.
5. Reopen the publication just closed.
6. Create a blank Publisher publication from Windows Explorer and then open the file.
7. Save a publication with a new file name.

To Run an App Using the Search Box

1 SIGN IN | 2 USE WINDOWS | 3 USE APPS | 4 FILE MANAGEMENT | 5 SWITCH APPS | 6 SAVE FILES
7 CHANGE SCREEN RESOLUTION | 8 EXIT APPS | 9 USE ADDITIONAL APP FEATURES | 10 USE HELP

The following steps, which assume Windows is running, use the search box to run Publisher based on a typical installation; however, you would follow similar steps to run any app. *Why? Sometimes an app does not appear on the Start screen, so you can find it quickly by searching.* You may need to ask your instructor how to run apps for your computer. If you are using Windows 7, skip these steps and instead perform the steps in the yellow box that immediately follows these Windows 8 steps.

1

- Swipe in from the right edge of the screen or point to the upper-right corner of the screen to display the Charms bar (Figure 65).

Q&A My Charms bar looks different. Did I do something wrong?

If you swipe in from the right edge of the screen, the Charms bar displays buttons on a black background with white labels.

Figure 65

2

- Tap or click the Search charm on the Charms bar to display the Search menu (Figure 66).

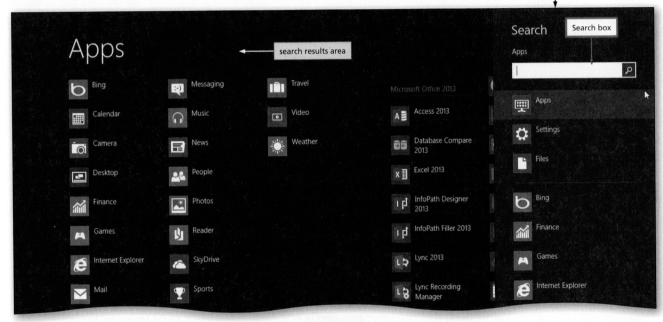

Figure 66

3

- Type **Publisher 2013** as the search text in the Search box and watch the search results appear in the Apps list (Figure 67).

Q&A Do I need to type the complete app name or use correct capitalization?

No, you need to type just enough characters of the app name for it to appear in the Apps list. For example, you may be able to type Publisher or publisher, instead of Publisher 2013.

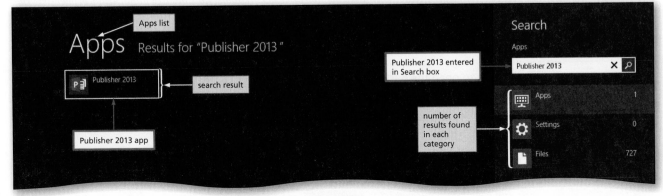

Figure 67

- Tap or click Publisher 2013 in the search results to run Publisher.

- Tap or click the Blank 8.5 × 11" thumbnail to create a blank publication and display it in the Publisher window.

- If the Publisher window is not maximized, tap or click the Maximize button on its title bar to maximize the window (Figure 68).

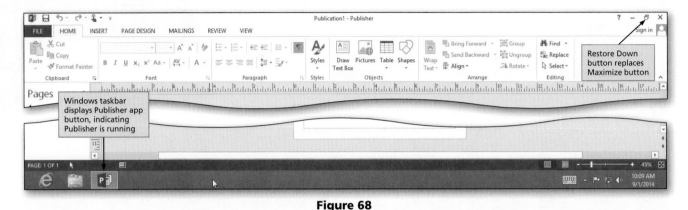

Figure 68

TO RUN AN APP USING THE SEARCH BOX USING WINDOWS 7

If you are using Windows 7, perform these steps to run an app using the search box instead of the previous steps that use Windows 8.

1. Click the Start button on the Windows 7 taskbar to display the Start menu.

2. Type **Publisher 2013** as the search text in the 'Search programs and files' text box and watch the search results appear on the Start menu.

3. Click Publisher 2013 in the search results on the Start menu to run Publisher.

4. Click the Blank 8.5 × 11" thumbnail to create a blank publication and display it in the Publisher window.

5. If the Publisher window is not maximized, click the Maximize button on its title bar to maximize the window.

To Open an Existing File

1 SIGN IN | 2 USE WINDOWS | 3 USE APPS | 4 FILE MANAGEMENT | 5 SWITCH APPS | 6 SAVE FILES
7 CHANGE SCREEN RESOLUTION | 8 EXIT APPS | 9 USE ADDITIONAL APP FEATURES | 10 USE HELP

As discussed earlier, the Backstage view contains a set of commands that enable you to manage publication and data about the publication. *Why? From the Backstage view in Publisher, for example, you can create, open, print, and save publication. You also can share publication, manage versions, set permissions, and modify publication properties. In other Office 2013 apps, the Backstage view may contain features specific to those apps.* The following steps open a saved file, specifically the Book Club Event Flyer file, that recently was saved.

- Tap or click FILE on the ribbon to open the Backstage view and then tap or click Open in the Backstage view to display the Open gallery in the Backstage view.

- Tap or click Computer to display recent folders accessed on your computer.

- Tap or click the Browse button to display the Open Publication dialog box.

- If necessary, navigate to the location of the file to open as described in Steps 4a and 4b on page OFF 30.

- Tap or click the file to open, Book Club Event Flyer in this case, to select the file (Figure 69).

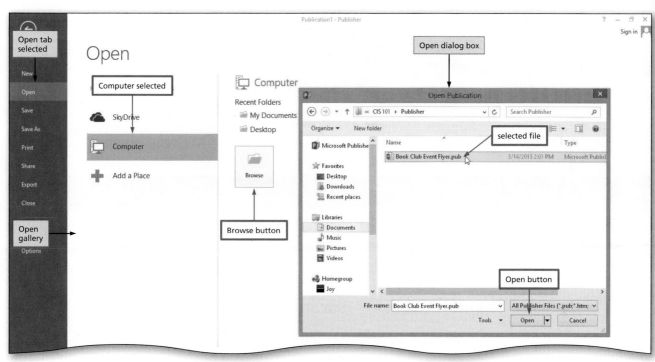

Figure 69

 2

- Tap or click the Open button (Open dialog box) to open the file (shown in Figure 47 on page OFF 30).

Other Ways
1. Press CTRL+O   2. Navigate to file in File Explorer window, double-tap or double-click file

To Create a New Publication from the Backstage View

1 SIGN IN | 2 USE WINDOWS | 3 USE APPS | 4 FILE MANAGEMENT | 5 SWITCH APPS | 6 SAVE FILES
7 CHANGE SCREEN RESOLUTION | 8 EXIT APPS | 9 **USE ADDITIONAL APP FEATURES** | 10 USE HELP

You can open multiple documents in an Office program, such as Publisher, so that you can work on the documents at the same time. The following steps create a file, a blank publication in this case, from the Backstage view. *Why? You want to create a new publication while keeping the current publication open.*

1

- Tap or click FILE on the ribbon to open the Backstage view.

- Tap or click the New tab in the Backstage view to display the New gallery (Figure 70).

Q&A Can I create documents through the Backstage view in other Office apps?
Yes. If the Office app has a New tab in the Backstage view, the New gallery displays various options for creating a new file.

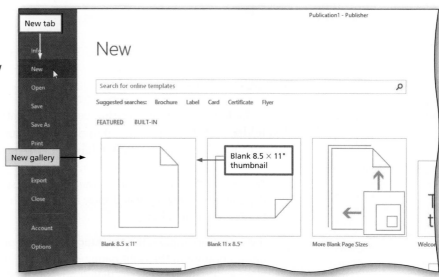

Figure 70

- Tap or click the Blank 8.5 × 11" thumbnail in the New gallery to create a new publication (Figure 71).

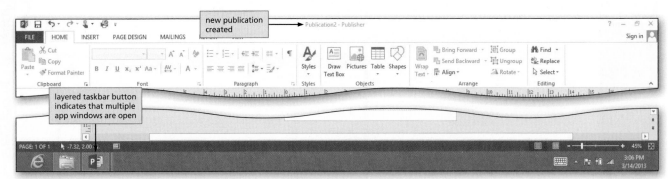

Figure 71

Other Ways

1. Press CTRL+N

To Enter Text in a Publication

The following steps enter text in a publication.

1 Tap or click the Draw a Text Box button (HOME tab | Objects group), and then drag a small text box at the top of the page layout.

2 Type **Hey girls! Let's celebrate!** and then press the ENTER key to move the insertion point to the beginning of the next line (Figure 72).

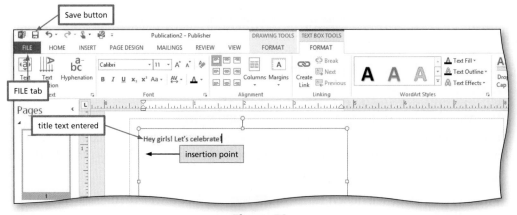

Figure 72

BTW

Customizing the Ribbon

In addition to customizing the Quick Access Toolbar, you can add items to and remove items from the ribbon. To customize the ribbon, click FILE on the ribbon to open the Backstage view, click Options in the Backstage view, and then click Customize Ribbon in the left pane of the Options dialog box. More information about customizing the ribbon is presented in a later chapter.

To Save a File in a Folder

The following steps save the second publication in the Publisher folder in the class folder (CIS 101, in this case) in the My Documents folder in the Documents library using the file name, Book Club Event Flyer 2.

1 Tap or click the Save button on the Quick Access Toolbar (shown in Figure 72), which depending on settings will display either the Save As gallery in the Backstage view or the Save As dialog box.

2 If your screen displays the Backstage view, tap or click Computer, if necessary, to display options in the right pane related to saving on your computer; if your screen already displays the Save As dialog box, proceed to Step 4.

3 Tap or click the Browse button in the right pane to display the Save As dialog box.

4 If necessary, type **Book Club Event Flyer 2** in the File name box (Save As dialog box) to change the file name. Do not press the ENTER key after typing the file name because you do not want to close the dialog box at this time.

5 If necessary, navigate to the desired save location (in this case, the Publisher folder in the CIS 101 folder [or your class folder] in the My Documents folder in the Documents library). For specific instructions, perform the tasks in Steps 4a and 4b on page OFF 30.

6 Tap or click the Save button (Save As dialog box) to save the publication in the selected folder on the selected drive with the entered file name.

To Close a File Using the Backstage View

1 SIGN IN | 2 USE WINDOWS | 3 USE APPS | 4 FILE MANAGEMENT | 5 SWITCH APPS | 6 SAVE FILES
7 CHANGE SCREEN RESOLUTION | 8 EXIT APPS | **9 USE ADDITIONAL APP FEATURES** | **10 USE HELP**

Sometimes, you may want to close an Office file, such as a Publisher publication, entirely and start over with a new file. *Why else would I close a file? You also may want to close a file when you are finished working with it so that you can begin a new file.* The following steps close the current active Publisher file, without exiting Publisher.

1

- Tap or click FILE on the ribbon (shown in Figure 72) to open the Backstage view (Figure 73).

2

- Tap or click Close in the Backstage view to close the open file (Book Club Event Flyer 2, in this case) without exiting the active app.

Q&A

What if Publisher displays a dialog box about saving?

Tap or click the Save button if you want to save the changes, tap or click the Don't Save button if you want to ignore the changes since the last time you saved, and tap or click the Cancel button if you do not want to close the publication.

Can I use the Backstage view to close an open file in other Office apps, such as PowerPoint and Excel?

Yes.

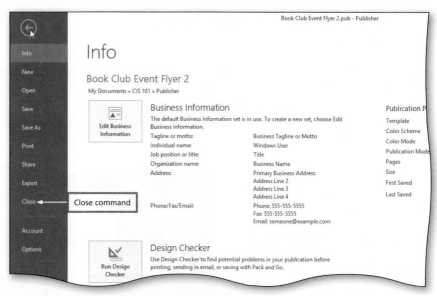

Figure 73

Other Ways

1. Press CTRL+F4

To Open a Recent File Using the Backstage View

1 SIGN IN | 2 USE WINDOWS | 3 USE APPS | 4 FILE MANAGEMENT | 5 SWITCH APPS | 6 SAVE FILES
7 CHANGE SCREEN RESOLUTION | 8 EXIT APPS | **9 USE ADDITIONAL APP FEATURES** | **10 USE HELP**

You sometimes need to open a file that you recently modified. *Why? You may have more changes to make, such as adding more content or correcting errors.* The Backstage view allows you to access recent files easily. The following steps reopen the Book Club Event Flyer 2 file just closed.

- Tap or click FILE on the ribbon to open the Backstage view.
- Tap or click the Open tab in the Backstage view to display the Open gallery (Figure 74).

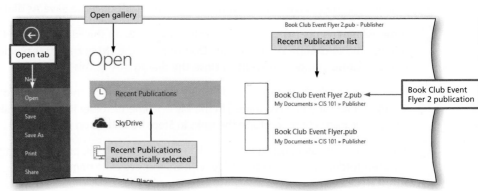

Figure 74

- Tap or click the desired file name in the Recent Publication list, Book Club Event Flyer 2 in this case, to open the file (shown in Figure 72).

Q&A | Can I use the Backstage view to open a recent file in other Office apps, such as PowerPoint and Excel?
Yes, as long as the file name appears in the list of recent files.

Other Ways

1. Tap or click FILE on ribbon, tap or click Open in Backstage view, tap or click Computer, tap or click Browse, navigate to file (Open dialog box), tap or click Open button

To Create a New Blank Publication from File Explorer

1 SIGN IN | 2 USE WINDOWS | 3 USE APPS | 4 FILE MANAGEMENT | 5 SWITCH APPS | 6 SAVE FILES
7 CHANGE SCREEN RESOLUTION | 8 EXIT APPS | 9 USE ADDITIONAL APP FEATURES | 10 USE HELP

File Explorer provides a means to create a blank Office document without running an Office app. The following steps use File Explorer to create a blank Publisher publication. *Why? Sometimes you might need to create a blank publication and then return to it later for editing.* If you are using Windows 7, skip these steps and instead perform the steps in the yellow box that immediately follows these Windows 8 steps.

- Double-tap or double-click the File Explorer app button on the taskbar to make the folder window the active window.
- If necessary, double-tap or double-click the Documents library in the navigation pane to expand the Documents library.
- If necessary, double-tap or double-click the My Documents folder in the navigation pane to expand the My Documents folder.
- If necessary, double-tap or double-click your class folder (CIS 101, in this case) in the navigation pane to expand the folder.
- Tap or click the Publisher folder in the navigation pane to display its contents in the file list.
- With the Publisher folder selected, press and hold or right-click an open area in the file list to display a shortcut menu.

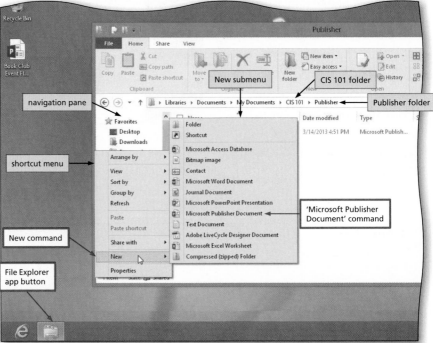

Figure 75

- Tap or point to New on the shortcut menu to display the New submenu (Figure 75).

- Tap or click 'Microsoft Publisher Document' on the New submenu to display an icon and text box for a new file in the current folder window with the file name, New Microsoft Publisher Document, selected (Figure 76).

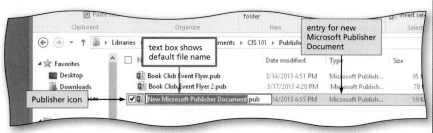

Figure 76

- Type **Book Club Invitation** in the text box and then press the ENTER key to assign a new name to the new file in the current folder (Figure 77).

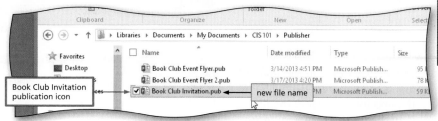

Figure 77

TO CREATE A NEW BLANK PUBLICATION FROM WINDOWS EXPLORER USING WINDOWS 7

If you are using Windows 7, perform these steps to create a new blank Office document from Windows Explorer instead of the previous steps that use Windows 8.

1. If necessary, click the Windows Explorer button on the taskbar to make the folder window the active window.

2. If necessary, double-click the Documents library in the navigation pane to expand the Documents library.

3. If necessary, double-click the My Documents folder in the navigation pane to expand the My Documents folder.

4. If necessary, double-click your class folder (CIS 101, in this case) in the navigation pane to expand the folder.

5. Click the Publisher folder in the navigation pane to display its contents in the file list.

6. With the Publisher folder selected, right-click an open area in the file list to display a shortcut menu.

7. Point to New on the shortcut menu to display the New submenu.

8. Click 'Microsoft Publisher Document' on the New submenu to display an icon and text box for a new file in the current folder window with the name, New Microsoft Publisher Document, selected.

9. Type **Book Club Invitation** in the text box and then press the ENTER key to assign a new name to the new file in the current folder.

To Run an App from File Explorer and Open a File

1 SIGN IN | 2 USE WINDOWS | 3 USE APPS | 4 FILE MANAGEMENT | 5 SWITCH APPS | 6 SAVE FILES
7 CHANGE SCREEN RESOLUTION | 8 EXIT APPS | 9 USE ADDITIONAL APP FEATURES | 10 USE HELP

Previously, you learned how to run Publisher using the Start screen and the Search charm. The following steps, which assume Windows is running, use File Explorer to run Publisher based on a typical installation. *Why? Another way to run an Office app is to open an existing file from File Explorer, which causes the app in which the file was created to run and then open the selected file.* You may need to ask your instructor how to run Publisher for your computer. If you are using Windows 7, follow the steps in the yellow box that immediately follows these Windows 8 steps.

- If necessary, display the file to open in the folder window in File Explorer (shown in Figure 77 on the previous page).

- Press and hold or right-click the file icon or file name (Book Club Invitation, in this case) to display a shortcut menu (Figure 78).

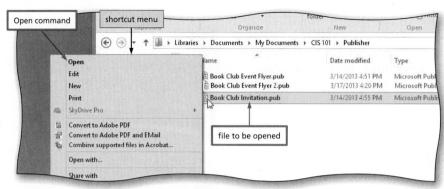

Figure 78

- Tap or click Open on the shortcut menu to open the selected file in the app used to create the file, Publisher in this case (Figure 79).

- If the Publisher window is not maximized, tap or click the Maximize button on the title bar to maximize the window.

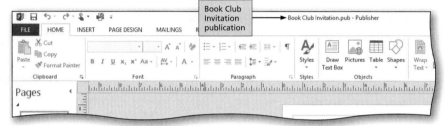

Figure 79

TO RUN AN APP FROM WINDOWS EXPLORER AND OPEN A FILE USING WINDOWS 7

If you are using Windows 7, perform these steps to run an app from Windows Explorer and open a file instead of the previous steps that use Windows 8.

1. Display the file to open in the folder window in Windows Explorer.

2. Right-click the file icon or file name (Book Club Invitation, in this case) to display a shortcut menu.

3. Click Open on the shortcut menu to open the selected file in the app used to create the file, Publisher in this case.

4. If the Publisher window is not maximized, click the Maximize button on the title bar to maximize the window.

To Enter Text in a Publication

The next step is to enter text in this blank Publisher publication. The following step enters a line of text.

1 Draw a text box and then type **Book Club Invitation** and then press the ENTER key to move the insertion point to the beginning of the next line (shown in Figure 80).

To Save an Existing File with the Same File Name

1 SIGN IN | 2 USE WINDOWS | 3 USE APPS | 4 FILE MANAGEMENT | 5 SWITCH APPS | 6 SAVE FILES
7 CHANGE SCREEN RESOLUTION | 8 EXIT APPS | 9 USE ADDITIONAL APP FEATURES | 10 USE HELP

Saving frequently cannot be overemphasized. *Why? You have made modifications to the file (publication) since you created it. Thus, you should save again. Similarly, you should continue saving files frequently so that you do not lose the changes you have made since the time you last saved the file.* You can use the same file name, such as Book Club Invitation, to save the changes made to the publication. The following step saves a file again with the same file name.

1

- Tap or click the Save button on the Quick Access Toolbar to overwrite the previously saved file (Book Club Invitation, in this case) in the Publisher folder (Figure 80).

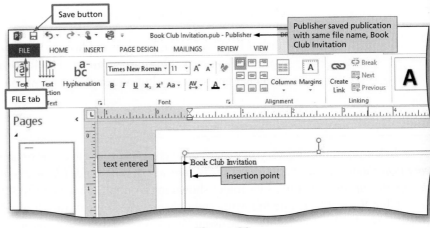

Figure 80

Other Ways

1. Press CTRL+S or press SHIFT+F12

To Save a File with a New File Name

You might want to save a file with a different name or to a different location. For example, you might start a homework assignment with a data file and then save it with a final file name for submission to your instructor, saving it to a location designated by your instructor. The following steps save a file with a different file name.

1 Tap or click the FILE tab to open the Backstage view.

2 Tap or click the Save As tab to display the Save As gallery.

3 If necessary, tap or click Computer to display options in the right pane related to saving on your computer.

4 Tap or click the Browse button in the right pane to display the Save As dialog box.

5 Type **Book Club Invitation List** in the File name box (Save As dialog box) to change the file name. Do not press the ENTER key after typing the file name because you do not want to close the dialog box at this time.

6 If necessary, navigate to the desired save location (in this case, the Publisher folder in the CIS 101 folder [or your class folder] in the My Documents folder in the Documents library). For specific instructions, perform the tasks in Steps 4a and 4b on page OFF 30.

7 Tap or click the Save button (Save As dialog box) to save the publication in the selected folder on the selected drive with the entered file name.

To Exit an Office App

You are finished using Publisher. The following steps exit Publisher. You would use similar steps to exit other Office apps.

1 Because you have multiple Publisher publications open, press and hold or right-click the app button on the taskbar and then tap or click 'Close all windows' on the shortcut menu to close all open publications and exit Publisher.

2 If a dialog box appears, tap or click the Save button to save any changes made to the file since the last save.

Renaming, Moving, and Deleting Files

Earlier in this chapter, you learned how to organize files in folders, which is part of a process known as **file management**. The following sections cover additional file management topics including renaming, moving, and deleting files.

To Rename a File

1 SIGN IN | 2 USE WINDOWS | 3 USE APPS | **4 FILE MANAGEMENT** | 5 SWITCH APPS | 6 SAVE FILES
7 CHANGE SCREEN RESOLUTION | 8 EXIT APPS | 9 USE ADDITIONAL APP FEATURES | **10 USE HELP**

In some circumstances, you may want to change the name of, or rename, a file or a folder. *Why? You may want to distinguish a file in one folder or drive from a copy of a similar file, or you may decide to rename a file to better identify its contents.* The Publisher folder shown in Figure 64 on page OFF 40 contains the Publisher publication, Book Club Event Flyer. The following steps change the name of the Book Club Event Flyer file in the Publisher folder to Book Club Flyer. If you are using Windows 7, skip these steps and instead perform the steps in the yellow box that immediately follows these Windows 8 steps.

1

- If necessary, tap or click the File Explorer app button on the taskbar to make the folder window the active window.

- If necessary, navigate to the location of the file to be renamed (in this case, the Publisher folder in the CIS 101 [or your class folder] folder in the My Documents folder in the Documents library) to display the file(s) it contains in the file list.

- Press and hold or right-click the Book Club Event Flyer icon or file name in the file list to select the Book Club Event Flyer file and display a shortcut menu that presents a list of commands related to files (Figure 81).

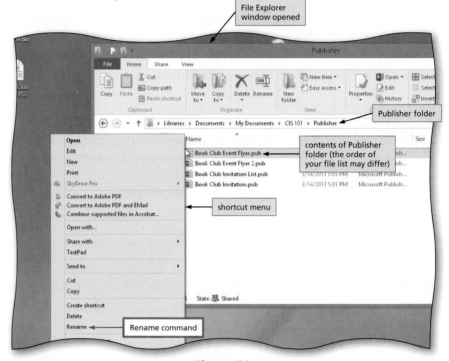

Figure 81

2

- Tap or click Rename on the shortcut menu to place the current file name in a text box.

- Type **Book Club Flyer** in the text box and then press the ENTER key (Figure 82).

Q&A

Are any risks involved in renaming files that are located on a hard disk?
If you inadvertently rename a file that is associated with certain apps, the apps may not be able to find the file and, therefore, may not run properly. Always use caution when renaming files.

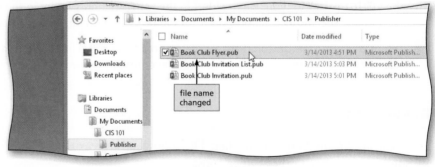

Figure 82

Can I rename a file when it is open?
No, a file must be closed to change the file name.

Other Ways

1. Select file, press F2, type new file name, press ENTER   2. Select file, tap or click Rename (Home tab | Organize group), type new file name, press ENTER

TO RENAME A FILE USING WINDOWS 7

If you are using Windows 7, perform these steps to rename a file instead of the previous steps that use Windows 8.

1. If necessary, click the Windows Explorer app button on the taskbar to make the folder window the active window.

2. Navigate to the location of the file to be renamed (in this case, the Publisher folder in the CIS 101 [or your class folder] folder in the My Documents folder in the Documents library) to display the file(s) it contains in the file list.

3. Right-click the Book Club Event Flyer icon or file name in the file list to select the Book Club Event Flyer file and display a shortcut menu that presents a list of commands related to files.

4. Click Rename on the shortcut menu to place the current file name in a text box.

5. Type **Book Club Flyer** in the text box and then press the ENTER key.

To Move a File

1 SIGN IN | 2 USE WINDOWS | 3 USE APPS | **4 FILE MANAGEMENT** | 5 SWITCH APPS | 6 SAVE FILES
7 CHANGE SCREEN RESOLUTION | 8 EXIT APPS | 9 USE ADDITIONAL APP FEATURES | **10 USE HELP**

Why? *At some time, you may want to move a file from one folder, called the source folder, to another, called the destination folder.* When you move a file, it no longer appears in the original folder. If the destination and the source folders are on the same media, you can move a file by dragging it. If the folders are on different media, then you will need to press and hold and then drag, or right-drag the file, and then click Move here on the shortcut menu. The following step moves the Book Club Flyer file from the Publisher folder to the CIS 101 folder. If you are using Windows 7, skip these steps and instead perform the steps in the yellow box that immediately follows these Windows 8 steps.

- In File Explorer, if necessary, navigate to the location of the file to be moved (in this case, the Publisher folder in the CIS 101 folder [or your class folder] in the Documents library).

- If necessary, tap or click the Publisher folder in the navigation pane to display the files it contains in the right pane.

- Drag the Book Club Flyer file in the right pane to the CIS 101 folder in the navigation pane and notice the ScreenTip as you drag the mouse (Figure 83).

🔎 **Experiment**

- Click the CIS 101 folder in the navigation pane to verify that the file was moved.

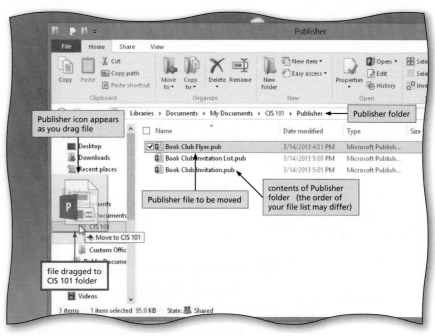

Figure 83

1. Press and hold or right-click file to move, tap or click Cut on shortcut menu, press and hold or right-click destination folder, tap or click Paste on shortcut menu   2. Select file to move, press CTRL+X, select destination folder, press CTRL+V

To Move a File Using Windows 7

If you are using Windows 7, perform these steps to move a file instead of the previous steps that use Windows 8.

1. In Windows Explorer, navigate to the location of the file to be moved (in this case, the Publisher folder in the CIS 101 folder [or your class folder] in the Documents library).

2. Click the Publisher folder in the navigation pane to display the files it contains in the right pane.

3. Drag the Book Club Flyer file in the right pane to the CIS 101 folder in the navigation pane.

To Delete a File

1 SIGN IN | 2 USE WINDOWS | 3 USE APPS | **4 FILE MANAGEMENT** | 5 SWITCH APPS | 6 SAVE FILES
7 CHANGE SCREEN RESOLUTION | 8 EXIT APPS | 9 USE ADDITIONAL APP FEATURES | **10 USE HELP**

A final task you may want to perform is to delete a file. Exercise extreme caution when deleting a file or files. When you delete a file from a hard disk, the deleted file is stored in the Recycle Bin where you can recover it until you empty the Recycle Bin. If you delete a file from removable media, such as a USB flash drive, the file is deleted permanently. The next steps delete the Book Club Flyer file from the CIS 101 folder. *Why? When a file no longer is needed, you can delete it to conserve space in your storage location.* If you are using Windows 7, skip these steps and instead perform the steps in the yellow box that immediately follows these Windows 8 steps.

- In File Explorer, navigate to the location of the file to be deleted (in this case, the CIS 101 folder [or your class folder] in the Documents library).

- Press and hold or right-click the Book Club Flyer icon or file name in the right pane to select the file and display a shortcut menu (Figure 84).

- Tap or click Delete on the shortcut menu to delete the file.

- If a dialog box appears, tap or click the Yes button to delete the file.

Q&A   Can I use this same technique to delete a folder?
Yes. Press and hold or right-click the folder and then tap or click Delete on the shortcut menu. When you delete a folder, all of the files and folders contained in the folder you are deleting, together with any files and folders on lower hierarchical levels, are deleted as well.

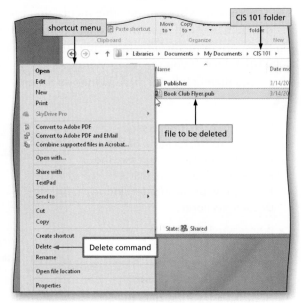

Figure 84

Other Ways

1. Select icon, press DELETE

To Delete a File Using Windows 7

If you are using Windows 7, perform these steps to delete a file instead of the previous steps that use Windows 8.

1. In Windows Explorer, navigate to the location of the file to be deleted (in this case, the CIS 101 folder [or your class folder] in the Documents library).

2. Right-click the Book Club Flyer icon or file name in the right pane to select the file and display a shortcut menu.

3. Click Delete on the shortcut menu to delete the file.

4. If a dialog box appears, click the Yes button to delete the file.

Microsoft Office and Windows Help

At any time while you are using one of the Office apps, such as Publisher, you can use Office Help to display information about all topics associated with the app. This section illustrates the use of Publisher Help. Help in other Office apps operates in a similar fashion.

In Office, Help is presented in a window that has browser-style navigation buttons. Each Office app has its own Help home page, which is the starting Help page that is displayed in the Help window. If your computer is connected to the Internet, the contents of the Help page reflect both the local help files installed on the computer and material from Microsoft's website.

To Open the Help Window in Publisher

1 SIGN IN | 2 USE WINDOWS | 3 USE APPS | 4 FILE MANAGEMENT | 5 SWITCH APPS | 6 SAVE FILES
7 CHANGE SCREEN RESOLUTION | 8 EXIT APPS | 9 USE ADDITIONAL APP FEATURES | 10 USE HELP

The following step opens the Publisher Help window. *Why? You might not understand how certain commands or operations work in Publisher, so you can obtain the necessary information using help.* The step to open a Help window in other Office programs is similar.

- Run Publisher and open a blank file.

- Tap or click the Microsoft Publisher Help button near the upper-right corner of the app window to open the Publisher Help window (Figure 85).

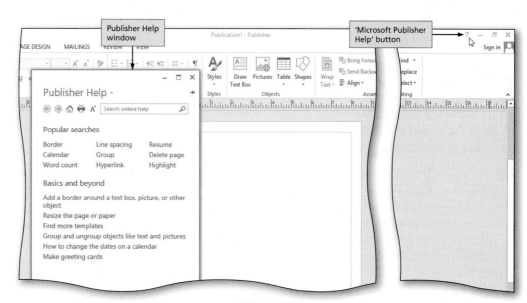

Figure 85

Other Ways
1. Press F1

Moving and Resizing Windows

At times, it is useful, or even necessary, to have more than one window open and visible on the screen at the same time. You can resize and move these open windows so that you can view different areas of and elements in the window. In the case of the Help window, for example, it could be covering publication text in the Publisher window that you need to see.

To Move a Window by Dragging

1 SIGN IN | 2 USE WINDOWS | 3 USE APPS | 4 FILE MANAGEMENT | 5 SWITCH APPS | 6 SAVE FILES
7 CHANGE SCREEN RESOLUTION | 8 EXIT APPS | 9 USE ADDITIONAL APP FEATURES | 10 USE HELP

You can move any open window that is not maximized to another location on the desktop by dragging the title bar of the window. *Why? You might want to have a better view of what is behind the window or just want to move the window so that you can see it better.* The following step drags the Publisher Help window to the upper-left corner of the desktop.

- Drag the window title bar (the Publisher Help window title bar, in this case) so that the window moves to the upper-left corner of the desktop, as shown in Figure 86.

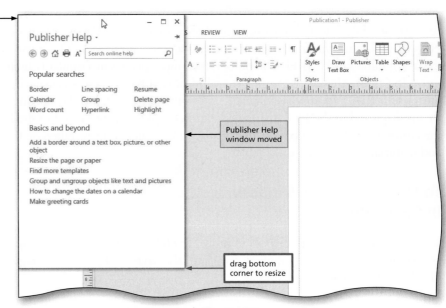

Figure 86

To Resize a Window by Dragging

1 SIGN IN | 2 USE WINDOWS | 3 USE APPS | 4 FILE MANAGEMENT | 5 SWITCH APPS | 6 SAVE FILES
7 CHANGE SCREEN RESOLUTION | 8 EXIT APPS | 9 USE ADDITIONAL APP FEATURES | 10 USE HELP

A method used to change the size of the window is to drag the window borders. The following step changes the size of the Publisher Help window by dragging its borders. *Why? Sometimes, information is not visible completely in a window, and you want to increase the size of the window.*

- If you are using a mouse, point to the lower-right corner of the window (the Publisher Help window, in this case) until the pointer changes to a two-headed arrow.

- Drag the bottom border downward to display more of the active window (Figure 87).

Q&A

Can I drag other borders on the window to enlarge or shrink the window?
Yes, you can drag the left, right, and top borders and any window corner to resize a window.

Will Windows remember the new size of the window after I close it?
Yes. When you reopen the window, Windows will display it at the same size it was when you closed it.

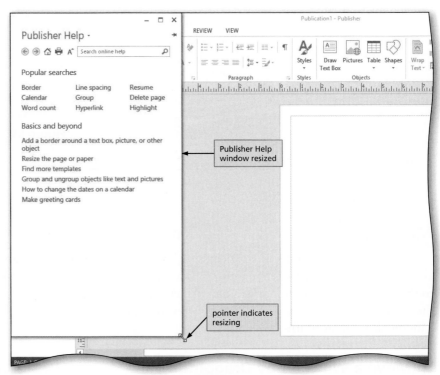

Figure 87

Using Office Help

Once an Office app's Help window is open, several methods exist for navigating Help. You can search for help by using any of the three following methods from the Help window:

1. Enter search text in the 'Search online help' text box.
2. Click the links in the Help window.
3. Use the Table of Contents.

To Obtain Help Using the 'Search online help' Text Box

1 SIGN IN | 2 USE WINDOWS | 3 USE APPS | 4 FILE MANAGEMENT | 5 SWITCH APPS | 6 SAVE FILES
7 CHANGE SCREEN RESOLUTION | 8 EXIT APPS | 9 USE ADDITIONAL APP FEATURES | 10 USE HELP

Assume for the following example that you want to know more about cropping. The following steps use the 'Search online help' text box to obtain useful information about cropping by entering the word, crop, as search text. *Why?* *You may not know the exact help topic you are looking to find, so using keywords can help narrow your search.*

1

- Type **crop** in the 'Search online help' text box at the top of the Publisher Help window to enter the search text.

- Tap or click the 'Search online help' button to display the search results (Figure 88).

Q&A Why do my search results differ?
If you do not have an Internet connection, your results will reflect only the content of the Help files on your computer. When searching for help online, results also can change as material is added, deleted, and updated on the online Help webpages maintained by Microsoft.

Why were my search results not very helpful?
When initiating a search, be sure to check the spelling of the search text; also, keep your search specific to return the most accurate results.

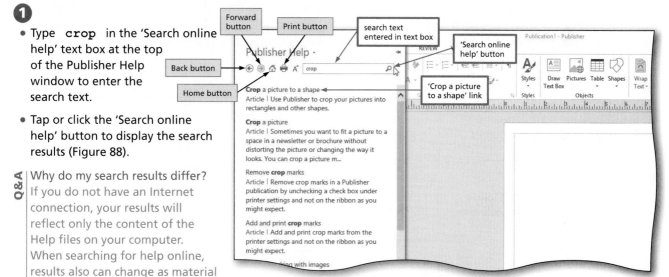

Figure 88

2

- Tap or click the 'Crop a picture to a shape' link to display the Help information associated with the selected topic (Figure 89).

Q&A What is the purpose of the Use Large Text button?
When you tap or click the Use Large Text button, the Help topics text displays in a larger font.

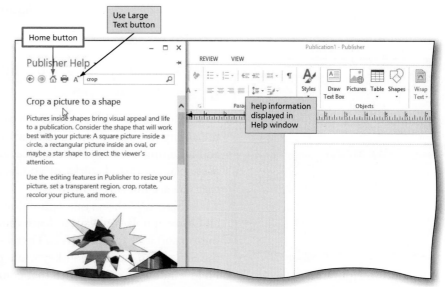

Figure 89

- Tap or click the Home button in the Help window to clear the search results and redisplay the Help home page (Figure 90).

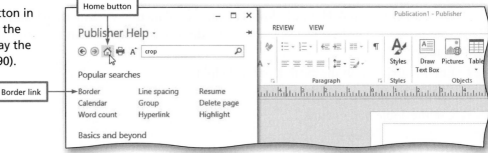

Figure 90

To Obtain Help Using Help Links

If your topic of interest is listed in the Help window, you can click the link to begin browsing the Help categories instead of entering search text. **Why?** *You browse Help just as you would browse a website. If you know which category contains your Help information, you may wish to use these links.* The following step finds the Border information using the Border link from the Publisher Help home page.

- Tap or click the Border link on the Help home page (shown in Figure 90) to display the Border help links (Figure 91).

- After reviewing the page, tap or click the Close button to close the Help window.

- Tap or click Publisher's Close button to exit Publisher.

Q&A Why does my Help window display different links?
The content of your Help window may differ because Microsoft continually updates its Help information.

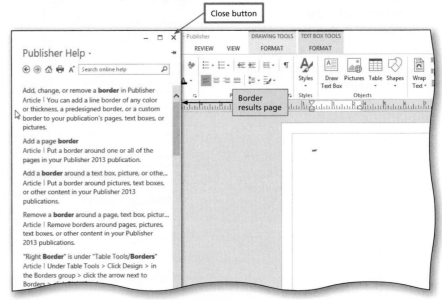

Figure 91

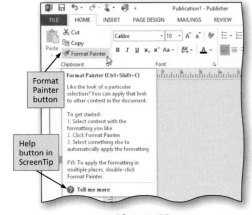

Figure 92

Obtaining Help while Working in an Office App

Help in the Office apps, such as Publisher, provides you with the ability to obtain help directly, without opening the Help window and initiating a search. For example, you may be unsure about how a particular command works, or you may be presented with a dialog box that you are not sure how to use.

Figure 92 shows one option for obtaining help while working in an Office app. If you want to learn more about a command, point to its button and wait for the ScreenTip to appear. If the Help icon appears in the ScreenTip, press the F1 key while pointing to the button to open the Help window associated with that command.

Figure 93 shows a dialog box that contains a Help button. Pressing the F1 key while the dialog box is displayed opens a Help window. The Help window contains help about that dialog box, if available. If no help file is available for that particular dialog box, then the main Help window opens.

Using Windows Help and Support

One of the more powerful Windows features is Windows Help and Support. **Windows Help and Support** is available when using Windows or when using any Microsoft app running in Windows. The same methods used for searching Microsoft Office Help can be used in Windows Help and Support. The difference is that Windows Help and Support displays help for Windows, instead of for Microsoft Office.

Figure 93

To Use Windows Help and Support

1 SIGN IN | 2 USE WINDOWS | 3 USE APPS | 4 FILE MANAGEMENT | 5 SWITCH APPS | 6 SAVE FILES
7 CHANGE SCREEN RESOLUTION | 8 EXIT APPS | 9 USE ADDITIONAL APP FEATURES | 10 USE HELP

The following steps use Windows Help and Support and open the Windows Help and Support window, which contains links to more information about Windows. *Why? This feature is designed to assist you in using Windows or the various apps.* If you are using Windows 7, skip these steps and instead perform the steps in the yellow box that immediately follows these Windows 8 steps.

● Swipe in from the right edge of the screen or point to the upper-right corner of the screen to display the Charms bar (Figure 94).

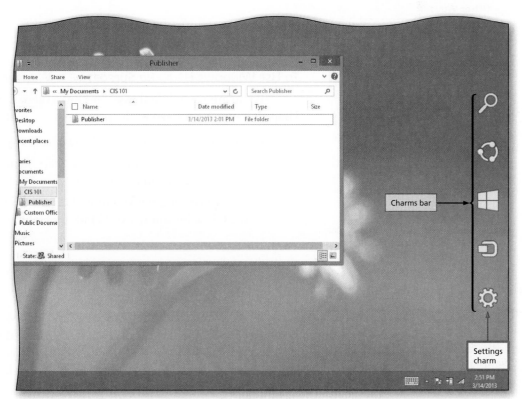

Figure 94

- Tap or click the Settings charm on the Charms bar to display the Settings menu (Figure 95).

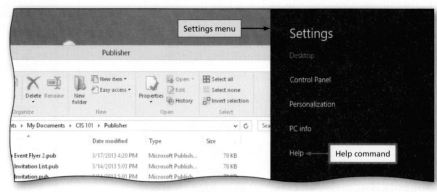

Figure 95

- Tap or click Help to open the Windows Help and Support window (Figure 96).

- After reviewing the Windows Help and Support window, tap or click the Close button to close the Windows Help and Support window.

Figure 96

Other Ways
1. Press WINDOWS + F1

TO USE WINDOWS HELP AND SUPPORT WITH WINDOWS 7

If you are using Windows 7, perform these steps to start Windows Help and Support instead of the previous steps that use Windows 8.

1. Click the Start button on the taskbar to display the Start menu.
2. Click Help and Support on the Start menu to open the Windows Help and Support window.
3. After reviewing the Windows Help and Support window, click the Close button to exit Windows Help and Support.

Chapter Summary

In this chapter, you learned how to use the Windows interface, several touch screen and mouse operations, and file and folder management. You also learned some basic features of Publisher and discovered the common elements that exist among Microsoft Office apps. The items listed below include all of the new Windows and Publisher skills you have learned in this chapter, with the tasks grouped by activity.

File Management

Create a Folder (OFF 24)
Create a Folder within a Folder (OFF 26)
Expand a Folder, Scroll through Folder Contents, and Collapse a Folder (OFF 27)
Copy a Folder to a USB Flash Drive (OFF 39)
Rename a File (OFF 50)
Move a File (OFF 51)
Delete a File (OFF 52)

Use Help

Open the Help Window in Publisher (OFF 53)
Obtain Help Using the 'Search online help' Text Box (OFF 55)
Obtain Help Using Help Links (OFF 56)
Use Windows Help and Support (OFF 57)

Use Windows

Sign In to an Account (OFF 7)
Run an App from the Start Screen (OFF 11)
Switch between an App and the Start Screen (OFF 13)
Maximize a Window (OFF 14)
Switch from One App to Another (OFF 29)
Minimize and Restore a Window (OFF 32)
Change the Screen Resolution (OFF 37)
Move a Window by Dragging (OFF 53)
Resize a Window by Dragging (OFF 54)

Use Publisher

Display a Different Tab on the Ribbon (OFF 18)
Collapse and Expand the Ribbon and Use Full Screen Mode (OFF 19)
Use a Shortcut Menu to Relocate the Quick Access Toolbar (OFF 20)
Customize the Quick Access Toolbar (OFF 21)
Enter Text in a Publication (OFF 22)
Save a File in a Folder (OFF 29)
Save a File on SkyDrive (OFF 33)
Sign Out of a Microsoft Account (OFF 35)
Exit an App with One Document Open (OFF 38)
Run an App Using the Search Box (OFF 40)
Open an Existing File (OFF 42)
Create a New Publication from the Backstage View (OFF 43)
Close a File Using the Backstage View (OFF 45)
Open a Recent File Using the Backstage View (OFF 45)
Create a New Blank Publication from File Explorer (OFF 46)
Run an App from File Explorer and Open a File (OFF 40)
Save an Existing File with the Same File Name (OFF 48)

What guidelines should you follow to plan your projects?

The process of communicating specific information is a learned, rational skill. Computers and software, especially Microsoft Office 2013, can help you develop ideas and present detailed information to a particular audience and minimize much of the laborious work of drafting and revising projects. No matter what method you use to plan a project, it is beneficial to follow some specific guidelines from the onset to arrive at a final product that is informative, relevant, and effective. Use some aspects of these guidelines every time you undertake a project, and others as needed in specific instances.

1. Determine the project's purpose.
   a) Clearly define why you are undertaking this assignment.
   b) Begin to draft ideas of how best to communicate information by handwriting ideas on paper; composing directly on a laptop, tablet, or mobile device; or developing a strategy that fits your particular thinking and writing style.

2. Analyze your audience.
   a) Learn about the people who will read, analyze, or view your work.
   b) Determine their interests and needs so that you can present the information they need to know and omit the information they already possess.
   c) Form a mental picture of these people or find photos of people who fit this profile so that you can develop a project with the audience in mind.

3. Gather possible content.
   a) Locate existing information that may reside in spreadsheets, databases, or other files.
   b) Conduct a web search to find relevant websites.
   c) Read pamphlets, magazine and newspaper articles, and books to gain insights of how others have approached your topic.
   d) Conduct personal interviews to obtain perspectives not available by any other means.
   e) Consider video and audio clips as potential sources for material that might complement or support the factual data you uncover.

CONSIDER THIS: PLAN AHEAD

4. Determine what content to present to your audience.

   a) Write three or four major ideas you want an audience member to remember after reading or viewing your project.

   b) Envision your project's endpoint, the key fact you wish to emphasize, so that all project elements lead to this final element.

   c) Determine relevant time factors, such as the length of time to develop the project, how long readers will spend reviewing your project, or the amount of time allocated for your speaking engagement.

   d) Decide whether a graph, photo, or artistic element can express or enhance a particular concept.

   e) Be mindful of the order in which you plan to present the content, and place the most important material at the top or bottom of the page, because readers and audience members generally remember the first and last pieces of information they see and hear.

✺ **How should you submit solutions to questions in the assignments identified with a ✺ symbol?**
Every assignment in this book contains one or more questions identified with a ✺ symbol. These questions require you to think beyond the assigned file. Present your solutions to the questions in the format required by your instructor. Possible formats may include one or more of these options: write the answer; create a document that contains the answer; present your answer to the class; discuss your answer in a group; record the answer as audio or video using a webcam, smartphone, or portable media player; or post answers on a blog, wiki, or website.

Apply Your Knowledge

Reinforce the skills and apply the concepts you learned in this chapter.

Creating a Folder and a Publication

Instructions: You will create a new folder and then create a publication and save it in the folder.

Perform the following tasks:

1. Open the File Explorer app and then double-tap or double-click to open the Documents library.

2. Tap or click the New folder button on the File Explorer Quick Access Toolbar to display a new folder icon and text box for the folder name.

3. Type **Apply Publisher** in the text box to name the folder. Press the ENTER key to create the folder in the Documents library.

4. Run Publisher.

5. Draw a text box and then enter the name(s) of the course(s) you are taking this semester (Figure 97).

6. If requested by your instructor, enter your name in the Publisher publication.

7. Tap or click the Save button on the Publisher Quick Access Toolbar. Navigate to the Apply Publisher folder in the Documents library and then save the publication using the file name, Apply 1 Class List.

8. If your Quick Access Toolbar does not show the Quick Print button, add the Quick Print button to the Quick Access Toolbar. Print the publication using the Quick Print button on the Quick Access Toolbar (Figure 97). When you are finished printing, remove the Quick Print button from the Quick Access Toolbar.

9. Submit the printout to your instructor and exit Publisher.

10. ✺ What other commands might you find useful to include on the Quick Access Toolbar?

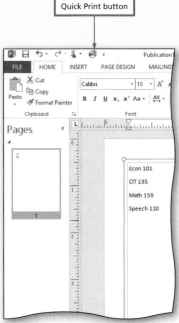

Figure 97

Extend Your Knowledge

Extend the skills you learned in this chapter and experiment with new skills. You will use Help to complete the assignment.

Using Help

Instructions: Use Publisher Help to perform the following tasks.

Perform the following tasks:

1. Run Publisher.
2. Tap or click the Microsoft Publisher Help button to open the Publisher Help window (Figure 98).
3. Search Publisher Help to answer the following questions.

   a. What are three features new to Publisher 2013?
   b. What type of training courses are available through Help?
   c. What are the steps to add a new group to the ribbon?
   d. What are Building Blocks?
   e. How do you insert clip art?
   f. What is a template?
   g. How do you insert a new page?
   h. What is a SmartArt graphic?
   i. What is cropping?
   j. Where is the Measurement toolbar?

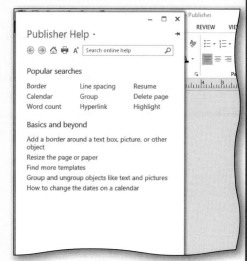

Figure 98

4. Type the answers from your searches in a new blank Publisher publication. If requested by your instructor, enter your name in the Publisher publication.
5. Save the publication with a new file name and then submit it in the format specified by your instructor.
6. Exit Publisher.
7. ✺ What search text did you use to perform the searches above? Did it take multiple attempts to search and locate the exact information for which you were searching?

Analyze, Correct, Improve

Analyze a file structure, correct all errors, and improve the design.

Organizing Vacation Photos

Note: To complete this assignment, you will be required to use the Data Files for Students. Visit www.cengage.com/ct/studentdownload for detailed instructions or contact your instructor for information about accessing the required files.

Instructions: Traditionally, you have stored photos from past vacations together in one folder. The photos are becoming difficult to manage, and you now want to store them in appropriate folders. You will create the folder structure shown in Figure 99. You then will move the photos to the folders so that they will be organized properly.

1. Correct Create the folder structure in Figure 99 so that you are able to store the photos in an organized manner. If requested by your instructor, add another folder using your last name as the folder name.

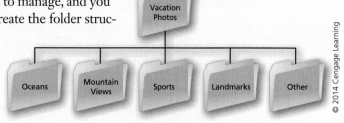

Figure 99

2. Improve View each photo and drag it to the appropriate folder to improve the organization. Submit the assignment in the format specified by your instructor.

3. ✺ In which folder did you place each photo? Think about the files you have stored on your computer. What folder hierarchy would be best to manage your files?

In the Labs

Use the guidelines, concepts, and skills presented in this chapter to increase your knowledge of Windows 8 and Publisher 2013. Labs 1 and 2, which increase in difficulty, require you to create solutions based on what you learned in the chapter; Lab 3 requires you to create a solution, which uses cloud and web technologies, by learning and investigating on your own from general guidance.

Lab 1: **Creating Folders for a Video Store**

Problem: Your friend works for Ebaird Video. He would like to organize his files in relation to the types of videos available in the store. He has six main categories: drama, action, romance, foreign, biographical, and comedy. You are to create a folder structure similar to Figure 100.

Instructions: Perform the following tasks:

1. Insert a USB flash drive in an available USB port and then open the USB flash drive window.

2. Create the main folder for Ebaird Video.

3. Navigate to the Ebaird Video folder.

4. Within the Ebaird Video folder, create a folder for each of the following: Drama, Action, Romance, Foreign, Biographical, and Comedy.

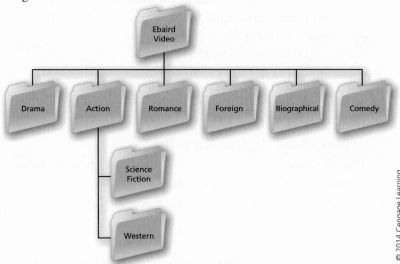

Figure 100

5. Within the Action folder, create two additional folders, one for Science Fiction and the second for Western.

6. If requested by your instructor, add another folder using your last name as the folder name.

7. Submit the assignment in the format specified by your instructor.

8. ☀ Think about how you use your computer for various tasks (consider personal, professional, and academic reasons). What folders do you think will be required on your computer to store the files you save?

Lab 2: **Saving Files in Folders**

Problem: You are taking a class that requires you to complete three Publisher chapters. You will save the work completed in each chapter in a different folder (Figure 101).

Instructions: Perform the following tasks:

1. Create a Publisher publication containing the text, First Publisher Chapter.

2. In the Backstage view, tap or click Save As and then tap or click Computer.

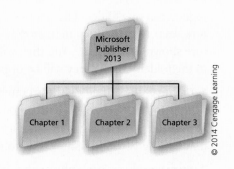

Figure 101

© 2014 Cengage Learning

3. Tap or click the Browse button to display the Save As dialog box.

4. Tap or click Documents to open the Documents library. Next, create the folder structure shown in Figure 101 using the New folder button.

5. Navigate to the Chapter 1 folder and then save the file in the Chapter 1 folder using the file name, Publisher Chapter 1 Publication.

6. Create another Publisher publication containing the text, Second Publisher Chapter, and then save it in the Chapter 2 folder using the file name, Publisher Chapter 2 Publication.

7. Create a third Publisher publication containing the text, Third Publisher Chapter, and then save it in the Chapter 3 folder using the file name, Publisher Chapter 3 Publication.

8. If requested by your instructor, add your name to each of the three Publisher files.

9. Submit the assignment in the format specified by your instructor.

10. ✺ Based on your current knowledge of Windows and Publisher, how will you organize folders for assignments in this class? Why?

Lab 3: Expand Your World: Cloud and Web Technologies
Creating Folders on SkyDrive

Problem: You are taking a class that requires you to create folders on SkyDrive (Figure 102).

Instructions: Perform the following tasks:

1. Sign in to SkyDrive in your browser.

2. Use the Create button to create the folder structure shown in Figure 102.

3. Create a blank publication. Draw a text box and enter the steps in this assignment.

4. If requested by your instructor, add your name to the publication.

5. Save the publication in the Word folder and then exit the app.

6. Submit the assignment in the format specified by your instructor.

7. ✺ Based on your current knowledge of SkyDrive, do you think you will use it? What about the Publisher Web App?

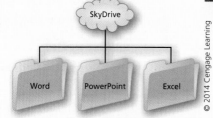

Figure 102

© 2014 Cengage Learning

✺ Consider This: Your Turn

Apply your creative thinking and problem solving skills to design and implement a solution.

1: Creating Beginning Files for Classes

Personal

Part 1:   You are taking the following classes: Introduction to Sociology, Chemistry, Calculus, and Marketing. Create folders for each of the classes. Create a folder structure that will store the documents for each of these classes. Use Publisher to create a separate publication for each class. Each publication should contain the name of each class and the class meeting locations and times: Introduction to Sociology meets on Mondays and Wednesdays from 8:00 a.m. to 10:00 a.m.; Chemistry meets on Tuesdays and Thursdays from 11:00 a.m. to 1:00 p.m.; Calculus meets on Mondays, Wednesdays, and Fridays from 1:30 p.m. to 3:00 p.m.; and Marketing meets on Tuesdays from 5:00 p.m. to 8:00 p.m. If requested by your instructor, add your name to each of the Publisher

Continued >

Consider This: Your Turn *continued*

publications. Use the concepts and techniques presented in this chapter to create the folders and files, and store the files in their respective locations. Submit your assignment in the format specified by your instructor.

Part 2: ❋ You made several decisions while determining the folder structure in this assignment. What was the rationale behind these decisions? Are there any other decisions that also might have worked?

2: Creating Folders

Professional

Part 1: Your boss at the media store where you work part-time has asked for help with organizing his files. After looking through the files, you decided upon a file structure for her to use, including the following folders: CDs, DVDs, and general merchandise. Use Publisher to create separate publications that list examples in each category. For example, CDs include music [blues, rock, country, new age, pop, and soundtracks], blank discs, books, and games; DVDs include movies [action, documentary, music videos, mystery, and drama], television series, and blank discs; and general merchandise includes clothing, portable media players, cases, earbuds, chargers, and cables. If requested by your instructor, add your name to each of the Publisher publications. Use the concepts and techniques presented in this chapter to create the folders. Submit your assignment in the format specified by your instructor.

Part 2: ❋ You made several decisions while determining the folder structure in this assignment. What was the rationale behind these decisions? Justify why you feel this folder structure will help your boss organize her files.

3: Using Help

Research and Collaboration

Part 1: You have just installed a new computer with the Windows operating system and want to be sure that it is protected from the threat of viruses. You ask two of your friends to help research computer viruses, virus prevention, and virus removal. In a team of three people, each person should choose a topic (computer viruses, virus prevention, and virus removal) to research. Use the concepts and techniques presented in this chapter to use Help to find information regarding these topics. Create a Publisher publication that contains steps to properly safeguard a computer from viruses, ways to prevent viruses, as well as the different ways to remove a virus should your computer become infected. Submit your assignment in the format specified by your instructor.

Part 2: ❋ You made several decisions while searching Windows Help and Support for this assignment. What decisions did you make? What was the rationale behind these decisions? How did you locate the required information about viruses in help?

Learn Online

Reinforce what you learned in this chapter with games, exercises, training, and many other online activities and resources.

Student Companion Site Reinforcement activities and resources are available at no additional cost on www.cengagebrain.com. Visit www.cengage.com/ct/studentdownload for detailed instructions about accessing the resources available at the Student Companion Site.

Office 365 Essentials

Objectives

You will have mastered the material in this chapter when you can:

- Describe the components of Office 365

- Compare Office 2013 to Office 365 subscription plans

- Understand the productivity tools of Office 365

- Sync multiple devices using Office 365

- Describe how business teams collaborate using SharePoint

- Describe how to use a SharePoint template to design a public website

- Describe how to conduct an online meeting with Lync

Explore Office 365

Introduction to Office 365

Microsoft Office 365 uses the cloud to deliver a subscription-based service offering the newest Office suite and much more. The Microsoft cloud provides Office software and information stored on remote servers all over the world. Your documents are located online or on the cloud, which provides you access to your information anywhere using a PC, Mac, tablet, mobile phone, or other device with an Internet connection. For businesses and students alike, Office 365 offers significant cost savings compared to the traditional cost of purchasing Microsoft Office 2013. In addition to the core desktop Office suite, Office 365 provides access to email, calendars, conferencing, file sharing, and website design, which sync across multiple devices.

Cloud Computing

Cloud computing refers to a collection of computer servers that house resources users access through the Internet (Figure 1). These resources include email messages, schedules, music, photos, videos, games, websites, programs, apps, servers, storage, and more. Instead of accessing these resources on your computer or mobile device, you access them on the cloud.

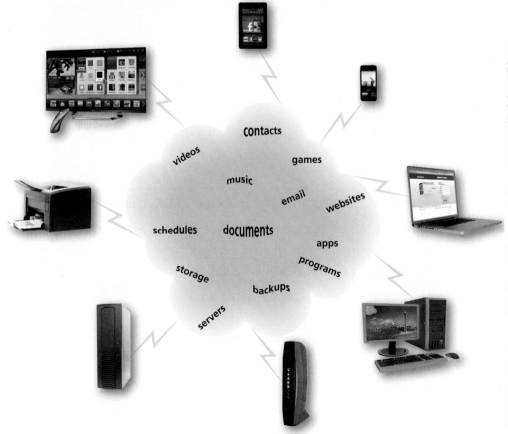

contacts
videos
games
music
email
websites
schedules
documents
apps
storage
programs
backups
servers

Figure 1

Cloud computing can help businesses be more efficient and save them money by shifting usage and the consumption of resources, such as servers and programs, from a local environment to the Internet. For example, an employee working during the day in California could use computing resources located in an office in London that is closed for the evening. When the company in California uses the computing resources, it pays a fee that is based on the amount of computing time and other resources it consumes, much in the same way that consumers pay utility companies for the amount of electricity they use.

Cloud computing is changing how users access and pay for software applications. Fading fast are the days when software packages were sold in boxes at a physical store location with a one-time purchase software license fee. Instead, the new pricing structure is a subscription-based model, where users pay a monthly or annual fee for the software that you can use on multiple devices. The cloud-based Office 365 offers the Office suite with added features that allow you to communicate and collaborate with others in real time.

When you create a free Microsoft account, do you get free cloud storage space?
Yes, when you create a free Microsoft account at Outlook.com, you have access to 7 GB of cloud storage for any type of files.

CONSIDER THIS

What Is Office 365?

Office 365 (Office365.com) is a collection of programs and services, which includes the Microsoft Office 2013 suite, file storage, online collaboration, and file synchronization, as shown in Figure 2 on the next page. You can access these services using your computer, browser, or supported mobile device. For example, a business has two options for providing Office to their employees. A business could purchase Office 2013 and install the software on company computers and servers; however, this traditional Office 2013 package with perpetual licensing does not include the communication and collaboration tools. Employees could not access the Office software if they were not using their work computers. In contrast, if the business purchases a monthly subscription to Office 365, each employee has access to the Office suite on up to five different computers, whether at home or work; company-wide email; web conferencing; website creation capabilities; cloud storage; and shared files. For a lower price, Office 365 provides many more features. In addition, a business may prefer a subscription plan with predictable monthly costs and no up-front infrastructure costs.

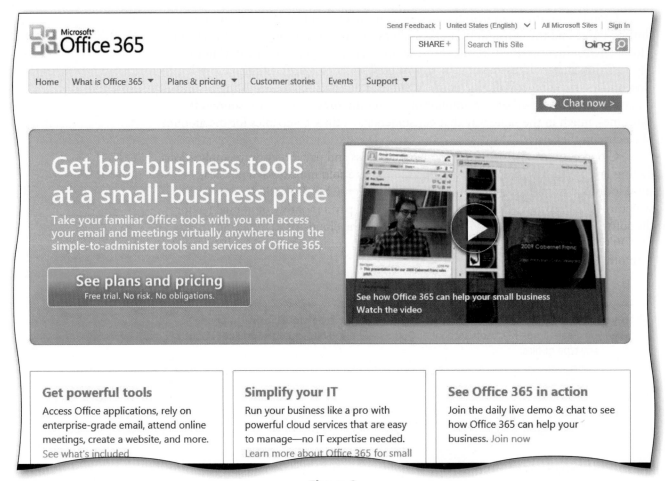

Figure 2

Office 2013 and Office 365 Features Comparison

Office 2013 is the name of the perpetual software package that includes individual applications that can be installed on a single computer. An Office 365 subscription comes with a license to install the software on multiple PCs or Macs at the same time, giving you more flexibility to use your Office products in your home, school, or workplace, whether on a computer or a mobile device. Office 365 provides the Office 2013 programs as part of a subscription service that includes online storage, sharing, and syncing via Microsoft cloud services as shown in Table 1.

Office 365 is available in business, consumer, education, and government editions. Office 365 combines the full version of the Microsoft Office desktop suite with cloud-based versions of Microsoft's communications and collaboration services. The subscription package includes:

- Microsoft Exchange online for shared email and calendars
- Microsoft SharePoint Online for shared file access and public website creation
- Microsoft Office Web apps for browser viewing
- Microsoft Lync Online for communication services

Table 1 Office 2013 and Office 365 Feature Comparison	
Office 2013 Professional (Installed on a single device)	**Office 365 Subscription (Installed on 2 to 5 devices)**
Microsoft Word	Microsoft Word
Microsoft Excel	Microsoft Excel
Microsoft PowerPoint	Microsoft PowerPoint
Microsoft Access	Microsoft Access
Microsoft Outlook	Microsoft Outlook
Microsoft Publisher	Microsoft Publisher
Microsoft OneNote	Microsoft OneNote
	email and calendars (Exchange Online)
	file sharing (SharePoint Online)
	public website design and publishing (SharePoint Online)
	browser-based Office Web Apps
	instant messaging (Lync Online)
	audio and video web conferencing (Lync Online)
	screen sharing with shared control (Lync Online)
	technical support

© 2014 Cengage Learning

Subscription-Based Office 365 Plans

Microsoft provides various subscription plans for Office 365 with different benefits for each individual or organization. Subscription plans include Office 365 Home Premium for home users, Office 365 University for students, Office 365 Small Business, Office 365 Small Business Premium, Office 365 Midsize Business, and Office 365 Enterprise and Government. During the Office 365 sign-up process, you create a Microsoft email address and password to use on your multiple devices. A single subscription to an Office 365 Home Premium account can cover an entire household. The Office 365 Home Premium subscription allows up to five concurrent installations by using the same email address and password combination. This means that your mother could be on the main family computer while you use your tablet and smartphone at the same time. You each can sign in with your individual Microsoft accounts using your settings and accessing your own documents using a single Office 365 subscription.

The Office 365 University subscription plan is designed for higher-education full-time and part-time students, faculty, and staff. By submitting the proper credentials, such as a school email address, students and faculty can purchase Office 365 University, including Word, PowerPoint, Excel, Access, Outlook, Publisher, and OneNote. A one-time payment covers a four-year subscription. In addition, Office 365 University provides users with 27 GB of SkyDrive cloud storage rather than the free 7 GB provided by a Microsoft account, and 60 Skype world minutes per month for videoconferencing. Students have the option of renewing for another four years, for a total of eight years. The Office 365 University edition is limited to two computers (PC or Mac).

The Microsoft Office 365 Business Plans can provide full support for employees to work from any location, whether they are in their traditional business office, commuting to and from work across the country, or working from a home office. Office 365 small business plans (Small Business and Small Business Premium) are best for companies with up to 10 employees, but can accommodate up to 25 users. Office 365 Midsize Business accommodates from 11 to 300 users. Office 365 Enterprise Plan fits organizations ranging in size from a single employee to 50,000-plus users. Each employee can install Microsoft Office 365 on five different computers.

First Look at Office 365

Microsoft Office 365 subscription plans offer all the same applications that are available in the Microsoft Office Professional 2013 suite in addition to multiple communication and collaboration tools. With Office 365 you can retrieve, edit, and save Office documents on the Office 365 cloud, coauthor documents in real time with others, and quickly initiate computer-based calls, instant messages, and web conferences with others.

Productivity Tools

Whether you are inserting audio and video into a Word document to create a high-impact business plan proposal or utilizing the visualization tools in Excel to chart the return on investment of a new mobile marketing program, Office 365 premium plans deliver the full Office product with the same features as the latest version of Microsoft Office. Office 365 uses a quick-start installation technology, called **Click-to-Run**, that downloads and installs the basics within minutes, so that users are able to start working almost immediately. It also includes **Office on Demand**, which streams Office to Windows 7- and Windows 8-based PCs for work performed on public computers. The single-use copy that is installed temporarily on the Windows computer does not count toward the device limit. No installation is necessary when using Office on Demand, and the applications disappear from the computer once you are finished using them. If you have a document on a USB drive or on SkyDrive that you need to edit on another PC, you can use Office on Demand to get the full version of Word in just a few minutes.

In effect, the Office 365 subscription provides access to the full Office applications wherever you are working. When you access your Office 365 account management panel, three choices are listed: 32- and 64-bit versions of Office 2013, and Office for Mac. Selecting the third option will initiate a download of an installer that must be run in the standard OS X fashion. When you install Office 365 on a Mac, the most current Mac version of Office is installed.

CONSIDER THIS

Unlike Google, which offers online documents, spreadsheets, and presentations called Google Docs, Microsoft Office 365 installs locally on your computer in addition to being available online. Google Docs is entirely browser based, which means if you are not connected to the Internet, you cannot access your Google Docs files.

Email and Calendars

In business, sharing information is essential to meeting the needs of your customers and staff. Office 365 offers shared access to business email, calendars, and contacts using **Exchange Online** from a computer, tablet, phone, and browser. The cloud-based Exchange Online enables business people to access Outlook information from anywhere at any time, while eliminating the cost of purchasing and maintaining servers to store data. If you need to meet with a colleague about a new project, you can compare calendars to view availability, confirm conference room availability, share project contacts, search email messages related to the project, and send email invitations to the project meeting. Exchange Online also allows you to search and access your company's address list.

Online Meetings

When you are working with a team on a project that requires interaction, email and text communications can slow the communications process. Microsoft Lync connects you with others by facilitating real-time, interactive presentations and meetings over the Internet using both video and audio calling. As shown in Figure 3, you can conduct an online meeting with a team member or customer that includes an instant messaging conversation, audio, high-definition video, virtual whiteboards, and screen sharing. If the customer does not have an Office 365 subscription, they still can join the meeting through the invitation link, which runs the Lync Web App.

Skype is another tool in the Office 365 subscription, which enables users to place video calls to computers and smartphones and voice calls to landlines. Skype also supports instant message and file sharing to computers and mobile devices. While Skype may be adequate for simple communication, Lync provides for more robust, comprehensive communications. These robust features include high-definition (HD) videoconferencing capabilities, a whiteboard, and a larger audience. Using Lync, meeting attendees simultaneously can view up to five participants' video, identify the active speaker, and associate names with faces. Lync supports up to 250 attendees per meeting. Unlike Skype, Lync meetings can be recorded for replaying at a later time. This enables businesses and schools to schedule meetings or organize online classes using Lync capabilities.

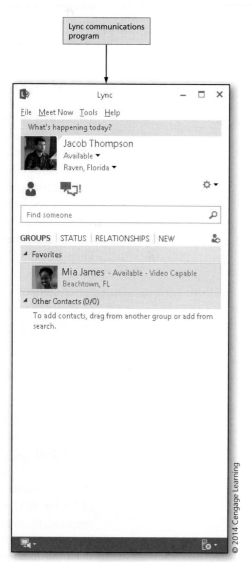

Figure 3

File Sharing

Office 365 includes a team site, which is a password-protected portal that supports sharing of large, difficult-to-email files and provides a single location for the latest versions of documents. In business, for example, colleagues working on common projects can save valuable time by being able to access instantly the latest master copy of each document. Security can be managed through different levels of user access so that users see only what they are supposed to see. Office 365 provides access to shared files using the cloud, making writing, editing, and sharing documents easier. If a construction company creates a commercial bid for a building project, the customers can be invited to view an Excel spreadsheet bid, construction timetable with a shared calendar, and an Access database of all the materials needed using the file sharing feature online.

Website Creation

Office 365 business plan subscriptions include a built-in hosted public website, where customers and clients can find an online storefront of a company. This public website, called the Website, can be customized to market a company by using various templates within the Office 365 cloud. The website creation tools include those for adding a theme, graphics, fonts, maps, directions, blogs, stock tickers, slide shows, PayPal, weather, and videos to interact with the website's visitors.

Synchronization

Office 365 subscription plans provide a central place to store and access your documents and business information. A feature of Office 365 ensures the original and backup computer files in two or more locations are identical through a process called **Active Directory Synchronization**. For example, if you open a PowerPoint presentation on your smartphone while you are riding a city bus and then add a new slide as you head to school, the PowerPoint presentation automatically is synced with Office 365. When you arrive on campus and open the PowerPoint presentation on a school computer, your new slide already is part of the finished slide show. By storing your files in Office 365, you can access your files on another computer if your home computer fails, with no loss of time or important information. When using your mobile phone's data plan, you do not need to search for a Wi-Fi hot spot to connect to the Office 365 cloud. Computer labs in schools can be configured to synchronize automatically all student files to Office 365 online.

Multiple Device Access to Office 365

With a single sign-in process, Office 365 provides access to multiple computers and mobile devices, including Android smartphones and tablets, Apple iPhones and iPads, Windows phones, and Blackberry phones. After you configure your devices' email settings, you can view your Microsoft account calendar, contacts, and email. Your personalized settings, preferences, and documents can be synchronized among all the different devices included in your Office 365 premium subscription. With the mobility of Office 365, students and employees can work anywhere, accessing information and responding to email requests immediately. If you lose your phone, Office 365 includes a feature that allows you to remotely wipe your phone clean of any data. By wiping your phone's data, you can prevent any unauthorized access to sensitive information, such as your banking information, passwords, and contacts, as well as discourage identity theft. Because your phone contacts and other information are stored on the Microsoft cloud, damaged or lost equipment is never a problem.

A thief can be quite resourceful if he or she steals your phone. Before you can alert your parents or spouse to the theft, they might receive a text from "you" asking for your ATM or credit card PIN number. Your parents or spouse might then reply with the PIN number. Your bank account could be emptied in minutes.

Teams Using Office 365 in Business

In the business world, rarely does an employee work in isolation. Companies need their employees to collaborate, whether they work in the same office or in locations around the world. Telecommuters working from home can communicate as if they were on-site by using a common team website and conferencing software. SharePoint Online and Lync Online provide seamless communication.

Small business subscription plans as low as $6.00 per user per month allow employees to create and store Word documents, Excel spreadsheets, and PowerPoint presentations online and communicate with one another via email, instant messaging, or video chat as they work on projects together. As shown in Figure 4, a team portal page is shown when you subscribe at https://portal.microsoftonline.com. Larger companies and those requiring more features can take advantage of the Office 365 business premium package, which, in addition to the features listed above, provides access to the Office 365 portal website and eliminates the effort and cost of the users maintaining their own costly computer servers.

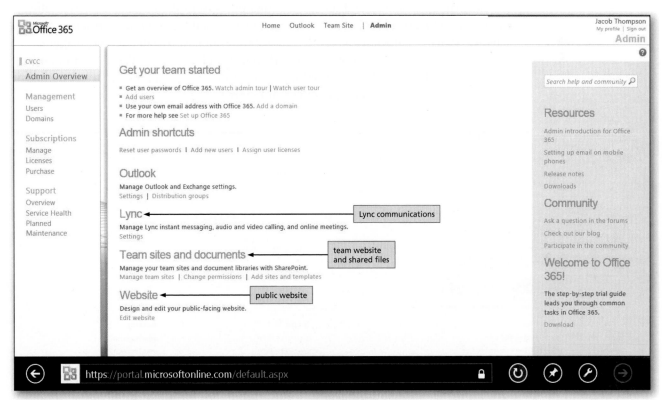

Figure 4

Email Communication Using Exchange

Office 365 includes Exchange Online, an email-based collaborative communications server for business. Exchange enables employees to be more productive by effectively managing email across multiple devices and facilitating teamwork.

Collaboration Using SharePoint

SharePoint Online, a part of Office 365 subscription plans, allows employees to collaborate with one another, share documents, post announcements, and track tasks, as shown in Table 2.

Table 2 Office 365 SharePoint Features	
Team Site Feature	**Description**
Calendar	Track important dates
Shared Document Library	Store related documents according to topic; picture, report, and slide libraries often are included
Task List	Track team tasks according to who is responsible for completion
Team Discussion Board	Discuss the topics at hand in an open forum
Contacts List	Share contact lists of employees, customers, contractors, and suppliers

© 2014 Cengage Learning

Office 365 provides the tools to plan meetings. Users can share calendars side by side, view availability, and suggest meeting times from shared calendars. Typically, a SharePoint team administrator or website owner establishes a folder structure to share and manage documents. The team website is fully searchable online, making locating and sharing data more efficient than using a local server. With a team website, everyone on the team has a central location to store and find all the information for a project, client, or department, as shown in Figure 5.

Figure 5

Website Design Using SharePoint

SharePoint provides templates to create a professional looking, public website for an online presence to market your business. As shown in Figure 6, a local pet sitting business is setting up a business website by customizing a SharePoint template. SharePoint Public Website includes features within the Design Manager that you use to customize and design your website by adding your own images, forms, style sheets, maps, themes, and social networking tools. When you finish customizing your business site, you can apply your own domain name to the site. A **domain** is a unique web address that identifies where your website can be found. Office 365 SharePoint hosts your website as part of your subscription. Your customers easily can find your business online and learn about your services.

BTW

Creating SharePoint Intranet Sites

A SharePoint website also can be customized to serve as an internal company website for private communications within the company.

Figure 6

Real-Time Communications Using Lync

Lync Online is Microsoft's server platform for online team communications and comes bundled with Office 365 business subscriptions. As shown in Figure 7, Lync connects in real time to allow instant messaging, videoconferencing, and voice communications; it also integrates with email and Microsoft Office applications.

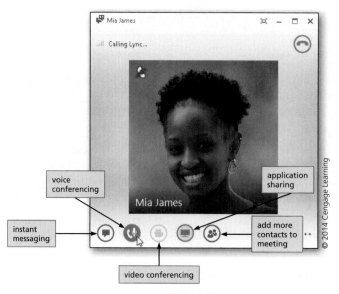

Figure 7

Lync allows you to connect with staff at remote locations using instant messaging capabilities, desktop sharing, videoconferencing, and shared agendas or documents. Lync is integrated into Office 365, which allows staff to start communicating from within the applications in which they currently are working. For example, while an employee is creating a PowerPoint presentation for a new product line, as shown in Figure 8, Lync enables him or her to collaborate with the entire team about the details of the product presentation. The team can view the presenter's screen displaying the PowerPoint presentation. The presenter can share control with any member of the team and can share his or her screen at any time during the Lync meeting.

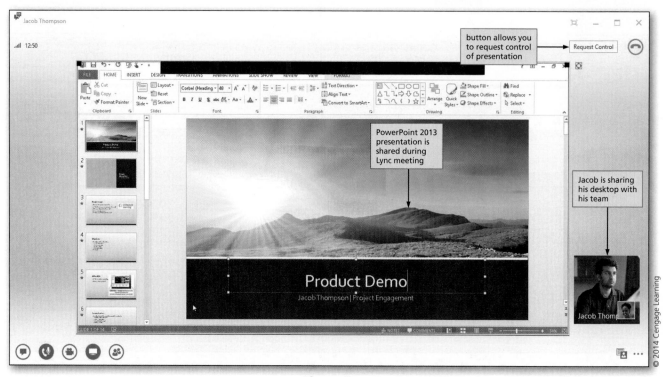

Figure 8

Users can send a Lync meeting request to schedule a team meeting, or an impromptu conversation can be started immediately using the Meet Now feature. Participants receive a Lync meeting request link via an email message, and when they click the meeting request link, Lync automatically connects them to the online conference. If the participant does not have Lync installed, the Lync Web App automatically connects to the Lync meeting through the user's PC or Mac OS X browser. If a participant is away from his or her computer, he or she still can participate using the Lync Mobile apps for Windows Phone, iOS, and Android. As shown in Figure 9, Lync utilizes **instant messaging** (IM), allowing two or more people to share text messages. They can communicate in real time, similar to a voice conversation. In addition to a simple instant message, Lync provides a feature called **persistent chat**, which allows end-users to participate in a working session of instant messages that is persistent or sustained over a specified amount of time in a moderated chat room. Consider having an instant messaging session with a group of colleagues in different parts of your organization, regardless of geographic region, where you all are working on the same project. Over the course of the project, different people post questions and concerns, and others are able to respond to all those who have subscribed to your topic or been admitted to the chat room. Instead of a long trail of email messages, a team can keep information in a controlled environment with a full history of the discussion in one location.

Figure 9

Lync also delivers support for full high-definition (HD) videoconferencing, so that a team can have a clear view of the participants, products, and demos. Before you join the video feed, you can preview your video feed to make sure your video camera is at the correct angle, your image is centered within the video frame, and that your room lighting provides for a clear image. The Lync preview option is important in creating a positive first impression over video. Your audio devices can be tested for clarity to make sure your headset, microphone, and speakers are functioning properly.

Lync provides a polling feature that presenters can use to ask the participants' opinions during a meeting (Figure 10). The poll question can consist of up to seven possible choices. The presenter has the option to view the results privately or share the results with the entire group.

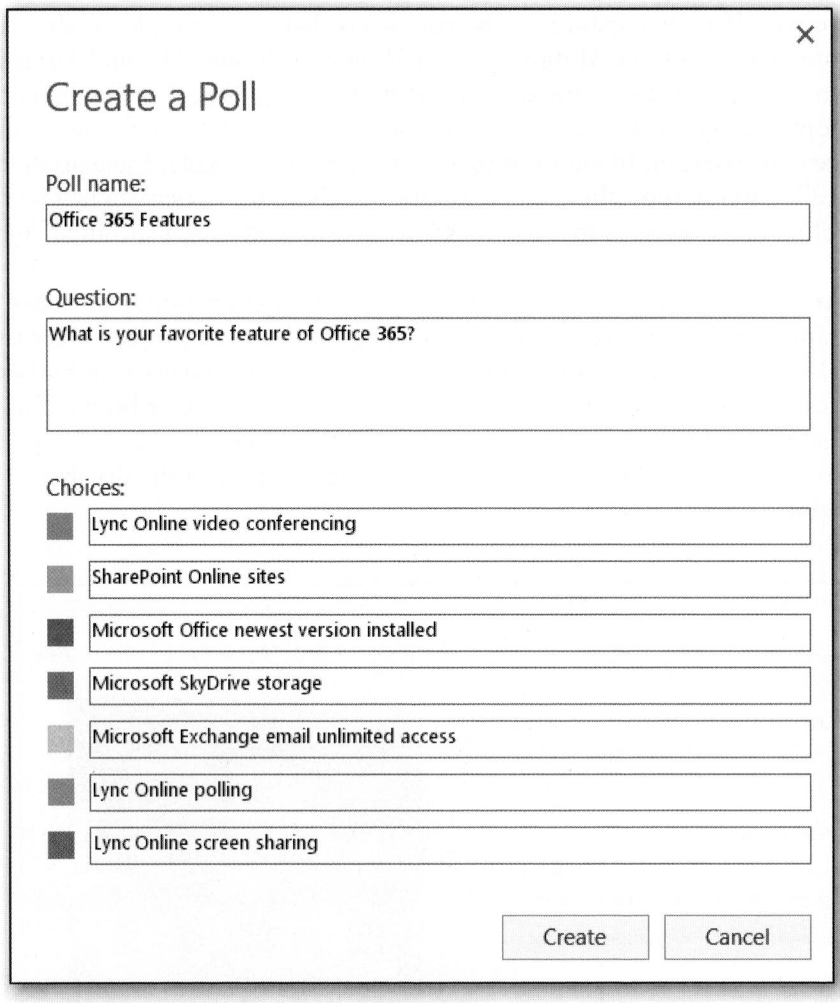

Figure 10

Finally, by enabling the recording feature, Lync meetings and conversations can be captured for viewing at a later time. For instance, you can capture the audio, video, instant messaging (IM), screen sharing, Microsoft PowerPoint presentations, whiteboard, and polling portions of the Lync session and then play them back just as they transpired during the live Lync event. The meeting recordings can be made available to others so that they can view all or part of the Lync event. Instructors can record Lync online class sessions for students who were unable to attend the original presentation. The recording starts in Microsoft Lync; recordings then can be viewed within the Recording Manager feature.

Chapter Summary

In this chapter, you have learned how to subscribe to Office 365, which provides local and online access to Office applications, email, document sharing, web conferencing, and business websites. You also learned how a business can utilize Office 365 features on the cloud to facilitate teamwork. Finally, you learned about the features of SharePoint and Lync, which provide collaboration and communications for business teams using Office 365.

✳ Consider This: Your Turn

Apply your creative thinking and problem solving skills to design and implement a solution.

1: Comparing Office 365 Personal Plans

Personal

Part 1: You are a freshman in college living at home with your family. You are considering if it would be a better value to subscribe to Office 365 University or Office 365 Home Premium. Write a one-page document comparing the pros and cons of the two subscription plans. Research the different subscriptions in detail at Office365.com. Submit your assignment in the format specified by your instructor.

Part 2: ✳ Which type of computer and/or devices would you use with your Office 365 subscription? If you are at a friend's home that does not have Office 365, how could you access your Office files if you do not have your computer or mobile device with you?

2: Upgrading a Local Business to Office 365

Professional

Part 1: You are an employee at Impact Digital Marketing, a small marketing firm with 12 employees. The firm is setting up an Office 365 Small Business subscription next week, and you need to compose an email message with multiple paragraphs to explain the features of this new subscription plan to the members of your firm. Research the Office 365 Small Business subscription plan in detail at Office365.com, and compile your findings in an email message. Submit your assignment in the format specified by your instructor.

Part 2: ✳ Give three examples of how a marketing firm could use Lync. How could a marketing firm use the SharePoint Websites feature?

3: Conducting a Lync Meeting

Research and Collaboration

* Students need an Office 365 subscription to complete the following assignment.

Part 1: Using your Office 365 subscription, conduct a meeting using Lync. Working with a partner, use your Office 365 subscription to research how to use Lync. Then, conduct a 15-minute Lync meeting, including instant messaging, to discuss the features of Lync. Use the concepts and techniques presented in this chapter to create the Lync meeting. Submit your assignment in the format specified by your instructor.

Part 2: ✳ When using Lync in business, when would the video feature best be utilized?

1 | Creating a Flyer

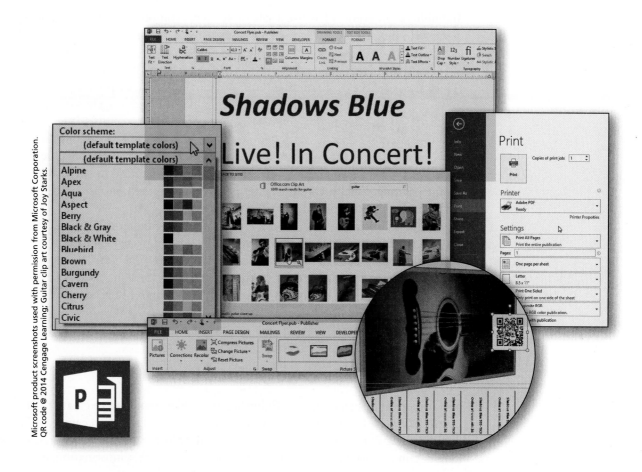

Objectives

You will have mastered the material in this chapter when you can:

- Choose Publisher template options
- Describe the Publisher window
- Select objects and zoom
- Replace Publisher placeholder text
- Check spelling as you type
- Delete objects
- Format text and autofit

- Insert and format a photo
- Move, align, and resize objects
- Print a publication
- Open and modify a publication
- Create a hyperlink
- Change the background
- Save a print publication as a web publication

1 | Creating a Flyer

Introduction

To publicize an event, advertise a sale or service, promote a business, or convey a message to the community, you may want to create a flyer and post it in a public location. A **flyer** is a single-page publication, which may be printed on various sizes of paper, announcing personal items for sale or rent (car, boat, apartment); garage or block sales; services being offered (housecleaning, lessons, carpooling); membership, sponsorship, or donation requests (club, religious organization, charity); and other messages. Flyers are an inexpensive means of reaching the community, yet many go unnoticed because they are designed poorly. A good flyer, or any publication, must deliver a message in the clearest, most attractive and effective way possible. You must clarify your purpose and know your target audience. You need to gather ideas and plan for the printing. Finally, you must edit, proofread, and then publish your flyer. Flyers must stand out to be noticed.

Flyers also can be posted on the web. Electronic bulletin boards, social networking sites, and online auction websites are good places to reach people with flyers, advertising everything from a bake sale to a part-time job.

To illustrate the features of Publisher, this book presents a series of projects that create publications similar to those you will encounter in academic and business environments.

Project—Concert Flyer

The project in this chapter uses Publisher and a flyer template to create the flyer shown in Figure 1–1. This attractive flyer advertises a concert on campus. The **headline** clearly identifies the purpose of the flyer, using large, bold letters. Below that, to maintain consistency, the same font is used for the ticket information, date, time, and location. In the upper-right portion of the flyer, the phone number and title of the series appear. The photo of the guitar is formatted to be eye-catching and entices people to stop and look at the flyer. The QR code graphic allows mobile devices to access the band's webpage quickly. The tear-offs, aligned at the bottom of the flyer, include the name, phone number, and website of the band. Finally, the font and color schemes support the topic and make the text stand out.

Campus Concerts

▶ 555-TICKETS

Shadows Blue

Live! In Concert!

For tickets, visit www.utix.biz

Saturday, October 4

8:00 p.m. at the Campus Auditorium

Online at www.utix.biz   Shadows Blue 555-TICKETS

Online at www.utix.biz   Shadows Blue 555-TICKETS

Online at www.utix.biz   Shadows Blue 555-TICKETS

Online at www.utix.biz   Shadows Blue 555-TICKETS

Online at www.utix.biz   Shadows Blue 555-TICKETS

Online at www.utix.biz   Shadows Blue 555-TICKETS

Online at www.utix.biz   Shadows Blue 555-TICKETS

Online at www.utix.biz   Shadows Blue 555-TICKETS

Online at www.utix.biz   Shadows Blue 555-TICKETS

Online at www.utix.biz   Shadows Blue 555-TICKETS

Online at www.utix.biz   Shadows Blue 555-TICKETS

Figure 1–1

Roadmap

In this chapter, you will learn how to create the flyer shown in Figure 1–1 on the previous page. The following roadmap identifies general activities you will perform as you progress through this chapter:

1. CUSTOMIZE the TEMPLATE options such as choice, color scheme, and font scheme.
2. NAVIGATE the interface and SELECT objects.
3. REPLACE placeholder TEXT.
4. DELETE OBJECTS you do not plan to use in the publication, if any.
5. FORMAT the TEXT in the flyer.
6. INSERT GRAPHICS in placeholders and in other locations, as necessary.
7. FORMAT PICTURES by adding borders and styles.
8. ENHANCE the PAGE by repositioning and aligning objects.
9. PRINT and EXIT the publication.
10. OPEN and REVISE the publication.

At the beginning of step instructions throughout the chapter, you will see an abbreviated form of this roadmap. The abbreviated roadmap uses colors to indicate chapter progress: gray means the chapter is beyond that activity, blue means the task being shown is covered in that activity, and black means that activity is yet to be covered. For example, the following abbreviated roadmap indicates the chapter would be showing a task in the Format Text activity.

1 CUSTOMIZE TEMPLATES | 2 NAVIGATE & SELECT | 3 REPLACE TEXT | 4 DELETE OBJECTS | **5 FORMAT TEXT**
6 INSERT GRAPHICS | 7 FORMAT PICTURE | 8 ENHANCE PAGE | 9 PRINT & EXIT | 10 OPEN & REVISE

Use the abbreviated roadmap as a progress guide while you read or step through the instructions in this chapter.

To Run Publisher

If you are using a computer to step through the project in this chapter and you want your screens to match the figures in this book, you should change your screen's resolution to 1366 × 768. For information about how to change a computer's resolution, refer to the Office and Windows chapter at the beginning of this book.

The following steps, which assume Windows 8 is running, use the Start screen or the search box to run Publisher based on a typical installation. You may need to ask your instructor how to run Publisher on your computer. For a detailed example of the procedure summarized below, refer to the Office and Windows chapter.

1 Scroll the Start screen and search for a Publisher 2013 tile. If your Start screen contains a Publisher 2013 tile, tap or click it to run Publisher and then proceed to Step 5. If the Start screen does not contain the Publisher 2013 tile, proceed to the next step to search for the Publisher app.

2 Swipe in from the right edge of the screen or point to the upper-right corner of the screen to display the Charms bar and then tap or click the Search charm on the Charms bar to display the Search menu.

3 Type **Publisher** as the search text in the Search box and watch the search results appear in the Apps list.

4 Tap or click Publisher 2013 in the search results to run Publisher.

5 If the Publisher window is not maximized, tap or click the Maximize button on its title bar to maximize the window (Figure 1–2).

For an introduction to Windows 8 and instruction about how to perform basic Windows 8 tasks, read the Office and Windows chapter at the beginning of this book, where you can learn how to resize windows, change screen resolution, create folders, move and rename files, use Windows Help, and much more.

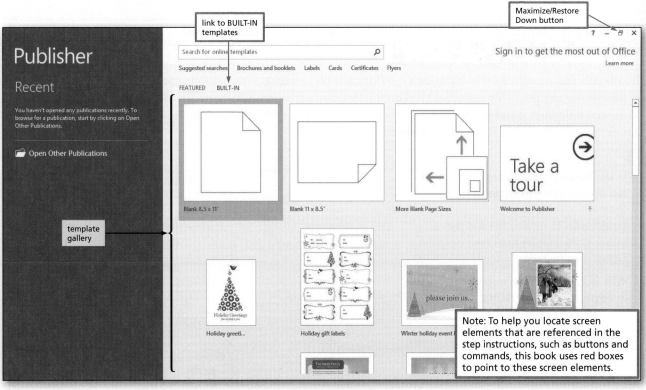

Figure 1–2

Creating a Flyer

Publisher provides many ways to begin the process of creating and editing a publication. You can:

- Create a new publication from a design template.
- Create a new publication or a webpage from scratch.
- Create a new publication based on an existing one.
- Open an existing publication.

Choosing the appropriate method depends on your experience with desktop publishing and on how you have used Publisher in the past.

Templates

Because many people find that composing and designing from scratch is a difficult process, Publisher provides templates to assist in publication preparation. Publisher has hundreds of templates to create professionally designed and unique publications. A template is a tool that helps you through the design process by offering you publication options and changing your publication accordingly. A **template** is similar to a blueprint you can use over and over, filling in the blanks, replacing prewritten text as necessary, and changing the art to fit your needs. In this first project, as you begin to learn about the features of Publisher, a series of steps is presented to create a publication using a design template.

When you run Publisher or when you tap or click the New tab in the Backstage view, Publisher displays the **template gallery**. Publisher provides two kinds of templates. Featured templates are downloaded from Office.com and customized for specific situations. Built-in templates are more generic and require no downloading. If you choose a template from the BUILT-IN template gallery, Publisher displays the **template information pane** on the right, with a larger preview of the selected template, along with some customization options.

BTW
Featured Template Gallery
You may have to wait a few minutes for Publisher to populate the FEATURED template gallery, as the gallery is updated from Microsoft every day.

BTW
Templates
Choose a template that suits the purpose of the publication, with headline and graphic placement that attracts your audience. Choose a style that has meaning for the topic.

To Select a Template

Templates are displayed as **thumbnails,** or small images of the template, in the template gallery. The thumbnails are organized by publication type (for example, Flyers); within publication type, they are organized by purpose or category (for example, Marketing) and then alphabetically by design type. Publisher groups additional templates into folders. The following steps select an event flyer template. *Why? An event flyer template contains many of the objects needed to create the desired concert flyer.*

1

- In the Publisher start screen, tap or click BUILT-IN to display the built-in templates.
- Scroll down to display the desired publication type (in this case, Flyers) (Figure 1–3).

Q&A Why does my list look different?
It may be that someone has downloaded additional folders of templates on your system. Or, the resolution on your screen may be different. Thus, the size and number of displayed folders may vary.

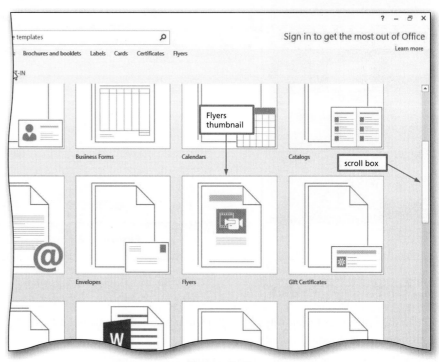

Figure 1–3

2

- Tap or click the Flyers thumbnail to display the Flyer templates and folders of additional templates (Figure 1–4).

Q&A Can I go back and choose a different category of templates?
Yes, you can tap or click the Back button in the upper-left corner of the template gallery, or you can tap or click Home or Flyers in the breadcrumb trail to move back to those previous locations.

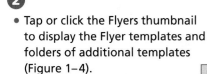 **Experiment**

- Scroll through the available templates and tap or click various flyers in the list. Watch the preview change in the template information pane.

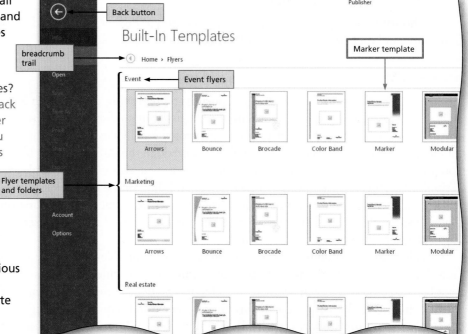

Figure 1–4

3

- Tap or click the Marker thumbnail in the Event category (Figure 1–5).

Q&A Could I use a different template? You could, but it does not have the same features as the template used in this chapter.

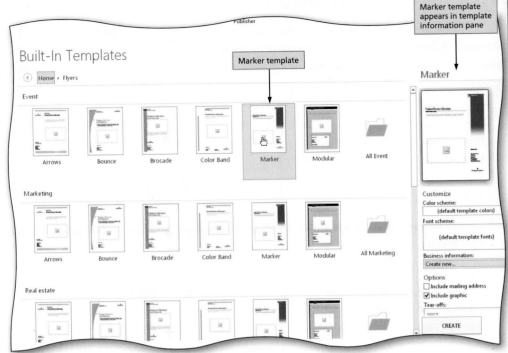

Figure 1–5

Does it make any difference which color scheme and font scheme you use?
Yes. The choice of an appropriate template, font, and color scheme is determined by the flyer's purpose and intended audience. For example, in this concert flyer about a blues band, the Navy color scheme helps connect the audience with the name of the band. The Flow font scheme uses a Calibri rounded font for the heading. Calibri is a sans serif font, meaning it has no flourishes on individual letters, and is suitable for print publications.

Customizing Templates

Once you choose a template, you should make choices about the color scheme, font scheme, and other components of the publication. A **color scheme** is a defined set of colors that complement each other when used in the same publication. Each Publisher color scheme provides four complementary colors. A **font scheme** is a defined set of fonts associated with a publication. A **font**, or typeface, defines the appearance and shape of the letters, numbers, and special characters. A font scheme contains one font for headings and another font for body text and captions. Font schemes make it easy to change all the fonts in a publication to give it a new look. Other customization options allow you to choose to include business information, a mailing address, a graphic, or tear-offs.

BTW
Font Schemes
Choose a font scheme that gives your flyer a consistent, professional appearance and characterizes your subject. Make intentional decisions about the font style and type. Avoid common reading fonts such as Arial, Times New Roman, and Helvetica that are used in other kinds of print publications. Flyers are more effective with stronger or unusual font schemes.

To Choose Publication Options

The following steps choose publication options. *Why? You typically will want to customize a template with an appropriate font and color scheme, determined by the flyer's purpose and intended audience.* The following steps choose customization options and change the preview in the template information pane to reflect your choices.

1

- Tap or click the Color scheme button in the Customize area to display the Color scheme gallery (Figure 1–6).

Q&A What are the individual colors used for in each scheme?
By default, the text will be black and the background will be white in each color scheme. Publisher uses the first and second scheme colors for major color accents within a publication. The third and fourth colors are used for shading and secondary accents.

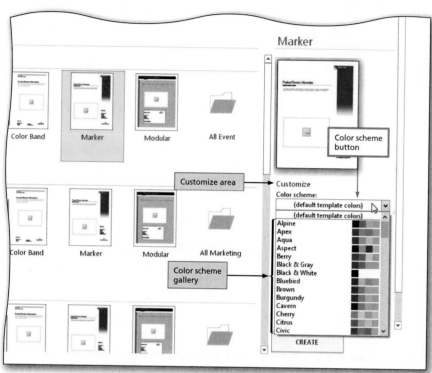

Figure 1–6

2

- Scroll as necessary and then tap or click Navy in the Color scheme gallery to select it (Figure 1–7).

Experiment

- Tap or click various color schemes and watch the changes in all of the thumbnails. When you finish experimenting, tap or click the Navy color scheme.

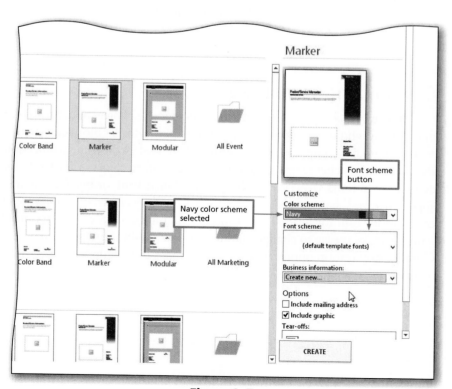

Figure 1–7

3

- Tap or click the Font scheme button in the Customize area to display the Font scheme gallery (Figure 1–8).

Q&A What are the three items listed in each scheme?

The first line is the generic name of the scheme. Below that, both a major font and a minor font are specified. Generally, a major font is used for titles and headings, and a minor font is used for body text.

Figure 1–8

4

- If necessary, scroll in the list and then tap or click Flow in the Font scheme gallery to select it.
- If necessary, scroll to display the Options area of the template information pane (Figure 1–9).

Q&A How are the font schemes organized?

The font schemes are organized alphabetically by the generic name of the scheme.

 Experiment

- Tap or click various font schemes and watch the changes in all of the thumbnails. When you finish experimenting, tap or click the Flow font scheme.

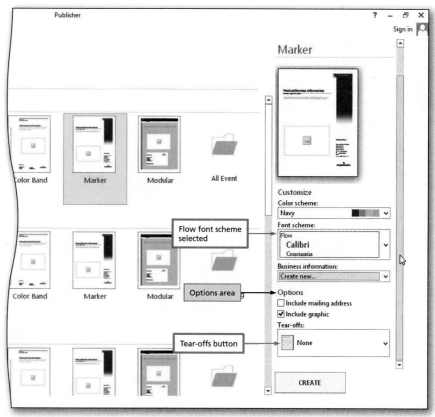

Figure 1–9

5

- Tap or click the Tear-offs button in the Options area to display the Tear-offs gallery (Figure 1–10).

Q&A What are the other kinds of tear-offs?
You can choose to display tear-offs for coupons, order forms, response forms, and sign-up forms.

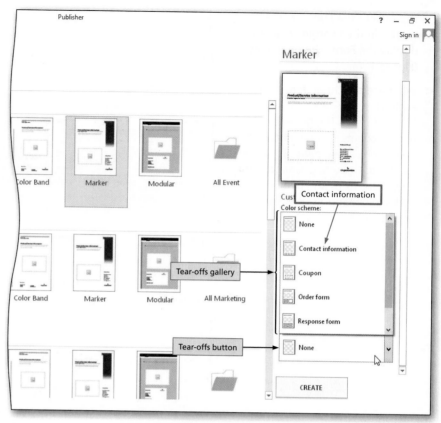

Figure 1–10

6

- Tap or click Contact information in the Tear-offs gallery to select tear-offs that will display contact information (Figure 1–11).

Q&A Should I change the check boxes?
No, the flyer you create in this chapter uses the default value of no mailing address, but includes a graphic.

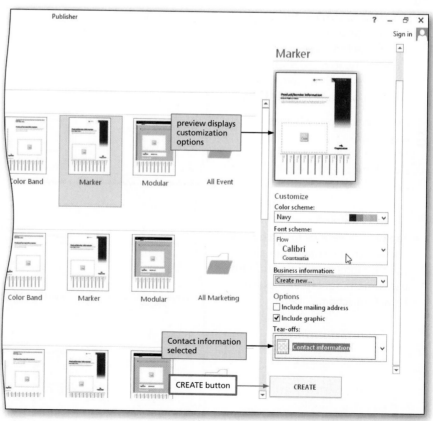

Figure 1–11

7

● Tap or click the CREATE button to create the publication using the selected template and options (Figure 1–12).

Q&A Is there a way to go back if I change my mind?

You can tap or click FILE on the ribbon and start a new publication, or you can make changes to the template, font scheme, color scheme, and other options using the ribbon, as you will see in this and subsequent chapters.

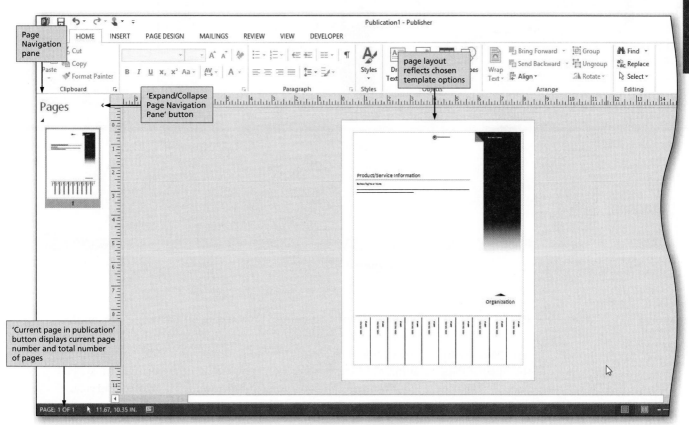

Figure 1–12

The Publisher Window

The Publisher window consists of a variety of components to make your work more efficient and your publication more professional. The following sections discuss these components.

The Workspace

The **workspace** contains several elements similar to the document windows of other applications, as well as some elements unique to Publisher. For more information on common window elements, read the Office and Windows chapter at the beginning of this book. In Publisher, as you create a publication, the page layout, rulers, scroll bars, guides, the Page Navigation pane, and the status bar are displayed in the gray workspace (Figure 1–13 on the next page). Objects can be placed on the page layout or in the light gray workspace.

For an introduction to Office and instruction about how to perform basic tasks in Office apps, read the Office and Windows chapter at the beginning of this book, where you can learn how to run an application, use the ribbon, save a file, open a file, exit an application, use Help, and much more.

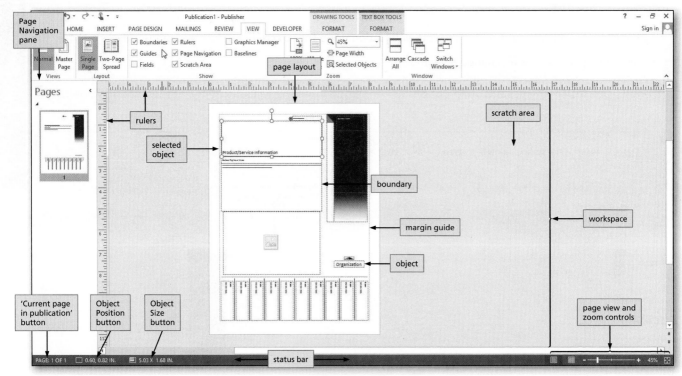

Figure 1–13

PAGE LAYOUT The **page layout** contains a view of the publication page, all the objects contained therein, plus the guides and boundaries for the page and its objects. The page layout can be changed to accommodate multipage spreads. You also can use the Special Paper command to view your page layout as it will be printed on special paper or see the final copy after preparing your publication for a printing service.

RULERS Two rulers outline the workspace at the top and left. A **ruler** is used to measure and place objects on the page. Although the vertical and horizontal rulers are displayed at the left and top of the workspace, they can be moved and placed anywhere you need them. You use the rulers to measure and align objects on the page, set tab stops, adjust text frames, and change margins. Additionally, the rulers can be hidden to show more of the workspace. You will learn more about rulers in a later chapter.

OBJECTS The elements you want to place in your publication are called **objects**, including, text, WordArt, tear-offs, graphics, pictures, bookmarks, bullets, lines, and web tools.

GUIDES AND BOUNDARIES Publisher's page layout displays guides and boundaries of the page and selected objects. A **boundary** is the gray, dotted line surrounding an object. Boundaries are useful when you want to move or resize objects on the page. Boundaries and guides can be turned on and off using the VIEW tab. They do not display on printed copies. **Margin guides** automatically are displayed in blue at all four margins. Other guides include grid guides, which you can turn on to help organize objects in rows and columns, visual layout guides that display as you move objects, and baseline guides that help you align text horizontally across text boxes.

STATUS BAR As with other Office 2013 applications, Publisher displays a status bar at the bottom of the workspace. The Publisher status bar contains the 'Current page in publication' button, the Object Position button, and the Object Size button on the left; on the right side of the status bar, Publisher includes buttons and controls you can use to change the view of a publication and adjust the size of the displayed publication.

One of the few differences between Windows 7 and Windows 8 occurs in the steps to run Publisher. If you are using Windows 7, click the Start button, type `Publisher` in the 'Search programs and files' box, click Publisher 2013, and then, if necessary, maximize the Publisher window. For detailed steps to run Publisher in Windows 7, refer to the Office and Windows chapter at the beginning of this book. For a summary of the steps, refer to the Quick Reference located at the back of this book.

The **Object Position button** and **Object Size button** serve as guidelines for lining up objects from the left and top margins. The exact position and size of a selected object is displayed in inches as you create or move it. You may choose to have the measurement displayed in pica, points, or centimeters. If no object is selected, the Object Position button displays the location of the pointer. Tapping or clicking either button will display the Measurements toolbar. You will learn more about the Measurements toolbar in a later chapter.

The right side of the status bar includes the Single Page, 'Two-Page Spread', and 'Show Whole Page' buttons, as well as the zoom controls. If you press and hold or right-click the status bar, you can choose which controls to display.

PAGE NAVIGATION PANE The Page Navigation pane displays all of the current pages in the publication as thumbnails in a panel on the left side of the workspace. Tapping or clicking a thumbnail displays that page in the workspace.

BTW

The Ribbon and Screen Resolution
Publisher may change how the groups and buttons within the groups appear on the ribbon, depending on the computer's screen resolution. Thus, your ribbon may look different from the ones in this book if you are using a screen resolution other than 1366 × 768.

To Hide the Page Navigation Pane

1 CUSTOMIZE TEMPLATES | 2 NAVIGATE & SELECT | 3 REPLACE TEXT | DELETE OBJECTS | FORMAT TEXT
6 INSERT GRAPHICS | 7 FORMAT PICTURE | 8 ENHANCE PAGE | 9 PRINT & EXIT | 10 OPEN & REVISE

Because the flyer contains only one page, you will hide the Page Navigation pane using the 'Current page in publication' button on the status bar. *Why?* *Hiding the pane gives you more room on the screen for viewing and editing the flyer.* The following step hides the Page Navigation pane.

- Tap or click the 'Current page in publication' button on the status bar to hide the Page Navigation pane (Figure 1–14).

Q&A I do not see the Page Navigation pane. What did I do wrong?
It may be that someone has hidden the Page Navigation pane already. The 'Current page in publication' button opens and closes the Page Navigation pane. Tap or click it again.

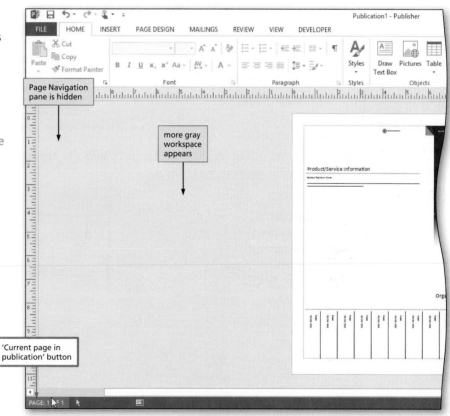

Figure 1–14

Other Ways

1. Tap or click Page Navigation check box (VIEW tab | Show group)

To Collapse and Expand the Page Navigation Pane

An alternative to hiding the Page Navigation pane is to collapse or minimize it. If you wanted to collapse the Page Navigation pane, you would perform the following steps.

1. If the Page Navigation pane is not open, click the 'Current page in publication' button on the status bar to display the Page Navigation pane.

2. Tap or click the 'Collapse Page Navigation Pane' button in the upper-right corner of the pane.

3. If you want to expand a collapsed Page Navigation pane, click the 'Expand Page Navigation Pane' button in the upper-right corner of the pane.

Selecting Objects and Zooming

Pointing to an object in Publisher causes the object to display its boundary, helping you to determine the edges and general shape of the object. When you **select** an object by clicking it, the object appears surrounded by a solid **selection rectangle**, which has small squares and circles, called **handles**, at each corner and middle location. Many objects also display a green **rotation handle** connected to the top of the object or a yellow **adjustment handle** used to change the shape of some objects. A selected object can be resized, rotated, moved, deleted, or grouped with other objects. Often it is easier to select and edit objects by zooming.

Objects such as photos, clip art, and shapes are easy to select. You simply tap or click them. With other objects such as text boxes, logos, and placeholders, you first must point to them—to display their boundaries—and then tap or click the boundary. Selecting text does not necessarily select the text box object that holds the text; rather, it may select the text itself. Tapping or clicking the boundary is the best way to select a text box object.

To Select

1 CUSTOMIZE TEMPLATES | 2 NAVIGATE & SELECT | 3 REPLACE TEXT | 4 DELETE OBJECTS | 5 FORMAT TEXT
6 INSERT GRAPHICS | 7 FORMAT PICTURE | 8 ENHANCE PAGE | 9 PRINT & EXIT | 10 OPEN & REVISE

In the following step, you will select the box that surrounds the headline in the flyer by tapping or clicking it. *Why? Before you can edit an object, you first must select it.*

- Tap near the desired object or click the boundary of the desired object (in this case, the headline text box) to select the object rather than the text (Figure 1–15).

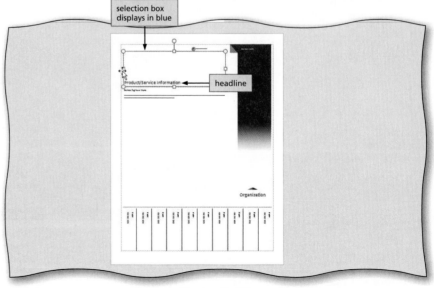

Figure 1–15

Other Ways

1. With no object selected, press TAB until desired object is selected

Zooming

Once selected, the size of the object might be small and, therefore, difficult to edit. Publisher provides several ways to **zoom**, or change the magnification of an object, to facilitate viewing and editing.

Table 1–1 shows several zoom methods.

Table 1–1 Zoom Methods

Tool	Method	Result
function key	To zoom in on an object, press the F9 key on the keyboard, press the F9 key again to return to the previous magnification.	Selected object appears centered in the workspace at 100% magnification.
mouse wheel	To change the magnification, press and hold the CTRL key and then move the mouse wheel down or up.	Page layout appears 20% smaller or larger.
Page Width button	To zoom to page width, tap or click the Page Width button (VIEW tab | Zoom group).	Page layout expands to fill the workspace horizontally.
ribbon	To use the ribbon, tap or click the VIEW tab. In the Zoom group, tap or click the desired button.	Page layout appears at selected magnification.
Selected Objects button	To zoom to objects, tap or click the Selected Objects button (VIEW tab | Zoom group).	Selected object is magnified as large as possible to fit on the screen.
shortcut keys	To zoom to page width, press CTRL+SHIFT+L.	Page layout is magnified as large as possible in the workspace.
shortcut menu	To zoom in on an object, press and hold or right-click the object, tap or point to Zoom on the shortcut menu, tap or click the desired magnification.	Object appears at selected magnification.
Show Whole Page button	To zoom to whole page, tap or click the Show Whole Page button on the status bar.	Page layout is magnified as large as possible in the workspace.
Whole Page button	To zoom to whole page, tap or click the Whole Page button (VIEW tab | Zoom group).	Page layout is magnified as large as possible in the workspace.
Zoom box	To change the magnification, enter a magnification percentage in the Zoom box (VIEW tab | Zoom group).	Page layout appears at entered magnification.
Zoom arrow	To change the magnification, tap or click Zoom box arrow (VIEW tab | Zoom group) and then tap or click desired magnification.	Page layout appears at selected magnification.
Zoom Out button Zoom In button	To increment or decrement magnification, tap or click the Zoom Out or Zoom In button on the status bar.	Page layout appears 10% smaller or larger with each tap or click.
Zoom slider	To change the magnification of the entire page, drag the Zoom slider on the status bar.	Objects appear at selected magnification.
100% button	To zoom to page width, tap or click the 100% button (VIEW tab | Zoom group).	Page layout is magnified to 100%.

© 2014 Cengage Learning

To Zoom

1 CUSTOMIZE TEMPLATES | 2 NAVIGATE & SELECT | 3 REPLACE TEXT | 4 DELETE OBJECTS | 5 FORMAT TEXT
6 INSERT GRAPHICS | 7 FORMAT PICTURE | 8 ENHANCE PAGE | 9 PRINT & EXIT | 10 OPEN & REVISE

When viewing an entire printed page, 8½ by11 inches, the magnification is approximately 45%, which makes reading small text difficult. If your keyboard has function keys, you press the F9 key to enlarge selected objects to 100% and center them in the Publisher window. Pressing the F9 key a second time returns the layout to its previous magnification. If you are using touch gestures, you can stretch to zoom in. The following step zooms in on the headline. *Why? Editing small areas of text is easier if you use zooming techniques to enlarge the view of the publication.*

1

- Stretch the text box or press the F9 key to zoom the selected object to approximately 100% (Figure 1–16).

Q&A What is the best way to zoom to 100%? If you have a keyboard with function keys, pressing the F9 key toggles between a zoom of 100% and the previous zoom percentage. You also can tap or click settings in the Zoom group on the VIEW tab on the ribbon.

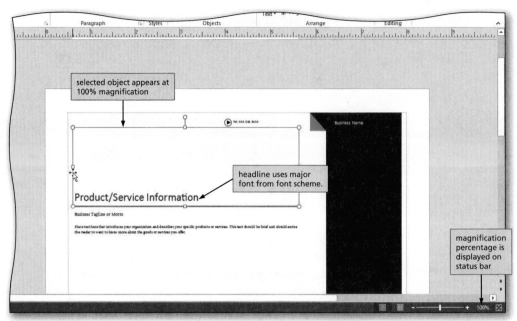

Figure 1–16

Other Ways

1. Press and hold or right-click object, tap or point to Zoom on shortcut menu, tap or click desired magnification on Zoom menu

2. Tap or click Zoom arrow (VIEW tab | Zoom group), tap or click desired magnification

3. Tap or click 100% button (VIEW tab | Zoom group)

4. Tap or click Selected Objects button (VIEW tab | Zoom group)

5. Drag Zoom slider on status bar

6. Tap or click Zoom In button or Zoom Out button on status bar

Selecting and Entering Text

The first step in editing a publication template is to replace its text by typing on the keyboard. You may have to scroll and zoom in the page layout to make careful edits. In a later section of this chapter, you will learn how to format, or change the appearance of the entered text.

Text Boxes

Most of Publisher's templates come with text already inserted into text boxes. A **text box** is an object in a publication designed to hold text in a specific shape, size, and style. Text boxes also can be drawn on the page using the Draw Text Box button (HOME tab | Objects group). Text boxes can be formatted using the ribbon, the mini toolbar, or the shortcut menu. A text box has changeable properties. A **property** is an attribute or characteristic of an object. Within text boxes, you can **edit**, or make changes to, many properties such as font, spacing, alignment, line/border style, fill color, and margins, among others. As you type, if you make a mistake you can backspace or use the DELETE key as you do in word processing. You also can **undo** by clicking the Undo button on the Quick Access Toolbar or by pressing CTRL+Z.

To Replace Placeholder Text

Publisher templates use two types of text in template text boxes. You select **placeholder text,** such as that in the flyer headline, with a single tap or click. ***Why?*** *Tapping or clicking once to select text allows you to begin typing immediately without having to select the text or press the* DELETE *key.* Other text, such as the business name, address, or tag line, is selected by dragging through the text, double-tapping or double-clicking specific words, or by pressing CTRL+A to select all of the text in the text box. Then, you simply type to replace the text.

The following steps select and replace placeholder text in the headline.

1

• Tap or click the headline text to select it (Figure 1–17).

Q&A | **What are the extra tabs on the ribbon?**
Those additional tabs appear when performing certain tasks with objects such as text boxes, pictures, or tables. You will use tool tabs later in this chapter and in subsequent chapters.

What toolbar was displayed when I selected the text?
Recall from the Office 2013 and Windows 8 chapter that the mini toolbar appears automatically and contains commands related to changing the appearance of text in a publication. If you do not use the mini toolbar, it disappears from the screen.

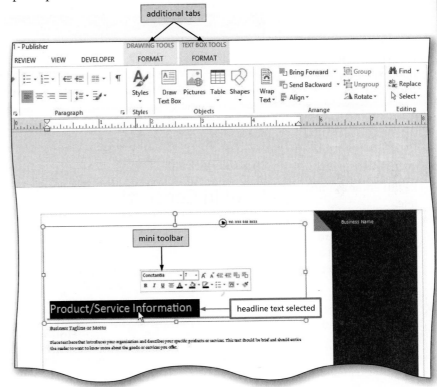

Figure 1–17

2

• Type `Shadows Blue` and then press the ENTER key to enter the first line of the heading.
• Type `Live! In Concert!` to complete the text (Figure 1–18).

Q&A | **What if I make an error while typing?**
Common word processing techniques work in Publisher text boxes. For example, you can press the BACKSPACE key until you have deleted the text in error and then retype the text correctly.

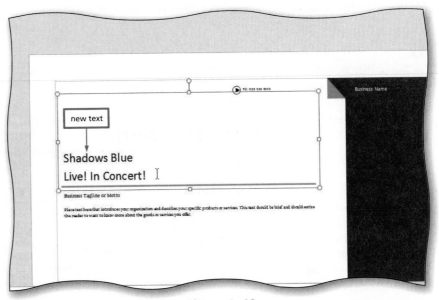

Figure 1–18

- Below the Business Tagline or Motto box, tap or click the text in the introduction text box to select the placeholder text.
- Stretch or click the Zoom In button on the status bar to zoom to approximately 200% (Figure 1–19).

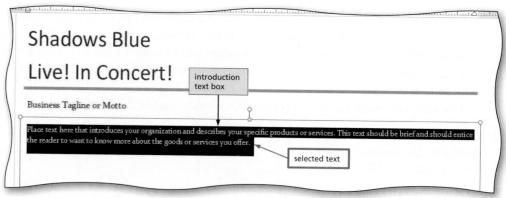

Figure 1–19

- Type **Saturday, October 4** and then press the ENTER key to enter the first line.
- Type **8:00 p.m. at the Campus Auditorium** to complete the text (Figure 1–20).

Q&A Am I skipping the Business Tagline or Motto text box?

The text in the Business Tagline or Motto text box is not selected with a single tap or click. You will edit that text later in the chapter.

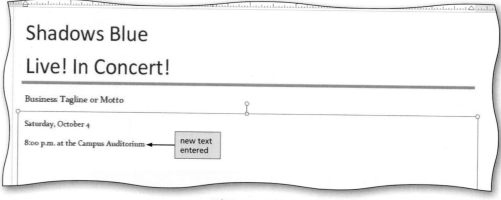

Figure 1–20

To Deselect an Object

1 CUSTOMIZE TEMPLATES | 2 NAVIGATE & SELECT | 3 REPLACE TEXT | 4 DELETE OBJECTS | 5 FORMAT TEXT
6 INSERT GRAPHICS | 7 FORMAT PICTURE | 8 ENHANCE PAGE | 9 PRINT & EXIT | 10 OPEN & REVISE

When a Publisher object is selected, scrolling is limited. *Why? Publisher assumes you would not want to scroll past the end of the object.* The following step deselects the object by clicking outside of its boundaries.

- Tap or click outside of the selected object (in this case, the text box) to deselect it (Figure 1– 21).

Q&A Exactly where should I click?

As long as you do not select another object, anywhere in the workspace is fine. You may want to click just to the right of the text box selection rectangle.

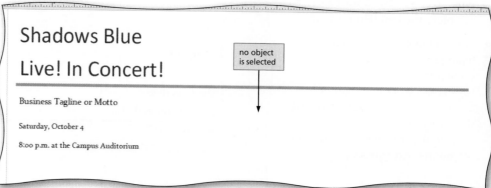

Figure 1–21

Other Ways

1. Press ESC

To Replace More Placeholder Text

1 Scroll to the upper portion of the template and then tap or click the text in the phone number text box to select the placeholder text

2 Type `555-TICKETS` to replace the text (Figure 1–22).

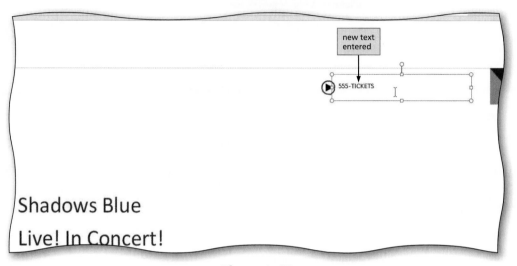

Figure 1–22

To Replace Other Text

1 CUSTOMIZE TEMPLATES | 2 NAVIGATE & SELECT | **3 REPLACE TEXT** | **4 DELETE OBJECTS** | **5 FORMAT TEXT**
6 INSERT GRAPHICS | **7 FORMAT PICTURE** | **8 ENHANCE PAGE** | **9 PRINT & EXIT** | **10 OPEN & REVISE**

In the following steps, you replace the **default**, or preset, text in other template text boxes by selecting all of the text and then typing the new text. ***Why?*** *Default text is different from placeholder text that is selected with a single click.*

1

• Scroll down and then tap or click the text in the Business Tagline or Motto text box to position the insertion point inside the text box (Figure 1–23).

 What is the button that displays the letter, i?

It is a smart tag button. If you click it, Publisher offers to fill in the text for you with various options. **Smart tag buttons** appear when you point to certain text boxes that are part of the business information set or when you click a logo.

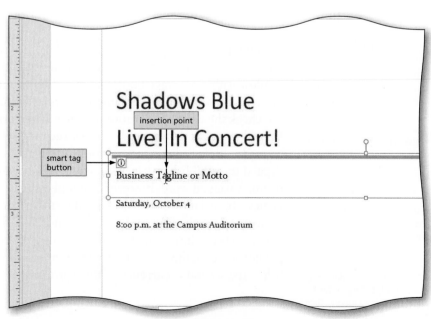

Figure 1–23

- Drag through the text in the Business Tagline or Motto text box to select all of the text in the text box (Figure 1–24).

 Could I press CTRL+A?

Yes, as long as the insertion point is positioned inside the text box, CTRL+A will select all of the text in the text box.

Figure 1–24

- Type **For tickets, visit www.utix.biz** to complete the text (Figure 1–25).

 Should I press the DELETE key before typing?

It is not necessary to press the DELETE key; the text you type deletes the selected text automatically.

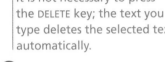

- Deselect the text box by tapping or clicking outside of its boundary.

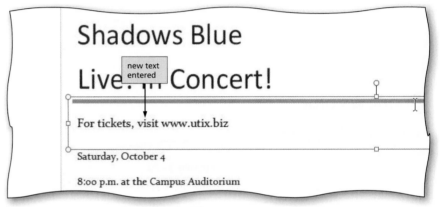

Figure 1–25

Other Ways

1. Select text box, tap or click Select button (HOME tab | Editing group), tap or click Select All Text in Text Box, type new text

---

BTW

Automatic Spelling Correction

As you type, Publisher automatically corrects some misspelled words. For example, if you type, recieve, Publisher automatically corrects the misspelling and displays the word, receive, when you press the spacebar or type a punctuation mark.

BTW

Automatically Corrected Words

To see a complete list of automatically corrected words, click FILE on the ribbon to open the Backstage view, click Options in the Backstage view, click Proofing in the left pane (Publisher Options dialog box), click the AutoCorrect Options button, and then scroll through the list near the bottom of the dialog box.

Checking the Spelling

As you type text in a publication, Publisher checks your typing for possible spelling errors. As mentioned earlier, Publisher **flags** the potential error in the publication window with a red wavy underline. A red wavy underline means the flagged text is not in Publisher's dictionary (because it is a proper name or misspelled). Although you can check the entire publication for spelling errors at once, you also can check these flagged errors as they appear on the screen.

To display a list of corrections for flagged text, press and hold or right-click the flagged text. Publisher displays a list of suggested spelling corrections on the shortcut menu. A flagged word, however, is not necessarily misspelled. For example, many names, abbreviations, and specialized terms are not in Publisher's main dictionary. In these cases, you instruct Publisher to ignore the flagged word. As you type, Publisher also detects duplicate words while checking for spelling errors. For example, if your publication contains the phrase, to the the store, Publisher places a red wavy underline below the second occurrence of the word, the.

To Check Spelling as You Type

In the following steps, the word, Concerts, has been misspelled intentionally as Conerts to illustrate Publisher's check spelling as you type feature. If you are doing this project on a computer, your flyer may contain different misspelled words. *Why? You may have made spelling or typographical errors, if your typing was not accurate.*

- Scroll to the upper-right portion of the flyer.
- Tap or click the text in the Business Name text box to position the insertion point inside the text box.
- Drag through the text, or press CTRL+A, to select all of the text in the text box (Figure 1–26).

Q&A
Why does my template list a different business name?
The person who installed Microsoft Office 2013 on your computer or network may have set or customized the field.

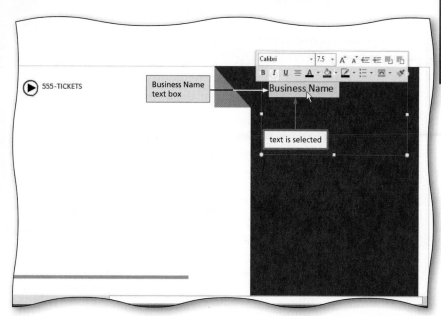

Figure 1–26

- Type **Campus Conerts** and then press the SPACEBAR so that a red wavy line appears below the misspelled word (Figure 1–27).

Q&A
What if Publisher does not flag my spelling errors with wavy underlines?
To verify that the check spelling as you type features are enabled, click FILE on the ribbon to open the Backstage view and then click Options. When the Publisher Options dialog box is displayed, click Proofing in the left pane, and then ensure the 'Check spelling as you type' check box contains a check mark. Also ensure the 'Hide spelling and grammar errors' check box does not have a check mark. Tap or click the OK button.

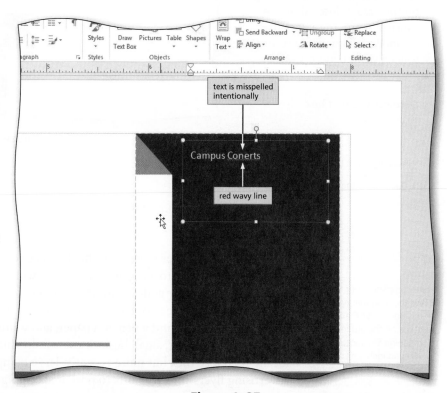

Figure 1–27

3

- Press and hold or right-click the flagged word (Conerts, in this case) to display a shortcut menu that presents a list of suggested spelling corrections for the flagged word (Figure 1–28).

What if, when I right-click the misspelled word, my desired correction is not in the list on the shortcut menu?

You can click outside the shortcut menu to close the shortcut menu and then retype the correct word, or you can click Spelling on the shortcut menu to display the Spelling dialog box. Chapter 2 discusses the Spelling dialog box.

What if a flagged word actually is, for example, a proper name and spelled correctly?

Press and hold or right-click it and then click Ignore All on the shortcut menu to instruct Publisher not to flag future occurrences of the same word in this publication.

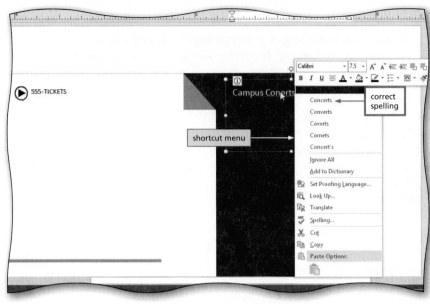

Figure 1–28

4

- Tap or click the correct spelling (in this case, Concerts) on the shortcut menu to replace the misspelled word with a correctly spelled word (Figure 1–29).

5

- Deselect the text box.

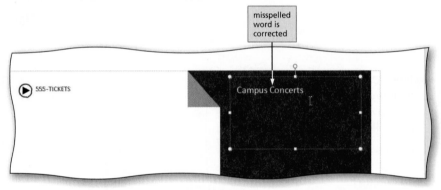

Figure 1–29

Other Ways

1. Tap or click Spelling button (REVIEW tab | Proofing group)

Tear-Offs

BTW
BTWs
For a complete list of the BTWs found in the margins of this book, visit the BTW resource on the Student Companion Site located on www.cengagebrain.com. For detailed instructions about accessing available resources, visit www.cengage.com/ct/studentdownload or see the inside back cover of this book.

Across the lower portion of the flyer are contact information tear-offs. **Tear-offs** are small, ready-to-be scored text boxes with some combination of name, phone number, fax, email, or address information. Designed for customer use, tear-offs typically are perforated so that a person walking by can tear off a tab to keep, rather than having to stop, find a pen and paper, and write down the name and phone number. Traditionally, small businesses or individuals wanting to advertise something locally used tear-offs, but more recently, large companies are mass-producing advertising flyers with tear-offs to post at shopping centers, display in offices, and advertise on college campuses.

Publisher tear-offs contain placeholder text and are **synchronized**, which means when you finish editing one of the tear-off text boxes, the others change to match it automatically.

To Enter Tear-Off Text

The following steps edit the tear-off text boxes. **Why?** *The tear-offs must contain information to contact the flyer's creator or to request more information.*

1

- Scroll to display the lower portion of the flyer.
- Tap or click the text in one of the tear-off text boxes to select it (Figure 1–30).

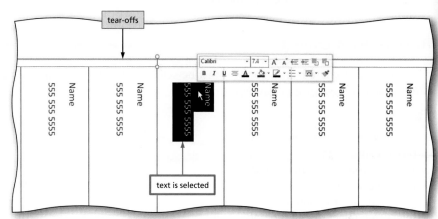

Figure 1–30

2

- Type **Shadows Blue 555-TICKETS** and then press the ENTER key.
- Type **Online at www.utix. biz** to complete the tear-off (Figure 1–31).

If requested by your instructor, enter your phone number instead of 555-TICKETS in the tear-off.

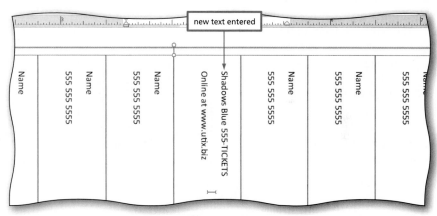

Figure 1–31

3

- Tap or click outside of the text box to synchronize the other tear-offs (Figure 1–32).

Q&A

What if I want to make each tear-off different?

Typically, all of the tear-offs are the same, but you can undo synchronization by tapping or clicking the Undo button on the Quick Access Toolbar and then entering the text for other tear-offs.

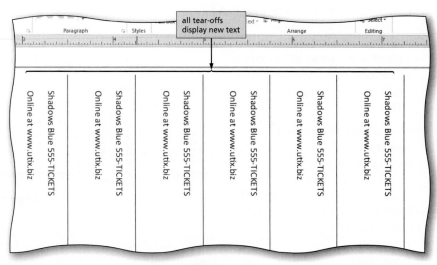

Figure 1–32

Deleting Objects

Templates may display objects in the page layout that you do not wish to use. In those cases, or when you change your mind about including an inserted object, you must delete objects.

To Delete an Object

In order to delete an object, it must be selected. In the following steps, you delete the organization logo. *Why? The logo is not used in this flyer.*

- Scroll as necessary to display the organization logo.
- Tap near the icon or point to the logo to display the boundary and then click the boundary to select the object. Avoid tapping or clicking the text in the logo (Figure 1–33).

Q&A What if I want to delete just part of the logo?
The template logo, in this case, is a small picture and the word, Organization, grouped together. To delete one or the other, select the logo first, and then tap or click only the part of the object you wish to delete. Press the DELETE key to delete that part of the grouped object.

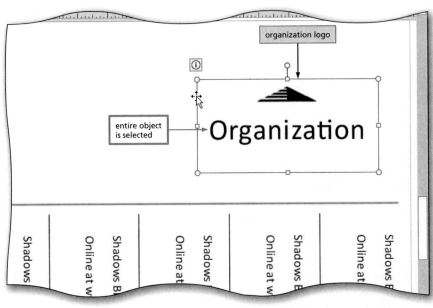

Figure 1–33

- Press the DELETE key to delete the selected object (Figure 1–34).

Q&A Why did only the text disappear?
You may have selected the text, or the boundary of the text box, instead of the boundary of the entire logo. Select the remaining object and then press the DELETE key.

What if I delete an object accidentally?
Press CTRL+Z to undo the most recent step, or tap or click the Undo button on the Quick Access Toolbar. The object will reappear in the original location.

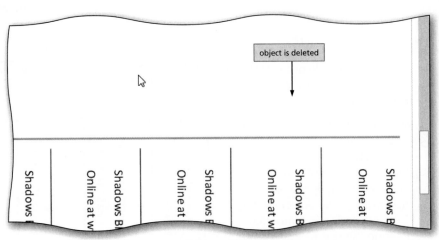

Figure 1–34

Other Ways

1. Press and hold or right-click, tap or click Delete Object on shortcut menu
2. Select object, press BACKSPACE

To Save a Publication with a New File Name

You have performed many tasks while creating this publication and do not want to risk losing work completed thus far. Accordingly, you should save the publication on your hard disk, SkyDrive, or a location that is most appropriate to your situation.

The following steps assume you already have created folders for storing your files, for example, a CIS 101 folder (for your class) that contains a Publisher folder (for your assignments). Thus, these steps save the publication in the Publisher folder in the CIS 101 folder on your desired save location. For a detailed example of the procedure for saving a file in a folder or saving a file on SkyDrive, refer to the Office and Windows chapter at the beginning of this book.

1 Tap or click the Save button on the Quick Access Toolbar, which depending on settings, will display either the Save As gallery in the Backstage view or the Save As dialog box.

2 To save on a hard disk or other storage media on your computer, proceed to Step 2a. To save on SkyDrive, proceed to Step 2b.

2a If your screen opens the Backstage view and you want to save on storage media on your computer, tap or click Computer in the left pane, if necessary, to display options in the right pane related to saving on your computer. If your screen already displays the Save As dialog box, proceed to Step 3.

2b If your screen opens the Backstage view and you want to save on SkyDrive, tap or click SkyDrive in the left pane to display SkyDrive saving options or a Sign In button. If your screen displays a Sign In button, tap or click it and then sign in to SkyDrive.

3 Tap or click the Browse button in the right pane to display the Save As dialog box associated with the selected save location (i.e., Computer or SkyDrive).

4 Type `Concert Flyer` in the File name text box to change the file name. Do not press the ENTER key after typing the file name because you do not want to close the dialog box at this time.

5 Navigate to the desired save location (in this case, the Publisher folder in the CIS 101 folder [or your class folder] on your computer or SkyDrive).

6 Tap or click the Save button (Save As dialog box) to save the file in the selected save folder on the selected location with the entered file name.

> **BTW**
> **Organizing Files and Folders**
> You should organize and store files in folders so that you easily can find the files later. For example, if you are taking an introductory computer class called CIS 101, a good practice would be to save all Publisher files in a Publisher folder in a CIS 101 folder. For a discussion of folders and detailed examples of creating folders, refer to the Office and Windows chapter at the beginning of this book.

Break Point: If you wish to take a break, this is a good place to do so. To resume at a later time, run Publisher, open the file called Concert Flyer, and continue following the steps from this location forward.

Formatting Text

Although you can format text before you type, many Publisher users enter text first and then format the existing text. Publisher provides many ways to modify the appearance, or **format**, of selected text. Some formatting options include editing the font, paragraph, alignment, typography, copy fitting, and text effects. The more common formatting commands are shown in the Font group on the HOME tab on the ribbon (Figure 1–35) or on the TEXT BOX TOOLS FORMAT tab. These include the capability to change the font size, color, style, and effects. You will learn more about each of the formatting options in the Font group as you use them.

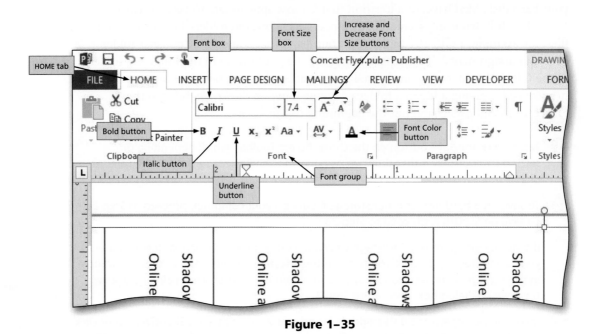

Figure 1–35

BTW
Touch Screen Differences
The Office and Windows interfaces may vary if you are using a touch screen. For this reason, you might notice that the function or appearance of your touch screen differs slightly from this chapter's presentation.

Many of these formatting tools also appear on a mini toolbar when you point to text. Recall that the mini toolbar, which appears automatically based on the tasks you perform, contains commands related to changing the appearance of text or graphics in a publication. The purpose of the mini toolbar is to minimize mouse movement.

A third way to format text involves using the shortcut menu, which appears when you press and hold or right-click an object, or when you press SHIFT+F10. The shortcut menu is a list of frequently used commands that relate to the selected object. If you press and hold or right-click some items, Publisher displays both the mini toolbar and a shortcut menu.

Formatting Text

Characters that appear on the screen are a specific shape and size, determined by the template you choose or the settings you apply. Recall that the font, or typeface, defines the appearance and shape of the letters, numbers, and special characters. The name of the font appears in the Font box (HOME tab | Font group). You can leave characters in the default font or change them to a different font. **Font size** specifies the size of the characters and is determined by a measurement system called points. A single **point** is about 1/72 of one inch in height. Thus, a character with a font size of 12 is about 12/72 or 1/6 of one inch in height. You can increase or decrease the font size of characters in a publication, as well as change the capitalization.

In addition to the common bold, italic, and underline formatting options, Publisher also allows you to apply special text effects and highlights.

Formatting Single versus Multiple Characters and Words

To format a single character, the character must be selected. To format a word, however, you simply can position the insertion point in the word, to make it the current word, and then format the word. You will learn in a later chapter that paragraph formatting, such as alignment and bullets, also can be applied without first selecting it; however, if you want to format multiple characters or words, you first must select the words you want to format and then format the selection.

To Bold Text

Bold characters appear somewhat thicker and darker than those that are not bold. To format the name of the band, you first will select the line. ***Why?*** *Multiple words or lines must be selected in order to apply formatting.* The following steps add bold formatting to the name of the band.

- Deselect any selected object, if necessary.
- Scroll to the upper portion of the flyer.
- Swipe or drag through the text you wish to format (in this case, the name of the band).
- With the text selected, tap or click the Bold button (HOME tab | Font group) to bold the selected text (Figure 1–36).

Q&A
How would I remove a bold format?
You would click the Bold button a second time, or you immediately could tap or click the Undo button on the Quick Access Toolbar, or press CTRL+Z.

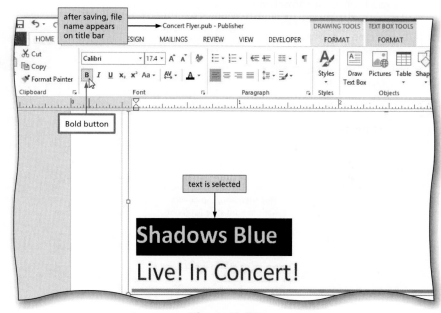

Figure 1–36

- Do not deselect the text.

Other Ways

1. Tap or click Bold button on mini toolbar	on shortcut menu, tap or click Font, tap or click Bold in Font style list (Font dialog box), tap or click OK button	3. Tap or click Font Dialog Box Launcher (HOME tab | Font group), tap or click Bold in Font style list (Font dialog box), tap or click OK button	4. Press CTRL+B
2. Press and hold or right-click selected text, tap or point to Change Text			

To Italicize Text

Italic text has a slanted appearance. The following steps format a word in italic. **Why?** *The italicized text draws attention and makes the text stand out.*

1

- With the text selected (Shadows Blue in this case), tap or click the Italic button (HOME tab | Font group) to italicize the selected text (Figure 1–37).

Q&A

How would I remove an italic format?
You would tap or click the Italic button a second time, or you immediately could tap or click the Undo button on the Quick Access Toolbar, or press CTRL+Z.

How can I tell what formatting has been applied to text?
The selected buttons and boxes on the HOME tab show formatting characteristics of the location of the insertion point.

2

- Deselect the text.

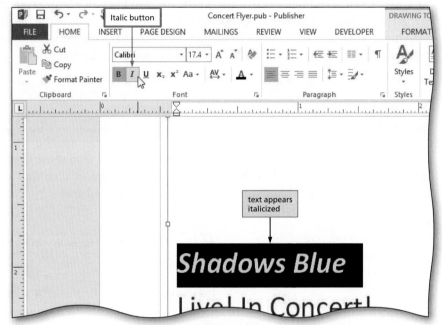

Figure 1–37

Other Ways

1. Tap or click Italic button on mini toolbar

2. Press and hold or right-click, point to Change Text on shortcut menu, | tap or click Font on Change Text submenu, tap or click Italic in Font style list (Font dialog box), tap or click OK button | 3. Tap or click Font Dialog Box Launcher (HOME tab | Font group), tap or click Italic in Font style list (Font dialog box), tap or click OK button | 4. Press CTRL+I

Autofitting Text

Other advanced text formatting commands are located on the TEXT BOX TOOLS FORMAT tab that is displayed when a text box is selected. You can autofit text, change the text direction, and hyphenate, as well as make changes to the alignment, styles, and typography.

Sometimes, the replacement text that you enter into a template does not fit the same way as the original template text—there might be too much text to fit, or too little text to fill the box. In those cases, you may want **autofit**, or **copy fit**, the text to adjust the way the text fits into the text box. Publisher autofitting choices are listed in Table 1–2.

Table 1–2 Autofitting Choices

Type of Autofitting	Result
Best Fit	Shrinks or expands text to fit in the text box, even when the text box is resized
Shrink Text On Overflow	Reduces the point size of text until no text is in overflow
Grow Text Box to Fit	Enlarges text box to fit all of the text at its current size
Do Not Autofit	Text appears at its current size

To Autofit Text

The following steps autofit the text in the headline. *Why?* *You want the headline to appear as large as possible.*

1

- If necessary, click the text in the desired text box (in this case the headline text) to position the insertion point in the text box.
- Tap or click TEXT BOX TOOLS FORMAT on the ribbon to display the TEXT BOX TOOLS FORMAT tab.
- Tap or click the Text Fit button (TEXT BOX TOOLS FORMAT tab | Text group) to display the Text Fit menu (Figure 1–38).

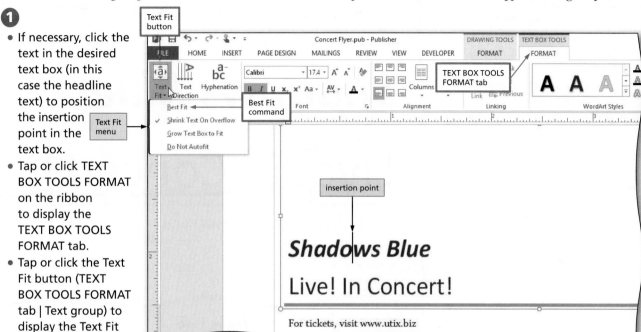

Figure 1–38

Q&A Do I have to select all of the text in a text box in order to autofit it?
No. Because all of the text in the text box is included automatically in autofitting, you do not need to select the text in order to autofit it.

2

- Tap or click Best Fit to autofit the text in the text box (Figure 1–39).

Q&A Could I use the Increase Font Size button to make the headline larger?
Yes, but you would have to estimate how big to make the text. Autofitting is different from using the Increase Font Size button. With autofitting, the text is increased, or decreased, to fit the given size of the text box automatically.

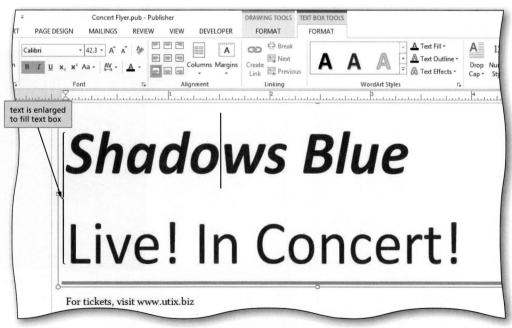

Figure 1–39

- Tap or click the text, For tickets, visit www.utix.biz.
- Tap or click the Text Fit button (TEXT BOX TOOLS FORMAT tab | Text group) to display the Text Fit menu.
- Tap or click Best Fit to autofit the text (Figure 1–40).

Figure 1–40

- Scroll if necessary and then tap or click the text, Campus Concerts, in the upper-right portion of the page.
- Tap or click the Text Fit button (TEXT BOX TOOLS FORMAT tab | Text group) to display the Text Fit menu.
- Tap or click Best Fit to autofit the text (Figure 1–41).

- Deselect the text box.

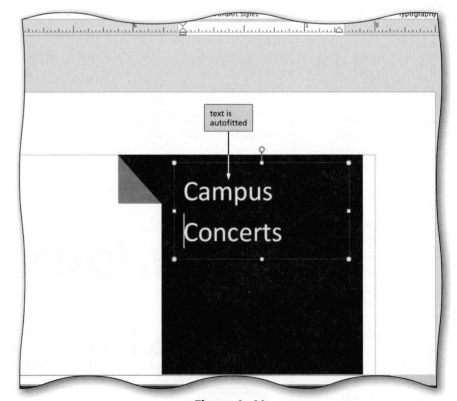

Figure 1–41

Other Ways

1. Press and hold or right-click selected text, tap or click Best Fit on shortcut menu

To Increase the Font Size

The following steps use the Increase Font Size button to enlarge the date and place text to make it easier to read. *Why not use autofit? The Best Fit command would fill the large text box, making the text even larger than the headline.*

- Scroll as necessary to display the text in the date and place text box.
- Tap or click the text and then press CTRL+A to select all of the text in the text box.
- Tap or click the 'Increase Font Size' button (HOME tab | Font group) several times until the text fills the text box without wrapping to a third line. If the line wraps, click the 'Decrease Font Size' button (HOME tab | Font group) (Figure 1–42).

Figure 1–42

Q&A Why did the ribbon change back to the HOME tab?
In the previous steps, you deselected the Campus Concerts text box. When no object is selected, Publisher redisplays the HOME tab.

- Deselect the text box.

Other Ways

1. Tap or click Increase Font Size button on mini toolbar
2. Tap or click Font Size arrow (HOME tab | Font group), tap or click larger font size
3. Press SHIFT+CTRL+>

To Underline Text

Underlines are used to emphasize or draw attention to specific text. **Underlined** text prints with an underscore (_) below each character. *Why? Underlining the spaces between words provides continuity.* In the flyer, the name of the series, Campus Concerts, is emphasized with an underline. The steps on the next page select the text and format it with an underline.

1

- Scroll as necessary and select the text, Campus Concerts, in the upper-right portion of the flyer.
- With the text selected, click the Underline button (HOME tab | Font group) to underline the selected text (Figure 1–43).

Q&A
How would I remove an underline?
You would click the Underline button a second time, or you immediately could tap or click the Undo button on the Quick Access Toolbar, or press CTRL+Z.

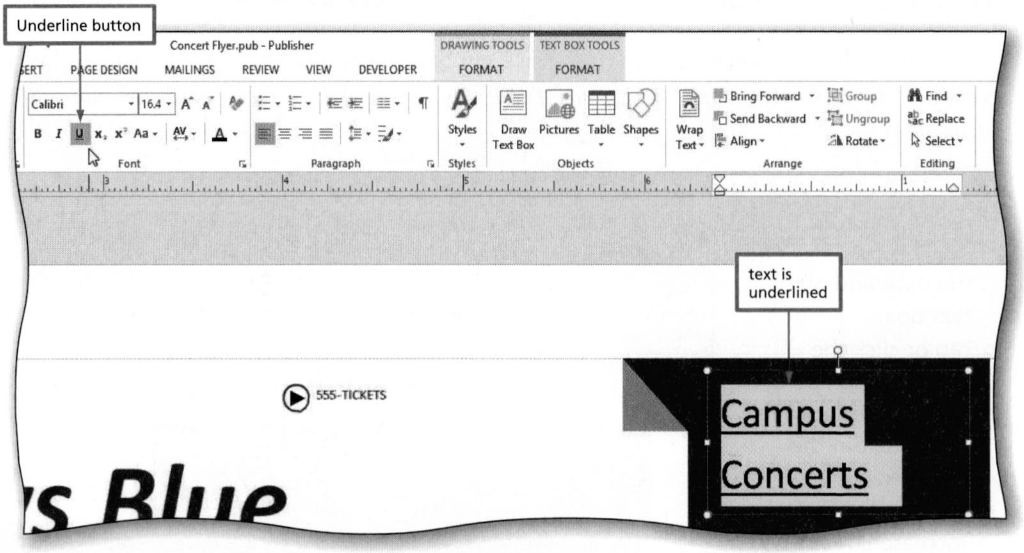

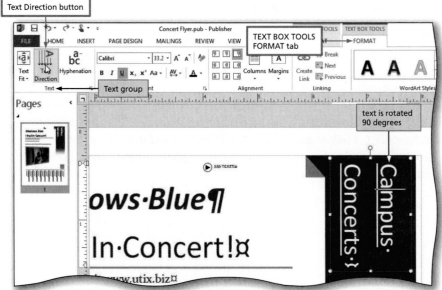

Figure 1–43

2

- Deselect the text.

Other Ways

1. Tap or click Underline button on mini toolbar	or click Font on Change Text submenu, tap or click Underline arrow (Font dialog box), tap or click desired underline style, tap or click OK button	3. Tap or click Font Dialog Box Launcher (HOME tab | Font group), tap or click Underline arrow (Font dialog box), tap or click desired underline style, tap or click OK button	4. Press CTRL+U
2. Press and hold or right-click selected text, point to Change Text on shortcut menu, tap			

To Change Text Direction

1 CUSTOMIZE TEMPLATES | 2 NAVIGATE & SELECT | 3 REPLACE TEXT | 4 DELETE OBJECTS | 5 FORMAT TEXT
6 INSERT GRAPHICS | 7 FORMAT PICTURE | 8 ENHANCE PAGE | 9 PRINT & EXIT | 10 OPEN & REVISE

The next step is to change the direction of the text in the upper-right portion of the flyer. *Why? Changing the direction adds interest.* Later in the chapter, you will enlarge the text box to make the text appear on one line. The following step changes direction of the text.

1

- Tap or click the text to be changed (in this case, Campus Concerts).
- If necessary, tap or click TEXT BOX TOOLS FORMAT on the ribbon to display the TEXT BOX TOOLS FORMAT tab.
- Tap or click the Text Direction button (TEXT BOX TOOLS FORMAT tab | Text group) to change the text direction (Figure 1–44).

Q&A
Do I have to select the text first?
No. As with single-word formatting, Publisher will apply the text direction to all of the text in the text box.

Figure 1–44

To View Whole Page

The following step views the entire page layout. *Why? Before you save the publication again, you may want to see how it looks so far.*

- Tap or click the 'Show Whole Page' button on the status bar to view the entire page (Figure 1–45).

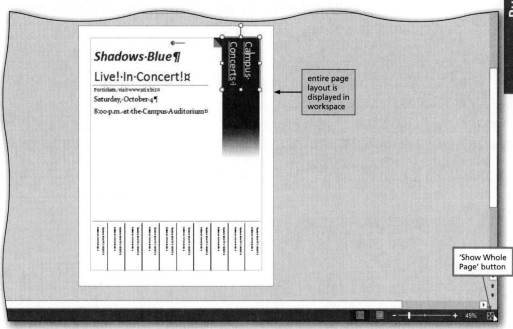

Figure 1–45

Other Ways

1. Tap or click Whole Page button (VIEW tab | Zoom group)　　2. Press SHIFT+CTRL+L

To Save an Existing Publication with the Same File Name

You have made several modifications to the publication since you last saved it. Thus, you should save it again. The following step saves the publication again. For an example of the step listed below, refer to the Office and Windows chapter at the beginning of this book.

 Tap or click the Save button on the Quick Access Toolbar to overwrite the previously saved file.

Break Point: If you wish to take a break, this is a good place to do so. To resume at a later time, run Publisher, open the file called Concert Flyer, and continue following the steps from this location forward.

Using Graphics

Files containing graphical images, also called **graphics**, are available from a variety of sources. Publisher provides access to Office.com Clip Art, a series of royalty-free, predefined graphics, such as drawings, photos, sounds, videos, and other media files, called clips. A **clip** is a single media file, such as art, sound, or animation, that you can insert and use in print publications, web publications, and other Microsoft Office documents. You also can insert pictures stored on your computer or storage location, or search for pictures on the web. **Picture** is a generic term for photos and clip art. You will learn about other kinds of graphics and illustrations in future chapters.

Many templates have picture placeholders that provide a size and shape to hold selected pictures. A **picture placeholder** has boundaries and a picture icon that is displayed only when you point to it. You can click the picture icon in a template to access the Insert Pictures dialog box. You also can insert an empty picture frame to reserve space for pictures you want to add later.

To Use the Picture Placeholder

1 CUSTOMIZE TEMPLATES | 2 NAVIGATE & SELECT | 3 REPLACE TEXT | 4 DELETE OBJECTS | 5 FORMAT TEXT
6 INSERT GRAPHICS | 7 FORMAT PICTURE | 8 ENHANCE PAGE | 9 PRINT & EXIT | 10 OPEN & REVISE

Many templates contain picture placeholders whose size and shape fit in with the template style. *Why? Publications with pictures attract attention and add a sense of realism; most users want pictures in their publications.* The following steps use the picture placeholder to access photos from Office.com Clip Art.

1
- Tap or click the area above the tear-offs to display the boundary of the picture placeholder and the picture placeholder icon.
- Stretch or press the F9 key to zoom to 100% (Figure 1–46).

Can I turn on the boundary so that I can see it without pointing to it?
Yes. Tap or click the Boundaries check box (VIEW tab | Show group), which will display the boundaries on all objects.

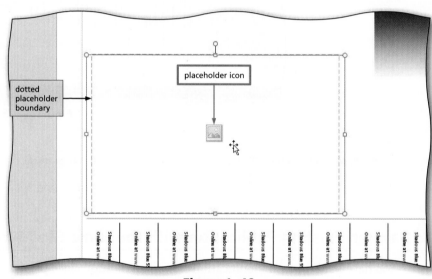

Figure 1–46

2
- Tap or click the placeholder icon to display the Insert Pictures dialog box.
- Tap or click Office.com Clip Art to place the insertion point in the search box.
- Type the desired search term (in this case, guitar) in the search box (Figure 1–47).

If I decide not to add a picture, will the placeholder print?
No. Graphic placeholders do not print. Placeholder text will print, however.

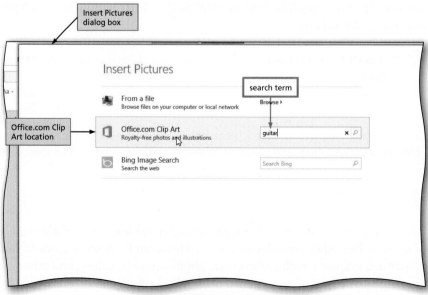

Figure 1–47

3

- Press the ENTER key to begin the search.
- When the results appear, tap or click the picture shown in Figure 1–48 or a similar picture.

 Experiment

- Scroll through the clip art gallery and notice it includes photos, drawings, and traditional clip art graphics. When you are finished, tap or click the desired picture.

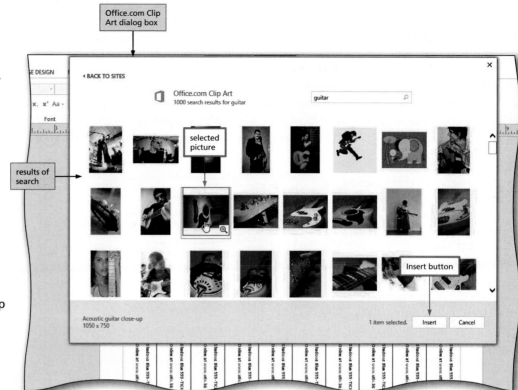

Figure 1–48

4

- Tap or click the Insert button (Office. com Clip Art dialog box) to insert the chosen picture into the publication (Figure 1–49).

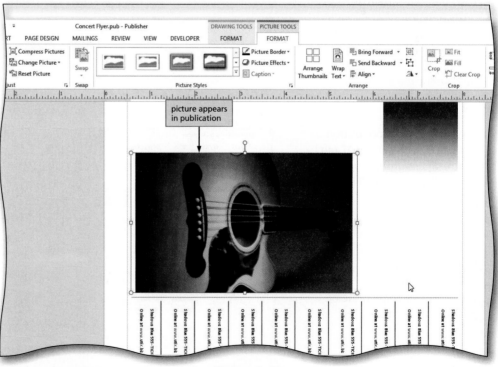

Figure 1–49

To Apply a Picture Style

Publisher provides **picture styles** that allow you easily to change the basic rectangle format to a more visually appealing style and designer look. The Picture Style gallery has more than 20 picture styles that include a variety of shapes, borders, and scallops. The flyer in this chapter uses a picture style slanting up and right. *Why?* *Some researchers say that an upward slant adds energy to a publication and directs the reader's eye toward the center of the publication with a 3-D look.* The following steps apply a picture style to the picture in the flyer.

1

- If necessary, select the picture.
- If necessary, tap or click PICTURE TOOLS FORMAT on the ribbon to display the PICTURE TOOLS FORMAT tab.
- Scroll slightly right to adjust the page layout.
- If you are using a mouse, point to the More button (PICTURE TOOLS FORMAT tab | Picture Styles group) to display the Enhanced ScreenTip (Figure 1–50).

Q&A Why did I scroll the page layout?
By scrolling, the Picture Styles gallery will not cover up the graphic in the next step.

What is an Enhanced ScreenTip?
An **Enhanced ScreenTip** is an on-screen note that provides the name of the command, a description, and sometimes instructions for how to obtain help about the command.

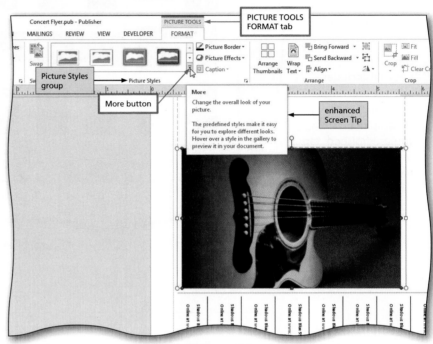

Figure 1–50

2

- Tap or click the More button (PICTURE TOOLS FORMAT tab | Picture Styles group) to display the Picture Styles gallery (Figure 1–51).

 Experiment

- Point to various picture styles in the Picture Styles gallery and watch the format of the picture change in the publication window.

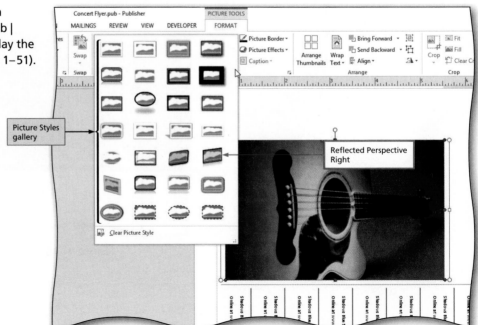

Figure 1–51

- Tap or click Reflected Perspective Right in the Picture Styles gallery to apply the selected style to the picture (Figure 1–52).

Q&A Should I be concerned that the picture overlaps the tear-offs slightly?
No. You will move the picture later in the chapter.

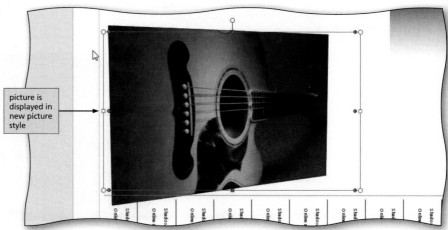

picture is displayed in new picture style

Figure 1–52

Borders

Similar to a frame around a picture on the wall, a **border** helps define the edge of an object on the page. Not only can you choose a color for the border, but Publisher also allows you to set a weight or size of the border and choose a tint, dashed line, or pattern.

To Set the Weight of a Border

1 CUSTOMIZE TEMPLATES | 2 NAVIGATE & SELECT | 3 REPLACE TEXT | 4 DELETE OBJECTS | 5 FORMAT TEXT
6 INSERT GRAPHICS | 7 FORMAT PICTURE | 8 ENHANCE PAGE | 9 PRINT & EXIT | 10 OPEN & REVISE

You will change the weight of the line around the picture to create a border. **Why?** *Adding a border defines the edges of a picture, makes it stand out from the background, and eliminates the perception of floating.* The following steps add a border to the picture in the flyer.

1

- If necessary, select the picture.
- Tap or click the Picture Border button (PICTURE TOOLS FORMAT tab | Picture Styles group) to display the Picture Border gallery.
- Tap or click Weight to display the Weight gallery (Figure 1–53).

Experiment

- Point to various weights in the list and watch the border size change in the publication window.

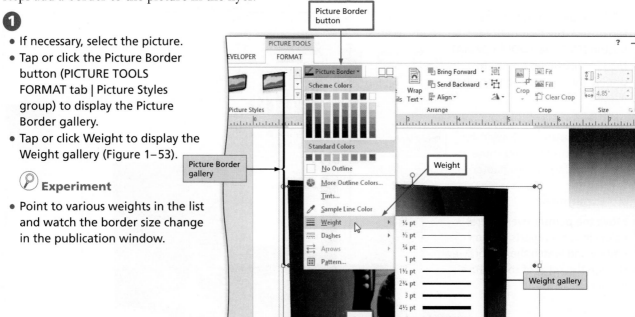

Figure 1–53

- Tap or click 6 pt to apply a 6-point line (Figure 1–54).

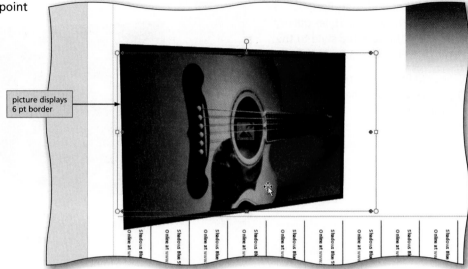

picture displays 6 pt border

Figure 1–54

Other Ways

1. Press and hold or right-click selected picture, tap or click Format Picture on shortcut menu, tap or click Colors and Lines tab, enter width

2. Tap or click Format Shape Dialog Box Launcher (PICTURE TOOLS FORMAT tab | Picture Styles group), tap or click Colors and Lines tab, enter width

To Change the Border Color

1 CUSTOMIZE TEMPLATES | 2 NAVIGATE & SELECT | 3 REPLACE TEXT | 4 DELETE OBJECTS | 5 FORMAT TEXT
6 INSERT GRAPHICS | 7 FORMAT PICTURE | 8 ENHANCE PAGE | 9 PRINT & EXIT | 10 OPEN & REVISE

The following steps change the border color to gray. *Why? The picture is dark; gray helps define the border better than the default black color.*

- With the picture still selected, tap or click the Picture Border button (PICTURE TOOLS FORMAT tab | Picture Styles group) to display the Picture Border gallery (Figure 1–55).

Q&A What is the first row of colors? Those colors are the Navy color scheme colors that you chose at the beginning of the chapter.

Experiment

- Move the pointer over several colors in various parts of the gallery and watch the live preview change the color of the picture border.

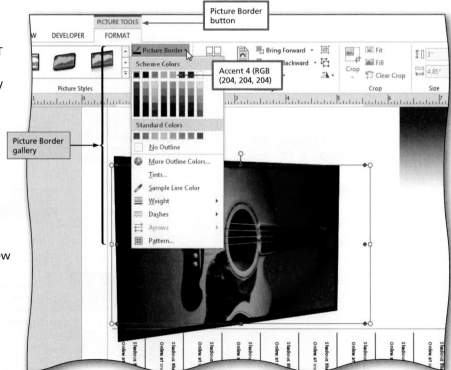

Figure 1–55

2

- Tap or click Accent 4 (RGB (204, 204, 204)) (first row, fifth column) to choose the gray color from the color scheme (Figure 1–56).

Q&A What do the numbers in the button name signify?
Those are the intensity values of red, green, and blue that define the color, gray.

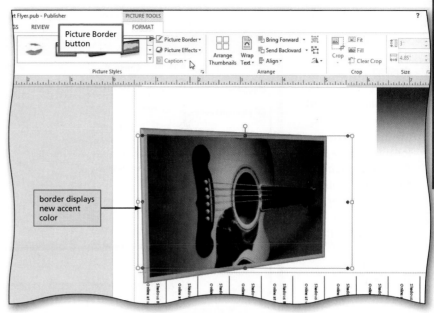

Figure 1–56

Other Ways

1. Tap or click Format Picture on shortcut menu, on Colors and Lines sheet, tap or click Color box in Line area, tap or click desired color

2. Tap or click Format Shape Dialog Box Launcher (PICTURE TOOLS FORMAT tab | Picture Styles group), on Colors and Lines sheet, tap or click Color box in Line area, tap or click desired color

To Insert a Picture from a Storage Device

1 CUSTOMIZE TEMPLATES | 2 NAVIGATE & SELECT | 3 REPLACE TEXT | 4 DELETE OBJECTS | 5 FORMAT TEXT
6 INSERT GRAPHICS | 7 FORMAT PICTURE | **8 ENHANCE PAGE** | 9 PRINT & EXIT | 10 OPEN & REVISE

You do not have to have a picture placeholder to insert pictures into a publication. *Why? You may want to use a picture as is and not have it conform to the size of the placeholder.* You can insert both online pictures and those from storage, using the Publisher ribbon.

The following steps insert a picture from a storage device. To complete this assignment, you will be required to use the Data Files for Students. Visit www.cengage.com/ct/studentdownload for detailed instructions or contact your instructor for information about accessing the required files.

1

- Tap or click outside the page layout so that no object is selected.
- Tap or click INSERT on the ribbon to display the INSERT tab (Figure 1–57).

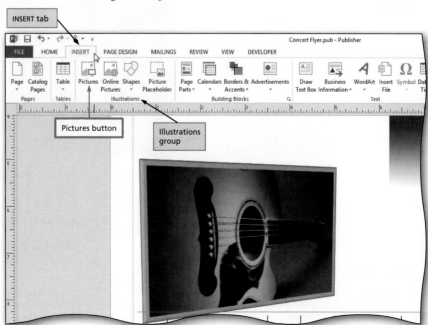

Figure 1–57

2

- Tap or click the Pictures button (INSERT tab | Illustrations group) to display the Insert Picture dialog box.
- Navigate to the location of the Data Files for Students (in this case, Chapter 01 in the Publisher folder [or your class folder]) on your computer or SkyDrive (Figure 1–58).

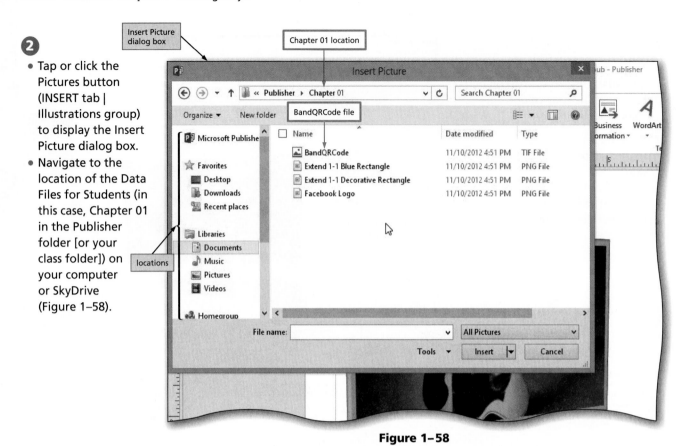

Figure 1–58

3

- Double-tap or double-click the desired picture (in this case, the BandQRCode file) to insert the file into the publication (Figure 1–59).

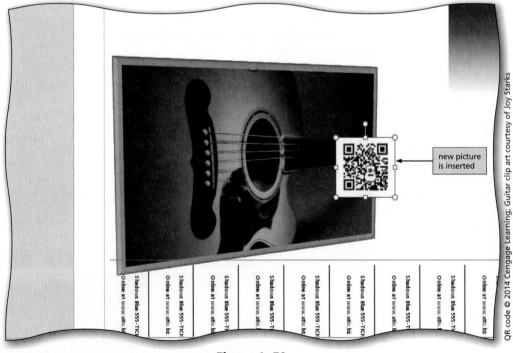

Figure 1–59

QR code © 2014 Cengage Learning; Guitar clip art courtesy of Joy Starks

Other Ways

1. Tap or click Pictures button (PICTURE TOOLS FORMAT tab | Insert Group), browse to folder (Insert Picture dialog box), double-tap or double-click desired picture

2. Tap or click placeholder icon, tap or click Browse button (Insert Pictures dialog box), browse to folder, double-tap or double-click desired picture

Moving, Aligning, and Resizing Objects

Many times, even when using a template, you will want to enhance the page by moving objects around on the page layout; or, you may want to change the size of objects as you did with the size of text. To move an object, it must be selected. The pointer changes to a double two-headed arrow, and you then drag the object to the new location or to the scratch area. If you press and hold the SHIFT key while dragging, the object moves in a straight line. Pressing the CTRL key while dragging creates a copy of the object. As you move an object, Publisher displays **visual layout guides** to help you place and align the object to other objects on the page layout. When you **align** an object to another object, its edge or center lines up, either vertically or horizontally. The visual layout guides display as pink lines that move from object to object as you drag. Visual layout guides appear when aligning to the left, right, top, bottom, or middle of objects.

Sometimes pictures and graphics are not the right size. In that case, you need to resize the object. To **resize** any object in Publisher, select the object, and then drag a handle. Recall that a handle is one of several small shapes displayed around an object when the object is selected. To resize by dragging, position the pointer over one of the handles and then drag the mouse. Pressing the CTRL key while dragging (CTRL+drag) keeps the center of the graphic in the same place during resizing. Pressing the SHIFT key while dragging (SHIFT+drag) maintains the graphic's proportions during resizing. Finally, pressing the SHIFT and CTRL keys while dragging (SHIFT+CTRL+drag) maintains the proportions and keeps the center in the same place.

BTW
QR Codes
A QR code, or Quick Reference code, can be generated by a variety of programs on the web. If a company wants to include a graphic in its QR code, the graphic designer needs to maintain the integrity of the code by inserting a graphic that covers less than 30% of the space.

To Move an Object

1 CUSTOMIZE TEMPLATES | 2 NAVIGATE & SELECT | 3 REPLACE TEXT | **4 DELETE OBJECTS** | 5 FORMAT TEXT
6 INSERT GRAPHICS | 7 FORMAT PICTURE | 8 ENHANCE PAGE | 9 PRINT & EXIT | 10 OPEN & REVISE

While text boxes need to be moved by dragging their borders, graphics can be moved by dragging from anywhere within the graphic. *Why? If you drag the text inside a text box, you may move the text, rather than the entire text box object.* The following steps move the QR code from its current location, the center, to a location above the tear-offs on the right.

- If necessary, select the object (in this case, the QR code).
- Drag the graphic to its new location (in this case, above the tear-offs on the right) until both the horizontal and vertical pink visual layout lines appear (Figure 1–60).

Q&A The graphic does not appear to be aligned. Did I do something wrong?
This particular graphic has a thick white border, which makes it hard to see the alignment.

- Release the mouse button to finish moving the object.

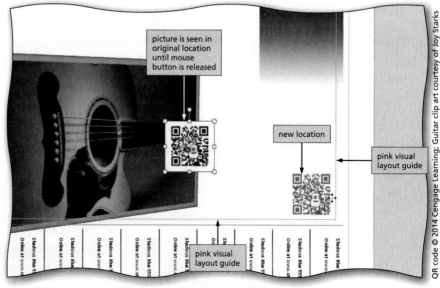

picture is seen in original location until mouse button is released

new location

pink visual layout guide

pink visual layout guide

QR code © 2014 Cengage Learning; Guitar clip art courtesy of Joy Starks

Figure 1–60

Other Ways

1. Select object, press ARROW key
2. Tap or click Object Position button on status bar, enter new x and y coordinates on Measurement toolbar

To Align an Object

The following steps align the guitar with the left margin as it is moved up on the page layout.
Why? *Moving the graphic up gives it a more prominent place in the flyer and keeps it from overlapping the tear-offs.*

- Select the object you wish to move (in this case, the guitar photo) by tapping or clicking it.
- Drag the object to its new location and align it using the visual layout guides. In this case, drag the guitar up and align it with the left margin (Figure 1–61).

- Deselect the picture.

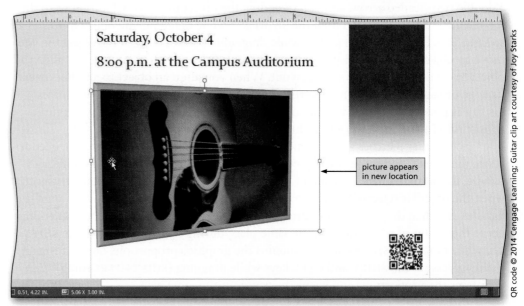

Figure 1–61

QR code © 2014 Cengage Learning; Guitar clip art courtesy of Joy Starks

To Resize an Object

The next step resizes the Campus Concerts text box to make it larger. ***Why?*** *Enlarging the text box causes the text to appear on one line.* Recall that selecting a text box involves clicking its border rather than its text.

- Scroll as necessary to display and then select the object to be resized (in this case, the Campus Concerts text box).
- Drag the lower-center sizing handle down to align it approximately with the top of the guitar (Figure 1–62).

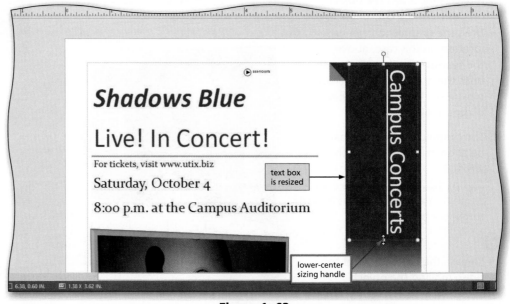

Figure 1–62

Other Ways

1. Tap or click Object size button on status bar, enter dimensions on Measurement toolbar

Publication Properties

Publisher helps you organize and identify your files by using **publication properties**, which are the details about a file, such as the project author, title, and subject. For example, a class name or publication topic can describe the file's purpose or content.

Why would you want to assign publication properties to a publication?
Publication properties are valuable for a variety of reasons:

- Users can save time locating a particular file because they can view a file's document properties without opening the publication.

- By creating consistent properties for files having similar content, users can better organize their publications.

- Some organizations require Publisher users to add document properties so that other employees can view details about these files.

The more common document properties are standard and automatically updated properties. **Standard properties** are associated with all Microsoft Office files and include author, title, and subject. **Automatically updated properties** include file system properties, such as the date you create or change a file, and statistics, such as the file size.

To Change Publication Properties

To change publication properties, you would follow these steps.

1 Tap or click FILE on the ribbon to open the Backstage view and then, if necessary, tap or click the Info tab in the Backstage view to display the Info gallery.

2 Tap or click the Publication Properties button in the right pane to display the Properties menu and then tap or click Advanced Properties on the Publication Properties menu to display the Publication Properties dialog box.

Q&A Why are some of the publication properties already filled in?
The person who installed Office 2013 on your computer or network may have set or customized the properties.

3 Type the desired text in the appropriate property text boxes in the Summary sheet.

Q&A What if the property I want to change is not displayed in the Document Information Panel?
Tap or click the Document Properties button in the Document Information Panel and then tap or click Advanced Properties on the menu to display the Properties dialog box. If necessary, tap or click the Summary tab (Properties dialog box) to display the Summary sheet, fill in the appropriate text boxes, and then tap or click the OK button.

4 Tap or click the OK button (Publication Properties dialog box) to save the properties.

BTW
Publisher Properties Keywords
Assigning keywords to a print publication allows you to search for publications based on those keywords. For example, you might enter the word, marketing, as a keyword in a flyer. In the future, you could search for all marketing publications on your company's storage device.

To Save an Existing Publication with the Same File Name

You have made several modifications to the publication since you last saved it. Thus, you should save it again. The following step saves the publication again. For an example of the step listed below, refer to the Office and Windows chapter at the beginning of this book.

 Tap or click the Save button on the Quick Access Toolbar to overwrite the previously saved file.

Break Point: If you wish to take a break, this is a good place to do so. To resume at a later time, run Publisher, open the file called Concert Flyer, and continue following the steps from this location forward.

Printing a Publication

After creating a publication, you may want to print it. Printing a publication enables you to distribute it to others in a form that can be read or viewed but typically not edited. It is a good practice to save a publication before printing it, in case you experience difficulties printing.

CONSIDER THIS

What is the best method for distributing a publication?
The traditional method of distributing a publication uses a printer to produce a hard copy. A **hard copy** or **printout** is information that exists on a physical medium such as paper. Hard copies can be useful for the following reasons:

- Some people prefer proofreading a hard copy of a publication rather than viewing it on the screen to check for errors and readability.
- Hard copies can serve as a backup reference if your storage medium is lost or becomes corrupted and you need to recreate the publication.

Instead of distributing a hard copy of a publication, users can distribute the publication as an electronic image that mirrors the original publication's appearance. The electronic image of the publication can be sent as an email attachment, posted on a website, or copied to a portable storage medium such as a USB flash drive. Two popular electronic image formats, sometimes called fixed formats, are PDF by Adobe Systems and XPS by Microsoft. In Publisher, you can create electronic image files through the Save As dialog box and the Export, Share, and Print tabs in the Backstage view. Electronic images of publications, such as PDF and XPS, can be useful for the following reasons:

- Users can view electronic images of publications without the software that created the original publication (e.g., Publisher). Specifically, to view a PDF file, you use a program called Adobe Reader, which can be downloaded free from Adobe's website. Similarly, to view an XPS file, you use a program called XPS Viewer, which is included in the latest versions of Windows and Internet Explorer.
- Sending electronic publications saves paper and printer supplies. Society encourages users to contribute to **green computing**, which involves reducing the electricity consumed and environmental waste generated when using computers, mobile devices, and related technologies.

To Print a Publication

1 CUSTOMIZE TEMPLATES | 2 NAVIGATE & SELECT | 3 REPLACE TEXT | 4 DELETE OBJECTS | 5 FORMAT TEXT
6 INSERT GRAPHICS | 7 FORMAT PICTURE | 8 ENHANCE PAGE | 9 PRINT & EXIT | 10 OPEN & REVISE

With the completed publication saved, you may want to print it. *Why? Because this flyer is being posted, you will print a hard copy on a printer.* The following steps print a hard copy of the contents of the saved Concert Flyer publication.

- Tap or click FILE on the ribbon to open the Backstage view.
- Tap or click the Print tab in the Backstage view to display the Print gallery.
- Verify the printer name listed on the Printer Status button will print a hard copy of the publication. If necessary, click the Printer Status button to display a list of available printer options and then click the desired printer to change the currently selected printer (Figure 1–63).

Q&A How can I print multiple copies of my publication?
Increase the number in the Copies box in the Print gallery.

What if I decide not to print the publication at this time?
Tap or click the Back button in the upper-left corner of the Backstage view to return to the publication window.

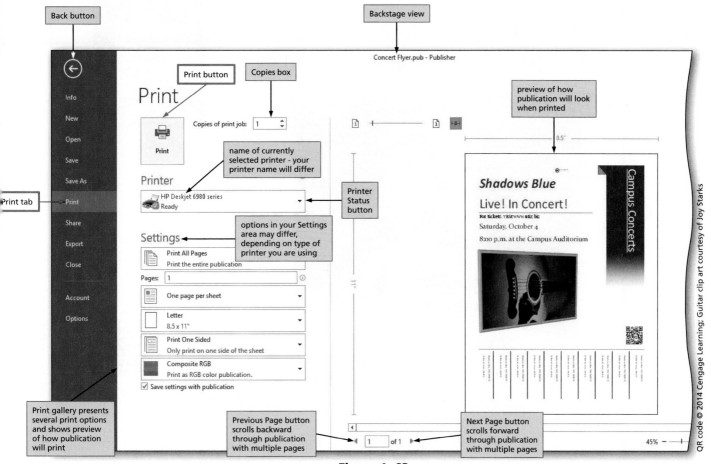

Figure 1–63

- Tap or click the Print button in the Print gallery to print the publication on the currently selected printer.
- When the printer stops, retrieve the hard copy (Figure 1–64 on the next page).

Q&A Do I have to wait until my publication is complete to print it?
No, you can follow these steps to print a publication at any time while you are creating it.

What if I want to print an electronic image of a publication instead of a hard copy?
In a later chapter, you will learn how to export the file to the PDF format; or, if it is installed, you can select Adobe PDF from the list of printers.

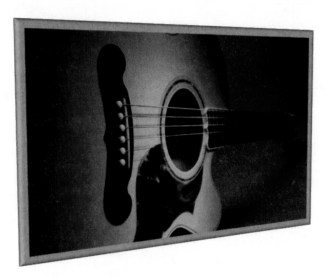

Figure 1–64

Other Ways

1. Press CTRL+P, press ENTER

To Exit Publisher

The print flyer is complete. The following steps exit Publisher. For a detailed example of the procedure summarized below, refer to the Office and Windows chapter at the beginning of this book.

1a If you have one Publisher publication open, tap or click the Close button on the right side of the title bar to close the open publication and exit Publisher.

1b If you have multiple Publisher publications open, press and hold or right-click the Publisher app button on the taskbar and then tap or click 'Close all windows' on the shortcut menu, or press ALT+F4 to close all open publications and exit Publisher.

Q&A Could I press and hold or repeatedly click the Close button to close all open publications and exit Publisher?
Yes.

2 If a Microsoft Publisher dialog box appears, tap or click the Save button to save any changes made to the publication since the last save.

Starting Publisher and Opening a Publication

Once you have created and saved a publication, you may need to retrieve it from your storage medium. For example, you might want to revise the publication or reprint it. Opening a publication requires that Publisher is running on your computer.

To Run Publisher

The following steps, which assume Windows 8 is running, use the Start screen or the search box to run Publisher based on a typical installation. You may need to ask your instructor how to run Publisher on your computer. For a detailed example of the procedure summarized below, refer to the Office and Windows chapter.

1 Scroll the Start screen and search for a Publisher 2013 tile. If your Start screen contains a Publisher 2013 tile, tap or click it to run Publisher and then proceed to Step 5. If the Start screen does not contain the Publisher 2013 tile, proceed to Step 2 to search for the Publisher app.

2 Swipe in from the right edge of the screen or point to the upper-right corner of the screen to display the Charms bar and then tap or click the Search charm on the Charms bar to display the Search menu.

3 Type **Publisher** as the search text in the Search text box and watch the search results appear in the Apps list.

4 Tap or click Publisher 2013 in the search results to run Publisher.

5 If the Publisher window is not maximized, tap or click the Maximize button on its title bar to maximize the window.

BTW
Conserving Ink and Toner
If you want to conserve ink or toner, you can instruct Publisher to print draft quality documents by tapping or clicking FILE on the ribbon to open the Backstage view, tapping or clicking Print in the Backstage view to display the Print gallery. Tap or click the Printer Properties link, and then, depending on your printer, click the Print Quality button and choose Draft in the list. Close the Printer Properties dialog box and then tap or click the Print button as usual.

BTW
Publisher Help
At any time while using Publisher, you can find answers to questions and display information about various topics through Publisher Help. Used properly, this form of assistance can increase your productivity and reduce your frustrations by minimizing the time you spend learning how to use Publisher. For instruction about Publisher Help and exercises that will help you gain confidence in using it, read the Office and Windows chapter at the beginning of this book.

To Open a Publication from Publisher

Earlier in this chapter, you saved your publication using the file name, Concert Flyer. The following steps open the Concert Flyer file from the Publisher folder in the CIS 101 folder. For a detailed example of the procedure summarized below, refer to the Office and Windows chapter at the beginning of this book.

1 If the file you wish to open is displayed in the Recent Publications list, tap or click the file name to open the file and display the opened publication in the Publisher window; then, skip the remaining steps. If the file you wish to open is not displayed in the Recent Publications list, proceed to the next step to locate the file.

2 Tap or click Open Other Publications and then navigate to the location of the file to be opened (in this case, the Publisher folder in the CIS 101 folder).

3 Tap or click Concert Flyer to select the file to be opened.

4 Tap or click the Open button (Open dialog box) to open the selected file and display the opened publication in the Publisher window.

Changing a Publication

BTW
Print Publications
When creating a print publication, you must consider paper type, color options, number of copies, and the plan for publishing. Does the publication have to be in print to reach the target audience? How will readers find the printed publication? Keep the limitations of printed material in mind when deciding what to include in the layout.

After creating a publication, you often will find that you must make changes to it. Changes can be required because the publication contains an error or because of new circumstances. The types of changes made to publications normally fall into one of the three following categories: deletions, additions, or modifications.

DELETIONS Sometimes deletions are necessary in a publication because objects are incorrect or no longer are needed. For example, to place this advertising flyer on a website, the tear-offs no longer are needed. In that case, you would delete them from the page layout.

ADDITIONS Additional text, objects, or formatting may be required in the publication. For example, in the Concert Flyer you may want to insert a text box that could be displayed when the flyer is published to the web.

MODIFICATIONS If you make modifications to text or graphics, normal techniques of inserting, deleting, editing, and formatting apply. Publisher provides several methods for detecting problems in a publication and making modifications, including spell checking and design checking.

In the following sections, you will make changes to the flyer to prepare it for publishing to the web.

To Insert a Hyperlink

1 CUSTOMIZE TEMPLATES | 2 NAVIGATE & SELECT | 3 REPLACE TEXT | 4 DELETE OBJECTS | 5 FORMAT TEXT
6 INSERT GRAPHICS | 7 FORMAT PICTURE | 8 ENHANCE PAGE | 9 PRINT & EXIT | 10 OPEN & REVISE

A **hyperlink**, or hypertext, is a computer link or reference to another location. A hyperlink can link to a page on the Internet, to an email address, to a location on a storage device, or another location within a publication. Users click links to navigate or browse to the location. The following steps create a hyperlink to the ticket website. *Why? This version of the flyer will be seen on the web, where users may want to click to buy tickets.*

- Select the text you wish to make a hyperlink (in this case, the web address) and then zoom to 100% (Figure 1–65).

Figure 1–65

- Tap or click INSERT on the ribbon to display the INSERT tab.
- Tap or click the 'Add a Hyperlink' button (INSERT tab | Links group) to display the Insert Hyperlink dialog box.
- If necessary, click the Address text box to position the insertion point and then type **www.utix.biz** to enter the web address (Figure 1–66).

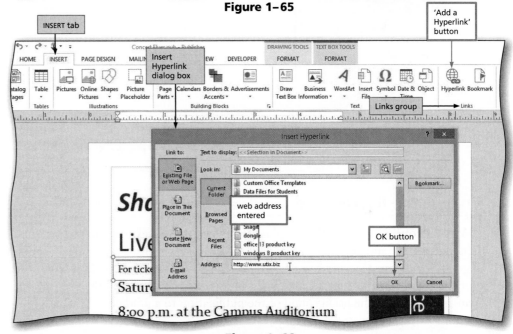

Figure 1–66

- Tap or click the OK button (Insert Hyperlink dialog box) to assign the hyperlink.
- Deselect the text to reveal the hyperlink (Figure 1–67).

Figure 1–67

Other Ways

1. Select text, press CTRL+K, enter web address in Address text box (Insert Hyperlink dialog box), click OK button

To Delete the Tear-Offs

If this flyer is displayed on a website, the tear-offs are unnecessary and should be deleted. The following steps delete the tear-offs using the shortcut menu.

1 Scroll to the lower portion of the flyer.

2 Press and hold or right-click any one of the tear-offs to display the shortcut menu and then tap or click Delete Object on the shortcut menu to delete the tear-offs (Figure 1–68).

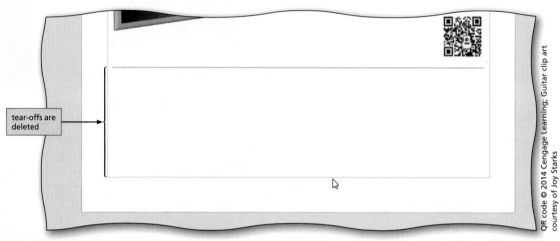

Figure 1–68

To Change the Background

| 1 CUSTOMIZE TEMPLATES | 2 NAVIGATE & SELECT | 3 REPLACE TEXT | 4 DELETE OBJECTS | 5 FORMAT TEXT |
| 6 INSERT GRAPHICS | 7 FORMAT PICTURE | 8 ENHANCE PAGE | 9 PRINT & EXIT | **10 OPEN & REVISE** |

A **background**, or page fill, is a color, gradient, pattern, texture, picture, or tint that fills the entire page, behind all text and graphics on the page layout. Many websites use a background to add interest. *Why? A background eliminates the sometimes harsh glare of a bright white webpage.* Gradient backgrounds use a progression of color shades to provide a subtle effect. They look more professional than solid colors or pictures. The following steps change the background of the publication to a gradient.

1

• Tap or click the 'Show Whole Page' button on the status bar to display the entire page layout.

• Tap or click PAGE DESIGN on the ribbon to display the PAGE DESIGN tab.

• Tap or click the Background button (PAGE DESIGN tab | Page Background group) to display the Background gallery (Figure 1–69).

(🔍) **Experiment**

• Point to each of the backgrounds and watch the live preview.

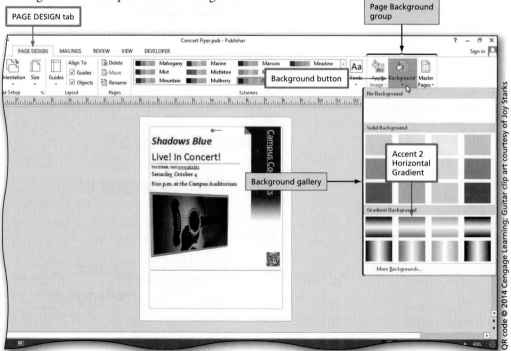

Figure 1–69

2

- Tap or click Accent 2 Horizontal Gradient to select a blue and white gradient for the webpage background (Figure 1–70).

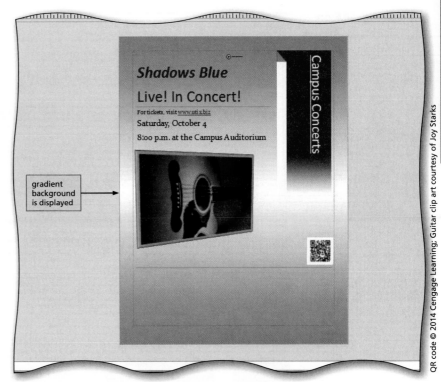

gradient background is displayed

QR code © 2014 Cengage Learning; Guitar clip art courtesy of Joy Starks

Figure 1–70

Creating a Webpage from a Publication

You can create several types of publications with Microsoft Publisher, other than standard print publications. A **web publication** is one suitable for publishing to the web, containing certain objects, formatting options, hyperlinks, and other features specific to webpages. You can create a web publication from scratch, or you can save the print publication as a web publication. The following sections create a web version of the flyer that might be posted on a campus website or social networking site.

BTW
Web publications
When converting to a web publication, determine which objects will work effectively on the web and which ones will not, modifying the publication as necessary. Will the publication be accessible on the web? Is the target audience common web users? If so, determine whether an email or website would be the most efficient means of communication.

To Save a Print Publication as a Web Publication

1 CUSTOMIZE TEMPLATES | 2 NAVIGATE & SELECT | 3 REPLACE TEXT | 4 DELETE OBJECTS | 5 FORMAT TEXT
6 INSERT GRAPHICS | 7 FORMAT PICTURE | 8 ENHANCE PAGE | 9 PRINT & EXIT | **10 OPEN & REVISE**

The Export tab in the Backstage view includes a group of commands that allow you to save publications as different file types or to package publications for sending to other users. In the following steps, you will export the publication by publishing it to the web. **Publishing HTML** or **publishing to the web** is the process of making webpages available to others, for example, on the World Wide Web or on a company's intranet. Files intended for use on the web, however, need a different format. A **Hypertext Markup Language (HTML)** file is a file capable of being stored and transferred electronically on a file server in order to display on the web.

In the steps on the next page, you will save the publication as a web flyer by publishing it as **MHTML** (Mime Hypertext Markup Language), a small single-file file format that does not create a supporting folder of resources. **Why?** *The MHTML file can be published to and downloaded from the web quickly.* For a detailed example of the procedure for using the Save As dialog box, refer to the Office 2013 and Windows 8 chapter at the beginning of this book.

1

- Tap or click FILE on the ribbon to open the Backstage view.
- Tap or click the Export tab to display the Export gallery.
- Tap or click Publish HTML to display its options.
- Tap or click the 'Web Page (HTML)' button to display options for publishing HTML (Figure 1–71).

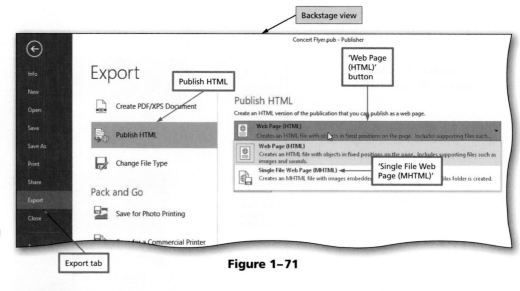

Figure 1–71

2

- Tap or click 'Single File Web Page (MHTML)' to select it (Figure 1–72).

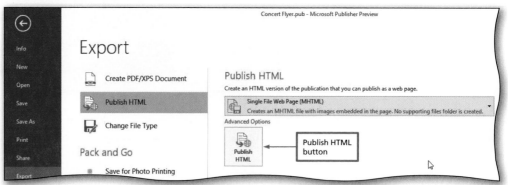

Figure 1–72

3

- Tap or click the Publish HTML button to display the Save As dialog box.
- Type **Concert Web Flyer** in the File name text box. Do not press the ENTER key after typing the file name.
- Navigate to your storage location (in this case, the Chapter 01 Folder of the Publisher Folder) (Figure 1–73).

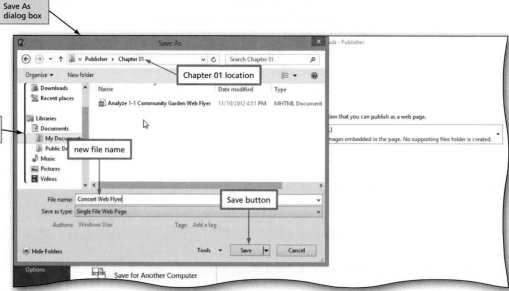

Figure 1–73

4

- Tap or click the Save button (Save As dialog box) to save the publication.

Other Ways

1. Tap or click Save As in Backstage view, tap or click storage location, enter file name, tap or click   'Save as type' button, tap or click 'Single File Web Page', tap or click Save button (Save As dialog box)

To Preview the Web Publication in a Browser

The following steps preview the web publication. *Why? Previewing is the best way to test the look and feel of the webpage and to test the hyperlink.* You will open the MHTML file from its storage location. For a detailed example of the procedure for navigating to a storage location, refer to the Office 2013 and Windows 8 chapter at the beginning of this book.

- Run the File Explorer app and navigate to your storage location (in this case, the Chapter 01 Folder of the Publisher Folder) (Figure 1–74).

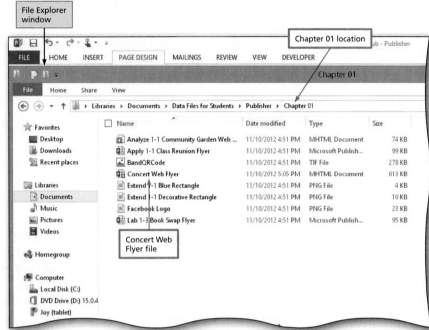

Figure 1–74

- Double-tap or double-click the Concert Web Flyer file.
- When the browser window opens, if necessary, maximize the window (Figure 1–75).

Q&A
Why does my display look different?
Each brand and version of browser software displays information in a slightly different manner. Additionally, your browser settings, such as text size and zoom level, may differ.

❸

- Tap or click the Close button on the browser window's title bar.
- Tap or click the Close button on the File Explorer window's title bar.

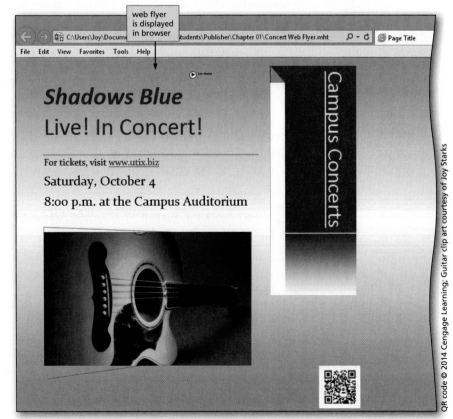

Figure 1–75

To Exit Publisher

This web flyer is complete. The following steps exit Publisher. For a detailed example of the procedure summarized below, refer to the Office and Windows chapter at the beginning of this book. The web flyer and print flyer were saved in previous steps, so you do not need to save the file again.

1a If you have one Publisher publication open, tap or click the Close button on the right side of the title bar to close the open publication and exit Publisher.

1b If you have multiple Publisher publications open, press and hold or right-click the Publisher app button on the taskbar and then tap or click 'Close all windows' on the shortcut menu, or press ALT+F4 to close all open publications and exit Publisher.

Q&A Could I press and hold or repeatedly click the Close button to close all open documents and exit Publisher?

Yes.

2 If a Microsoft Publisher dialog box appears, tap or click the Don't Save button to exit Publisher.

To Sign Out of a Microsoft Account

BTW

Quick Reference
For a table that lists how to complete the tasks covered in this book using touch gestures, the mouse, ribbon, shortcut menu, and keyboard, see the Quick Reference Summary at the back of this book, or visit the Quick Reference resource on the Student Companion Site located on www.cengagebrain.com. For detailed instructions about accessing available resources, visit www.cengage.com/ct/studentdownload or see the inside back cover of this book.

If you are signed in to a Microsoft account and are using a public computer or otherwise wish to sign out of your Microsoft account, you should sign out of the account from the Account gallery in the Backstage view before exiting Publisher. Signing out of the account is the safest way to make sure that nobody else can access SkyDrive files or settings stored in your Microsoft account. The following steps sign out of a Microsoft account from Publisher. For a detailed example of the procedure summarized below, refer to the Office and Windows chapter at the beginning of this book.

1 If you wish to sign out of your Microsoft account, tap or click FILE on the ribbon to open the Backstage view and then tap or click the Account tab to display the Account gallery.

2 Tap or click the Sign out link, which displays the Remove Account dialog box. If a Can't remove Windows accounts dialog box appears instead of the Remove Account dialog box, click the OK button and skip the remaining steps.

Q&A Why does a Can't remove Windows accounts dialog box appear?

If you signed in to Windows using your Microsoft account, then you also must sign out from Windows, rather than signing out from within Publisher. When you are finished using Windows, be sure to sign out at that time.

3 Tap or click the Yes button (Remove Account dialog box) to sign out of your Microsoft account on this computer.

Q&A Should I sign out of Windows after signing out of my Microsoft account?

When you are finished using the computer, you should sign out of your account for maximum security.

4 Tap or click the Back button in the upper-left corner of the Backstage view to return to the publication.

Chapter Summary

In this chapter, you learned to choose a publication template, set font and color schemes, enter text in a publication, delete objects in a publication, insert a picture with a style and border, print a publication, and save a print publication as a web publication. The items listed below include all the new Publisher skills you have learned in this chapter, with the tasks grouped by activity.

Enter and Format Text
Autofit Text (PUB 28)
Bold Text (PUB 27)
Change Text Direction (PUB 32)
Check Spelling as You Type (PUB 21)
Enter Tear-Off Text (PUB 23)
Increase the Font Size (PUB 31)
Italicize Text (PUB 28)
Replace Other Text (PUB 19)
Replace Placeholder Text (PUB 17)
Underline Text (PUB 31)

Graphics
Apply a Picture Style (PUB 36)
Change the Border Color (PUB 38)
Insert a Picture from a Storage Device (PUB 39)
Set the Weight of a Border (PUB 37)
Use the Picture Placeholder (PUB 34)

Prepare a Web Publication
Change Document Properties (PUB 43)
Change the Background (PUB 50)
Insert a Hyperlink (PUB 48)

Preview the Web Publication in a Browser
(PUB 53)
Save a Print Publication as a Web Publication
(PUB 51)

Print
Print a Publication (PUB 44)

Select, Zoom, and Manipulate Objects
Align an Object (PUB 42)
Collapse and Expand the Page Navigation Pane
(PUB 14)
Delete an Object (PUB 24)
Deselect an Object (PUB 18)
Hide the Page Navigation Pane (PUB 13)
Move an Object (PUB 41)
Resize an Object (PUB 42)
Select an Object (PUB 14)
View Whole Page (PUB 15)
Zoom (PUB 15)

Templates
Choose Publication Options (PUB 8)
Select a Template (PUB 6)

What decisions will you need to make when creating your next publication?
Use these guidelines as you complete the assignments in this chapter and create your own publications outside of this class.

1. Select template options.
    a) Select a template that matches your need.
    b) Choose font and color schemes determined by the flyer's purpose and audience.
2. Choose words for the text.
    a) Replace all placeholder and default text.
    b) Add other text boxes as necessary; delete unused items.
3. Identify how to format various objects in the flyer.
    a) Use bold, underline, and italics for emphasis.
    b) Autofit the text to make the flyer easy to read.
4. Find the appropriate graphic(s).
5. Determine whether the flyer will be more effective as a print publication, web publication, or both.
    a) Insert any necessary hyperlinks.
    b) Consider creating a background for web publication.

CONSIDER THIS

How should you submit solutions to questions in the assignments identified with a ✹ symbol?

Every assignment in this book contains one or more questions identified with a ✹ symbol. These questions require you to think beyond the assigned publication. Present your solutions to the questions in the format required by your instructor. Possible formats may include one or more of these options: write the answer; create a document that contains the answer; present your answer to the class; discuss your answer in a group; record the answer as audio or video using a webcam, smartphone, or portable media player; or post answers on a blog, wiki, or website.

Apply Your Knowledge

Reinforce the skills and apply the concepts you learned in this chapter.

Editing a Flyer with Text, Graphic, and Tear-Offs

Note: To complete this assignment, you will be required to use the Data Files for Students. Visit www.cengage.com/ct/studentdownload for detailed instructions or contact your instructor for information about accessing the required files.

Instructions: Your brother is in charge of advertising his 10-year class reunion. He has asked you to help him with editing the text, graphic, and tear-offs. You produce the flyer shown in Figure 1–76.

Perform the following tasks:

1. Run Publisher and open the file Apply 1-1 Class Reunion Flyer from the Data Files for Students.
2. Tap or click the Major Heading default text and drag to select it. Type `10-Year Reunion Gym Party!` to replace the text.
3. Tap or click the Subheading default text box and then drag the text to select it. Type `05/21/15` to replace the text.
4. Tap or click the default bulleted text and then press CTRL+A to select all of the text. Type the following text, pressing the ENTER key at the end of each line.

    `Wear your letter jacket!`

    `Show your school spirit!`

    `High School Gym!`

    `7:00 p.m.!`

    `RSVP to Jesse by 05/07/15!`

5. Tap or click one of the tear-offs, type `Jesse` and then press the ENTER key. Type `402-555-1306` to finish entering the text. Tap or click outside the tear-offs to synchronize them. If requested by your instructor, use your name in the tear-offs.
6. Select the text in the attention getter sunburst shape and replace it with the text shown in Figure 1–76.
7. Select the attention getter and change the border weight to 6 point, using the Shape Outline button (DRAWING TOOLS FORMAT tab | ShapeStyles group).
8. At the top of the flyer, select the picture placeholder. Tap or click the picture placeholder icon to display the Insert Pictures dialog box. Use Office.com Clip Art to search for a picture related to academics, similar to the one shown in Figure 1–76.

Figure 1–76

9. Tap or click the Background button (PAGE DESIGN tab | Page Background group) to display the Background gallery. Choose the Accent 3 Vertical Gradient.

10. Save the flyer on your storage device with the file name, Apply 1-1 Class Reunion Flyer Complete.

11. Print a hardcopy of the flyer by performing the following steps:

    a. Tap or click FILE on the ribbon to open the Backstage view and then tap or click the Print tab in the Backstage view to display the Print gallery.

    b. Verify the printer name that appears on the Printer Status button will print a hard copy of the publication. If necessary, click the Printer Status button to display a list of available printer options and then click the desired printer to change the currently selected printer.

    c. Tap or click the Print button in the Print gallery to print the publication on the currently selected printer. When the printer stops, retrieve the hard copy.

12. Submit the revised document in the format specified by your instructor.

13. ✺ What would you add or delete if you were to publish this flyer in the MHTML format on the web? Why?

Extend Your Knowledge

Extend the skills you learned in this chapter and experiment with new skills. You may need to use Help to complete the assignment.

Creating a Flyer from Scratch

Instructions: You have been asked to create a flyer to remind students to vote. You decide to start from scratch to create the flyer shown in Figure 1–77.

Perform the following tasks:

1. Run Publisher and select the Blank 8.5 × 11" template.

2. Tap or click the More button (PAGE DESIGN tab | Schemes group) and then select the Bluebird color scheme.

3. Tap or click the Scheme Fonts button (PAGE DESIGN tab | Schemes group) and then select the Office Classic 1 font scheme.

4. Tap or click the Pictures button (INSERT tab | Illustrations group) and then navigate to the Data Files for Students. Insert the graphic named, Extend 1-1 Decorative Rectangle. Move it as necessary to approximately the center of the page.

5. Insert a second picture from the Data Files for Students named, Extend 1-1 Blue Rectangle. Move it to the upper-center as shown in Figure 1–77.

6. Tap or click the Online Pictures button (INSERT tab | Illustrations group) and then search Office.com Clip Art for a graphic of an American flag. Move the graphic to the upper portion of the flyer and, if necessary, resize the graphic. Apply a picture style, such as Relaxed Perspective, White.

7. Use Help to read about drawing text boxes and then perform the following tasks:

   a. Use the Draw Text box button (HOME tab | Objects group) to create a text box on top of the blue rectangle, filling the area below the flag graphic.

Figure 1–77

b. Before typing the text, click the Font Color arrow (HOME tab | Font group) and then choose a white color. Type the text, `Register to Vote!` and then autofit it.

c. Draw another text box below the first one. Tap or click the Font Color arrow (HOME tab | Font group) and then choose a black color. Tap or click the Bold button (HOME tab | Font group). Tap or click the Center button (HOME tab | Paragraph group) and then type the text shown in Figure 1–77. If necessary, change the font size to 24 pt.

d. Repeat Step 7c for the next text box and format the text italic. Change the font size to 20 pt.

e. Repeat Step 7c for the last text box and format the text underlined. Change the font size to 14 pt.

f. If requested to do so by your instructor, add the name of your voting location to the flyer.

8. Save the file with the file name, Extend 1-1 Vote Flyer Complete.

9. Submit the file in the format specified by your instructor.

10. ✳ When would you use a template instead of creating a flyer from scratch that contains only the fields you need? Was formatting the font before you typed easier than selecting text and formatting it afterward?

Analyze, Correct, Improve

Analyze a publication, correct all errors, and improve the design.

Making Changes to a Web Flyer

Note: To complete this assignment, you will be required to use the Data Files for Students. Visit www.cengage.com/ct/studentdownload for detailed instructions or contact your instructor for information about accessing the required files.

Instructions: Your community is trying to promote its community garden. A former gardener created the website shown in Figure 1–78 using Publisher, but it has several issues. You decide to improve the flyer. Run Publisher and open the file, Analyze 1-1 Community Garden Web Flyer.

Figure 1–78

Continued >

Analyze, Correct, Improve *continued*

1. Correct   Correct the date on the flyer. This year's event is March 25. The flyer still has default text in the lower-left corner. If requested to do so by your instructor, insert your community and your phone number. The website listed in the lower-right corner should be a hyperlink. Resize any text boxes whose text wraps awkwardly.

2. Improve   Each of the text boxes seems to be a different font size. Choose a large size for the main heading. Change the description text to best fit and then increase or decrease the fonts in the lower text boxes so that they all match. Choose to make them all bold. Align objects horizontally with each other and with the margins. Correct the misspelled word. Change the color scheme to an all green color scheme such as Green or Floral. Experiment with different font schemes. Save the document using the file name, Analyze 1-1 Community Garden Flyer Complete. Submit the revised document in the format specified by your instructor.

3. ☀ What errors existed in the starting file? How did creating consistency in font sizes enhance the publication? Did changing the color scheme improve the effectiveness of the flyer? What other improvements would you make?

In the Labs

Design, create, modify, and/or use a publication following the guidelines, concepts, and skills presented in this chapter. Labs 1 and 2, which increase in difficulty, require you to create solutions based on what you learned in the chapter; Lab 3 requires you to create a solution, which uses cloud and web technologies, by learning and investigating on your own from general guidance.

Lab 1: Creating a Sign-Up Sheet

Problem: The Self-Defense Club on campus would like you to create a sign-up sheet for students who want to take classes in the Fall semester. You decide to look through Publisher's templates for an appropriate flyer to use as a starting point. You create the flyer shown in Figure 1–79.

Perform the following tasks:
1. Run Publisher. In the template gallery, click BUILT-IN and then click Flyers.
2. In the Event group, click the All Event folder to open it. Scroll down to the Other category at the end of the list and select the Company Sign Up template.
3. Customize the template with the Alpine color scheme and the Basis font scheme and create the publication.
4. Tap or click the Event Title placeholder text to select it. Type `Self-Defense` and then press the ENTER key. Type `Classes` to finish replacing the text.
5. Tap or click the description placeholder text to select it. Type the following text, pressing the ENTER key at the end of each line. The last line purposefully has a misspelled word.

   `Learn the techniques you need to protect yourself.`

   `Prepare now, for the event you hope will never happen.`

   `Classes will be held on Thursdays throughout the semester.`

   `Easy to learn. Gain confidfence. Become more self-aware.`
6. Press and hold or right-click the misspelled word and choose the correct spelling from the list.
7. Press and hold or right-click the text box and then click Best Fit on the shortcut menu.
8. Change the Date text, Date: 00/00/00, to `Fall Semester` to replace the text.
9. Change the Time text, Time: 00:00, to `7:00-8:00 p.m.` to replace the text.

10. Change the text, Contact person:, to **Aaron Gilbert** to replace the text. If requested by your instructor, type your name as the contact person.

11. Change the phone number to 303 555 9753.

12. Tap or click the boundary of the Sign up heading text box select the text box. Press the DELETE key to delete the object.

13. Select the graphic. Press the DELETE key to delete the object.

14. Tap or click the Online Pictures button (INSERT tab | Illustrations group). Use the concepts in the chapter to search for a self-defense graphic, similar to the one shown in Figure 1–79, from Office.com Clip Art. Insert the graphic.

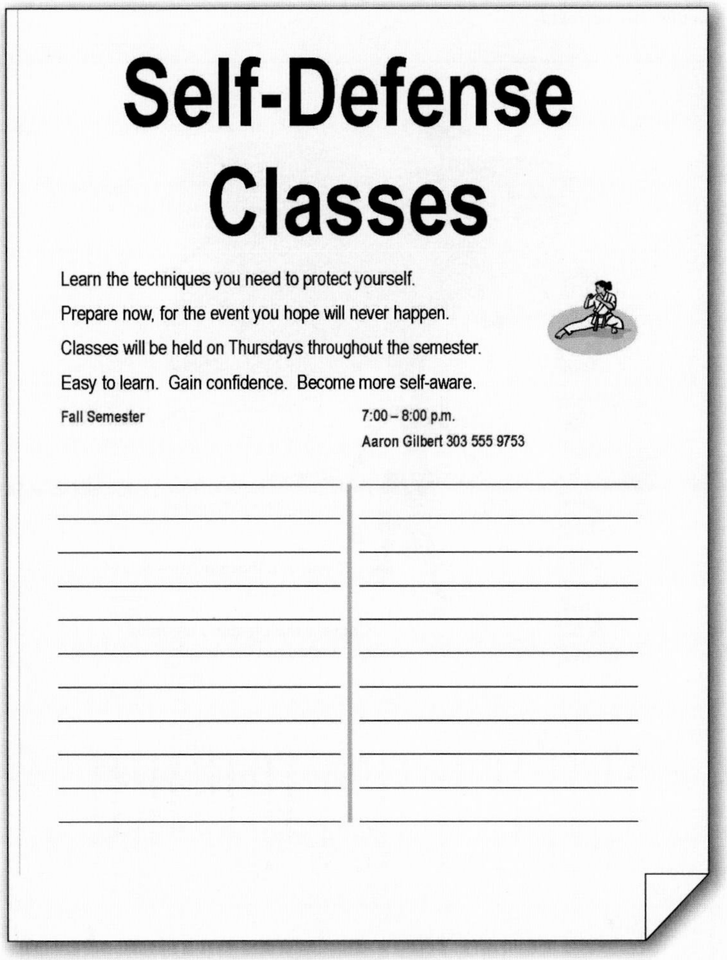

15. Using Figure 1–79 as a guide, move the graphic up and align it with the right margin. If necessary, resize the graphic by SHIFT+dragging the upper-left corner toward the center of the graphic, so that no text wraps in the description text box.

16. Save the flyer on your storage device with the file name, Lab 1-1 Self-Defense Flyer.

17. Print a hardcopy of the flyer.

18. Submit the file as directed by your instructor.

19. ✳ Would a page background make this flyer easier to read or harder to read? Which elements would you change if this were a flyer on the web?

Self-Defense Classes

Learn the techniques you need to protect yourself.

Prepare now, for the event you hope will never happen.

Classes will be held on Thursdays throughout the semester.

Easy to learn. Gain confidence. Become more self-aware.

Fall Semester   7:00 – 8:00 p.m.
                                 Aaron Gilbert 303 555 9753

Figure 1–79

Lab 2: Creating an Event Flyer

Problem: You have been asked to create a flyer for a flash mob event. A flash mob, usually triggered by a text message or web posting, describes a group of people who come together suddenly in a specified place to perform an unusual and sometimes pointless act for a brief time, often for the purpose of entertainment, parody, or artistic expression. You create the flyer shown in Figure 1–80 on the next page.

1. Run Publisher. In the template gallery, tap or click BUILT-IN and then tap or click Flyers.

2. In the Marketing group, tap or click the All Marketing folder to open it. Scroll down to the Other category and then select the Baby-Sitting template.

3. Customize the template with the Parrot color scheme and the Foundry font scheme and create the publication.

4. Select the text, Baby-Sitting. Type **Flash Mob** to replace the text. Autofit the text.

5. Select the description placeholder text. Type **Come on!** and then press the ENTER key. Type **You know you want to!** to replace the text.

Continued >

Figure 1–80

6. Select the hourly rate text. Type **Time and location area secret.** and then press the ENTER key twice. Resize the text box as necessary and type **Come to the planning meeting to find out the details.** to replace the text. Delete the $00.00 placeholder text.

7. Delete the Contact person text box.

8. Tap or click a tear-off. Type **September 17 - 7:00 p.m.** and then press the ENTER key. Type **Alpha Mu Sorority** to complete the tear-offs. If requested by your instructor, type the name of your (or a campus) sorority or fraternity in the text box.

9. Delete the two child graphics.

10. Tap or click the Online Pictures button (INSERT tab | Illustrations group). Use the concepts in the chapter to search Office.com Clip Art for a graphic similar to the first one shown in Figure 1–80. Search for dancers. Insert the graphic. Resize the graphic. Repeat the process to find two more graphics.

11. Save the flyer on your storage device with the file name, Lab 1-2 Flash Mob Flyer.

12. Print a hardcopy of the flyer.

13. Submit the file as directed by your instructor.

14. ☀ How did the Baby-Sitting flyer template work for you? Would it have been easier to choose a template with a picture placeholder rather than one with default pictures? Could you have found a different template and made the changes, such as text direction, yourself? Would that have been easier?

Lab 3: Expand Your World: Cloud and Web Technologies
Modifying and Exporting a Publication

Note: To complete this assignment, you will be required to use the Data Files for Students. Visit www.cengage.com/ct/studentdownload for detailed instructions or contact your instructor for information about accessing the required files.

Problem: Your school library is planning a book swap and has asked you to create a flyer. You want to share the final product with the library staff, so you have decided to store the file on SkyDrive so that the staff can access it easily. You are going to modify the flyer you have created thus far shown in Figure 1–81 and save on SkyDrive.

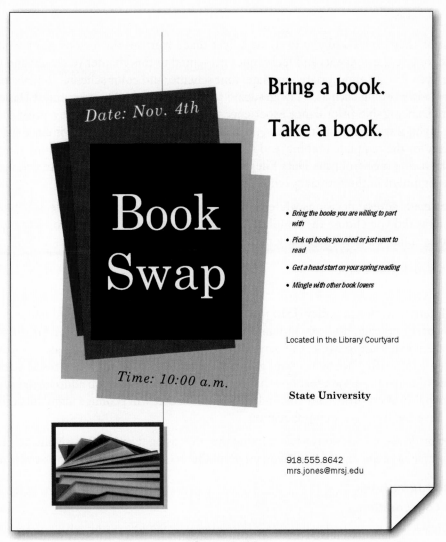

Figure 1–81

Instructions:

1. Open the file named, Lab 1-3 Book Swap Flyer, from the Data Files for Students.

2. Insert a picture and format it as shown in Figure 1 – 81.

3. If requested to do so by your instructor, change the email address to your email address.

4. Save the presentation on SkyDrive in the Publisher folder using the file name, Lab 1–3 Book Swap Flyer Complete.

5. Submit the assignment in the format specified by your instructor.

6. ✸ When would you save one of your files for school or your job on SkyDrive? Do you think using SkyDrive enhances collaboration efforts? Why?

✸ Consider This: Your Turn

Apply your creative thinking and problem solving skills to design and implement a solution.

1: Creating an Advertisement

Personal/Academic

Part 1: You attend a college that is famous for its Department of Dance. Students who major in dance are required to complete internships as dance instructors. Because you are a computer

Continued >

Consider This: Your Turn *continued*

technology major, they have asked you to create a flyer that advertises the lessons and includes a social media logo. Use the concepts and techniques presented in this chapter to design and create an advertising flyer. Use an appropriate template, font scheme, and color scheme. Replace place-holder text. Include wording such as, "The graduate students from the Department of Dance will teach Ballroom Dancing. No prior dance experience is necessary. Come and have a great time—it is a great date night, guys!!" Include the date and time of the dance lessons. Tap or click the picture placeholder icon for the template graphic, and search for a graphic related to ballroom dancing. Insert the social media logo from the Data Files for Students and use an appropriate text reference. Submit your assignment in the format specified by your instructor.

Part 2: ✳ You made several decisions while determining the appropriate template, schemes, text, and graphics. How did you choose the template? What did you consider when choosing the color and font schemes? Did you choose a ballroom dancing clip art graphic or a photo? Why?

2: Creating a Workplace Flyer
Professional

Part 1: Your Internet service provider (ISP) maintains an electronic bulletin board where customers may post one-page business announcements. Create an advertising flyer for the place you work or where you want to work. You may use one of Publisher's Flyer templates, or you can design one from scratch. Replace all text and graphics. Use font colors and font sizes to attract at-tention. Instead of tear-offs, draw a text box that includes the company's web address and phone number. Assign publication properties and include keywords that will produce many hits during web searches. Save the flyer as a web publication.

Part 2: ✳ You made several decisions while creating the advertising flyer in this assignment. How did your choices complement the topic? Would you use Publisher to create websites? Why or why not?

3: Researching Templates
Research and Collaboration

Part 1: Publisher has online templates and built-in templates. Within the built-in templates, each folder has a section of tailored templates labeled Other. Get together with your group and scroll through the template gallery. One at a time, click each of the built-in Flyer category folders and scroll down to the bottom of each list. Make a list of the Other flyer templates that are tailored toward a specific event, marketing advertisement, or real estate project. Ask your group if anyone recalls seeing any of these flyers or similar flyers posted around campus.

Part 2: ✳ How are these Other flyer templates different from the Built-in templates and the online Featured templates? When would you use each?

Learn Online

Reinforce what you learned in this chapter with games, exercises, training, and many other online activities and resources.

Student Companion Site Reinforce chapter terms and concepts using review questions, flash cards, practice tests, and interactive learning games, such as a crossword puzzle. These and other online activities and resources are available at no additional cost on www.cengagebrain.com. Visit www.cengage.com/ct/studentdownload for detailed instructions about accessing the resources available at the Student Companion Site.

2 | Publishing a Trifold Brochure

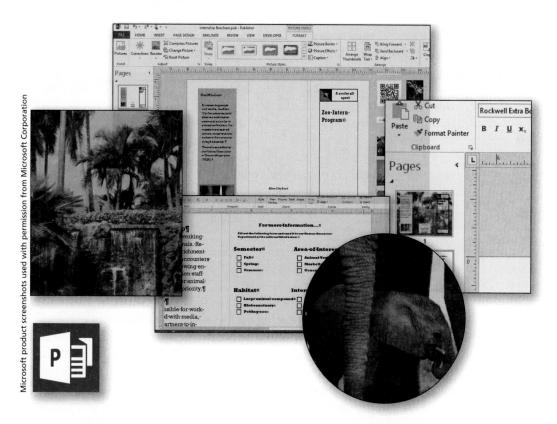

Microsoft product screenshots used with permission from Microsoft Corporation

Objectives

You will have mastered the material in this chapter when you can:

- Discuss advantages of the brochure medium
- Choose brochure options
- Copy and paste with paste options
- Wordwrap text
- Swap pictures using the scratch area and arrange thumbnails
- Use a picture as a background
- Copy formatting with the Format Painter
- Employ typography such as stylistic sets, ligatures, and drop caps

- Edit captions and caption styles
- Check the spelling of the entire publication
- Run the Design Checker
- Choose appropriate printing services, paper, and color libraries
- Package a publication for a printing service
- Explain the use of PostScript files

2 | Publishing a Trifold Brochure

Introduction

Whether you want to advertise a service, event, or product, or merely want to inform the public about a current topic of interest, brochures are a popular type of promotional publication. A **brochure**, or pamphlet, usually is a high-quality publication with lots of color and graphics, created for advertising purposes. Businesses that may not be able to reach potential clientele effectively through traditional advertising, such as newspapers and radio, can create a long-lasting advertisement with a well-designed brochure.

Brochures come in all shapes and sizes. Colleges and universities produce brochures about their programs. The travel industry uses brochures to entice tourists. In addition, service industries and manufacturers display their products using this visual, hands-on medium.

Project—Brochure

The project in this chapter shows you how to build the two-page, trifold brochure shown in Figure 2–1. The brochure informs students about professional internships at a zoo. Each side of the brochure has three panels. Page 1 (Figure 2–1a) contains the front and back panels, as well as the inside fold. Page 2 (Figure 2–1b) contains a three-panel display that, when opened completely, provides the reader with more details about the zoo and a response form.

On page 1, the front panel contains shapes, text boxes, a graphic, and a background designed to draw the reader's attention and inform the reader of the intent of the brochure. The back panel, which displays in the middle of page 1, contains the name of the business, the address, phone and fax numbers, and an email address. The inside fold, on the left, contains the zoo's mission statement.

The three inside panels on page 2 contain more information about the internships and a form the reader may use to request more information.

FILE   HOME   INSERT   PAGE DESIGN   MAILINGS

inside fold → | ← back panel | ← front of brochure

background image →

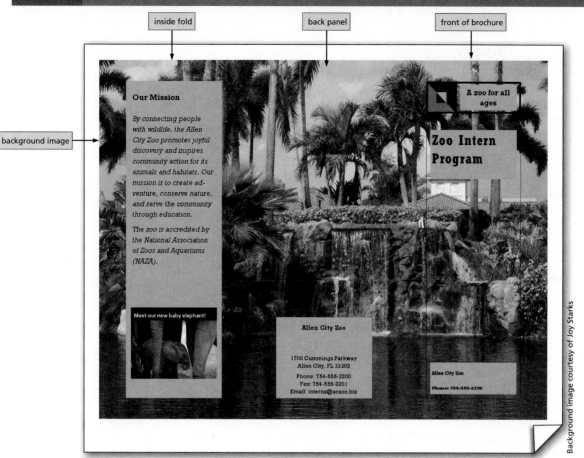

Our Mission

By connecting people with wildlife, the Allen City Zoo promotes joyful discovery and inspires community action for its animals and habitats. Our mission is to create adventure, conserve nature, and serve the community through education.

The zoo is accredited by the National Association of Zoos and Aquariums (NAZA).

Meet our new baby elephant!

A zoo for all ages

Zoo Intern Program

Allen City Zoo

1700 Cummings Parkway
Allen City, FL 33302

Phone: 754-555-2200
Fax: 754-555-2201
Email: interns@aczoo.biz

Allen City Zoo

Phone: 754-555-2200

Background image courtesy of Joy Starks

(a) Page 1

---

inside of brochure →

Internships

Learn how to "pinken" up the flamingos!

Our internship experience is an exciting and educational opportunity for students to participate in various departments at Allen City Zoo. Our interns achieve learning goals associated with their field of study.

Interns are monitored carefully by their managers to ensure that they have active opportunities to participate in a wide variety of learning experiences. The zoo works to meet the academic credit requirements of the intern's educational institution. The program features a learning agenda complete with objectives, observation, reflection, evaluation, assessment, and periodic performance evaluations. Internships last 12 weeks.

Animal Training Internship
Animal training interns establish a working relationship with the animals. Responsibilities include providing enrichment for the animals, presenting animal encounters to the public, researching and reviewing enrichment data, and assisting education staff with the show animals. Interns with prior animal handling experience will be given priority.

Marketing Internship
Marketing interns are responsible for working in all areas of the zoo, and with media, corporate, and community partners to increase public awareness, promote programs, plan special events, and coordinate corporate engagement. Allen City Zoo is seeking motivated individuals with good communication, computer, and writing skills.

General Education Internship
General education interns work to develop and improve educational opportunities for zoo patrons by contributing to the development and evaluation of new curriculum, including distance learning, outreach, and on-grounds programming.

Join us

Giraffes in the large animal compound

← response form

For more information...

Fill out the following form and send it to our Human Resources Department at the address listed below.

Semester	Area of Interest
☐ Fall	☐ Animal Training
☐ Spring	☐ Marketing
☐ Summer	☐ General Education

Habitat	Internship Type
☐ Large animal compound	☐ For credit only
☐ Bird sanctuary	☐ Paid only
☐ Petting zoo	☐ No preference

Comments:

Name

Address

Phone

Allen City Zoo

1700 Cummings Parkway
Allen City, FL 33302

Phone: 754-555-2200
Fax: 754-555-2201
Email: interns@aczoo.biz

QR code © 2014 Cengage Learning
Scott Dunlap/iStock Vectors/Getty Images

(b) Page 2

Figure 2–1

For an introduction to Windows and instruction about how to perform basic Windows tasks, read the Office and Windows chapter at the beginning of this book, where you can learn how to resize windows, change screen resolution, create folders, move and rename files, use Windows Help, and much more.

Roadmap

In this chapter, you will learn how to create the brochure shown in Figure 2–1 on the previous page. The following roadmap identifies general activities you will perform as you progress through this chapter:

1. CUSTOMIZE the BROCHURE template options such as choice, color scheme, and font scheme.
2. EDIT template TEXT and OBJECTS.
3. SWAP PICTURES and use picture backgrounds.
4. USE the FORMAT PAINTER.
5. EDIT a Publisher FORM.
6. USE TYPOGRAPHY to enhance brochure text.
7. INSERT CAPTIONS for each photo.
8. CHECK the PUBLICATION for errors.
9. PACK the PUBLICATION for a printing service.

At the beginning of step instructions throughout the chapter, you will see an abbreviated form of this roadmap. The abbreviated roadmap uses colors to indicate chapter progress: gray means the chapter is beyond that activity, blue means the task being shown is covered in that activity, and black means that activity is yet to be covered. For example, the following abbreviated roadmap indicates the chapter would be showing a task in the Use Format Painter activity.

1 CUSTOMIZE BROCHURE | 2 EDIT TEXT & OBJECTS | 3 SWAP PICTURES | 4 USE FORMAT PAINTER
5 EDIT FORM | 6 USE TYPOGRAPHY | 7 INSERT CAPTIONS | 8 CHECK PUBLICATION | 9 PACK PUBLICATION

Use the abbreviated roadmap as a progress guide while you read or step through the instructions in this chapter.

To Run Publisher

One of the few differences between Windows 7 and Windows 8 occurs in the steps to run Publisher. If you are using Windows 7, click the Start button, type Publisher in the 'Search programs and files' box, click Publisher 2013, and then, if necessary, maximize the Publisher window. For detailed steps to run Publisher in Windows 7, refer to the Office and Windows chapter at the beginning of this book. For a summary of the steps, refer to the Quick Reference located at the back of this book.

If you are using a computer to step through the project in this chapter and you want your screens to match the figures in this book, you should change your screen's resolution to 1366×768. For information about how to change a computer's resolution, refer to the Office and Windows chapter at the beginning of this book.

The following steps, which assume Windows 8 is running, use the Start screen or the search box to run Publisher based on a typical installation. You may need to ask your instructor how to run Publisher on your computer. For a detailed example of the procedure summarized below, refer to the Office and Windows chapter.

1 Scroll the Start screen and search for a Publisher 2013 tile. If your Start screen contains a Publisher 2013 tile, tap or click it to run Publisher and then proceed to Step 5. If the Start screen does not contain the Publisher 2013 tile, proceed to the next step to search for the Publisher app.

2 Swipe in from the right edge of the screen or point to the upper-right corner of the screen to display the Charms bar and then tap or click the Search charm on the Charms bar to display the Search menu.

3 Type **Publisher** as the search text in the Search box, and watch the search results appear in the Apps list.

4 Tap or click Publisher 2013 in the search results to run Publisher.

5 If the Publisher window is not maximized, tap or click the Maximize button on its title bar to maximize the window.

How do you decide on the purpose, shelf life, and layout of a brochure?

Spend time brainstorming ideas for the brochure. Think about why you want to create one. Decide on the purpose of the brochure. Is it to inform, sell, attract, or advertise an event? Adjust your template, fonts, colors, and graphics to match that purpose. Brochures commonly have a wider audience than flyers. They need to last longer, so carefully consider whether to add dated material or prices. Create a timeline of effectiveness and plan to have the brochure ready far in advance. Decide how many panels your brochure should be and how often you are going to produce it. If you are working for someone, draw a storyboard and get it approved before you begin. Think about alignment of objects, proximity of similar data, contrast, and repetition.

The Brochure Medium

Professionals commonly print brochures on special paper to provide long-lasting documents and to enhance the graphics. The brochure medium intentionally is tactile. Brochures are meant to be touched, carried home, passed along, and looked at, again and again. Newspapers and flyers usually have short-term readership on paper that readers throw away or recycle. Brochures, on the other hand, frequently use a heavier stock of paper so that they can stand better in a display rack.

The content of a brochure needs to last longer, too. On occasion, the intent of a brochure is to educate, such as a brochure on health issues in a doctor's office. More commonly, though, the intent is to market a product or sell a service. Prices and dated materials that are subject to frequent change affect the usable life of a brochure.

Typically, brochures use a great deal of color, and they include actual photos instead of drawings or clip art. Photos give a sense of realism to a publication and show people, places, or objects that are real, whereas images or drawings more appropriately are used to convey concepts or ideas.

Brochures, designed to be in circulation for longer periods as a type of advertising, ordinarily are published in greater quantities and on more expensive paper than other single-page publications, so they can be more costly. The cost, however, is less prohibitive when produced **in-house** using desktop publishing rather than hiring an outside service. The cost per copy is lower when producing brochures in mass quantities.

Table 2–1 lists some benefits and advantages of using the brochure medium.

For an introduction to Office and instruction about how to perform basic tasks in Office apps, read the Office and Windows chapter at the beginning of this book, where you can learn how to run an application, use the ribbon, save a file, open a file, exit an application, use Help, and much more.

BTW
How Brochures Differ
Each brochure template produces two pages of graphics, business information text boxes, and story boxes. Brochures are differentiated by the look and feel of the front panel, the location and style of the shapes and graphics, the design of any panel dividers, and the specific kind of decorations unique to each publication set.

Table 2–1 Benefits and Advantages of Using the Brochure Medium	
EXPOSURE	An attention getter in displays
	A take-along document encouraging second looks
	A long-lasting publication due to paper and content
	An easily distributed publication — mass mailings, advertising sites
INFORMATION	An in-depth look at a product or service
	An opportunity to inform in a nonrestrictive environment
	An opportunity for focused feedback using forms
AUDIENCE	Interested clientele and potential customers
COMMUNICATION	An effective medium to highlight products and services
	A source of free information to build credibility
	An easier method to disseminate information than a magazine

Creating a Trifold Brochure

BTW
Brochures
Brochures commonly have a wider audience than flyers. They need to last longer. Carefully consider whether to add dated material or prices. Create a timeline of effectiveness and plan to have the brochure ready far in advance.

Publisher-supplied templates use proven design strategies and combinations of objects, which are placed to attract attention and disseminate information effectively. The options for brochures differ from other publications in that they allow you to choose from page sizes, special kinds of forms, and panel/page layout options.

Making Choices about Brochure Options

For the Internship Brochure publication, you will use an informational brochure template, named Accent Box, making changes to its color scheme, font scheme, page size, and forms. **Page size** refers to the number of panels in the brochure. **Form options**, which appear on page 2 of the brochure, include Order form, Response form, and Sign-up form, or no form at all. The **Order form** displays fields for the description of items ordered as well as types of payment information, including blank fields for entering items, quantities, and prices. The **Response form** displays check box choices for up to four multiple-choice questions and a comment section. The **Sign-up form** displays check box choices, fields for time and price, and payment information. All three forms are meant to be detached as turnaround documents.

To Select a Brochure Template

1 CUSTOMIZE BROCHURE | 2 EDIT TEXT & OBJECTS | 3 SWAP PICTURES | 4 USE FORMAT PAINTER
5 EDIT FORM | 6 USE TYPOGRAPHY | 7 INSERT CAPTIONS | 8 CHECK PUBLICATION | 9 PACK PUBLICATION

The following step selects the Accent Box brochure template. *Why? You should use a template until you are more experienced in designing brochures.*

1
- In the template gallery, tap or click BUILT-IN to display the built-in templates.
- Tap or click the Brochures thumbnail within the BUILT-IN templates to display the Brochure templates.
- Scroll to the section labeled, More Installed Templates. Below that heading, in the Informational area, tap or click the Accent Box thumbnail (Figure 2–2).

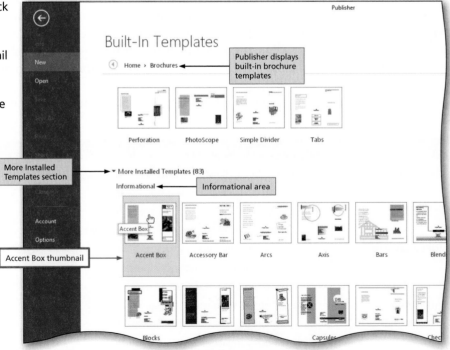

Figure 2–2

To Choose Brochure Options

The following steps choose brochure options.

1 Tap or click the Color scheme button in the template information pane. Scroll as necessary to tap or click Rain Forest to choose the color scheme.

2 Tap or click the Font scheme button, and then tap or click Foundry to choose the font scheme.

3 Do not tap or click the Business information button because it is not used in this publication.

4 Tap or click the Page size button in the Options area and then, if necessary, tap or click 3-panel to choose the number of panels.

5 If necessary, tap or click to remove the check mark in the 'Include customer address' check box.

6 Scroll down and then tap or click the Form button in the Options area. Tap or click Response form to choose the type of form (Figure 2–3).

7 Tap or click the CREATE button to create the publication based on the template settings.

BTW

Color Scheme

Choose a color scheme that is consistent with your company, client, or purpose. Do you need color, or black and white? Think about the plan for printing and the number of copies, in order to select a manageable color scheme. Remember that you can add more visual interest and contrast by bolding the color of text in the scheme; however, keep in mind that too many colors can detract from the flyer and make it difficult to read.

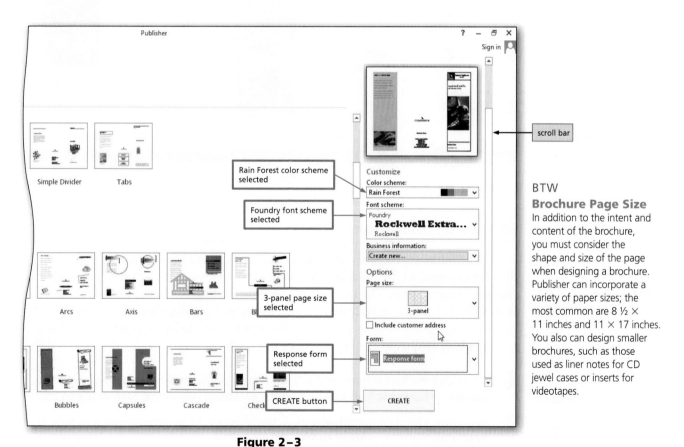

Figure 2–3

BTW

Brochure Page Size

In addition to the intent and content of the brochure, you must consider the shape and size of the page when designing a brochure. Publisher can incorporate a variety of paper sizes; the most common are 8 ½ × 11 inches and 11 × 17 inches. You also can design smaller brochures, such as those used as liner notes for CD jewel cases or inserts for videotapes.

BTW

Other Options

The template information pane contains additional options for brochures. Decide if you need a graphic or tear-offs. Will the publication need to be mailed? Might any specific information be difficult for your audience to remember? What kind of tear-off makes sense for your topic and message?

If you are using your finger on a touch screen and are having difficulty completing the steps in this chapter, consider using a stylus. Many people find it easier to be precise with a stylus rather than with a finger. In addition, with a stylus you see the pointer. If you still are having trouble completing the steps with a stylus, try using a mouse.

To Open the Page Navigation Pane

The following step opens the Page Navigation pane to display both pages of the brochure.

1 If the Page Navigation pane is not displayed, tap or click the 'Current page in publication' button on the status bar to open the Page Navigation pane. If the Page Navigation pane is minimized, tap or click the 'Expand Page Navigation Pane' button to maximize it (Figure 2–4).

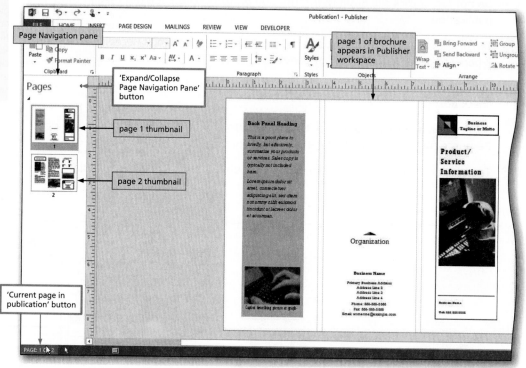

Figure 2–4

To Save a Publication

BTW
Organizing Files and Folders
You should organize and store files in folders so that you easily can find the files later. For example, if you are taking an introductory computer class called CIS 101, a good practice would be to save all Publisher files in a Publisher folder in a CIS 101 folder. For a discussion of folders and detailed examples of creating folders, refer to the Office and Windows chapter at the beginning of this book.

The following steps assume you already have created folders for storing your files, for example, a CIS 101 folder (for your class) that contains a Publisher folder (for your assignments). Thus, these steps save the publication in the Publisher folder in the CIS 101 folder on your desired save location. For a detailed example of the procedure for saving a file in a folder or saving a file on SkyDrive, refer to the Office and Windows chapter at the beginning of this book.

1 Tap or click the Save button on the Quick Access Toolbar, which depending on settings, will display either the Save As gallery in the Backstage view or the Save As dialog box.

2 To save on a hard disk or other storage media on your computer, proceed to Step 2a. To save on SkyDrive, proceed to Step 2b.

2a If your screen opens the Backstage view and you want to save on storage media on your computer, tap or click Computer in the left pane, if necessary, to display options in the right pane related to saving on your computer. If your screen already displays the Save As dialog box, proceed to Step 4.

2b If your screen opens the Backstage view and you want to save on SkyDrive, tap or click SkyDrive in the left pane to display SkyDrive saving options or a Sign In button. If your screen displays a Sign In button, tap or click it and then sign in to SkyDrive.

3 Tap or click the Browse button in the right pane to display the Save As dialog box associated with the selected save location (i.e., Computer or SkyDrive).

4 Type **Internship Brochure** in the File name text box to change the file name. Do not press the ENTER key after typing the file name because you do not want to close the dialog box at this time.

5 Navigate to the desired save location (in this case, the Publisher folder in the CIS 101 folder [or your class folder] on your computer or SkyDrive).

6 Tap or click the Save button (Save As dialog box) to save the publication in the selected folder on the selected save location with the entered file name.

To Delete Objects

You will not use some of the objects in the brochure template. The following steps delete the unused objects.

1 Tap or click the picture in the right panel of page 1 to select it. Press the DELETE key to delete the object.

2 Tap or click the boundary of the Organization logo in the middle panel to select it. Press the DELETE key to delete the object (Figure 2–5).

BTW
Automatic Saving
Publisher can save your publication at regular intervals for you. In the Backstage view, tap or click Options, and then tap or click Save (Publisher Options dialog box). Select the 'Save AutoRecover information every *10* minutes' check box. In the minutes box, specify how often you want Publisher to save files. Do not use AutoRecover as a substitute for regularly saving your work.

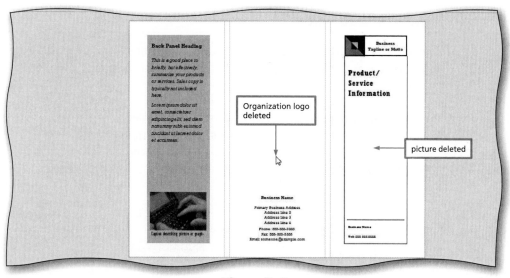

Figure 2–5

To Edit Text in the Right Panel

The front of the brochure displays in the right panel of page 1 and contains default text, placeholder text, and synchronized text. Recall that default text must be selected by dragging or pressing CTRL+A. Placeholder text is selected with a single tap or click. The following steps edit various text boxes on the front panel.

1 In the right panel, select the Business Tagline or Motto by dragging through the text. Type **A zoo for all ages** to replace the text.

BTW
The Ribbon and Screen Resolution
Publisher may change how the groups and buttons within the groups appear on the ribbon, depending on the computer's screen resolution. Thus, your ribbon may look different from the ones in this book if you are using a screen resolution other than 1366 × 768.

BTW
BTWs
For a complete list of the BTWs found in the margins of this book, visit the BTW resource on the Student Companion Site located on www.cengagebrain.com. For detailed instructions about accessing available resources, visit www.cengage.com/ct/studentdownload or see the inside back cover of this book.

2 Tap or click the Product/Service Information headline placeholder text to select it. Type `Zoo Intern Program` to replace the text (Figure 2–6).

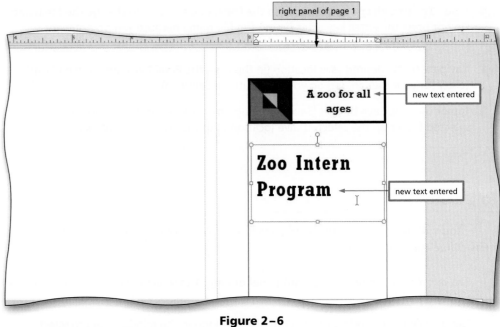

Figure 2–6

To Edit Synchronized Text

Edits to synchronized text change text in multiple locations. The following step edits the Business name at the bottom of the page. You will edit the phone number later in the chapter.

1 At the bottom of the right panel, select the synchronized Business Name text by dragging through the text. Stretch or press the F9 key to zoom to 100%. Type `Allen City Zoo` to replace the text. Deselect the text box to synchronize other locations in the brochure (Figure 2–7).

BTW
Brochure Features
Many brochures incorporate newspaper features, such as columns and a masthead, and add eye appeal with logos, sidebars, shapes, and graphics. Small brochures typically have folded panels. Larger brochures resemble small magazines, with multiple pages and stapled bindings.

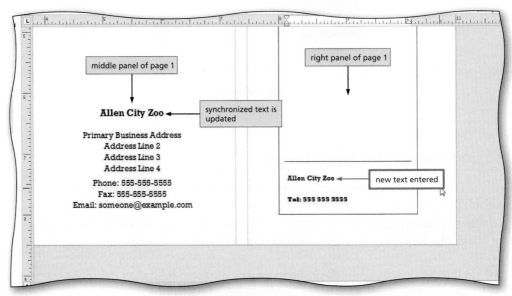

Figure 2–7

To Edit Text in the Middle Panel

When folded, the middle panel will display on the back of the trifold brochure. It contains text boxes for the business address, phone numbers, and email address. The following steps edit the text in the middle panel.

1 Scroll as necessary to display the middle panel. If necessary, stretch or press the F9 key to zoom to 100%.

2 Drag to select the all of the text in the Primary Business Address text box. Type `1700 Cummings Parkway` and then press the ENTER key to finish the first line of the address and advance to the next address line. Type `Allen City, FL 33302` to finish entering the address text.

If requested by your instructor, enter your address, city and state instead of the address in Step 2. Do not press the ENTER key after the last line.

3 Drag to select the phone and fax numbers and the email address text. Type `Phone: 754-555-2200` and then press the ENTER key to finish entering the first line. Type `Fax: 754-555-2201` and then press the ENTER key to finish entering the second line. Type `Email: interns@aczoo.biz` to finish entering the text. Do not press the ENTER key after the last line (Figure 2–8).

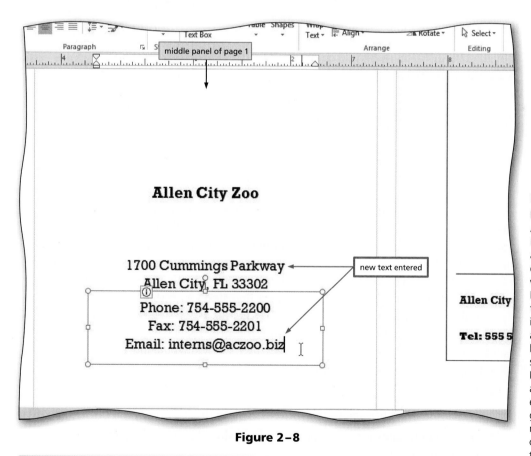

Figure 2–8

BTW
Publisher Help
At any time while using Publisher, you can find answers to questions and display information about various topics through Publisher Help. Used properly, this form of assistance can increase your productivity and reduce your frustrations by minimizing the time you spend learning how to use Publisher. For instruction about Publisher Help and exercises that will help you gain confidence in using it, read the Office and Windows chapter at the beginning of this book.

BTW
Superscripts and Subscripts
Two special font effects are superscript and subscript. A superscript is a character that appears slightly higher than other text on a line, such as that used in footnotes (reference[1]). A subscript is text that is slightly lower than other text on a line, such as that used in scientific formulas (H_2O).

To Edit Heading Text in the Left Panel

The left panel will appear when the brochure is first opened. It contains text boxes for a heading and summary text. The following steps edit the heading text.

1 Scroll to the top of the left panel and zoom to 100%.

2 In the left panel, tap or click to select the Back Panel Heading placeholder text. Type **Our Mission** to replace the text (Figure 2–9).

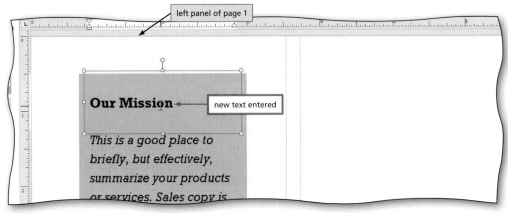

Figure 2–9

How do you decide on a brochure's content?

Gather all the information, such as stories, graphics, logos, colors, shapes, style information, and watermarks. Save copies or versions along the way. If you have to create objects from scratch, have someone else evaluate your work and give you constructive feedback. If you are using forms in your brochure, verify the manner in which the viewer will return the form. Check and double-check all prices, addresses, and phone numbers.

Typing Paragraphs of Text

BTW
Gate Folds
A gatefold is a 4-panel brochure where both ends fold toward the center. Gatefolds, also called foldouts, commonly are used in advertising, for menus, or as inserts in magazines.

When you type paragraphs of text, you will use Publisher's wordwrap feature. **Wordwrap** allows you to type words in a text box continually without pressing the ENTER key at the end of each line. When the insertion point reaches the right margin of a text box, Publisher automatically positions the insertion point at the beginning of the next line. As you type, if a word extends beyond the right margin, Publisher automatically positions that word on the next line along with the insertion point.

Publisher creates a new paragraph or **hard return** each time you press the ENTER key. Thus, as you type text in a text box, do not press the ENTER key when the insertion point reaches the right margin. Instead, press the ENTER key only in these circumstances:

- To insert blank lines in a text box
- To begin a new paragraph
- To terminate a short line of text and advance to the next line
- To respond to questions or prompts in Publisher dialog boxes, panes, and other on-screen objects

To view where in a publication you pressed the ENTER key or SPACEBAR key, you may find it helpful to display formatting marks. A **formatting mark**, sometimes called a **nonprinting character**, is a special character that Publisher displays on the screen, but one that is not visible on a printed publication. For example, the paragraph mark (¶) is a formatting mark that indicates where you pressed the ENTER key. A raised dot (·) appears where you pressed the spacebar. An end of field marker (¤) is displayed to indicate the end of text in a text box. Other formatting marks are discussed as they appear on the screen.

To Display Formatting Marks

The following step displays formatting marks, if they do not show already on the screen. *Why?* *The formatting marks help you see where you pressed the* ENTER *key and the* SPACEBAR *key, among other things.*

1

- If it is not selected already, tap or click the Special Characters button (HOME tab | Paragraph group) to display formatting marks (Figure 2–10).

Q&A What if I do not want formatting marks to show on the screen?
If you feel the formatting marks clutter the screen, you can hide them by tapping or clicking the Special Characters button again. The figures presented in the rest of this chapter show the formatting marks.

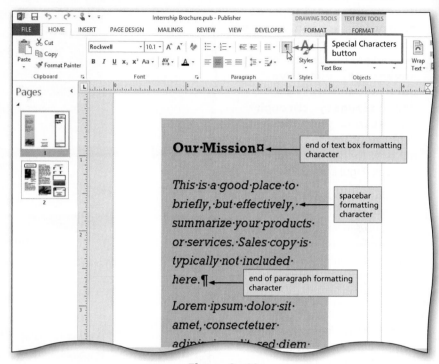

Figure 2–10

Other Ways

1. Press CTRL+SHIFT+Y

To Wordwrap Text as You Type

The next step in creating the flyer is to type the text in the left panel. The following steps wordwrap the text in the text box. *Why?* *Using wordwrap ensures consistent margins.*

1

- Tap or click to select the placeholder text in the text box below the title, Our Mission (Figure 2–11).

Q&A Should I delete the text before typing?
No, it is placeholder text that will disappear automatically when you begin to type.

Figure 2–11

- Type **By connecting people with wildlife, the Allen City Zoo promotes joyful discovery and inspires community action for its animals and habitats. Our mission is to create adventure, conserve nature, and serve the community through education.** and notice that Publisher wraps the text when you get close to the right edge of the text box (Figure 2–12).

Q&A

Why does my publication wrap on different words?

Differences in wordwrap relate to your printer. It is possible that the same publication could wordwrap differently if printed on different printers.

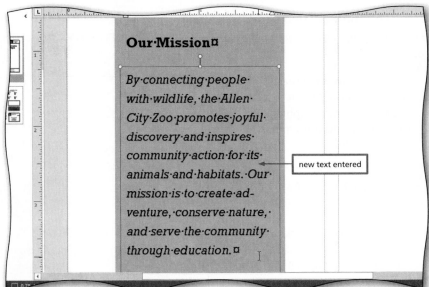

Figure 2–12

- Press the ENTER key to finish the first paragraph.
- Type **The zoo is accredited by the National Association of Zoos and Aquariums (NAZA).** to finish the text (Figure 2–13).

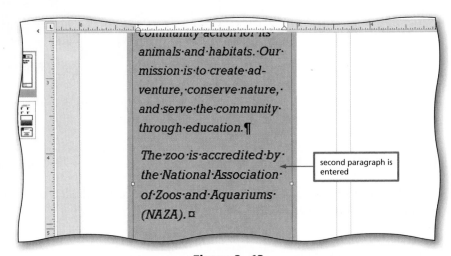

Figure 2–13

Copying, Cutting, and Pasting

BTW

Touch Galleries

If you are using a mouse or stylus, galleries such as the Font color gallery, display their choices in small colored squares. If you are touching to display the gallery, Windows 8 senses that touch and displays the gallery with much larger colored squares, making it easier to tap the one you want.

In each of the Office 2013 applications, you can store or copy text and objects for later use. The **Office Clipboard** is a temporary storage area that holds up to 24 items (text or graphics) copied from any Office program. The Office Clipboard is different from the **Windows Clipboard** associated with the operating system, which can contain only one item at a time. **Copying** is the process of placing items on the Office Clipboard, leaving the item in the publication. **Cutting**, by contrast, removes the item from the publication before placing it on the Office Clipboard. The copy and cut functions transfer text or objects to the Windows Clipboard as well as to the Office Clipboard. Cutting is different from deleting. Deleted items are not placed on either clipboard. **Pasting** is the process of copying an item from the Office Clipboard into the publication at the location of the insertion point or selection.

Table 2–2 describes various methods to copy, cut, paste, and delete selected text.

Table 2–2 Copy, Cut, Paste, and Delete Text

Method	Copy	Cut	Paste	Delete
shortcut menu	Press and hold or right-click to display the shortcut menu and then tap or click Copy	Press and hold or right-click to display the shortcut menu and then tap or click Cut	Press and hold or right-click to display the shortcut menu and then tap or click Paste	Press and hold or right-click to display the shortcut menu and then tap or click Delete Text
ribbon	Tap or click the Copy button (HOME tab | Clipboard group)	Tap or click the Cut button (HOME tab | Clipboard group)	Tap or click the Paste button (HOME tab | Clipboard group)	not available
keyboard	Press CTRL+C	Press CTRL+X	Press CTRL+V	Press the DELETE key or BACKSPACE key

In Publisher, you can copy, cut, paste, and delete objects as well as text. If you are copying text, it is advisable to select from the beginning letter of the text and include any ending spaces, tabs, punctuation, or paragraph marks. That way, when you cut or paste, the text will be spaced properly. If you are copying, cutting, pasting, and deleting objects, the object must be selected. Publisher normally pastes objects from either clipboard into the center of the displayed page layout if no object is selected.

The next step in editing the brochure is to replace the phone number at the bottom of the right panel. One way to enter this information in the brochure is to type it. Recall, however, that you already typed this information on the center panel. Thus, a timesaving alternative would be to copy and paste the text.

1 CUSTOMIZE BROCHURE | 2 EDIT TEXT & OBJECTS | 3 SWAP PICTURES | 4 USE FORMAT PAINTER

To Copy and Paste

5 EDIT FORM | 6 USE TYPOGRAPHY | 7 INSERT CAPTIONS | 8 CHECK PUBLICATION | 9 PACK PUBLICATION

In the brochure, you want to copy the phone number from one panel to the other. ***Why? Copying and pasting reduces errors that might result from retyping information.*** The following steps copy and paste the phone number.

- Scroll to the lower portion of the middle panel.
- Tap or click the phone number text box to select it.
- Drag to select the item to be copied (the word, Phone, and the phone number in this case).
- Tap or click the Copy button (HOME tab \| Clipboard group) to copy the selected item in the publication to the Office Clipboard (Figure 2–14).

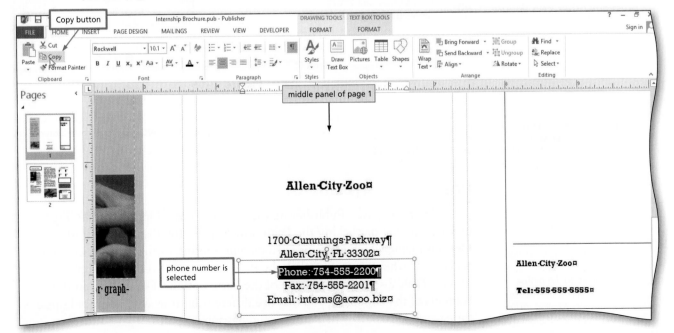

Figure 2–14

● Tap or click the text in the phone number text box on the right panel to select it (Figure 2–15).

Q&A Do I always have to select text before pasting?
No. If you are not replacing text, you position the insertion point at the desired location and then paste.

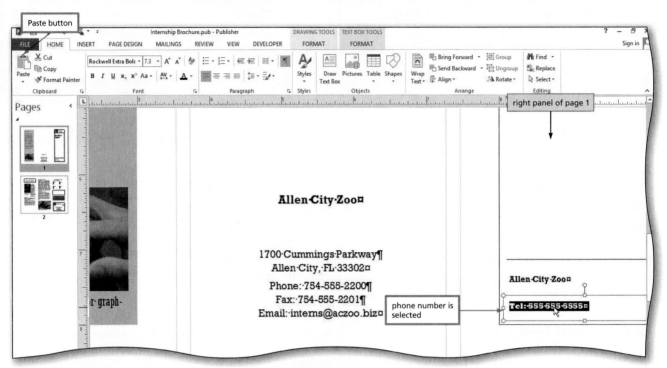

Figure 2–15

● Tap or click the Paste button (HOME tab | Clipboard group) to paste the copied item in the publication and replace the selected phone number. Do not press any other keys (Figure 2–16).

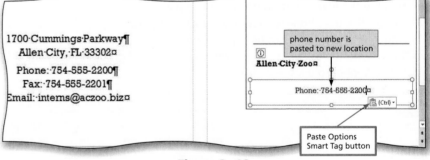

Figure 2–16

Other Ways

1. Press and hold or right-click selected item, tap or click Copy on shortcut menu, press and hold or right-click at paste location, tap or click desired formatting in Paste Options area on shortcut menu

2. Select item, press CTRL+C, position insertion point at paste location, press CTRL+V

BTW

Moving Text

If you want to use your mouse to move text from one location to another, you can select the text and the drag it to the new location. Publisher will display a small rectangle attached to the mouse pointer as you position the mouse in the new location. Moving text or objects also can be accomplished by cutting and then pasting.

Paste Options Button

After you paste, Publisher may display the Paste Options Smart Tag button. Tapping or clicking the **Paste Options** button displays the Paste Options menu, which contains buttons representing formatting choices. They also appear when you tap or click the Paste arrow (HOME tab | Clipboard group). Table 2–3 describes some of the Paste options. Depending on the contents of the clipboard, you may see different buttons with advanced options for pasting, especially when cutting and pasting graphics.

Table 2–3 Paste Options		
Button	**Option**	**Result**
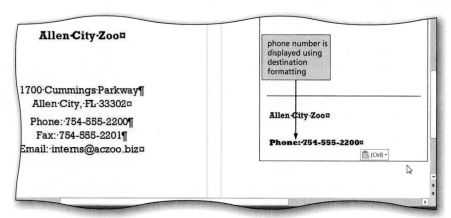	Paste	Pastes the copied content as is, without any formatting changes
	Keep Source Formatting	Pastes the copied content as is, without any formatting changes
	Merge Formatting	Changes the formatting so that it matches the text around it
	Keep Text Only	Pastes the copied text as plain unformatted text and removes any styles or hyperlinks

© 2014 Cengage Learning

To Select a Paste Option

1 CUSTOMIZE BROCHURE | 2 EDIT TEXT & OBJECTS | 3 SWAP PICTURES | 4 USE FORMAT PAINTER
5 EDIT FORM | 6 USE TYPOGRAPHY | 7 INSERT CAPTIONS | 8 CHECK PUBLICATION | 9 PACK PUBLICATION

The following steps select the Keep Text Only Paste Option. *Why? The phone number should match the font style in the right panel.*

1

- Tap or click the Paste Options Smart Tag button that appears below the pasted information to display the Paste Options menu (Figure 2–17).

Experiment

- Point to each of the Paste Options buttons to see their ScreenTips.

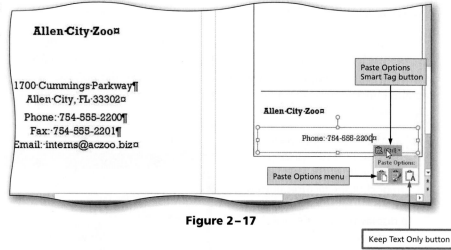

Figure 2–17

2

- Tap or click the Keep Text Only button to paste using the destination formatting (Figure 2–18).

Q&A
Can I change my mind and choose a different paste option?
Yes, if you change it before typing anything else. Otherwise you would have to delete and paste again.

Figure 2–18

Other Ways		
1. Press CTRL key, tap or click Paste Options button	2. Tap or click Paste arrow (HOME tab | Clipboard group), tap or click Paste Options button	3. Press and hold or right-click pasted text, tap or click desired paste option button on shortcut menu.

Swapping Pictures

BTW
Q&As
For a complete list of the Q&As found in many of the step-by-step sequences in this book, visit the Q&A resource on the Student Companion Site located on www.cengagebrain.com. For detailed instructions about accessing available resources, visit www.cengage.com/ct/studentdownload or see the inside back cover of this book.

A new feature in Publisher 2013 is the use of the scratch area to manipulate and swap pictures. The **scratch area** is the gray area that appears outside the publication page. It is used as a temporary holding area; if you are not sure where you want to move an item, you can drag it to the scratch area. When inserting a single picture, you can drag it to the scratch area. When you insert multiple pictures at one time, Publisher arranges the thumbnails or puts them in a column in the scratch area, instead of on top of one another on your page. Unlike the clipboard, the scratch area is saved with the publication. The pictures in the scratch area will still be there the next time you open the publication. The scratch area does not print and contains the same items, regardless of which page of the publication is displayed.

Many templates include picture placeholders, each with a placeholder icon. After the placeholder is replaced with a picture, the icon changes to a **swap icon**. Pictures in the scratch area also have swap icons. You can drag the swap icon to swap pictures with one another, or press and hold or right-click the swap icon to display a shortcut menu with more options.

To Insert Multiple Pictures from a Storage Device

1 CUSTOMIZE BROCHURE | 2 EDIT TEXT & OBJECTS | 3 SWAP PICTURES | 4 USE FORMAT PAINTER
5 EDIT FORM | 6 USE TYPOGRAPHY | 7 INSERT CAPTIONS | 8 CHECK PUBLICATION | 9 PACK PUBLICATION

The following steps insert multiple pictures from a storage device. *Why? Selecting and placing multiple pictures in the scratch area allows you to see what different pictures might look like in the publication.* To complete these steps, you will be required to use the Data Files for Students. Visit www.cengage.com/ct/studentdownload for detailed instructions or contact your instructor for information about accessing the required files.

1
- Zoom to Whole Page view.
- Tap or click INSERT on the ribbon to display the INSERT tab.
- Tap or click the Pictures button (INSERT tab | Illustrations group) to display the Insert Picture dialog box.
- Navigate to the Data Files for Students and the Chapter 02 folder.
- One at a time, CTRL+tap or CTRL+click the files, Social Media, Zoo Scene, and ZooQRcode to select the three pictures (Figure 2–19).

Q&A Why do I have to use the CTRL key? CTRL+tapping or CTRL+clicking allows you to select multiple items, rather than selecting them one at a time.

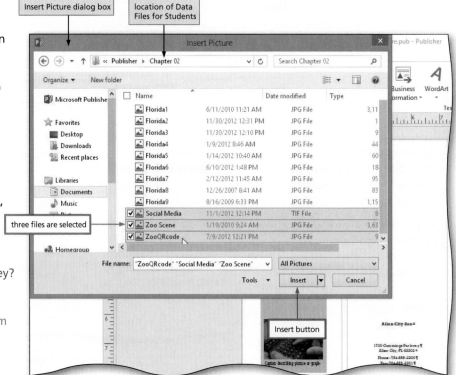

Figure 2–19

2

- Tap or click the Insert button (Insert Picture dialog box) to place the pictures in the scratch area (Figure 2–20).

Q&A
My picture displays in the middle of the publication rather than scratch area. What did I do wrong? If you choose just one picture, it is displayed in the middle of the publication. Multiple selections appear in the scratch area. You can drag your picture to the scratch area, if necessary.

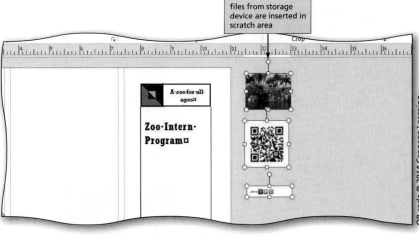

files from storage device are inserted in scratch area

Figure 2–20

QR code © 2014 Cengage Learning

To Insert Online Pictures

The following steps select pictures from Office.com Clip Art and place them in the Publisher scratch area. The size of your pictures may vary.

1 Tap or click the scratch area, away from the pictures to deselect them.

2 Pinch or use the zoom controls on the status bar to zoom to approximately 40%.

3 If necessary, tap or click the INSERT tab and then, with no object selected, tap or click the Online Pictures button (INSERT tab | Illustrations group) to display the Insert Pictures dialog box.

4 Type `giraffes` in the Office.com Clip Art search box to enter the search term. Press the ENTER key to display pictures of giraffes. Tap or click a picture of giraffes similar to the one shown in Figure 2–21.

5 Tap or click the Insert button (Office.com Clip Art dialog box) to place the selected picture in the publication.

6 Drag the picture to the scratch area.

7 Repeat Steps 3 through 6 to insert a picture of elephants and a picture of flamingos. Scroll as necessary to view all of the pictures (Figure 2–21).

BTW

Clip Art Sources
In addition to the clip art images included with Publisher, other sources for clip art include retailers specializing in computer software, the Internet, bulletin board systems, and online information systems. A bulletin board system is a computer service that allows users to communicate with each other and share files.

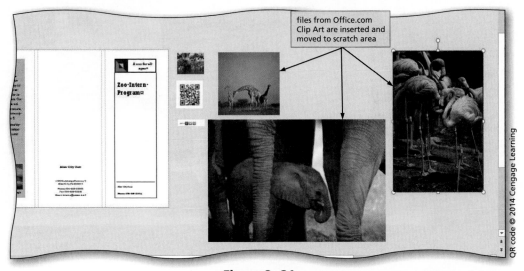

files from Office.com Clip Art are inserted and moved to scratch area

QR code © 2014 Cengage Learning

Figure 2–21

To Select Multiple Objects

The following steps select all of the pictures in the scratch area. *Why? They must be selected in order to arrange them in the next series of steps.*

- In the scratch area, drag, starting above and to the left of the first thumbnail, moving down and to the right, to include all of the pictures. Do not lift your finger or release the mouse button (Figure 2–22).

Figure 2–22

- Release the drag to select all of the pictures (Figure 2–23).

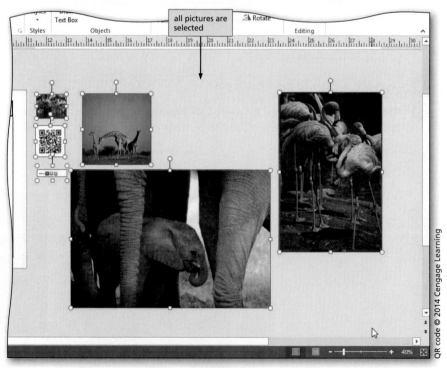

Figure 2–23

Other Ways

1. CTRL+tap or CTRL+click each picture in scratch area

To Arrange Thumbnails

1 CUSTOMIZE BROCHURE | 2 EDIT TEXT & OBJECTS | 3 SWAP PICTURES | 4 USE FORMAT PAINTER
5 EDIT FORM | 6 USE TYPOGRAPHY | 7 INSERT CAPTIONS | 8 CHECK PUBLICATION | 9 PACK PUBLICATION

The scratch area displays pictures as thumbnails. *Why? A* **thumbnail** *is a reduced-size version of a larger graphic image used to help recognize and organize pictures, and to save space.* When you **arrange thumbnails**, all of the pictures are reduced to thumbnail size and are aligned in rows and columns. The following step arranges thumbnails.

1

- If necessary, tap or click PICTURE TOOLS FORMAT on the ribbon to display the PICTURE TOOLS FORMAT tab.
- Tap or click the Arrange Thumbnails button (PICTURE TOOLS FORMAT tab | Arrange group) to arrange the thumbnails (Figure 2–24).

Q&A My tab disappeared. Did I do something wrong?
No. The PICTURE TOOLS FORMAT tab displays only when a picture is selected. Arranging the thumbnails may have deselected the pictures.

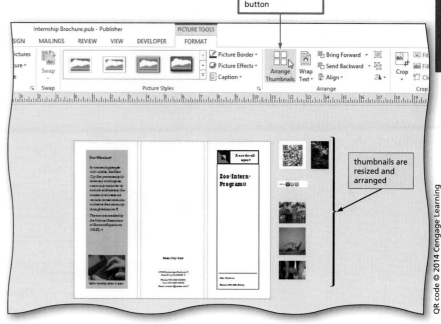

Figure 2–24

Other Ways

1. Select pictures in scratch area, press and hold or right-click any picture, tap or click Arrange Thumbnails on shortcut menu

To Swap Pictures

1 CUSTOMIZE BROCHURE | 2 EDIT TEXT & OBJECTS | 3 SWAP PICTURES | 4 USE FORMAT PAINTER
5 EDIT FORM | 6 USE TYPOGRAPHY | 7 INSERT CAPTIONS | 8 CHECK PUBLICATION | 9 PACK PUBLICATION

When you decide to swap one picture for another, you drag the new picture toward the old picture. When Publisher displays a pink boundary, lift your finger away from the screen or release the mouse button. It is a good idea to swap pictures that have the same orientation. *Why? Pictures with the same orientation as the template fit the area better and are not scaled disproportionately.* **Portrait** pictures are taller than they are wide. Pictures that are **landscape** oriented are wider than they are tall. The following steps swap the picture on the left panel of page 1 in the brochure.

1

- Zoom to Whole Page view.
- In the scratch area, tap or click the photo you wish to use in the brochure (in this case the picture of the elephants) to display the swap icon. (Figure 2–25).

Q&A The swap icon disappeared. Did I do something wrong?
You may have moved your finger or the pointer away from the picture. Tap the picture or move the pointer back over the top of the selected picture to display the swap icon.

Figure 2–25

2

- From the scratch area, drag the swap icon of the photo you wish to swap to a location over a current graphic on the page. In this case, you are dragging the picture of the elephant to a location over the picture of the keyboard in the left panel. Do not lift your finger or release the mouse button (Figure 2–26).

Q&A What should I do with the other pictures?
You will use them later in the project.

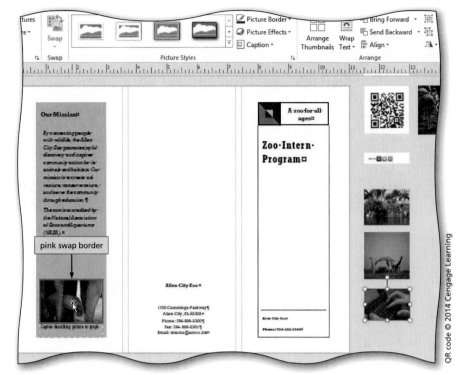

Figure 2–26

QR code © 2014 Cengage Learning

3

- When the pink boundary is displayed, lift your finger or release the mouse button to swap the pictures (Figure 2–27).

Q&A Should I edit the caption?
No, you will edit the caption later in the chapter.

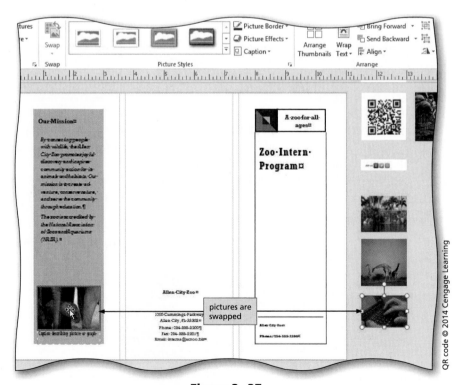

Figure 2–27

QR code © 2014 Cengage Learning

To Use a Picture as a Background

Many brochures use pictures in the background. *Why? A picture adds interest and removes the stark white color around objects in the brochure.* Recall that in Chapter 1 you used a gradient background for the web flyer. In this brochure, you will apply a picture to the background, using a picture from the scratch area and the shortcut menu. The following steps apply a picture to the background of page 1 of the brochure.

 1

- Press and hold or right-click the picture you wish to use as a background (in this case, the Zoo Scene picture) to display the shortcut menu.
- Tap or click 'Apply to Background' to display the Apply to Background submenu (Figure 2–28).

Q&A Will the picture also be placed on page 2?
No, not unless you go to page 2 and apply it there. Each page of a publication has a unique background area.

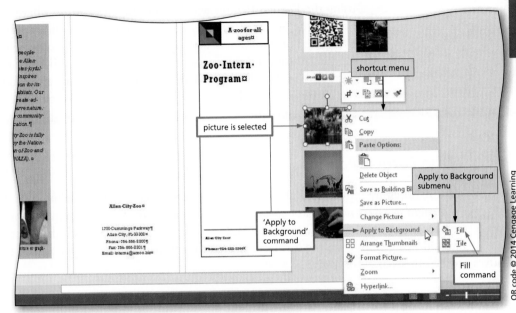

Figure 2–28

2

- Tap or click Fill on the Apply to Background submenu to place the picture in the background of the page (Figure 2–29).

Q&A Should I change the white background behind the text boxes?
You will format that later in the chapter.

Should I delete the extra vertical lines on the right panel?
The vertical lines are a rectangle that helps keep the two text box concepts together. They do not need to be deleted.

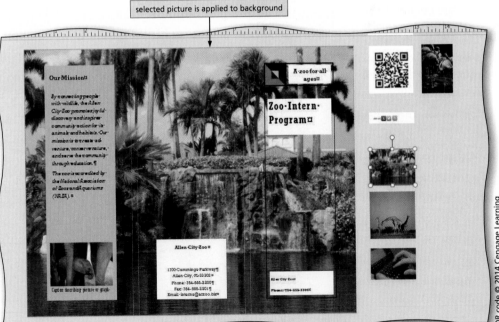

Figure 2–29

Other Ways

1. Tap or click Background button (PAGE DESIGN tab | Page Background group), tap or click More Backgrounds in Background gallery, tap or click 'Picture or texture fill', tap or click File, navigate to picture, double-tap or double-click picture, tap or click OK button (Format Background dialog box)

Using the Format Painter

A convenient way to apply specific formatting is to copy the formatting from existing text or objects using the Format Painter button (HOME tab | Clipboard group). The **Format Painter** copies formatting such as color, border, font, font size, and special effects, from a **source** object (the object whose formatting you wish to copy) to a **destination** object (the object that will be reformatted to match the source). When using the Format Painter with objects, tap or click anywhere in the source object, tap or click the Format Painter button, and then tap or click the destination object. When using the Format Painter with text, tap or click the source text, tap or click the Format Painter button, and then select the destination text. To apply formatting to multiple destinations, double-tap or double-click the Format Painter button so that it stays on. In those cases, when you finish formatting, tap or click the Format Painter button again to turn it off.

To Use the Format Painter

1 CUSTOMIZE BROCHURE | 2 EDIT TEXT & OBJECTS | 3 SWAP PICTURES | 4 USE FORMAT PAINTER
5 EDIT FORM | 6 USE TYPOGRAPHY | 7 INSERT CAPTIONS | 8 CHECK PUBLICATION | 9 PACK PUBLICATION

In many brochure templates, Publisher places a white rectangle shape behind text. *Why? If the background of the page is changed to a dark color, for example, the text still is visible.* In the Internship Brochure, you decide to change the white background of the text boxes in the middle and right panels to match the color of the left panel.

The following steps copy the formatting from the left panel shape, which is pale green, to the white text boxes on the other panels of page 1.

1

- In the left panel, tap or click the edge of the rectangle shape behind the text boxes to select the shape. Do not select any of the text boxes or the picture (Figure 2–30).

Q&A

How do I know that I have the shape selected and not a text box?
The sizing handles should appear at the four corners of the light green rectangle shape.

Could I copy the formatting of the text box?
You should not. Besides the color, text boxes have font, font sizes, and perhaps other formatting that would be copied. In this case, you want to copy only the color from the shape.

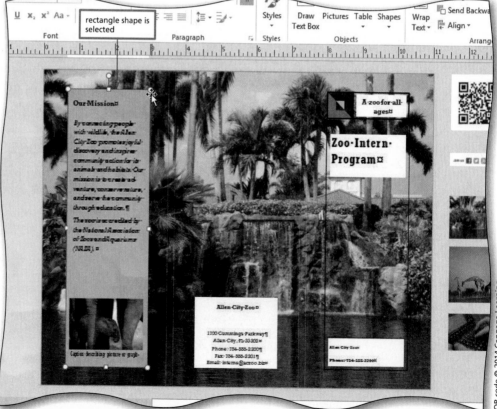

Figure 2–30

2

- Double-tap or double-click the Format Painter button (HOME Tab | Clipboard group) to copy the formatting.
- Move the pointer into the workspace (Figure 2–31).

Q&A Why does the pointer display a paintbrush icon?

The pointer changes when a format has been copied. Once you turn off the Format Painter, the paintbrush icon will disappear.

Do I always have to double-tap or double-click the Format Painter button?

No. You only double-tap or double-click to apply the format to multiple locations. If you have only one place to format, a single click will do. After a single click application of formatting, the Format Painter turns off automatically.

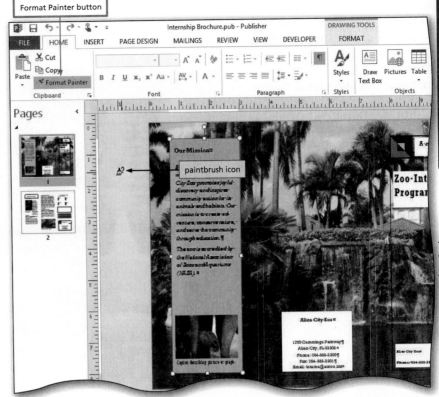

Figure 2–31

Background image courtesy of Joy Starks

3

- Tap or click one of the white text boxes in the middle panel (Figure 2–32).

Q&A Should I try to tap or click the shape behind the text box?

Ideally, yes; however, the text boxes in the middle panel completely fill the shape behind them, making it nearly impossible to tap or click the shape alone. Formatting the text boxes with the color will achieve the same effect.

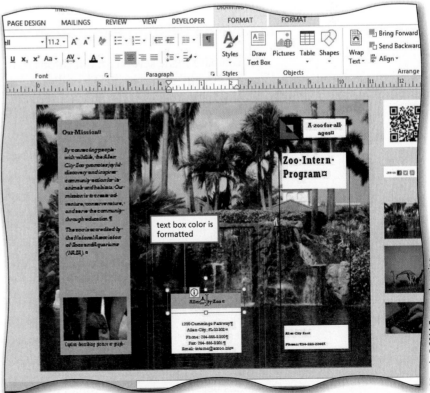

Figure 2–32

QR code © 2014 Cengage Learning
Background image courtesy of Joy Starks

4

- One at a time, tap or click each of the other white text boxes in the middle panel and in the right panel.
- Tap or click the Format Painter button (HOME Tab | Clipboard group) to turn it off (Figure 2–33).

Q&A
Can I use the Format Painter button on objects other than shapes?
Yes. You can copy applied formatting of text, a graphic, WordArt, shapes, fills, or any object from the Design Gallery. If you can change an object's style or set its formatting options, you can copy the formatting from that object to another.

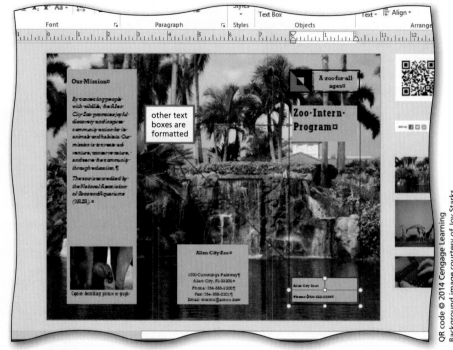

other text boxes are formatted

Figure 2–33

Other Ways

1. Select source, press and hold or right-click selection, tap or click Format Painter button on mini toolbar, tap or click destination

To Save an Existing Publication with the Same File Name

You have made several modifications to the publication since you last saved it. Thus, you should save it again. The following step saves the publication again. For an example of the step listed below, refer to the Office and Windows chapter at the beginning of this book.

1 Tap or click the Save button on the Quick Access Toolbar to overwrite the previously saved file.

Break Point: If you wish to take a break, this is a good place to do so. To resume at a later time, run Publisher, open the file called Internship Brochure, and continue following the steps from this location forward.

Editing the Inside Panels of a Brochure

As you edit the inside panels of the brochure, you will change text, edit the form text boxes, and change the pictures and captions. Headings introduce information about the topic and describe specific products or services. Secondary headings and the stories below them organize topics to make it easier for readers to understand the information.

To Switch to Page 2

The following step uses the Page Navigation pane to move to page 2. *Why? The Page Navigation pane is the only way to move among pages by tapping or clicking; however, you can press the* F5 *key and enter the new page number.*

1

- Tap or click the Page 2 icon in the Page Navigation pane to display page 2.
- If necessary, zoom to Whole Page view (Figure 2–34).

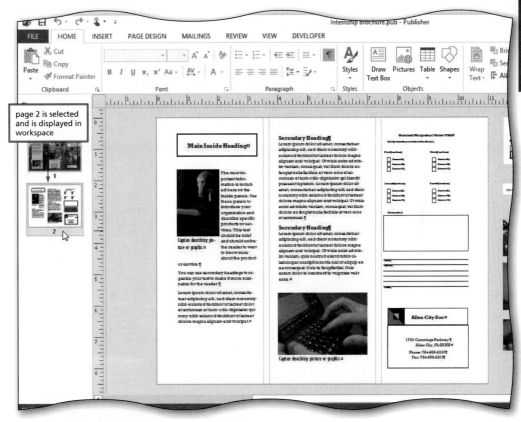

Figure 2–34

Other Ways

1. Press F5, enter page number, tap or click OK button

To Edit the Left Panel on Page 2

The following steps edit the text on the left panel of page 2. As you edit the text, zoom and scroll as necessary to view the text.

1 In the left panel of page 2, tap or click the placeholder text in the Main Inside Heading text box to select it.

2 Type **Internships** to complete the heading.

3 Tap or click the placeholder text for the story in the left panel.

4 Type **Our internship experience is an exciting and educational opportunity for students to participate in various departments at Allen City Zoo. Our interns achieve learning goals associated with their field of study.** and then press the ENTER key to create the first paragraph.

5 Type `Interns are monitored carefully by their managers to ensure that they have active opportunities to participate in a wide variety of learning experiences. The zoo works to meet the academic credit requirements of the intern's educational institution. The program features a learning agenda complete with objectives, observation, reflection, evaluation, assessment, and periodic performance evaluations. Internships last 12 weeks.`

6 Press and hold or right-click the text to display the shortcut menu. Click Best Fit on the shortcut menu to make the text fit the text box (Figure 2–35).

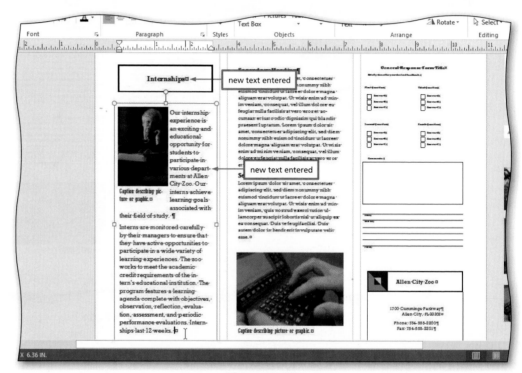

Figure 2–35

To Edit the Middle Panel on Page 2

The following steps edit the text in the middle panel of page 2. As you edit the text, zoom and scroll as necessary to view the text. Later in the chapter, you will format the text.

1 In the middle panel of page 2, tap or click the first Secondary Heading placeholder text in the middle panel to select it.

2 Type `Animal Training Internship` to complete the text.

3 Tap or click the story below the heading to select the placeholder text.

4 Type `Animal training interns establish a working relationship with the animals. Responsibilities include providing enrichment for the animals, presenting animal encounters to the public, researching and reviewing enrichment data, and assisting education staff with the show animals. Interns with prior animal handling experience will be given priority.`

5 Tap or click the second Secondary Heading placeholder text on the middle panel to select it.

6 Type `Marketing Internship` to complete the text.

7 Tap or click the story below the heading to select the placeholder text.

8 Type `Marketing interns are responsible for working with all areas of the zoo, and with media, corporate, and community partners to increase public awareness, promote programs, plan special events, and coordinate corporate engagement. Allen City Zoo is seeking motivated individuals with good communication, computer, and writing skills.` and then press the ENTER key to finish the paragraph.

9 Type `General Education Internship` and then press the ENTER key to create a third heading.

10 Type `General education interns work to develop and improve educational opportunities for zoo patrons by contributing to the development and evaluation of new curriculum, including distance learning, outreach, and on-grounds programming.` (Figure 2–36).

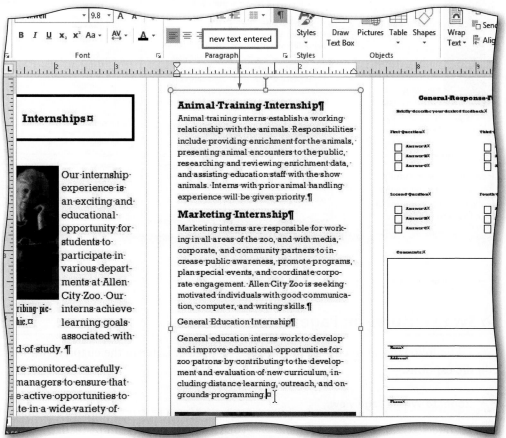

Figure 2–36

BTW
Touch Screen Differences
The Office and Windows interfaces may vary if you are using a touch screen. For this reason, you might notice that the function or appearance of your touch screen differs slightly from this chapter's presentation.

To Copy the Heading Format

The following steps use the Format Painter to copy the heading format to the third heading in the middle panel.

1 Tap or click the heading, Animal Training Internship, to specify the source of the formatting style.

2 Tap or click the Format Painter button (HOME Tab | Clipboard group) to copy the formatting.

3 Drag through the text, General Education Internship, to paste the formatting to the third heading (Figure 2–37).

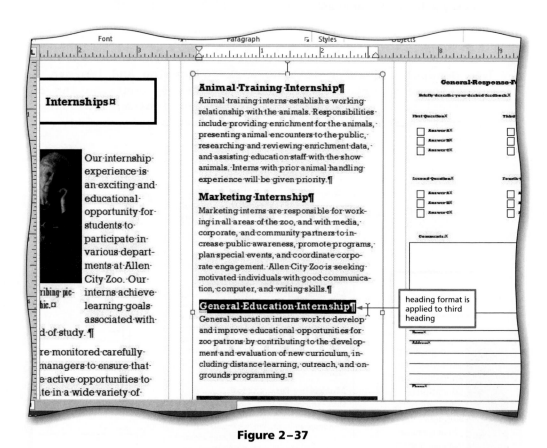

Figure 2–37

To Swap Pictures on Page 2

The following steps change the pictures on page 2. Later in the chapter, you will edit the captions.

1 Zoom to Whole Page view.

2 In the scratch area, tap or click the photo you wish to use in the left panel of the brochure (in this case, the picture of the flamingos) to display the swap icon.

3 From the scratch area, drag the swap icon of the photo to a location over the graphic in the left panel. When you see a pink boundary, drop the picture.

4 Repeat steps 2 and 3 swapping the giraffes picture with the picture of the keyboard in the middle panel (Figure 2–38).

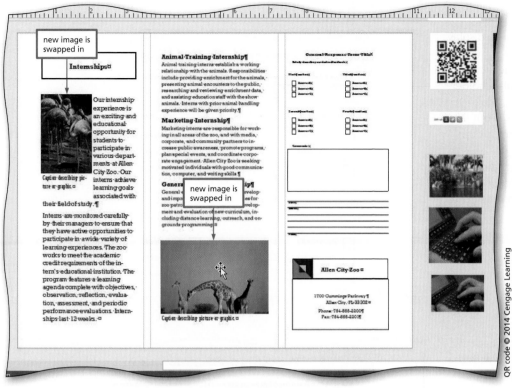

Figure 2–38

QR code © 2014 Cengage Learning

To Edit the Form

1 CUSTOMIZE BROCHURE | 2 EDIT TEXT & OBJECTS | 3 SWAP PICTURES | 4 USE FORMAT PAINTER
5 EDIT FORM | 6 USE TYPOGRAPHY | 7 INSERT CAPTIONS | 8 CHECK PUBLICATION | 9 PACK PUBLICATION

Publisher forms consist of text boxes, graphic boxes, and lines grouped together in an attractive and usable format. As you edit the text in the text boxes, you may have to tap or click the check box text twice to select the placeholder text. *Why? The check boxes consist of a graphic and a text box grouped together; if you tap or click the text, the placeholder text will be selected. However, if you tap or click on the square shape, the check box will be selected. You will have to tap or click the text again to select the placeholder text.*

The following steps edit the text boxes and check boxes in the form in the right panel of page 2.

1

- On the right panel of page 2, tap or click the text in the General Response Form Title text box to select the placeholder text.
- Stretch or click the Zoom In button on the status bar to zoom to approximately 200%.
- Type `For more information...` to complete the text.
- Tap or click the instruction text box below the heading to select the placeholder text.
- Type `Fill out the following form and send it to our Human Resources Department at the address listed below.` to finish entering the text (Figure 2–39).

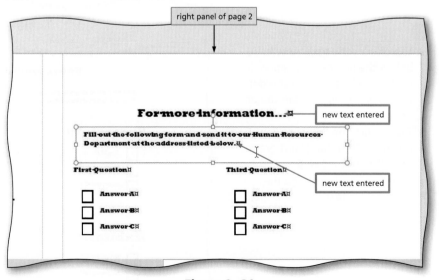

Figure 2–39

2

- If necessary, scroll down to display the check box area.
- Tap or click the First Question heading to select the placeholder text.
- Tap or click the 'Increase Font Size' button (HOME tab | Font group) until the font is size 9.
- Type `Semester` to change the heading and then click outside the text box to deselect it (Figure 2–40).

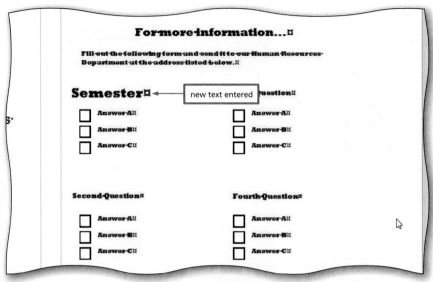

Figure 2–40

3

- Repeat Step 2 to replace each of the other three headings with the headings shown in Figure 2–41.

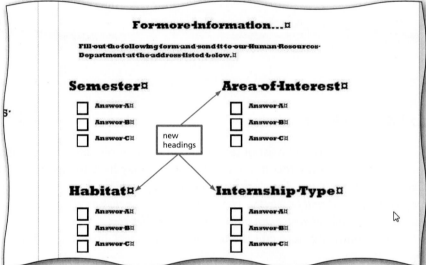

Figure 2–41

4

- Tap or click the text, Answer A, below the Semester heading, in order to select the placeholder text only. Do not double-tap or double-click.
- Tap or click the 'Increase Font Size' button (HOME tab | Font group) until the font is size 6.
- Type `Fall` to change the placeholder text (Figure 2–42).

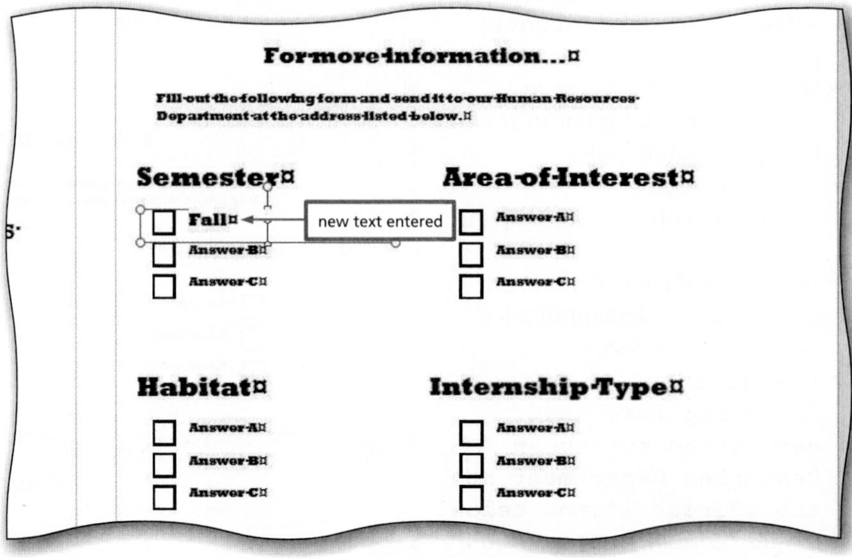

Figure 2–42

5
- Repeat Step 4 for each of the other 11 choices as shown in Figure 2–43. If necessary, resize the Large animal compound text box, so that all of the text is displayed.

new choices are entered in each category

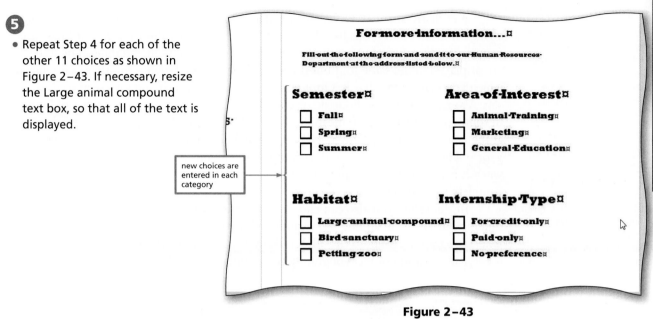

Figure 2–43

To Save an Existing Publication with the Same File Name

You have made several modifications to the publication since you last saved it. Thus, you should save it again. The following step saves the publication again. For an example of the step listed below, refer to the Office and Windows chapter at the beginning of this book.

1 Tap or click the Save button on the Quick Access Toolbar to overwrite the previously saved file.

BTW
Character Typography
Typography also includes scaling, tracking, and kerning of characters. You will learn about these spacing options in a future chapter.

Break Point: If you wish to take a break, this is a good place to do so. To resume at a later time, run Publisher, open the file called Internship Brochure, and continue following the steps from this location forward.

Typography

In Publisher, **typography** refers to specialized effects and fonts, including stylistic sets, drop caps, number styles, and glyphs. A **glyph** is a special stroke that appears in text that is not part of the normal font set. Diacritical marks, such as the umlaut (ä) or cedilla (ç), use glyphs. Ligatures, stylistic sets, swashes, and stylistic alternates, as well as some alphabetic characters that are not part of the English language, also are created with glyphs (Figure 2–44).

BTW
Swashes
A swash is an exaggerated serif or glyph that typically runs into the space above or below the next letter. Some swashes can cause an unattractive appearance when used with adjacent descending letters such as g, j, or y; however, when used correctly, a swash produces a flowing, linear appearance that adds interest to the font.

glyph

Figure 2–44

BTW
Serif Fonts
Serif fonts are considered Oldstyle when they display a slanted serif. Fonts are considered Modern when they use horizontal serifs.

BTW
Stylistic Alternate Sets
If you use a script font that looks like cursive writing, a stylistic alternate can simulate handwriting by using of a set of randomly chosen glyphs with slight differences in appearance.

A **stylistic set** is an organized set of alternate letters and glyphs, allowing you to change what the font looks like. Besides its regular display, almost every font has three common stylistic sets: bold, italic, and the combination of bold and italic. The letters are displayed in the same font but use a heavier or slanted glyph. Another example with which you may be familiar is a font family that has both serif and sans serif stylistic sets. A **serif** is small line, flourish, or embellishment, that crosses the strokes of letters in some fonts. A **sans serif**, meaning without flourish, set has no extra embellishment at the end of characters. Other stylistic sets include alternates for characters such as e, j, g, or y. The extra characters with accompanying glyphs have to be a part of the font set when it is installed. On a typical Publisher installation only a few font families contain complete stylistic sets.

In Publisher, you also can choose a **stylistic alternate** set, which creates a random pattern from among the various stylistic sets available for the current font. The Typography group on the TEXT BOX TOOLS FORMAT tab displays choices for stylistic sets and other typography commands (Figure 2–45).

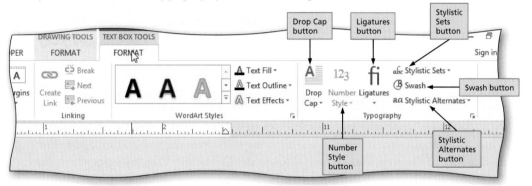

Figure 2–45

To Edit the Font Family

1 CUSTOMIZE BROCHURE | 2 EDIT TEXT & OBJECTS | 3 SWAP PICTURES | 4 USE FORMAT PAINTER
5 EDIT FORM | 6 USE TYPOGRAPHY | 7 INSERT CAPTIONS | 8 CHECK PUBLICATION | 9 PACK PUBLICATION

Recall that in Chapter 1 you formatted text with bold, underline, and italics. You also increased the font size of text. In the following steps you will change the font itself. *Why? The Gabriola font family has a wide variety of stylistic sets.*

- On page 2, drag to select the heading, For more information…, in the right panel.
- Tap or click the Font arrow (HOME tab | Font group) to display the Font gallery (Figure 2–46).

🔎 **Experiment**

- Point to each of the font names and watch the live preview.

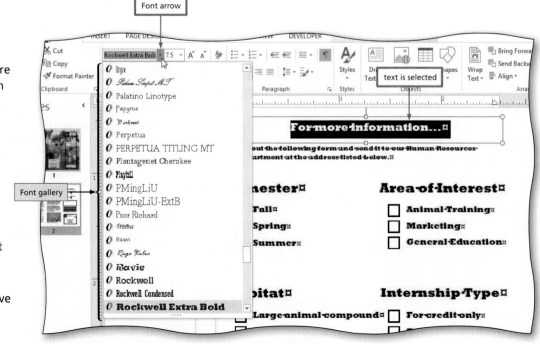

Figure 2–46

2
- Scroll to display the desired font (in this case, Gabriola), and then tap or click the font name to choose the font.
- Do not deselect the heading text (Figure 2–47).

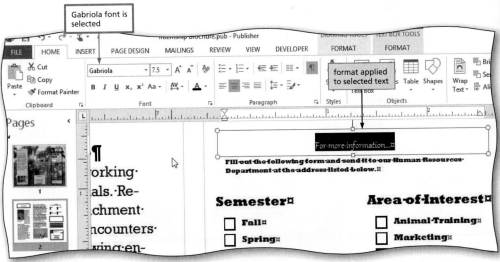

Figure 2–47

Other Ways

1. Tap or click Font arrow on mini toolbar, select desired font

2. Press and hold or right-click selected text, tap or click Change Text on shortcut menu, tap or click Font on Change Text menu, tap or click desired font in Font list (Font dialog box), tap or click OK button

3. Tap or click Font Dialog Box Launcher (HOME tab | Font group), tap or click desired font in Font list (Font dialog box), tap or click OK button

To Resize the Text Box and the Font

The following steps resize the text box and increase the font size in preparation for typography changes.

1 With the text still selected, drag the upper-center sizing handle up to approximately the 1/8 inch mark on the vertical ruler to increase the size of the box.

2 Tap or click the 'Increase Font Size' button (HOME tab | Font group) several times until the Font Size box displays 22.

3 Do not deselect the text (Figure 2–48).

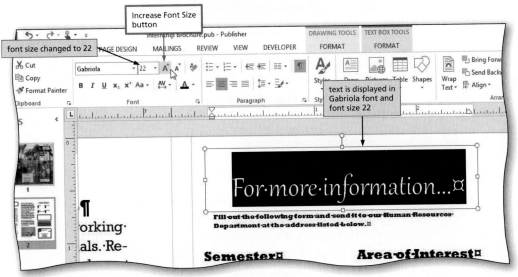

Figure 2–48

To Format with a Stylistic Set

The following steps choose a stylistic set for the heading. *Why? Stylistic sets add interest and flair to headings.*

- Tap or click TEXT BOX TOOLS FORMAT on the ribbon to display the TEXT BOX TOOLS FORMAT tab.
- With the text selected, tap or click the Stylistic Sets button (TEXT BOX TOOLS FORMAT tab | Typography group) to display the Stylistic Sets gallery. Scroll in the gallery to display more stylistic sets (Figure 2–49).

🔍 **Experiment**

- Point to each stylistic set and watch the live preview in the text box.

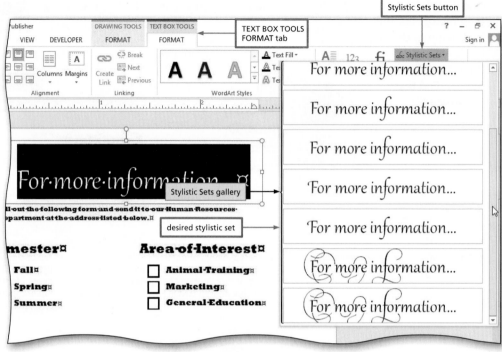

Figure 2–49

Q&A Do all fonts have fancy stylistic sets?

No, usually only **OpenType** or scalable fonts contain stylistic sets other than bold and italic.

- Tap or click the desired set (in this case, the third one from the bottom) to apply the stylistic set to the selected text (Figure 2–50).

Q&A Could I use one of the fancier stylistic sets?

You could, but the fancier stylistic sets with large glyphs will not fit in with the style of the brochure.

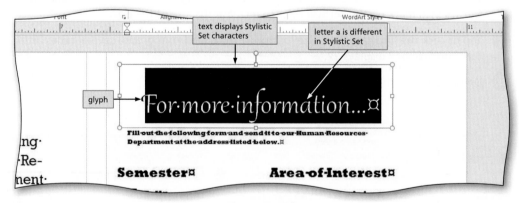

Figure 2–50

BTW
Other Ligatures
The standard ligatures are fi, ffi, and fl; however, in some font families, Publisher offers discretionary ligatures that you may create, including all of the ascending letters that might follow the letter, f, as well as ligatures such as ki, th, or ae.

Ligatures

Ligatures are two or more characters grouped together without glyphs in order to create a more readable font, especially in larger font sizes. A common ligature is a combination of the letter f, followed by the letter i. The glyph of the f may overlap the i slightly in some fonts; as a result, an awkward bulge may appear on the f as it runs into the dot of the i. The fi ligature creates a cleaner line. Figure 2–51 shows the fi combination, first without the ligature and then with the ligature. Most ligatures turn off glyphs to improve readability. Because stylistic sets have more glyphs than standard fonts, they also have more ligatures. By default, ligatures are **enabled,** or turned on.

BTW
Ligatures
When a program automatically changes a typed fraction, for example, 1/2 to ½, it is creating a ligature for you. The 1/2 requires three spaces, whereas the ½ requires only one.

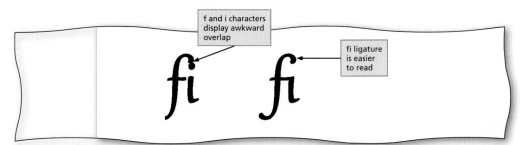

Figure 2–51

To Examine Ligatures

1 CUSTOMIZE BROCHURE | 2 EDIT TEXT & OBJECTS | 3 SWAP PICTURES | 4 USE FORMAT PAINTER
5 EDIT FORM | 6 USE TYPOGRAPHY | 7 INSERT CAPTIONS | 8 CHECK PUBLICATION | 9 PACK PUBLICATION

The following steps look at letters with ligatures disabled. *Why? Examining ligature letters and the same letters with glyphs helps you understand the concept.*

- In the form heading, select the letters, atio, in the word, information.
- Tap or click the Ligatures button (TEXT BOX TOOLS FORMAT tab | Typography group) to display the Ligatures gallery (Figure 2–52).

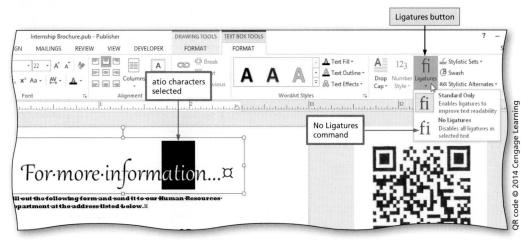

Figure 2–52

2
- Tap or click No Ligatures to disable the ligature.
- Deselect the letters to better view the effect of no ligatures (Figure 2–53).

Q&A | What changed?
Without ligatures, all of the glyphs for those letters display. They run into each other, making the text more difficult to read.

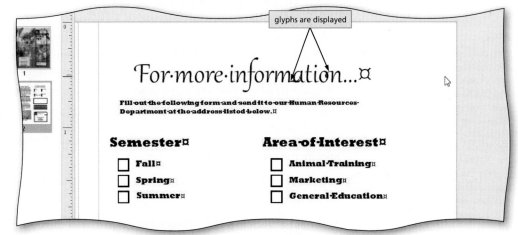

Figure 2–53

Other Ways

1. Tap or click Symbol button (INSERT tab | Text group), tap or click More Symbols, tap or click desired ligature, tap or click Insert button (Symbol dialog box)

To Undo an Action

Publisher provides a means of canceling your recent command(s) or action(s). ***Why?*** *If you format text incorrectly, you can undo the format and try it again.* When you point to the Undo button, Publisher displays the action you can undo as part of a ScreenTip. If, after you undo an action, you decide you did not want to perform the undo, you can redo the undone action. Publisher does not allow you to undo or redo some actions, such as copying, saving, or printing a publication. The next step undoes the No Ligatures formatting performed in the previous steps.

- Click the Undo button on the Quick Access Toolbar to reverse your most recent action (in this case, disabling the ligatures) (Figure 2–54).

Experiment

- Tap or click the Undo arrow to view recent actions.

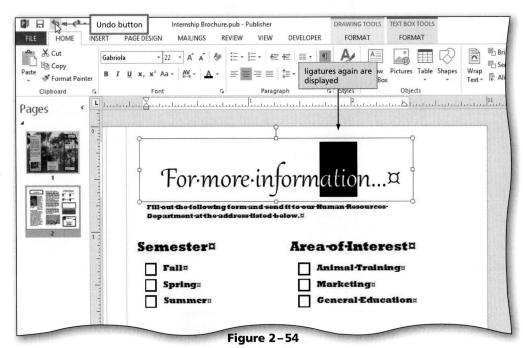

Figure 2–54

Other Ways	
1. Press CTRL+Z	2. Tap or click Undo arrow, tap or click undo action

To Copy the Stylistic Set Formatting

When you make a major change to the formatting of text, as you did in previous steps, it is a good idea to use that formatting more than once, so that it does not look like a mistake. Reusing font styles or stylistic sets also provides continuity in the publication. The following steps copy the stylistic set formatting from the form heading to the heading on the left panel of page 2.

1. If necessary, tap or click the text in the form heading, For more information... to specify the source formatting.

2. Tap or click the Format Painter button (HOME tab | Clipboard group) to copy the formatting.

3. Scroll as necessary to the left panel of page 2, and then drag to select and apply the copied format to the heading, Internships.

4. If necessary, tap or click the Center button (HOME tab | Paragraph group) to center the heading (Figure 2–55).

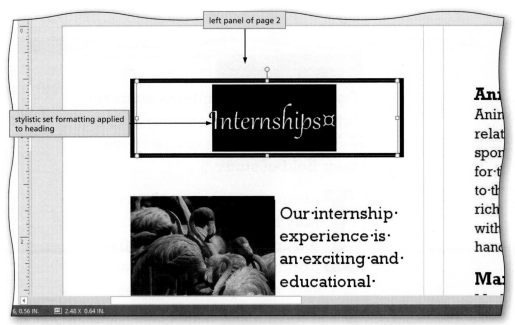

left panel of page 2

stylistic set formatting applied to heading

Internships¤

Our·internship· experience·is· an·exciting·and· educational·

Figure 2–55

To Create a Drop Cap

1 CUSTOMIZE BROCHURE | 2 EDIT TEXT & OBJECTS | 3 SWAP PICTURES | 4 USE FORMAT PAINTER
5 EDIT FORM | 6 USE TYPOGRAPHY | 7 INSERT CAPTIONS | 8 CHECK PUBLICATION | 9 PACK PUBLICATION

A dropped capital letter, or **drop cap**, is a decorative large initial capital letter extending down below the other letters in the line. If the text wraps to more than one line, the paragraph typically wraps around the dropped capital letter. The following steps create a dropped capital letter I to begin the word, Interns, in the second paragraph. *Why? A drop cap will set off the paragraph and draw the reader's eye toward an important part of the brochure.*

1

- If necessary, scroll to the middle portion of the left panel and then tap or click to the left of the letter, I, at the beginning of the second paragraph.
- Tap or click TEXT BOX TOOLS FORMAT on the ribbon to display the TEXT BOX TOOLS FORMAT tab.
- Tap or click the Drop Cap button (TEXT BOX TOOLS FORMAT tab | Typography group) to display the Drop Cap gallery (Figure 2–56).

Experiment

- Point to each of the available drop caps to preview the different styles.

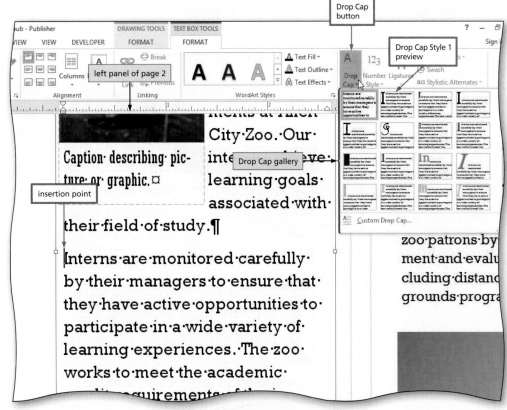

Figure 2–56

2

- Tap or click the Drop Cap Style 1 preview to select it (Figure 2–57).

Q&A Will this drop cap look inconsistent with the other fonts on the page? The font is still Rockwell, which will match the rest of the paragraph.

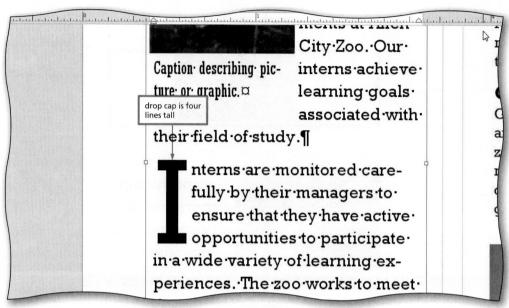

Figure 2–57

To Customize a Drop Cap

1 CUSTOMIZE BROCHURE | 2 EDIT TEXT & OBJECTS | 3 SWAP PICTURES | 4 USE FORMAT PAINTER
5 EDIT FORM | 6 USE TYPOGRAPHY | 7 INSERT CAPTIONS | 8 CHECK PUBLICATION | 9 PACK PUBLICATION

The Drop Cap dialog box allows you to customize the drop cap. You can format the number of lines in the drop cap or even change it to an **up cap**, in which the larger letter extends up above the rest of the text. You also can change the font, font style, and color of the text.

Once created, the customized style is added to the Available drop caps list. *Why? Publisher makes it available to use in other portions of the publication, if desired.* The following steps change the drop cap size to two lines.

1

- With the insertion point still positioned before the desired letter (in this case, the I of Interns), tap or click the Drop Cap button (TEXT BOX TOOLS FORMAT tab | Typography group) again to display the Drop Cap gallery (Figure 2–58).

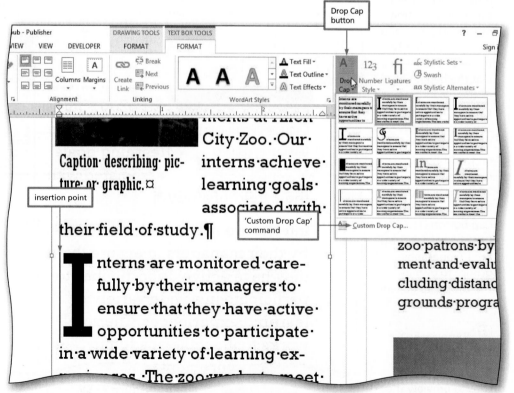

Figure 2–58

2

- Tap or click Custom Drop Cap at the bottom of the gallery to display the Drop Cap dialog box.
- Tap or click the 'Size of letters' down arrow twice, to change the height of the drop cap to 2 lines of text (Figure 2–59).

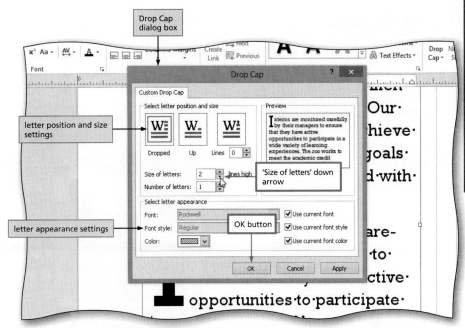

Figure 2–59

3

- Tap or click the OK button (Drop Cap dialog box) to apply the formatting (Figure 2–60).

Q&A

Is a drop cap limited to a single letter?
No, you can format up to 15 contiguous letters and spaces as drop caps at the beginning of each paragraph.

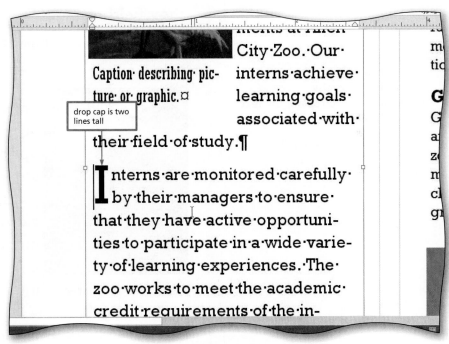

Figure 2–60

Captions

A **caption** is explanatory or identification text or a title that accompanies a graphic, figure, or photo. A caption can be as simple as a figure number, as you see in the figures of this book, or a caption can identify people, places, objects, or actions occurring in the graphic. When using Publisher templates, some captions already exist near a graphic. In those cases, the caption is a text box grouped with a graphic. If a graphic or photo does not have a caption, you can add one using the Caption gallery.

To Edit Captions

The following steps edit the text in the captions on page 2. *Why?* *A caption explains the graphic to the reader.*

1

- Scroll to the desired caption (in this case, the left panel of page 2).
- Tap or click the caption text below the photo to select it (Figure 2–61).

Q&A

Can you delete a caption?
Yes, but be sure to delete the text box as well as the text. If the caption is part of a group, tap or click once to select the group, then point to the border of the text box and tap or click to select it. Finally, press the DELETE key to delete the caption text box.

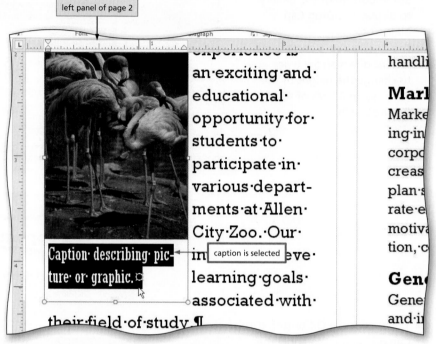

Figure 2–61

2

- Type `Learn how to "pinken" up the flamingos!` to replace the text (Figure 2–62).

Q&A

Should I fix the red wavy line below the word, pinken?
No. You will run the spell checker later in the chapter.

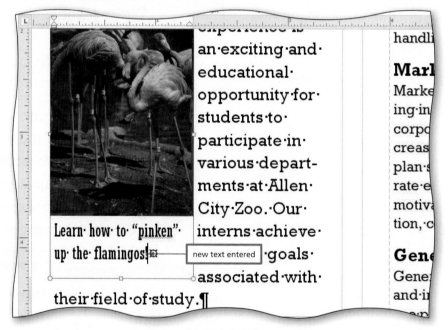

Figure 2–62

To Edit Other Captions

The following steps edit the other captions in the brochure.

1 Scroll to the caption on the middle panel of page 2.

2 Tap or click the caption text below the photo to select it.

3 Type `Giraffes in the large animal compound` to complete the caption.

④ Go to page 1 of the brochure, and select the caption text in the left panel. Zoom as necessary.

⑤ Type **Meet our new baby elephant!** to replace the caption. If necessary, delete the paragraph mark at the end of the caption, so that the caption contains just one line of text (Figure 2–63).

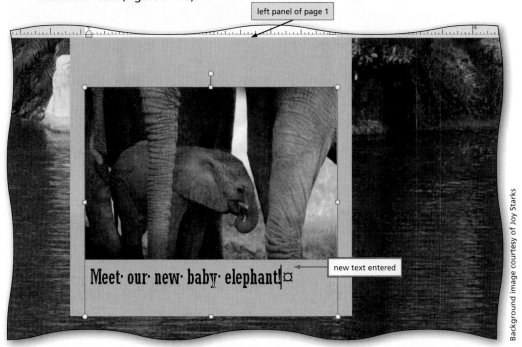

left panel of page 1

new text entered

Meet our new baby elephant!¤

Background image courtesy of Joy Starks

Figure 2–63

To Use the Caption Gallery

1 CUSTOMIZE BROCHURE | 2 EDIT TEXT & OBJECTS | 3 SWAP PICTURES | 4 USE FORMAT PAINTER
5 EDIT FORM | 6 USE TYPOGRAPHY | 7 INSERT CAPTIONS | 8 CHECK PUBLICATION | 9 PACK PUBLICATION

The following step adds a decorative caption to an existing photo using the Caption gallery. *Why? A decorative caption adds interest and color to the back panel.*

1

- Select the elephant photo above the newly added caption.
- Tap or click PICTURE TOOLS FORMAT on the ribbon to display the PICTURE TOOLS FORMAT tab.
- Tap or click the Caption button (PICTURE TOOLS FORMAT tab | Picture Styles group) to display its gallery (Figure 2–64).

🔍 **Experiment**

- Point to each caption style in the gallery to see its effect on the publication.

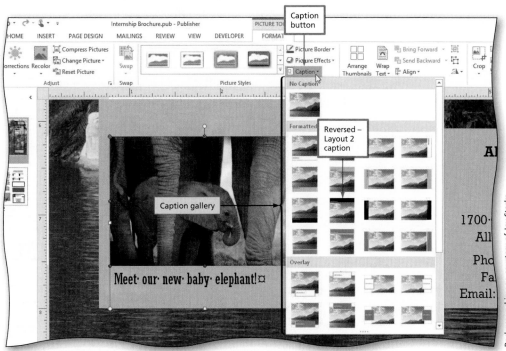

Caption button

Reversed – Layout 2 caption

Caption gallery

Meet our new baby elephant!¤

Background image courtesy of Joy Starks

Figure 2–64

2

• Tap or click the Reversed – Layout 2 thumbnail (column 2, row 3) to apply the caption style to the picture (Figure 2–65).

caption is displayed in new format

Background image courtesy of Joy Starks

Figure 2–65

To Insert Graphics

BTW

The Undo Button
The Undo button on the Quick Access Toolbar displays different ScreenTips depending upon the previous task. For example, if you have just changed the font scheme, the ScreenTip will say Undo Font Schemes. In Figure 2–66, the button's ScreenTip will read Undo Move Object. The same is true of the Redo button.

The final new content will be to add two graphics to page 2 of the brochure as shown in the following steps.

1 Go to page 2 and zoom to Whole Page view.

2 Drag the QR code to a location on the right panel, just above the name of the zoo and aligned with the right side as shown in Figure 2–66. SHIFT+drag a corner sizing handle of the picture to resize it to approximately one inch square.

3 Drag the social media graphic to a location on the middle panel, on top of the current picture. As you drag, you can center the graphic by releasing the drag when you see the pink vertical guide as shown in Figure 2–66.

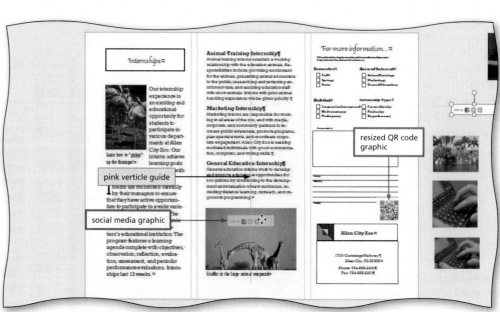

pink verticle guide

social media graphic

resized QR code graphic

Figure 2–66

What is the best way to eliminate errors in the brochure?

If possible, proofread the brochure with a fresh set of eyes, that is, at least one to two days after completing the first draft. Insert repeated elements and special objects, such as watermarks and logos, which need to be placed around, or behind, other objects. Look at text wrapping on every graphic. Ask someone else to proofread the brochure and give you suggestions for improvements. Revise it as necessary and then use the spelling and design checking features of the software.

Checking the Publication

Recall that you checked a publication for spelling errors as you typed in Chapter 1. A wavy, red line indicated a word that was not in Publisher's dictionary. You then used the shortcut menu to choose the correct word. Additionally, Publisher can check the entire publication once you have finished editing it. The process of checking your entire publication for spelling errors, moves from text box to text box and offers suggestions for words it does not find in its dictionary. Publisher does not look for grammatical errors.

A second kind of publication check is called the Design Checker. The **Design Checker** finds potential design problems in the publication such as objects hidden behind other objects, text that does not fit in its text box, or a picture that is scaled disproportionately. As with the spelling check, you can choose to correct or ignore each design problem.

BTW

Proper Nouns, Titles, and Headings

If a flagged word is spelled correctly, tap or click the Ignore button to ignore the flag, or tap or click the Ignore All button if the word occurs more than once.

To Check the Spelling of the Entire Publication

1 CUSTOMIZE BROCHURE | 2 EDIT TEXT & OBJECTS | 3 SWAP PICTURES | 4 USE FORMAT PAINTER
5 EDIT FORM | 6 USE TYPOGRAPHY | 7 INSERT CAPTIONS | **8 CHECK PUBLICATION** | **9 PACK PUBLICATION**

The following steps check the entire publication for spelling errors. *Why? You should check the spelling on every publication after you finish editing it.*

- Click REVIEW on the ribbon to display the REVIEW tab.
- Tap or click the Spelling button (REVIEW tab | Spelling group) to begin the spelling check in the current location, which in this case, is inside the caption text box (Figure 2–67).

Q&A

Can I check spelling of just a section of a publication?

Yes, select the text before starting the spelling check.

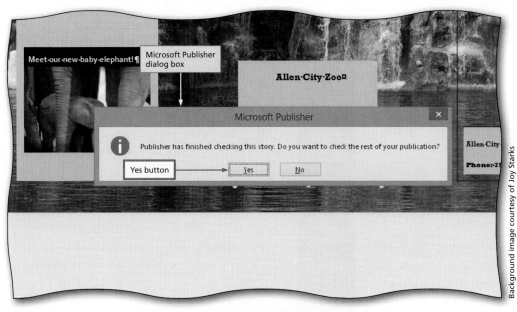

Figure 2–67

Background image courtesy of Joy Starks

2

- Tap or click the Yes button (Microsoft Publisher dialog box) to tell Publisher to check the rest of the publication. If your publication displays a different error, accept or ignore it as necessary (Figure 2–68).

3

- Tap or click the Ignore button (Check Spelling dialog box) to ignore the misspelled word (in this case, pinken).

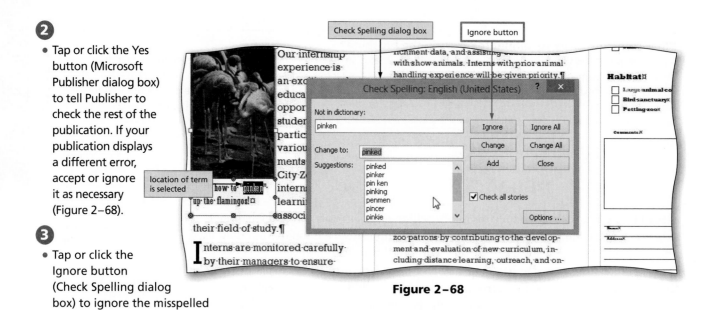

Figure 2–68

4

- If Publisher flags any other words, choose the correct spelling in the Suggestions list, click the Change button, and then continue the spelling check until the next error is identified or the end of the publication is reached. Tap or click the OK button to close the dialog box.

Other Ways
1. Press the F7 key   2. Press and hold or right-click flagged word, tap or click Spelling on shortcut menu

To Run the Design Checker

The following steps run the Design Checker. *Why? The Design Checker troubleshoots and identifies potential design problems in the publication.*

1

- Tap or click FILE on the ribbon to open the Backstage view and, by default, select the Info tab (Figure 2–69).

Q&A

Will the Design Checker fix the problems automatically?
In some cases, you will have the option of choosing an automatic fix for the issue; in other cases, you will have to fix the problem manually.

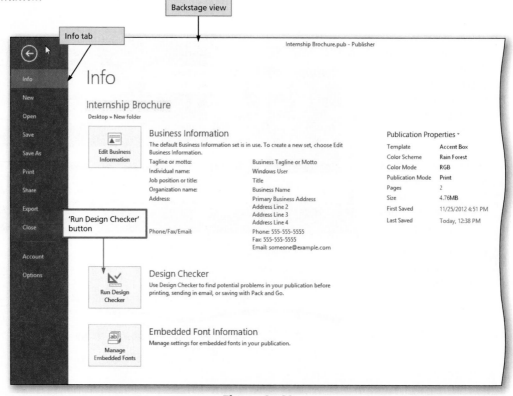

Figure 2–69

2

- Tap or click the Run Design Checker button in the Info gallery to display the Design Checker task pane (Figure 2–70).

Q&A What are the links at the bottom of the Design Checker task pane?
You can tap or click the link, Design Checker Options, to specify the order in which the Design Checker checks the pages of your publication, or to specify which kinds of design issues to include. The second link offers tips from the Publisher Help system about running the Design Checker.

What are the listed design problems?
A small amount of space appears between the margin of the page and the closest object to the margin. This is intentional and was part of the template, but the Design Checker notes the problem for your information only. Two of the publication objects are close to the printable area margin. This also is just a warning. The brochure will print correctly.

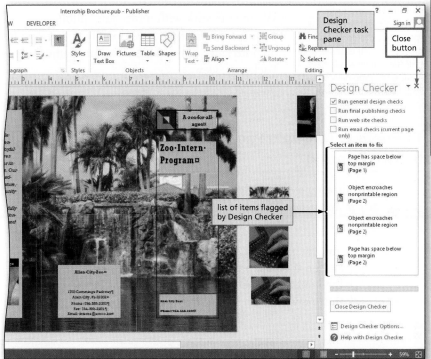

Figure 2–70

3

- If your publication has problems other than margin spacing or objects near the margin, point to the problem in the 'Select an item to fix' box. When a button appears on the right side of the problem, tap or click the button and then tap or click the provided Fix command.

4

- Tap or click the Close button on the Design Checker task pane to close the Design Checker and return to the publication.

To Save an Existing Publication with the Same File Name

You have made several modifications to the publication since you last saved it. Thus, you should save it again. The following step saves the publication again. For an example of the step listed below, refer to the Office and Windows chapter at the beginning of this book.

1 Tap or click the Save button on the Quick Access Toolbar to overwrite the previously saved file.

BTW

Design Problems
If you want to learn more about specific design problems, tap or click the problem in the 'Select an item to fix' box (Design Checker task pane). Tap or click the arrow that appears, and then tap or click Explain to obtain more information.

How do you make wise, professional printing choices?
Make a firm decision that quality matters, and consult with several commercial printers ahead of time. Get prices, color modes, copies, paper, and folding options in writing before you finish your brochure. Brochures are more effective on heavier paper, with strong colors and a glossy feel. Together with the commercial printer, select a paper that is going to last. Check to make sure the commercial printer can accept Microsoft Publisher 2013 files.

CONSIDER THIS

Background image courtesy of Joy Starks

**BTW
Storage**
Graphic files and fonts
require a great deal of disk
space, but should fit on
most USB flash drives. If your
USB flash drive is full, have
another storage device ready.
Publisher will prompt you to
insert it.

Previewing and Printing

When you work with multi-page publications, it is a good idea to preview each page before printing. Additionally, if you decide to print on special paper, or print on both sides of the paper, you must adjust certain settings on the Print tab in the Backstage view.

To Preview Multiple Pages before Printing

1 CUSTOMIZE BROCHURE | 2 EDIT TEXT & OBJECTS | 3 SWAP PICTURES | 4 USE FORMAT PAINTER
5 EDIT FORM | 6 USE TYPOGRAPHY | 7 INSERT CAPTIONS | 8 CHECK PUBLICATION | 9 PACK PUBLICATION

The following steps preview both pages of the brochure before printing. ***Why?*** *Previewing is the first step in getting the publication ready for outside printing as you examine what the printed copy will look like from your desktop.*

- If necessary, display page 1.
- Tap or click FILE on the ribbon to open the Backstage view.
- Tap or click the Print tab in the Backstage view to display the Print gallery.
- Tap or click the 'View Multiple Sheets' button to display the Multiple Sheets gallery (Figure 2–71).

Q&A

What are the rulers in the Print gallery?

Publisher displays rulers at the top and left of the print preview to help you verify the size of the printed page. You can turn off the ruler display by tapping or clicking the Ruler button.

If the brochure has only two pages, why do all of those preview grids exist?

Publisher allows for more pages in every kind of publication, should you decide to add them. If you tap or click a button in the grid for more than two pages — either horizontally or vertically — the size of the preview is reduced.

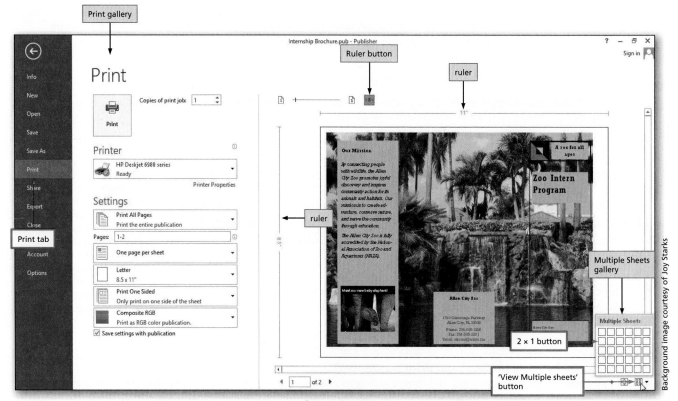

Figure 2–71

2

- Tap or click the 2 × 1 button to display the pages above one another (Figure 2–72).

Q&A Is that the best way to preview the brochure?

Viewing two full pages with intensive graphics and text may give you a good overview of the publication; however, do not substitute the preview for checking the publication for errors by reading the content carefully and running the spelling and design checking tools.

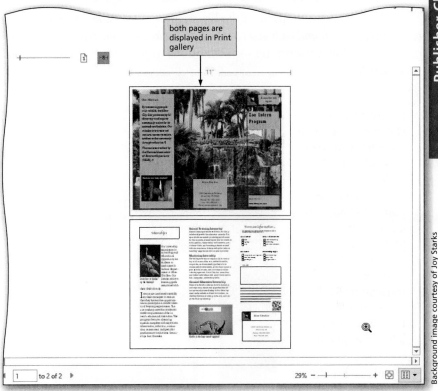

Figure 2–72

Other Ways

1. Press CTRL+P, tap or click 'View Multiple Sheets' button, tap or click desired preview

---

Print Settings

Printing the brochure on a high grade of paper results in a professional look. A heavier stock paper helps the brochure to stand up better in display racks, although any paper will suffice. **Brochure paper** is a special paper with creases that create a professional-looking fold, and with a paper finish that works well with color and graphics.

TO PRINT ON SPECIAL PAPER

If you have special paper, you would perform the following steps to choose that special paper before printing. See your instructor for assistance in choosing the correct option associated with your printer.

1. Open the Backstage view and then tap or click the Print tab.
2. Tap or click the Printer Properties link below the Printer Status box to display your printer's Properties dialog box.
3. Find the paper or quality setting and then choose your paper.
4. Tap or click the OK button in that dialog box to return to the Backstage view.

BTW

Distributing a Document

Instead of printing and distributing a hard copy of a document, you can distribute the document electronically. Options include sending the document via email; posting it on cloud storage (such as SkyDrive) and sharing the file with others; posting it on a social networking site, blog, or other website; and sharing a link associated with an online location of the document. You also can create and share a PDF or XPS image of the document, so that users can view the file in Acrobat Reader or XPS Viewer instead of in Publisher.

BTW

Printer Memory

Some printers do not have enough memory to print a wide variety of images and colors. In these cases, the printer prints up to a certain point on a page and then stops — resulting in only the top portion of the publication printing. Check with your instructor to see if your printer has enough memory to work with colors.

To Print on Both Sides

The following steps print the brochure on both sides. ***Why?*** *Printing on both sides gives you the opportunity to check your panels and folds and to view the brochure as your readers will view it.* If your printer does not have that capability, follow your printer's specifications to print one side of the brochure, turn it over, and then print the reverse side.

- If necessary, tap or click the Print tab in the Backstage view to display the Print gallery.
- Verify the printer name that appears on the Printer Status button will print a hard copy of the publication. If necessary, click the Printer Status button to display a list of available printer options and then click the desired printer to change the currently selected printer.
- Tap or click the 'Print One Sided' button to display the list of options (Figure 2–73).

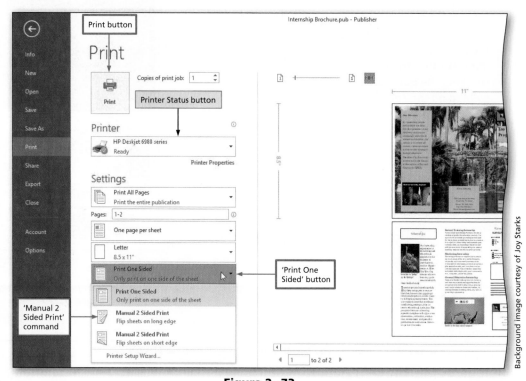

Figure 2–73

Background image courtesy of Joy Starks

- If your list displays a Print On Both Sides (Flip sheets on long edge) command, tap or click it to select automatic printing of both sides.
- If your list displays a Manual 2 Sided Print (Flip sheets on long edge) command, tap or click it to select manual printing.
- Tap or click the Print button to print the brochure.
- When the printer stops, retrieve the printed publication.

Other Ways

1. Press CTRL+P, choose settings, tap or click Print button (Print gallery)

BTW

Conserving Ink and Toner
If you want to conserve ink or toner, you can instruct Publisher to print draft quality documents by tapping or clicking FILE on the ribbon to open the Backstage view, and then tapping or clicking Print in the Backstage view to display the Print gallery. Tap or click the Printer Properties link, and then, depending on your printer, click the Print Quality button and choose Draft in the list. Close the Printer Properties dialog box and then tap or click the Print button as usual.

Printing Considerations

When they need mass quantities of publications, businesses generally **outsource**, or submit their publications to an outside printer, for duplicating. You must make special considerations when preparing a publication for outside printing.

If you start a publication from scratch, it is best to **set up** the publication for the type of printing you want before you place objects on the page. Otherwise, you may be forced to make design changes at the last minute. You also may set up an existing publication for a printing service. In order to provide you with experience in setting up a publication for outside printing, this project guides you through the preparation steps — even if you are submitting this publication only to your instructor.

Printing options, such as whether to use a copy shop or commercial printer, have advantages and limitations. You may have to make some trade-offs before deciding on the best printing option. Table 2–4 shows some of the questions you can ask yourself about printing.

Table 2–4 Choosing a Printing Option			
Consideration	**Questions to Ask**	**Desktop Option**	**Professional Options**
Color	Is the quality of photos and color a high priority?	Low to medium quality	High quality
Convenience	Do I want the easy way?	Very convenient and familiar	Time needed to explore different methods, unfamiliarity
Cost	How much do I want to pay?	Printer supplies and personal time	High-resolution color/high quality is expensive; the more you print, the less expensive the per-copy price
Quality	How formal is the purpose of my publication?	Local event; narrow, personal audience	Business, marketing, professional services
Quantity	How many copies do I need?	1 to 10 copies	10 to 500 copies: use a copy shop; 500+ copies: use a commercial printer
Turnaround	How soon do I need it?	Immediate	Rush outside printing is probably an extra cost

© 2014 Cengage Learning

Paper Considerations

Professional brochures are printed on a high grade of paper to enhance the graphics and provide a longer lasting document. Grades of paper are based on weight. Desktop printers commonly use **20 lb. bond paper**, which means they use a lightweight paper intended for writing and printing. A commercial printer might use 60 lb. glossy or linen paper.

The finishing options and their costs are important considerations that may take additional time to explore. **Glossy paper** is a coated paper, produced using a heat process with clay and titanium. **Linen paper**, with its mild texture or grain, can support high-quality graphics without the shine and slick feel of glossy paper. Users sometimes choose a special stock of paper, such as cover stock, card stock, or text stock. This textbook is printed on 45 lb., blade-coated paper. **Blade-coated paper** is coated and then skimmed and smoothed to create the pages you see here.

These paper and finishing options may seem burdensome, but they are becoming conveniently available to desktop publishers. Local office supply stores have shelf after shelf of special computer paper specifically designed for laser and ink-jet printers. Some of the paper you can purchase has been prescored for special folding.

Color Considerations

When printing colors, Publisher uses a color scheme called RGB. **RGB** stands for the three colors — red, green, and blue — that are used to print the combined colors of your publication. RGB provides the best color matching for graphics and photos. Desktop printers may convert the RGB specifications to CMYK, which stands for Cyan, Magenta, Yellow, and Key (black). Professional printers, on the other hand, can print your publication using color scheme processes, or **libraries**. These processes include black and white, spot color, and process color.

In **black-and-white printing**, the printer uses only one color of ink (usually black, but you can choose a different color if you want). You can add accent colors to your publication by using different shades of gray or by printing on colored paper. Your publication can have the same range of subtleties as a black-and-white photo.

BTW
CMYK Colors
When Process Colors are selected, Publisher converts all colors in text, graphics, and other objects to CMYK values and then creates four plates, regardless of the color scheme originally used to create the publication. Some RGB colors, including some of Publisher's standard colors, cannot be matched exactly to a CMYK color. After setting up for process-color printing, be sure to evaluate the publication for color changes. If a color does not match the color you want, you will have to include the new color library when you pack the publication.

BTW

Embedding Font Sets
To embed the fonts for a commercial printing service, tap or click Info in Backstage view, and then tap or click the Manage Embedded Fonts button. Select the 'Embed TrueType fonts when saving publication' check box (Fonts dialog box) Deselect any other check boxes.

BTW

Spot Colors
If you choose black plus one spot color in a publication, Publisher converts all colors except for black to tints of the selected spot color. If you choose black plus two spot colors, Publisher changes only exact matches of the second spot color to 100 percent of the second spot color. All other colors in the publication, other than black, are changed to tints of the first spot color. You then can apply, manually, tints of the second spot color to objects in the publication.

A **spot color** is used to accent a black-and-white publication. Newspapers, for example, may print their masthead in a bright, eye-catching color on page 1 but print the rest of the publication in black and white. A printing service may apply up to two spot colors with a color matching system called **Pantone**. **Spot-color printing** uses semitransparent, premixed inks typically chosen from standard color-matching guides, such as Pantone. Choosing colors from a **color-matching library** helps ensure high-quality results, because printing professionals who license the libraries agree to maintain the specifications, control, and quality.

In a spot-color publication, each spot color is **separated** on its own plate and printed on an offset printing press. The use of spot colors has become more creative in the last few years. Printing services use spot colors of metallic or florescent inks, as well as screen tints, to provide color variations without increasing the number of color separations and cost. If your publication includes a logo with one or two colors, or if you want to use color to emphasize line art or text, then consider using spot-color printing.

Process-color printing means your publication can include color photos and any color or combination of colors. One of the process-color libraries, called **CMYK**, or **four-color printing**, is named for the four semitransparent process inks — cyan, magenta, yellow, and key (black). CMYK process-color printing can reproduce a full range of colors on a printed page. The CMYK color model defines color as it is absorbed and reflected on a printed page rather than in its liquid state.

Process-color printing is the most expensive proposition; black-and-white printing is the cheapest. Using color increases the cost and time it takes to process the publication. When using either the spot-color or process-color method, the printer first must output the publication to film on an **image setter**, which recreates the publication on film or photographic paper. The film then is used to create color **printing plates**. Each printing plate transfers one of the colors in the publication onto paper in an offset process. Publisher can print a preview of these individual sheets showing how the colors will separate before you take your publication to the printer.

A new printing technology called **digital printing** uses toner instead of ink to reproduce a full range of colors. Digital printing does not require separate printing plates. Although not yet widely available, digital printing promises to become cheaper than offset printing without sacrificing any quality.

Publisher supports all three kinds of printing and provides the tools commercial printing services need to print the publication. You should ask your printing service which color-matching system it uses.

Packaging the Publication for the Printing Service

The publication file can be packaged for the printing service in two ways. The first way is to give the printing service the Publisher file in Publisher format using the Pack and Go Wizard. The second way is to save the file in a format called Encapsulated PostScript. Both of these methods are discussed in the following sections.

To Use the Pack and Go Wizard

1 CUSTOMIZE BROCHURE | 2 EDIT TEXT & OBJECTS | 3 SWAP PICTURES | 4 USE FORMAT PAINTER
5 EDIT FORM | 6 USE TYPOGRAPHY | 7 INSERT CAPTIONS | 8 CHECK PUBLICATION | 9 PACK PUBLICATION

The **Pack and Go Wizard** guides you through the steps to collect and pack all the files the printing service needs and then compresses the files. *Why? Publisher checks for and embeds the TrueType fonts used in the publication, in case the printing service does not have those fonts available.* The following steps use the Pack and Go Wizard to ready the publication for submission to a commercial printing service. These steps create a compressed, or zipped, folder on your storage device.

1

- Click FILE on the ribbon to open the Backstage view.
- Tap or click the Export tab in the Backstage view to display the Export gallery.
- In the 'Pack and Go' area, tap or click the 'Save for a Commercial Printer' tab (Figure 2–74).

Q&A

Should I save my file first?

You do not have to save it again; however, if you plan to store the publication on a storage device other than the one on which you previously saved the brochure, save it again on the new medium before beginning the process.

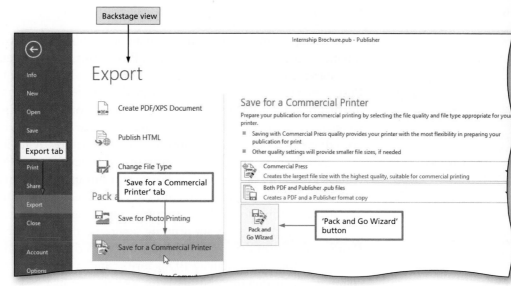

Figure 2–74

2

- Tap or click the 'Pack and Go Wizard' button to begin the Pack and Go Wizard.
- If necessary, browse to your storage location (Figure 2–75).

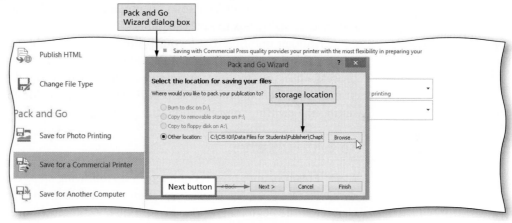

Figure 2–75

3

- Tap or click the Next button to save the file.
- When the final dialog box is displayed, remove the check mark in the 'Print a composite proof' check box (Figure 2–76).

Q&A

What if I make a change to the publication after running the Pack and Go Wizard?

The file is saved in a compressed format on your storage location, with the same file name as your Publisher file. If you make changes to the publication after packing the files, be sure to run the Pack and Go Wizard again so that the changes are part of the packed publication.

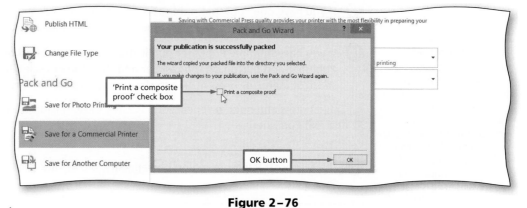

Figure 2–76

4

- Tap or click the OK button to close the Pack and Go Wizard dialog box.

BTW
Offset Printing
Your printing service may use the initials SWOP, which stand for Standard for Web Offset Printing — a widely accepted set of color standards used in web offset printing. Web offset printing has nothing to do with the World Wide Web. It is merely the name for an offset printing designed to print thousands of pieces in a single run from a giant roll of paper.

BTW
PostScript Files
If you decide to submit a PostScript dump, or file, to an outside printer or service bureau, include a copy of the original document as well — for backup purposes. Many shops slowly are changing over from Macintosh-based to cross-platform based operations. If an error occurs, the printer technician can correct the error from the original document without requiring you to make another trip to the print shop.

Using PostScript Files

If your printing service does not accept Publisher files, you can hand off, or submit, your files in PostScript format. **PostScript** is a page definition language that describes the document to be printed in language that the printer can understand. The PostScript printer driver includes a page definition language translator to interpret the instructions and print the document on a printer or a PostScript output device, such as an image setter. Because you cannot open or make changes directly to a PostScript file, everything in the publication must be complete before saving it.

Nearly all printing services can work with some type of PostScript file, either regular PostScript files, known as **PostScript dumps**, or **Encapsulated PostScript** (**EPS**) files, which are graphic pictures of each page. If you hand off a PostScript file, you are responsible for updating graphics, including the necessary fonts, and ensuring that you have all the files your printing service needs. Publisher includes several **PostScript printer drivers** (**PPDs**) and their description files to facilitate printing at the print shop. You must install a PPD before saving in PostScript form. Because the most common installation of Publisher is for a single user in a desktop environment, this project does not provide the steps involved in installing a PostScript printer driver. That process would require using original operating system disks and advanced knowledge of PostScript printers. Ask your printing service representative for the correct printer driver, and refer to your Windows documentation installation instructions. Then, use the Save As dialog box to save the publication in PostScript format.

Another question to ask your printing service is whether it performs the **prepress tasks** or a **preflight check**. These kinds of checks include the typesetting process, checking the page layout and other tasks performed before the publication is printed on paper. You may be responsible for making color corrections, separations, setting the printing options, and other printing tasks.

To Exit Publisher

This brochure now is complete. The following steps exit Publisher. For a detailed example of the procedure summarized below, refer to the Office and Windows chapter at the beginning of this book. The brochure was saved in previous steps, so you do not need to save the file again.

1a If you have one Publisher publication open, tap or click the Close button on the right side of the title bar to close the open publication and exit Publisher.

1b If you have multiple Publisher publications open, press and hold or right-click the Publisher app button on the taskbar and then tap or click 'Close all windows' on the shortcut menu, or press ALT+F4 to close all open publications and exit Publisher.

Q&A Could I press and hold or repeatedly click the Close button to close all open publications and exit Publisher?
Yes.

2 If a Microsoft Publisher dialog box appears, tap or click the Don't Save button to exit Publisher.

BTW
Subsetting
A file prepared for submission to a commercial printer includes all fonts from the publication. If you use only a small number of characters from a font, such as for drop caps or for headlines, you can instruct Publisher to embed only the characters you used from the font. Embedding only part of a font is called subsetting. The advantage of font subsetting is that it decreases the overall size of the file. The disadvantage is that it limits the ability to make corrections at the printing service. If the printing service does not have the full font installed on its computer, corrections can be made only by using the characters included in the subset.

To Sign Out of a Microsoft Account

If you are signed in to a Microsoft account and are using a public computer or otherwise wish to sign out of your Microsoft account, you should remove the account from the Account gallery in the Backstage view before exiting Publisher. Signing out of the account is the safest way to make sure that nobody else can access SkyDrive files or settings stored in your Microsoft account. The following steps sign out of a Microsoft account from Publisher. For a detailed example of the procedure summarized below, refer to the Office and Windows chapter at the beginning of this book.

1 If you wish to sign out of your Microsoft account, tap or click FILE on the ribbon to open the Backstage view and then tap or click the Account tab to display the Account gallery.

2 Tap or click the Sign out link, which displays the Remove Account dialog box. If a Can't remove Windows accounts dialog box appears instead of the Remove Account dialog box, click the OK button and skip the remaining steps.

Q&A Why does a Can't remove Windows accounts dialog box appear?
If you signed in to Windows using your Microsoft account, then you also must sign out from Windows, rather than signing out from within Publisher. When you are finished using Windows, be sure to sign out at that time.

3 Tap or click the Yes button (Remove Account dialog box) to sign out of your Microsoft account on this computer.

Q&A Should I sign out of Windows after signing out of my Microsoft account?
When you are finished using the computer, you should sign out of your account for maximum security.

4 Tap or click the Back button in the upper-left corner of the Backstage view to return to the publication.

Chapter Summary

In this chapter, you have learned how to choose make choices about brochures and brochure templates, edit headings and paragraphs, swap pictures, edit Publisher forms, use Publisher typography tools, insert captions, check the publication for errors, and pack the publication for a printing service. The items listed below include all the new Publisher skills you have learned in this chapter.

Editing Text and Options
Copy and Paste (PUB 79)
Display Formatting Marks (PUB 77)
Select a Brochure Template (PUB 70)
Select a Paste Option (PUB 81)
Switch to Page 2 (PUB 91)
Undo an Action (PUB 102)
Use the Format Painter (PUB 88)
Wordwrap Text as You Type (PUB 77)

Forms
Edit the Form (PUB 95)

Graphics
Arrange Thumbnails (PUB 85)
Insert Multiple Pictures from a Storage Device (PUB 82)
Select Multiple Objects (PUB 84)
Swap Pictures (PUB 82)
Use a Picture as a Background (PUB 87)

Publication Checking and Packing
Check the Spelling of the Entire Publication (PUB 109)
Preview Multiple Pages before Printing (PUB 112)
Print on Special Paper (PUB 113)
Print on Both Sides (PUB 114)
Run the Design Checker (PUB 110)
Use the Pack and Go Wizard (PUB 116)

Typography
Create a Drop Cap (PUB 103)
Customize a Drop Cap (PUB 104)
Edit Captions (PUB 106)
Edit the Font Family (PUB 98)
Examine Ligatures (PUB 101)
Format with a Stylistic Set (PUB 100)
Use the Caption Gallery (PUB 107)

CONSIDER THIS

What decisions will you need to make when creating your next publication?
Use these guidelines as you complete the assignments in this chapter and create your own publications outside of this class.

1. Decide on the purpose, shelf life, and layout.
    a) Select a template that matches your need.
    b) Choose font and color schemes determined by the brochure's purpose and audience.

2. Create the brochure.
    a) Replace all placeholder and default text.
    b) Copy and paste text when possible to prevent the introduction of new errors.
    c) Edit forms.
    d) Use appropriate pictures with captions.
    e) Swap pictures when possible so they will fit in the space.

3. Identify how to format various objects in the brochure.
   a) Use the Format Painter to copy formats for consistency.
   b) Use typography tools to enhance the brochure.

4. Proofread and check the publication.
   a) Read the brochure.
   b) Ask another person to read it.
   c) Use the spell checking feature.
   d) Use the Design Checker.

5. Plan for printing and packaging.
   a) Choose correct printing options.
   b) Consult with a commercial printing service.
   c) Use the Pack and Go Wizard.

How should you submit solutions to questions in the assignments identified with a ✳ symbol?
Every assignment in this book contains one or more questions identified with a ✳ symbol. These questions require you to think beyond the assigned publication. Present your solutions to the questions in the format required by your instructor. Possible formats may include one or more of these options: write the answer; create a document that contains the answer; present your answer to the class; discuss your answer in a group; record the answer as audio or video using a webcam, smartphone, or portable media player; or post answers on a blog, wiki, or website.

Apply Your Knowledge

Reinforce the skills and apply the concepts you learned in this chapter.

Swapping Graphics

Note: To complete this assignment, you will be required to use the Data Files for Students. Visit www.cengage.com/ct/studentdownload for detailed instructions or contact your instructor for information about accessing the required files.

Instructions: You decide to create a collage of pictures from your recent Florida vacation. You produce the publication shown in Figure 2–77.

Perform the following tasks:
1. Run Publisher and open the file Apply 2-1 Picture Collage from the Data Files for Students.

2. Tap or click the Pictures button (INSERT tab | Illustrations group). Navigate to the Data Files for Students and CTRL-tap or CTRL-click each of the Florida pictures to select them. Tap or click the Insert button to insert the multiple pictures into the scratch area.

All images Courtesy of Joy Starks

Figure 2–77

3. One at a time, swap the pictures for the empty picture placeholders.

4. Arrange the pictures on the page layout as desired.

5. Choose one picture for the background. To apply it, press and hold or right-click its swap icon, tap or click 'Apply to Background', and then tap or click Fill.

6. Save the collage on your storage device with the file name, Apply 2-1 Picture Collage Complete.

7. Submit the revised document in the format specified by your instructor.

8. ✳ Do you think a caption on each picture would make the publication look cluttered? Why or why not?

Extend Your Knowledge

Extend the skills you learned in this chapter and experiment with new skills. You may need to use Help to complete the assignment.

Creating a Brochure from Scratch

Instructions: The local county park provides a stargazing program for families and those interested in learning more about astronomy. They need a brochure to promote the event. They have supplied you with the content for page 1. You decide to start from scratch to create the brochure shown in Figure 2–78.

Perform the following tasks:

1. Run Publisher. Tap or click BUILT-IN, and then tap or click Brochures. Scroll to the Blank Sizes area, and then tap or click the Letter (Landscape) thumbnail.

2. Choose the Office color scheme and the Office 1 font scheme. Tap or click the CREATE button to create the publication.

3. Use Help to read about creating guides and then perform the following tasks:

   a. To create panel guides, drag from the vertical ruler into the publication creating a non-printing guide, stopping at 3 5/8" as measured on the horizontal ruler. Drag another guide from the vertical ruler into the publication, stopping at 7 3/8".

Figure 2–78

   b. In the Page Navigation pane, press and hold or right-click the page 1 icon, and then click Insert Duplicate Page on the shortcut menu. You will leave page 2 blank for future content.

   c. If necessary, tap or click the page 1 icon to return to page 1 in the brochure.

   d. Save the publication on your storage device with the file name, `Extend 2-1 Night Sky Tours Brochure`.

4. Tap or click the Online Pictures button (INSERT tab | Illustrations group). Use Office.com Clip Art to insert a picture of the moon. Drag the picture to the scratch area and then tap or click the Arrange Thumbnails button (PICTURE TOOLS FORMAT tab | Arrange group) to reduce the size of the thumbnail.

5. Repeat Step 4 to insert five or six photos of stars, meteors, and constellations.

6. To create the right panel, which serves as the front of the brochure, do the following:

   a. Drag an appropriate picture to the right panel. Position it in the center, vertically; resize it so that it almost fills the panel horizontally. Deselect the picture.

   b. Tap or click the Draw Text Box button (HOME tab | Objects group). Drag to create a text box at the top of the right panel, approximately ½" tall. Stay within the margin and guides. Tap or click the Shape Fill arrow (DRAWING TOOLS FORMAT tab | Shape Styles group), and then click a black color in the gallery. Tap or click the Font Color arrow (HOME tab | Font group) and then click a white color in the gallery. Type `Clay County Park` to enter the text. Press and hold or right-click the text, and then tap or click Best Fit on the shortcut menu.

   c. Tap or click the Draw Text Box button (HOME tab | Objects group). Drag to create another text box to fill the area between the previous text box and the picture. Type `Night Sky Tours` to enter the text. Press and hold or right-click the text, and then tap or click Best Fit on the shortcut menu. Format the text bold.

Continued >

Extend Your Knowledge *continued*

   d. Create another text box below the graphic. Type **Tours available on clear Saturday nights in April, May, and June.** Format the text italic and use Best Fit to make the text fill the text box.

7. On the middle panel of page 1, create a text box with the name, address, and phone number of the park. If requested to do so by your instructor, use your name and address in the brochure.

   ```
   Clay County Park
   540 County Line Road
   Mayfield, OK 74109
   Phone: (918) 555-PARK
   ```

8. To create the left panel of page 1:

   a. Drag an appropriate picture onto the left panel. Position it in the lower portion of the left panel; resize it so that it almost fills the panel horizontally.

   b. Click the Caption button (PICTURE TOOLS FORMAT tab | Picture Styles group) and choose an appropriate caption style. Edit the caption to say **Meteor showers are most prevalent in the spring!**

   c. Create a text box above the picture. Type the following text and format it appropriately:

   ```
   Night Sky Tours
   Unique, memorable, fascinating!
   An evening out under the blanket of the heavens above – bring a
   blanket for the earth below. We meet at approximately 10:00 p.m. to
   learn about the universe and see it up close.
   Your Night Sky Tour is accompanied by a personalized, educational,
   inspirational, and humorous dialogue with an astronomy professor and
   longtime astronomer, making it a truly stellar experience.
   ```

9. Using the techniques presented in this chapter, select all of the pictures in the scratch area. Press the DELETE key to delete the extra pictures.

10. Check the brochure for spelling errors and design errors and fix them as necessary. Save the file again.

11. Submit the file in the format specified by your instructor.

12. ✳ When would you use a template instead of creating a brochure from scratch? Would formatting the font before you type be easier than selecting text and formatting it afterward?

Analyze, Correct, Improve

Analyze a publication, correct all errors, and improve the design.

Making Typography Changes

Note: To complete this assignment, you will be required to use the Data Files for Students. Visit www.cengage.com/ct/studentdownload for detailed instructions or contact your instructor for information about accessing the required files.

Instructions: You have been given page 1 of the proposed brochure for a campus fraternity, Sigma Sigma. The brochure is shown in Figure 2–79, but it has several issues. You decide to improve the brochure. Run Publisher and open the file, Analyze 2–1 Fraternity Brochure.

1. Correct The publication has spelling and design errors. Use Publisher tools to help you correct those errors. The text in the left panel uses too many different font sizes. Use the Format Painter to standardize the font. Use the address of your school and your phone number.

2. Improve The graphic in the left panel is not very exciting. Search for a replacement picture using Office.com Clip Art. Insert an appropriate caption and caption style. In the right panel, the picture border helps set off the picture. Use the Format Painter to copy the formatting of that picture to the graphics in the center panel. Check the publication for spelling errors and design errors. Ignore any errors about space below the top margin. Save the document using the file name, Analyze 2-1 Fraternity Brochure Complete. Submit the revised document in the format specified by your instructor.

3. ✷ What errors existed in the starting file? How did creating consistency in font sizes enhance the publication? Did changing the graphic improve the effectiveness of the brochure? What other improvements would you make? Why?

Figure 2–79

In the Labs

Design, create, or modify a publication using the guidelines, concepts, and skills presented in this chapter. Labs 1 and 2, which increase in difficulty, require you to create a solution based on what you learned in the chapter; Lab 3 requires you to create a solution, which uses cloud and web technologies, by learning and investigating on your own from general guidance.

Lab 1: **Creating a Brochure**

Problem: The Students Against Bullying group has asked you to create a brochure they can distribute to students, teachers, and parents. You create the brochure shown in Figure 2–80.

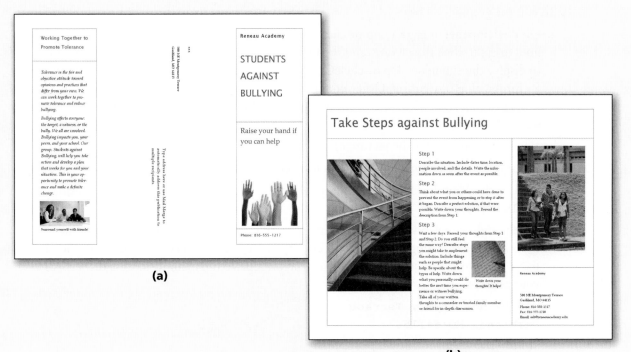

(a)

(b)

Figure 2–80

Continued >

In the Labs *continued*

1. Run Publisher. In the template gallery, click BUILT-IN and then click Brochures.

2. In the More Installed Templates section, choose the Frames template in the Informational area.

3. Select a 3-panel design with the Sunset color scheme and the Apex font scheme. Choose to include a customer address but no form. Create the publication.

4. As you make changes to the brochure, scroll and zoom as necessary. Turn on the display of formatting characters if desired.

5. To edit the text on page 1:

    a. On the right panel, drag through the Business Name text to select it. Type `Reneau Academy`. Tap or click outside the text box to synchronize the text.

    b. Tap or click the Product/Service Information placeholder text to select it. Type `STUDENTS AGAINST BULLYING`, all in capital letters.

    c. Drag through the Business Tagline or Motto text to select it. Type `Raise your hand if you can help.`

    d. Do not change the phone number; you will copy and paste it later in the steps.

    e. On the left panel, tap or click the Back Panel Heading placeholder text to select it. Type `Working Together to Promote Tolerance.`

    f. Use wordwrap as you replace the text in the story on the left panel. Type `Tolerance is the fair and objective attitude toward opinions and practices that differ from your own. We can work together to promote tolerance and reduce bullying.` and then press the ENTER key to complete the first paragraph.

    g. Type `Bullying affects everyone: the target, a witness, or the bully. We all are involved. Bullying impacts you, your peers, and your school. Our group, Students Against Bullying, will help you take action and develop a plan that works for you and your situation. This is your opportunity to promote tolerance and make a definitive change.` to complete the text.

6. To edit the graphics on page 1:

    a. On the left panel of page 1, tap or click the picture twice to select only the picture. Press and hold or right-click the picture, and then tap or click Change Picture on the shortcut menu to display the submenu. Tap or click Change Picture on the submenu to display the Insert Pictures dialog box. Search Office.com Clip Art for the term, students, and insert a picture similar to Figure 2–80 on the previous page. Edit the caption to say `Surround yourself with friends!`

    b. Repeat the process for the picture on the right panel, using the search term, raise hands.

7. Go to page 2 of the brochure. To edit the text on page 2, do the following:

    a. Replace the Main Inside Heading placeholder text with the text, `Take Steps against Bullying.`

    b. On the right panel, select the text in the Primary Business Address text box. Type the following text, pressing the ENTER key after the first line. It will synchronize with the middle panel on page 1. If requested by your instructor, replace the mailing address text box with your address.

    `500 NE Montgomery Terrace`
    `Gashland, MO 64115`

c. Select the text in the Phone, Fax, and Email text box. Type the following text, pressing the ENTER key after each line, except the last.

> Phone: 816-555-1217

> Fax: 816-555-1218

> Email: sab@reneauacademy.edu

d. On the middle panel, replace the first Secondary Heading with the text, `Step 1.` Replace the story under the Step 1 heading with the text, `Describe the situation. Include dates, time, location, people involved, and the details. Write the information down as soon after the event as possible.`

f. Replace the second Secondary Heading with the text, `Step 2.`

g. Replace the story under the Step 2 heading with the text, `Think about what you or others could have done to prevent the event from happening or to stop it after it began. Describe a perfect solution, if that were possible. Write down your thoughts. Reread the description from Step 1.` and then press the ENTER key to finish the paragraph.

h. Type `Step 3` and then press the ENTER key to finish the third heading. You will format it later.

i. Type `Wait a few days. Reread your thoughts from Step 1 and Step 2. Do you still feel the same way? Describe steps you might take to implement the solution. Include things such as people that might help. Be specific about the types of help. Write down what you personally could do better the next time you experience or witness bullying. Take all of your written thoughts to a counselor or trusted family member or friend for in-depth discussion.`

j. Tap or click the Step 1 text. Tap or click the Format Painter button (HOME tab | Clipboard group). Drag through the text, Step 3, to apply the formatting.

8. Replace the graphic on the middle panel with a picture from Office.com searching for the term, **pen.** Edit the caption to say, `Write down your thoughts! It helps!`

9. Delete the text, text box, graphic, and caption on the left panel. Replace it with a picture from Office.com Clip Art, searching for the term, **staircase.** Choose a portrait-oriented picture. Move the inserted graphic to the left panel and resize it to fit the panel as necessary. Repeat the process to insert a picture in the upper portion of the right panel. Use the search term, **students.**

10. Use the copy and paste techniques presented in the chapter to copy the phone number from the right panel of page 2 to the right panel of page 1. Use the Keep Text Only button on the Paste Options menu.

11. Check your publication for spelling and design errors, and fix or ignore the flagged items as necessary.

12. Save the brochure on your storage device with the file name, Lab 2-1 Students Against Bullying Brochure.

13. Submit the file as directed by your instructor.

14. ✳ Would a page background make this brochure easier to read or harder to read? Would you use a picture background, or a gradient as you did in Chapter 1? Why?

Lab 2: Editing an Order Form

Note: To complete this assignment, you will be required to use the Data Files for Students. Visit www.cengage.com/ct/studentdownload for detailed instructions or contact your instructor for information about accessing the required files.

Problem: The Biology Club is selling poinsettias and wreaths for the Christmas season. The members started a form, but they would like you to make it more appealing. You create the form shown in Figure 2–81.

1. Run Publisher and open the file Lab 2-2 Order Form from the Data Files for Students.
2. Tap or click the heading. Type **Biology Club Order Form** to replace the text. Change the font to Gabriola. Change the font size to 22. Change the font color to red. Resize the text box as necessary to display all of the text.
3. With the heading text still selected, tap or click the Stylistic Sets button (TEXT BOX TOOLS FORMAT tab | Typography group). Select a fancy stylistic set. Resize the text box as necessary to display all of the glyphs.

Figure 2–81

4. Select the text in the Item # text box. Change the font to Gabriola and the font size to 11. Double-tap or double-click the Format Painter (HOME tab | Clipboard group) to copy the formatting.
5. One at a time, select each of the other text boxes on the form to apply the formatting. It is OK if the alignment changes. If necessary, resize any text boxes that are too small to accommodate the font change.
6. Select the picture. Tap or click the Caption button (PICTURE TOOLS FORMAT tab | Picture Styles group) to display the Caption gallery. Choose the Offset – Layout 3 caption style. Edit the caption to say **We deliver on campus!**
7. Check the brochure for spelling errors and design errors, and fix them as necessary. Save the order form on your storage device with the file name, Lab 2-2 Order Form Complete.
8. Submit the file as directed by your instructor.
9. ✳ How might you have created this order form from scratch? Does Publisher have the individual components that you could add? Would that have been easier than trying to customize a built-in form?

Lab 3: Expand Your World: Cloud and Web Technologies
Creating a Google Drive

Problem: Many company websites include a link to download a print copy of various brochures. You would like to create a webpage with a link to download one of your brochures stored on the cloud.

Instructions:

1. If you do not have a SkyDrive account, create one. For a detailed example of the procedure, refer to the Office and Windows chapter.

2. Save one of your brochures on SkyDrive.

3. Run the Notepad app or other text editor app on your computer. Enter the code from Figure 2–82, leaving the ninth line blank, as shown.

4. If requested to do so by your instructor, change the words, My Web Page, to your name in line five.

```
MyWebPage - Notepad
File  Edit  Format  View  Help
<!DOCTYPE html>
<html lang ="en">
        <head>
                <meta charset="utf-8" />
                <title>My Web Page</title>          line 5
        </head>
        <body>
line 9      <h1>Download my brochure here</h1>

        </body>
</html>
```

Notepad window

insertion point in ninth line

Figure 2–82

5. Save the file on your storage device, using `MyWebPage.html` as the file name. Do not close the text editor window.

6. Run a browser and navigate to your SkyDrive account.

7. Press and hold or right-click the stored brochure file to display the shortcut menu. Tap or click Embed on the shortcut menu. When prompted, tap or click the Generate button. When SkyDrive displays the HTML code, press CTRL+C to copy the highlighted code.

8. Go back to the text editor window and position the insertion point on line nine. Press CTRL+V to paste the code into the file. If necessary, click Format on the menu bar and then click Word Wrap to enable the feature. Save the HTML file again, and then close the window.

9. To view your webpage, open a File Explorer window and then navigate to the location of your saved HTML file. Double-tap or double-click the MyWebPage.html file. If your browser asks permission to run the ActiveX content, tap or click the 'Allow blocked content' button.

10. Submit the assignment in the format specified by your instructor.

11. ❂ Does your school provide a brochure about its program? Can you download the brochure from the school's website? Do you think it still is good to have a hard copy? Why?

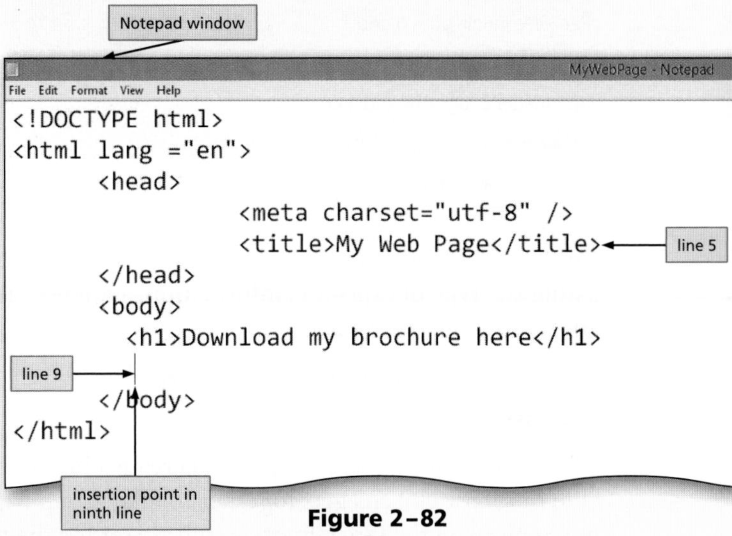

❂ Consider This: Your Turn

Apply your creative thinking and problem solving skills to design and implement a solution.

1: Creating a Youth Baseball League Brochure
Personal/Academic

Part 1: Your brother belongs to a youth baseball league. Use the Ascent Event brochure template to create a brochure announcing the Youth Baseball League. Pick an appropriate color and font scheme, and include a sign-up form. Type `Preseason Sign-Up` as the brochure title. Type `Youth Baseball League,` to replace the Business Name text. Type your address and phone number in the appropriate text boxes. Delete the logo. Replace all graphics with sports-related clip art. Edit the captions to match. The league commissioner will send you content for the stories at a later date. Edit the sign-up form event boxes as displayed in Table 2–5 on the next page.

Continued >

Consider This: Your Turn *continued*

Table 2–5 Sign-Up Form Check Box Content		
Event Name	Time	Price
Preschool T-Ball: ages 4 and 5	10:00 a.m.	$35.00
Pee-Wee T-Ball: ages 6 and 7	11:00 a.m.	$35.00
Coach Pitched: ages 8 and 9	1:00 p.m.	$50.00
Intermediate: ages 10 and 11	2:30 p.m.	$50.00
Advanced: ages 12 and 13	4:00 p.m.	$50.00
City Team: audition only	6:00 p.m.	TBA

© 2014 Cengage Learning

Part 2: ✸ On a separate piece of paper, make a table similar to Table 2–1 on page PUB 69, listing the type of exposure, information, audience, and purpose of the communication. Turn in the table with your printout.

2: Creating a Travel Club Brochure

Professional

Part 1: Use the Voyage template to create a brochure for the Seniors Abroad Club. This local club of senior citizens gets together to take group trips. Use the Casual font scheme. For the title, use Seniors on the Go. Choose a stylistic set for the title. On page 2, include an article describing last year's trip to London (you may use the default text in the story itself), and a secondary article heading that tells how to pack lightly for trips overseas. Insert the social media logo from the Data Files for Students. On page 1, replace the story on the left panel with a list of dates for the upcoming trips to Paris, the Caribbean, and Tokyo. Replace the graphics with suitable pictures and caption styles. Submit your assignment in the format specified by your instructor.

Part 2: ✸ You made several decisions while creating the travel brochure in this assignment. How did your choices complement the topic?

3: Researching Templates

Research and Collaboration

Part 1: Individually, visit or call several local copy shops or commercial printers in your area, or visit the websites of several commercial printers. Ask them the following questions: What kind of paper stock do your customers choose for brochures? What is the most commonly used finish? Do you support all three color processes? Will you accept files saved with the Microsoft Publisher Pack and Go Wizard or EPS files? What prepress tasks do you perform? Come back together as a group and create a blank Publisher publication to record your answers. Create a table with the Insert Table button (INSERT tab | Tables group). Insert the questions down the left side. Insert the names of the print shops across the top. Fill in the grid with the answers they provide.

Part 2: ✸ Which commercial printer would be the best one to print the Internship Brochure created in this chapter? What information made you choose it? How would you recommend finding a commercial printer to someone who has not studied desktop publishing?

Learn Online

Reinforce what you learned in this chapter with games, exercises, training, and many other online activities and resources.

Student Companion Site Reinforce chapter terms and concepts using review questions, flash cards, practice tests, and interactive learning games, such as a crossword puzzle. These and other online activities and resources are available at no additional cost on www.cengagebrain.com. Visit www.cengage.com/ct/studentdownload for detailed instructions about accessing the resources available at the Student Companion Site.

3 | Designing a Newsletter

Microsoft product screenshots used with permission from Microsoft Corporation.

Objectives

You will have mastered the material in this chapter when you can:

- Describe the advantages of using the newsletter medium and identify the steps in its design process

- Edit a newsletter template and navigate pages

- Set page options

- Edit a masthead

- Import text files

- Continue a story across pages and insert continued notices

- Customize the ribbon

- Use Publisher's Edit Story in Microsoft Word feature

- Insert Marginal Elements

- Insert and edit coupons

- Duplicate a graphic

- Revise a newsletter

- Drag-and-drop text

- Check hyphenation in stories

- Create a template with property changes

3 | Designing a Newsletter

Introduction

Desktop publishing is becoming an increasingly popular way for businesses of all sizes to produce their printed publications. The desktop aspects of design and production make it easy and inexpensive to produce high-quality publications in a short time. **Desktop publishing** (DTP) encompasses performing all publishing tasks from a desk, including the planning, designing, writing, and layout, as well as printing, collating, and distributing. With a personal computer and a software program, such as Publisher, you can create a professional publication from your computer without the cost and time of using a professional printer.

Project—Newsletter

Newsletters are a popular way for offices, businesses, schools, and other organizations to distribute information to their clientele. A **newsletter** usually is a double-sided multipage publication with newspaper features, such as columns and a masthead, and the added eye appeal of sidebars, pictures, and other graphics.

Newsletters have several advantages over other publication media. Typically, they are cheaper to produce than brochures. Brochures, designed to be in circulation longer as a type of advertising, are published in greater quantities and on more expensive paper than newsletters, making brochures more costly. Newsletters also differ from brochures in that newsletters commonly have a shorter shelf life, making newsletters a perfect forum for information with dates. Newsletters are narrower and more focused in scope than newspapers; their eye appeal is more distinctive. Many companies distribute newsletters to interested audiences; however, newsletters also are becoming an integral part of many marketing plans to widen audiences, because they offer a legitimate medium by which to communicate services, successes, and issues.

The project in this chapter uses a Publisher newsletter template to produce the Tech Talk newsletter shown in Figure 3 – 1. This monthly publication informs readers about the Campus Technology Club. The club's four-page newsletter contains a masthead, headings, stories, sidebars, pull quotes, a coupon, and graphics.

Campus Technology Club
Newsletter

School of Technology
Banner Area Community College
8400 Walker Lane
Banner, IL 50024

Phone: 618-555-8662
Fax: 618-555-8663
Email: ctc@bacc.edu

Join us on Facebook!

The **Campus Technology Club** is the premier club for School of Technology students who want to experience all that today's leading technology companies have to offer. The Club sponsors a variety of events with other clubs and campus schools to prepare our members to lead today's technology companies. Members get priority access to round tables with the Executive Speaker Series.

If you have any interest in working in the technology field, the **Campus Technology Club** is for you!

Page 2

Spotlight on Students

This month we are proud to turn the spotlight on Latisha Druze. Latisha is earning her Associate of Science Degree in Health Information Technology and is an active member of the Campus Technology Club.

Latisha wanted to take most classes online so that she could be at home with her small children and save gas. Banner Area Community College was a perfect fit. Also, she knew joining CTC would look good on her resume as well as provide career planning opportunities.

"Health information technology is very marketable," Latisha says. "And, I can use technology while helping people. That's my goal."

Studying online enables her to be a mom, a wife, and a student, allowing her to earn her Health Information Technology degree in a short amount of time.

Way to go Latisha!

What are treks?

Students who have a strong passion for technology should seek professional opportunities beyond the traditional recruiting avenues. To this end, the Campus Technology Club partners with the School of Technology Career Center and the Alumni Office to organize networking "treks" to areas that have a high concentration of technology-related employers.

Treks provide students the opportunity

to gain a broade... information. St... about compani... ni to understan... converse with ... understand tec... Treks are organ... by students on ...

Come to the CT... about the next t...

Come to the CTC meeting to find out about the next trek!

It is clear that tech careers are a good choice, with strong potential for growth

Tech Talk

Outlook Good for T...

(Continued from page 1)

on-the-job training, making it a great fit for those who cannot attend college full-time, or temporarily must leave college to work. The work experience will prove invaluable, however, as you complete a degree and seek higher levels of employment.

Those who com... several good em... programmer ca... ry of $71,380 p... a system manag... experience com... nual salary of $... projects an 18%... er positions. Th... goal for technol...

Volume 7 Issue 2

Page 3

New Exciting Web Technologies (NEWT)

E-sensing technology strives to emulate all five senses by using electronic means. While sight and sound are mainstream, the other senses soon will follow. Over the last decade, "electronic sensing" or "e-sensing" technologies have undergone important developments from a technical and commercial point of view. The expression "electronic sensing" re...

What's the next greatest thing? Well, it may very well be electronic noses! An electronic nose is a hardware device used to detect...

Campus
Technology Club
Newsletter

Special points of interest:

- Oct. 7 Executive Speaker Series

- Oct. 10 CTC meeting: Outsmarting Your Smartphone

- Oct. 27 Spring registration begins

- Oct. 31 Halloween party

Tech Talk

Volume 7 Issue 2   September 22, 2014

Executive Speaker Series Announces John Patmos, Hollywood Animator

The Campus Technology Club (CTC) is proud to announce that Mr. John Patmos from Revelation Animation Studios will be on campus Tuesday, October 7 to meet with students majoring in computer graphics. Mr. Patmos also will give a presentation entitled "The Moving Picture – Unlocking a Career in Animation," at 3:00 p.m. in Shylock Auditorium, as part of the renowned Executive Speaker Series.

John Patmos of Revelation Animation Studios

Mr. Patmos is an American animator, film director, and entrepreneur. He founded Revelation Animation Studios in 2010 and still leads the company as

chairman and chief executive. He is best known as the creator of the *Green World* animated cartoon series.

Campus Technology Club members get priority access to the round table with Mr. Patmos. Sign up at ctc_roundtable.edu.

Executive Speaker Series presentations are open to the general public. Arrive early for a good seat.

Revelation Animation Studios, located in La Jacinta Verde, California, employs more than 50 animators in full-time positions.

Outlook Good for Tech Jobs

Students, educators, and employers have been discussing the general worth of a college degree, especially in technology — both in dollars and job growth. After all, college is time-consuming and expensive.

The website of the Bureau of Labor Statistics is a useful source to examine the job and salary outlook problem. At the low end of the scale are computer support specialists. While it is the fastest growth area in

technology (a projected need of 110,000 new positions by 2020), it is one of the lower-paying jobs at $46,000 per year. Only some college education is required, combined with
(Continued on page 2)

Figure 3–1

For an introduction to Windows and instruction about how to perform basic Windows tasks, read the Office and Windows chapter at the beginning of this book, where you can learn how to resize windows, change screen resolution, create folders, move and rename files, use Windows Help, and much more.

Roadmap

In this chapter, you will learn how to create the newsletter shown in Figure 3–1 on the previous page. The following roadmap identifies general activities you will perform as you progress through this chapter:

1. Select a newsletter template and EDIT publication OPTIONS.
2. IMPORT text from files and CONNECT STORIES across pages.
3. USE CONTINUED NOTICES.
4. CUSTOMIZE the RIBBON.
5. EDIT USING Microsoft WORD when necessary.
6. CREATE sidebars, pull quotes, coupons, and other MARGINAL ELEMENTS.
7. IMPORT GRAPHICS from files and clip art and REVISE.
8. CREATE and change TEMPLATE properties.

At the beginning of step instructions throughout the chapter, you will see an abbreviated form of this roadmap. The abbreviated roadmap uses colors to indicate chapter progress: gray means the chapter is beyond that activity, blue means the task being shown is covered in that activity, and black means that activity is yet to be covered. For example, the following abbreviated roadmap indicates the chapter would be showing a task in the Customize Ribbon activity.

1 EDIT OPTIONS | 2 IMPORT & CONNECT STORIES | 3 USE CONTINUED NOTICES | 4 CUSTOMIZE RIBBON
5 EDIT USING WORD | 6 CREATE MARGINAL ELEMENTS | 7 IMPORT GRAPHICS & REVISE | 8 CREATE TEMPLATE

Use the abbreviated roadmap as a progress guide while you read or step through the instructions in this chapter.

One of the few differences between Windows 7 and Windows 8 occurs in the steps to run Publisher. If you are using Windows 7, click the Start button, type Publisher in the 'Search programs and files' box, click Publisher 2013, and then, if necessary, maximize the Publisher window. For a summary of the steps, refer to the Quick Reference located at the back of this book.

To Run Publisher

If you are using a computer to step through the project in this chapter and you want your screens to match the figures in this book, you should change your screen's resolution to 1366 × 768. For information about how to change a computer's resolution, refer to the Office and Windows chapter at the beginning of this book.

The following steps, which assume Windows 8 is running, use the Start screen or the search box to run Publisher based on a typical installation. You may need to ask your instructor how to run Publisher on your computer. For a detailed example of the procedure summarized below, refer to the Office and Windows chapter.

1 Scroll the Start screen and search for a Publisher 2013 tile. If your Start screen contains a Publisher 2013 tile, tap or click it to run Publisher and then proceed to Step 5; if the Start screen does not contain the Publisher 2013 tile, proceed to the next step to search for the Publisher app.

2 Swipe in from the right edge of the screen or point to the upper-right corner of the screen to display the Charms bar, and then tap or click the Search charm on the Charms bar to display the Search menu.

3 Type **Publisher** as the search text in the Search box, and watch the search results appear in the Apps list.

4 Tap or click Publisher 2013 in the search results to run Publisher.

5 If the Publisher window is not maximized, tap or click the Maximize button on its title bar to maximize the window.

How do you decide on the purpose and audience of a newsletter?

Designing an effective newsletter involves a great deal of planning in order to deliver a message in the clearest, most attractive, and most effective way possible. Spend time brainstorming ideas for the newsletter with other members of the organization. Ask yourself why you want to create a newsletter in the first place and what message you want to convey. Remember that newsletters both communicate and educate. Identify the scope of the newsletter, and whether you want the topic to be general in nature or more specific — perhaps about only one aspect of the organization. Use the phrase, "I want to tell <audience> about <topic> because <purpose>." Decide on one purpose, and adjust your plans to match that purpose.

As you decide on your audience, ask yourself these questions:

- Who will be reading the stories?

- What are the demographics of this population? That is, what are their characteristics, such as gender, age, educational background, and heritage?

- Why do you want those people to read your newsletter?

Decide if the audience is composed of local, interested clientele, patrons, employees, prospective customers, or family members. Keep in mind the age of your readers and their backgrounds, including both present and future readers.

Benefits and Advantages of Newsletters

Table 3–1 lists some benefits and advantages of using the newsletter medium.

Table 3–1 Benefits and Advantages of Using a Newsletter	
Purpose	**Benefits and Advantages**
Exposure	An easily distributed publication via office mail, by bulk mail, or electronically A pass-along publication for other interested parties A coffee-table reading item in reception areas
Education	An opportunity to inform in a nonrestrictive environment A directed education forum for clientele Increased, focused feedback that is unavailable in most advertising
Contacts	A form of legitimized contact A source of free information to build credibility An easier way to expand a contact database than other marketing tools
Communication	An effective medium to highlight the inner workings of a company A way to create a discussion forum A method to disseminate more information than a brochure
Cost	An easily designed medium using desktop publishing software An inexpensive method of mass production A reusable design using a newsletter template

© 2014 Cengage Learning

Publisher's newsletter templates include stories, graphics, sidebars, and other elements typical of newsletters using a rich collection of intuitive design, layout, typography, and graphic tools. Because Publisher takes care of many of the design issues, using a template to begin a newsletter gives you the advantage of proven layouts with fewer chances of publication errors.

BTW
BTWs
For a complete list of the BTWs found in the margins of this book, visit the BTW resource on the Student Companion Site located on www.cengagebrain.com. For detailed instructions about accessing available resources, visit www.cengage.com/ct/ studentdownload or see the inside back cover of this book.

Newsletter Design Choices

Publisher's many design-planning features include more than 100 different newsletter templates from which you may choose, each with its own set of design, color, font, and layout schemes. Each newsletter template produces four pages of stories, graphics, and other objects in the same way. The difference is the location and style of the shapes and graphics, as well as the specific kind of decorations unique to each publication set. A **publication set** is a predefined group of shapes, designed in patterns to create a template style. A publication set is constant across publication

For an introduction to Windows and instruction about how to perform basic Windows tasks, read the Office and Windows chapter at the beginning of this book, where you can learn how to resize windows, change screen resolution, create folders, move and rename files, use Windows Help, and much more.

types; for example, the Bars newsletter template has the same shapes and style of objects as does the Bars brochure template. A publication set helps in branding a company across publication types.

To Choose a Newsletter Template and Options

The following steps choose a newsletter template and change its options.

1 In the template gallery, tap or click BUILT-IN to display the built-in templates.

2 Scroll as necessary and then tap or click the Newsletters thumbnail within the BUILT-IN templates to display the Newsletter templates.

3 Scroll to the section labeled, More Installed Templates, and then tap or click the Banded thumbnail to choose the template.

4 Tap or click the Color scheme button in the template information pane. Scroll as necessary and tap or click Solstice to choose the color scheme.

5 Tap or click the Font scheme button, scroll as necessary, and then tap or click Civic to choose the font scheme.

6 Do not tap or click the Business information button because it is not used in this publication.

7 Tap or click the Page size button in the Options area and then, if necessary, tap or click Two-page spread to choose how the template will display.

8 If necessary, tap or click to remove the check mark in the 'Include customer address' check box (Figure 3–2).

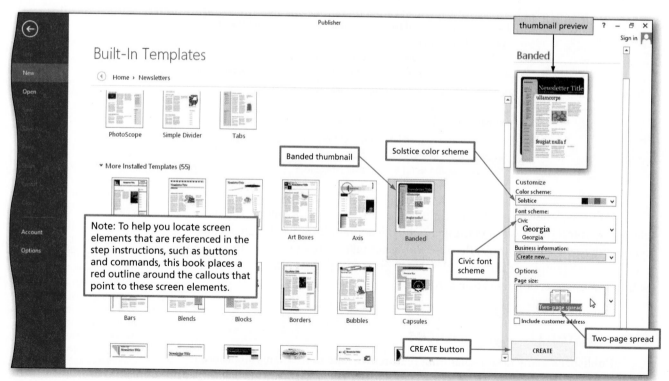

Figure 3–2

9 Tap or click the CREATE button to create the publication based on the template settings.

To Open the Page Navigation Pane

The following step opens the Page Navigation pane to display all of the pages of the newsletter.

1 If the Page Navigation pane is not displayed, tap or click the 'Current page in publication' button on the status bar to open the Page Navigation pane. If the Page Navigation pane is minimized, tap or click the 'Expand Page Navigation Pane' button to maximize it.

To Display Formatting Marks

As discussed in Chapter 2, it is helpful to display formatting marks, which indicate where in the publication you pressed the ENTER key, the SPACEBAR key, and other keys. The following step displays formatting marks.

1 If the Special Characters button (HOME tab | Paragraph group) is not selected already, tap or click it to display formatting marks on the screen.

How do you decide about options for the layout and printing?

Choosing a layout and printing options before you even write the stories is a daunting, yet extremely important, task. The kind of printing process and paper you will be using will affect the cost and, therefore, the length of the newsletter. Depending on what you can afford to produce and distribute, the layout may need more or fewer stories, graphics, columns, and sidebars. Base your decisions on content that will be repeated in future newsletters

Make informed decisions about the kind of alignment you plan to use. Choose the paper size and determine how columns, a masthead, and graphics will affect your layout. Decide what kinds of features in the newsletter should be close to each other. A consistent look and feel with simple, eye-catching graphics normally is the best choice for the publication set. Plan to include one graphic with each story. Because newsletters usually are mass-produced, collated, and stapled, you should make a plan for printing and decide if you are going to publish it in-house or externally. Choose a paper that is going to last until the next newsletter.

CONSIDER THIS

To Set Page Options

1 EDIT OPTIONS | 2 IMPORT & CONNECT STORIES | 3 USE CONTINUED NOTICES | 4 CUSTOMIZE RIBBON
5 EDIT USING WORD | 6 CREATE MARGINAL ELEMENTS | 7 IMPORT GRAPHICS & REVISE | 8 CREATE TEMPLATE

Publisher newsletters can display one, two, or three columns of story text, or mix the format. *Why? Changing the number of columns in a story or mixing the format adds visual interest.* The following steps select page options for the various pages in the newsletter.

1

- With Page 1 of the newsletter displayed in the workspace, tap or click PAGE DESIGN on the ribbon to display the PAGE DESIGN tab.

- Tap or click the Options button (PAGE DESIGN tab | Template group) to display the Page Content dialog box.

- Tap or click the Columns button to display its list (Figure 3–3).

Q&A Does the column choice affect the objects down the left side of the newsletter page?
No, the number of columns that you choose will be displayed in the stories only, and the choice affects only the current page.

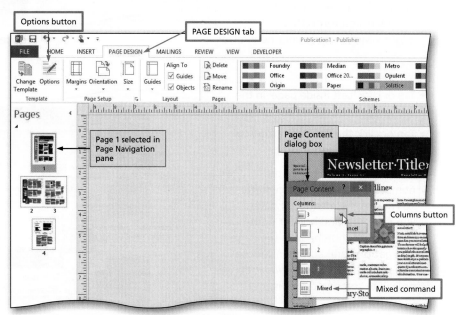

Figure 3–3

2

- Tap or click Mixed in the list to choose a mixed number of columns for the stories on page 1.

- Tap or click the OK button (Page Content dialog box) to change the options for the page (Figure 3–4).

 Q&A Is one choice better than another one?

No, it is a personal or customer preference. Longer stories may need to be continued at different places, depending upon how many columns of text you have. The more columns you have, the more white space is created on the page.

lead story displays two columns

secondary story displays three columns

Figure 3–4

3

- Tap or click the 'Page 2 and Page 3' thumbnail in the Page Navigation pane to display the pages in the workspace.

- Tap or click the Options button (PAGE DESIGN tab | Template group) to display the Page Content dialog box.

- Tap or click the 'Select a page to modify' arrow to display its list (Figure 3–5).

 Q&A What is the Content for page list?

The 'Content for page' list is a list of other objects, including calendars and forms that you might want to use in your newsletter.

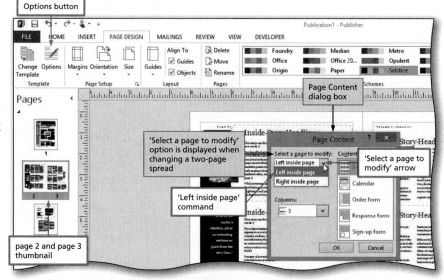

Options button

Page Content dialog box

'Select a page to modify' option is displayed when changing a two-page spread

'Select a page to modify' arrow

'Left inside page' command

page 2 and page 3 thumbnail

Figure 3–5

4

- Tap or click 'Left inside page' in the list to adjust the columns on page 2.

- Tap or click the Columns arrow to display its list (Figure 3–6).

 Q&A What if I want to change the number of pages in my newsletter?

To change the number of pages, you can press and hold or right-click a page thumbnail in the Page Navigation pane and then choose either the Insert Page command or Delete command on the shortcut menu.

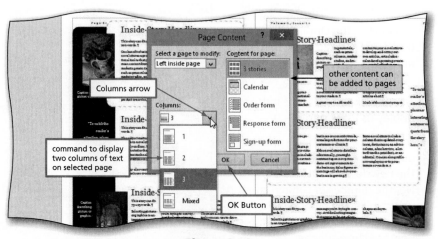

Columns arrow

other content can be added to pages

command to display two columns of text on selected page

OK Button

Figure 3–6

⑤

- Tap or click 2 in the list to choose a two-column format for the stories on page 2.

- Tap or click the OK button (Page Content dialog box) to close the dialog box (Figure 3–7).

Q&A Can I move pages around in my newsletter?

Yes, you can press and hold or right-click in the Page Navigation pane and then choose Move on the shortcut menu. Publisher will display a dialog box, allowing you to specify which page to move and the new location.

stories on page 2 are displayed in a two-column format

Figure 3 – 7

⑥

- Repeat Steps 3 through 5 to set a two-column format for Page 3, the right inside page of the two-page spread (Figure 3–8).

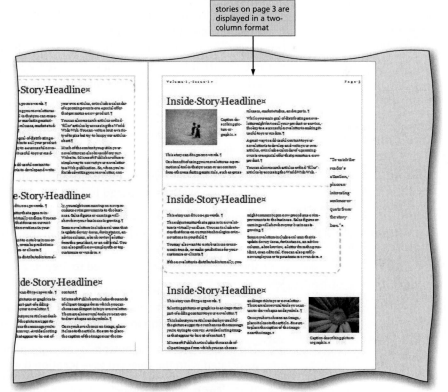

stories on page 3 are displayed in a two-column format

Figure 3 – 8

Changing the Number of Pages in a Newsletter

Not all newsletters are four pages long. Some will have more or fewer pages. The sections on the next page describe how to add pages to or delete them from a newsletter template.

For an introduction to Office and instruction about how to perform basic tasks in Office apps, read the Office and Windows chapter at the beginning of this book, where you can learn how to run an application, use the ribbon, save a file, open a file, exit an application, use Help, and much more.

TO DELETE PAGES FROM A NEWSLETTER

If you were designing a newsletter with only two pages, it would be best to delete pages 2 and 3 because page 4 already is formatted to be a back page in most templates. Pages 2 and 3 have inside page numbers and graphics. You would perform the following steps to delete pages 2 and 3.

1. Press and hold or right-click the 'Page 2 and Page 3' thumbnail in the Page Navigation pane to display the shortcut menu.
2. Tap or click Delete to delete pages 2 and 3. When Publisher displays the Delete Page dialog box for confirmation, tap or click Both pages and then click the OK button (Delete Page dialog box).

TO ADD PAGES TO A NEWSLETTER

If you wanted to add extra pages to a newsletter, you would perform the following steps.

1. Press and hold or right-click the 'Page 2 and Page 3' thumbnail in the Page Navigation pane to display the shortcut menu.
2. Tap or click Insert Page to insert a new page. Follow the directions in the dialog box to insert either a left-hand or right-hand page, or both, and then click the OK button (Insert Newsletter Pages dialog box).

To Save a Publication

The following steps assume you already have created folders for storing your files, for example, a CIS 101 folder (for your class) that contains a Publisher folder (for your assignments). Thus, these steps save the publication in the Publisher folder in the CIS 101 folder on your desired save location. For a detailed example of the procedure for saving a file in a folder or saving a file on SkyDrive, refer to the Office and Windows chapter at the beginning of this book.

BTW
Organizing Files and Folders
You should organize and store files in folders so that you easily can find the files later. For example, if you are taking an introductory computer class called CIS 101, a good practice would be to save all Publisher files in a Publisher folder in a CIS 101 folder. For a discussion of folders and detailed examples of creating folders, refer to the Office and Windows chapter at the beginning of this book.

1. Tap or click the Save button on the Quick Access Toolbar, which, depending on settings, will display either the Save As gallery in the Backstage view or the Save As dialog box.

2. To save on a hard disk or other storage media on your computer, proceed to Step 2a. To save on SkyDrive, proceed to Step 2b.

2a. If your screen opens the Backstage view and you want to save on storage media on your computer, tap or click Computer in the left pane, if necessary, to display options in the right pane related to saving on your computer. If your screen already displays the Save As dialog box, proceed to Step 4.

2b. If your screen opens the Backstage view and you want to save on SkyDrive, tap or click SkyDrive in the left pane to display SkyDrive saving options or a Sign In button. If your screen displays a Sign In button, tap or click it and then sign in to SkyDrive.

3. Tap or click the Browse button in the right pane to display the Save As dialog box associated with the selected save location (i.e., Computer or SkyDrive).

4. Type **Tech Talk Newsletter** in the File name text box to change the file name. Do not press the ENTER key after typing the file name because you do not want to close the dialog box at this time.

5. Navigate to the desired save location (in this case, the Publisher folder in the CIS 101 folder [or your class folder] on your computer or SkyDrive).

6. Tap or click the Save button (Save As dialog box) to save the publication in the selected folder on the selected save location with the entered file name.

Editing the Masthead

Most newsletters and brochures contain a masthead similar to those used in newspapers. A **masthead** is a box or section printed in each issue that lists information, such as the name, publisher, location, volume, and date. The Publisher-designed masthead, included in the Bars newsletter publication set, contains several text boxes and color-filled shapes that create an attractive, eye-catching graphic to complement the set.

1 EDIT OPTIONS | 2 IMPORT & CONNECT STORIES | 3 USE CONTINUED NOTICES | 4 CUSTOMIZE RIBBON
5 EDIT USING WORD | 6 CREATE MARGINAL ELEMENTS | 7 IMPORT GRAPHICS & REVISE | 8 CREATE TEMPLATE

To Edit the Masthead

The following steps edit text in the masthead, including the volume and issue number. *Why? Publications typically use volume numbers to indicate the number of years the publication has been in existence. The issue number indicates its sequence. Volume numbers and issue numbers do not necessarily correlate to the calendar year and months. Schools, for example, sometimes start in the fall with Volume 1, Issue 1.*

- Tap or click Page 1 in the Page Navigation pane to change the display to page 1.

- Tap or click the text, Newsletter Title, to select it.

- Zoom to 150%.

- Type `Tech Talk` to replace the text (Figure 3–9).

Q&A Why does my font look different?
Publisher replaces the selected text with the font from the publication set. Your font may differ from the one shown.

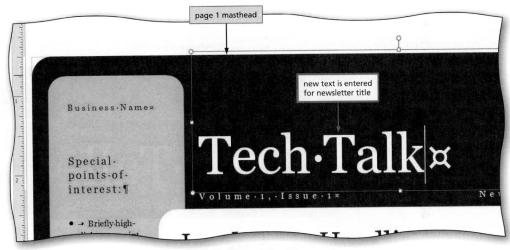

Figure 3 – 9

- If necessary, scroll to the left and tap or click the default text in the Business Name text box, and then press CTRL+A to select all of the text.

- Type `Campus Technology Club Newsletter` to replace the text (Figure 3–10).

Q&A What if my text does not fit in the box?
Template text boxes for business information components, headlines, and other special boxes use autofitting techniques. Publisher should decrease the font size for longer text as you type. If it does not, someone has turned off the autofitting option; press and hold or right-click the text and then click Best Fit on the shortcut menu to autofit the text.

Figure 3 – 10

- Tap or click the placeholder text in the Volume 1, Issue 1 text box to select it.

- Type **Volume 7 Issue 2** to replace the text (Figure 3–11).

Figure 3–11

- Tap or click the placeholder text in the Newsletter Date text box to select it.

- Type **September 22, 2014** to replace the text (Figure 3–12).

Figure 3–12

Newsletter Text

BTW
Touch Screen Differences
The Office and Windows interfaces may vary if you are using a touch screen. For this reason, you might notice that the function or appearance of your touch screen differs slightly from this chapter's presentation.

Newsletter content may be submitted to you in various ways. Authors may submit their stories in email or as attachments. Others may post a Microsoft Word document or a graphic on the company's common storage drive. Still other authors may handwrite their stories or record them on a recording device. In those cases, you will have to type the story yourself.

Publisher allows users to import text and graphics from many sources, from a variety of different programs, and in many different file formats. Publisher uses the term, **importing**, to describe inserting text or objects from any other source into the Publisher workspace. Publisher uses the term, **story**, when referring to text that is contained within a single text box or a chain of linked text boxes. Each newsletter template provides **linked text boxes**, or text boxes whose text flows from one to another. In the templates, two or three text boxes may be linked automatically; however, if a story is too long to fit in the linked text boxes, Publisher will offer to link even more text boxes for easy reading.

How do you gather topics and research stories?

Gather credible, relevant information in the form of stories, pictures, dates, figures, tables, and discussion threads. Plan far enough ahead so that you have time to take pictures or gather graphics for each story — even if you end up not using them. Stay organized; keep folders of information and store pictures and stories together. If you have to write a story from scratch, gather your data, do your research, and have an informed reader go over your content.

The same principles of audience, purpose, and topic apply to individual stories, just as they do for the newsletter as a whole. Evaluate your sources for authority, timeliness, and accuracy. Be especially wary of information obtained from the web. Any person, company, or organization can publish a webpage on the Internet. Ask yourself these questions about the source:

- Authority: Does a reputable institution or group support the source? Is the information presented without bias? Are the author's credentials listed and verifiable?

- Timeliness: Is the information up to date? Are the dates of sources listed? What is the last date that the information was revised or updated?

- Accuracy: Is the information free of errors? Is it verifiable? Are the sources clearly identified?

Identify the sources for your text and graphics. Notify all writers of important dates, and allow time for gathering the data. Make a list for each story: include the author's name, the approximate length of the story, the electronic format, and associated graphics. Ask the author for suggestions for headlines. Consult with colleagues about other graphics, features, sidebars, and the masthead.

Acknowledge all sources of information; do not **plagiarize**. Not only is plagiarism unethical, but it also is considered an academic crime that can have severe consequences, such as failing a course or being expelled from school.

When you summarize, paraphrase (rewrite information in your own words), present facts, give statistics, quote exact words, or show a map, chart, or other graphical image, you must acknowledge the source. Information that commonly is known or accessible to the audience constitutes **common knowledge** and does not need to be acknowledged. If, however, you question whether certain information is common knowledge, you should document it — just to be safe.

Replacing Placeholder Text Using an Imported File

Publisher suggests that 175 to 225 words will fit in the space allocated for the lead story. The story is displayed in a two-column text box format that **connects**, or links, the running text from one text box to the next. Publisher links text boxes according to your settings and displays arrow buttons to navigate to the next and previous text boxes.

This edition of Tech Talk contains several stories, some of which have been typed previously and stored using Microsoft Word. The stories, stored on the Data Disk that accompanies this book, are ready to be used in the newsletter. The final story you will type yourself. Each story will include a **headline**, which is a short phrase printed at the top of a story, usually in a bigger font than the story. A headline summarizes the story that follows it.

To Edit the Lead Story Headline

The following steps edit the Lead Story Headline placeholder text.

1 Tap or click the placeholder text, Lead Story Headline, on page 1 to select it.

2 Type `Executive Speaker Series Announces John Patmos, Hollywood Animator` to replace the text (Figure 3–13).

BTW
Publisher Help
At any time while using Publisher, you can find answers to questions and display information about various topics through Publisher Help. Used properly, this form of assistance can increase your productivity and reduce your frustrations by minimizing the time you spend learning how to use Publisher. For instruction about Publisher Help and exercises that will help you gain confidence in using it, read the Office and Windows chapter at the beginning of this book.

Figure 3–13

To Import a Text File

The following steps import a text file to replace the Publisher-supplied placeholder text. ***Why?*** *Importing the story prevents typographical errors created by typing the text.* The text file is included in the Data Files for Students. To complete these steps, you will be required to use the Data Files for Students. Visit www.cengage.com/ct/studentdownload for detailed instructions or contact your instructor for information about accessing the required files.

1
- Scroll down to display the story below the headline.
- Tap or click the placeholder text in the story to select it (Figure 3–14).

 Experiment
- Scroll as necessary to read the placeholder text in order to learn about design suggestions related to newsletter publications.

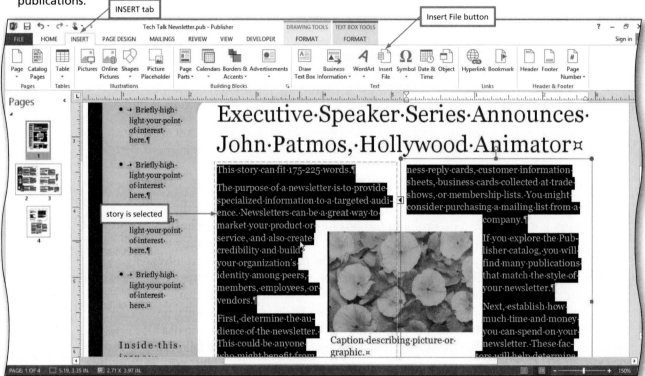

Figure 3–14

2
- Display the INSERT tab.

- Tap or click the Insert File button (INSERT tab | Text group) to display the Insert Text dialog box (Figure 3–15).

- Navigate to the location of the file to be opened (in this case, the Chapter 03 folder in the Publisher folder in the CIS 101 folder).

Q&A | What kinds of text files can Publisher import?
Publisher can import files from most popular applications. If you click the 'All Text Formats' button, you can see a list of all of the file types.

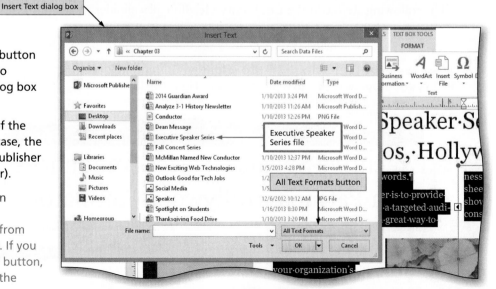

Figure 3–15

- Double-tap or double-click the 'Executive Speaker Series' file to insert the text into the newsletter (Figure 3–16).

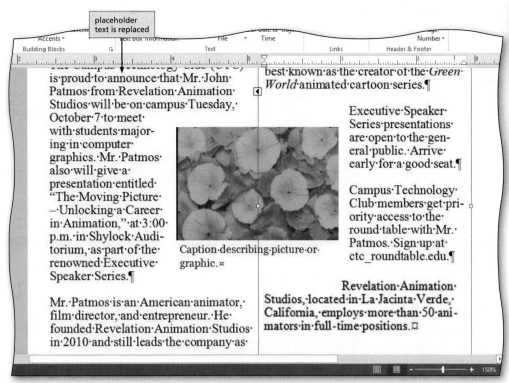

Figure 3–16

Other Ways

1. Press and hold or right-click story, tap or click Change Text, tap or click Text File, select File, tap or click OK button (Insert Text dialog box)

To Edit the Secondary Story Headline

The following steps edit the Secondary Story Headline placeholder text.

1 Tap or click the placeholder text, Secondary Story Headline, on page 1 to select it.

2 Type `Outlook Good for Tech Jobs` to replace the text (Figure 3–17).

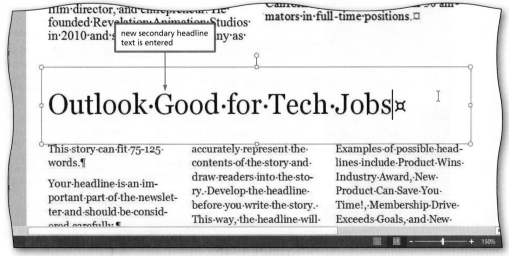

Figure 3–17

To Continue a Story across Pages

As you import text, if a story contains more text than will fit in the default text box, Publisher displays a message to warn you. *Why? You then have the option to allow Publisher to connect or* **autoflow** *the text to another available text box, or to flow the text yourself, manually.* The following steps import a story and continue it from page 1 to page 2, using Publisher dialog boxes. To complete these steps, you will be required to use the Data Files for Students. Visit www.cengage.com/ct/studentdownload for detailed instructions or contact your instructor for information about accessing the required files.

1

- Tap or click the secondary story placeholder text on page 1 to select it.

- Tap or click the Insert File button (INSERT tab | Text group) to display the Insert Text dialog box.

- If necessary, navigate to the location of the file to be opened (in this case, the Chapter 03 folder in the Publisher folder in the CIS 101 folder) (Figure 3–18).

Figure 3–18

2

- Double-tap or double-click the file named, Outlook Good for Tech Jobs, to insert the text file (Figure 3–19).

Q&A Why did Publisher display a dialog box and move to page 2? The story was too large to fit in the space provided on page 1. Publisher moved to the first available text box with default or placeholder story text.

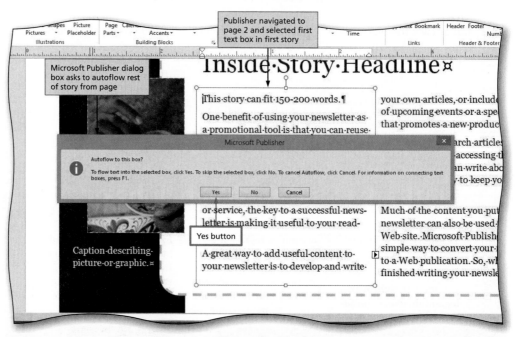

Figure 3–19

- In the Microsoft Publisher dialog box, tap or click the Yes button to autoflow the story to the selected text box (Figure 3–20).

Q&A What do the three buttons do?
If you click the Yes button, Publisher will insert the rest of the text in the currently selected text box. If you click the No button, Publisher will move to the next story text box and ask again. If you click the Cancel button, you will have to flow the text manually.

What if I have no more spare text boxes in which to flow the text?
Publisher will ask if you want new text boxes created. If you answer yes, Publisher automatically will create a new page with new text boxes.

Figure 3–20

To Follow a Story across Pages

1 EDIT OPTIONS | 2 IMPORT & CONNECT STORIES | 3 USE CONTINUED NOTICES | 4 CUSTOMIZE RIBBON
5 EDIT USING WORD | 6 CREATE MARGINAL ELEMENTS | 7 IMPORT GRAPHICS & REVISE | 8 CREATE TEMPLATE

Publisher provides a way to move quickly back and forth through a continued story. *Why? While reading the story online, you may forget where the rest of the story is located or want to jump to its location quickly.* The following steps use the Next and Previous buttons to follow the story from text box to text box, across pages.

- Click Page 1 in the Page Navigation pane and navigate to the Outlook Good for Tech Jobs story at the bottom of the page.

- Tap or click the third text box in the story to display the Previous and Next buttons (Figure 3–21).

Q&A Do all text boxes have Previous and Next buttons?
No. Only text boxes that contain a linked story display the buttons.

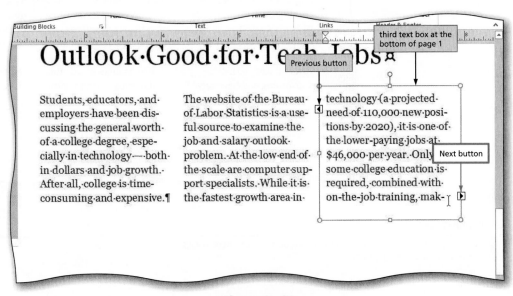

Figure 3–21

2

- Tap or click the Next button to move to the rest of the story (Figure 3–22).

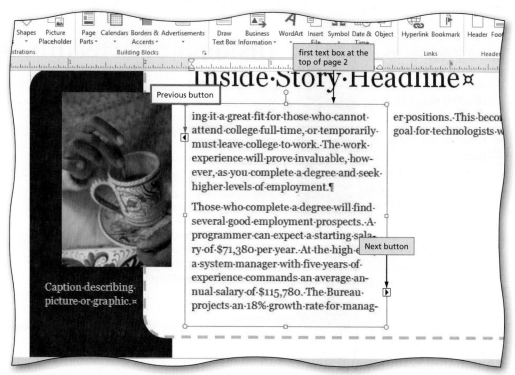

Figure 3–22

3

- Tap or click the Previous button to move back to the first part of the story, the third text box on page 1 (Figure 3–23).

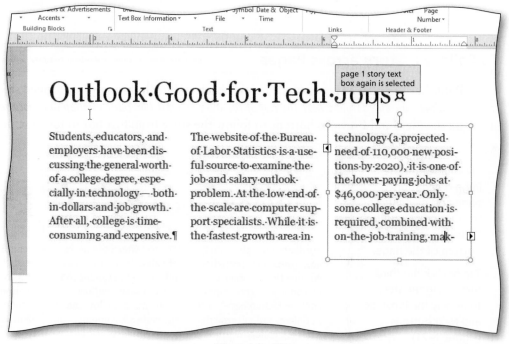

Figure 3–23

Other Ways

1. Select text box, tap or click Previous or Next button (TEXT BOX TOOLS FORMAT tab | Linking group)

To Break a Text Box Link

Sometimes you change your mind about where to continue a story. In that case, you have two choices. You can undo the previous insertion and autoflow again, or you can break the connection and create a manual one. When you break a connection, the extra text that cannot fit in the text box is placed in **overflow**. *Why? Unlike the Clipboard, the overflow area is maintained when you save the publication, allowing you to access it at any time.* The following step breaks the connection between the story at the bottom of page 1 and its continuation at the top of page 2.

1

- If necessary, navigate to page 1 and the story at the bottom of the page.

- Tap or click the rightmost column in the story to select the text box.

- Display the TEXT BOX TOOLS FORMAT tab.

- Tap or click the Break button (TEXT BOX TOOLS FORMAT tab | Linking group) to break the connection to the rest of the story (Figure 3–24).

Figure 3–24

Q&A Where is the rest of the story now?
Publisher places it in a special overflow area as indicated by the 'Text in Overflow' button in Figure 3–24. The text box on page 2 becomes blank.

To Manually Continue the Story across Pages

The following steps manually move the text from the overflow area to another text box. *Why? You cannot see the text while it is in overflow.*

1

- If necessary, select the text box that displays the 'Text in Overflow' button.

- Tap or click the 'Text in Overflow' button to display the pitcher mouse pointer (Figure 3–25).

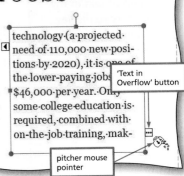

Q&A My text wraps at different places. Did I do something wrong?
Your story may wrap differently depending upon your printer's capability of reproducing the font. You will hyphenate all of the stories later in the chapter.

Figure 3–25

2

- Tap or click 'Page 2 and Page 3' in the Page Navigation pane to display the pages.

- Scroll as necessary to display the third story on page 2.

- With the pitcher mouse pointer, tap or click the placeholder text in the third story to continue the "Outlook Good for Tech Jobs" text (Figure 3–26).

Figure 3–26

Q&A What if I change my mind and want to continue to a different text box?
You can tap or click the Undo button on the Quick Access Toolbar, or you can tap or click the last column of the story on page 1 and then tap or click the Break button (TEXT BOX TOOLS FORMAT tab | Linking Group). You then can tap or click the 'Text in Overflow' button again.

To Format with Continued Notices

1 EDIT OPTIONS | 2 IMPORT & CONNECT STORIES | 3 **USE CONTINUED NOTICES** | 4 **CUSTOMIZE RIBBON**
5 **EDIT USING WORD** | 6 **CREATE MARGINAL ELEMENTS** | 7 **IMPORT GRAPHICS & REVISE** | 8 **CREATE TEMPLATE**

In print publications for stories that flow from one page to another, it is good practice to add **continued notices**, or **jump lines**, to guide readers through the story. *Why? A jump line helps readers find the rest of the story easily.* The following steps format the last box on page 1 with a continued on notice. Then, on page 3, the first text box in the rest of the story is formatted with a continued from notice.

1

- Tap or click the Page 1 icon in the Page Navigation pane, and then navigate to the bottom of the page.

- Press and hold or right-click the third column of text in the lead story to display the shortcut menu (Figure 3–27).

Q&A Will Publisher ask me what page number to use?
The placement of the notices and the page numbering are automatic.

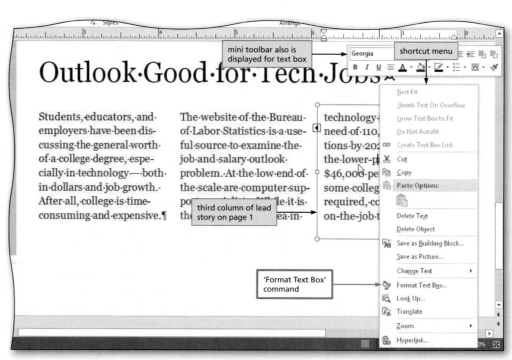

Figure 3–27

2

- Tap or click 'Format Text Box' to display the Format Text Box dialog box.

- Tap or click the Text Box tab to display its settings.

- Tap or click to display a check mark in the 'Include "Continued on page …"' check box (Figure 3–28).

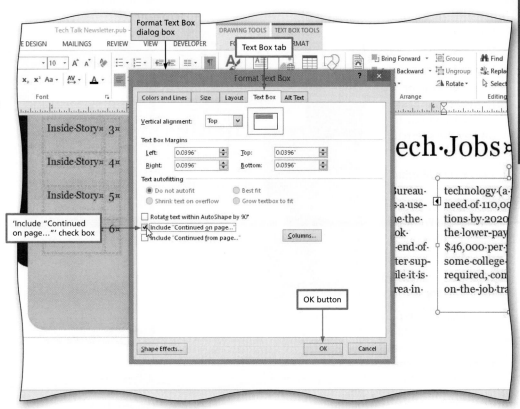

Figure 3–28

3

- Tap or click the OK button (Format Text Box dialog box) to insert the continued notice (Figure 3–29).

Outlook·Good·for·Tech·Jobs ¤

Students,·educators,·and· employers·have·been·discussing·the·general·worth· of·a·college·degree,·especially·in·technology——·both· in·dollars·and·job·growth.· After·all,·college·is·time-consuming·and·expensive.¶

The·website·of·the·Bureau· of·Labor·Statistics·is·a·useful·source·to·examine·the· job·and·salary·outlook· problem.·At·the·low-end·of· the·scale·are·computer·support·s[...]· the·fas[...]

technology·(a·projected· need·of·110,000·new·positions·by·2020),·it·is·one·of· the·lower-paying·jobs·at· $46,000·per·year.·Only· some·college·education·is· required,·combined·with· *(Continued·on·page·2)*

Figure 3–29

4

- Tap or click the Next button to move to the rest of the story on page 2.

- Press and hold or right-click the text in the first text box to display the shortcut menu.

- Tap or click 'Format Text Box' on the shortcut menu to display the Format Text Box dialog box.

- If necessary, tap or click the Text Box tab to display its settings.

- Tap or click to display a check mark in the 'Include "Continued from page …"' check box (Figure 3–30).

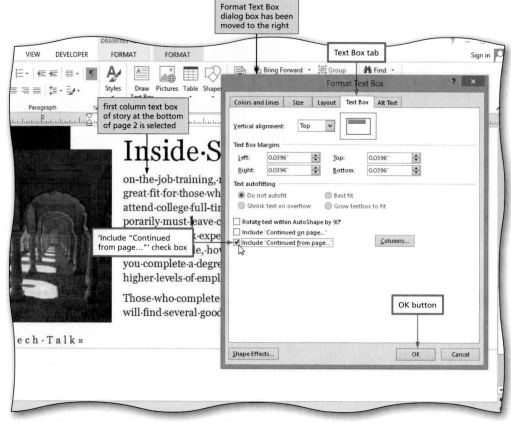

Figure 3–30

Q&A What do I do if my dialog box is covering up the text box?

The setting changes will take place when you click the OK button. If you want to see both the dialog box and the text box, you can drag the title bar of the dialog box to the right, as shown in Figure 3–30.

5

- Tap or click the OK button (Format Text Box dialog box) to insert the continued from notice (Figure 3–31).

Experiment

- Use the next and previous buttons to move between the linked text boxes on pages 1 and 2. Examine the jump lines with the supplied page numbers.

Figure 3–31

Other Ways

1. Select text box, tap or click Format Text Box Dialog Box Launcher (TEXT BOX TOOLS FORMAT tab | Text group), tap or click Text Box tab, tap or click desired continued notice check box

To Edit the Headlines for the Continued Story

The following step edits the inside headlines for the continued story.

1 Tap or click the Inside Story Headline placeholder text to select it, and then type `Outlook Good for Tech Jobs` to replace the text (Figure 3–32).

BTW
Text in Overflow
The overflow area is an invisible storage location within a publication that holds extra text. You can move text out of overflow and back into a publication by one of several means: flowing text into a new text box, autofitting text, enlarging the text box, changing the text size, changing the margins within the text box, or deleting some of the text in the text box.

new headline in third story on page 2

Outlook·Good·for·Tech·Jobs¤

(Continued·from·page·1)¤

on-the-job·training,·making·it·a· great·fit·for·those·who·cannot· attend·college·full-time,·or·tem- porarily·must·leave·college·to· work.·The·work·experience·will· prove·invaluable,·however,·as· you·complete·a·degree·and·seek· higher·levels·of·employment.¶

Those·who·complete·a·degree·will·find· several·good·employment·prospects.·A· programmer·can·expect·a·starting·sala- ry·of·$71,380·per·year.·At·the·high·end,· a·system·manager·with·five·years·of· experience·commands·an·average·an- nual·salary·of·$115,780.·The·Bureau· projects·an·18%·growth·rate·for·manag- er·positions.·This·becomes·a·desirable· goal·for·technologists·with·degrees.¤

ech·Talk¤

Figure 3–32

To Import Other Stories on Page 2

The following steps edit the headline and import the text for the second story on page 2. To complete these steps, you will be required to use the Data Files for Students. Visit www.cengage.com/ct/studentdownload for detailed instructions or contact your instructor for information about accessing the required files.

BTW
The Ribbon and Screen Resolution
Publisher may change how the groups and buttons within the groups appear on the ribbon, depending on the computer's screen resolution. Thus, your ribbon may look different from the ones in this book if you are using a screen resolution other than 1366 × 768.

1 Scroll to display the top portion of page 2, and then click the Inside Story Headline placeholder text above the first story to select it. Recall that the first story text box is blank because of the autoflow change.

2 Type `Spotlight on Students` to replace the selected headline.

3 Tap or click inside the empty story text box to position the insertion point.

4 Tap or click the Insert File button (INSERT tab | Text group) to display the Insert Text dialog box.

5 If necessary, navigate to the location of the file to be opened (in this case, the Chapter 03 folder in the Publisher folder in the CIS 101 folder).

6 Double-tap or double-click the file named, Spotlight on Students, to insert the text file.

7 Repeat steps 1 through 6 on the previous page for the second story on the page entitled, What are treks?, inserting the file named, 'What are treks.'

8 Zoom to approximately 80% to display both stories and headlines (Figure 3–33).

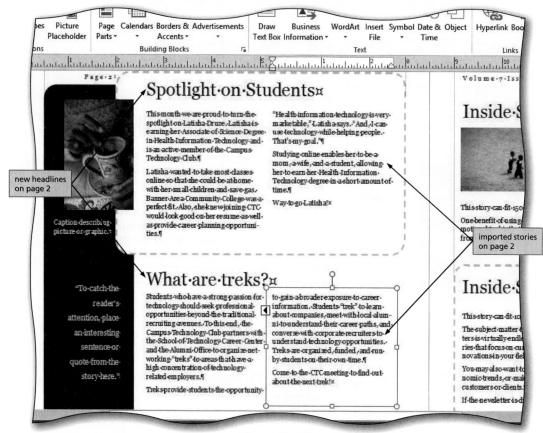

Figure 3–33

To Import a Story on Page 4

BTW

Zooming
Recall that the F9 key toggles between the current page view and 100% magnification or actual size. **Toggle** means the same key will alternate views, or turn a feature on and off. Editing text is easier if you view the text at 100% magnification or higher.

The following steps edit the headline and import the text for the story in the lower portion of page 4. To complete these steps, you will be required to use the Data Files for Students. Visit www.cengage.com/ct/studentdownload for detailed instructions or contact your instructor for information about accessing the required files.

1 Navigate to the lower portion of page 4, and then click the Back Page Story Headline placeholder text to select it.

2 Type `From the desk of the dean...` to replace the selected headline.

3 Tap or click the placeholder text inside the story text box to select it.

4 Tap or click the Insert File button (INSERT tab | Text group) to display the Insert Text dialog box.

5 If necessary, navigate to the location of the file to be opened (in this case, the Chapter 03 folder in the Publisher folder in the CIS 101 folder).

6 Double-tap or double-click the file named, Dean Message to insert the text file (Figure 3–34).

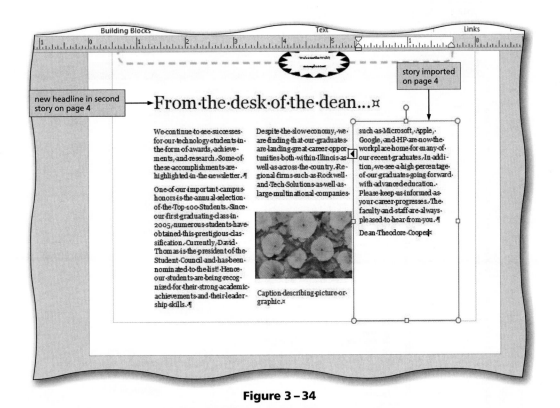

Figure 3 – 34

Customizing the Ribbon

It is easy to **customize**, or personalize, the ribbon the way that you want it. You can

- Create custom groups and custom tabs to contain frequently used commands
- Rearrange or rename buttons, groups, and tabs to fit your work style
- Rename or remove buttons and boxes from an existing tab and group
- Add new buttons to a custom group

When you add new buttons to the ribbon, you may choose from a list that includes commands that you may use elsewhere in Publisher such as those on shortcut menus, commands from the Backstage view, or other commands that are not on the ribbon. Or, you can create a new button that executes a command or set of commands that you record. You will create such a button later in this book. In this chapter, you will create a custom group on the Review tab and add a command that is not currently on the ribbon. The command will appear as a button in the new custom group.

You can customize the ribbon in all of the Microsoft Office applications, but the customizations are application-specific. The changes you make to the Publisher ribbon will not change the ribbon in any other Microsoft Office application. When you no longer need the customization, it can be removed individually, or the entire ribbon can be reset to its default settings, removing all customizations.

BTW

Whole Page View
The Show Whole Page button on the right side of the Publisher status bar displays the entire page. Page editing techniques such as moving graphics, inserting new objects, and aligning objects are performed more easily in Whole Page view. You also may choose different magnifications and views by clicking the Zoom arrow (VIEW tab | Zoom group).

To Customize the Publisher Ribbon

1 EDIT OPTIONS | 2 IMPORT & CONNECT STORIES | 3 USE CONTINUED NOTICES | 4 CUSTOMIZE RIBBON
5 EDIT USING WORD | 6 CREATE MARGINAL ELEMENTS | 7 IMPORT GRAPHICS & REVISE | 8 CREATE TEMPLATE

The steps on the next page add the 'Edit Story in Microsoft Word' button to a new group on the Review tab on the ribbon. **Why?** *The Review tab has empty space to hold custom groups. The other tabs are full. Adding a custom group to one of the other tabs would compress the existing groups, which might make it more difficult to locate buttons and boxes.*

1

- Tap or click FILE on the ribbon to open the Backstage view, and then click Options to display the Publisher Options dialog box.

- Tap or click Customize Ribbon in the left pane (Publisher Options dialog box) to display the options for customizing the ribbon.

- Tap or click the 'Choose commands from' button to view the list of commands (Figure 3–35).

Q&A Why are some commands not in the ribbon?
Publisher is a powerful program with many commands. Including all of the available commands on the ribbon would be overwhelming to many users. Publisher includes the most used or popular commands in its default set.

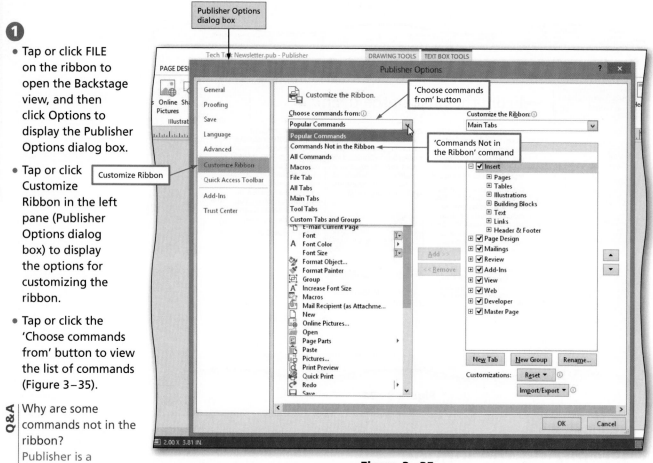

Figure 3–35

2

- Tap or click 'Commands Not in the Ribbon' to display the list.

- Tap or click the command you want to add (in this case, the 'Edit Story in Microsoft Word' command) (Figure 3–36).

Q&A Can I add more than one command to the ribbon?
Yes, but you have to add them one at a time.

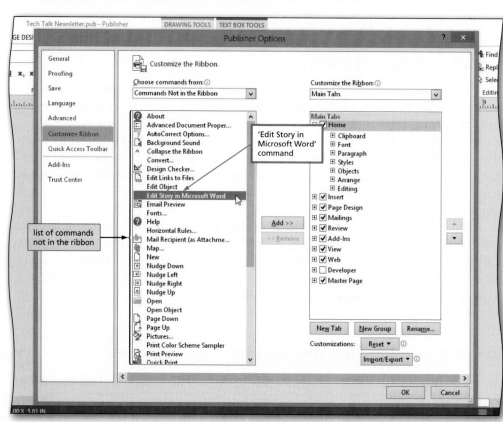

Figure 3–36

3

- Tap or click Review in the list of Main Tabs to select it.
- Tap or click the New Group button to create a custom group (Figure 3–37).

Q&A Do I have to add commands to a new group?
Yes. Commands only can be added to custom groups. The default tabs and groups cannot be changed.

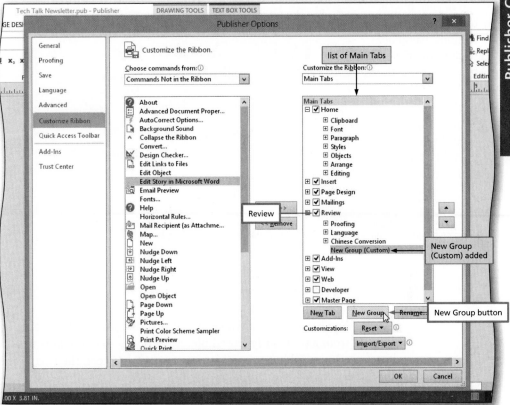

Figure 3–37

4

- Tap or click the Add button to add the chosen command to the new group (Figure 3–38).

Q&A Can I rename the custom group?
Yes, you can rename any group or command by tapping or clicking the Rename button and then entering a new name in the Rename dialog box. You even can choose an icon for the command.

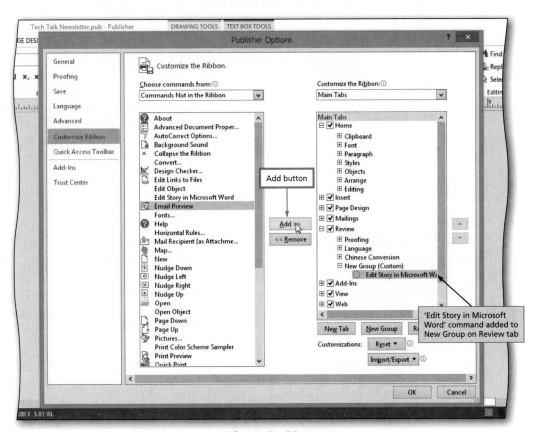

Figure 3–38

5

- Tap or click the OK button (Publisher Options dialog box) to close the dialog box and create the custom group.

- Tap or click REVIEW on the ribbon to display the REVIEW tab and its new group and button (Figure 3–39).

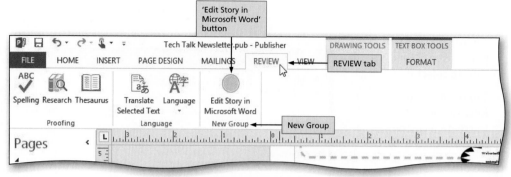

Figure 3–39

Other Ways

1. Press and hold or right-click ribbon, tap or click Customize the Ribbon, choose or create groups, add commands, tap or click OK (Publisher Options dialog box)

Editing Stories in Microsoft Word

You have seen that you can edit text directly in Microsoft Publisher or import text from a previously stored file. A third way to edit text is to use Microsoft Word as your editor. Publisher provides an easy link between the two applications.

If you need to edit only a few words, it is faster to continue using Publisher. If you need to edit a longer story or one that is not available on your storage device, it sometimes is easier to edit the story in Word. Many users are accustomed to working in Word and want to take advantage of available Word features, such as grammar checking and revision tracking. It may be easier to drag-and-drop paragraphs in a Word window than to perform the same task in a Publisher window, especially when it involves moving across pages in a larger Publisher publication. Editing your stories in Word allows you to manipulate the text using the full capabilities of a word processing program.

While you are editing a story in Word, you cannot edit the corresponding text box in Publisher; Publisher displays a gray box instead of the text. When you close Word, control returns to Publisher and the text appears.

Occasionally, if you have many applications running, such as virus protection and other memory-taxing programs, Publisher may warn you that you are low on computer memory. In that case, close the other applications and try editing the story in Word again.

To Edit a Story Using Microsoft Word

1 EDIT OPTIONS | 2 IMPORT & CONNECT STORIES | 3 USE CONTINUED NOTICES | 4 CUSTOMIZE RIBBON
5 EDIT USING WORD | 6 CREATE MARGINAL ELEMENTS | 7 IMPORT GRAPHICS & REVISE | 8 CREATE TEMPLATE

The following steps use Microsoft Word in conjunction with Publisher to create the text on the back page of the newsletter. *Why? Some people find it easier to edit stories using Microsoft Word.* Microsoft Word version 6.0 or later must be installed on your computer for this procedure to work.

1

- If necessary, navigate to page 4.

- Scroll to display the story text box in the upper portion of page 4.

- Select all of the text.

- Display the REVIEW tab (Figure 3–40).

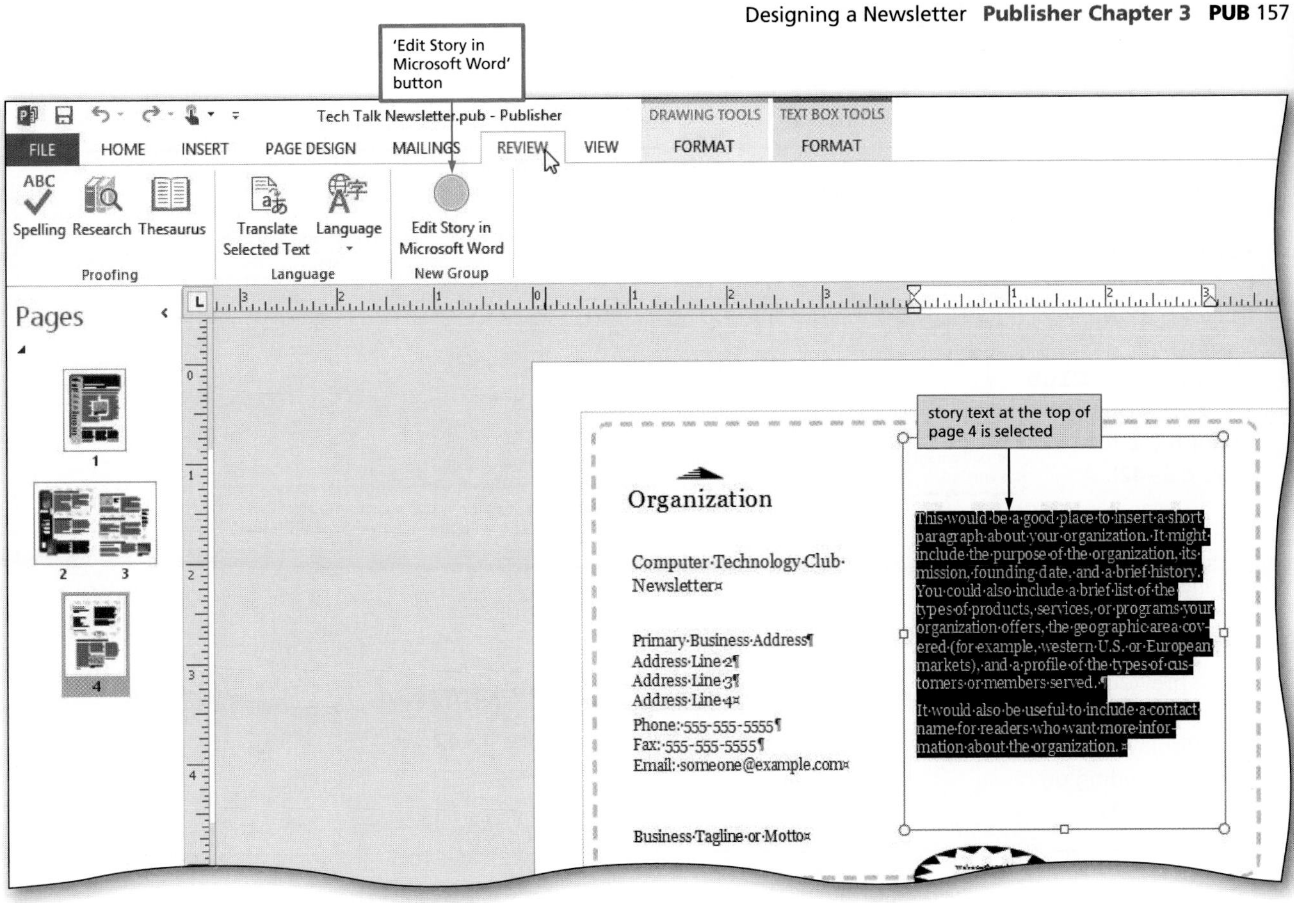

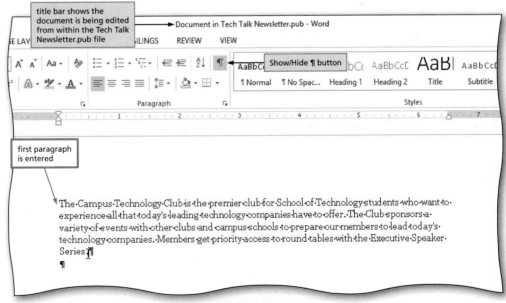

'Edit Story in Microsoft Word' button

story text at the top of page 4 is selected

Figure 3–40

2

- Tap or click the 'Edit Story in Microsoft Word' button (REVIEW tab | New Group) to start the Word program.

- Press CTRL+A to select all of the text, and then type **The Campus Technology Club is the premier club for School of Technology students who want to experience all that today's leading technology companies have to offer. The Club sponsors a variety of events with other clubs and campus schools to prepare our members to lead today's technology companies. Members get priority access to round tables with the Executive Speaker Series.** and then press the ENTER key to finish the first paragraph (Figure 3–41).

title bar shows the document is being edited from within the Tech Talk Newsletter.pub file

Show/Hide ¶ button

first paragraph is entered

Figure 3–41

- Type `If you have any interest in working in the technology field, the Campus Technology Club is for you!` to finish the text (Figure 3–42).

Why are my fonts different?

Usually, the Word text displays the same formatting as the previous text in Publisher. Your display may differ depending on available fonts.

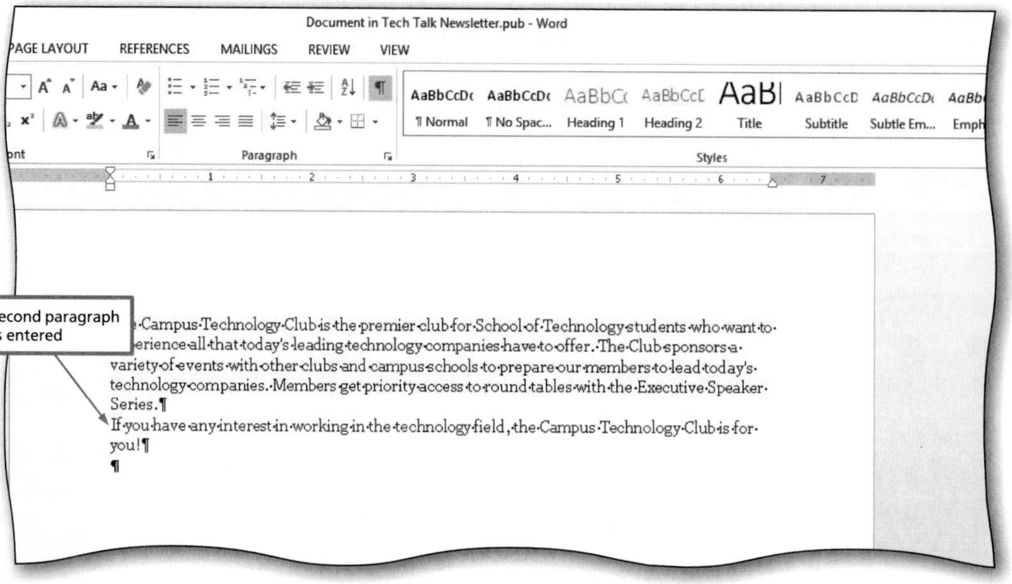

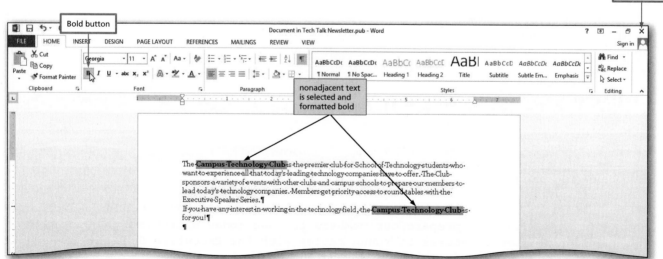

Figure 3–42

To Format while Editing in Microsoft Word

1 EDIT OPTIONS | 2 IMPORT & CONNECT STORIES | 3 USE CONTINUED NOTICES | 4 CUSTOMIZE RIBBON
5 EDIT USING WORD | 6 CREATE MARGINAL ELEMENTS | 7 IMPORT GRAPHICS & REVISE | 8 CREATE TEMPLATE

The following step uses the CTRL key to select multiple sections of nonadjacent text and format them in Microsoft Word. *Why? You cannot select nonadjacent text in Publisher.*

- Drag to select the words, Campus Technology Club, in the first paragraph.
- CTRL+drag to select the same words in the second paragraph.
- Tap or click the Bold button (HOME tab | Font group) on the Word ribbon (Figure 3–43).

Figure 3–43

To Exit Word and Return to Publisher

The following step exits Word and returns to Publisher. ***Why?*** *You must exit Word in order to edit the text box in Publisher.*

- Tap or click the Close button on the title bar of the Document in Tech Talk Newsletter.pub – Word window to quit Word (Figure 3–44).

Q&A

Why do I see only gray lines instead of the text?
Starting Microsoft Word from within Microsoft Publisher is a drain on your system's memory and on the refresh rate of your screen. Try navigating to page 1 and then back to page 4 to refresh the screen.

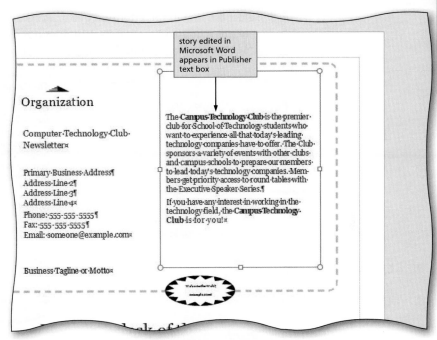

Figure 3–44

To Edit Other Objects on Page 4

Table 3–2 lists text for the other objects on page 4.

Table 3–2 Text for Page 4	
Location	**Text**
Organization logo	<delete>
Primary Business Address	School of Technology Banner Area Community College 8400 Walker Lane Banner, IL 50024
Phone, Fax, Email text box	Phone: 618-555-8662 Fax: 618-555-8663 Email: ctc@bacc.edu
Business Tagline or Motto	Join us on Facebook!
Attention getter	We meet the 2nd Friday of each month

BTW

Q&As

For a complete list of the Q&As found in many of the step-by-step sequences in this book, visit the Q&A resource on the Student Companion Site located on www.cengagebrain.com. For detailed instructions about accessing available resources, visit www.cengage.com/ct/ studentdownload or see the inside back cover of this book.

The following steps delete the logo and edit other text boxes on page 2. As you edit the text boxes, zoom and scroll as necessary.

1. In the upper-left portion of page 4, select the organization logo and delete it.

2. Tap or click the default text in the Primary Business Address text box. Press CTRL+A to select all of the text. Enter the text from Table 3–2.

3 Select the default text in the Phone, Fax, Email text box, and then enter the text from Table 3–2 on the previous page.

4 Select the business tagline or motto placeholder text, and then enter the text from Table 3–2.

5 Select the text in the attention getter. Press and hold or right-click to display the shortcut menu and then, if Best Fit does not display a check mark, tap or click Best Fit. Enter the text from Table 3–2 (Figure 3–45).

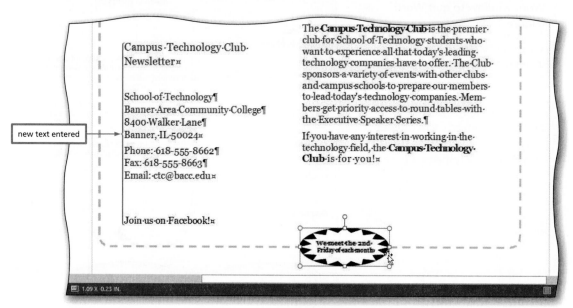

Figure 3–45

To Save the Publication Again

The following step saves the publication again.

1 Tap or click the Save button on the Quick Access Toolbar to save the file again with the same name, and in the same location.

Break Point: If you wish to take a break, this is a good place to do so. Exit Publisher. To resume at a later time, run Publisher, open the file called Tech Talk Newsletter, and continue following the steps from this location forward.

Marginal Elements

BTW
Left and Right Pages
In printing and publishing, the left page of a two-page spread is called **verso**. The right page is called **recto**. Typically the first page of a newsletter, book, or chapter is a recto page; thus, all recto pages will have odd page numbers and all verso pages will have even page numbers.

Publisher newsletter templates include marginal elements and layout features to make the newsletter more attractive and add interest to the page. A **sidebar**, or breakout, is a small piece of text, set off with a box or graphic, and placed beside a story. It contains text that is not vital for understanding the main text but usually adds interest or additional information. Tables of contents, art boxes, and bulleted points of interest are examples of sidebars. A newsletter **table of contents**, or margin table, usually is a narrow, short list that is used to refer readers to specific pages or to present listed or numeric items in the margin area. A **pull quote, or pullout,** is an excerpt from the main story used to highlight the concepts within the story or to attract readers. Pull quotes, like sidebars, can be set off with a box or graphic. Shapes and borders also are used sometimes as marginal elements.

To Edit Sidebars

The Banded newsletter template includes two sidebars on page 1. The first one is a bulleted list about special points of interest. The second is a table of contents. *Why? Some newsletters use a sidebar table as an index to locate stories in longer newsletters; sidebars also are used to break up a page with lots of text and attract readers to inside pages. Other newsletters use sidebar tables to display numerical data and lists.* Table 3–3 lists the text for the sidebars.

Table 3–3 Text for Sidebars		
SPECIAL POINTS OF INTEREST:	Oct. 7 Executive Speaker Series	
	Oct. 10 CTC meeting: Outsmarting Your Smartphone	
	Oct. 27 Spring registration begins	
	Oct.31 Halloween party	
INSIDE THIS ISSUE:	Student Spotlight	2
	Treks	2
	E-smells	3
	Coupon	3
	About Our Club	4
	Dean's Message	4

The following steps edit the sidebars. Recall that a hard return is created when you press the ENTER key. A hard return also causes a bullet to appear on the next line in a bulleted list. To create a new line within a bulleted item, you will use a **soft return** by pressing the SHIFT+ENTER keys. Neither hard returns nor soft returns print on hard copies.

- Navigate to page 1.
- Locate the Special points of interest sidebar, and zoom to approximately 120% magnification.
- Tap or click the bulleted list to select it (Figure 3–46).

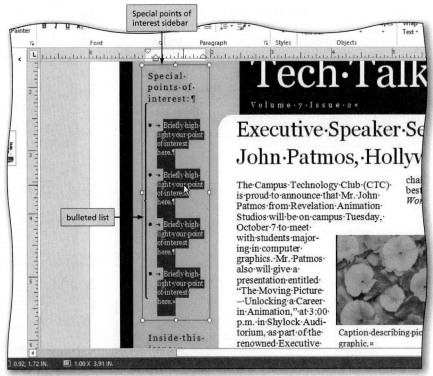

Figure 3–46

2

- Type the list as shown in Table 3–3 on the previous page. Press the SHIFT+ENTER keys after each line within the bullet item to create soft returns. Press the ENTER key at the end of each bulleted item, except the last, to create hard returns (Figure 3–47).

Q&A Why do I need to use soft returns? The bulleted list is very narrow and might hyphenate awkwardly if you use wordwrap.

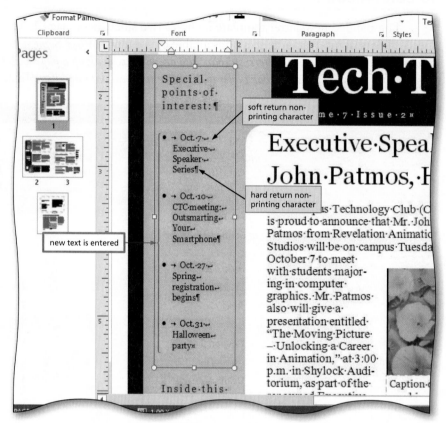

Figure 3–47

3

- Scroll down to the second sidebar, Inside this issue.
- Tap or click the default text, Inside Story, just below the heading to select the text (Figure 3–48).

Q&A Is the heading part of the table? No, the heading is a text box grouped with subsequent rows, which comprise a table. You will learn more about tables in a future chapter.

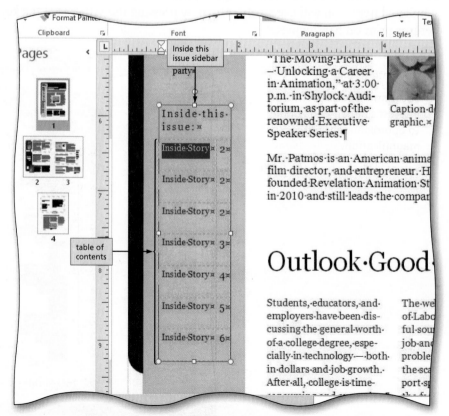

Figure 3–48

4

- Type **Student Spotlight** to replace the text (Figure 3–49).

Q&A What are the dotted gray lines in the table?

Publisher displays dotted gray lines to indicate the size of each cell in the table. A **cell** is the text box located where a table column and table row intersect. The lines do not print.

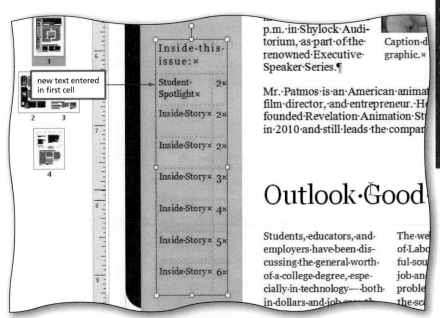

new text entered in first cell

Figure 3–49

5

- If necessary, type **2** to replace the page number just to the right of the Student Spotlight text.

- Complete the table with the data from Table 3–3 on page PUB 161. Use the TAB key to move from cell to cell. Delete the default text in the last row because it will be blank (Figure 3–50). If necessary, add a soft return after the word, Dean's, in Dean's Message, so a hyphen is not created.

Q&A Could I click the next cell instead of using the TAB key?

You could click the cell, but you then would need to select the page number and type to replace it. Pressing the TAB key both advances to and selects the data in the next cell.

Figure 3–50

To Insert a Pull Quote

People often make reading decisions based on the size of the story. Using a pull quote brings a small portion of the text to their attention. *Why? Pull quotes invite the reader to read the story, and are useful for breaking the monotony of long columns of text and for adding visual interest.* The following steps insert a pull quote using function keys to copy and paste the quote from the story.

1

- Navigate to the second story, What are treks?, on page 2.

- Drag to select the text in the last sentence.

- Press CTRL+C to copy the sentence to the Clipboard (Figure 3–51).

Q&A How should I choose the text for the pull quote?
Layout specialists say pull quotes should summarize the intended message in one or two sentences.

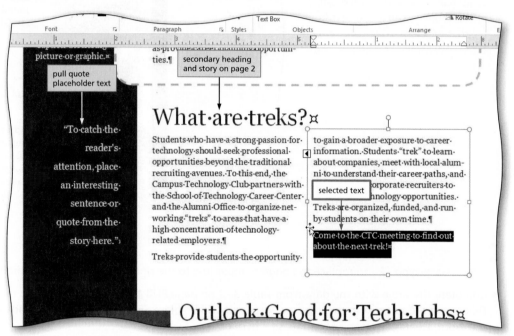

Figure 3–51

2

- Tap or click to select the pull quote placeholder text to the left of the story (Figure 3–52).

Q&A What if there is no pull quote on the page?
You can insert a pull quote from the Page Parts gallery. You will learn about the gallery in a later chapter.

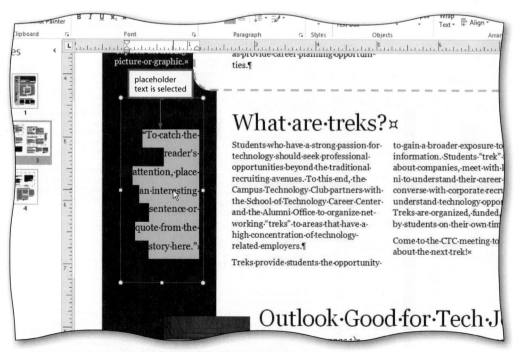

Figure 3–52

3

- Press CTRL+V to paste the sentence from the Clipboard.

- Tap or click the Paste Options button, and then click the 'Keep Text Only' button to accept the destination formatting (Figure 3–53).

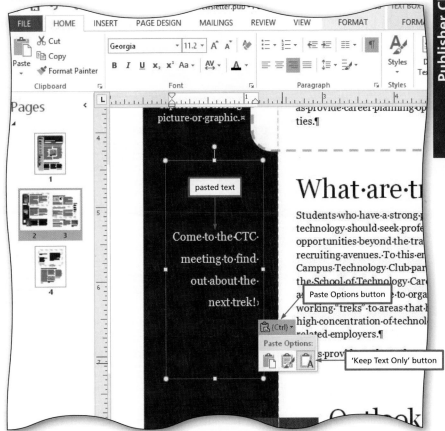

Figure 3–53

To Delete Objects on Page 3

The following steps delete the first and third stories on page 3. Recall that dragging around multiple objects selects them automatically.

1 Navigate to the top of page 3.

2 Tap or click the border of the first heading to select it.

3 Press the DELETE key to delete the text box.

4 Drag around the first story text boxes, graphic, and caption to select them.

5 Press the DELETE key to delete the selected items.

6 Delete the pull quote text box on the right.

7 Scroll to the bottom of the page, and then tap or click the border of the third heading to select it.

8 Press the DELETE key to delete the text box.

BTW

Deleting Objects
If you think there is even a remote possibility that you might use an object again, do not delete it. Simply drag it to the scratch area. That way, it is saved with the publication, but will not appear on the page layout itself, and it will not print. When you are certain that you no longer will need an object, delete it to lower the size of your Publisher file.

9 Drag around the third story text boxes, graphic, and caption to select them all.

10 Press the DELETE key to delete the selected items.

11 Zoom to Whole Page (Figure 3–54).

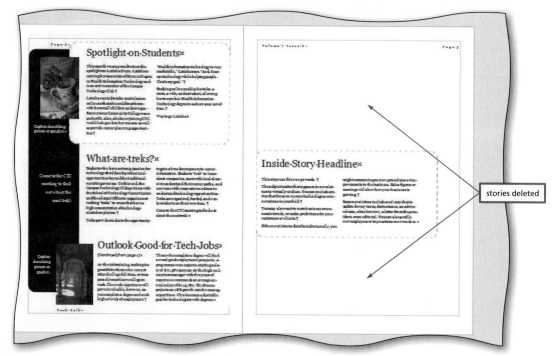

Figure 3–54

To Resize and Move Objects

The following steps move the border, headline, and story on page 3. The border and text boxes also are resized. In the Banded template, the border is a white, rectangular shape with a yellow, dotted line along the edge. You will learn more about creating borders in a later chapter.

1 On page 3, drag around the border, headline text box, and story text boxes to select them.

2 Drag the selection to the top of the page, approximately 1.5 inch from the top of the page.

3 Deselect.

4 Tap or click the border to select it, and then drag the lower-center sizing handle down to approximately the 7-inch mark on the vertical ruler.

5 Drag around the two story text boxes to select them. If you have trouble dragging around only the text boxes, SHIFT+click each one to select them.

6 Drag one of the lower-center sizing handles down to approximately the 6.5-inch mark on the vertical ruler (Figure 3–55).

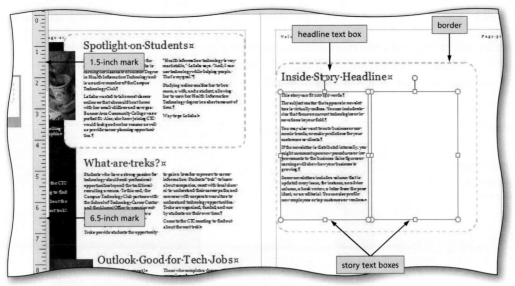

Figure 3–55

To Edit the Story on Page 3

The following steps edit the headline and import the remaining story on page 3. To complete these steps, you will be required to use the Data Files for Students. Visit www.cengage.com/ct/studentdownload for detailed instructions or contact your instructor for information about accessing the required files.

1 On page 3, tap or click the headline placeholder text. Type **New Exciting Web Technologies (NEWT)** to replace the selected headline.

2 Tap or click the placeholder text in the inside story text box to select it.

3 Tap or click the Insert File button (INSERT tab | Text group) to display the Insert Text dialog box.

4 If necessary, navigate to the location of the file to be opened (in this case, the Chapter 03 folder in the Publisher folder in the CIS 101 folder).

5 Double-tap or double-click the file, New Exciting Web Technologies, to insert the text file (Figure 3–56).

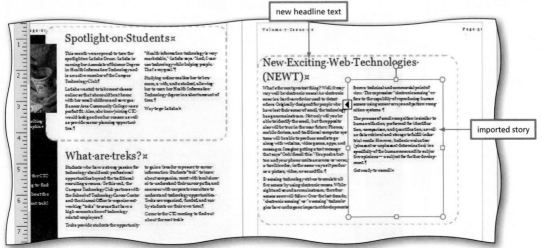

Figure 3–56

To Duplicate an Object

1 EDIT OPTIONS | 2 IMPORT & CONNECT STORIES | 3 USE CONTINUED NOTICES | 4 CUSTOMIZE RIBBON
5 EDIT USING WORD | 6 CREATE MARGINAL ELEMENTS | 7 IMPORT GRAPHICS & REVISE | 8 CREATE TEMPLATE

When you **duplicate** an object, you use a shortcut method to create a copy, rather than the traditional copy-and-paste method. ***Why?*** *A duplicate does not use the Clipboard.* The following step duplicates the brown shape on page 2 to use as a marginal element. You will learn more about shapes in a later chapter.

- Tap or click the brown shape on page 2.

- CTRL+ drag the brown shape from page 2 to the lower-right corner of page 3, within the margin (Figure 3–57).

Q&A

Why do I need to press the CTRL the key while dragging?
The CTRL key creates the duplicate copy.

Why is the duplicate copy so much bigger than the original?
It is not bigger. The original shape is partially obscured by the text boxes in front of it.

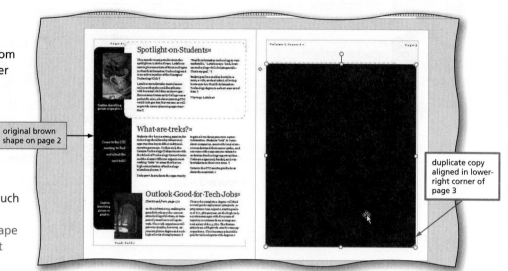

original brown shape on page 2

duplicate copy aligned in lower-right corner of page 3

Figure 3–57

To Send an Object to the Back

1 EDIT OPTIONS | 2 IMPORT & CONNECT STORIES | 3 USE CONTINUED NOTICES | 4 CUSTOMIZE RIBBON
5 EDIT USING WORD | 6 CREATE MARGINAL ELEMENTS | 7 IMPORT GRAPHICS & REVISE | 8 CREATE TEMPLATE

Layering involves determining which objects should be displayed in front or behind other objects. Obviously, you do not want to layer an object that would obstruct text or necessary graphics; however, sometimes shapes and colors can be layered to provide interesting backgrounds. On page 2 of the Banded template, the brown shape is layered behind the other text boxes and objects on the page. ***Why?*** *It creates a marginal element of color.* The following steps send the brown shape on page 3 to the back, behind the other objects, creating symmetry across the pages.

- Display the DRAWING TOOLS FORMAT tab.

- Tap or click the Send Backward arrow (DRAWING TOOLS FORMAT tab | Arrange group) to display the list (Figure 3–58).

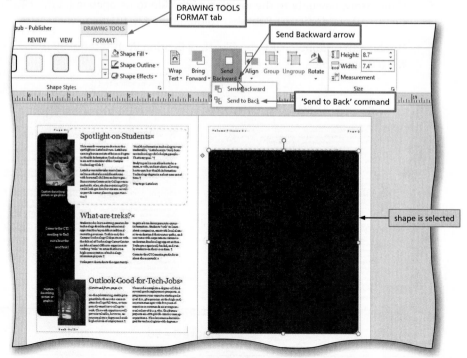

DRAWING TOOLS FORMAT tab

Send Backward arrow

'Send to Back' command

shape is selected

Figure 3–58

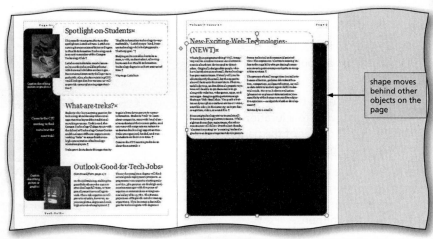

- Tap or click the 'Send to Back' command to move the brown shape behind the other objects on the page (Figure 3–59).

shape moves behind other objects on the page

Figure 3–59

Advertisements

Publisher **advertisements** include a group of promotional templates used to market a product or service, including ads that might be placed in newspapers, attention getters, and coupons. Advertisements can be stand-alone publications or inserted as building block items in larger publications. On page 3 of the newsletter, the club will offer a coupon. A **coupon** is a promotional device used to market a product or service. Customers exchange coupons for discounts when purchasing a product. Some coupons offer rebates or free items to attract customers. Coupons often are distributed widely as small printed documents through mail, magazines, newspapers, and newsletters. More recently, however, they are distributed as electronic tags collected through preferred customer cards via the Internet and mobile devices such as cell phones.

To Insert a Coupon

1 EDIT OPTIONS | 2 IMPORT & CONNECT STORIES | 3 USE CONTINUED NOTICES | 4 CUSTOMIZE RIBBON
5 EDIT USING WORD | 6 CREATE MARGINAL ELEMENTS | 7 IMPORT GRAPHICS & REVISE | **8 CREATE TEMPLATE**

The following steps insert a coupon on page 3 of the newsletter. *Why? A coupon is an excellent marketing tool to help track who is reading your publications.*

- Navigate to the lower portion of page 3 in the newsletter and zoom to approximately 150%.

- Display the INSERT tab.

- Tap or click the Advertisements button (INSERT tab | Building Blocks group) to display the Advertisements gallery (Figure 3–60).

Q&A Why does my gallery look different?
Your Advertisements gallery may have an area of recently used items. If necessary, scroll down in the gallery to display the Coupons area.

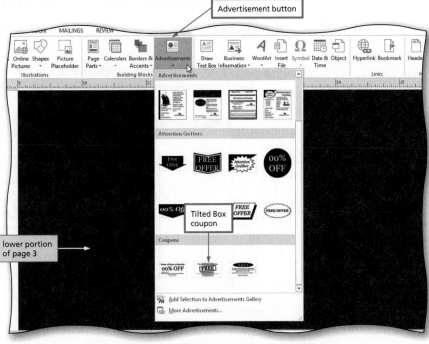

Advertisement button

lower portion of page 3

Tilted Box coupon

Figure 3–60

- In the Coupons area, tap or click the Tilted Box coupon to insert it in the newsletter.

- Drag the border of the inserted coupon to move it to a location in the lower-left corner of the page, as shown in Figure 3–61.

- SHIFT+drag the upper-right sizing handle to approximately the 8-inch mark on the vertical ruler, to resize the coupon.

Q&A

My coupon looks different. Did I do something wrong?
No, depending upon your printer and fonts, the coupon may be displayed slightly differently.

coupon inserted in lower-left corner of page 3

Figure 3–61

Other Ways

1. Tap or click Show Building Block Library Dialog Box Launcher (INSERT tab | Building Blocks group), tap or click Advertisements folder, tap or click desired coupon

To Edit the Coupon

The following steps edit the text boxes in the coupon.

1. Replace the 'Name of Item or Service' placeholder text with the words `Pizza and Pop` as the new text

2. Replace the Organization Name placeholder text with the words `Campus Technology Club` as the new text.

3. Replace the 'Describe your location by landmark or area of town.' placeholder text with the words `Just come to our next meeting!` as the new text.

4. Replace the telephone number with the text, `October 10, 2014 at 3:00 p.m.` as the new text.

5. Zoom as necessary and delete the text in the expiration date text boxes. The end of text formatting marks may remain (Figure 3–62).

new text entered

Figure 3–62

Using Graphics in a Newsletter

Most graphic designers employ an easy technique for deciding how many graphics are too many. They hold the publication at arm's length and glance at it. Then, closing their eyes, they count the number of things they remember. Remembering more than five graphics indicates too many; less than two indicates too few. Without question, graphics can make or break a publication. The world has come to expect them. Used correctly, graphics enhance the text, attract the eye, and brighten the look of the publication.

You can use Publisher's clip art images and photos in any publication you create, including newsletters. Publisher also accepts graphics and pictures created by other programs, as well as scanned photos and digital photos. You can import and replace graphics in publications in the same way that you imported stories and replaced template text. Once inserted, graphics can be resized and moved to appropriate locations. In newsletters, you should use photos as true-to-life representations, such as pictures of employees and products. Drawings, on the other hand, can explain, instruct, entertain, or represent images for which you have no picture. The careful use of graphics can add flair and distinction to your publication.

How do you decide on the best layout?

As you insert graphics and arrange stories, follow any guidelines from the authors or from the company for which you are creating the newsletter. Together, determine the best layout for visual appeal and reliable dissemination of content. Make any required changes. Print a copy and mark the places where sidebars and pull quotes would make sense. Verify that all photos have captions.

CONSIDER THIS

The following sections import graphics from the Data Files for Students, edit the captions and sidebar text, and insert a pull quote.

To Replace a Graphic Using the Shortcut Menu

1 EDIT OPTIONS | 2 IMPORT & CONNECT STORIES | 3 USE CONTINUED NOTICES | 4 CUSTOMIZE RIBBON
5 EDIT USING WORD | 6 CREATE MARGINAL ELEMENTS | **7 IMPORT GRAPHICS & REVISE** | **8 CREATE TEMPLATE**

The following steps replace a graphic using the shortcut menu. ***Why?*** *Using the shortcut menu is a quick way to change a picture without having to navigate the ribbon.* To complete these steps, you will be required to use the Data Files for Students. Visit www.cengage.com/ct/studentdownload for detailed instructions or contact your instructor for information about accessing the required files.

1

- Navigate to page 1.

- Scroll and zoom as necessary to display the graphic in the lead story.

- Press and hold or right-click the graphic to display the shortcut menu and then tap or click Change Picture to display its submenu (Figure 3–63).

Q&A What is the toolbar that appeared on the screen?
When a picture is selected, Publisher displays a mini toolbar in case you want to make changes to the picture.

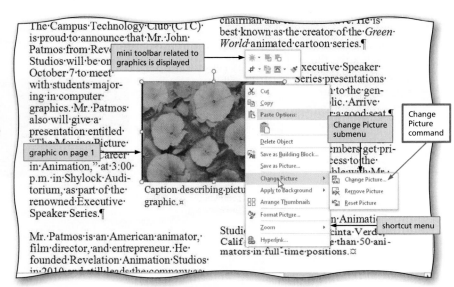

Figure 3–63

- Tap or click Change Picture on the submenu to display the Insert Pictures dialog box (Figure 3–64).

Q&A What do the other choices on the Change Picture submenu do?
The Remove Picture command deletes the picture but retains the picture placeholder. The Reset Picture command removes any previous cropping or resizing.

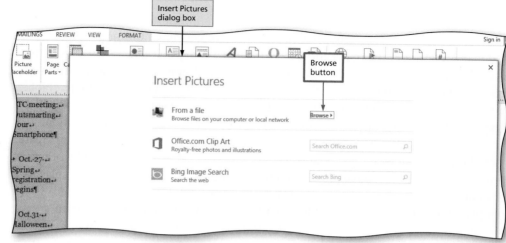

Figure 3–64

- Tap or click the Browse button in the From a file area to display the Insert Picture dialog box.

- Navigate to the location of the Data Files for Students (in this case, the Chapter 03 folder in the Publisher folder in the CIS 101 folder) (Figure 3–65).

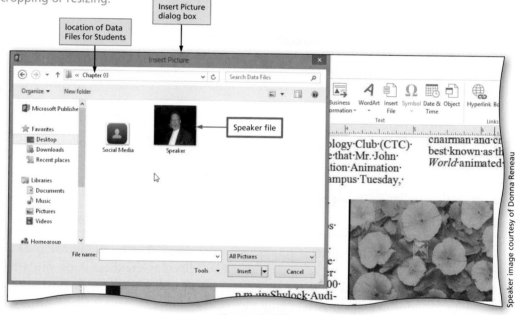

Figure 3–65

- Double-tap or double-click the file named, Speaker, to replace the picture. If necessary, zoom to 150% (Figure 3–66).

Q&A What if I choose a bigger or smaller picture?
Because you are replacing the graphic, rather than inserting a picture, Publisher resizes the picture to fit the space. The picture automatically is scaled in proportion.

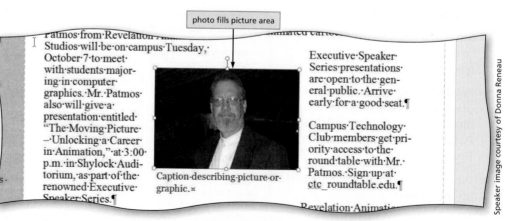

Figure 3–66

To Edit the Caption

The following steps edit the picture caption.

1 Select the placeholder text in the caption in order to replace it.

2 Type `John Patmos of` and then press the ENTER key to finish the first line of the caption. Type `Revelation Animation Studios` to finish the caption (Figure 3–67).

Figure 3–67

To Replace the Graphic on Page 2

The following steps replace other graphics in the newsletter.

1 Navigate to the top of page 2.

2 Press and hold or right-click the graphic beside the first story to display the shortcut menu, and then tap or click Change Picture to display its submenu.

3 Tap or click Change Picture on the submenu to display the Insert Pictures dialog box.

4 Type `spotlight` in the Office.com Clip Art search box, and then press the ENTER key to begin the search.

5 Scroll as necessary in the Office.com Clip Art dialog box, and then double-tap or double-click a picture similar to the one in Figure 3–68 to replace the graphic. If necessary, zoom to 100%.

6 Delete the caption for the picture at the top of page 2.

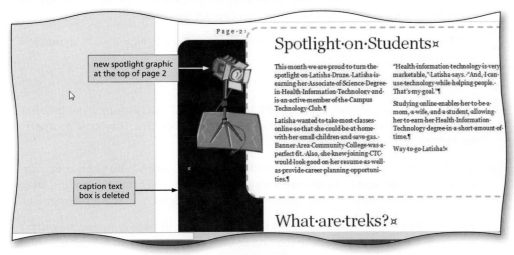

Figure 3–68

To Replace the Graphic and Caption on Page 2

The following steps replace other graphics in the newsletter.

1 Navigate to the bottom of page 2.

2 Use the shortcut menu to replace the graphic, searching Office.com Clip Art for the term, `network`. Use a graphic similar to the one in Figure 3–69. If necessary, zoom to 100%.

3 Replace the caption by typing, `It is clear that tech careers are a good choice with strong potential for growth` as the caption text.

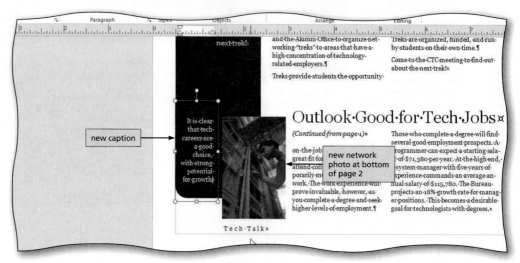

Figure 3–69

To Insert a Graphic and Caption on Page 3

The following steps insert a graphic and caption for the story on page 3 of the newsletter.

1 Navigate to the top of page 3.

2 Display the INSERT tab.

3 Tap or click the Online Pictures button (INSERT tab | Illustrations group) to display the Insert Pictures dialog box. Search Office.com Clip Art for the term, `smell`.

4 Scroll as necessary then choose a picture similar to the one in Figure 3–70 to replace the graphic.

5 If necessary, display the PICTURE TOOLS FORMAT tab.

6 Tap or click the Caption button (PICTURE TOOLS FORMAT tab | Picture Styles group) to display the Caption gallery. In the Overlay area, tap or click 'Box - Layout 4' to insert the caption text box.

7 With the caption placeholder text selected, type `An e-smell button coming soon to your app!` to change the caption. If the entire caption is not displayed, press and hold or right-click the caption and then click Best Fit on the shortcut menu.

8 Drag the picture and its caption to the upper-left corner of page 3. Resize the picture as necessary to fill the area above the first column of text, as shown in Figure 3–70.

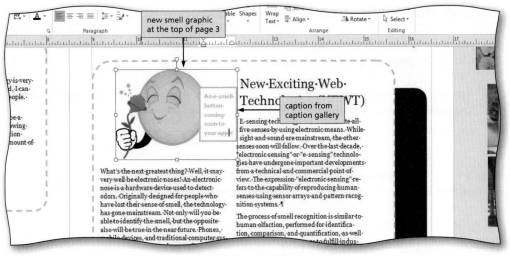

Figure 3–70

To Insert Graphics on Page 4

The following steps insert a graphic and caption for the story on page 4 of the newsletter.

1 Navigate to the top of page 4.

2 Display the INSERT tab.

3 Tap or click the Pictures button (INSERT tab | Illustrations group) to display the Insert Picture dialog box.

4 Navigate to the Data Files for Students, and insert the Social Media graphic.

5 In the publication, drag the graphic to a location near the reference to Facebook.

6 Press and hold or right-click the graphic in the lower portion of Page 4, and use the shortcut menu and Office.com Clip Art to insert a picture related to the search term, **pen**.

7 Delete the caption placeholder text (Figure 3–71).

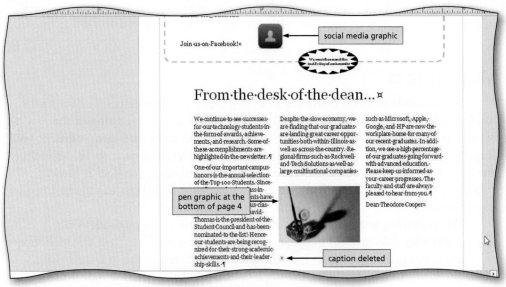

Figure 3–71

To Save the Publication before Revising

It is a good idea to save the newsletter before going back and revising it. The following step saves the publication again.

 Tap or click the Save button on the Quick Access Toolbar to save the file again, with the same file name and in the same location.

Break Point: If you wish to take a break, this is a good place to do so. Exit Publisher. To resume at a later time, run Publisher, open the file called Tech Talk Newsletter, and continue following the steps from this location forward.

Revising a Newsletter

As discussed in Chapter 1, once you complete a publication, you may find it necessary to make changes to it. Before submitting a newsletter to a customer or printing service, you should proofread it. While **proofreading**, you look for grammatical errors and spelling errors. You want to be sure the layout, graphics, and stories make sense. If you find errors, you must correct, make changes to, or edit the newsletter. Other readers, perhaps customers or editors, may want to proofread your publication and make changes, such as moving text. You also should check how Publisher has hyphenated your stories.

CONSIDER THIS

How should you proofread and revise a newsletter?
As you proofread the newsletter, look for ways to improve it. Check all grammar, spelling, and punctuation. Be sure the text is logical and transitions are smooth. Where necessary, add text, delete text, reword text, and move text to different locations. Ask yourself these questions:

• Does the title suggest the topic?

• Does the first line of the story entice the reader to continue?

• Is the purpose of the newsletter clear?

• Are all sources acknowledged?

The final phase of the design process is a synthesis involving proofreading, editing, and publishing. Publisher offers several methods to check for errors in your newsletter. None of these methods is a replacement for careful reading and proofreading.

Moving Text

If you decide to move text, such as words, characters, sentences, or paragraphs, you first select the text to be moved and then use drag-and-drop editing or the cut-and-paste technique to move the selected text. With **drag-and-drop editing**, you drag the selected item to the new location and then insert, or *drop*, it there. Moving text in this manner does not transfer data to either Clipboard, nor does it cause Publisher to display the Paste Options button. Any format changes to the text must be made manually.

When moving text between pages, use the cut-and-paste method. When moving text a long distance or between application programs, use the Office Clipboard task pane to cut and paste. When moving text a short distance, the drag-and-drop technique is more efficient. Thus, the steps on the following pages demonstrate drag-and-drop editing.

To Drag-and-Drop Text

1 EDIT OPTIONS | 2 IMPORT & CONNECT STORIES | 3 USE CONTINUED NOTICES | 4 CUSTOMIZE RIBBON
5 EDIT USING WORD | 6 CREATE MARGINAL ELEMENTS | 7 IMPORT GRAPHICS & REVISE | 8 CREATE TEMPLATE

The editor of the newsletter has decided that two paragraphs on page 3 should be inverted. *Why? The editor feels that the story will read better with the change.* The following steps move paragraphs by dragging and dropping.

- Navigate to the first story on page 1.

- Triple-tap or triple-click to select the penultimate (next to the last) paragraph (Figure 3–72).

Q&A Could I drag to select the paragraph?
Yes; however, it is more efficient to triple-tap or triple-click, which automatically selects the entire paragraph and the paragraph mark at the end of it.

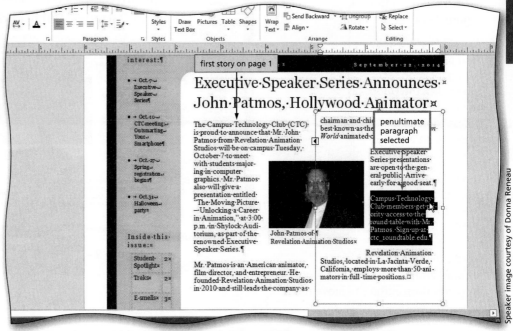

Figure 3–72

Speaker image courtesy of Donna Reneau

- Drag the selection to the beginning of the previous paragraph. Do not release the mouse button (Figure 3–73).

Q&A My drag is not working. What did I do wrong?
It may be that someone has turned off drag-and-drop editing. Tap or click FILE on the ribbon to open the Backstage view. Tap or click Options and then click Advanced. Tap or click to display a check mark in the 'Allow text to be dragged and dropped' check box.

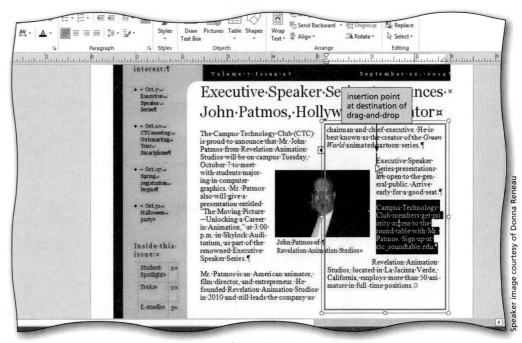

Figure 3–73

Speaker image courtesy of Donna Reneau

3

- Lift your finger or release the mouse button to move the selected text to the location of the mouse pointer (Figure 3–74).

Q&A

What if I accidentally drag text to the wrong location?
Tap or click the Undo button on the Quick Access Toolbar, or press CTRL+Z and try again.

Can I use drag-and-drop editing to move any selected item?
Yes, you can select words, sentences, phrases, and graphics and then use drag-and-drop editing to move them.

Figure 3–74

Speaker image courtesy of Donna Reneau

Other Ways

1. Select item, tap or click Cut button (HOME tab | Clipboard group), tap or click where text is to be pasted, tap or click Paste button (HOME tab | Clipboard group)

2. Press and hold or right-click selected item, tap or click Cut on shortcut menu, press and hold or right-click where text is to be pasted, tap or click Paste Option button on shortcut menu

3. Select item, press CTRL+X, position insertion point where text is to be pasted, press CTRL+V

To Insert a Text Box Marginal Element

Another revision may be to add a marginal text element to balance the two-page spread. The following step inserts a text box, formats the font, and enters the text.

1 Navigate to the middle of page 3.

2 Tap or click the Draw Text Box button (HOME tab | Objects group), and then drag to create a text box that approximately fills the area between the story and the coupon.

3 If necessary, display the HOME tab.

4 Change the font size to 20.

5 Change the alignment to Align Right.

6 Change the font color to white.

7 Type **Tech Talk** and then press the ENTER key. Type **Campus Technology Club Newsletter** to finish the text (Figure 3–75).

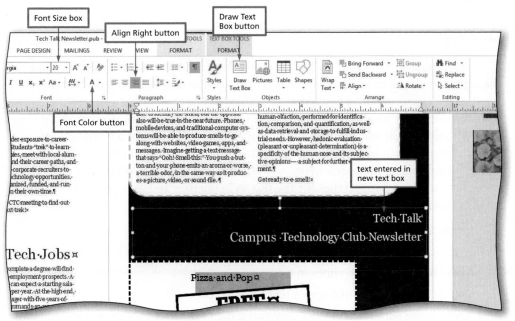

Figure 3–75

To Check the Spelling of the Entire Publication

The following steps check the entire publication for spelling errors.

1. Display the REVIEW tab.

2. Tap or click the Spelling button (REVIEW tab | Proofing group) to begin the spelling check in the current location, which in this case, is inside the caption text box.

3. If Publisher flags any words, choose the correct spelling in the Suggestions list, tap or click the Change button, and then continue the spelling check until the next error is identified or the end of the text box is reached.

4. Tap or click the Yes button (Microsoft Publisher dialog box) to tell Publisher to check the rest of the publication. If your publication displays a different error, correct or ignore it as necessary.

5. Tap or click the OK button (Microsoft Publisher dialog box) to close the dialog box.

To Run the Design Checker

The following steps run the Design Checker.

1. Tap or click FILE on the ribbon to open the Backstage view and, by default, select the Info tab.

2. Tap or click the Run Design Checker button in the Info gallery to display the Design Checker task pane.

3. If your publication has problems other than margin spacing, low resolution pictures, or objects near the margin, point to the problem in the 'Select an item to fix' box. When an arrow appears on the right side of the problem, tap or click the arrow and then tap or click the 'Go to this Item' command. Fix or ignore the flagged item as necessary.

4. Tap or click the Close button on the Design Checker task pane to close the Design Checker and return to the publication.

Hyphenation

Hyphenation refers to splitting a word that otherwise would extend beyond the right margin. Because Publisher bases hyphenation on words in its dictionary, it is a good idea to review the hyphenation. Publisher's hyphenation feature allows you to automatically or manually hyphenate the text, insert optional or **nonbreaking hyphens**, and set the maximum amount of space allowed between a word and the right margin without hyphenating the word. When you use automatic hyphenation, Publisher automatically inserts hyphens where they are needed. When you use manual hyphenation, Publisher searches for the text to hyphenate and asks you whether you want to insert the hyphens in the text. Some rules for hyphenation include:

- Hyphenate at standard syllable breaks.
- Do not change the hyphen location of words that already are hyphenated.
- Avoid hyphenating two lines in a row.
- Avoid hyphenating a line across text boxes or pages.
- Avoid hyphenations that leave only two letters at the beginning of the second line, when possible.
- Avoid hyphenating proper nouns.

To Check Hyphenation

1 EDIT OPTIONS | 2 IMPORT & CONNECT STORIES | 3 USE CONTINUED NOTICES | 4 CUSTOMIZE RIBBON
5 EDIT USING WORD | 6 CREATE MARGINAL ELEMENTS | 7 IMPORT GRAPHICS & REVISE | **8 CREATE TEMPLATE**

The following steps hyphenate the stories. *Why? Hyphenating allows you to make decisions about where the hyphens will be placed.* You will choose to hyphenate manually, which means you can specify where the hyphen should occur, rather than have Publisher hyphenate the story automatically.

- Navigate to page 1 and tap or click in the first column of the lead story.

- Display the TEXT BOX TOOLS FORMAT tab.

- Tap or click the Hyphenation button (TEXT BOX TOOLS FORMAT tab | Text group) to display the Hyphenation dialog box (Figure 3–76).

Q&A What is the hyphenation zone? The **hyphenation zone** is the maximum amount of space Publisher allows between a word and the right margin without hyphenating the word. To reduce the number of hyphens, increase the hyphenation zone. To reduce the ragged edge of the right margin, decrease the hyphenation zone.

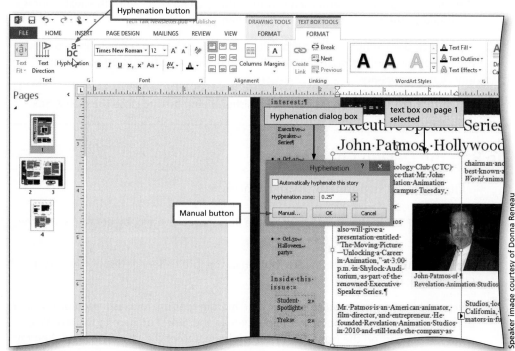

Figure 3–76

- If necessary, tap or click to remove the check mark in the 'Automatically hyphenate this story' check box.

- Tap or click the Manual button (Hyphenation dialog box) to hyphenate the story manually and to display the first hyphenation choice (Figure 3–77).

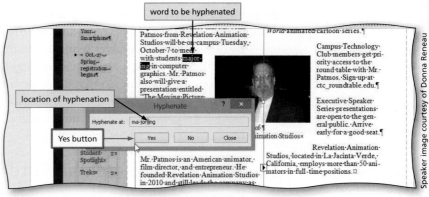

Figure 3 – 77

- Tap or click the Yes button to hyphenate the word, majoring, at the recommended place.

- Continue to tap or click the Yes button to accept Publisher's hyphenation until you get to the word, Series (Figure 3–78).

Q&A

Why is the text already hyphenated?
The default value is automatic hyphenation. Publisher hyphenates after the standard syllables.

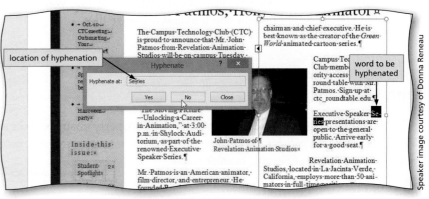

Figure 3 – 78

- Tap or click the No button so Publisher will not hyphenate the word, series, as proper nouns are not supposed to be hyphenated.

- Continue to tap or click the Yes or No button using the hyphenation rules listed previously.

- When Publisher finishes hyphenating the lead story, manually hyphenate the other stories in the newsletter.

Other Ways

1. Press CTRL+SHIFT+H, tap or click OK button (Hyphenation dialog box)

To Save the Revised Publication

The following step saves the publication again.

1 Tap or click the Save button on the Quick Access Toolbar to overwrite the previously saved file.

Creating a Template

Newsletters typically retain their masthead, color scheme, font scheme, and other graphics from issue to issue. In a first issue, you must make design choices and implement them to make sure the newsletter is displayed correctly — reviewing that takes time. You do

BTW

Quick Reference
For a table that lists how to complete the tasks covered in this book using touch gestures, the mouse, ribbon, shortcut menu, and keyboard, see the Quick Reference Summary at the back of this book, or visit the Quick Reference resource on the Student Companion Site located on www.cengagebrain.com. For detailed instructions about accessing available resources, visit www.cengage.com/ct/studentdownload or see the inside back cover of this book.

BTW

Tags
Tags are one of many file properties to help you find and organize the files. In addition to tags, other properties include the Date Modified, Author, and Subject. They become the keywords in the Properties dialog box. Unlike some predefined properties, tags can be anything you choose, such as "Newsletters," "Vacation," or even "My Stuff."

not have to do all of that for subsequent issues. Once the decisions have been made and the publication has been distributed, you can reuse the same publication as a template. Additionally, Publisher allows you to add it to the templates on your computer.

By default, Publisher saves templates in the My Templates folder for easy access from the Backstage view. When you open a saved template, a new publication is created from the template, so that users do not overwrite the template file. In lab situations, you should not save a personal template in the My Templates folder. You should save it on your own storage device and change the system properties to prevent overwriting, as shown in the next set of steps.

Saving the Template and Setting File Properties

Recall that in Chapter 1, you set file properties using the Properties command from the File menu. Two specific properties can be set at the time you create a publication or template. The author and tag properties can be entered into any of the Save As dialog boxes, which can save you several steps. A **tag** is a custom property used to help you find and organize files.

To Create a Template with Property Changes

1 EDIT OPTIONS | 2 IMPORT & CONNECT STORIES | 3 USE CONTINUED NOTICES | 4 CUSTOMIZE RIBBON
5 EDIT USING WORD | 6 CREATE MARGINAL ELEMENTS | 7 IMPORT GRAPHICS & REVISE | **8 CREATE TEMPLATE**

The following steps create a template with property changes and save it on a personal storage device. *Why? Even though Publisher has a folder specifically for templates, it is not recommended to save templates on lab computers or computers belonging to other people.*

1

- Tap or click FILE on the ribbon to open the Backstage view.

- Tap or click the Save As command and then double-tap or double-click Computer or SkyDrive to display the Save As dialog box.

- Type **Newsletter Template** to change the name of the publication. Do not press the ENTER key.

- Tap or click the 'Save as type' button to display the list of file types (Figure 3–79).

 Experiment

- Scroll through the many types of file formats available for publications.

Q&A Where should a company store its templates?

On a business computer, for an organization that routinely uses templates, you should save templates in the default location. Publisher stores templates within the program data in a folder named, Custom Office Templates. Templates stored in the default location are displayed in the catalog when you click the My Templates button. Templates, however, can be stored in several places: on a personal computer, on a web server, or on a common drive for use by multiple employees or students.

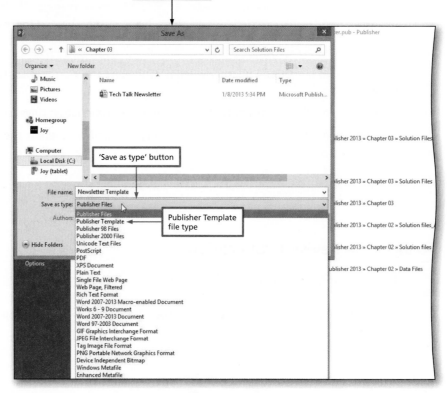

Figure 3–79

- Tap or click Publisher Template to choose to save the publication as a template.

- Navigate to your preferred storage location.

  If requested by your instructor, double-tap or double-click in the Authors text box in the lower portion of the dialog box, and then type your name to replace the text.

- Tap or click in the Tags text box, and then type **monthly newsletter** to add the tag words (Figure 3–80). The current text in the Tags text box will disappear as you start to type.

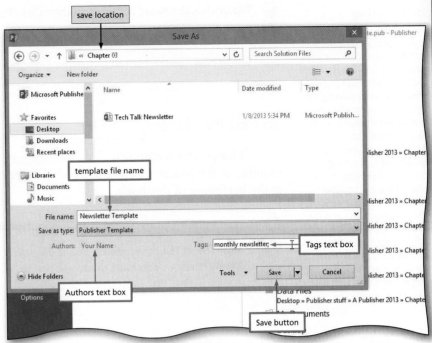

Figure 3 – 80

- Tap or click the Save button (Save As dialog box) to save the template.

To Print the Newsletter

If you have access to a printer that can accept 17×11.5 inch paper, you can print double-sided and then fold the paper to create the newsletter. If you want to print double-sided on 8.5×11 inch paper, the newsletter will print on the back and front of two pages that you then can staple. For a detailed example of the procedure summarized below, refer to Chapter 2.

The following steps print the newsletter.

1. Ready the printer according to the printer instructions. Tap or click FILE on the ribbon to open the Backstage view.

2. Tap or click the Print tab in the Backstage view to display the Print gallery.

3. Tap or click the Print button in the Print gallery to print the document.

4. Make any necessary changes to the print settings for your paper size and duplex printing.

5. When the printer stops, retrieve the printed document.

To Remove All Ribbon Customization

When working in a lab environment, it is advisable to remove the ribbon customization. The following steps remove all ribbon customization.

1. Tap or click FILE on the ribbon to open the Backstage view, and then click Options to display the Publisher Options dialog box.

2. Tap or click Customize Ribbon in the left pane (Publisher Options dialog box) to display the options for customizing the ribbon.

BTW

Conserving Ink and Toner
If you want to conserve ink or toner, you can instruct Publisher to print draft quality documents by tapping or clicking FILE on the ribbon to open the Backstage view, and tapping or clicking Print in the Backstage view to display the Print gallery. Tap or click the Printer Properties link, and then, depending on your printer, click the Print Quality button and choose Draft in the list. Close the Printer Properties dialog box and then tap or click the Print button as usual.

BTW

Distributing a Document
Instead of printing and distributing a hard copy of a document, you can distribute the document electronically. Options include sending the document via email; posting it on cloud storage (such as SkyDrive) and sharing the file with others; posting it on a social networking site, blog, or other website; and sharing a link associated with an online location of the document. You also can create and share a PDF or XPS image of the document, so that users can view the file in Acrobat Reader or XPS Viewer instead of in Publisher.

3 Tap or click the Reset button and then click 'Reset all customizations' in the list.

4 Tap or click the Yes button (Microsoft Office dialog box).

5 Tap or click the OK button (Publisher Options dialog box) to close the dialog box.

To Exit Publisher

This project is complete. The following steps exit Publisher. For a detailed example of the procedure summarized below, refer to the Office and Windows chapter at the beginning of this book.

1 To exit Publisher, tap or click the Close button on the right side of the title bar.

2 If a Microsoft Publisher dialog box is displayed, tap or click the Don't Save button so that any changes you have made are not saved.

Chapter Summary

In this chapter, you learned how to select template options for a newsletter, edit the masthead and sidebars, import stories, insert continued notices across pages, and create original stories using the Edit Story in Microsoft Word command. You edited sidebars and inserted a coupon. In revising the newsletter, you used drag-and-drop editing techniques, hyphenated the stories, checked the spelling, and ran the Design Checker. The items listed below include all the new Publisher skills you have learned in this chapter.

Change Settings
Create a Template with Property Changes (PUB 182)
Customize the Publisher Ribbon (PUB 153)
Remove All Ribbon Customization (PUB 183)
Set Page Options (PUB 135)

Change the Layout
Add Pages to a Newsletter (PUB 138)
Delete Pages in a Newsletter (PUB 138)
Duplicate an Object (PUB 168)
Send an Object to the Back (PUB 168)

Edit Text
Drag-and-Drop Text (PUB 177)
Edit a Story Using Microsoft Word (PUB 156)
Edit Sidebars (PUB 161)
Edit the Masthead (PUB 139)

Format Text
Break a Text Box Link (PUB 147)
Check Hyphenation (PUB 180)
Continue a Story across Pages (PUB 144)
Format while Editing in Microsoft Word (PUB 158)
Format with Continued Notices (PUB 148)

Insert Objects
Insert a Coupon (PUB 169)
Insert a Pull Quote (PUB 164)
Replace a Graphic Using the Shortcut Menu (PUB 171)

Import Text
Import a Text File (PUB 142)

Navigate the Publication
Follow a Story across Pages (PUB 145)
Manually Continue the Story across Pages (PUB 147)
Exit Word and Return to Publisher (PUB 159)

What decisions will you need to make when creating your next newsletter?
Use these guidelines as you complete the assignments in this chapter and create your own publications outside of this class.

1. Decide on the layout.
    a) Select a template and options that matches your need.
    b) Set columns and options for each page purpose and audience.
2. Edit the masthead.

3. Gather the text content.

    a) Import stories when possible.

    b) Edit stories in Microsoft Word when necessary.

    c) Flow long stories to other text boxes.

    d) Format continued stories with jump lines.

4. Create and edit marginal elements.

5. Insert other elements such as advertisements.

6. Edit graphics and captions.

7. Revise as necessary.

    a) Proofread and check the publication.

    b) Run an hyphenation check.

8. Create a template for future use.

CONSIDER THIS

How should you submit solutions to questions in the assignments identified with a symbol?

Every assignment in this book contains one or more questions identified with a symbol. These questions require you to think beyond the assigned publication. Present your solutions to the questions in the format required by your instructor. Possible formats may include one or more of these options: write the answer; create a document that contains the answer; present your answer to the class; discuss your answer in a group; record the answer as audio or video using a webcam, smartphone, or portable media player; or post answers on a blog, wiki, or website.

Apply Your Knowledge

Reinforce the skills and apply the concepts you learned in this chapter.

Creating a Newsletter

Note: To complete this assignment, you will be required to use the Data Files for Students. Visit www.cengage.com/ct/studentdownload for detailed instructions or contact your instructor for information about accessing the required files.

Instructions: The local food pantry would like you to create a newsletter for them. They have provided some stories and will give you others at a later time. You produce the publication shown in Figure 3–81.

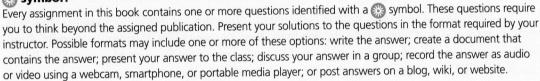

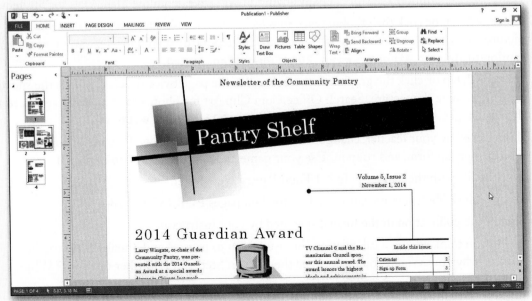

Figure 3–81

Continued >

Apply Your Knowledge *continued*

Perform the following tasks:

1. Run Publisher. Tap or click BUILT-IN, and then tap or click Newsletters.

2. Choose the Blends newsletter template, the Parrot color scheme, and the Oriel font scheme. Set the Page size to 'Two-page spread'.

3. Create the publication. Use the Options button (PAGE DESIGN tab | Template group) to choose a mixed format on pages 1 and 4. On page 2, include a calendar and a 3 column format. The date of your calendar may differ. On page 3, include a sign-up form and a 1 column format.

4. Edit the masthead as shown in Figure 3–81 on the previous page.

5. For the lead story, use the headline, `2014 Guardian Award`. Import the story, 2014 Guardian Award, from the Data Files for Students.

6. If necessary, customize the ribbon to display the 'Edit Story in Microsoft Word' button (REVIEW tab | New Group). See pages PUB 153 through 156 for instructions.

7. For the secondary story on page 1, press and hold or right-click the headline and then tap or click Best Fit on the shortcut menu. Type the headline `New Counseling Center to Open Soon`. Tap or click the placeholder text of the story. Tap or click the 'Edit Story in Microsoft Word' button (REVIEW tab | New Group). When Word is displayed, press CTRL+A to select all of the text. Type the following text, pressing the ENTER key at the end of each paragraph except the last:

`The Community Pantry will open a new counseling and referral center for its patrons on December 1. Counselors will be available to help with housing needs, utility assistance, transportation, and job placement, as well as our normal food services.`

`Through gracious donations from the Community Foundation, the Pantry has expanded its physical space as well. Trained counselors are available during our normal Pantry hours. If you need assistance with any of these programs, please stop by the Community Pantry and talk to a counselor.`

`The Pantry wants to be there when help is needed.`

Exit Word to return to Publisher.

8. Navigate to the bottom of page 2. Change the Inside Story Headline to `Thanksgiving Food Drive`. Import the story, Thanksgiving Food Drive, from the Data Files for Students.

9. On page 1, tap or click the graphic twice to select it. Use the shortcut menu to change the picture. Search Office.Com Clip Art for photos related to the search term, award. Change the caption to `Larry Wingate wins 2014 Guardian Award`.

10. On page 2, tap or click the graphic at the bottom of the page twice to select it. Use the shortcut menu to change the picture. Search Office.Com Clip Art for photos related to the search term, thanksgiving. Change the caption to `Share your blessings with others`.

11. If instructed by your teacher, change other text and graphics such as the table of contents sidebar, sign-up form, and coupon. Use your name and address at the top of page 4.

12. Save the file with the name Apply 3-1 Food Pantry Newsletter.

13. Remove the ribbon customization as described on pages PUB 183 and 184.

14. Submit the publication in the format specified by your instructor.

15. ✳ Do you think adding a calendar and sign-up form to pages 2 and 3 make them too busy? Why or why not? Would you rather type the story in Step 7 in Publisher or Word? Why?

Extend Your Knowledge

Extend the skills you learned in this chapter and experiment with new skills. You may need to use Help to complete the assignment.

Creating Page 1 of a Newsletter from Scratch

Instructions: Your school had a first-time callout for the Extreme Sports Club. You have been asked to create a layout for page 1 of a proposed newsletter. They need a newsletter to promote meetings and events. You decide to start from scratch to create the newsletter page shown in Figure 3–82.

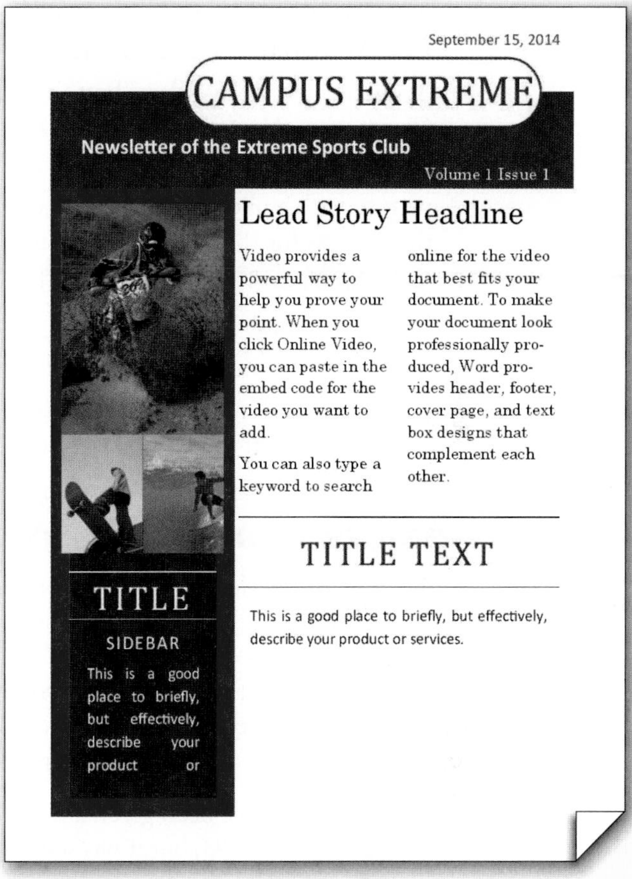

Perform the following tasks:

1. Run Publisher. Tap or click BUILT-IN, and then tap or click Newsletters. Scroll to the Blank Sizes area, and then tap or click the 1/2 A4 Booklet 5.827 × 8.268 thumbnail to choose a paper size.

2. Choose the Clay color scheme and the Textbook font scheme. Tap or click the CREATE button to create the publication. When Publisher asks to insert pages automatically, click the Yes button.

3. Use Help to read about inserting Page Parts. Tap or click the Page Parts button (INSERT tab | Building Blocks group) to display the gallery, and then choose the Portal heading to use as a masthead. When Publisher inserts the heading, resize it to fit within the margins.

4. Press and hold or right-click the Title text, and choose Best Fit on the shortcut menu. Type **CAMPUS EXTREME** to change the title. Press and hold or right-click the subtitle text, and choose Best Fit on the shortcut menu. Change the subtitle to **Newsletter of the Extreme Sports Club**. Change the date to **September 15, 2014**. If requested to do so by your instructor, use the current date in the newsletter.

Figure 3–82

5. Use the Draw Text Box button (HOME tab | Objects group) to add a text box in the lower-right portion of the masthead. Insert the text, **Volume 1, Issue 1**, and then change the text color to white.

6. Again using the Page Parts button (INSERT tab | Building Blocks group), insert the Convention (Layout 3) sidebar. Resize the sidebar to fit the space below the masthead and at the left margin as shown in Figure 3–82. Your display may differ, depending on how you resize the sidebar.

7. Draw a text box below the masthead, approximately .5 inches tall and 3 inches wide. Insert the text, **Lead Story Headline**. Press and hold or right-click the text, and then click Best Fit on the shortcut menu.

8. Draw a text box below the lead story headline, approximately 1.5 inches wide and 2.5 inches tall. Position the text box in the upper-left corner of the blank area of the page. Create another text box, the same size and place it in the upper-right corner of the blank area. Tap or click the first text box, and then click the Create Link button (TEXT BOX TOOLS FORMAT tab | Linking group). Tap or click the second text box to link the two.

Continued >

Extend Your Knowledge *continued*

9. If necessary, customize the ribbon to display the 'Edit Story in Microsoft Word' button (REVIEW tab | New group). See pages PUB 153 through 156 for instructions.

10. Tap or click the first empty text box. Tap or click the 'Edit Story in Microsoft Word' button (REVIEW tab | New group). When Word is displayed, type `=rand(2,2)` and then press the ENTER key to generate random text. Delete any extra hard returns at the end of the text. Exit Word to return to Publisher.

11. Again using the Page Parts button (INSERT tab | Building Blocks group), insert the Convention (Layout 1) story. Resize the story to fit the empty space at the bottom of the page.

12. Tap or click one of the pictures in the side bar twice, to select only the picture. Replace the picture with a photo from Office.com Clip Art using the search term, extreme sports. Repeat the process for the other two pictures.

13. Save the file with the name Extend 3-1 Extreme Sports Newsletter.

14. Remove the ribbon customization as described on pages PUB 183 and 184.

15. Submit the file in the format specified by your instructor.

16. ✸ When would you use a template instead of creating a newsletter from scratch? What other page parts might you add to subsequent pages? Why?

Analyze, Correct, Improve

Analyze a publication, correct all errors, and improve the design.

Formatting Long Stories

Note: To complete this assignment, you will be required to use the Data Files for Students. Visit www.cengage.com/ct/studentdownload for detailed instructions or contact your instructor for information about accessing the required files.

Instructions: You have been given a newsletter for a local historical society. The newsletter is shown in Figure 3–83, but it has several issues. You decide to improve the newsletter. Run Publisher and open the file, Analyze 3-1 History Newsletter.

(a) Page 1

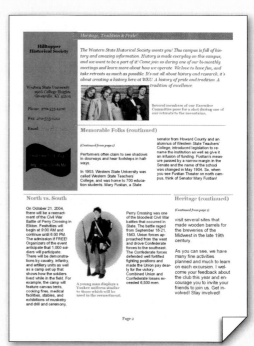

(b) Page 2

Figure 3–83

1. Correct   The publication has formatting errors related to text in overflow. Use Publisher tools to help you find those locations. Manually continue overflow stories to blank text boxes in the newsletter. Add headings to the continued stories. Use the format painter to match the headings to others in the newsletter.

2. Improve   None of the continued stories has jump lines to guide the reader to the appropriate page. Use the Next and Previous buttons to find the rest of the story. Add jump lines to every continued story. Hyphenate all stories. Check the sidebars for hyphenation issues and use soft returns where necessary. Save the document using the file name, Analyze 3-1 History Newsletter Complete. Submit the revised document in the format specified by your instructor.

3. ☀ How did you make decisions about where to hyphenate? Which rules of hyphenation did you use? Was changing the hyphenated sidebar difficult? Why?

In the Labs

Design, create, or modify a publication using the guidelines, concepts, and skills presented in this chapter. Labs 1 and 2, which increase in difficulty, require you to create a solution based on what you learned in the chapter; Lab 3 requires you to create a solution, which uses cloud and web technologies, by learning and investigating on your own from general guidance.

Lab 1: **Creating a Newsletter Template**

Problem: The symphonic orchestra has asked you to create a newsletter they can distribute to their patrons. Currently, they have given you content for page 1 and page 4. You are to leave place-holder text and graphics on the inside pages. You create the newsletter shown in Figure 3–84.

(a) Page 1

(b) Page 2

Director image courtesy of Joy Starks

Figure 3–84

1. Run Publisher. In the template gallery, tap or click BUILT-IN and then tap or click Newsletters.

2. In the More Installed Templates area, choose the Eclipse template.

3. Select the Aspect color scheme and the Etched font scheme. Choose to use a two-page spread. Create the publication.

Continued >

In the Labs *continued*

4. As you make changes to the newsletter, scroll and zoom as necessary. Turn on the display of formatting characters if desired.

5. Use the following text to edit the masthead on page 1.

    Newsletter Title: `Music Among the Maples`

    Volume and Issue: `Volume 3 Issue 4`

    Newsletter Date: `August 3, 2014`

    Business Name: `The Newsletter of the Williams Symphony Orchestra`

6. For the lead story, use the headline `Fall Concert Series Announced`. Import the lead story, Fall Concert Series, from the Data Files for Students.

7. Replace the graphic on page 1 using the shortcut menu. Search Office.com Clip Art for the term, maples. Edit the caption to read `Outdoor concerts, weather permitting`.

8. For the second story on page 1, use the headline, `McMillan Named New Conductor`. Import the story, McMillan Named New Conductor, from the Data Files for Students. When Publisher prompts you, flow the story to the last story on page 4. Use the same headline on page 4.

9. Add continued notices on page 1 and page 4 as appropriate.

10. At the bottom of page 4, tap or click the graphic twice to select it. Replace the graphic using the shortcut menu. Browse to the Data Files for Students and insert the Conductor graphic. Click the Fit button (PICTURE TOOLS FORMAT tab | Crop group) to make the graphic fit the area. If requested to do so by your instructor, use your picture instead of the one supplied in the Data Files for Students. Edit the caption to read `Anita McMillan, artistic director-conductor`.

11. Check your publication for spelling and design errors, and fix or ignore the flagged items as necessary. Hyphenate the stories according to the hyphenation rules on page PUB 180.

12. Save the newsletter on your storage device with the file name, Lab 3-1 Symphony Newsletter. Save the file again, this time as a Publisher template, named Lab 3-1 Symphony Newsletter Template.

13. Submit the file as directed by your instructor.

14. ✳ How do the font scheme and color scheme compliment the topic of the newsletter? How do you think page 1 would have looked if you had changed it to a mixed column format? Why might you want to change the format?

Lab 2: Publisher Newsletter Choices

Note: To complete this assignment, you will be required to use the Data Files for Students. Visit www.cengage.com/ct/studentdownload for detailed instructions or contact your instructor for information about accessing the required files.

Problem: Use a copy of a newsletter that you regularly receive, or obtain one from a friend, company, or school. Using the principles in this chapter, analyze the newsletter.

Run Publisher. Open the publication, Lab 3-2 Newsletter Analysis Table, from the Data Files for Students. Use the skills you learned in editing sidebars to fill in each of the empty cells in the table as it applies to your selected newsletter. The topics to look for are listed below:

- Purpose
- Audience
- Paper
- Distribution

- Font and color scheme
- Consistency
- Alignment
- Repeated elements

- Continued notices and ease of navigation
- Sidebars, pull quotes, patterns, etc.

Print the publication and attach a copy of the newsletter. Turn in both to your instructor.

Lab 3: Expand Your World: Cloud and Web Technologies
Converting Files

Problem: You would like to explore converting your newsletter to formats other than the .pub Publisher format. While Publisher has many formats in the Save As type list, a cloud tool may have even more choices.

Instructions:

1. Open a browser and go to zamzar.com (Figure 3–85).

2. In Step 1 of the Convert Files section, tap or click the Browse button, or the Choose Files button depending on your browser, and navigate to one of your completed newsletters.

3. In Step 2, tap or click the 'Convert files(s) to:' box and choose a conversion format such as html or an e-book format.

4. In Step 3, enter your email address.

5. In Step 4, tap or click the Convert button to send the converted file to your email. If you receive a message indicating the conversion is about to happen, tap or click the OK button.

6. When you receive the email from Zamzar, tap or click the link provided, and then tap or click the Download Now button. Your browser should direct you to save the download.

7. If your download is a compressed file, press and hold or right-click the zipped file to display a shortcut menu. Tap or click Extract or Extract All to extract the file.

8. Open the converted file.

9. Submit the assignment in the format specified by your instructor.

10. ✱ What format might you use to post your newsletter on the web? Would an HTML file be better than a download link? Why or why not? When might you convert to a PDF format?

Figure 3–85

✸ Consider This: Your Turn

Apply your creative thinking and problem solving skills to design and implement a solution.

1: Using Publisher vs. Word

Personal/Academic

Part 1: Using Publisher, create a blank print publication with a large text box that fills the page. Using the Edit Story in Microsoft Word feature, type an assignment, such as an essay or short report, for one of your classes.

Part 2: ✸ As you have worked in Publisher, make a list of things you found easier to do in Publisher and three things you found easier to do in Word.

2: Creating a Money Newsletter

Professional

Part 1: Use the Cascade newsletter template to create a newsletter template about the wise use of money and spending. Use the Green Color Scheme and the Trek font scheme. Use the title, You and Your Money. On page 1, change the lead story headline to The Road to Financial Freedom (you may use the default text in the story itself). Change the secondary story headline to You Take Over the Wheel (you may use the default text in the story itself). Link the story to one of the stories on page 2, and change the headline there as well. Replace the graphics with suitable pictures and caption. Submit your assignment in the format specified by your instructor.

Part 2: ✸ What other kinds of stories might you include in a money newsletter such as this one? Where might those stories come from? Who might be the author/organization for this newsletter? Who might be the audience?

3: Researching Templates

Research and Collaboration

Part 1: Many clubs and organizations publish their newsletters on the web. Browse the web and look for examples of newsletters. Choose a newsletter that you think displays good desktop publishing practices. Print the newsletter or copy its web address to distribute to each team member. Make a list of each object in the newsletter, such as the masthead, graphics, captions, stories, headlines, marginal elements, continued notices, etc. Discuss the newsletters and note which parts were most effective. List three things that stand out as good examples of newsletter content. List three things that need to be improved.

Part 2: ✸ How did you evaluate effectiveness? Did the marginal elements add value to the newsletter? How so? What elements caused you to read further into the newsletter and its stories? Why?

Learn Online

Reinforce what you learned in this chapter with games, exercises, training, and many other online activities and resources.

Student Companion Site Reinforce chapter terms and concepts using review questions, flash cards, practice tests, and interactive learning games, such as a crossword puzzle. These and other online activities and resources are available at no additional cost on www.cengagebrain.com. Visit www.cengage.com/ct/studentdownload for detailed instructions about accessing the resources available at the Student Companion Site.

4 Creating a Custom Publication from Scratch

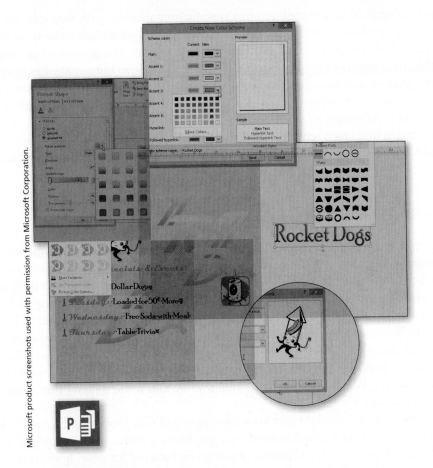

Objectives

You will have mastered the material in this chapter when you can:

- Create a custom publication size
- Create color and font schemes
- Group and ungroup objects
- Convert a picture to a drawing object and edit
- Rotate and flip graphics
- Add to the building block library
- Change the line spacing of text
- Align objects and wrap text
- Use WordArt

- Customize a bullet
- Insert a shape
- Format an object with a gradient fill, differentiating among text, patterns, pictures, tints, and shades
- Fill a shape with a picture and format a picture with a shape
- Recolor a graphic
- Delete customizations

4 | Creating a Custom Publication from Scratch

Introduction

Customizing publications, tailored to a specific organization, with font schemes, color schemes, page dimensions, and margins, allows desktop publishers to be more creative and provide made-to-order publications for their clients. The process of developing a publication that communicates a company brand and specific requirements entails careful analysis and planning. Coordinating design choices with the customer and gathering necessary information will determine the design and style that will be most successful in delivering the company's message. Whether you are creating a publication from scratch or using a template, many settings and preferences can be customized and saved. Once saved, the publication can be reused, resulting in increased productivity.

Project—Table Card

Chapter 4 uses Publisher to create a restaurant table card. **Table cards** commonly are displayed in acrylic stands on counters and tables in many kinds of businesses. Sometimes they are folded to create tent cards. This table card advertises daily specials and events for a hot dog emporium named Rocket Dogs, and includes graphics, bulleted items, and WordArt. The completed image is displayed in Figure 4–1.

To illustrate some of the customizable features of Microsoft Publisher, this project presents a series of steps to create the table card with a customized color scheme that uses the company colors: red, tan, and gold. A customized font scheme will include the Poor Richard font for the heading and the secondary font, Magneto, for the body text.

The graphics combine clip art with shapes and fills, repeating the color scheme. With a solid color in the background, two graphics are edited and repurposed as a logo for Rocket Dogs. Finally, a WordArt object and a bulleted list provide the text content as shown in Figure 4–1. Similar graphics appear within shapes in the lower-right corner.

Figure 4–1

Roadmap

BTW

Blank Publications
If you want Publisher to start with a blank publication, rather than the list of templates, each time you start the program, do the following. Tap or click the File tab and then tap or click Options. Tap or click the General tab (Publisher Options dialog box) and then remove the check mark in the 'Show the New template gallery when starting Publisher' check box.

In this chapter, you will learn how to create the publication shown in Figure 4–1 on the previous page. The following roadmap identifies general activities you will perform as you progress through this chapter:

1. CUSTOMIZE the page size, margins, font schemes, and color schemes.
2. EDIT GRAPHICS.
3. Create and USE BUILDING BLOCKS.
4. EDIT and FORMAT TEXT with line spacing, text effects, and other formatting.
5. CREATE BULLETED LISTS.
6. Insert and FORMAT SHAPES.
7. APPLY CUSTOMIZATIONS.
8. DELETE CUSTOMIZATIONS.

At the beginning of step instructions throughout the chapter, you will see an abbreviated form of this roadmap. The abbreviated roadmap uses colors to indicate chapter progress: gray means the chapter is beyond that activity, blue means the task being shown is covered in that activity, and black means that activity is yet to be covered. For example, the following abbreviated roadmap indicates the chapter would be showing a task in the Edit and Format Text activity.

1 CUSTOMIZE | 2 EDIT GRAPHICS | 3 USE BUILDING BLOCKS | **4 EDIT & FORMAT TEXT**
5 CREATE BULLETED LISTS | 6 FORMAT SHAPES | 7 APPLY CUSTOMIZATIONS | 8 DELETE CUSTOMIZATIONS

Use the abbreviated roadmap as a progress guide while you read or step through the instructions in this chapter.

To Run Publisher

One of the few differences between Windows 7 and Windows 8 occurs in the steps to run Publisher. If you are using Windows 7, click the Start button, type **Publisher** in the 'Search programs and files' box, click Publisher 2013, and then, if necessary, maximize the Publisher window. For a summary of the steps to run Publisher in Windows 7, refer to the Quick Reference located at the back of this book.

If you are using a computer to step through the project in this chapter and you want your screens to match the figures in this book, you should change your screen's resolution to 1366×768. For information about how to change a computer's resolution, refer to the Office and Windows chapter at the beginning of this book.

The following steps, which assume Windows 8 is running, use the Start screen or the search box to run Publisher based on a typical installation. You may need to ask your instructor how to run Publisher on your computer. For a detailed example of the procedure summarized below, refer to the Office and Windows chapter.

1 Scroll the Start screen and search for a Publisher 2013 tile. If your Start screen contains a Publisher 2013 tile, tap or click it to run Publisher and then proceed to Step 5. If the Start screen does not contain the Publisher 2013 tile, proceed to the next step to search for the Publisher app.

2 Swipe in from the right edge of the screen or point to the upper-right corner of the screen to display the Charms bar and then tap or click the Search charm on the Charms bar to display the Search menu.

3 Type **Publisher** as the search text in the Search box, and watch the search results appear in the Apps list.

4 Tap or click Publisher 2013 in the search results to run Publisher.

5 If the Publisher window is not maximized, tap or click the Maximize button on its title bar to maximize the window.

Custom-Sized Publication

Publications come in many different sizes and shapes. Customers and designers do not always want to use one of the preset sizes, such as 8 1/2 × 11. In those cases, you may want to create a **custom-sized publication** with specific dimensions, orientation, and margins. Custom-sized publications are used for everything from newspaper advertisements to greeting cards to church bulletins.

CONSIDER THIS

What steps should I take when creating a custom publication?
Define the purpose of the publication. Choose a font scheme and color scheme to match the customer's logo or company colors. Define which pieces of business information you plan to use. Does the proposed publication fulfill the need? If you are working from scratch, look at similar publication templates. Choose margins and a paper size that will help standardize the publication with others used in the industry.

To Select a Blank Publication

1 CUSTOMIZE | 2 EDIT GRAPHICS | 3 USE BUILDING BLOCKS | 4 EDIT & FORMAT TEXT
5 CREATE BULLETED LISTS | 6 FORMAT SHAPES | 7 APPLY CUSTOMIZATIONS | 8 DELETE CUSTOMIZATIONS

When you first start Publisher, the template gallery displays a list of featured and built-in templates, as well as blank publications. Most users select a publication template and then begin editing. It is not always the case, however, that a template will fit every situation. *Why? Sometimes you want to think through a publication while manipulating objects on a blank page, trying different shapes, colors, graphics, and effects. Other times you may have specific goals for a publication, such as size or orientation, that do not match any of the templates.* For these cases, Publisher provides **blank publications** with no preset objects or design, allowing you to start from scratch.

The following step selects a blank print publication.

- Tap or click the Blank 8.5 × 11" thumbnail in the template gallery to create a blank publication in the Publisher window (Figure 4–2).

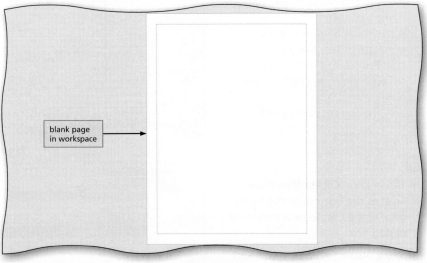

blank page in workspace

Figure 4–2

To Display Formatting Marks

As discussed in a previous chapter, it is helpful to display formatting marks, which indicate where in the publication you pressed the ENTER key, SPACEBAR, and other keys. The following step displays formatting marks.

1 If the Special Characters button (HOME tab | Paragraph group) is not selected already, tap or click it to display formatting marks on the screen.

To Hide the Page Navigation Pane

The following step hides the Page Navigation pane.

 If the Page Navigation pane is displayed, tap or click the 'Current page in publication' button on the status bar to hide the Page Navigation pane.

To Create a Custom Page Size

1 CUSTOMIZE | 2 EDIT GRAPHICS | 3 USE BUILDING BLOCKS | 4 EDIT & FORMAT TEXT
5 CREATE BULLETED LISTS | 6 FORMAT SHAPES | 7 APPLY CUSTOMIZATIONS | 8 DELETE CUSTOMIZATIONS

The following steps create a new, custom page size. **Why?** *The customer has requested a table card that measures 5 × 7.* Publisher and other Office applications use the term **page setup** to refer to the process of changing the document margins, orientation, and size, among other settings.

❶

- Tap or click PAGE DESIGN on the ribbon to display the PAGE DESIGN tab.

- Tap or click the 'Choose Page Size' button (PAGE DESIGN tab | Page Setup group) to display the list of standard page sizes and options for other sizes (Figure 4–3).

Q&A How does the 'Create New Page Size' command differ from the Page Setup command?

When you chose the 'Create New Page Size' command, you can name and save the settings. A new thumbnail will appear in the template gallery every time you start Publisher, which allows you to reuse the page size for other publications. Page Setup affects only the current publication.

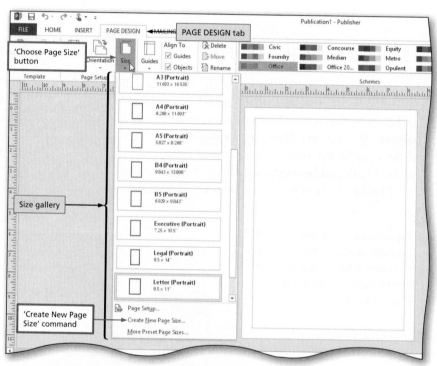

Figure 4–3

❷

- Tap or click 'Create New Page Size' at the bottom of the list to display the Create New Page Size dialog box.

- In the Name text box, type `5x7 Table Card` (Create New Page Size dialog box) to name the custom size.

- Tap or click the Layout type button to display the list of layouts (Figure 4–4).

 Experiment

- One at a time, tap or click each of the layout types in the list to view additional settings that may appear. Note how the preview changes.

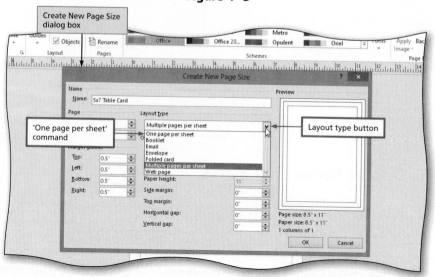

Figure 4–4

- Tap or click 'One page per sheet' to display the settings associated with single publications on a sheet of paper.

- Select the text in the Width text box, and then type 5 to set the width for the publication.

- Select the text in the Height text box, and then type 7 to set the height for the publication.

- One at a time, select the text in each of the four Margin guides text boxes and type 0 to remove the margin on each side of the publication (Figure 4–5).

Q&A Why are the margins set to zero?
The table card color will go all the way to the edge of the paper.

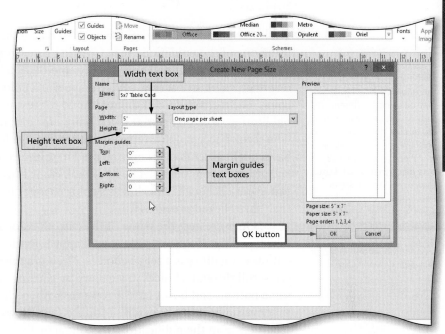

Figure 4–5

- Tap or click the OK button to save the page layout, size, and margins (Figure 4–6).

Q&A Where will the custom layout be saved?
The saved layout will appear in the template gallery when you first start Publisher, or when you click FILE on the ribbon and then tap or click the New tab. To view custom sizes in the template gallery, click the 'More Blank Page Sizes' thumbnail.

Experiment

- Tap or click the 'Choose Page Size' button (PAGE DESIGN tab | Page Setup group) to verify the new page size has been saved.

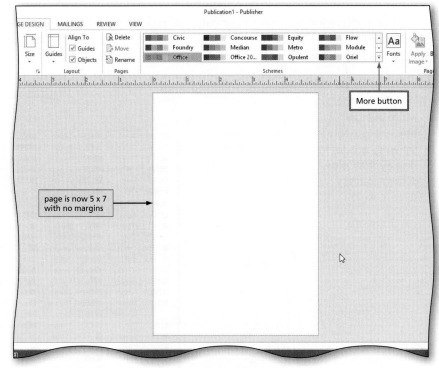

Figure 4–6

Other Ways

1. In template gallery, tap or click 'More Blank Page Sizes' thumbnail, tap or click 'Create new page size' thumbnail, enter values, tap or click OK button (Create New Page Size dialog box)

2. To change margins, tap or click Adjust Margins button (PAGE DESIGN tab | Page Setup group), tap or click Custom Margins, enter margin values on Margin Guides tab, tap or click OK button (Layout Guides dialog box)

Custom Color Schemes

BTW
Color Palette
If your color palette contains fewer colors than shown in this book, your computer may be using a different color setting. To check your setting, tap or click the Start button on the Windows 8 taskbar and then type **adjust screen resolution**. Tap or click Adjust Screen Resolution in the search list, and then tap or click the Advanced settings link. Tap or click the Colors button on the Monitor tab, and then tap or click True Color (32 bit).

Publisher provides an option for users to create their own color schemes rather than using one of the predefined sets. Creating a **custom color scheme** means choosing your own colors that will apply to text and objects in a publication. You may choose one main color, five accent colors, a hyperlink color, and a followed hyperlink color. The main color commonly is used for text in major, eye-catching areas of the publication. The first accent color is used for graphical lines, boxes, and separators. The second accent color typically is used as fill color in prominent publication shapes. Subsequent accent colors may be used in several ways, including shading, text effects, and alternate font colors. The hyperlink color is used as the font color for hyperlink text. After clicking a hyperlink, its color changes to show users which path, or trail, they have clicked previously.

Once created, the name of the custom color scheme appears in the list of color schemes. The chosen colors also will appear in the galleries related to shapes, fills, and outlines. A **gallery** is a set of choices, often graphical, arranged in a grid or in a list. You can scroll through choices in a gallery by clicking the gallery's scroll arrows. Recall that some buttons and boxes have arrows that, when clicked, also display a gallery. Most galleries support **live preview**, a feature that allows you to point to a gallery choice and see its effect in the publication, without actually selecting the choice.

To Create a New Color Scheme

1 CUSTOMIZE | 2 EDIT GRAPHICS | 3 USE BUILDING BLOCKS | 4 EDIT & FORMAT TEXT
5 CREATE BULLETED LISTS | 6 FORMAT SHAPES | 7 APPLY CUSTOMIZATIONS | 8 DELETE CUSTOMIZATIONS

The publication will use accent colors of red, gold, and tan, as well as a black main color for text. *Why?* *The customer wants to emulate the colors of his product, red for the hotdog, and tan for the bun.* The following steps create a custom color scheme.

1

• Tap or click the More button (PAGE DESIGN tab | Schemes group) to display the Colors Scheme gallery (Figure 4–7).

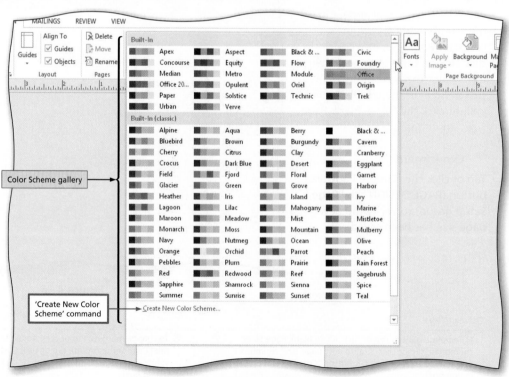

Figure 4–7

2

- Tap or click 'Create New Color Scheme' to display the Create New Color Scheme dialog box.

- Type **Rocket Dogs** in the Color scheme name text box (Create New Color Scheme dialog box) to name the color scheme with the same name as the company (Figure 4–8).

Q&A What if I do not enter a name for the modified color scheme?
Publisher assigns a name that begins with the word, Custom, followed by a number (i.e., Custom 8).

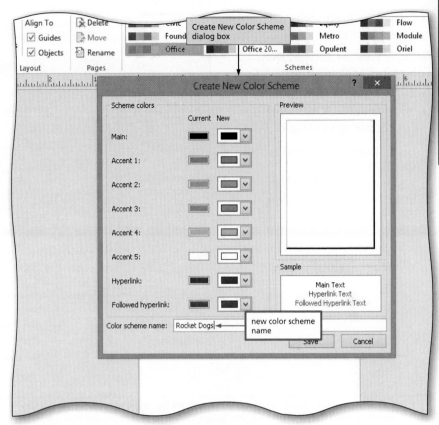

Figure 4–8

3

- In the Scheme colors area, click the New button next to the Accent 1 color to display a gallery of color choices (Figure 4–9).

🔎 **Experiment**

- Point to each color in the gallery to display its name

Q&A Why is this color gallery different from others?
This color gallery is a general palette of colors. It does not display the typical accent colors across the top, because you are choosing the accent colors in this dialog box.

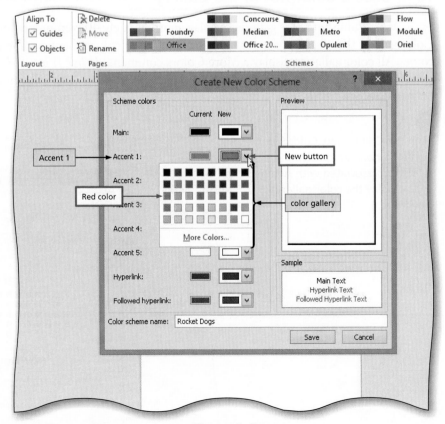

Figure 4–9

- Tap or click Red to select the Accent 1 color.

- Tap or click the Accent 2, New button, and then tap or click Gold to select the Accent 2 color.

- Do not close the Create New Color Scheme dialog box (Figure 4–10).

Q&A Can I delete a color scheme once I create it?

Yes. To delete a color scheme, first display the list of color schemes, and then press and hold or right-click the custom color scheme. Tap or click Delete Scheme on the shortcut menu.

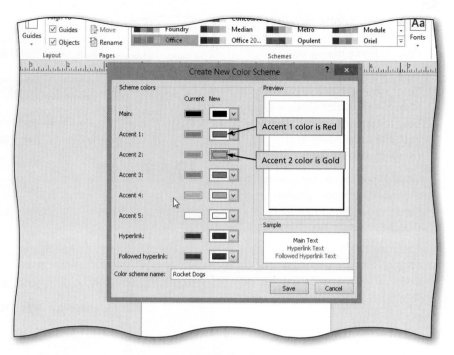

Figure 4–10

Other Ways

1. In template information pane, tap or click Color scheme box, scroll to end of list, tap or click Create new, enter values, tap or click Save button (Create New Color Scheme dialog box)

To Choose a Color not in the Gallery

1 CUSTOMIZE | 2 EDIT GRAPHICS | 3 USE BUILDING BLOCKS | 4 EDIT & FORMAT TEXT
5 CREATE BULLETED LISTS | 6 FORMAT SHAPES | 7 APPLY CUSTOMIZATIONS | 8 DELETE CUSTOMIZATIONS

Most Publisher color galleries display approximately 40 common colors. For example, in the Font Color gallery the 40 colors are variations of the chosen color scheme. Some galleries also display recently used colors. All color galleries display a More Colors command. *Why? When clicked, the command allows the user to choose from other Standard colors, Custom colors, and Pantone colors.* The following steps choose a color from the Standard colors.

- In the Create New Color Scheme dialog box, tap or click the New button associated with Accent 3 to display the color gallery (Figure 4–11).

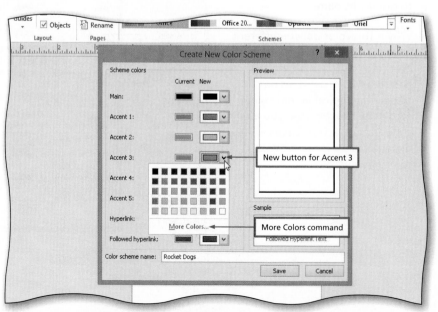

Figure 4–11

- Tap or click More Colors to display the Colors dialog box.
- If necessary, tap or click the Standard tab, and then tap or click the desired color (in this case, the tan color, second from the left, in the next-to-the-last row) (Figure 4–12).

- Tap or click the OK button (Colors dialog box) to select the chosen color.
- Tap or click the Save button (Create New Color Scheme dialog box) to save the new color scheme.

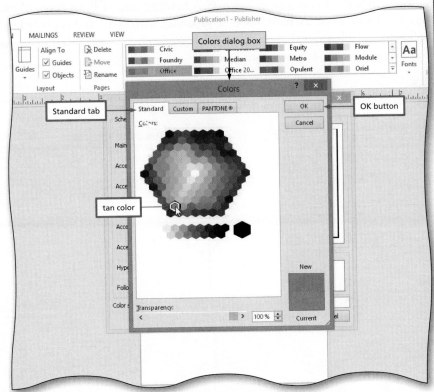

Figure 4–12

Other Ways

1. In any color gallery, tap or click More Colors, tap or click desired color, tap or click OK button (Colors dialog box)

Custom Font Schemes

Publisher provides an option for users to create their own font schemes rather than using one of the predefined sets. Creating a **custom font scheme** means choosing your own fonts to use in a publication. You may choose one heading font and one body font. Choosing complimentary fonts takes practice. In general, either the heading font and body font should match exactly but perhaps appear in different sizes or formats (such as italics), or the two fonts should contrast with each other dramatically in features such as size, type ornamentation, and direction. **Type ornamentation** refers to serif, structure, form, or style.

Custom font schemes contain a name that will appear in the font scheme list. The chosen fonts also will appear in the Styles list. The body font will be the default font for new text boxes.

BTW
The Ribbon and Screen Resolution
Publisher may change how the groups and buttons within the groups appear on the ribbon, depending on the computer's screen resolution. Thus, your ribbon may look different from the ones in this book if you are using a screen resolution other than 1366 × 768.

1 CUSTOMIZE | 2 EDIT GRAPHICS | 3 USE BUILDING BLOCKS | 4 EDIT & FORMAT TEXT

To Create a New Font Scheme

5 CREATE BULLETED LISTS | 6 FORMAT SHAPES | 7 APPLY CUSTOMIZATIONS | 8 DELETE CUSTOMIZATIONS

Because the Rocket Dogs company wants to portray motion and activity as well as good food, a customized font scheme will include the Magneto font, which implies motion. Magneto fonts have been used in the transportation industry and as title fonts in magazines. Magneto is a **script font**, which looks like handwriting, as all characters are connected. Script fonts should not be used for all-caps text. ***Why?*** *All capital letters written in script are difficult to read.* A heading font of Poor Richard provides a nice contrast with the Magneto font. Poor Richard is a TrueType font with serifs and is easily legible in print publications. **TrueType** refers to scalable fonts that produce high-quality characters on both computer screens and printers. The following steps create a new font scheme.

- Tap or click the Scheme Fonts button (PAGE DESIGN tab | Schemes group) to display the Scheme Fonts gallery (Figure 4–13).

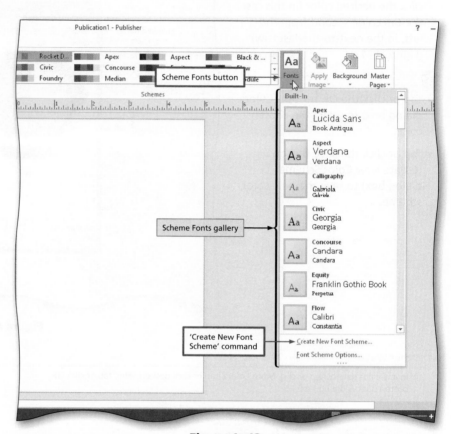

Figure 4–13

- Tap or click 'Create New Font Scheme' to display the Create New Font Scheme dialog box.

- Type **Rocket Dogs** in the Font scheme name text box (Create New Font Scheme dialog box) to name the font scheme with the same name as the company (Figure 4–14).

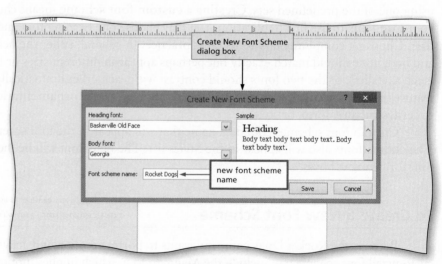

Figure 4–14

3

- Tap or click the Heading font arrow to display the list of fonts (Figure 4–15).

Experiment

- Tap or click different fonts and watch the Sample box change. When you are finished, click the Heading font arrow again.

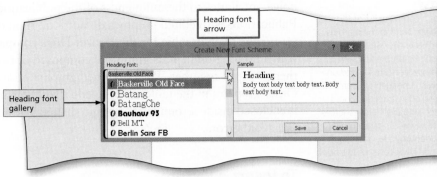

Figure 4–15

4

- Scroll as necessary and then tap or click the Poor Richard font or a similar serif font to select it.

- Tap or click the Body font arrow, and then tap or click Magneto or a similar script font to select the body font (Figure 4–16).

 Can I delete a font scheme once I create it?

Yes. To delete a font scheme, display the list of font schemes and press and hold or right-click the custom font scheme. Tap or click Delete Scheme on the shortcut menu. You also can rename or duplicate the scheme.

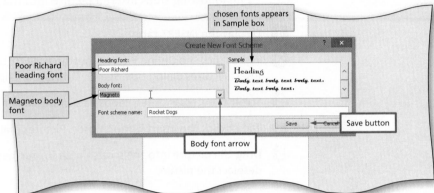

Figure 4–16

5

- Tap or click the Save button (Create New Font Scheme dialog box) to save the new font scheme.

 Where is the new font scheme stored?

Each font scheme that you create will appear at the top of the gallery, alphabetized by name.

Other Ways

1. In template information pane, click Color scheme box, scroll to end of list, click Create new, enter values, click Save button (Create New Color Scheme dialog box)

What is the best way to choose a layout and elements?

Carefully consider the necessary elements and their placement. Choose margins and a paper size that will help standardize the publication. Decide whether to add dated material or prices. Think about alignment of elements and proximity of similar data. Create appropriate contrast or repetition when using fonts and colors.

If you are working for someone, draw a storyboard and get it approved before you begin. If you need to create objects from scratch, have someone else evaluate your work and give you constructive feedback.

CONSIDER THIS

Editing Graphics

Recall that you have inserted graphics or pictures into publications by choosing them online and by importing them from a file. Graphics add value and visual flair to publications; however, to create a unique publication for a business, it is good to enhance and customize the graphic through editing. Many times customers are bored

BTW

BTWs

For a complete list of the BTWs found in the margins of this book, visit the BTW resource on the Student Companion Site located on www.cengagebrain.com. For detailed instructions about accessing available resources, visit www.cengage.com/ct/studentdownload or see the inside back cover of this book.

by stock graphics and clip art because of their overuse. A well-edited graphic not only contributes to the uniqueness of the publication, but also adds a personal touch. Publications with edited graphics do not look rigid or computer-generated.

The main graphic for the Rocket Dogs company is a picture of a traveling rocket with a hot dog on it. This graphic is composed of two separate graphics, edited, and then grouped together. The combined graphic is saved as a picture for future use. Other graphics in the table card include a soda can and a package of french fries. Each is enclosed inside a rounded rectangle shape. Editing graphics in the scratch area helps you avoid errors.

To Insert a Picture

The following steps insert a picture into the publication.

1 Display the INSERT tab.

2 Tap or click the Online Pictures button (INSERT tab | Illustrations group) to display the Insert Pictures dialog box. Search Office.com Clip Art for the term, `rocket`.

3 Scroll as necessary, then choose a picture similar to the one in Figure 4–17.

4 Tap or click the Insert button (Insert Pictures dialog box) to insert the picture.

5 Drag the picture into the scratch area for further editing. Zoom to 150%. Do not deselect the picture.

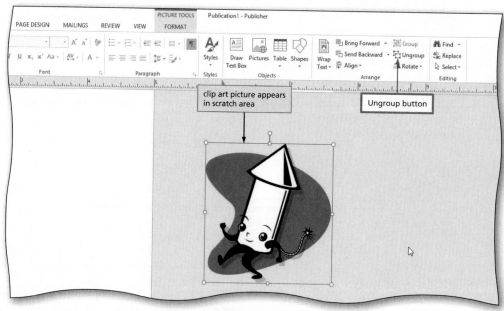

Figure 4–17

BTW

Touch Screen Differences

The Office and Windows interfaces may vary if you are using a touch screen. For this reason, you might notice that the function or appearance of your touch screen differs slightly from this chapter's presentation.

Grouping and Ungrouping Objects

Many clip art graphics are a combination of line drawings and shapes. If you want to edit the graphic, you have to ungroup the graphic. When you **ungroup** objects, their parts can be selected and manipulated individually. Alternately, when multiple objects are selected, you can **group** them, which means they stay together for purposes such as cutting, pasting, moving, and formatting. Some clip art pictures must first be converted to a different format, the Microsoft Office drawing object format, before ungrouping.

To Convert a Picture into a Drawing Object

1 CUSTOMIZE | 2 EDIT GRAPHICS | 3 USE BUILDING BLOCKS | 4 EDIT & FORMAT TEXT
5 CREATE BULLETED LISTS | 6 FORMAT SHAPES | 7 APPLY CUSTOMIZATIONS | 8 DELETE CUSTOMIZATIONS

The following step changes the picture into a Microsoft Office drawing object. ***Why?*** *Publisher provides more ways to edit drawing objects than it does for pictures.*

1

- If necessary, select the picture and display the PICTURE TOOLS FORMAT tab.
- Tap or click the Ungroup button (PICTURE TOOLS FORMAT tab | Arrange group) to begin the ungroup process.
- When the Microsoft Publisher dialog box is displayed, click the Yes button to convert the picture into a Microsoft Office drawing object. Do not deselect (Figure 4–18).

Figure 4–18

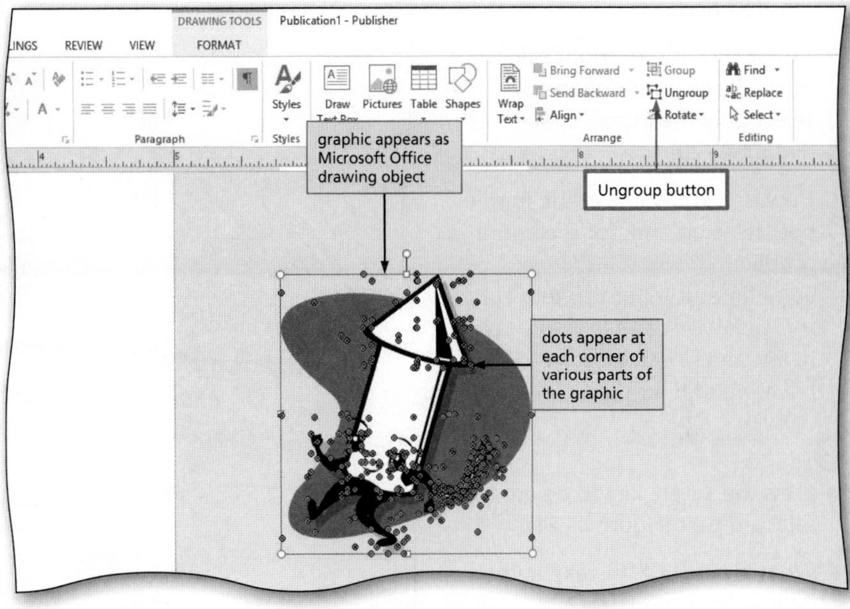

Q&A What are all of the little dots on the graphic?
Those dots are place markers that occur at the corners of individual parts of the graphic.

Why do I have to click the Ungroup button to change the format of a picture?
Beginning the ungroup process provides easy access to the conversion dialog box.

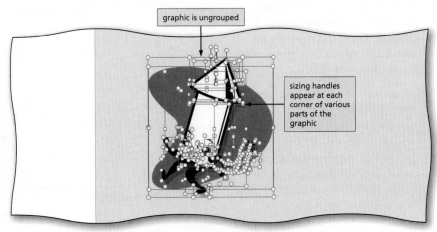

Other Ways

1. Press and hold or right-click graphic, tap or click Ungroup on shortcut menu
2. Select graphic, press SHIFT+CTRL+G

To Ungroup the Graphic

1 CUSTOMIZE | 2 EDIT GRAPHICS | 3 USE BUILDING BLOCKS | 4 EDIT & FORMAT TEXT
5 CREATE BULLETED LISTS | 6 FORMAT SHAPES | 7 APPLY CUSTOMIZATIONS | 8 DELETE CUSTOMIZATIONS

The following step ungroups the rocket graphic. ***Why?*** *To create the logo for Rocket Dogs, you need to edit specific parts of the graphic, rather than the graphic as a whole.*

1

- Display the DRAWING TOOLS FORMAT tab.
- Tap or click the Ungroup button (DRAWING TOOLS FORMAT tab | Arrange group) to ungroup the graphic (Figure 4–19).

Figure 4–19

Q&A Is this Ungroup button different from the one in the previous steps?
Yes. This Ungroup button is on the DRAWING TOOLS FORMAT tab, which displays more editing tools than does the PICTURE TOOLS FORMAT tab in the previous steps.

Other Ways

1. Press and hold or right-click graphic, tap or click Ungroup on shortcut menu
2. Select graphic, press SHIFT+CTRL+G

To Edit an Ungrouped Graphic

The following steps delete the purple parts of the graphic. **Why?** *The purple color is not part of the Rocket Dogs color scheme; the customer does not wish to include it in the new logo.*

- Deselect by clicking outside of the selected parts.

- Tap or click the far-right side of the large purple shape to select only the purple shape (Figure 4–20).

Q&A How do I know I have the purple part selected and not the entire graphic?
Sometimes it is hard to tell, but in this case, you can see the foot is below the selection, so you do not have the entire graphic selected.

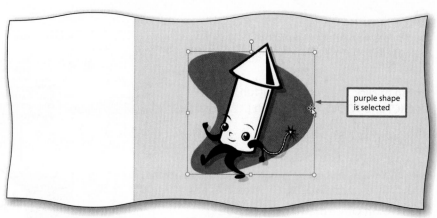

purple shape is selected

Figure 4–20

- Press the DELETE key to delete the selected part (Figure 4–21).

Q&A What if I make a mistake and delete the wrong part?
Tap or click the Undo button (Quick Access tool bar) to undo and select again.

purple shape is deleted

Figure 4–21

- Repeat Steps 1 and 2 to delete the other purple portions of the graphic. Zoom as necessary to select and delete only the purple parts. (Figure 4–22).

Q&A What is the best way to ensure that I have the correct part selected before I delete?
You should zoom in, and then tap or click an area completely separate from other parts of the graphic, such as the purple end of the rocket's fuse in this case.

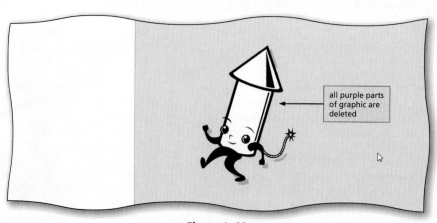

all purple parts of graphic are deleted

Figure 4–22

Other Ways

1. Select object, press TAB key until desired part is selected, press DELETE key

To Insert Another Picture and Resize It

The following steps insert a picture into the publication.

1 Display the INSERT tab

2 Tap or click the Online Pictures button (INSERT tab | Illustrations group) to display the Insert Pictures dialog box. Search Office.com Clip Art for the term, `hot dog`.

3 Scroll as necessary then choose a picture similar to the one in Figure 4–23.

4 Tap or click the Insert button (Insert Pictures dialog box) to insert the picture.

5 SHIFT+drag the lower-right sizing handle to resize the picture to be approximately .75 inches wide and .41 inches tall.

6 Drag the image into the scratch area, close to, but not obstructing, the rocket image (Figure 4–23).

BTW

Scaling

The term, **scaling**, when it applies to graphics, means changing the vertical or horizontal size of the graphic by a percentage. Scaling can create interesting graphic effects. Caricature drawings and intentionally distorted photographs routinely use scaling. When used for resizing, scaling is appropriate to make a graphic fit in tight places.

hot dog graphic is resized

Figure 4–23

To Convert, Ungroup, and Edit Another Picture

The following steps convert the hot dog image to a Microsoft Office drawing object, ungroup it, and then edit out the blue part of the graphic.

1 With the picture selected, tap or click the Ungroup button (PICTURE TOOLS FORMAT tab | Arrange group) to start the process.

2 When the Microsoft Publisher dialog box is displayed, tap or click the Yes button to convert the picture into a Microsoft Office drawing object. Do not deselect.

3 Tap or click the Ungroup button (DRAWING TOOLS FORMAT tab | Arrange group) to ungroup the graphic again.

4 Deselect by tapping or clicking outside of all selected parts.

5 Tap or click the blue area to select it.

6 Press the DELETE key to delete the selected part (Figure 4–24).

BTW

Q&As

For a complete list of the Q&As found in many of the step-by-step sequences in this book, visit the Q&A resource on the Student Companion Site located on www.cengagebrain.com. For detailed instructions about accessing available resources, visit www.cengage.com/ct/studentdownload or see the inside back cover of this book.

blue part of ungrouped hot dog graphic is deleted

Figure 4–24

To Group

The following steps drag around the hot dog image to select all its parts and then regroup them. *Why? It is easier to move and save the graphic if it is grouped.*

- Select the objects you wish to group (in this case, drag around the entire hot dog image to create a selection of the multiple parts) (Figure 4–25).

- Tap or click the Group button (DRAWING TOOLS FORMAT tab | Arrange group) to regroup the graphic.

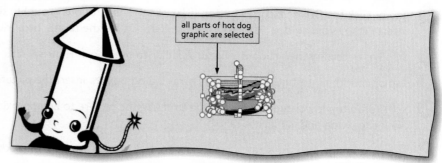

all parts of hot dog graphic are selected

Figure 4–25

Other Ways

1. Press and hold or right-click selected objects, tap or click Group on shortcut menu   2. Select objects, press CTRL+SHIFT+G

Rotating and Flipping Objects

When you **rotate** an object in Publisher, you turn it so that the top of the object faces a different direction. For example, a picture of a person could be rotated to look like that person was standing on his or her head. Each selected object in Publisher displays one or more green rotation handles used to rotate the object freely. To rotate in 15-degree increments, hold down the SHIFT key while dragging a rotation handle. To rotate an object on its base, hold down the CTRL key and drag the green rotation handle — the object will rotate in a circle by pivoting around the handle. You can enter other rotation percentages using the More Rotation Options command.

Publisher also allows you to **flip** objects. For example, a picture of a person facing left could be flipped horizontally so that it would appear the person is facing right.

To Rotate

The following steps rotate the graphic. *Why? The hot dog graphic needs to fit within the margins of the rocket when combined.*

- With the graphic still selected, tap or click the Rotate Objects button (DRAWING TOOLS FORMAT tab | Arrange group) to display the Rotate gallery (Figure 4–26).

Experiment

- Point to each rotation and flip option and watch how the graphic changes in the page layout.

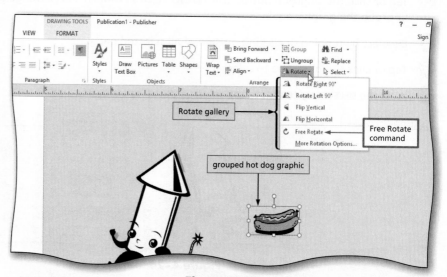

Rotate gallery

Free Rotate command

grouped hot dog graphic

Figure 4–26

2
- Tap or click Free Rotate to display the rotation handles (Figure 4–27).

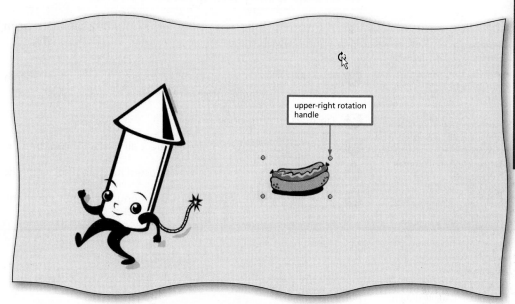

Figure 4–27

3
- Point to the upper-right rotation handle. When the pointer changes to a rotation symbol, drag the handle up and to the left, until the hot dog is at approximately a 45-degree angle as shown in Figure 4–28.

Q&A
Can I rotate objects other than drawing objects?
Yes, you can rotate all objects including text boxes and tables. Rotate Objects buttons appear on many tabs on the ribbon

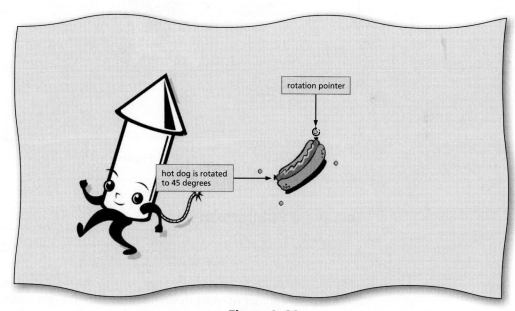

Figure 4–28

Other Ways

1. Tap or click Rotate Objects button (PICTURE TOOLS FORMAT tab | Arrange group) or (HOME tab | Arrange group), tap or click Free Rotate, rotate object

2. Press and hold or right-click object, tap or click Format Object on shortcut menu, tap or click Size tab, enter rotation percentage, tap or click OK button (Format Object dialog box)

3. Tap or click Object Size button (status bar), enter rotation percentage on Measurement toolbar

To Group Using the Shortcut Menu

The following steps position the hot dog graphic in front of the rocket graphic and group the two together.

1 If necessary, select the hot dog graphic. Drag the graphic to a location on top of the rocket as shown in Figure 4–29.

2 Deselect the hot dog graphic.

3 Drag around both graphics to select all parts of both graphics.

4 Press and hold or right-click the selected items to display the shortcut menu (Figure 4–29).

5 Tap or click Group on the shortcut menu to group the graphics.

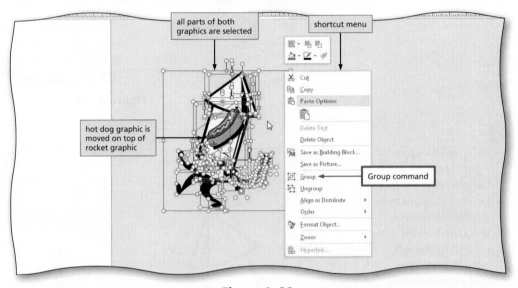

Figure 4–29

To Save a Publication

The following steps assume you already have created folders for storing your files, for example, a CIS 101 folder (for your class) that contains a Publisher folder (for your assignments). Thus, these steps save the publication in the Publisher folder in the CIS 101 folder on your desired save location. For a detailed example of the procedure for saving a file in a folder or saving a file on SkyDrive, refer to the Office and Windows chapter at the beginning of this book.

1 Tap or click the Save button on the Quick Access Toolbar, which, depending on settings, will display either the Save As gallery in the Backstage view or the Save As dialog box.

2 To save on a hard disk or other storage media on your computer, proceed to Step 2a. To save on SkyDrive, proceed to Step 2b.

2a If your screen opens the Backstage view and you want to save on storage media on your computer, tap or click Computer in the left pane, if necessary, to display options in the right pane related to saving on your computer. If your screen already displays the Save As dialog box, proceed to Step 4.

2b If your screen opens the Backstage view and you want to save on SkyDrive, tap or click SkyDrive in the left pane to display SkyDrive saving options or a Sign In button. If your screen displays a Sign In button, tap or click it and then sign in to SkyDrive.

3 Tap or click the Browse button in the right pane to display the Save As dialog box associated with the selected save location (i.e., Computer or SkyDrive).

4 Type `Rocket Dogs Table Card` in the File name text box to change the file name. Do not press the ENTER key after typing the file name because you do not want to close the dialog box at this time.

5 Navigate to the desired save location (in this case, the Publisher folder in the CIS 101 folder [or your class folder] on your computer or SkyDrive).

6 Tap or click the Save button (Save As dialog box) to save the publication in the selected folder on the selected save location with the entered file name.

Break Point: If you wish to take a break, this is a good place to do so. To resume at a later time, run Publisher, open the file called Rocket Dogs Table Card, and continue following the steps from this location forward.

Building Blocks

Building blocks are graphical elements that you can insert in a publication, including advertisement items, business information components, calendars, design accents, and page parts. To insert a building block into a publication, you tap or click the appropriate button on the INSERT tab, such as Calendars or Advertisements. Recall that you inserted a coupon building block in a previous chapter. You also can create your own building blocks and add them to the Building Block Library. The **Building Block Library** displays folders of building block components. When saving a building block, you can enter a title, description, and keywords to help you find the building block later. You also can choose the gallery and category in which you wish to save.

Alternately, you can save edited graphics on your storage device as pictures. Saving the graphic as a picture allows you to use that graphic in other applications, whereas building blocks are only available in Publisher.

BTW
Building Block Categories
In the Create New Building Block dialog box, you cannot change the Gallery list, but you can enter a new category and save your graphic to that new category. Once you tap or click the OK button, the new category will appear each time you access the Building Block Library.

To Save a Building Block

1 CUSTOMIZE | 2 EDIT GRAPHICS | 3 USE BUILDING BLOCKS | 4 EDIT & FORMAT TEXT
5 CREATE BULLETED LISTS | 6 FORMAT SHAPES | 7 APPLY CUSTOMIZATIONS | 8 DELETE CUSTOMIZATIONS

The following steps save the grouped graphic as a building block to use as a company logo. *Why? The graphic becomes reusable across multiple publications.*

1
• Press and hold or right-click the desired graphic or object (in this case, the grouped rocket and hot dog) to display the shortcut menu (Figure 4–30).

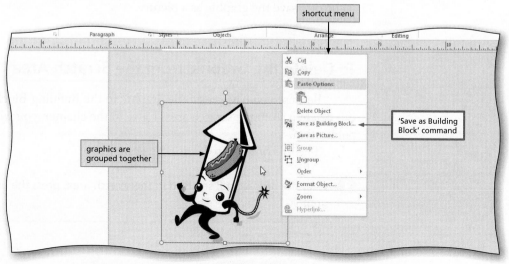

Figure 4–30

- Tap or click 'Save as Building Block' to display the Create New Building Block dialog box.

- Type **Rocket Dogs Logo** in the Title text box.

- Press the TAB key to move to the Description text box, and then type **This logo is a grouped graphic of a hot dog and a rocket clip art.**

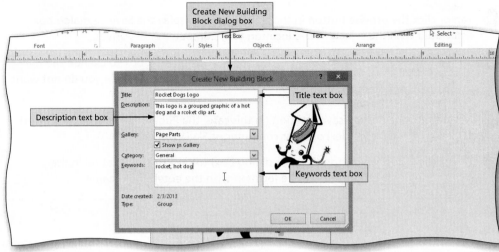

Figure 4–31

- Tap or click the Keywords text box. Type **rocket, hot dog** to enter keywords (Figure 4–31).

- Tap or click the OK button (Create New Building Block dialog box) to save the building block.

Other Ways
1. Tap or click Page Parts button (INSERT tab | Building Blocks group), tap or click Add Selection to Pages Parts Gallery, enter information (Create New Building Block dialog box), tap or click OK button

TO SAVE THE GRAPHIC AS A PICTURE

If you wanted to use the logo in another application, such as Microsoft Word or Microsoft PowerPoint, you would perform the following steps to save the graphic as a picture on your storage device.

1. Press and hold or right-click the object, and then tap or click 'Save as Picture' to open the Save As dialog box.
2. Type the name of your graphic in the File name text box.
3. Navigate to your storage location.
4. Edit property tags as desired, and then tap or click the Save button (Save As dialog box) to save the graphic as a picture.

To Delete the Graphic from the Scratch Area

Because you have saved the graphic to the Building Blocks Library, you can delete it from the scratch area. Later in the chapter, you will insert it into the publication.

The following step deletes the graphic.

1 With the graphic still selected in the scratch area, press the DELETE key to delete the graphic.

To Create a Solid Background

In Publisher, **layering**, or **ordering**, means to make purposeful decisions on how objects appear in front of one another. When objects are layered, the most forward object will eclipse the objects below it. Building a publication in layers from the back to the front ensures that you will be aware of any objects that might obstruct one another, and that your choices provide interesting backgrounds. Otherwise, to change the layering order, you must select the object and then choose to either bring it forward or send it backward. You can reorder most objects, including shapes, tables, text boxes, pictures, and clip art.

The following steps insert a solid color in the background of the table card.

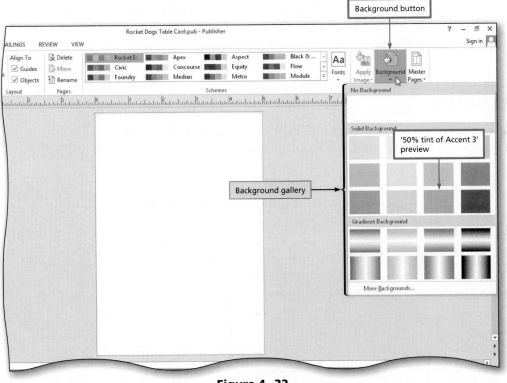

1 Zoom to Whole Page view.

2 Display the PAGE DESIGN tab.

3 Tap or click the Background button (PAGE DESIGN tab | Page Background group) to display the Background gallery (Figure 4–32).

4 Tap or click '50% tint of Accent 3' to apply the scheme color to the background.

Figure 4–32

BTW
Background Transparency
If the shape or text box has white in the background, you may want to remove it so the objects behind show through. Select the shape or text box and then press CTRL+T to make the object transparent.

Line Spacing

Line spacing is the amount of space from the bottom of one line of text to the bottom of the next line, which determines the amount of vertical space between lines of text in a paragraph. By default, the Normal style is single spaced, but because Publisher accommodates the largest font in any given line, plus a small amount of extra space, the actual line spacing value is 1.19 inches. To change the line spacing, you tap or click the

Line Spacing button (HOME tab | Paragraph group) on the ribbon (Figure 4–33). The Paragraph group includes buttons and boxes to help you format lines of text, including line spacing, alignment, columns, bullets, and numbering.

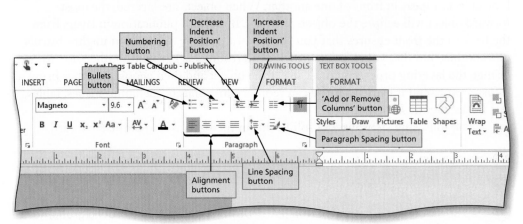

Figure 4–33

In the table card, in front of the solid color background, is a text box with the letters R and D. The letters are centered horizontally and are formatted with line spacing so that they overlap slightly. They also display a gradient fill. The other text and graphics will appear in front of those background elements.

To Change the Line Spacing

1 CUSTOMIZE | 2 EDIT GRAPHICS | 3 USE BUILDING BLOCKS | 4 EDIT & FORMAT TEXT
5 CREATE BULLETED LISTS | 6 FORMAT SHAPES | 7 APPLY CUSTOMIZATIONS | 8 DELETE CUSTOMIZATIONS

The following steps create a text box, and then reduce the line spacing. *Why? To create a stylistic letter sequence in the background of the table card, the R and D touch each other, which requires a very small line spacing.*

1
- Display the HOME tab.

- Tap or click the 'Draw a Text Box' button (HOME tab | Objects group) and then SHIFT+drag a text box in the scratch area, at least 4.5 inches square. Watch the Object Size button on the status bar as you drag.

- With the insertion point inside the text box, tap or click the Line Spacing button (HOME tab | Paragraph group) to display the Line Spacing gallery (Figure 4–34).

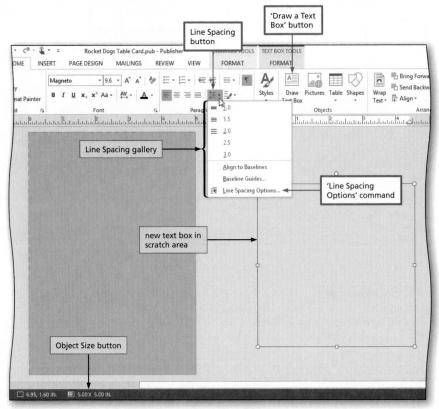

Figure 4–34

2

- Tap or click 'Line Spacing Options' to display the Paragraph dialog box.

- Select the text in the After paragraphs text box, and then type `0pt` to replace the text.

- Select the text in the Between lines text box, and then type `.5sp` to replace the text (Figure 4–35).

Q&A What do pt and sp stand for?
The letters pt stand for **point**, which is a physical measurement approximately equal to 1/72nd of an inch. The letters sp stand for **space**, which is measured in inches by default.

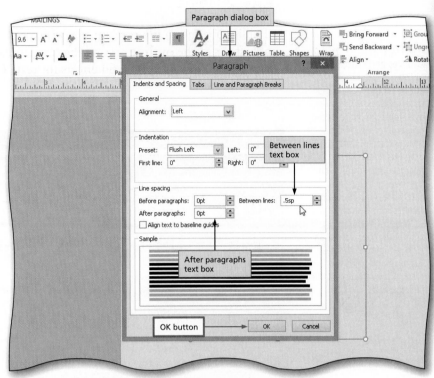

Figure 4–35

3

- Tap or click the OK button to close the Paragraph dialog box.

- Press CTRL+I to format with italics.

- Tap or click the Font Size text box. Type `175` and then press the ENTER key to change the font size.

- Within the text box, press the ENTER key to insert a blank line.

- Type the letter `R` and then press the ENTER key.

- Press the SPACEBAR key and then type the letter `D` to finish the text.

- Tap or click outside the text box to view the overlapped letters (Figure 4–36).

 Experiment

- Tap or click the Special Characters button (HOME tab | Paragraph group) to view the letters without special characters. If you want to see the special characters, tap or click the Special Characters button (HOME tab | Paragraph group) again.

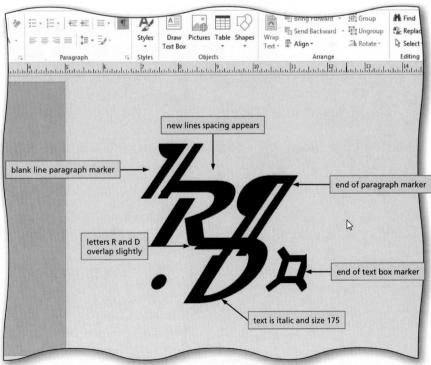

Figure 4–36

Other Ways

1. Tap or click Paragraph Settings Dialog Box Launcher (HOME tab | Paragraph group), enter settings, tap or click OK button (Paragraph dialog box)

2. Press and hold or right-click text, tap or click Change Text on shortcut menu, tap or click Paragraph, enter settings, click OK button (Paragraph dialog box)

Text Effects

BTW
Desktop Publishing
Advances in desktop publishing, combined with the convenience and quality of desktop printers, have created a surge in the popularity of programs such as Microsoft Publisher 2013. Some businesses that once used programs such as Adobe InDesign and QuarkXpress are switching to Publisher because of the Windows intuitive commands, the more than 3,000 templates, the easy learning curve, and the integration with other Office applications.

In Publisher, you can **fill**, or paint text with a color or with a special effect. You also can apply effects to the **outline** around the text, similar to adding a border around each letter. Table 4–1 displays the fill effects for text. Table 4–2 displays the outline effects for text.

Table 4–1 Text Fill Effects

Fill Effect	Settings	Result
No fill	none	text is transparent (best used over a solid color)
Solid fill	Color button Transparency slider	text appears with a solid color (default setting)
Gradient fill	Preset gradients button Type button Direction button Angle arrows Gradient stops Color button Position arrows Transparency slider and arrows Rotate with shape check box	gradual progression of colors and shades

© 2014 Cengage Learning

Table 4–2 Text Outline Effects

Fill Effect	Settings	Result
No fill	none	text displays fill effect or default settings with no outline
Solid fill	Color button Transparency slider Width arrows Compound type Dash type button Cap type button Join type button	outline appears as a solid color at specified width and type settings
Gradient fill	Preset gradients button Type button Direction button Angle arrows Gradient stops Color button Position arrows Transparency slider and arrows Width button Compound type button Dash type button Cap type button Join type button	outline appears with gradual progression of colors and shades at specified width and type settings

© 2014 Cengage Learning

To Apply a Gradient to Text

A **gradient** is a gradual progression of colors and shades, usually from one color to another color, or from one shade to another shade of the same color. Recall that you used a gradient background from the Background gallery in a previous chapter. When editing a gradient, you either can choose a preset or you can make specific choices about the type of gradient, the direction, and the colors. A **color stop** is a button on a slider to set exactly where the color should start to change in the gradient.

The following steps apply a gradient fill to the text. *Why? Gradient fills create a sense of movement to draw attention and add dimension to a publication.*

1

- Select the desired text (in this case, the letters, R and D)

- Tap or click the Font Color arrow (HOME tab | Font group) to display the Font Color gallery (Figure 4–37).

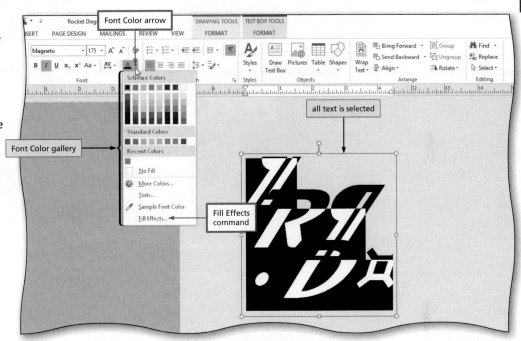

Figure 4–37

2

- Tap or click Fill Effects to display the Format Shape dialog box.

- Tap or click the Gradient fill button (Format Shape dialog box) to display the gradient settings. Drag the lower-right corner of the dialog box down, to view all of the settings.

- Tap or click the Preset gradients button to display the Preset gradients gallery (Figure 4–38).

Q&A

What is the purpose of the Transparency sliders?
When you choose one color for your gradient, the Transparency sliders allow you to specify what percentage of **transparency**, or opacity, for the beginning and end of the gradient. A 100% transparency appears white. A 0% transparency displays the chosen color.

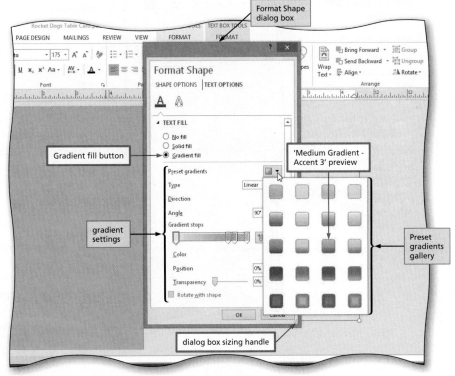

Figure 4–38

- Tap or click the desired gradient (in this case, 'Medium Gradient - Accent 3') to select the preset.
- Tap or click the Direction button to display the Direction gallery (Figure 4–39).

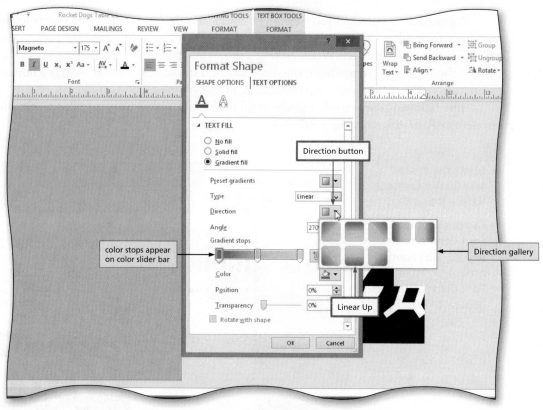

Figure 4–39

- Tap or click the desired direction (in this case, Linear Up) to select the direction.
- Tap or click the gradient stop you wish to change (in this case, Stop 3 of 3).
- Tap or click the Position down arrow until it reaches 75%, to change the location of the stop (Figure 4–40).

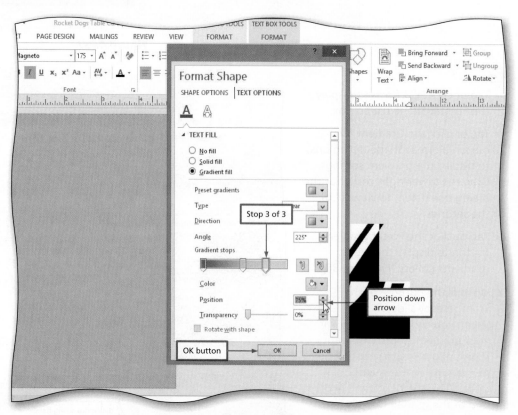

Figure 4–40

5
- Tap or click the OK button to close the Format Shape dialog box.
- Tap or click outside the text box to view the fill effect (Figure 4–41).

Q&A Do fill effects work on all text?
Yes, but it is more effective with larger font sizes.

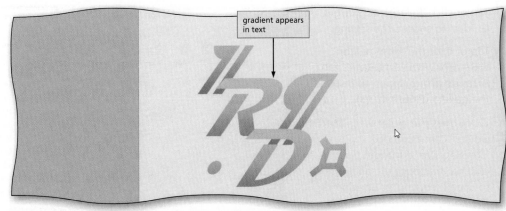

Figure 4–41

Other Ways

1. Tap or click Format Shape Dialog Box Launcher (DRAWING TOOLS FORMAT tab | Shape Styles group), tap or click Colors and Lines tab (Format Text Box dialog box), tap or click Fill Effects button, choose settings, click OK button (Format Shape dialog box), tap or click OK button (Format Text Box dialog box)

2. Press and hold or right-click selection, tap or click Format Text box on shortcut menu, tap or click Colors and Lines tab (Format Text Box dialog box), tap or click Fill Effects button, choose settings, tap or click OK button (Format Shape dialog box), tap or click OK button (Format Text Box dialog box)

Aligning and Distributing Objects

The alignment buttons (HOME tab | Paragraph group) are used to align text within the text box. For the text box itself, and other objects on the page, Publisher uses Align and Distribute tools (DRAWING TOOLS tab | Arrange group). **Align** means to line up an object relative to the page margin or relative to another object. **Distribute** means to adjust the spacing evenly among objects.

1 CUSTOMIZE | 2 EDIT GRAPHICS | 3 USE BUILDING BLOCKS | 4 EDIT & FORMAT TEXT
5 CREATE BULLETED LISTS | 6 FORMAT SHAPES | 7 APPLY CUSTOMIZATIONS | 8 DELETE CUSTOMIZATIONS

To Align an Object

The following steps center the text box horizontally on the page. **Why?** *Using a command to align an object is much better than estimating.*

1
- Select the object you wish to align (in this case, the text box).
- Display the DRAWING TOOLS FORMAT tab.
- Tap or click the Align button (DRAWING TOOLS FORMAT tab | Arrange group) to display the Align gallery (Figure 4–42).

Q&A Why are the align and distribute commands grayed out?
Only one object is selected. If you had multiple objects selected, the other commands could be applied.

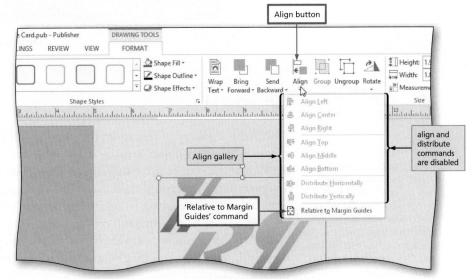

Figure 4–42

- Tap or click 'Relative to Margin Guides' to choose the setting.

- Tap or click the Align button (DRAWING TOOLS FORMAT tab | Arrange group) again to display the gallery (Figure 4–43).

Q&A What does the 'Relative to Margin Guides' command do?
The 'Relative to Margin Guides' command applies the alignment to the object and its position on the page, rather than its position relative to another object.

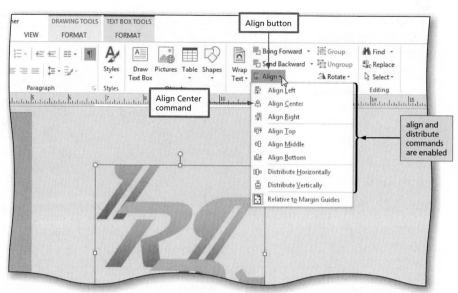

Figure 4–43

- Tap or click Align Center to choose the setting (Figure 4–44).

Q&A What is the difference between Align Center and Align Middle?
Align Center aligns horizontally. Align Middle aligns vertically.

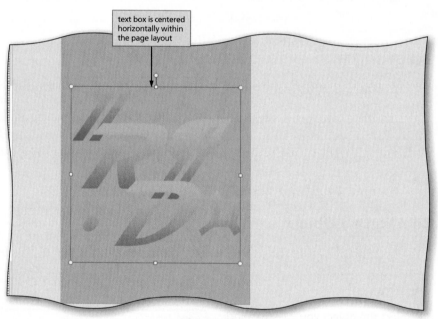

Figure 4–44

WordArt

BTW
WordArt Spelling
Keep in mind that WordArt objects are drawing objects; they are not Publisher text. Thus, if you misspell the contents of a WordArt object and then check the publication, Publisher will not flag the misspelled word(s) in the WordArt text.

WordArt is a gallery of text styles that works with Publisher to create fancy text effects. A WordArt object actually is a graphic, not text. Publication designers typically use WordArt to create eye-catching headlines, banners, or watermark images. Most designers agree that you should use WordArt sparingly and, at most, only once per page, unless you are trying to achieve some kind of special effect or illustration.

WordArt has its own tab on the ribbon that is displayed only when a WordArt object is selected. On the WordArt tab, you can change many settings such as the fill, outline, warp, height, and alignment, as well as edit the color, shape, and shape effect.

To Insert a WordArt Object

The following steps add a WordArt object at the top of the table card. *Why? While a formatted text box with font effects might create a similar effect, using WordArt increases the number of special effect possibilities and options.*

- If necessary, deselect any selected objects on the page or in the scratch area.
- Display the INSERT tab.
- Tap or click the WordArt button (INSERT tab | Text group) to display the WordArt gallery (Figure 4–45).

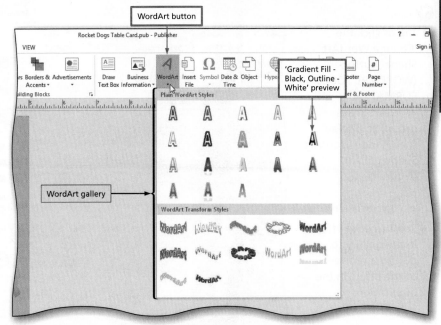

Figure 4–45

- Tap or click the desired style (in this case, 'Gradient Fill – Black, Outline - White') in the WordArt gallery to select it.
- Type **Rocket Dogs** (Edit WordArt Text dialog box) to enter the text.
- Tap or click the Font arrow, scroll as necessary, and then tap or click Poor Richard in the list of fonts.
- Tap or click the Size arrow, scroll as necessary, and then tap or click 66 in the list of sizes (Figure 4–46).

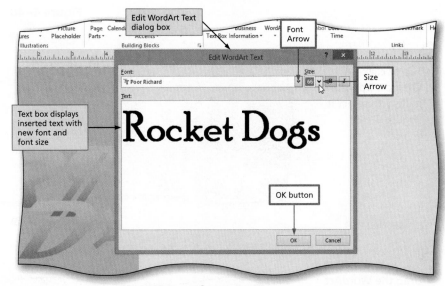

Figure 4–46

❸

- Tap or click the OK button to close the Edit WordArt Text dialog box and insert the WordArt graphic (Figure 4–47). If necessary, move the WordArt object to the scratch area.

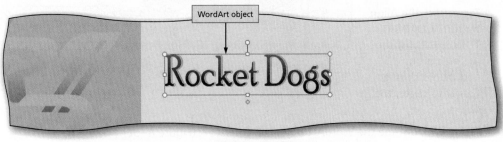

Figure 4–47

To Change the WordArt Shape

The following steps change the shape of the WordArt. *Why? The owner of Rocket Dogs wants an upward pointing shape to help enforce the rocket concept.*

1

- Tap or click the 'Change WordArt Shape' button (WORDART TOOLS FORMAT tab | WordArt Styles group) to display the Change WordArt Shape gallery (Figure 4–48).

Experiment

- Point to each effect in the gallery to display a preview of the effect in the publication.

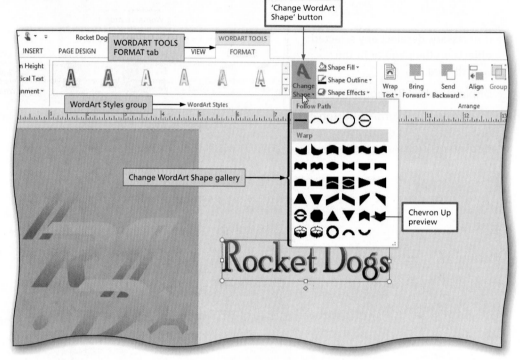

Figure 4–48

2

- Tap or click Chevron Up in the gallery to select it (Figure 4–49).

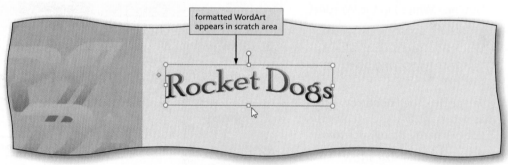

Figure 4–49

3

- Drag the WordArt object to the top of the page layout.

- Tap or click the Align button (WORDART TOOLS FORMAT tab | Arrange group), and then click Align Center to center the object.

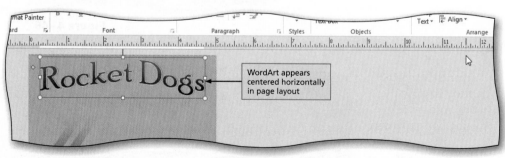

Figure 4–50

- Tap or click outside the WordArt object to deselect it (Figure 4–50).

To Insert a Building Block

The following steps insert the Rocket Dogs Logo that you created earlier in the chapter, and place it below the WordArt heading. *Why?* *Building the publication from the back to the front, and then from the top to the bottom is a good design technique.*

1

- Display the INSERT tab.

- Tap or click the Page Parts button (INSERT tab | Building Blocks group) to display the gallery (Figure 4–51).

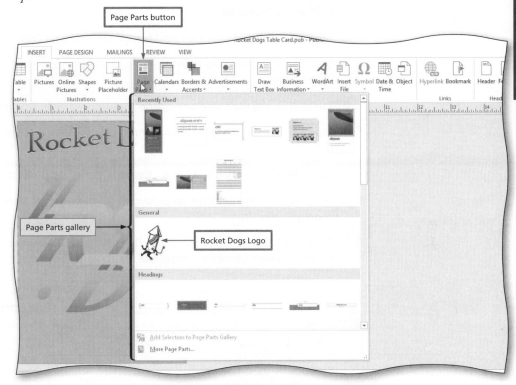

Figure 4–51

2

- Tap or click the desired building block (in this case, the Rocket Dogs Logo) to insert it into the publication.

- Drag the logo to a location just below the WordArt.

- Display the DRAWING TOOLS FORMAT tab.

- Tap or click the Align button (DRAWING TOOLS FORMAT tab | Arrange group) and then tap or click Align Center to center the logo (Figure 4–52).

Figure 4–52

To Create a Subheading

The following steps draw a text box at the top of the publication that will contain the heading.

1 Display the Home tab.

2 Tap or click the 'Draw a Text Box' button (HOME tab | Objects group) to select it.

3 Drag in the scratch area to draw a text box approximately 4.5 inches wide and .5 inches tall.

4 Tap or click the Font Size arrow, and then choose 22 in the list.

5 Tap or click the Font Color arrow, and then choose the Accent 1 (Red) color in the Font Color gallery.

6 Type **Nightly Specials & Events** to enter the text.

7 Drag the text box onto the page layout, so it appears just below the Rocket Dogs Logo graphic (Figure 4–53).

8 Tap or click the Align button (DRAWING TOOLS FORMAT tab | Arrange group) and then click Align Center to center the text box horizontally.

Figure 4–53

Text Wrapping

Text wrapping refers to how objects wrap themselves around other objects on the page. Typically, text wrapping is used when wrapping text boxes around pictures; however, it also is used when wrapping text boxes with other text boxes. Wrapping tightly means there is not much space around the margins of the object, allowing text to appear very close. Wrapping loosely means there is more space. Other options include Square, Top and Bottom, Through, and None.

To Set the Text Wrapping

The following steps set the text wrapping of the subheading text box to None. *Why? If text wrapping is on, text boxes will not appear in front of one another.*

1

- With the text box selected, display the DRAWING TOOLS FORMAT tab.

- Tap or click the Wrap Text button (DRAWING TOOLS FORMAT tab | Arrange group) (Figure 4–54).

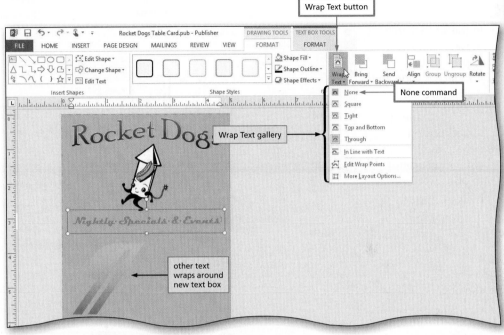

Figure 4–54

2

- Tap or click the desired text wrapping choice (in this case, None) in the Wrap Text gallery (Figure 4–55).

Figure 4–55

Other Ways

1. Tap or click Format Text Box Dialog Box Launcher (TEXT BOX TOOLS FORMAT tab | Text group), tap or click Layout tab, tap or click desired wrapping style, tap or click OK button (Format Text Box dialog box)

2. Press and hold or right click text, tap or click Format Text box on shortcut menu, tap or click Layout tab, tap or click desired wrapping style, tap or click OK button (Format Text Box dialog box)

Bulleted Lists

A **bulleted list** is a series of lines, each beginning with a bullet character. When you click the Bullets button (Home tab | Paragraph group), Publisher displays the Bullet Styles gallery, which is a clickable list of thumbnails and commands that show different bullet styles. You can choose a standard bullet character (•) and adjust its size and how far the text is indented. You also can customize the bullet by choosing a different character or symbol.

To Create a Custom Bullet

The following steps create a bulleted list using a custom character. *Why? The owner of Rocket Dogs wants a rocket shape bullet.*

1

- In the scratch area, draw a text box approximately 4.75 inches wide and 2.25 inches tall.

- Tap or click the Bullets button (HOME tab | Paragraph group) to display the Bullets gallery (Figure 4–56).

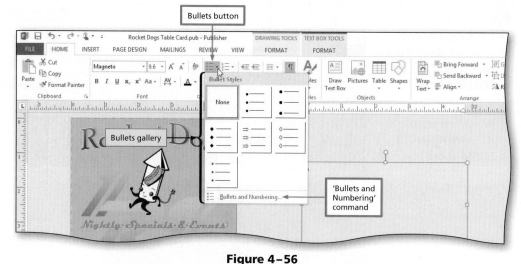

Figure 4–56

2

- Tap or click 'Bullets and Numbering' to display the Bullets and Numbering dialog box (Figure 4–57).

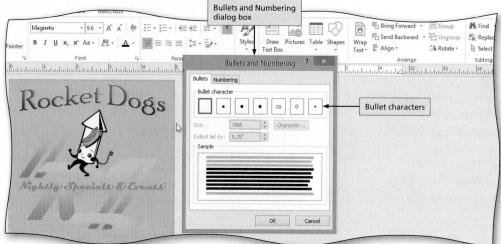

Figure 4–57

3

- If necessary, tap or click any Bullet character, other than a blank one.

- Tap or click the Character button (Bullets and Numbering dialog box) to display the Bullet Character dialog box.

- Tap or click the Font arrow (Bullet Character dialog box) to disiplay its list (Figure 4–58).

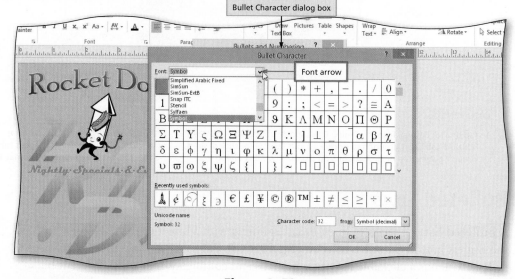

Figure 4–58

4

- Scroll as necessary, and then tap or click Webdings in the list.
- Scroll as necessary in the character list, and then tap or click the rocket ship, character code 249 (Figure 4–59).

Q&A Could I enter the character code to find the character faster?
Yes.

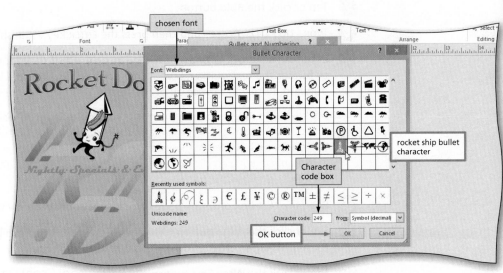

Figure 4–59

5

- Tap or click the OK button (Bullet Character dialog box) to choose the character and return to the Bullets and Numbering dialog box.
- Tap or click the Size box and then type **22pt** to enter the size (Figure 4–60).

6

- Tap or click the OK button (Bullets and Numbering dialog box) to apply the settings.

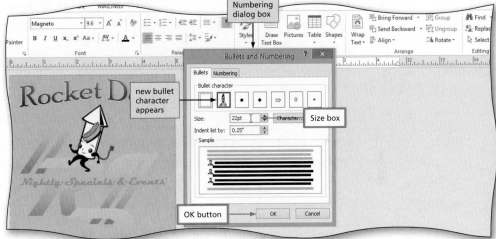

Figure 4–60

To Enter Text

The following steps enter bulleted text.

1 Zoom to 100%.

2 With the insertion point in the text box, click the Font Size arrow and then choose 22 in the list.

3 Tap or click the Font Color arrow, and then tap or click Accent 1 (Red) in the Font Color gallery.

4 Type **Monday:** and then press the SPACEBAR key to enter the first part of the line.

5 Tap or click the Font Color arrow, and then tap or click Main (Black) in the Font Color gallery.

6 Tap or click the Font arrow, and then choose Poor Richard from the list.

7 Tap or click the Bold button.

8 Type **Dollar Dogs** and then press the ENTER key to finish the first line.

9 Enter the next four lines as shown in Figure 4–61. If desired, use the format painter to format the text quicker. If your text does not fit, drag the lower-right sizing handle outward, until you can see all of the text.

Q&A My keyboard does not have a cent sign (¢). How do I type it?

If you have a numeric keypad, make sure your Num Lock is turned on, and then you can press and hold the ALT key and then type the character code 0162 to generate the cent sign. Or, you can click the Symbol button (INSERT tab | Text group), and choose the cent sign from the gallery.

10 Drag the text box onto the page layout, so it appears below the subheading.

11 Tap or click the Align button (DRAWING TOOLS FORMAT tab | Arrange group) and then click Align Center to center the text box horizontally.

12 Tap or click the Wrap Text button (DRAWING TOOLS FORMAT tab | Arrange group), and then tap or click None to turn off text wrapping (Figure 4–61).

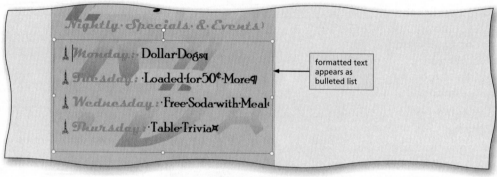

Figure 4–61

To Save an Existing Publication with the Same File Name

The following step saves the publication again.

1 Tap or click the Save button on the Quick Access Toolbar to save the file again with the same name and in the same location.

Break Point: If you wish to take a break, this is a good place to do so. To resume at a later time, run Publisher, open the file called Rocket Dogs Table Card, and continue following the steps from this location forward.

Shapes

Publisher has more than 150 shapes that you can use to create logos, graphics, banners, illustrations, and other ornamental objects. You can apply fill effects, shadows, reflections, glows, and other special effects to shapes. An interesting fill effect is to fill a shape with a picture. Alternately, you can insert the picture first, and then apply the shape. You will do both as you create two shapes in the lower-left corner of the table card.

To Insert a Shape

The following steps insert a rounded rectangle shape in the publication. *Why? You will fill the rounded rectangle shape with a graphic.*

1

- Deselect any selected objects, and display the INSERT tab.

- Tap or click the Shapes button (INSERT tab | Illustrations group) to display the Shapes gallery (Figure 4–62).

 Why is my gallery different?
Publisher displays the most recently used shapes at the top of the gallery. The recently used shapes on your system may differ.

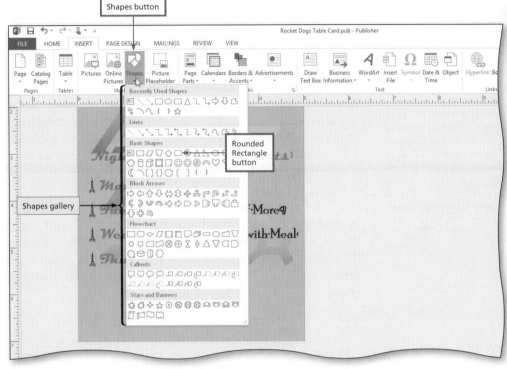

Figure 4–62

2

- Tap or click the desired shape button (in this case, Rounded Rectangle) in the Basic Shapes category to select it.

- Move the mouse pointer into the scratch area and then SHIFT+drag a shape, approximately 1-inch square (Figure 4–63).

 Why use the SHIFT key?
SHIFT+dragging maintains the proportions of any shape. If you SHIFT+drag a rectangular shape, it will create a square; to create a circle, you can SHIFT+drag an oval.

My rounded rectangle looks different. Did I do something wrong?
No, your default color and outline may differ. You will format the shape in the next series of steps.

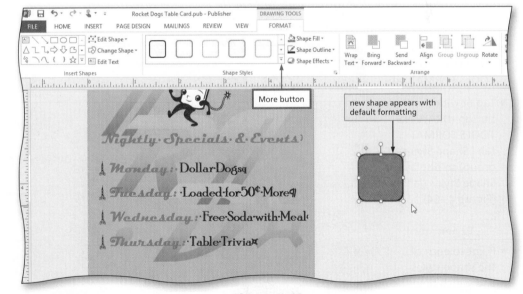

Figure 4–63

Other Ways

1. Tap or click More button (DRAWING TOOLS FORMAT tab | Insert Shapes group), tap or click the desired shape button

Shape Fills

Shape fills include fill colors, shape styles, gradients, textures, patterns, pictures, and tints/shades. Shape fills add subtle contrast and create an illusion of texture and depth.

A **shape style** is a predefined color, fill, and outline based on the chosen color scheme.

A **texture fill** is a combination of color and patterns without gradual shading. Publisher provides 24 different textures from which you may choose.

Patterns include variations of repeating designs such as lines, stripes, checks, and bricks. Publisher uses the base color and a second color to create the pattern. When publications are destined for commercial printing, patterns usually are more expensive than tints and shades because they increase the time it takes to process the file.

A **picture fill** is a special effect that inserts clip art or your own graphic to create a unique and personal shape. A picture fill gives the appearance of a picture, cropped to a specific shape, such as a star or circle.

A **tint** is a color created from a base color mixed with a percentage of white. A **shade**, on the other hand, is a mixture of a base color and black. You use tints and shades to create a more sophisticated color scheme. Tints and shades are applied in 10-percent increments. For example, the first tint of red is nine parts red and one part white. Therefore, Publisher displays 10 tints and 10 shades of each basic color on the Tints sheet in the Fill Effects dialog box.

To Choose a Shape Style

1 CUSTOMIZE | 2 EDIT GRAPHICS | 3 USE BUILDING BLOCKS | 4 EDIT & FORMAT TEXT
5 CREATE BULLETED LISTS | 6 FORMAT SHAPES | **7 APPLY CUSTOMIZATIONS** | 8 DELETE CUSTOMIZATIONS

The following steps choose a style for the shape from the shape styles gallery. *Why?* *The shape styles gallery uses colors from the custom color scheme you created at the beginning of the chapter.*

1

- If necessary, display the DRAWING TOOLS FORMAT tab.

- Tap or click the More button (DRAWING TOOLS FORMAT tab | Shape Styles group) to display the Shape Styles gallery (Figure 4–64).

🔍 **Experiment**

- Point to each of the shape styles and watch how the graphic changes.

Q&A
Do I have to choose a scheme color?
No, you do not have to choose a scheme color, but using scheme colors provides consistency in your publication.

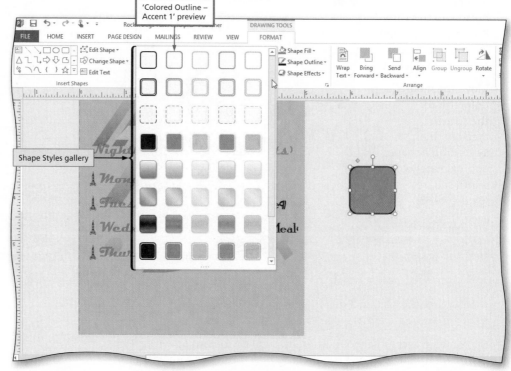

Figure 4–64

2

- Tap or click 'Colored Outline – Accent 1' to select the style (Figure 4–65).

Q&A

Is the fill color white?

No, there is no fill color; Publisher displays white to help you differentiate the inside of the shape from the scratch area.

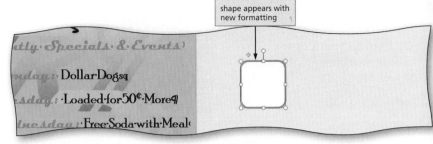

Figure 4–65

To Create a Picture Fill

1 CUSTOMIZE | 2 EDIT GRAPHICS | 3 USE BUILDING BLOCKS | 4 EDIT & FORMAT TEXT
5 CREATE BULLETED LISTS | 6 FORMAT SHAPES | 7 APPLY CUSTOMIZATIONS | 8 DELETE CUSTOMIZATIONS

The following steps insert a picture in the shape. *Why? Adding a picture to the shape will add more visual weight to the table card and create balance between the logo and the added shape.*

1

- Tap or click the Shape Fill button (DRAWING TOOLS FORMAT tab | Shape Styles group) to display the Shape Fill gallery (Figure 4–66).

Experiment

- Point to each of the fill colors and watch how the graphic changes.

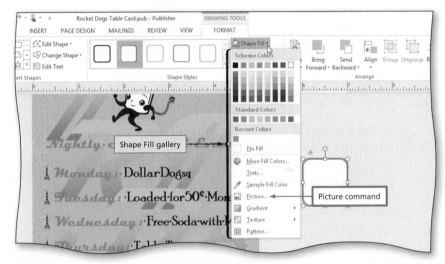

Figure 4–66

2

- Tap or click Picture in the gallery to display the Insert Pictures dialog box.

- Type **soda** in the Office.com Clip Art search box, and then press the ENTER key to begin the search.

- Tap or click a graphic similar to the one shown in Figure 4–67.

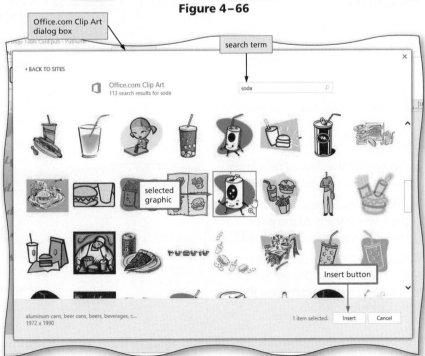

Figure 4–67

③

- Tap or click the Insert button (Office.com Clip Art dialog box) to insert the picture into the shape (Figure 4–68).

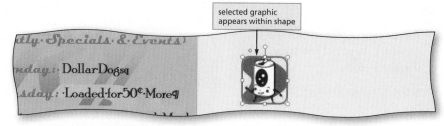

selected graphic appears within shape

Figure 4–68

Other Ways

1. Press and hold or right-click shape, tap or click Format AutoShape on shortcut menu, tap or click Fill Effects button (Colors and Lines tab), tap or click 'Picture or texture fill' button (Format Shape dialog box), tap or click File button or Online button, choose picture

To Recolor a Graphic

1 CUSTOMIZE | 2 EDIT GRAPHICS | 3 USE BUILDING BLOCKS | 4 EDIT & FORMAT TEXT
5 CREATE BULLETED LISTS | 6 FORMAT SHAPES | **7 APPLY CUSTOMIZATIONS** | 8 DELETE CUSTOMIZATIONS

When you **recolor** a graphic, you make a large-scale color change to the entire graphic. The chosen color is applied to all parts of the graphic, with the option of leaving the black parts black. *Why? It is an easy way to convert a color graphic to a black and white line drawing in order to print more clearly. The reverse also is true; if you have a black and white graphic, you can convert it to a tint or shade of any one color.*

The following steps recolor the clip art of the soda can.

①

- Display the PICTURE TOOLS FORMAT tab.

- Tap or click the Recolor button (PICTURE TOOLS FORMAT tab | Adjust group) to display the Recolor gallery (Figure 4–69).

🔍 Experiment

- Point to each of the color modes and variations and watch how the graphic changes.

Q&A What does the More Variations command do?
The More Variations command displays the same Colors dialog box, as it did when you chose a color for the color scheme, allowing you to choose colors based on a color number, palette, or coloring system.

Recolor button

Grayscale preview

Recolor gallery

Figure 4–69

②

- Tap or click the desired recoloring (in this case, Grayscale) to select it.

- Drag the shape to a location in the lower portion of the page layout as shown in Figure 4–70.

- Tap or click the Wrap Text button (PICTURE TOOLS FORMAT tab | Arrange group) and change the text wrapping to None.

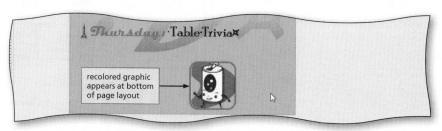

recolored graphic appears at bottom of page layout

Figure 4–70

Other Ways

1. Press and hold or right-click graphic, tap or click Format Picture on shortcut menu, tap or click Picture tab (Format Picture dialog box), tap or click Color button in Recolor area, choose settings, tap or click OK button

To Insert Another Graphic

The following steps insert another graphic into the publication. You will format and apply a shape later in the chapter.

1 Display the INSERT tab.

2 Tap or click the Online Pictures button (INSERT tab | Illustrations group) to display the Insert Pictures dialog box.

3 Type **French fries** in the Office.com Clip Art search box, and then press the ENTER key to begin the search.

4 Insert a graphic similar to the one shown in Figure 4–71.

5 Drag the graphic to the scratch area.

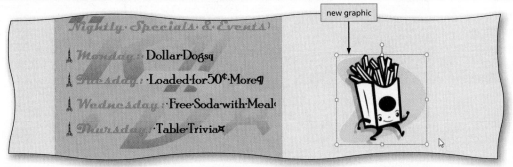

Figure 4–71

To Format the graphic

The following steps format the graphic by resizing it, flipping it, changing the border, and recoloring the graphic.

1 With the graphic still selected, SHIFT+drag a corner sizing handle until the picture is approximately 1-inch square.

2 If necessary, zoom to 100%.

3 Tap or click the Rotate Objects button (PICTURE TOOLS FORMAT tab | Arrange group), and then tap or click Flip Horizontal in the gallery.

4 Tap or click the Picture Border button (PICTURE TOOLS FORMAT tab | Picture Styles group), and then tap or click 'Accent 1 (Red)' in the gallery.

5 Tap or click the Recolor button (PICTURE TOOLS FORMAT tab | Adjust group), and then tap or click Grayscale in the gallery (Figure 4–72).

BTW
Fitting Graphics
The Fit button (PICTURE TOOLS FORMAT tab | Crop group) places the entire, original graphic within the cropping handle dimensions, even if that means creating a disproportional image. The Fill command places the original graphic within the cropping handles maintaining proportions, which sometimes means a slight cropping occurs if the cropping handle dimensions are not the same shape as the original. The Clear Crop command resets the graphic to its original size and dimension with no cropping. The commands become enabled after an initial crop.

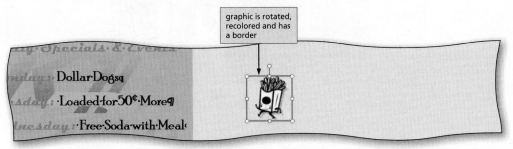

Figure 4–72

To Crop to a Shape

Earlier in the chapter, you filled a shape with a picture. Now you will apply a shape to an existing picture, in this case the French fries graphic. The graphic currently displays the default shape, which is rectangular. Publisher allows you to **crop**, or trim, the edges of a graphic or picture to a different shape. *Why? Cropping can focus attention on a particular area, or remove background clutter and unwanted portions of the picture.*

The following steps crop the graphic to a different shape.

1

- With the graphic still selected, tap or click the Crop button (PICTURE TOOLS FORMAT tab | Crop group), and then tap or click 'Crop to Shape' to display the Crop to Shape gallery (Figure 4–73).

 Q&A
What does the Crop command do?
The Crop command crops to a rectangular shape using cropping handles. You will learn more about cropping in a later chapter.

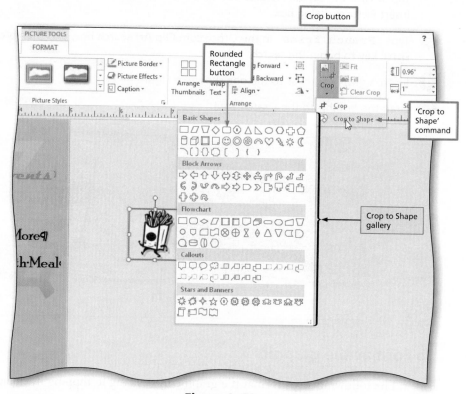

Figure 4–73

2

- Tap or click the desired shape (in this case, Rounded Rectangle) to select it.

- Tap or click the Crop button (PICTURE TOOLS FORMAT tab | Crop group) again to complete the crop.

- Drag the graphic to the lower-right portion of the page layout (Figure 4–74).

Figure 4–74

Other Ways

1. Press and hold or right-click shape, tap or click Format AutoShape on shortcut menu, tap or click Colors and Lines tab (Format AutoShape dialog box), tap or click Color button, tap or click color

To Check the Publication for Errors

The following steps check the publication for errors.

1 Press the F7 key to begin checking the publication for spelling errors. If Publisher flags any words, fix or ignore them as appropriate.

2 When Publisher displays a dialog box asking if you want to check the rest of your publication, click the Yes button.

3 When the spell check is complete, click the OK button.

4 Tap or click FILE on the ribbon to open the Backstage view and, by default, select the Info tab.

5 Tap or click the 'Run Design Checker' button.

6 Ignore any errors related to the spacing around margins. If the Design Checker identifies any other errors, fix them as necessary.

7 Close the Design Checker task pane.

To Save the Publication Again

You are finished editing the publication. Thus, you should save it again. The following step saves the publication again.

1 Tap or click the Save button on the Quick Access Toolbar to overwrite the previously saved file.

TO PRINT THE TABLE CARD

If you wanted to print the table card, you would perform the following steps.

1. Ready the printer according to the printer instructions. Tap or click FILE on the ribbon to open the Backstage view.

2. Tap or click the Print tab in the Backstage view to display the Print gallery.

3. Tap or click the Print button in the Print gallery to print the publication.

4. When the printer stops, retrieve the printed publication (shown in Figure 4–1 on page PUB 195).

To Close a Publication without Exiting Publisher

The following steps close the publication without exiting Publisher.

1 Tap or click FILE on the ribbon to open the Backstage view.

2 Tap or click Close to close the publication without exiting Publisher and to return to the template gallery.

Break Point: If you wish to take a break, this is a good place to do so. To resume at a later time, run Publisher, and then continue following the steps from this location forward.

Using Customized Sizes, Schemes, and Building Blocks

Earlier in this chapter, you created a custom blank page for a 5 × 7 table card, a customized font scheme, a customized color scheme, and a graphic that you stored as a building block. These customizations are meant to be used again. They also can be deleted if you no longer need them.

In the following sections, you will open and access the customizations as if you were going to create a second publication for the same company. You then will delete them.

To Open a Customized Blank Page

1 CUSTOMIZE | 2 EDIT GRAPHICS | 3 USE BUILDING BLOCKS | 4 EDIT & FORMAT TEXT
5 CREATE BULLETED LISTS | 6 FORMAT SHAPES | **7 APPLY CUSTOMIZATIONS** | **8 DELETE CUSTOMIZATIONS**

The following steps open a customized blank page. *Why? The previously stored page size was stored in the custom area.*

1

- With Publisher running, if necessary, click FILE on the ribbon to open the Backstage view.

- Tap or click New to display the template gallery (Figure 4–75).

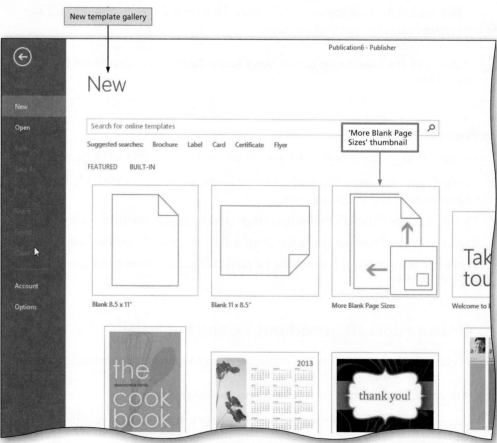

Figure 4–75

2

- Tap or click the 'More Blank Page Sizes' thumbnail to view the Standard and Custom page sizes.

- Tap or click the '5 × 7 Table Card' thumbnail to select it (Figure 4–76).

 Q&A My thumbnails look different. Did I do something wrong? No, you did not do anything wrong. The custom sizes on your machine will differ depending on the users and previous customizations.

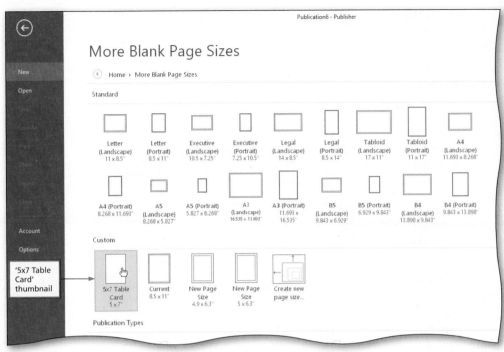

Figure 4–76

Other Ways

1. Tap or click 'Choose Page Size' button (PAGE DESIGN tab | Page Setup group), tap or click custom size

To Apply Customized Color and Font Schemes

1 CUSTOMIZE | 2 EDIT GRAPHICS | 3 USE BUILDING BLOCKS | 4 EDIT & FORMAT TEXT
5 CREATE BULLETED LISTS | 6 FORMAT SHAPES | **7 APPLY CUSTOMIZATIONS** | **8 DELETE CUSTOMIZATIONS**

The following steps apply customized color and font schemes. *Why? Your publication colors and fonts need to adhere to company schemes.*

1

- Tap or click the Color scheme button (template information pane), and then scroll to the top of the list (Figure 4–77).

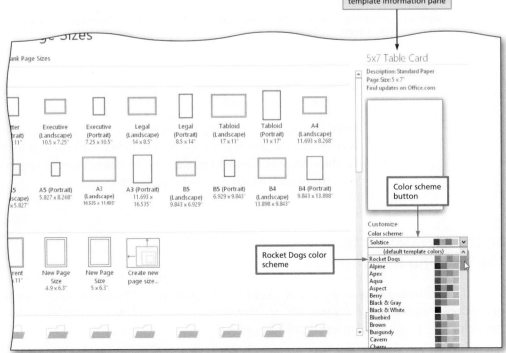

Figure 4–77

- Tap or click the Rocket Dogs color scheme to select it.

- Tap or click the Font scheme button (template information pane), and then scroll to the top of the list (Figure 4–78).

- Tap or click the Rocket Dogs font scheme to select it.

- Tap or click the CREATE button (template information pane) to create the publication.

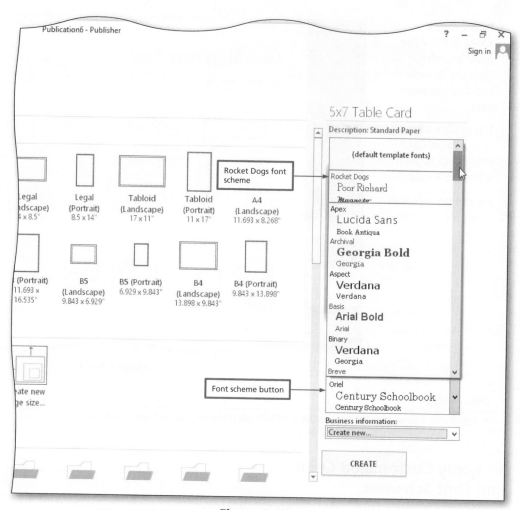

Figure 4–78

Other Ways

1. Tap or click More button (PAGE DESIGN tab | Schemes group), tap or click custom color scheme

2. Tap or click Fonts button (PAGE DESIGN tab | Schemes group), tap or click custom font scheme

Deleting Customizations

In laboratory environments, where many students work on the same computers throughout the day, it is a good idea to delete content you have created that is stored on the computer. You also might want to delete customization and content for companies with which you no longer do business.

To Delete Content from the Building Block Library

1 CUSTOMIZE | 2 EDIT GRAPHICS | 3 USE BUILDING BLOCKS | 4 EDIT & FORMAT TEXT
5 CREATE BULLETED LISTS | 6 FORMAT SHAPES | 7 APPLY CUSTOMIZATIONS | **8 DELETE CUSTOMIZATIONS**

The following steps delete the Rocket Dogs Logo from the Building Block Library. *Why? Many logos are proprietary or copyrighted. It is a good idea to delete them when you no longer need them.* Deleting from the library does not delete the graphics from saved publications.

1

- Display the INSERT tab.

- Tap or click the Show Building Block Library Dialog Box Launcher (INSERT tab | Building Blocks group) to display the Building Block Library dialog box (Figure 4–79).

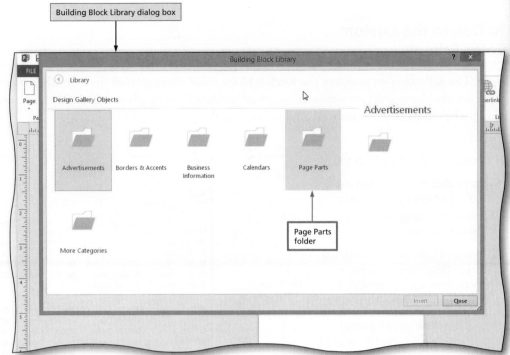

Figure 4–79

2

- Tap or click the Page Parts folder (Building Block Library dialog box) to open it.

- Press and hold or right-click the Rocket Dogs Logo to display its shortcut menu (Figure 4–80).

🔍 **Experiment**

- Tap or click Edit Properties on the shortcut menu and view the Edit Building Block Properties dialog box and its fields of information that Publisher saves. When finished, click the OK button to close the dialog box, and then press and hold or right-click again to display the graphic's shortcut menu.

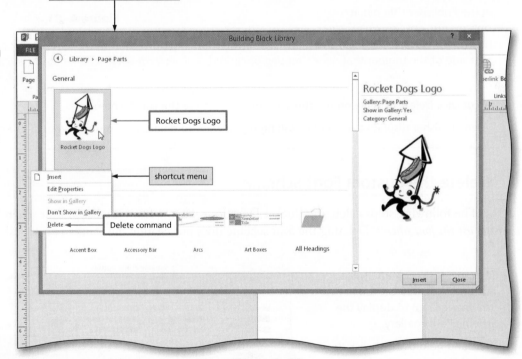

Figure 4–80

3

- Tap or click Delete on the shortcut menu to delete the graphic.

- If Publisher displays a dialog box asking if you want to delete the building block permanently, tap or click the Yes button.

- Tap or click the Close button (Building Block Library dialog box) to close the dialog box.

To Delete the Custom Color Scheme

The following steps delete the Rocket Dogs color scheme from the Publisher list of color schemes. **Why?** *If you are working in a lab environment, you should delete all custom schemes.* Deleting the color scheme does not change the colors in previously created publications.

- Display the PAGE DESIGN tab.

- Tap or click the More button (PAGE DESIGN tab | Schemes group) to display the Color Scheme gallery.

- Press and hold or right-click the Rocket Dogs color scheme in the Custom area to display the shortcut menu (Figure 4–81).

Q&A How does the 'Add Gallery to Quick Access Toolbar' command work?
Recall that the Quick Access Toolbar appears above the ribbon on the Publisher title bar. It contains buttons for commonly used commands and settings, and it is customizable. Tapping or clicking the command will add a button on the right side of the toolbar that, when tapped or clicked, will set your color scheme automatically.

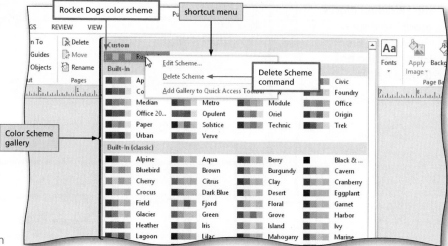

Figure 4–81

- Tap or click Delete Scheme on the shortcut menu to delete the color scheme.

- When Publisher displays a dialog box asking if you want to delete the color scheme, tap or click the Yes button.

To Delete the Custom Font Scheme

The following steps delete the Rocket Dogs font scheme from the list of font schemes. **Why?** *You no longer need to use the font scheme.* Deleting the font scheme does not change the fonts in previously created publications.

- Tap or click the Scheme Fonts button (PAGE DESIGN tab | Schemes group) to display the Scheme Fonts gallery.

- Press and hold or right-click the Rocket Dogs font scheme in the Scheme Fonts gallery to display the shortcut menu (Figure 4–82).

Q&A How does the 'Update Scheme from Publication Styles' command work?
If you change the font in some of your text boxes and like it better than the original one in the font scheme, you can click the command to change the font scheme permanently.

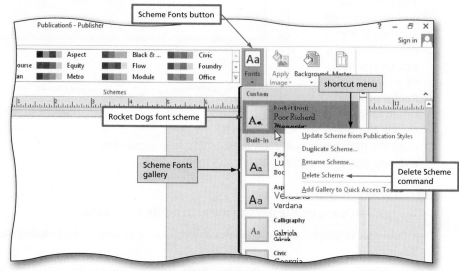

Figure 4–82

- Tap or click Delete Scheme on the shortcut menu to delete the font scheme.

- When Publisher displays a dialog box asking if you want to delete the building block, tap or click the Yes button.

To Delete the Custom Blank Page

The following steps delete the customized blank page size named 5 × 7 Table Card. Deleting the page size does not change the size of previously created publications. *Why? Publisher does not go back and change settings in a saved publication.*

- Tap or click the 'Choose Page Size' button (PAGE DESIGN tab | Page Setup group) to display the Page Size gallery.

- Press and hold or right-click '5 × 7 Table Card' to display the shortcut menu (Figure 4–83).

- Tap or click Delete on the shortcut menu to delete the page size.

- When Publisher displays a dialog box asking if you want to delete the size permanently, tap or click the Yes button.

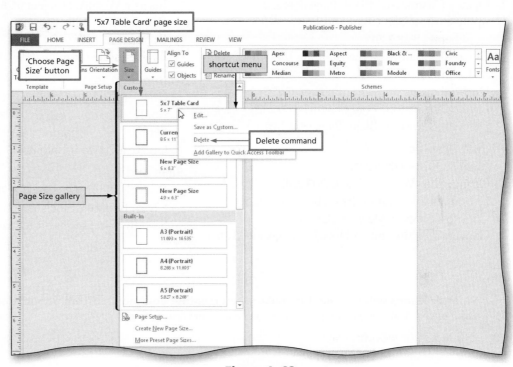

Figure 4–83

Other Ways

1. In template gallery, press and hold or right-click custom template, tap or click Delete on shortcut menu

To Exit Publisher

This project is complete. The following steps exit Publisher. For a detailed example of the procedure summarized below, refer to the Office and Windows chapter at the beginning of this book.

1. To exit Publisher, tap or click the Close button on the right side of the title bar.

2. If a Microsoft Publisher dialog box is displayed, tap or click the Don't Save button so that any changes you have made are not saved.

BTW

Quick Reference
For a table that lists how to complete the tasks covered in this book using touch gestures, the mouse, ribbon, shortcut menu, and keyboard, see the Quick Reference Summary at the back of this book, or visit the Quick Reference resource on the Student Companion Site located on www.cengagebrain .com. For detailed instructions about accessing available resources, visit www.cengage.com/ct/ studentdownload or see the inside back cover of this book.

Chapter Summary

In this chapter, you learned how to create a custom publication, editing the size, margins, color scheme, and font scheme. You formatted text with gradients and changed the line spacing, alignment, and distribution. You grouped, rotated, and edited graphics and shapes. You created a WordArt object and a bulleted list with a custom bullet. The items listed below include all the new Publisher skills you have learned in this chapter.

Customize Publications
Create a Custom Page Size (PUB 198)
Create a New Color Scheme (PUB 200)
Create a New Font Scheme (PUB 203)
Select a Blank Publication (PUB 197)
Open a Customized Blank Page (PUB 238)
Apply Customized Color and Font
    Schemes (PUB 239)
Delete Content from the Building Block
    Library (PUB 240)
Delete the Custom Color Scheme (PUB 242)
Delete the Custom Font Scheme (PUB 242)
Delete the Custom Blank Page (PUB 243)

Format Graphics
Align an Object (PUB 221)
Change the WordArt Shape (PUB 224)
Choose a Color not in the Gallery (PUB 202)
Choose a Shape Style (PUB 232)
Convert a Picture into a Drawing Object (PUB 207)

Create a Picture Fill (PUB 233)
Crop to Shape (PUB 236)
Edit an Ungrouped Graphic (PUB 208)
Insert a Building Block (PUB 225)
Insert a Shape (PUB 231)
Insert a WordArt Object (PUB 223)
Recolor a Graphic (PUB 234)
Rotate (PUB 210)
Ungroup the Graphic (PUB 207)

Manipulate Text
Change the Line Spacing (PUB 216)
Apply a Gradient to Text (PUB 219)
Set the Text Wrapping (PUB 227)
Create a Custom Bullet (PUB 228)

Save and Print
Print the Table Card (PUB 237)
Save a Building Block (PUB 213)
Save the Graphic as a Picture (PUB 214)

CONSIDER THIS

What decisions will you need to make when creating your next custom publication?

Use these guidelines as you complete the assignments in this chapter and create your own publications outside of this class.

1. Decide on the customization.
   a) Create a custom page size.
   b) Create a custom color scheme.
   c) Create a custom font scheme.
2. Choose your graphics.
   a) Edit and format pictures and clip art to create custom graphics.
3. Save reusable graphics as building blocks.
4. Create headings and text.
   a) Change the line spacing as necessary.
   b) Wrap text.
   c) Apply text effects.
   d) Align and distribute objects.
   e) Create bulleted lists.
5. Use WordArt sparingly.
6. Insert shapes for emphasis and interest.
   a) Use color, gradient, and picture fills as necessary.
   b) Crop pictures to shapes as needed.
7. Delete customizations in lab settings.

CONSIDER THIS

How should you submit solutions to questions in the assignments identified with a symbol?

Every assignment in this book contains one or more questions identified with a symbol. These questions require you to think beyond the assigned publication. Present your solutions to the questions in the format required by your instructor. Possible formats may include one or more of these options: write the answer; create a document that contains the answer; present your answer to the class; discuss your answer in a group; record the answer as audio or video using a webcam, smartphone, or portable media player; or post answers on a blog, wiki, or website.

Apply Your Knowledge

Reinforce the skills and apply the concepts you learned in this chapter.

Editing Drawing Objects

Note: To complete this assignment, you will be required to use the Data Files for Students. Visit www.cengage.com/ct/studentdownload for detailed instructions or contact your instructor for information about accessing the required files.

Instructions: The local hobby shop, Hobby Express would like you to create a logo for them. You produce the logo shown in Figure 4–84.

Figure 4–84

Perform the following tasks:

1. Run Publisher. Open the file named Apply 4-1 Hobby Express. Zoom to 150%.
2. To separate the parts of the graphic:
   a. Select the graphic, and then tap or click the Ungroup button (PICTURE TOOLS FORMAT tab | Arrange group). When Publisher asks if you want to convert the picture to a Microsoft Office drawing object, tap or click the Yes button (Microsoft Publisher dialog box).
   b. Press and hold or right-click the drawing object, and then tap or click Ungroup on the shortcut menu.

Continued >

c. Tap or click outside the graphic to deselect it. One at a time, select and delete each of the light blue lines that comprise the tracks, the smoke, and the railroad crossing sign.

d. Drag around the remaining parts of the graphic, and then tap or click the Group button (DRAWING TOOLS FORMAT tab | Arrange group) to regroup the graphic.

3. Flip the graphic horizontally by using the Rotate button (DRAWING TOOLS FORMAT tab | Arrange group).

4. To save the graphic as a picture, press and hold or right-click the grouped object, and then tap or click 'Save as Picture' on the shortcut menu. Save the file on your storage device with the name Apply 4-1 Engine. Delete the graphic from the publication.

5. To insert and format a shape:

a. Tap or click the Shapes button (INSERT tab | Illustrations group.

b. Tap or click the Oval button in the Basic Shapes area of the Shapes gallery, and SHIFT+drag a circle approximately 2 inches by 2 inches.

c. Tap or click the Shape Fill button (DRAWING TOOLS FORMAT tab | Shape Styles group), and then tap or click Picture in the Shape Fill gallery.

d. Tap or click Browse next to From a file (Insert Pictures dialog box), navigate to your storage location, and then double-tap or double-click the Apply 4-1 Engine graphic.

e. Tap or click the Shape Outline button (DRAWING TOOLS FORMAT tab | Shape Styles group), and choose a dark blue color, such as Accent 1 (RGB(91,155,213)), Darker 50%.

f. Tap or click the Shape Outline button (DRAWING TOOLS FORMAT tab | Shape Styles group) again, tap or click Weight, and then choose 3 pt in the list.

6. To create a text box:

a. If necessary, zoom out and then draw a text box on the page approximately .75 inches tall, from margin to margin. Type the words, **Hobby Express**. Press and hold or right-click the text, and tap or click Best Fit on the shortcut menu.

b. Tap or click the Shape Fill button (DRAWING TOOLS FORMAT tab | Shape Styles group) and then choose a dark blue color.

c. Select the text, and then tap or click the Font Color arrow (HOME tab | Font group). Choose a white color.

d. Tap or click the Wrap Text button (DRAWING TOOLS FORMAT tab | Arrange group), and then tap or click Square.

7. To position the graphics:

a. Zoom to Whole Page view. Drag the graphic to the top of the page approximately 2 inches from the left margin.

b. Drag the text box up so the bottom of the text box roughly aligns with the bottom of the graphic.

c. Tap or click the Send Backward button (DRAWING TOOLS FORMAT tab | Arrange group).

8. Save the file with the name Apply 4-1 Hobby Express Complete.

9. Submit the revised publication in the format specified by your instructor.

10. ✳ Why do you think the instructions ask you to save the graphic as a picture in Step 4? Why might you save the graphic and the text box as a building block? What other things would you add to the publication to make it usable as letterhead?

Extend Your Knowledge

Extend the skills you learned in this chapter and experiment with new skills. You may need to use Help to complete the assignment.

Creating a Custom Graphic

Note: To complete this assignment, you will be required to use the Data Files for Students. Visit www.cengage.com/ct/studentdownload for detailed instructions or contact your instructor for information about accessing the required files.

Instructions: It is Mardi Gras time! The tourism board has asked you to create a newspaper advertisement about the Mardi Gras parade. In the broadsheet newspaper format, a 1/8-page advertisement would be 3 columns wide (approximately 5.25 inches) by 5 inches tall with 1/8-inch (or .125-inch) margins. You decide to start from scratch to create the ad shown in Figure 4–85.

Figure 4–85

Continued >

Extend Your Knowledge *continued*

Perform the following tasks:

1. Run Publisher. Choose a blank publication template.

2. Create a new page size named 1/8 Page Advertisement. Set the width to 5.25 inches and the height to 5 inches. Set all margins to zero. Tap or click the Layout type arrow, and then tap or click 'One page per sheet'.

3. Create a custom color scheme named Mardi Gras with the Black as the main color and accent colors of violet, green, gold, and red.

4. Create a custom font scheme named Mardi Gras with Jokerman as the heading font and Imprint MT Shadow as the body font.

5. Change the background to 10% tint of Accent 3.

6. Insert several pictures from Office.com Clip Art, related to Mardi Gras, beads, fleur-de-lis, and feathers similar to those shown in Figure 4–85. Move the pictures to the scratch area. Insert the Extend 4-1 Mask graphic from the Data Files for Students.

7. Use Help to read about tips for working with images. Select the beads graphic. Tap or click the Corrections button (PICTURE TOOLS FORMAT tab | Adjust group), and choose a very light preview. Tap or click the Recolor button (PICTURE TOOLS FORMAT tab | Adjust group), and then tap or click the 'Set Transparent Color' command. Tap or click the white background in the beads graphic to make that color transparent. Move the graphic into the page layout.

8. Ungroup the mask to create a Microsoft Office drawing object, and then ungroup to separate the graphic. Tap or click away from the graphic to deselect its parts. Drag around half of the mask and recolor the selection. Drag around the other half of the mask and recolor it using a different color. Regroup the mask, and then move it into the page layout.

9. Select the fleur-de-lis and recolor it. Tap or click the Picture Effects button (PICTURE TOOLS FORMAT tab | Picture styles group). Tap or click Glow in the gallery and choose an appropriate glow. Use the gallery again to choose a reflection similar to Figure 4–85. Move the graphic into the page layout.

10. Recolor and rotate the feathers and move them into the page layout.

11. Create a text box in the scratch area, approximately 4 inches square. Set the text wrapping on the text box to Through. Set the font size to 24. Press CTRL+E to center the text. Type the following text, pressing the ENTER key after each line except the last.

```
Mardi Gras Parade!
February 17
8:00 p.m.
17th & Main
to
38th & Main
```

12. Format the first line with the Jokerman font, and then move the text box into the page layout.

13. Save the file with the name Extend 4-1 Mardi Gras Advertisement.

14. If you are working in a lab environment, delete any customization.

15. Submit the file in the format specified by your instructor.

16. ✸ What are some differences between Text Fill effects and Picture effects? Why do you think the Picture Effects gallery has more options and settings? How many picture and fill effects are too many?

Analyze, Correct, Improve

Analyze a publication, correct all errors, and improve it.

Correcting Text Formatting

Note: To complete this assignment, you will be required to use the Data Files for Students. Visit www.cengage.com/ct/studentdownload for detailed instructions or contact your instructor for information about accessing the required files.

Instructions: Your father started to create a meme to post on Facebook or other social media sites, but then he ran into trouble when the text would not display in front of the graphics (Figure 4–86). He has asked you to fix it. Run Publisher and open the file, Analyze 4-1 Social Media Graphic.

Figure 4–86

Continued >

Analyze, Correct, Improve *continued*

Perform the following tasks:

1. Correct The publication has formatting errors related to layering, line spacing, and text wrapping. Move objects into the scratch area to format them individually. Set the text wrapping of the black and white rectangles to Through. Set the text wrapping of the text box to Square. Change the line spacing of the text box to 1sp. One at a time, move the objects on to the page layout, bringing them forward or sending them backward as necessary.

2. Improve The white rectangle and the text box would look better if they were both at an angle. Free rotate each approximately 15 degrees counterclockwise. Save the document using the file name, Analyze 4-1 Social Media Graphic Complete. Submit the revised document in the format specified by your instructor.

3. What objects might you group together for formatting purposes? Why?

In the Labs

Design, create, or modify a publication using the guidelines, concepts, and skills presented in this chapter. Labs 1 and 2, which increase in difficulty, require you to create a solution based on what you learned in the chapter; Lab 3 requires you to create a solution, which uses cloud and web technologies, by learning and investigating on your own from general guidance.

Lab 1: Designing a Recipe Card

Problem: You enjoy the Student Chef Club on campus. They are holding a recipe exchange at the next meeting, so you decide to create the recipe card shown in Figure 4–87. You plan to print 20 copies.

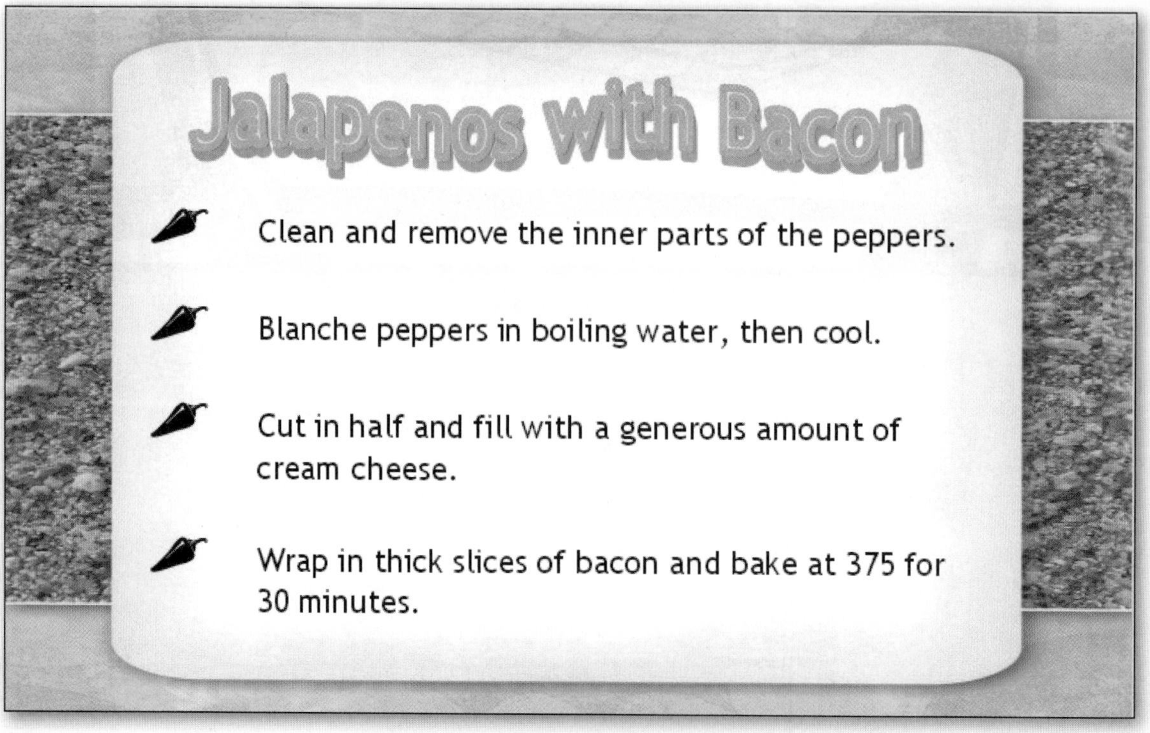

Figure 4–87

1. Run Publisher. Choose a blank 8.5 × 11 publication. Select the Fjord color scheme and the Opulent font scheme. Create the publication.

2. Tap or click the 'Choose Page Size' button (PAGE DESIGN tab | Page Setup group). Create a new page size named 3 × 5 Recipe Card (Create New Page Size dialog box). Set the width to 5 inches and the height to 3 inches. Set all margins to zero. Tap or click the Layout type arrow, and then tap or click 'Multiple pages per sheet' in the list. In the Options area, set the side and top margins to 1 inch. Tap or click the OK button to close the Create New Page Size dialog box.

3. Tap or click the Online Pictures button (INSERT tab | Illustrations group) and use Office.com Clip Art searching for the term, `border.` Choose a graphic with four sides and white space in the middle, similar to the one shown in Figure 4–87 on the previous page.

4. Resize the graphic to fill the page layout.

5. Insert a WordArt object into the scratch area. Use the 'Fill - Light Orange, Outline – Orange' WordArt Style. Type the text, `Jalapenos with Bacon.` Choose the Trebuchet font and size 20.

6. Change the shape of the WordArt to 'Double Wave 1,' and then drag the WordArt to a location across the top of the white area of the border graphic.

7. Draw a text box in the scratch area, approximately 4 inches wide and 2.25 inches tall. Create a custom bullet character using the Webdings character set, and the pepper character, code 44. Set the bullet character to be size 22. Select the text in the 'Indent list by' text box (Bullets and Numbering dialog box), and then type .5 for the indenture.

8. In the text box, change the font size to 10. Enter the following lines of text, pressing the ENTER key after each line except the last:

   `Clean and remove the inner parts of the peppers.`

   `Blanche peppers in boiling water, then cool.`

   `Cut in half and fill with a generous amount of cream cheese.`

   `Wrap in thick slices of bacon and bake at 375 for 30 minutes.`

9. Drag the text box into the publication and align it relative to the margins.

10. Check your publication for spelling and design errors.

11. Save the publication on your storage device with the file name, Lab 4-1 Recipe Card.

12. If you are working in a lab situation, delete any customization.

13. Submit the file as directed by your instructor.

14. ✴ Are custom bullet characters distracting? Why or why not? How hard is it to find the character you want in the Bullet Character dialog box? Can you think of other ways to create or find custom bullets?

Continued >

In the Labs *continued*

Lab 2: Editing a Save the Date Card

Note: To complete this assignment, you will be required to use the Data Files for Students. Visit www.cengage.com/ct/studentdownload for detailed instructions or contact your instructor for information about accessing the required files.

Problem: Your best friend has started a Save the Date card for her upcoming wedding. She has asked you to enhance the text with a gradient fill and put rounded corners on the picture (Figure 4–88).

1. Run Publisher and open the file Lab 4-2 Save the Date Card from the Data Files for Students.
2. Select the picture of the ring. Crop it to the shape of a heart.
3. Select the picture of the two people embracing on the right. Crop it to a rounded rectangle.
4. Select the text, Laura & Fredrick. Create a text fill with a gradient, and then add a text outline.
5. Check the publication for spelling errors and design errors, and fix them as necessary.
6. Save the publication on your storage device with the file name, Lab 4-2 Save the Date Card Complete.
7. Submit the file as directed by your instructor.
8. ✳ Why do you think this publication is 4 × 6 inches? Would it make sense to create a second page to this publication? Why?

Figure 4–88

Photos courtesy of Fredrick Starks

Lab 3: Expand Your World: Cloud and Web Technologies
Choosing Colors

Problem: You would like to create a color scheme that exactly matches your school colors. You decide to explore Web 2.0 color tools.

Instructions:

1. Locate a picture with your school colors, or the web address (URL) of your school logo. The picture should be in the .gif, .png, or .jpg format. The web address might be something like www.myschool.edu/logo.gif.

2. Open a browser and go to www.imagecolorpicker.com (Figure 4–89). The website may differ slightly.

3. If you have the web address of your school logo, type it in the 'URL to Image' text box. If you have a picture, tap or click the 'Upload your image' button, browse to and open the image; and then tap or click Submit Query button (File upload dialog box).

4. When the image is displayed, tap or click the main color of the image. Write down the RGB codes. Tap or click two other prominent colors in the logo and write down their RGB codes.

5. Open Publisher and create a blank publication. Tap or click the More button (PAGE DESIGN tab | Schemes group) to display the Color Schemes gallery. Tap or click 'Create New Color Scheme' to display the Create New Color Scheme dialog box. Enter a name for your new color scheme.

Figure 4–89

© www.imagecolorpicker.com 2006–2013

Continued >

In the Labs *continued*

6. Tap or click the Accent 1 New button, and then tap or click the More Colors button to display the Colors dialog box. Tap or click the Custom tab and enter the RGB numbers. Tap or click the OK button (Colors dialog box).

7. Repeat Step 6 for the Accent 2 and Accent 3 colors.

8. Save the color scheme. Use the color scheme to create a shape, WordArt, or text fill.

9. Submit the assignment in the format specified by your instructor.

10. If you are working in a lab environment, delete any customizations.

11. ✳ In what other situations might you want to search for exact colors? Make a list of companies that probably copyright their logo and its colors. Do you know of any colors that commonly are referred to by a company name, such as "Facebook blue"?

✳ Consider This: Your Turn

Apply your creative thinking and problem solving skills to design and implement a solution.

1: Creating a Custom Building Block

Personal/Academic

Part 1: The American Sign Language Club has a chapter at your school. They would like to create a building block that includes the signs for the letters, A, S, and L. They plan to use the building block in several ways, including on their correspondence, website, and flyers. Open a blank publication. Set the color scheme to Metro. Use Office.com Clip Art to look for graphics related to sign language. One at a time, insert the signs for A, S, and L into the publication. Recolor each one differently. Rotate the A and the L at 45-degree angles on either side of the letter S, creating a kind of triangle. Select the three graphics and group. Add the group to the Building Block Library. Save the publication. Remember to include a description and searchable keywords. If you create the building block on a lab computer, remember to delete it after submitting the assignment to your instructor.

Part 2: ✳ Why do you think the assignment called for setting the color scheme? How did it affect required steps after that? What recolor options did you choose, and why?

2: Creating a Banner

Professional

Part 1: A local farmer's market has asked you to create a banner. They would like a wave shape that fills the banner, with a gradient fill to serve as a background for the words, The Merry Market. Create a blank page publication approximately 17 inches wide and 8.5 inches tall. Insert a Wave shape and resize it to fill the banner. Use a one-color gradient any shade of green. Use a large text box and style for the company name, placed in front of the wave shape. Insert a text box in the lower-left corner of the banner that displays the address and telephone number: `1350 Gentry Avenue, Blue Dust, IA 50382, (515) 555-3770.` If you are working in a lab environment, delete any customization.

Part 2: ✳ Did you save this page size and give it a name, or did you just change the size of the page for this publication only? Why?

3: Researching Templates

Research and Collaboration

Part 1: As a group, find a local not-for-profit agency that needs a custom publication. Discuss with the agency manager the needs of the agency and the skills of your group. As a group, decide on consistent fonts, colors, logos, and other elements of the publication. Individually, use the concepts and techniques presented in this chapter to create the publication for the agency. Bring the publications to the group, discuss each one, and make recommendations for change. Edit the publications and submit them in the format specified by your instructor. If you are working in a lab environment, delete any customization. Submit all final copies to the agency.

Part 2: ✹ You made several decisions while creating the publication in this assignment: How did you decide on a color and font scheme? What was the hardest part of working with the customer? What was the easiest? Which publication did the agency choose to use and why?

Learn Online

Reinforce what you learned in this chapter with games, exercises, training, and many other online activities and resources.

Student Companion Site Reinforce chapter terms and concepts using review questions, flash cards, practice tests, and interactive learning games, such as a crossword puzzle. These and other online activities and resources are available at no additional cost on www.cengagebrain.com. Visit www.cengage.com/ct/studentdownload for detailed instructions about accessing the resources available at the Student Companion Site.

5 | Using Business Information Sets

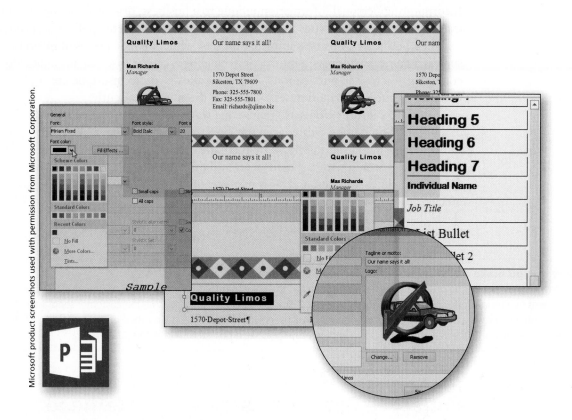

Objectives

You will have mastered the material in this chapter when you can:

- Design a letterhead
- Create a business information set
- Insert business information fields into a publication
- Use the Measurement toolbar to position and scale objects
- Create and apply a new text style
- Insert an automatically updated date and time

- Apply the read-only attribute to a publication
- Add user-friendly features to an interactive publication
- Create a fax cover
- Create an envelope
- Create and print business cards
- Publish a portable PDF/XPS file
- Embed fonts in a publication

5 | Using Business Information Sets

Introduction

Incorporating personal information unique to a business, organization, or individual user expands the possibilities for using Publisher as a complete application product for small businesses. Business information sets, which include pieces of information such as a name, an address, a motto, or even a logo, can be inserted automatically and consistently across all publications. Publisher allows you to insert, delete, and save multiple business information sets and apply them independently.

Business information sets are just one way that people expand Publisher's capabilities. Some users create large text boxes and use Publisher like a word processor. Others create a table and perform mathematical and statistical operations or embed charts as they would with a spreadsheet. Still others create a database and use Publisher for mass mailings, billings, and customer accounts. Publisher's capabilities make it an efficient tool in small business offices — without the cost and learning curve of some of the high-end dedicated application software.

Project — Business Cards and Letterhead

Storing permanent information about a business facilitates the customization of publications such as business cards and letterhead. A **business information set** is a group of customized information fields about an individual or an organization that can be used to generate information text boxes across publications. Many of the Publisher templates automatically create business information text boxes to incorporate data from the business information set. Publications created from scratch also can integrate a business information set by including one or more pieces in the publication. For example, you can save your name, address, and telephone number in a business information set. Whenever you need that information, you can insert it in a publication without retyping it.

To illustrate some of the business features of Microsoft Publisher, this project presents a series of steps to create a business information set. You will use the business information set in a letterhead, fax cover, envelope, and business card. You also will create a portable file for easy viewing, and embed fonts in the Publisher file for editing on a different computer. The project creates publications for a business named Quality Limos, as shown in Figure 5–1.

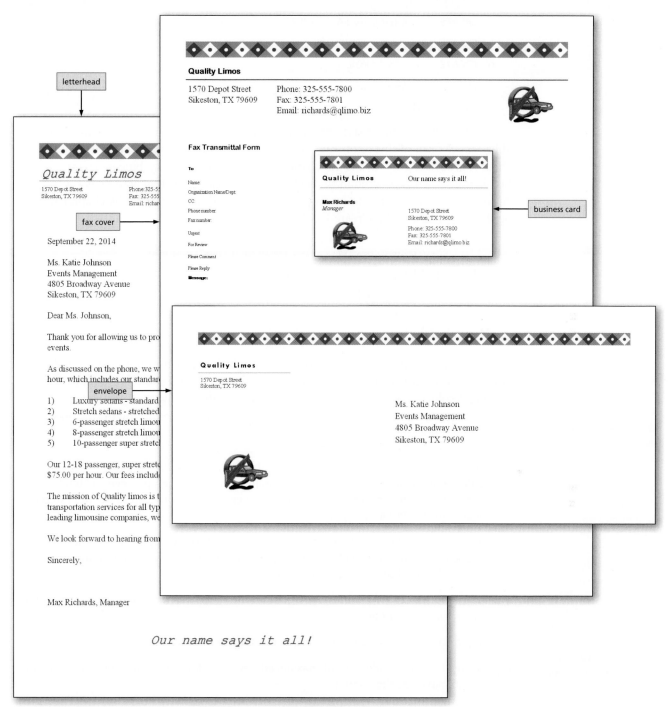

Figure 5–1

Roadmap

In this chapter, you will learn how to create the publication shown in Figure 5–1. The following roadmap identifies general activities you will perform as you progress through this chapter:

1. CREATE letterhead using a BUSINESS INFORMATION SET.

2. CREATE a NEW STYLE.

3. CUSTOMIZE business LETTERHEAD for ease of use.

4. CREATE a user-friendly FAX COVER.
5. CREATE a single-use ENVELOPE.
6. CREATE BUSINESS CARDS.
7. CREATE PORTABLE FILES.
8. EMBED FONTS.

At the beginning of step instructions throughout the chapter, you will see an abbreviated form of this roadmap. The abbreviated roadmap uses colors to indicate chapter progress: gray means the chapter is beyond that activity, blue means the task being shown is covered in that activity, and black means that activity is yet to be covered. For example, the following abbreviated roadmap indicates the chapter would be showing a task in the Create Fax Cover activity.

1 CREATE BUSINESS INFORMATION SET | 2 CREATE NEW STYLE | 3 CUSTOMIZE LETTERHEAD | **4 CREATE FAX COVER**
5 CREATE ENVELOPE | 6 CREATE BUSINESS CARDS | 7 CREATE PORTABLE FILES | 8 EMBED FONTS

Use the abbreviated roadmap as a progress guide while you read or step through the instructions in this chapter.

To Run Publisher

If you are using a computer to step through the project in this chapter and you want your screens to match the figures in this book, you should change your screen's resolution to 1366×768. For information about how to change a computer's resolution, refer to the Office and Windows chapter at the beginning of this book.

The following steps run Publisher.

One of the few differences between Windows 7 and Windows 8 occurs in the steps to run Publisher. If you are using Windows 7, click the Start button, type **Publisher** in the 'Search programs and files' box, click Publisher 2013, and then, if necessary, maximize the Publisher window. For a summary of the steps to run Publisher in Windows 7, refer to the Quick Reference located at the back of this book.

1 Scroll the Start screen and search for a Publisher 2013 tile. If your Start screen contains a Publisher 2013 tile, tap or click it to run Publisher, and then proceed to Step 5. If the Start screen does not contain the Publisher 2013 tile, proceed to the next step to search for the Publisher app.

2 Swipe in from the right edge of the screen or point to the upper-right corner of the screen to display the Charms bar, and then tap or click the Search charm on the Charms bar to display the Search menu.

3 Type **Publisher** as the search text in the Search box, and watch the search results appear in the Apps list.

4 Tap or click Publisher 2013 in the search results to run Publisher.

5 If the Publisher window is not maximized, tap or click the Maximize button on its title bar to maximize the window.

Creating Letterhead

In many businesses, **letterhead** is preprinted paper with important facts about the company and blank space to contain the text of the correspondence. Letterhead, typically used for official business communication, is an easy way to convey company information to the reader and quickly establish a formal and legitimate mode of correspondence. The company information may be displayed in a variety of places — across the top, down the side, or split between the top and bottom of the page. Although most business letterhead is $8\frac{1}{2} \times 11$ inches, other sizes are becoming more popular, especially with small agencies and not-for-profit organizations.

Generally, it is cost effective for companies to outsource the printing of their letterhead; however, designing the letterhead in-house and then sending the file to a commercial printer saves design consultation time, customization, and money. Black-and-white or spot-color letterhead is more common and less expensive than composite or process color. Businesses sometimes opt not to purchase preprinted letterhead because of its expense, color, or the limited quantity required. In those cases, companies design their own letterhead and save it in a file. In some cases, businesses print multiple copies of their blank letterhead and then, using application software, they prepare documents to print on the letterhead paper.

To Create a Letterhead Template

The following steps open a letterhead template and apply color and font schemes.

1 In the template gallery, tap or click BUILT-IN to display the BUILT-IN templates.

2 Scroll as necessary and then tap or click the Letterhead thumbnail within the BUILT-IN templates to display the Letterhead templates.

3 In the section labeled, More Installed Templates, tap or click the Accessory Bar thumbnail to choose the template.

4 Tap or click the Color scheme button in the template information pane. Scroll as necessary, and tap or click Orange to choose the color scheme.

5 Tap or click the Font scheme button, scroll as necessary, and then tap or click Galley to choose the font scheme.

6 If necessary, tap or click to display the check mark in the Include logo check box (Figure 5–2).

7 Tap or click the CREATE button to create the publication based on the template settings.

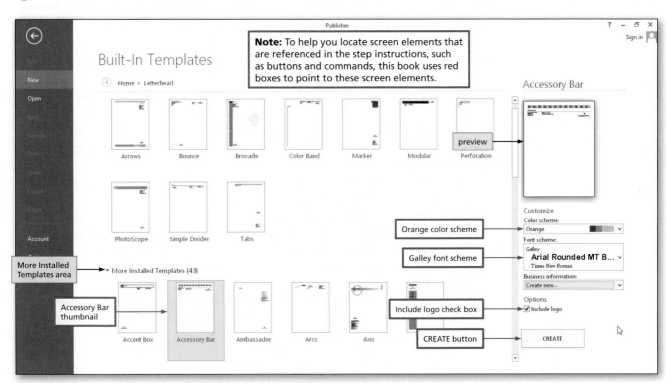

Figure 5–2

To Hide the Page Navigation Pane

The following step hides the Page Navigation pane.

1 If the Page Navigation pane is displayed, tap or click the 'Current page in publication' button on the status bar to hide the Page Navigation pane.

To Display Formatting Marks

The following step displays formatting marks.

1 If the Special Characters button (HOME tab | Paragraph group) is not selected already, tap or click it to display formatting marks on the screen.

Creating a Business Information Set

Business information sets store data about a company. This data then is used in publications whenever you need it or when a Publisher template incorporates it. For example, rather than typing the name of the company multiple times, you can insert the data from a field in the business information set. A **field** is a specific component in the set, such as an individual's name, job position or title, organization name, address, telephone and fax numbers, email address, tagline, or logo. When inserting a field, Publisher places a text box in your publication and supplies the text.

Publisher allows you to create and save as many different business information sets as you want. If you have more than one set saved, you can choose the set you need from a list. The sets are stored within the Publisher application files on your computer. When you create a new publication, the business information set used most recently populates the new publication. When Publisher first is installed, the business information is generic, with words such as Title and Business Name. In a laboratory situation, the business information set may be populated with information about your school, which was provided when Microsoft Office 2013 was installed.

If you edit a text box within a publication that contains personal information, you change the set for that publication only, unless you choose to update the set. To affect changes for all future publications, you edit the business information set itself. You can edit the stored business information set at any time — before, during, or after performing other publication tasks.

Many types of publications use logos to identify and distinguish the page. A **logo** is a recognizable symbol that identifies a person, business, or organization. A logo may be composed of a name, a picture, or a combination of text, symbols, and graphics. The Building Block Library contains many logo styles from which you may choose, or you can create a logo from a picture, from a file, or from scratch. Although Publisher's logo styles are generic, commercial logos typically are copyrighted. Consult with a legal representative before you commercially use materials bearing clip art, logos, designs, words, or other symbols that could violate third-party rights, including trademarks.

Table 5–1 displays the data for each of the fields in the business information set that you will create in this project.

Table 5–1 Data for Business Information Fields

Fields	Data
Individual name	Max Richards
Job or position or title	Manager
Organization name	Quality Limos
Address	1570 Depot Street Sikeston, TX 79609
Phone, fax, and e-mail	Phone: 325-555-7800 Fax: 325-555-7801 Email: richards@qlimo.biz
Tagline or motto	Our name says it all!
Business Information set name	Quality Limos
Logo	Quality Limos Logo.gif from Data Files for Students

©2014 Cengage Learning

To Create a Business Information Set

1 CREATE BUSINESS INFORMATION SET | 2 CREATE NEW STYLE | 3 CUSTOMIZE LETTERHEAD | 4 CREATE FAX COVER
5 CREATE ENVELOPE | 6 CREATE BUSINESS CARDS | 7 CREATE PORTABLE FILES | 8 EMBED FONTS

The following steps create a business information set for Quality Limos and apply it to the current publication. You will enter data for each field. *Why? Entering the data fields and saving them will allow you to reuse the content in other publications.* To complete these steps, you will be required to use the Data Files for Students. Visit www.cengage.com/ct/studentdownload for detailed instructions or contact your instructor for information about accessing the required files.

1

- Zoom to Page Width.

- Display the INSERT tab.

- Tap or click the Business Information button (INSERT tab | Text group) to display the list of business information fields and commands (Figure 5–3).

Q&A
Why does my screen look different?
If you have any saved business information sets on your computer, your list may contain other data in each field.

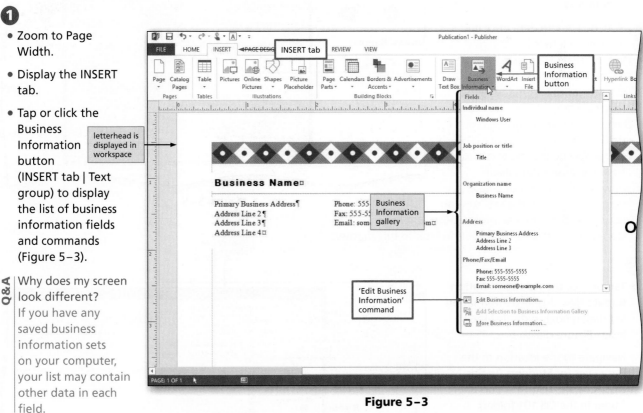

Figure 5–3

• Tap or click 'Edit Business Information' to display the Create New Business Information Set dialog box (Figure 5–4).

Q&A

Why does the Individual name text box already have a name in it?
The person or company that installed Publisher may have supplied data for the business information set. You will replace the data in the next step.

How do you use the other commands in the list?
The 'Add Selection to Business Information Gallery' command allows you to add selected text and graphics as a Publisher building block. The 'More Business Information' command opens the Building Block Library from which you can add objects to your publication.

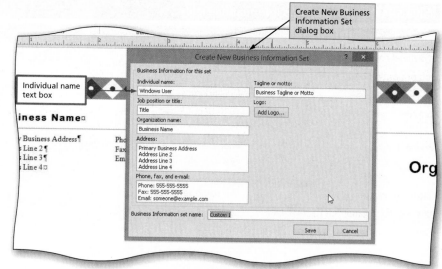

Figure 5–4

• Enter the data from Table 5–1, pressing the TAB key to advance from one field to the next (Figure 5–5).

Q&A

How do I delete data once it is inserted in a field?
In the Create New Business Information Set dialog box, you can select the text in the field and then press the DELETE key. To remove a business information field while editing a publication, you simply delete the text box from the publication itself; however, this does not delete it permanently from the set. You can remove entire business information sets once they are stored; you will see how to do this later in this chapter.

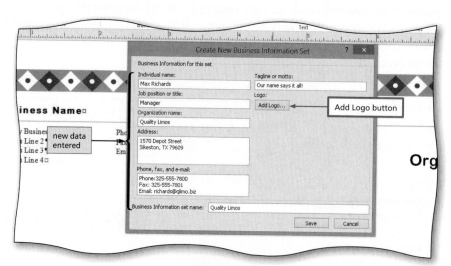

Figure 5–5

4

• Tap or click the Add Logo button (Create New Business Information Set dialog box) to display the Insert Picture dialog box.

• Navigate to the location of the Data Files for Students (in this case, Chapter 05 in the Publisher folder in the CIS 101 folder) on your computer or SkyDrive (Figure 5–6).

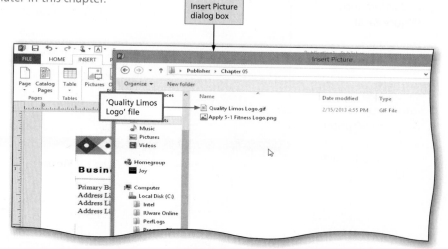

Figure 5–6

5

- Double-tap or double-click the desired file (in this case the 'Quality Limos Logo' file) (Insert Picture dialog box) to insert the logo (Figure 5–7).

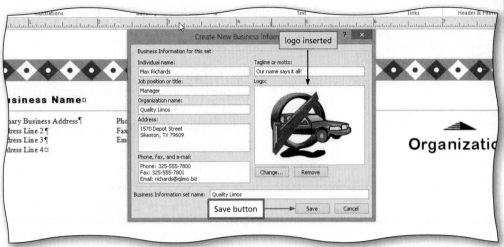

Figure 5–7

6

- Tap or click the Save button (Create New Business Information Set dialog box) to save the business information set and to display the Business Information dialog box (Figure 5–8).

Q&A Does saving the business information set also save the publication?
No, you are saving a separate, internal data file that contains only the data in the fields.

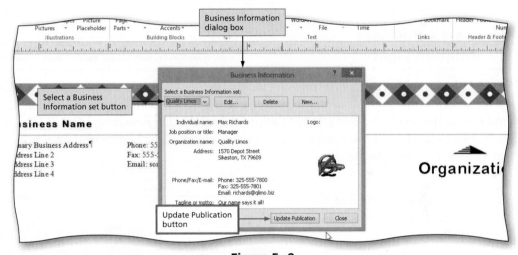

Figure 5–8

7

- Tap or click the Update Publication button (Business Information dialog box) (Figure 5–9).

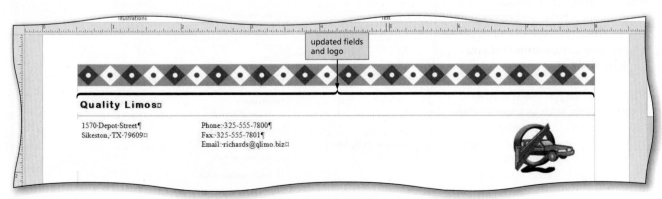

Figure 5–9

Other Ways

1. In publication, tap or click smart tag button, tap or click 'Edit Business Information', enter data, tap or click Update Publication button (Business Information dialog box)

2. In template gallery, tap or click 'Edit Business Information' button, tap or click New button, enter data, tap or click Save button (Create New Business Information Set dialog box)

BTW

Previous Business Information Set

If other people have used the computer you are working on, it is possible that other business information sets appear in your list. If you need to delete a business information set, tap or click the 'Select a business information set' box arrow (Figure 5–8 on the previous page), select the set, and then tap or click the Delete button (Business Information dialog box).

TO CHANGE THE BUSINESS INFORMATION SET OF AN EXISTING PUBLICATION

If you wanted to apply a different business information set to a publication, you would perform the following tasks.

1. Open a publication.
2. Display the INSERT tab.
3. Tap or click the Business Information button (INSERT tab | Text group) to display the list of business information fields and commands.
4. Tap or click the 'Edit Business Information' command to open the Business Information dialog box.
5. Tap or click the 'Select a Business Information set' button to display the available business information sets.
6. Tap or click the business information set (Business Information dialog box) you wish to use.
7. Tap or click the Update Publication button (Business Information dialog box).

To Insert a Business Information Field

1 CREATE BUSINESS INFORMATION SET | 2 CREATE NEW STYLE | 3 CUSTOMIZE LETTERHEAD | 4 CREATE FAX COVER
5 CREATE ENVELOPE | 6 CREATE BUSINESS CARDS | 7 CREATE PORTABLE FILES | 8 EMBED FONTS

When you insert an individual field, Publisher places either a text box with the information in the center of the screen with a preset font and font size, or a picture box with the logo. You then may position the field and format the text as necessary. *Why? Publisher uses the default formatting. Applied formatting affects the current publication only.* The following steps insert a field, in this case the tagline or motto, from the business information set into the current publication.

- Scroll to the lower portion of the page layout and display the INSERT tab.
- Tap or click the Business Information button (INSERT tab | Text group) to display the Business Information gallery (Figure 5–10).

🔎 **Experiment**

- Scroll through the various information fields and commands in the gallery to see the kinds of fields and components that you might insert.

Q&A When would you use the other components, such as those in the Content Information area?

Content Information components are similar to building block items that can be inserted as objects into the current publication. Content Information components are populated with appropriate business information fields from the current set.

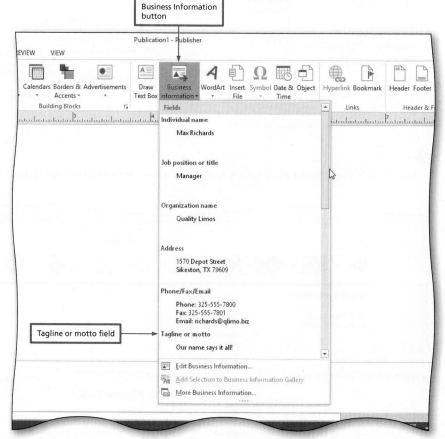

Figure 5–10

- Tap or click the desired field (in this case, the Tagline or motto field) to insert it into the publication (Figure 5–11).

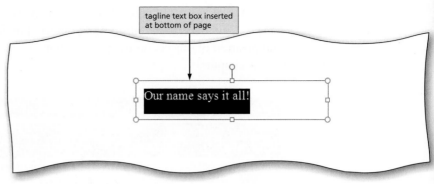

Figure 5–11

TO CREATE A BUSINESS INFORMATION SET FROM A PUBLICATION

If you have typed business information manually into a letterhead, you still can save it as a business information set. To do so, you would perform the following steps. If you currently are performing the steps in this chapter, do not perform these steps until you are finished, as creating a business information set from a publication overwrites the current business information set.

1. Choose a letterhead template and create the publication.
2. Tap or click the text in the Business Name text box, and then type the name of the business.
3. To add the field to the current business information set, which will overwrite the current information, tap or click the information smart tag, and then tap or click the 'Save to Business Information Set' command to save the data.
4. Repeat Steps 2 and 3 for the address, phone, tagline (if it exists), and logo.

BTW

The Ribbon and Screen Resolution
Publisher may change how the groups and buttons within the groups appear on the ribbon, depending on the computer's screen resolution. Thus, your ribbon may look different from the ones in this book if you are using a screen resolution other than 1366 x 768.

Using the Measurement Toolbar

To place and scale objects precisely, rather than estimating by dragging and resizing, you use the **Measurement toolbar** to enter the exact values for the horizontal position, vertical position, width, and height of the object. The Measurement toolbar not only sets the location and size of an object but also sets the angle of rotation. If the object is text, the Measurement toolbar offers additional character spacing or typesetting options. The Measurement toolbar is a floating toolbar with eight text boxes (Figure 5–12). Entries can be typed in each box by tapping or clicking the appropriate arrows.

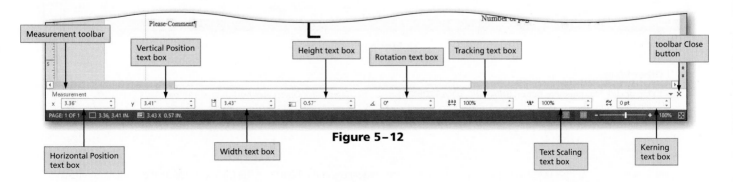

Figure 5–12

Table 5–2 lists the text boxes on the Measurement toolbar that are used to edit the position, size, and rotation of an object. The first five text boxes edit the location and position of objects on the page layout. You will learn about the other text boxes in a later chapter.

Table 5–2 Position, Size, and Rotation Boxes on the Measurement Toolbar		
Box Name	**Specifies**	**Preset Unit of Measurement**
Horizontal Position	Horizontal distance from the left edge of the page to the upper-left corner of the object	Inches
Vertical Position	Vertical distance from the top of the page to the upper-left corner of the object	Inches
Width	Width of the object	Inches
Height	Height of the object	Inches
Rotation	Rotation of the object counterclockwise from the original orientation	Degrees
Tracking	General spacing between all selected characters	Percentages
Text Scaling	Width of selected characters	Percentages
Kerning	Spacing between two selected characters to improve readability	Points

©2014 Cengage Learning

To Display the Measurement Toolbar

1 CREATE BUSINESS INFORMATION SET | 2 CREATE NEW STYLE | 3 CUSTOMIZE LETTERHEAD | 4 CREATE FAX COVER
5 CREATE ENVELOPE | 6 CREATE BUSINESS CARDS | 7 CREATE PORTABLE FILES | 8 EMBED FONTS

The following step displays the Measurement toolbar. *Why? You can choose the exact size and location of any object using the Measurement toolbar.*

- Tap or click the Object Position button on the status bar to display the Measurement toolbar (Figure 5–13).

- If necessary, drag the toolbar's title to the status bar to anchor it.

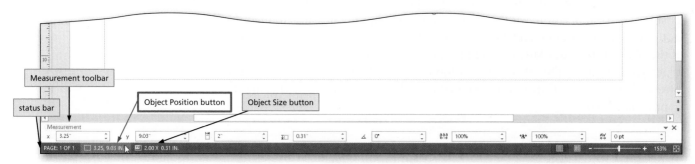

Figure 5–13

Other Ways	
1. Tap or click Measurement button (DRAWING TOOLS FORMAT tab | Size group)	2. Tap or click Object Size button on status bar

BTW
Q&As
For a complete list of the Q&As found in many of the step-by-step sequences in this book, visit the Q&A resource on the Student Companion Site located on www.cengagebrain.com. For detailed instructions about accessing available resources, visit www.cengage.com/ct/studentdownload or see the inside back cover of this book.

To Position Objects Using the Measurement Toolbar

1 CREATE BUSINESS INFORMATION SET | 2 CREATE NEW STYLE | 3 CUSTOMIZE LETTERHEAD | 4 CREATE FAX COVER
5 CREATE ENVELOPE | 6 CREATE BUSINESS CARDS | 7 CREATE PORTABLE FILES | 8 EMBED FONTS

The following steps position and scale the motto precisely using the Measurement toolbar. *Why?* *The customer has asked that the Quality Limos tagline appear more prominently at the bottom of the letterhead.*

- With the Tagline or motto text box selected, on the Measurement toolbar, select the text in the Horizontal Position text box and then type **2** to replace it. Press the TAB key to advance to the next text box.

- Type **9.75** in the Vertical Position text box, and then press the TAB key.

- Type **4.5** in the Width text box, and then press the TAB key.

- Type **.5** in the Height text box, and then press the ENTER key (Figure 5–14).

Q&A Should I change the value in the Rotation box?
No. A zero value is appropriate for an object that should appear straight up and down.

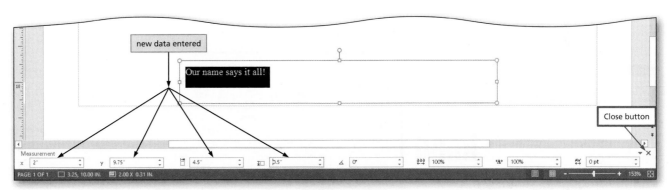

new data entered

Our name says it all!

Close button

Figure 5–14

- Tap or click the Close button on the Measurement toolbar to close it.

- Press CTRL+E to center the text within the text box.

Creating a New Style

Publisher allows you to create a new text and formatting style from scratch or one based on a current style or text selection. A **style** is a named group of formatting characteristics, including font, font size, font color, character spacing, bullets, and shadows, among other attributes. The default style in Publisher is called the **Normal style**, which includes the body font from the current font scheme in a black font color with left-justified alignment.

Styles also can be used as branding for a business; for example, many people recognize the James Bond font. It has become a brand for the movie series. Some companies even copyright their text styles or brands. Creating a new style is a good idea when you want to change those defaults or you have multiple text passages that must be formatted identically and the desired attributes are not saved as a current style. For the customer in this chapter, you will create and apply a new style to both the name of the company and the tagline or motto.

BTW

Styles
When creating a new text style, consult with the customer about company colors and/or font schemes. Sample colors from the company logo to make sure the colors match. Keep in mind reusability when assigning font formats. Remind the customer of possible formatting features such as shadow, engrave, emboss, and others. Save the style with the name of the company. If you are creating multiple styles, include the type of data in the style name, such as My Company Footnote Style.

To Sample a Font Color

The first step in creating a new style will be to choose a font color. You will sample the red color in the logo. ***Why?*** *The font color of your new style will match the company logo.* When you **sample** a color, the mouse pointer changes to an eyedropper; then, any color that you tap or click in the publication is added to all color galleries, just below the color scheme palette. The following steps sample the font color.

1

- Scroll to the top of the page.

- Triple-tap or triple-click the text, Quality Limos, to select it.

- Display the TEXT BOX TOOLS FORMAT tab.

- Tap or click the Font Color arrow (TEXT BOX TOOLS FORMAT tab | Font group) to display the Font Color gallery (Figure 5–15).

Q&A Does it make any difference whether I use the Font Color arrow on the HOME tab or on the TEXT BOX TOOLS FORMAT tab?

You may use either one. Typically, when you select text, Publisher automatically displays the TEXT BOX TOOLS FORMAT tab, so that Font Color arrow would be quicker to use.

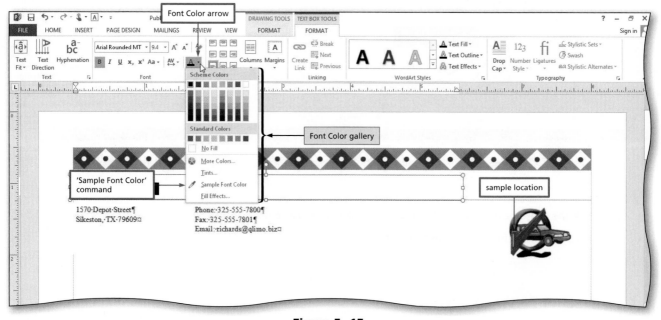

Figure 5–15

2

- Tap or click 'Sample Font Color' in the Font Color gallery to display the eyedropper pointer.

- Tap or click the red color in the logo to apply the sampled color to the selected text.

- Deselect to view the result (Figure 5–16).

Figure 5–16

Using Business Information Sets **Publisher Chapter 5 PUB** 271

1 CREATE BUSINESS INFORMATION SET | 2 CREATE NEW STYLE | 3 CUSTOMIZE LETTERHEAD | 4 CREATE FAX COVER
5 CREATE ENVELOPE | 6 CREATE BUSINESS CARDS | 7 CREATE PORTABLE FILES | 8 EMBED FONTS

Publisher Chapter 5

To Create a New Style

The following steps display the New Style Dialog box to create a new style. *Why? Using a style is easier than using the Format Painter when copying formats across pages.*

1

- Display the HOME tab.

- Tap or click the Styles button (HOME tab | Styles group) to display the Styles gallery (Figure 5–17).

Figure 5–17

2

- Tap or click New Style to display the New Style dialog box.

- In the 'Enter new style name' text box, type **Quality Limos** to name the style (Figure 5–18).

Q&A Why did the name also appear in the 'Style for the following paragraph' list?
Publisher assumes you will want to use the same style for subsequent paragraphs. If you want to change that setting, you can tap or click the 'Style for the following paragraph' list (New Style dialog box), and then tap or click a different style.

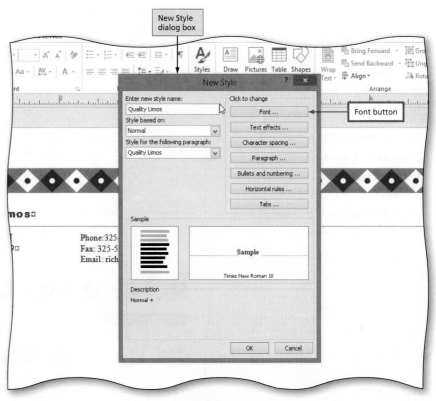

Figure 5–18

- Tap or click the Font button (New Style dialog box) to display the Font dialog box.

- Tap or click the Font arrow (Font dialog box), and then select the Miriam Fixed font in the list of fonts.

- Tap or click the Font style button, and then select **Bold Italic** in the list.

- Enter 20 in the Font size text box to set the font size.

- Tap or click the Font color button to display its gallery (Figure 5–19).

- Tap or click the added red color in the middle of the gallery.

- Tap or click the OK button (Font dialog box) to close the Font dialog box.

- Tap or click the OK button (New Style dialog box) to close the New Style dialog box.

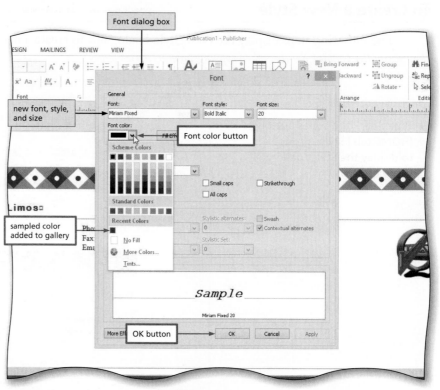

Figure 5–19

To Apply the New Style

1 CREATE BUSINESS INFORMATION SET | 2 CREATE NEW STYLE | 3 CUSTOMIZE LETTERHEAD | 4 CREATE FAX COVER
5 CREATE ENVELOPE | 6 CREATE BUSINESS CARDS | 7 CREATE PORTABLE FILES | 8 EMBED FONTS

The following steps apply the new style to both the name of the company and the tagline. *Why? Repeating the new style at the top and bottom of the publication ties the page together and provides consistency.*

- Select the Quality Limos text.

- Tap or click the Styles button (HOME tab | Styles group) to display the Styles gallery.

- Scroll to display the Quality Limos style (Figure 5–20).

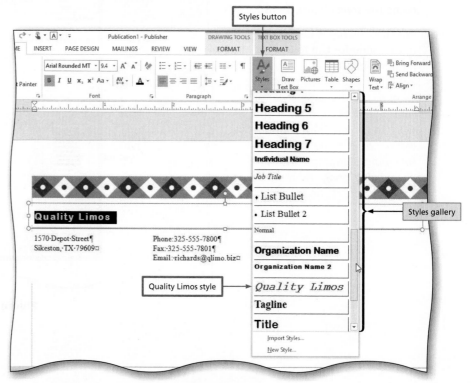

Figure 5–20

2

- Tap or click the Quality Limos style to apply it to the text.

- If necessary, select the Quality Limos text, then tap or click the 'Increase Font Size' button (HOME tab | Font group) until the text is size 18.

- Tap or click outside the selection to view the change (Figure 5–21).

Figure 5–21

Q&A Will I be able to use this style in a different publication?

Publisher attaches new styles only to the publication in which they are created; however, you can import styles from one publication to another. The process copies all of the styles, not just the new ones.

3

- Scroll in the workspace to display the lower portion of the letterhead.

- Triple-tap or triple-click the text in the tagline text box to select it.

- Tap or click the Styles button (HOME tab | Styles group) to display the Styles gallery, and then tap or click the Quality Limos style to apply it to the selected text.

- Tap or click outside the selection to view the new formatting (Figure 5–22).

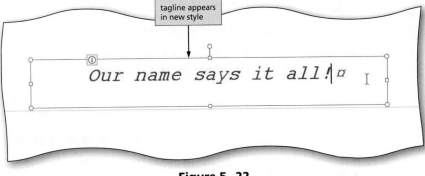

Figure 5–22

Q&A Could I use the Format Painter to copy the formatting attributes?

Yes, you can edit the formatting either way.

TO IMPORT STYLES

Because styles are publication-specific, if you want to use a style in a different publication, you would have to perform the following steps to import the style.

1. Tap or click the Styles button (HOME tab | Styles group) to display the Styles gallery.

2. Tap or click Import Styles.

3. Navigate to the publication that contains the desired style (Import Styles dialog box).

4. When Publisher asks if you wish to make changes to the Normal style, tap or click the No button (Microsoft Publisher dialog box).

5. As Publisher goes through each of the font styles, tap or click the No button until you see the desired style. In that case, tap or click the Yes button (Microsoft Publisher dialog box).

BTW
Touch Screen Differences
The Office and Windows interfaces may vary if you are using a touch screen. For this reason, you might notice that the function or appearance of your touch screen differs slightly from this chapter's presentation.

Customizing the Letterhead for Interactivity

When creating publications that are designed to be edited by others, or publications with which users must interact, it is important to make the publication as user-friendly as possible. Prepare the publication with the novice user in mind. Always place the interactive components in the front, or on top, of other objects in the publication. Use updatable fields when possible, and insert blank lines or tabs to help users know where to type. In a later chapter, you also will learn how to create customized code to turn on and off certain Publisher features and create dialog box reminders for the user.

To Create a Text Box for Users

To make the letterhead more functional for the company, you will insert a large text box in which users can type their text.

1 Tap or click the 'Show Whole Page' button on the status bar, and then tap or click the scratch area so no object is selected.

2 Tap or click the 'Draw Text Box' button (HOME tab | Objects group) to select it.

3 Drag to create a large rectangle that fills the white area in the center of the letterhead (Figure 5–23).

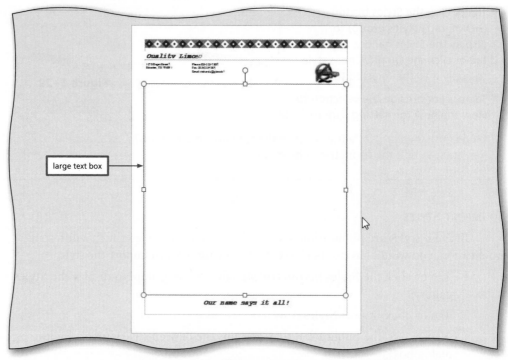

Figure 5–23

To Change the Font Size and Line Spacing

The default settings for line and paragraph settings are determined by the font or style used; however, in general, the default line spacing for text boxes is greater than 1 because Publisher accommodates the largest character of the font family and adds an additional amount of space for the text box margin. The default spacing after paragraphs varies. Many business letters use the Times New Roman font with a font size of 12. In addition, most users press the ENTER key twice at the end of a paragraph. Because you want to make the letterhead as user-friendly as possible, the following steps change the font size to 12 and set the line spacing to insert no extra spacing when the user presses the ENTER key.

1 Press the F9 key to zoom the text box to 100%.

2 Tap or click the Font Size arrow (HOME tab | Font group), and then tap or click 12 in the Font Size gallery.

3 Tap or click the Paragraph Settings Dialog Box Launcher (HOME tab | Paragraph group) to display the Paragraph dialog box.

4 On the Indents and Spacing tab, select the text in the After paragraphs text box. Type 0 to change the line spacing after each paragraph (Figure 5–24).

5 Tap or click the OK button (Paragraph dialog box) to save the settings.

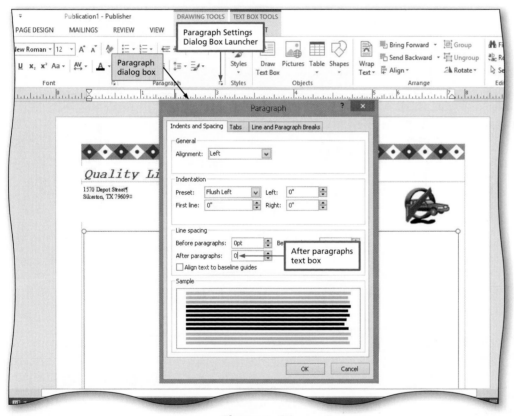

Figure 5–24

1 CREATE BUSINESS INFORMATION SET | 2 CREATE NEW STYLE | 3 CUSTOMIZE LETTERHEAD | 4 CREATE FAX COVER
5 CREATE ENVELOPE | 6 CREATE BUSINESS CARDS | 7 CREATE PORTABLE FILES | 8 EMBED FONTS

To Insert an Automatic Date

Publisher and other Microsoft Office applications can access your computer's stored date and time. You can retrieve the current date and/or time and display it in a variety of formats. Additionally, you can choose to update the date and time automatically each time the file is accessed. *Why? The date will be current whenever the user opens the letterhead to prepare a new letter.* The steps on the next page insert an automatic date.

- With the insertion point inside the text box, display the INSERT tab.
- Tap or click the 'Date & Time' button (INSERT tab | Text group) to display the Date and Time dialog box (Figure 5–25).

🔍 **Experiment**

- Scroll in the list of Available formats to view the various ways that Publisher can insert the date or time.

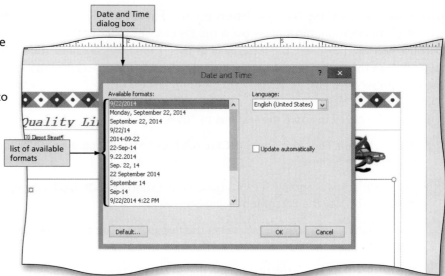

Figure 5–25

- Tap or click the third format in the Available formats list to select it.
- Tap or click the Update automatically check box so that it contains a check mark (Figure 5–26).

Q&A What does the Default button do? When you tap or click the Default button, the current settings for date and time are chosen automatically every time you insert the date or time.

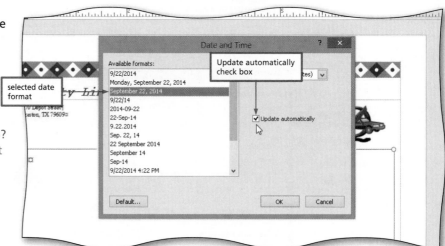

Figure 5–26

- Tap or click the OK button (Date and Time dialog box) to close the dialog box.
- Press the ENTER key twice to create a blank line after the date (Figure 5–27).

Q&A Why is my date different? Checking the Update automatically check box causes Publisher to access your computer's system date. The publication will display your current date.

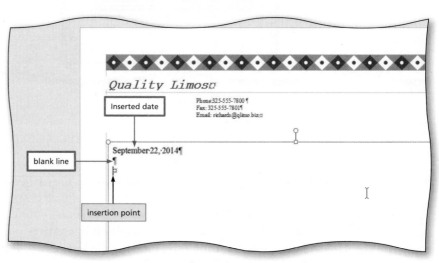

Figure 5–27

To Save the Letterhead

The following step saves the letterhead.

1 Save the publication on your desired save location, using the file name, `Quality Limos Letterhead`.

To Close a Publication without Exiting Publisher

The following steps close the publication without exiting Publisher.

1 Tap or click FILE on the ribbon to open the Backstage view.

2 Tap or click Close to close the publication without exiting Publisher and to return to the template gallery.

To Set the Read-Only Attribute

1 CREATE BUSINESS INFORMATION SET | 2 CREATE NEW STYLE | 3 CUSTOMIZE LETTERHEAD | **4 CREATE FAX COVER**
5 CREATE ENVELOPE | 6 CREATE BUSINESS CARDS | 7 CREATE PORTABLE FILES | 8 EMBED FONTS

Once a generic letterhead is created, it is a good idea to change the file's attribute, or classification, to read-only. With a **read-only** file, you can open and access the file normally, but you cannot make permanent changes to it. *Why? That way, users will be forced to save the publication with a new file name, keeping the original letterhead intact and unchanged for the next user.*

While you can view system properties in Publisher 2013, you cannot change the read-only attribute from within Publisher. Setting the read-only attribute is a function of the operating system. Therefore, the following steps set the read-only attribute to true, using File Explorer and the Properties dialog box.

1

- Tap or click the File Explorer button on the Windows 8 taskbar. Navigate to your storage location.

- Press and hold or right-click the file named Quality Limos Letterhead to display the shortcut menu (Figure 5–28).

Q&A

I show multiple files named Quality Limos Letterhead. Which one should I choose?
Choose the top or most recent one in the list. It is possible that another person has created the file using your computer, which would result in multiple listings. Your file should be the most recent and appear at the top of the list, provided you saved the document recently.

Why is my shortcut menu different?
You may have different programs installed on your computer that affect the shortcut menu.

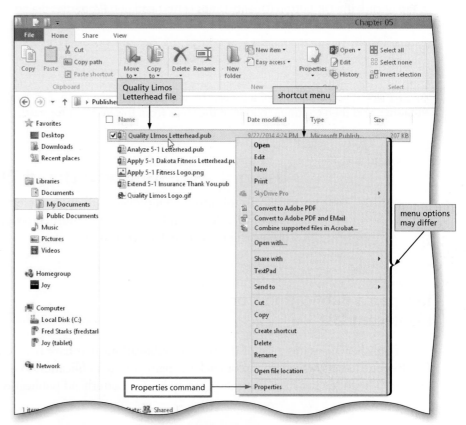

Figure 5–28

2

- Tap or click Properties on the shortcut menu to display the Quality Limos Letterhead.pub Properties dialog box.

- If necessary, tap or click the General tab (Quality Limos Letterhead.pub Properties dialog box) to display its settings.

- Verify that the file is the one you previously saved on your storage device by looking at the Location information.

- Tap or click to place a check mark in the Read-only check box in the Attributes area (Figure 5–29).

Q&A What is the difference between applying a read-only attribute and creating a Publisher template? Publisher templates do not prevent users from saving over the template with the same name, which would destroy the default settings and user text box features. The read-only attribute keeps the file unchanged and the same for every user.

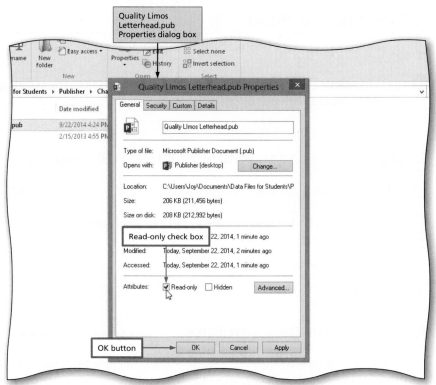

Figure 5–29

3

- Tap or click the OK button (Quality Limos Letterhead.pub Properties dialog box) to close the dialog box and apply the read-only attribute.

Break Point: If you wish to take a break, this is a good place to do so. Exit Publisher. To resume at a later time, run Publisher, and then continue following the steps from this location forward.

Using the Custom Letterhead Template

In this project, employees will open the letterhead file in Publisher, type the text of their letter, and then save the finished product with a new file name — thus preserving the original letterhead file.

To Open a Publication from the Recent List

1 CREATE BUSINESS INFORMATION SET | 2 CREATE NEW STYLE | 3 CUSTOMIZE LETTERHEAD | 4 CREATE FAX COVER
5 CREATE ENVELOPE | 6 CREATE BUSINESS CARDS | 7 CREATE PORTABLE FILES | 8 EMBED FONTS

Publisher maintains a list of the last few publications that have been opened or saved on your computer. The **Recent list** allows you to tap or click the name of the publication to open it, without browsing to the location. The following steps open the Quality Limos Letterhead publication from the Recent list.

1

- Tap or click the Publisher button on the Windows 8 taskbar to return to Publisher and the template gallery.

- Tap or click the Open tab to display the recent publications (Figure 5–30).

 My list of recent publications is different. Did I do something wrong?
No, your list will differ depending on what publications you have opened in the past.

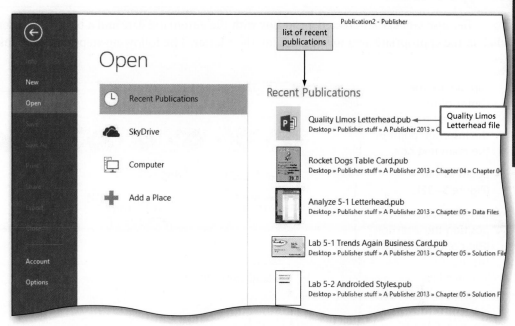

Figure 5–30

Can I change the total number of publications listed in the Recent Publications list?
Yes. In the Backstage view, tap or click Options, tap or click Advanced, and then in the Display area, change the number in the 'Show this number of Recent Publications' text box.

2

- Tap or click the 'Quality Limos Letterhead' file in the Recent Publications list to open the file (Figure 5–31).

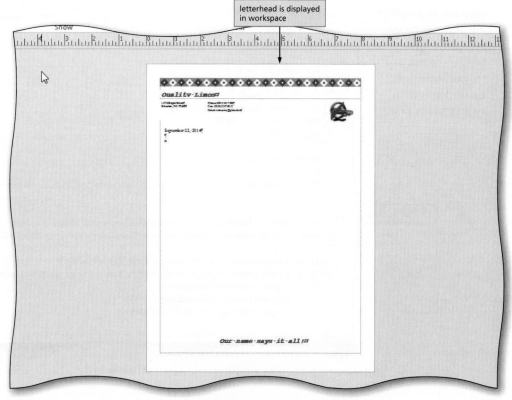

Figure 5–31

Other Ways

1. In Backstage view, tap or click Open, tap or click desired file (Recent Publications list)

To Type a Letter

Because you earlier created a text box with the automatic date and a blank line, users can simply tap or click in the appropriate area to begin typing their letter. The following steps enter the text of a letter.

● Tap or click the center of the letterhead to place the insertion point in the main text box.

● Zoom to 150% (Figure 5–32).

Is there a way to position the insertion point automatically for the user?
Yes. In a later chapter, you will learn how to write a macro event to help streamline data entry.

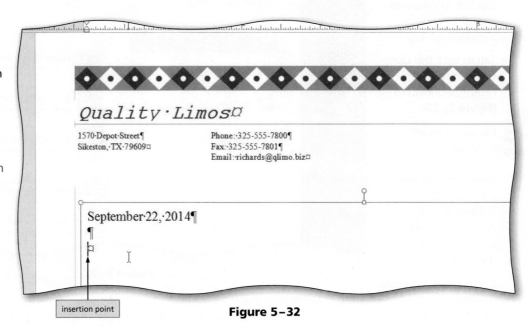

insertion point

Figure 5–32

● Type the first half of the letter as shown in Figure 5–33. Press the ENTER key only to complete a paragraph or to insert a blank line.

new text entered

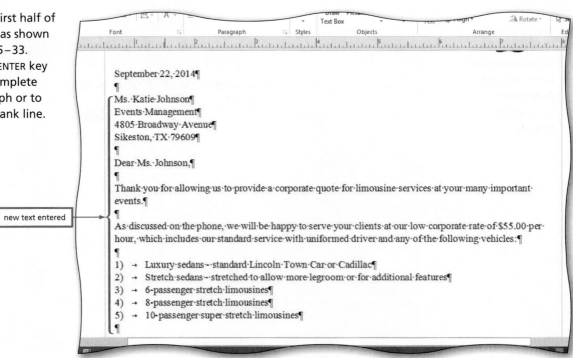

Figure 5–33

③

- Type the second half of the letter as shown in Figure 5–34. Press the ENTER key only to complete a paragraph or to insert a blank line. If necessary, increase the size of the text box, to fit the text.

new text entered

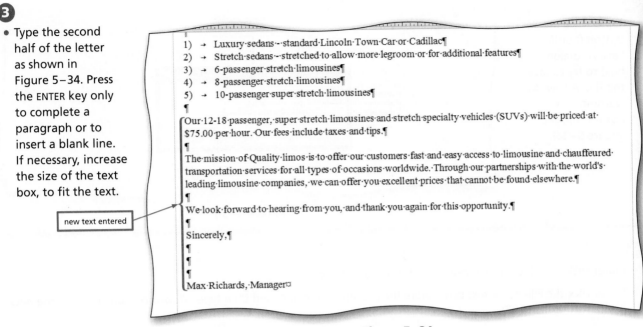

1) → Luxury·sedans·--standard·Lincoln·Town·Car·or·Cadillac¶
2) → Stretch·sedans·--stretched·to·allow·more·legroom·or·for·additional·features¶
3) → 6-passenger·stretch·limousines¶
4) → 8-passenger·stretch·limousines¶
5) → 10-passenger·super·stretch·limousines¶
¶
Our·12-18·passenger,·super-stretch·limousines·and·stretch·specialty·vehicles·(SUVs)·will·be·priced·at·$75.00·per·hour.·Our·fees·include·taxes·and·tips.¶
¶
The·mission·of·Quality·limos·is·to·offer·our·customers·fast·and·easy·access·to·limousine·and·chauffeured·transportation·services·for·all·types·of·occasions·worldwide.·Through·our·partnerships·with·the·world's·leading·limousine·companies,·we·can·offer·you·excellent·prices·that·cannot·be·found·elsewhere.¶
¶
We·look·forward·to·hearing·from·you,·and·thank·you·again·for·this·opportunity.¶
¶
Sincerely,¶
¶
¶
¶
Max·Richards,·Manager□

Figure 5–34

1 CREATE BUSINESS INFORMATION SET | 2 CREATE NEW STYLE | 3 CUSTOMIZE LETTERHEAD | 4 CREATE FAX COVER
5 CREATE ENVELOPE | 6 CREATE BUSINESS CARDS | 7 CREATE PORTABLE FILES | 8 EMBED FONTS

To Save the Letter

To illustrate the read-only properties of the letter, you will try to save the publication in the same place with the same file name, Quality Limos Letterhead. Because you have changed the publication to read-only, Publisher will generate an error message. You then will choose a new file name and save the file. The following steps save the file with a new file name.

①

- Tap or click the Save button on the Quick Access Toolbar to display the Save As dialog box. Do not navigate to another location.

- Tap or click the Save button (Save As dialog box) to display the Confirm Save As dialog box (Figure 5–35).

Q&A What would happen if the file were not read-only?
Tapping or clicking the Save button would save the edited letter, replacing the custom template.

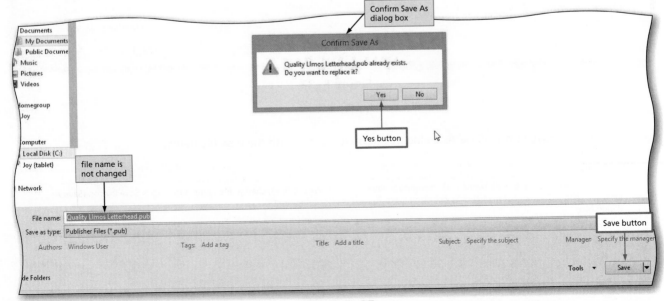

Confirm Save As dialog box

Confirm Save As

⚠ Quality Limos Letterhead.pub already exists.
Do you want to replace it?

Yes   No

Yes button

Documents
My Documents
Public Docume
Music
Pictures
Videos

Homegroup
Joy

Computer
Local Disk (C:)
Joy (tablet)   file name is not changed

Network

File name: Quality Limos Letterhead.pub
Save as type: Publisher Files (*.pub)

Authors: Windows User   Tags: Add a tag   Title: Add a title   Subject: Specify the subject   Manager: Specify the manager

Save button

Tools ▼   Save ▼

Hide Folders

Figure 5–35

- Tap or click the Yes button (Confirm Save As dialog box) to try to save the file. A Save As warning dialog box is displayed (Figure 5–36).

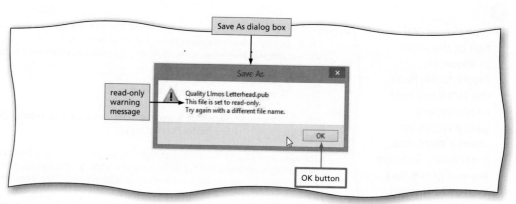

Figure 5–36

- Tap or click the OK button to return to the Save As dialog box.
- Tap or click the File name text box, delete the previous file name, and then type **Johnson Letter** as the new file name (Figure 5–37).

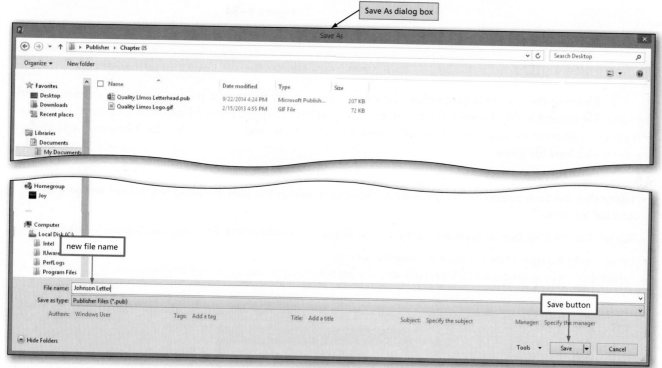

Figure 5–37

- Tap or click the Save button (Save As dialog box) to save the file with the new file name.

Other Ways

1. Tap or click FILE tab, tap or click Save As tab, navigate to save location, change file name, tap or click Save button (Save As dialog box)

2. Press CTRL+S, change file name, tap or click Save button (Save As dialog box)

To Print the Letter

The following steps print a hard copy of the contents of the saved Johnson letter publication.

1 Tap or click FILE on the ribbon to open the Backstage view.

2 Tap or click the Print tab in the Backstage view to display the Print gallery.

3 Verify the printer name that appears on the Printer Status button will print a hard copy of the publication. If necessary, tap or click the Printer Status button to display a list of available printer options and then tap or click the desired printer to change the currently selected printer.

4 Tap or click the Print button in the Print gallery to print the publication on the currently selected printer.

5 When the printer stops, retrieve the hard copy (Figure 5–38).

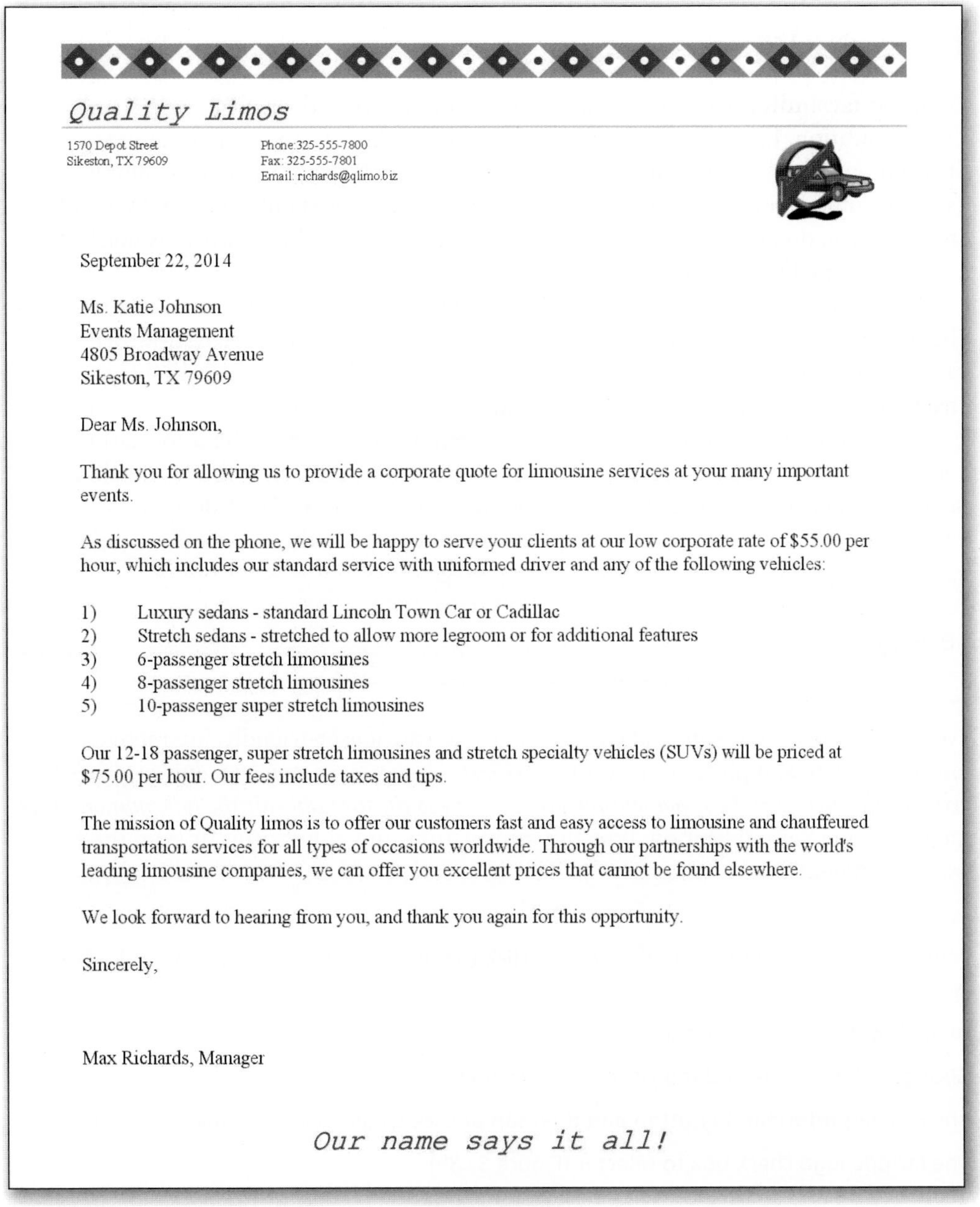

Quality Limos

1570 Depot Street   Phone: 325-555-7800
Sikeston, TX 79609   Fax: 325-555-7801
                 Email: richards@qlimo.biz

September 22, 2014

Ms. Katie Johnson
Events Management
4805 Broadway Avenue
Sikeston, TX 79609

Dear Ms. Johnson,

Thank you for allowing us to provide a corporate quote for limousine services at your many important events.

As discussed on the phone, we will be happy to serve your clients at our low corporate rate of $55.00 per hour, which includes our standard service with uniformed driver and any of the following vehicles:

1)   Luxury sedans - standard Lincoln Town Car or Cadillac
2)   Stretch sedans - stretched to allow more legroom or for additional features
3)   6-passenger stretch limousines
4)   8-passenger stretch limousines
5)   10-passenger super stretch limousines

Our 12-18 passenger, super stretch limousines and stretch specialty vehicles (SUVs) will be priced at $75.00 per hour. Our fees include taxes and tips.

The mission of Quality limos is to offer our customers fast and easy access to limousine and chauffeured transportation services for all types of occasions worldwide. Through our partnerships with the world's leading limousine companies, we can offer you excellent prices that cannot be found elsewhere.

We look forward to hearing from you, and thank you again for this opportunity.

Sincerely,

Max Richards, Manager

Our name says it all!

Figure 5–38

To Close a Publication without Quitting Publisher

The following step closes the letter without quitting Publisher.

1 Open the Backstage view.

2 Tap or click Close to close the publication without quitting Publisher and to return to the template gallery.

3 If a Microsoft Publisher dialog box is displayed, tap or click the Don't Save button so that any changes you have made are not saved.

Break Point: If you wish to take a break, this is a good place to do so. Exit Publisher. To resume at a later time, run Publisher and continue following the steps from this location forward.

Fax Covers

A **fax** (or **facsimile**) is a copy of a document sent or received via electronic communication. Faxes can be sent using a fax machine or from most computers. It commonly is used when the document is not in an electronic format. Examples of faxed documents include contracts, forms, records, or signed publications. With a fax machine, you do not have to scan or print the document, and because a fax machine uses telephone lines, you do not need to be online on a computer.

The first page of a fax is usually a **fax cover** that includes information about the sender, receiver, subject, and date. A fax cover also tells the receiver how many faxed pages to expect. Some companies have copies of blank fax covers beside the fax machine, and users handwrite this information; however, creating the fax cover on the computer has several advantages. With a computerized fax cover, the information is more legible. The user either can print the cover and insert it into the fax machine, or send it via a fax program on his or her computer. In addition, a well-designed fax cover makes it easy for the user to fill in the blanks and complete the information quickly.

To Create a User-Friendly Fax Cover

1 CREATE BUSINESS INFORMATION SET | 2 CREATE NEW STYLE | 3 CUSTOMIZE LETTERHEAD | 4 CREATE FAX COVER
5 CREATE ENVELOPE | 6 CREATE BUSINESS CARDS | 7 CREATE PORTABLE FILES | 8 EMBED FONTS

The following steps open a fax cover template and customize it to create a user-friendly, interactive fax cover. You will include an automatic date and places to insert text. *Why? The fax cover templates display placeholder text that cannot be edited directly by the user; therefore, you will replace that text so the user can edit the information easily.* Ultimately, the user will open the fax cover publication, type the information, and either print or send the fax cover along with the necessary documents.

1

- In the new template gallery, tap or click BUILT-IN, and then tap or click the Business Forms thumbnail to display the Business Forms templates.

- In the Fax Cover area, tap or click the Accessory Bar thumbnail.

- If necessary, choose the Orange color scheme and the Galley font scheme.

- If necessary, tap or click the Business information button and then tap or click Quality Limos to select the set.

- If necessary, tap or click the Include logo check box to select it (Figure 5–39).

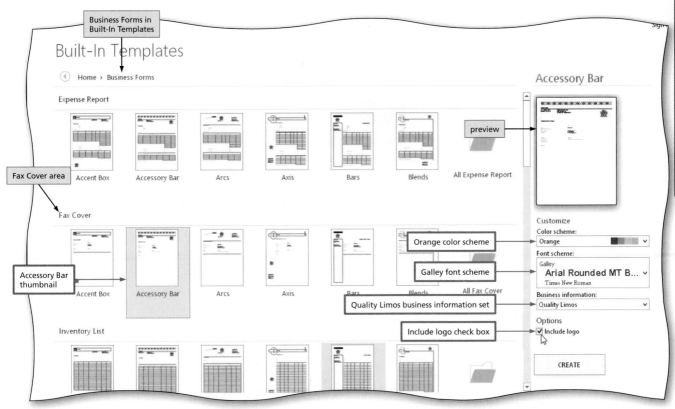

Figure 5–39

2

- Tap or click the CREATE button to create the fax cover.

- Zoom to 100% and scroll to the top of the publication (Figure 5–40).

🅟 **Experiment**

- Tap or click the text in various text boxes on the page to see which text boxes are placeholder text (automatically selected), and which text boxes are editable immediately.

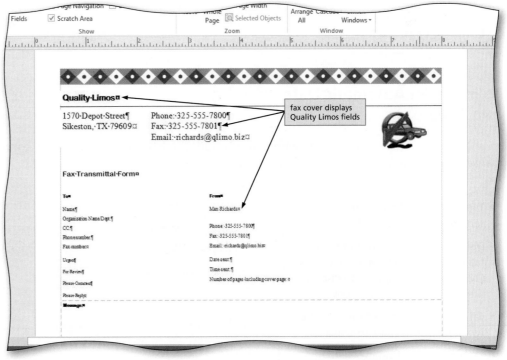

Figure 5–40

- Tap or click the text in the date and time text box and zoom to 200%.
- Press CTRL+C to copy the selected text (Figure 5–41).

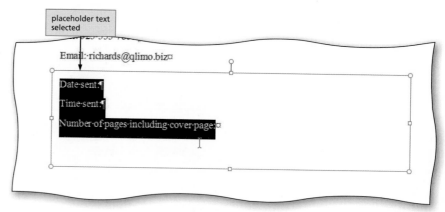

Figure 5–41

- Press CTRL+V to paste the text, and then tap or click the Paste Options smart tag button to display the Paste Options gallery (Figure 5–42).

Q&A

Why do I have to copy and paste the exact same text?

Users cannot edit placeholder text — it must be replaced. Copying and pasting the text, rather than retyping it, will save you time in designing the form.

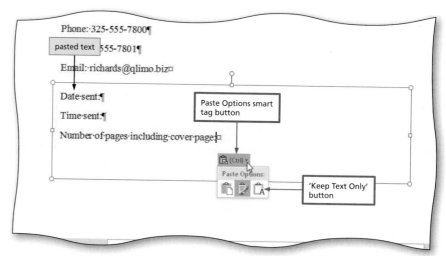

- Tap or click the 'Keep Text Only' button to paste the text.

Figure 5–42

To Insert an Automatic Date and Time

1 CREATE BUSINESS INFORMATION SET | 2 CREATE NEW STYLE | 3 CUSTOMIZE LETTERHEAD | 4 CREATE FAX COVER
5 CREATE ENVELOPE | 6 CREATE BUSINESS CARDS | 7 CREATE PORTABLE FILES | 8 EMBED FONTS

The following steps insert an automatically updated date and time in the fax cover. **Why?** *The date and time will be correct when the user opens the fax cover file.*

- Tap or click at the end of the Date sent line. Press the TAB key.
- Display the INSERT tab, and then tap or click the 'Date & Time' button (INSERT tab | Text group) to display the Date and Time dialog box.
- Tap or click the third format in the Available formats list to select it.
- Tap or click the Update automatically check box so that it contains a check mark.
- Tap or click the OK button (Date and Time dialog box) to close the dialog box (Figure 5–43).

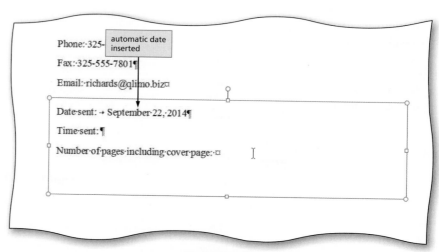

Figure 5–43

2

- Tap or click at the end of the Time sent line. Press the TAB key.

- Display the INSERT tab, and then tap or click the 'Date & Time' button (INSERT tab | Text group) to display the Date and Time dialog box.

- Scroll in the Available formats list, and then tap or click the time shown in hour and minute format as shown in Figure 5–44.

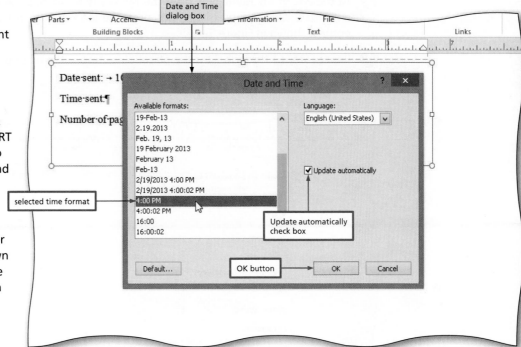

Figure 5–44

3

- Tap or click the Update automatically check box so that it contains a check mark.

- Tap or click the OK button (Date and Time dialog box) to close the dialog box (Figure 5–45).

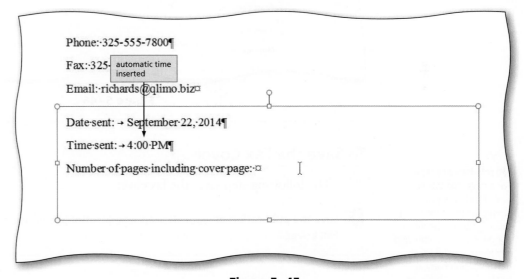

Figure 5–45

To Replace Other Text

The following steps replace other placeholder text with user-friendly, editable text boxes.

1 Tap or click the placeholder text in the text box that begins with the word, Name.

2 Press CTRL+C to copy the selected text. Press CTRL+V to paste the selected text. Tap or click the Paste Options button, then tap or click the 'Keep Text Only' button (Paste Options gallery).

③ At the end of the Name line, press the TAB key twice to help the user see where to enter data. On the subsequent lines, press the TAB key once or twice to align data entry as shown in Figure 5–46.

④ Repeat Steps 1 through 3 for the placeholder text in the text box that begins with the word, Urgent (Figure 5–46).

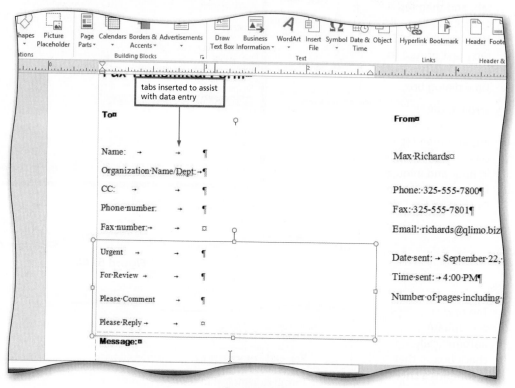

Figure 5–46

BTW
Quick Reference
For a table that lists how to complete the tasks covered in this book using touch gestures, the mouse, ribbon, shortcut menu, and keyboard, see the Quick Reference Summary at the back of this book, or visit the Quick Reference resource on the Student Companion Site located on www.cengagebrain.com. For detailed instructions about accessing available resources, visit www.cengage.com/ct/studentdownload or see the inside back cover of this book.

To Save the Fax Cover

The following step saves the fax cover.

① Save the publication on your desired save location, using the file name, Quality Limos Fax Cover.

To Print the Fax Cover

The following steps print a hard copy of the contents of the saved fax cover.

① Open the Backstage view.

② Tap or click the Print tab in the Backstage view to display the Print gallery.

③ Verify the printer name that appears on the Printer Status button will print a hard copy of the publication.

④ Tap or click the Print button in the Print gallery to print the publication on the currently selected printer.

⑤ When the printer stops, retrieve the hard copy (Figure 5–47).

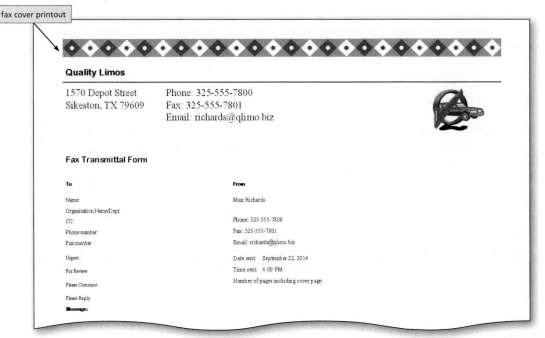

fax cover printout

Quality Limos

1570 Depot Street
Sikeston, TX 79609

Phone: 325-555-7800
Fax: 325-555-7801
Email: richards@qlimo.biz

Fax Transmittal Form

To

Name:
Organization Name/Dept:
CC:
Phone number:
Fax number:
Urgent
For Review
Please Comment
Please Reply
Message:

From

Max Richards

Phone: 325-555-7800
Fax: 325-555-7801
Email: richards@qlimo.biz

Date sent: September 22, 2014
Time sent: 4:00 PM
Number of pages including cover page:

Figure 5–47

To Close a Publication without Exiting Publisher

The following steps close the publication without exiting Publisher.

1 Open the Backstage view.

2 Tap or click Close to close the publication without exiting Publisher and to return to the template gallery.

3 If a Microsoft Publisher dialog box is displayed, tap or click the Don't Save button so that any changes you have made are not saved.

To Set the Read-Only Attribute on the Fax Cover

The following steps set the read-only attribute on the fax cover to prevent users from saving their information over the template file.

1 Tap or click the File Explorer button on the status bar. Navigate to your storage location.

2 Press and hold or right-click the file named Quality Limos Fax Cover to display the shortcut menu.

3 Tap or click Properties on the shortcut menu to display the Quality Limos Fax Cover.pub Properties dialog box. If necessary, tap or click the General tab (Quality Limos Fax Cover.pub Properties dialog box) to display its settings.

4 Verify that the file is the one you previously saved on your storage device by looking at the Location information.

5 Tap or click to place a check mark in the Read-only check box in the Attributes area.

6 Tap or click the OK button (Quality Limos Fax Cover.pub Properties dialog box) to close the dialog box and apply the read-only attribute.

BTW

Using Read-Only Files
Read-only files can be deleted and moved, but Windows will prompt you with a special dialog box asking you to confirm that you want to move or delete the read-only file.

Break Point: If you wish to take a break, this is a good place to do so. Exit Publisher. To resume at a later time, run Publisher and continue following the steps from this location forward.

BTW
Envelopes
Microsoft has many envelope templates for occasions such as holidays, weddings, parties, and graduations stored in their online templates. On a computer that is connected to the Internet, start Publisher and then, in the New template gallery, tap or click Envelopes. Tap or click any template to see a preview before downloading.

Envelopes

Envelopes are manufactured in a variety of sizes and shapes. The most common sizes are #6 personal envelopes that measure $3\frac{5}{8} \times 6\frac{1}{2}$ inches, and #10 business envelopes that measure $4\frac{1}{8} \times 9\frac{1}{2}$ inches. You also can customize the page layout to instruct Publisher to print envelopes for invitations, cards, and mailers, or to merge an address list with an envelope template to avoid using labels.

Although the majority of businesses outsource the production of their preprinted envelopes, most desktop printers have an envelope-feeding mechanism that works especially well for business envelopes. Check your printer's documentation for any limitations on the size and shape of envelopes. For testing purposes, you can print the envelope on $8\frac{1}{2} \times 11$-inch paper, if necessary.

To Create an Envelope

1 CREATE BUSINESS INFORMATION SET | 2 CREATE NEW STYLE | 3 CUSTOMIZE LETTERHEAD | 4 CREATE FAX COVER
5 CREATE ENVELOPE | 6 CREATE BUSINESS CARDS | 7 CREATE PORTABLE FILES | 8 EMBED FONTS

The following steps use the template gallery to produce a business-sized envelope for Quality Limos. The envelope automatically uses information from the business information set created earlier in this project.

- With the template gallery still displayed, tap or click BUILT-IN, and then tap or click Envelopes to display the available templates.

- Scroll down to the More Installed Templates area, and then tap or click the Accessory Bar thumbnail.

- If necessary, choose the Orange color scheme and the Galley font scheme.

- If necessary, tap or click the Business information button and then tap or click Quality Limos to select the set.

- Tap or click the Page size button to display the list of page sizes (Figure 5–48).

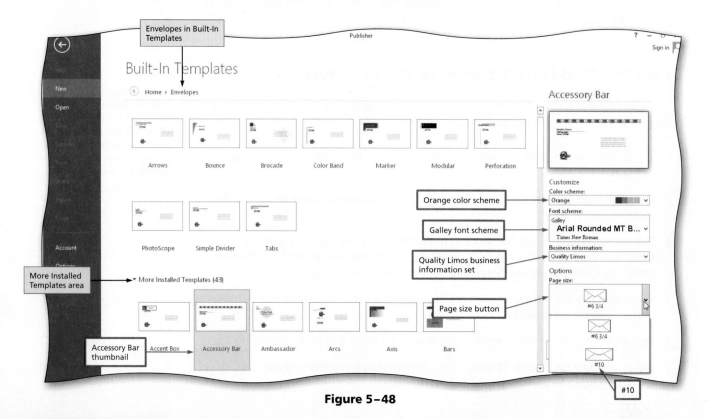

Figure 5–48

2

- Tap or click #10 to choose a business-size envelope.

- If necessary, tap or click to place a check mark in the Include logo check box (Figure 5–49).

Q&A What if I want a different size envelope?

In the template gallery, scroll down to Blank Sizes and choose the size from the list. Otherwise, you could change the size using the Size button (PAGE DESIGN tab | Page Setup group).

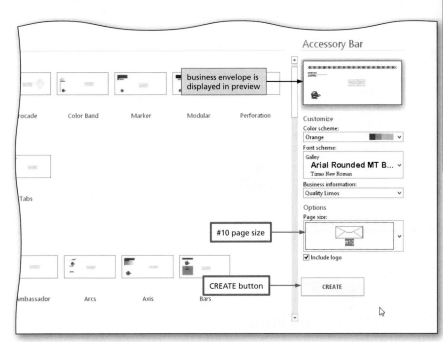

Figure 5–49

3

- Tap or click the CREATE button (Figure 5–50).

Q&A Why is there a different number on my title bar after the word, Publication?

Depending on how many publications you have opened or created during the current Publisher session, the number will vary.

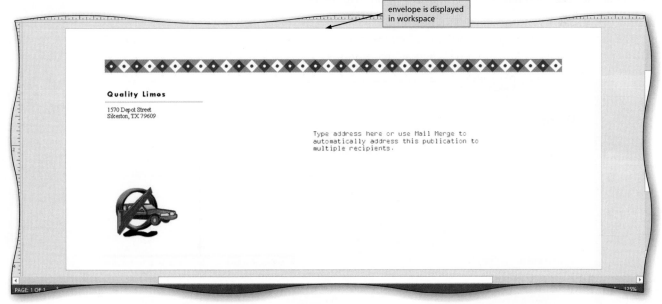

Figure 5–50

To Save the Envelope

The following step saves the envelope.

1 Save the publication on your desired save location, using the file name Quality Limos Envelope.

To Address the Envelope

The envelope is ready to use. The following step fills in the name and address on this envelope.

1

- Tap or click the placeholder text in the address text box to select it.

- Type the address as shown in Figure 5–51.

- If the text does not fit in the text box, resize the text box.

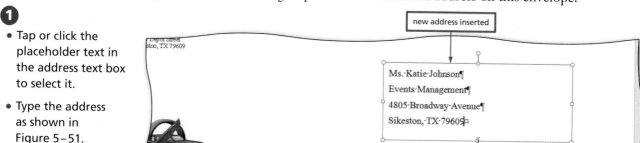

new address inserted

Ms.·Katie·Johnson¶
Events·Management¶
4805·Broadway·Avenue¶
Sikeston,·TX·79609¤

Figure 5–51

Q&A Could I use a mailing label instead of typing the address?
Yes. In later chapters, you will learn how to create both mailing labels and a mail merge for customers on a mailing list.

To Set Options and Print the Envelope

The following steps print a hard copy of the envelope with special settings.

1

- Open the Backstage view, and then tap or click the Print tab to display the Print gallery.

- Verify that the printer listed on the Printer Status button will print a hard copy of the publication.

- Tap or click the Tiled button to display the options (Figure 5–52).

Q&A Why is the envelope displayed across two pages?
The default value for page settings is to place the publication on an 8½ × 11-inch piece of paper. The envelope will not fit, so Publisher tiles it until you change the setting.

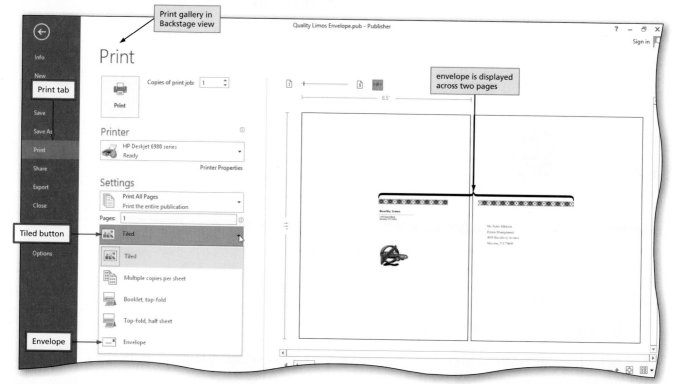

Figure 5–52

2

- Scroll as necessary and then tap or click Envelope in the list (Figure 5–53).

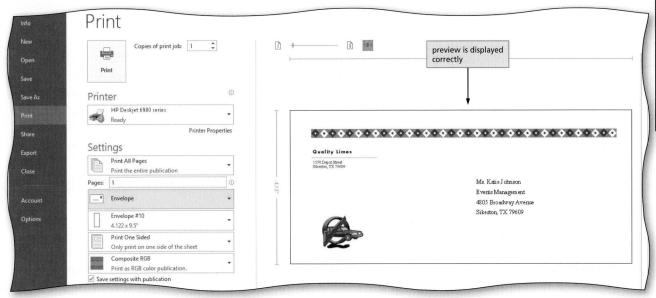

Figure 5–53

3

- Tap or click the Print button in the Print gallery to print the envelope on the currently selected printer (Figure 5–54).

Figure 5–54

Other Ways

1. Press CTRL+P, choose settings, tap or click Print button

To Close a Publication without Saving

The following step closes the envelope without saving the current address.

1 Open the Backstage view, and then tap or click the Close button to close the publication. When Publisher asks if you want to save the changes to the envelope, tap or click the Don't Save button to return to the template gallery.

Break Point: If you wish to take a break, this is a good place to do so. Exit Publisher. To resume at a later time, run Publisher and continue following the steps from this location forward.

Business Cards

Another way companies are reducing publishing costs is by designing their own business cards. A **business card** is a small publication, 3½ × 2 inches, printed on heavy stock paper. It usually contains the name, title, business, and address information for an employee, as well as a logo, distinguishing graphic, or color to draw attention to the card. Many employees want their telephone, pager, and fax numbers on their business cards in addition to their email and web addresses, so that colleagues and customers can reach them quickly.

Business cards can be saved as files to send to commercial printers or printed by desktop color printers on special perforated paper.

To Create a Business Card

1 CREATE BUSINESS INFORMATION SET | 2 CREATE NEW STYLE | 3 CUSTOMIZE LETTERHEAD | 4 CREATE FAX COVER
5 CREATE ENVELOPE | 6 CREATE BUSINESS CARDS | 7 CREATE PORTABLE FILES | 8 EMBED FONTS

Because the business information set contains information about the Quality Limos company and its manager, using a Publisher business card template is the quickest way to create a business card. Not only does the template set the size and shape of a typical business card, but it also presets page and printing options for easy production.

The following steps use the template gallery to produce a business card for the manager of Quality Limos.

- With the template gallery still displayed, tap or click BUILT-IN, and then tap or click the Business Cards thumbnail.
- Scroll down to the More Installed Templates area, and then tap or click the Accessory Bar thumbnail.
- If necessary, choose the Orange color scheme, the Galley font scheme, and a Landscape page size.
- If necessary, tap or click the Business information button, and then tap or click Quality Limos to select the set.
- If necessary, place a check mark in the Include logo check box (Figure 5–55).

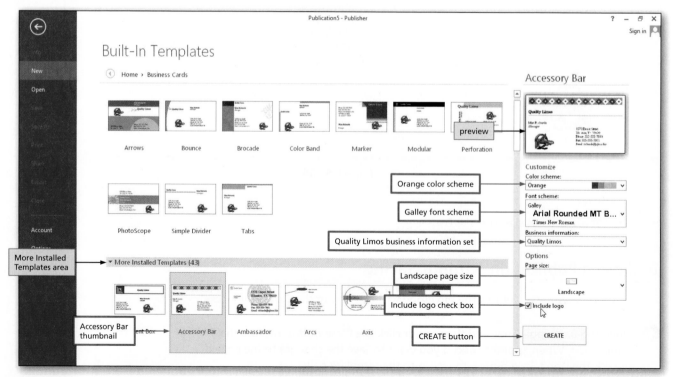

Figure 5–55

- Tap or click the CREATE button to create the business card.

- Zoom as necessary to display the entire business card in the Publisher workspace (Figure 5–56).

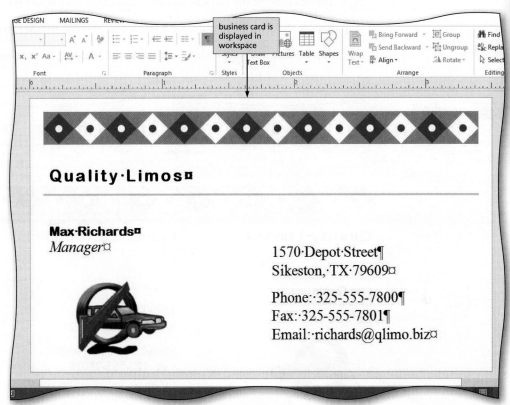

Figure 5–56

To Insert and Edit the Tagline or Motto Field

The following steps insert the Tagline or motto field from the business information set and then position, scale, and fit the text in the text box.

1 If necessary, tap or click the scratch area so that no objects are selected in the page layout, and display the INSERT tab.

2 Tap or click the Business Information button (INSERT tab | Text group) to display the list of business information fields and commands.

3 Scroll as necessary and then tap or click the Tagline or motto field to insert it into the publication.

4 Tap or click the Object Position button on the status bar to display the Measurement toolbar. Select the text in the Horizontal Position text box and then type **1.78** to replace it. Press the TAB key to advance to the next text box.

5 Type **.41** in the Vertical Position text box, and then press the TAB key.

6 Type **1.62** in the Width text box, and then press the TAB key.

7 Type **.2** in the Height text box, and then press the ENTER key.

⑧ Do not change the default values in the other text boxes (Figure 5–57).

⑨ Tap or click the Close button on the Measurement toolbar to close it.

⑩ Tap or click in the scratch area outside the text box to deselect the text.

Figure 5–57

To Set Publication Properties

Because you also plan to send the business cards to a commercial printer, it is important to set publication properties. The following steps set publication properties.

① Open the Backstage view and, by default, select the Info tab.

② Tap or click the Publication Properties button in the right pane of the Info gallery, and then tap or click Advanced Properties to display the properties dialog box for your publication. If necessary, tap or click the Summary tab.

③ Type **Business Card** in the Title text box.

④ Type **Max Richards** in the Author text box.

If requested by your instructor, type your name to replace the text in the Author text box.

⑤ Type **Quality Limos** in the Company text box (Figure 5–58).

⑥ Tap or click the OK button (Publication Properties dialog box) to save the settings.

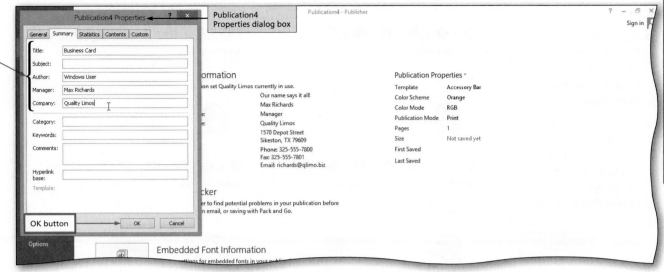

Figure 5–58

To Save the Business Card

The following step saves the business card with the file name, Quality Limos Business Card.

 Save the publication on your desired save location, using the file name Quality Limos Business Card.

To Print the Business Card

1 CREATE BUSINESS INFORMATION SET | 2 CREATE NEW STYLE | 3 CUSTOMIZE LETTERHEAD | 4 CREATE FAX COVER
5 CREATE ENVELOPE | 6 CREATE BUSINESS CARDS | **7 CREATE PORTABLE FILES** | **8 EMBED FONTS**

You have the choice of printing multiple business cards per sheet or only one card per sheet. Layout options allow you to set specific margins to match specialized business card paper. The following steps print the business cards.

1

- Open the Backstage view, and then tap or click the Print tab to display the Print gallery.

- If necessary, verify the printer name that appears on the Printer Status button will print a hard copy of the publication.

- If necessary, tap or click the Pages button to display the Pages list, and then tap or click 'Multiple copies per sheet' to select the option.

- If necessary, type 10 in the 'Copies of each page' text box.

- Tap or click the Layout Options button to display the Layout Options dialog box.

- Make sure your settings match those in Figure 5–59.

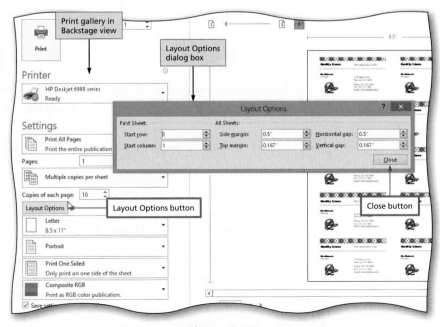

Figure 5–59

2

- Tap or click the Close button (Layout Options dialog box) to close the dialog box.

- Tap or click the Print button in the Print gallery to print the business cards on the currently selected printer (Figure 5–60).

multiple business cards print on single page

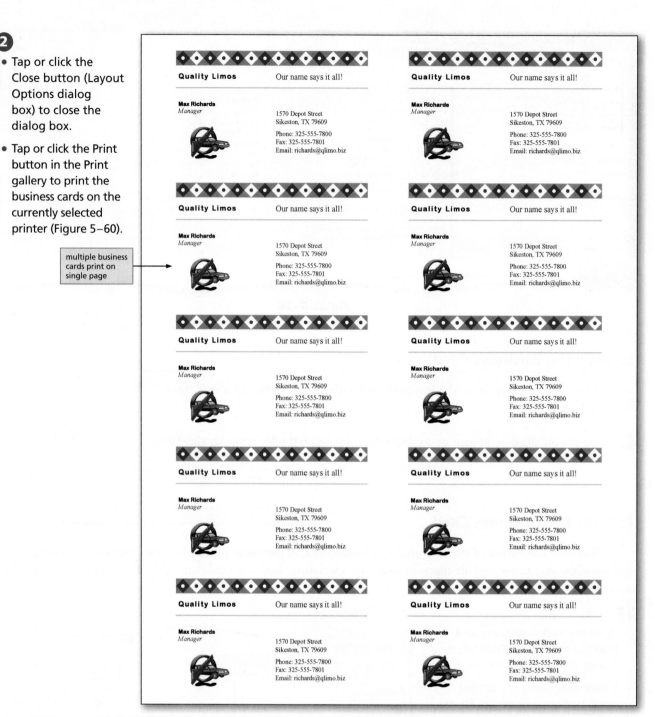

Figure 5–60

CONSIDER THIS

Why do I need to create portable files?

You might have to distribute your artwork in a variety of formats for customers, print shops, webmasters, and email attachments. The format you choose depends on how the file will be used, but portability is always a consideration. The publication might need to be used with various operating systems, monitor resolutions, computing environments, and servers.

It is a good idea to discuss with your customer the types of formats he or she might need. It usually is safe to begin work in Publisher and then use the Save As command or Print command to convert the files. PDF is a portable format that can be read by anyone using a free reader, which is available on the web. The PDF format is platform- and software-independent. Commonly, PDF files are virus free and safe as email attachments.

Creating Portable Files

The final step is to create a portable file of the business card for document exchange between computers. Publisher offers two choices: PDF or XPS. **PDF** stands for **Portable Document Format**, a flexible file format based on the PostScript imaging model that is cross-platform and cross-application. PDF files accurately display and preserve fonts, page layouts, and graphics. The content in a PDF file is not changed easily, but it can be viewed by everyone with a free viewer available on the web. **XPS** stands for **XML Paper Specification** and is also a format that preserves document formatting and enables file sharing. XPS is Microsoft's portable format similar to PDF. When the XPS file is viewed online or printed, it retains exactly the format that you intended. Like PDF files, the data in XPS files cannot be changed easily.

You might want to create a portable file for an outside printing service or to display your publication on the web. Publisher allows you to set additional options for quality, graphics, and document properties when creating portable files.

To Publish in a Portable Format

1 CREATE BUSINESS INFORMATION SET | 2 CREATE NEW STYLE | 3 CUSTOMIZE LETTERHEAD | 4 CREATE FAX COVER
5 CREATE ENVELOPE | 6 CREATE BUSINESS CARDS | 7 CREATE PORTABLE FILES | 8 EMBED FONTS

The following steps publish the business card in a portable format using high-quality settings and maintaining document properties.

- Open the Backstage view and select the Export tab (Figure 5–61).

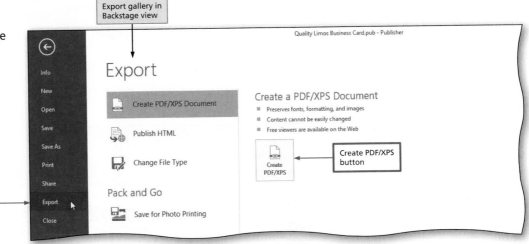

Figure 5–61

- Tap or click the 'Create PDF/XPS' button to display the Publish as PDF or XPS dialog box.

- If necessary, navigate to your storage device and appropriate folder (Figure 5–62).

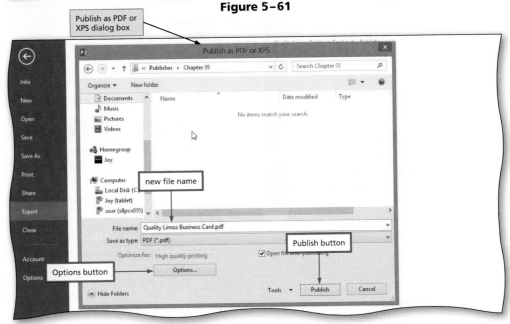

Figure 5–62

- Tap or click the Options or Change button (Publish as PDF or XPS dialog box) to display the Publish Options dialog box.

- If necessary, in the Specify how this publication will be printed or distributed area, tap or click 'High quality printing' (Publish Options dialog box).

- If necessary, in the Include non-printing information area, tap or click both check boxes to select them.

- Do not change any of the other default values (Figure 5–63).

 **Experiment**

- Tap or click each choice in the Specify how this publication will be printed or distributed list to view the descriptions and other settings. When you are done, tap or click 'High quality printing'.

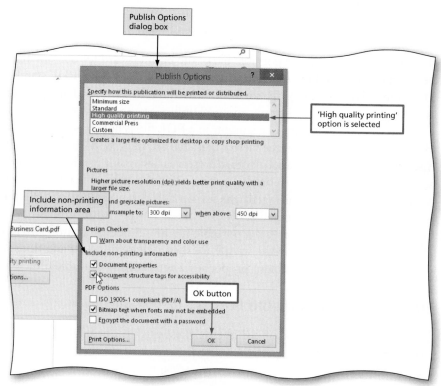

Figure 5–63

- Tap or click the OK button (Publish Options dialog box) to close the dialog box.

- Tap or click the Publish button (Publish as PDF or XPS dialog box) to create the portable file.

- When the PDF file opens, maximize the window (Figure 5–64).

Q&A Why does my display look different?
Your computer may not have the PDF reader installed. In that case, the file opens with an XPS reader.

❺

- Tap or click the Close button on the PDF or XPS title bar to close the display of the portable file.

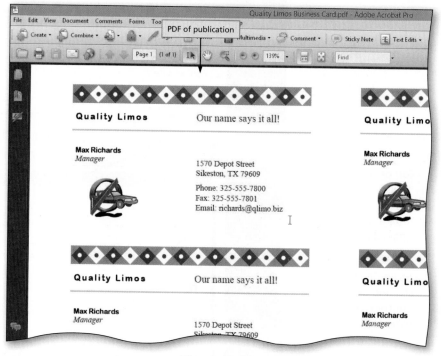

Figure 5–64

Other Ways

1. In Backstage view, tap or click Save As button, choose your save location, and then tap or click 'Save as type' button (Save As dialog box), tap or click PDF (*.pdf), tap or click Options or Change button, select options, tap or click OK button (Publish Options dialog box), tap or click Save button (Save As dialog box)

Embedding Fonts

If you plan to send the Publisher file to a professional printing service or to other users, they may or may not have the same fonts available on their computers as you do on yours. Thus, any fonts peculiar to your printer or new font styles that you created may have to be substituted. When the publication is opened, Publisher usually displays a dialog box that informs the user of the substitution. Publisher tries to find a similar font based on the text ornamentation, but your publication will not look exactly as it did. One option is to create a PDF or XPS as you did earlier in the chapter, which would maintain the look of the publication; however, the PDF or XPS user cannot make significant changes to the design. If you want to preserve your font settings and create a fully editable file, you should **embed** or save the fonts with the publication. Optionally, you can embed a **subset** of the font, which means that it will embed only the specific characters you used in the publication.

Most common fonts, such as Times New Roman, do not have to be embedded because most users already will have that font. In general, TrueType fonts can be embedded only if their licensing allows embedding; however, all of the TrueType fonts that are included in Publisher allow licensed embedding.

Embedded fonts increase the file size of your publication, so you may want to limit the number of fonts or subsets that you embed; however, embedding fonts is one of the best ways to ensure that a font is always available.

Table 5–3 displays some of Publisher's embedding options.

BTW
Pack and Go Wizard
Publisher automatically embeds TrueType fonts by default when you use the Pack and Go Wizard as you did in Chapter 2. If you do not use the Pack and Go Wizard, you have to make choices related to embedding.

Table 5–3 Embedding Options

Type of Embedding	Kinds of Fonts (If Any)	Advantages	Restrictions
Full Font Embedding		The recipient does not need the same font to view or edit the file.	You must own the embedded font by owning your printer or by purchasing the font. Fully embedded fonts create a large file size.
	Print And Preview Fonts	Viewable fonts are embedded in the publication.	The recipient cannot edit the publication.
	Licensed, Installable Fonts	Embedded fonts, licensed as installable, may be installed permanently for use in other publications and programs.	No restrictions exist.
	Licensed, Editable Fonts	Embedded fonts that are licensed as editable are available for use in other publications and programs.	The publication with the editable fonts must remain open in order for the recipient to use the font.
	TrueType Fonts	TrueType fonts include permissions defined by the original publisher of the font that detail when and how the font may be embedded.	The TrueType fonts can be applied to a publication only if the embedded fonts are installed on the local computer.
Subset Font Embedding		The recipient does not have to own the font to view it.	Only the characters that you use in the publication are included in the font family. Subset font embedding creates a file that is larger than one with no embedding but smaller than one with full font embedding.
No Font Embedding		File size does not change.	The recipient needs to have the same fonts installed or accept a substitution.
Save as PDF or XPS		Fonts, layout, and design are maintained.	Recipient has limited editing capabilities.

To Embed Fonts

The following steps embed the fonts with the business card. Because other workers at Quality Limos may want to use this file to create their own business cards, you will embed all of the characters in the heading font, rather than just a subset. You will not embed the common system fonts that most users have, in this case Times New Roman, in order to reduce the file size slightly.

- With the Quality Limos Business Card still displayed in the workspace, tap or click the FILE tab to open the Backstage view and, by default, select the Info tab.

- Tap or click the 'Manage Embedded Fonts' button to display the Fonts dialog box.

- Tap or click to place a check mark in the 'Embed TrueType fonts when saving publication' check box (Fonts dialog box).

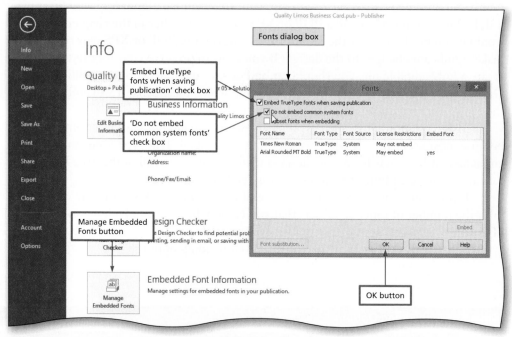

- If necessary, tap or click to place a check mark in the 'Do not embed common system fonts' check box (Figure 5–65).

Figure 5–65

Q&A

What will users see when they open the file?

A dialog box will verify that some fonts were embedded and allow the user to substitute those if necessary.

What does the Embed/Don't Embed button do?

If you own the font but do not want others to use it, you can tap or click to select the specific font in the list and then tap or click the Don't Embed button. In that case, the yes column changes to no, and the button changes to the Embed button. You must select a specific font in the list to enable the button.

- Tap or click the OK button (Fonts dialog box) to close the dialog box.

- Tap or click the Back button (Backstage view) to return to the publication.

To Save the File Again

The following step saves the business card file again, this time with the embedded font settings.

 Tap or click the Save button (Quick Access Toolbar) to save the file again, with the same name.

To Delete the Business Information Set

The following steps delete the Quality Limos business information set. Deleting the business information set does not delete the information from saved publications.

- Display the INSERT tab.

- Tap or click the Business Information button (INSERT tab | Text group) to display the list of business information fields and commands.

- Tap or click the 'Edit Business Information' command to display the Business Information dialog box.

- If necessary, tap or click the 'Select a Business Information set' box and then tap or click Quality Limos to select the set (Figure 5–66).

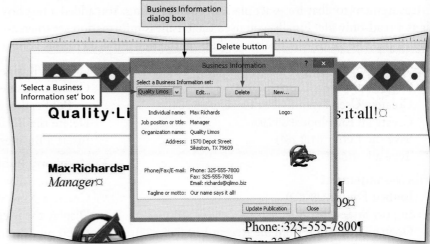

Figure 5–66

- Tap or click the Delete button (Business Information dialog box) to delete the business information set (Figure 5–67).

Q&A

Will this delete the fields from the current business card?

No. It will delete only the set. All publications containing that data will remain unchanged.

- When Publisher displays a dialog box asking you to confirm the deletion, tap or click the Yes button.

- Tap or click the Close button (Business Information dialog box) to close the dialog box.

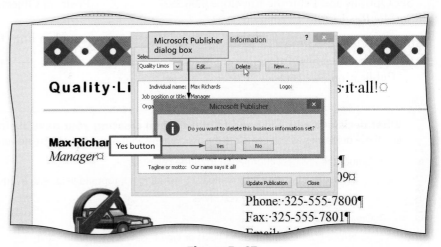

Figure 5–67

To Exit Publisher

This project is complete. The following steps exit Publisher. For a detailed example of the procedure summarized below, refer to the Office and Windows chapter at the beginning of this book.

1. To exit Publisher, tap or click the Close button on the right side of the title bar.

2. If a Microsoft Publisher dialog box is displayed, tap or click the Don't Save button so that any changes you have made are not saved.

Chapter Summary

In this chapter, you have learned how to personalize and customize publications with business information sets. You created the business information set with its many components and then used the business information set to create a letterhead. You created a new style and applied it to text boxes in the letterhead, using the Measurement toolbar for exact placement and scaling. You added a text box with an automatic date, and saved it as a read-only file. Finally, you used the business information set to create a fax cover, business card, and envelope. The items listed below include all the new Publisher skills you have learned in this chapter.

Creating New Publications
Create a Business Card (PUB 294)
Create a User-Friendly Fax Cover (PUB 284)
Create an Envelope (PUB 290)
Save the Letter (PUB 281)
Type a Letter (PUB 280)

File Management
Embed Fonts (PUB 302)
Import Styles (PUB 273)
Open a Publication from the Recent List (PUB 278)
Print the Business Card (PUB 297, 298)
Publish in a Portable Format (PUB 299)
Set Options and Print the Envelope (PUB 292)
Set the Read-Only Attribute (PUB 277)

Using Business Information Sets
Change the Business Information Set of an Existing Publication (PUB 266)

Create a Business Information Set (PUB 263)
Create a Business Information Set from a Publication (PUB 267)
Delete the Business Information Set (PUB 303)
Insert a Business Information Field (PUB 266)

Customizing Publications
Apply the New Style (PUB 272)
Create a New Style (PUB 271)
Display the Measurement Toolbar (PUB 268)
Insert an Automatic Date (PUB 275)
Insert an Automatic Date and Time (PUB 286)
Position Objects Using the Measurement Toolbar (PUB 269)
Sample a Font Color (PUB 270)

CONSIDER THIS

What decisions will you need to make when creating your next business publications?
Use these guidelines as you complete the assignments in this chapter and create your own publications outside of this class.

1. Gather the business information from the customer.
   a) Create a business information set including appropriate fields and a logo, if applicable.
   b) Create any necessary text styles.

2. Create letterhead.
   a) Use business information fields or type business information text.
   b) Create an automatic date and user-friendly text box for future use.
   c) Set the read-only attribute.

3. Create fax covers.
   a) Insert an automatic date.
   b) Edit other text boxes as necessary.

4. Create envelopes.
   a) Use business information sets when possible.
   b) Include a location for addresses or future labels.
   c) Set publication properties.

5. Create business cards.
   a) Insert a tagline or motto.
   b) Set publication properties.

6. Publish portable files.
   a) Proofread and check the publication.
   b) Save as PDF or XPS.

7. Embed fonts.

How should you submit solutions to questions in the assignments identified with a ✹ symbol?

Every assignment in this book contains one or more questions identified with a ✹ symbol. These questions require you to think beyond the assigned publication. Present your solutions to the questions in the format required by your instructor. Possible formats may include one or more of these options: write the answer; create a document that contains the answer; present your answer to the class; discuss your answer in a group; record the answer as audio or video using a webcam, smartphone, or portable media player; or post answers on a blog, wiki, or website.

Apply Your Knowledge

Reinforce the skills and apply the concepts you learned in this chapter.

Creating Letterhead

Note: To complete this assignment, you will be required to use the Data Files for Students. Visit www.cengage.com/ct/studentdownload for detailed instructions or contact your instructor for information about accessing the required files.

Instructions: Start Publisher. Open the publication, Apply 5-1 Dakota Fitness Letterhead, from the Data Files for Students. The publication is a letterhead that contains default business information fields. You will create a new business information set, publish the file in a portable format, and create an envelope. Figure 5–68 shows the completed letterhead and envelope.

Perform the following tasks:

1. Tap or click the Business Information button (INSERT tab | Text group), and then tap or click the 'Edit Business Information' command. If necessary, tap or click the New button (Business Information dialog box).

2. Enter the information from Table 5–4 and insert the logo file. The picture for the logo is available on the Data Files for Students. If instructed to do so, use your email address in the business information set.

3. Tap or click the Save button (Create New Business Information Set dialog box) to save the business information set with the company's name, Dakota Fitness.

4. Tap or click the Update Publication button (Business Information dialog box) to change the fields in the current letterhead.

Figure 5–68

Table 5–4 Dakota Fitness Business Information Set

Field Name	Company Data
Individual name	Devin Sturgis
Job position or title	Manager
Organization name	Dakota Fitness
Address	3177 Stanley Blvd. Munster, SD 57904
Phone, fax, and e-mail	Phone: 605-555-2400 Fax: 605-555-2401 E-mail: devin@sturgis.biz
Business Information set name	Dakota Fitness
Tagline or motto	Fitness is a life style!
Logo	Apply 5-1 Fitness Logo.png

Continued >

Apply Your Knowledge *continued*

5. Select the logo and then tap or click the Measurement button (DRAWING TOOLS FORMAT tab | Size group) to display the Measurement toolbar.

   a. Select the text in the Horizontal Position text box and then type **6.67** to replace it. Press the TAB key to advance to the next box.

   b. Type **.5** in the Vertical Position text box, and then press the TAB key.

   c. Type **1.3** in the Width text box, and then press the TAB key.

   d. Type **1.3** in the Height text box, and then press the ENTER key.

   e. Close the Measurement toolbar.

6. Zoom to 100% and then scroll to the bottom of the page. Tap or click the Business Information button (INSERT tab | Text group) to display its list. Tap or click the Individual name text box and position it at the bottom of the letterhead. Repeat the process for the Job position or title field and the Tagline or motto field, as shown in Figure 5–68 on the previous page.

7. One at a time, apply the Heading 4 style to each of the three text boxes by selecting the text and then tapping or clicking the Styles button (HOME tab | Styles group).

8. Open the Backstage view and then tap or click Save As. Save the publication using the file name, Apply 5-1 Dakota Fitness Letterhead Complete.

9. To publish the letterhead as a PDF in order to send it to a commercial printer, open the Backstage view and then tap or click the Export tab. Tap or click the 'Create PDF/XPS' button to display the Publish as PDF or XPS dialog box.

10. Navigate to your storage device and appropriate folder, if necessary.

11. Tap or click the Options button (Publish as PDF or XPS dialog box) to display the Publish Options dialog box. If necessary, in the Specify how this publication will be printed or distributed area, tap or click 'High quality printing'. If necessary, in the Include non-printing information area, tap or click both check boxes to select them. Do not change any of the other default values.

12. Tap or click the OK button (Publish Options dialog box) to close the dialog box. Tap or click the Publish button (Publish as PDF or XPS dialog box) to create the portable file. View the PDF (or XPS) file and then close the Adobe Reader (or XPS Reader) window.

13. Close the letterhead publication without quitting Publisher, to display the template gallery.

14. Tap or click BUILT-IN, tap or click the Envelopes thumbnail, and then choose the Bars envelope template in size #10. Use the Aqua color scheme and the Modern font scheme. Tap or click the CREATE button to display the publication in the Publisher workspace. If necessary, update the publication with the business information set.

15. Print the envelope with appropriate printer settings.

16. Tap or click the Business Information button (INSERT tab | Text group), and then tap or click the 'Edit Business Information' command. Tap or click the Delete button (Business Information dialog box), and then tap or click the Yes button (Microsoft Publisher dialog box) to delete the Dakota Fitness business information set. Tap or click the Close button (Business Information dialog box).

17. Save the envelope with the file name, Apply 5-1 Dakota Fitness Envelope, and then exit Publisher.

18. Submit the files as specified by your instructor.

19. ✳ When would it be more advantageous to send the letterhead out for printing, rather than just typing text on the template and printing it on a desktop printer? If a company uses preprinted letterhead, how do they create content? Would there be an advantage to running the paper through the printer and just using a Publisher text box with proper dimensions? Or do you think most companies use a copy machine?

Extend Your Knowledge

Extend the skills you learned in this chapter and experiment with new skills. You may need to use Help to complete the assignment.

Adding Styles to the Quick Access Toolbar

Note: To complete this assignment, you will be required to use the Data Files for Students. Visit www.cengage.com/ct/studentdownload for detailed instructions or contact your instructor for information about accessing the required files.

Instructions: Open the publication, Extend 5-1 Insurance Thank You from the Data Files for Students. You will add the Styles button to the Quick Access Toolbar, apply styles to the publication, and then remove the button from the Quick Access Toolbar.

Perform the following tasks:

1. Use Help to learn more about customizing the Quick Access Toolbar.

2. If necessary, tap or click the 'Current page in publication' button on the status bar to show the Page Navigation pane.

3. Press and hold or right-click the Styles button (HOME tab | Styles group) to display the shortcut menu.

4. Tap or click the 'Add to Quick Access Toolbar' command to add the Styles button to the Quick Access Toolbar.

5. Select the text on Page 1 of the thank you card. Tap or click the Styles button on the Quick Access Toolbar, and then choose the 'Pete Hayes Insurance' style.

6. Tap or click the 'Page 2 and Page 3' thumbnail in the Page Navigation pane to display the inside pages in the Publisher workspace.

7. Select the text on Page 2 (in the upper portion of the page layout). Tap or click the Styles button on the Quick Access Toolbar, and then choose the Heading 4 style, if necessary.

8. Select the text on Page 3 (in the lower portion of the page layout). Tap or click the Styles button on the Quick Access Toolbar, and then choose the 'Body Text 5' style.

9. Tap or click the Page 4 icon in the Page Navigation pane to display the back page in the Publisher workspace.

10. Select the text on Page 4 of the thank you card. Tap or click the Styles button on the Quick Access Toolbar, and then choose the 'Pete Hayes Insurance' style.

11. Tap or click the 'Customize Quick Access Toolbar' button on the right side of the Quick Access Toolbar to display its menu, and then tap or click More Commands to display the Publisher Options dialog box and, by default, the Quick Access Toolbar settings.

12. Tap or click the Styles button in the Customize Quick Access Toolbar list (Figure 5–69).

13. Tap or click the Remove button (Publisher Options Dialog box) to remove the Styles button from the Quick Access Toolbar. Tap or click the OK button to return to the publication.

14. Save the revised publication with the name Extend 5-1 Insurance Thank You Complete, and then submit it in the format specified by your instructor.

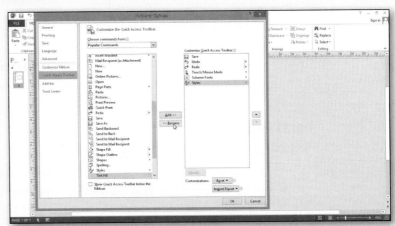

Figure 5–69

Continued >

Extend Your Knowledge *continued*

15. Exit Publisher.

16. ✷ Would you consider adding the Styles button to the Quick Access Toolbar on a permanent basis? Why or why not? What other features do you use so often that you might want to add them to the Quick Access Toolbar?

Analyze, Correct, Improve

Analyze a publication, correct all errors, and improve the design.

Inserting User-Friendly Features

Note: To complete this assignment, you will be required to use the Data Files for Students. Visit www.cengage.com/ct/studentdownload for detailed instructions or contact your instructor for information about accessing the required files.

Instructions: You have been given a letterhead that is not user-friendly, as shown in Figure 5–70. You decide to improve the letterhead. Run Publisher and open the file, Analyze 5-1 Letterhead.

1. Correct The large text box in the center of the publication has characteristics that are not convenient for most users. Change the font to Times New Roman, size 10. Change the line spacing to single spacing. Change the spacing after paragraphs to zero.

2. Improve The large text box in the center of the publication is difficult to see. Insert text to help the user determine where to type. Include an automatic date, and the words, ENTER TEXT HERE to help guide the user. Change the document properties, including keywords, as specified by your instructor. Save the publication using the file name, Analyze 5-1 Letterhead Complete. Set the read-only attribute so that the user cannot save the edited file and overwrite the template file accidentally. Submit the revised document in the format specified by your instructor.

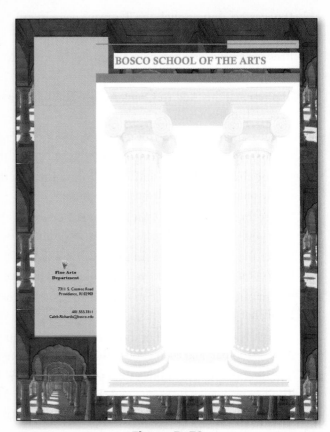

Figure 5–70

3. ✷ Can you think of some other ways to make a letterhead template user-friendly? Might you create a standard signature block at the bottom of the page? Why or why not?

In the Labs

Design, create, or modify a publication using the guidelines, concepts, and skills presented in this chapter. Labs 1 and 2, which increase in difficulty, require you to create a solution based on what you learned in the chapter; Lab 3 requires you to create a solution that uses cloud and web technologies, by learning and investigating on your own from general guidance.

Lab 1: **Creating a Business Card**

Problem: Your friend has just opened a clothing resale shop. She wants you to create a business card for her. You prepare the business card shown in Figure 5–71. Because this is the only publication she needs, it is not necessary to save the business information set.

Figure 5–71

Perform the following tasks:

1. Run Publisher. In the template gallery, tap or click BUILT-IN and then tap or click Business Cards.

2. Choose the Retro Business card, the Lilac color scheme, the Breve font scheme, and the Landscape page size option.

3. Select the text in the Business Name text box. Change the font to French Script MT and the font size to 20. Type `Trends Again` to change the name of the business.

4. Change the name to `Amanda Renfro` and, if necessary, change the position to Manager. If instructed to do so, use your name instead of Amanda Renfro.

5. Change the address, phone, fax, and email as shown in Figure 5–71.

6. Delete the logo.

7. Draw a text box in the lower-right portion of the business card. Insert the text `Specializing in vintage clothing`. Use the Format Painter to copy the formatting from the business name text box. Autofit the text.

8. Press and hold or right-click the small flower picture over the business name. Tap or click Change picture and then use Office.com Clip Art to replace the picture with one related to the term `fashion`. Delete the replaced file from the scratch area.

9. Embed the fonts and then save the publication using the file name, Lab 5-1 Trends Again Business Card, and then print a copy.

10. Submit the file as directed by your instructor.

11. Exit Publisher.

12. ✳ With business cards being fairly inexpensive to have produced professionally and online, why do you think people still buy the business card paper and print them out? What other kinds of paper do people buy to do their own desktop publishing? Is that a good use of their time and money?

Lab 2: **Creating Styles**

Problem: Your friend creates Android apps using Java. As part of his marketing plan, he wants a distinctive branding font that he can use in all of his publications. You decide to present him with several styles and colors from which he may choose (Figure 5–72). Table 5–5 on the next page displays the style settings.

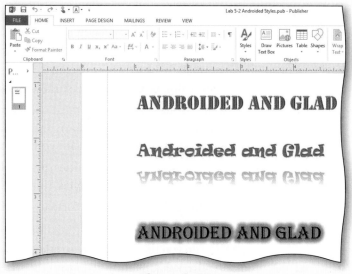

Figure 5–72

Perform the following tasks:

1. Run Publisher. In the template gallery, tap or click the Blank 8.5 × 11" template to open a blank publication. If necessary, choose the Office color scheme.

2. Draw a large text box and enter the text, `Androided and Glad,` three times, pressing the ENTER key twice after each instance.

Continued >

In the Labs continued

Table 5–5 Style Settings			
Style Name	Android 1	Android 2	Android 3
Font	Stencil	Ravie	Algerian
Font style	Regular	Regular	Regular
Font size	26	20	24
Font color	Green (in Standard Colors)	Dark Red	Black
Text Effects	<none>	Reflection Presets: Full Reflection, 8 pt offset	Glow Presets: Accent 4, 18 pt glow Color: Accent 2 (RGB (237, 125, 49)), Darker 50%

©2014 Cengage Learning

3. Select the first occurrence of the text.

    a. Tap or click the Styles button (HOME tab | Styles group). Tap or click the New Style command in the gallery.

    b. In the 'Enter new style name' text box (New Style dialog box), type Android 1 to name the style.

    c. Tap or click the Font button and select the settings as shown in Table 5–5. Tap or click the OK button (Font Dialog box).

    d. Tap or click the OK button (New Style dialog box) to save the style.

    e. Apply the new style to the first occurrence of the text.

4. Select the second occurrence of the text.

    a. Create a new style with the name and font settings shown in Table 5–5.

    b. Tap or click the Text Effects button (New Style dialog box), and then tap or click Reflection (Format Text Effects dialog box). Tap or click the Presets button (Reflection area) and select Full Reflection, 8 pt offset.

    c. Tap or click the OK button (Format Text Effects dialog box). Tap or click the OK button (Font dialog box). Tap or click the OK button (New Style dialog box) to save the style.

    d. Apply the new style to the second occurrence of the text.

5. Select the third occurrence of the text.

    a. Create a new style with the name and font settings shown in Table 5–5.

    b. Tap or click the Text Effects button (New Style dialog box), and then tap or click Glow (Format Text Effects dialog box). Tap or click the Presets button (Glow area), and select Accent 4, 18 pt glow. Tap or click the Color button, and choose a dark brown color.

    c. Tap or click the OK button (Format Text Effects dialog box). Tap or click the OK button (Font dialog box). Tap or click the OK button (New Style dialog box) to save the style.

    d. Apply the new style to the third occurrence of the text. If directed by your instructor, create a fourth occurrence of the text, and choose a different font and formatting when creating the new style. Name the style with your name.

6. Change the publication properties, as specified by your instructor. Save the publication with the file name, Lab 5-2 Android Styles.

7. Submit the publication in the format specified by your instructor.

8. Exit Publisher.

9. ✳ Why do you think this exercise asked you to create styles, rather than just to format the text differently? What might you do with the styles in the future? Considering the nature of the business that requested the styles, do you think the font choices were appropriate? Why or why not?

Lab 3: Expand Your World: Cloud and Web Technologies
Sharing Ideas

Problem: You work online from home as a desktop publisher for a business. You would like to discuss your ideas for a new company letterhead with a coworker, but it has become tedious and time-consuming sending files back and forth. You decide to try a screen-sharing program.

Instructions:

1. Open a browser and go to http:// join.me. Tap or click the basic button (Figure 5–73).

2. Tap or click the Start button. After a few moments, when the join.me website asks if you want to run the application, tap or click the Run button (Application Run - Security Warning dialog box). (*Hint:* The website requires the .Net framework, which commonly is installed already on many computers. If you do not have the .Net framework, join.me will offer to download it for you.)

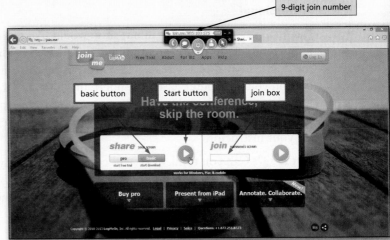

Figure 5–73   ©Join.me 2006–2013

3. The join.me website will start the screen-sharing applet and provide you with a nine-digit number to share with others (Figure 5–73).

4. Contact another student in your class or a friend, and ask him or her to navigate to the join.me website and enter the number in the join box.

5. Once the user has joined you, open Publisher and demonstrate how to create a simple letterhead.

6. When you are finished, tap or click the Exit button.

7. Write a paragraph about your experience with the screen-sharing program. Include several advantages and disadvantages for collaborating in this manner.

8. Submit the assignment in the format specified by your instructor.

9. ✳ What other screen-sharing programs have you heard about or used? What are the advantages to a web-based, free service such as join.me? Do you think screen sharing is an important tool in business? Why or why not?

✳ Consider This: Your Turn

Apply your creative thinking and problem solving skills to design and implement a solution.

1: Creating a Personal Business Card

Personal/Academic

Part 1:   As part of an internship search, you need to create a business card for yourself to give potential employers. Start Publisher and choose a Business Card template from the list. Choose a color and font scheme. Edit the business information set to include your personal data. Use your own name and the title of the job you would like to have. Enter the name and address of your school or workplace as the organization. Update the publication. Print the business card using appropriate printer settings. Delete your business information set if you used a laboratory computer.

Continued >

Consider This: Your Turn *continued*

Part 2: ✸ If you decide to send business cards out for professional printing, what kind of file will you submit, a publisher file, PDF, or XPS? Give several advantages and disadvantages of each choice.

2: Branding Text
Professional

Part 1: The Baker's Dozen donut shop would like you to create a text style that employees can import into all of their current publications. Using a blank page, create a text box with the name of the donut shop as text. Create a new style using the Harlow Solid Italic font or a decorative italic font on your computer. Use a 48-point, bright red font. Add the Engrave font effect. Save the style with the name, Baker's Dozen. Create another text box with your name in it, and apply the new style. Embed all possible fonts and then save the publication for the donut shop to use. Print a copy for your instructor.

Part 2: ✸ Can you think of several companies that have distinct formatting for the business name? How is branding the text different from branding a logo? Search the web for third-party providers of specific font styles such as the James Bond font or the IBM font.

3: Researching How People Use Faxes
Research and Collaboration

Part 1: Find a local company or a department at your school that sends faxes. Alternatively, find a business that sends faxes for other people as part of their office-related services. Ask them the following questions:

- How often do you use a fax machine?
- Do you pay for a separate phone line for your fax machine?
- Does your copy machine have fax capabilities?
- Do you ever use a fax app on your computer or mobile device?
- What kind of documents do you fax?
- Is the fax number listed on your letterhead?
- Do you use a fax cover, and if so, how is that generated?
- Why do people still fax?

Create a publication summarizing your answers and submit it to your instructor. Compare answers with others in the class.

Part 2: ✸ What answers surprised you? What did you learn about faxes? Was this exercise useful in preparing you for a career as a desktop publisher?

Learn Online

Reinforce what you learned in this chapter with games, exercises, training, and many other online activities and resources.

Student Companion Site Reinforce chapter terms and concepts using review questions, flash cards, practice tests, and interactive learning games, such as a crossword puzzle. These and other online activities and resources are available at no additional cost on www.cengagebrain.com. Visit www.cengage.com/ct/studentdownload for detailed instructions about accessing the resources available at the Student Companion Site.

6 | Working with Publisher Tables

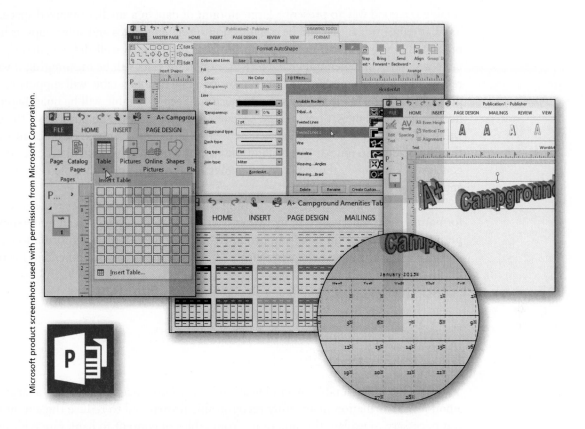

Objectives

You will have mastered the material in this chapter when you can:

- Change page orientation
- Apply shape effects
- Snap objects to margin guides
- Create tables and enter data
- Insert and delete rows and columns in tables
- Apply table formats
- Select table rows, columns, and cells
- Center and align table data
- Format tables with borders

- Merge, split, and divide cells diagonally
- Create a 12-month calendar
- Use the Master Page
- Edit BorderArt
- Select all and set the transparency
- Embed an Excel table in a Publisher publication
- Use Excel tools on the Publisher ribbon to format a table

6 | Working with Publisher Tables

Introduction

A table is a good way to present a large amount of data in a small, organized space. Tabular data, or data that can be organized into related groups and subgroups, is best presented in rows and columns with appropriate headings. A well-defined, descriptive table will have three general characteristics. First, the data will be meaningful; it will relate closely to the purpose of the publication. The data in a table will support or provide evidence of any analyses or conclusions. Second, a table will be unambiguous — it will have clear labels, titles, headings, legends, or footnotes. The purpose of the table will be clear, and the scale will be well defined. Third, a table should be efficient so that the reader can quickly understand the data and its presentation, in order to draw conclusions and apply the data to a particular situation. An efficient table is formatted appropriately and read quickly.

While many tables are created using Microsoft Excel, Publisher tables are formatted easily and fit well in many kinds of publications. Readers can understand the purpose of a publication table and promptly retrieve the important information. As you also will learn in this chapter, many of Excel's features can be embedded for use in Publisher tables.

Project — Amenities Table, Calendar, and Business Table

The decision to use a table in a publication is based on a need to organize a large amount of information in an easily recognizable format and to reduce the amount of text necessary to explain the situation. From tables of content to bank rate tables to timetables, you may need to display text, graphics, dates, or color in many different tabular ways. Publisher allows you to create tables from scratch or use tables that already are organized for specific purposes.

In this project, you will create three different publications that incorporate tables for a chain of campgrounds called A+ Campgrounds, as shown in Figure 6–1. A WordArt object with special shape effects will serve as a common element across publications. An amenities table (Figure 6–1a) will show which services are available at which campgrounds. A promotional calendar (Figure 6–1b) will present each month as a table. Finally, a letter to the campground managers (Figure 6–1c) will contain an embedded table with totals and formatting.

Campground Amenities

Services:\ Camp	Full Hookups	Electricity	Water	Pool	Playground	Cabins	Wi-Fi	Bike Rentals
Big Fox	X			X	X	X	X	X
Middle Creek	X						X	
Winding River		X	X		X		X	
Crossroads			X		X			X

(a)

(b)

651 Michigan Street
Suite 501
Dugan, NH 03033
Phone: 603-555-3123
Fax: 603-555-3125
E-mail:
associates@walker.biz

October 16, 2014

To All Managers:

Below please find the Third Quarter Revenue for July through September 2014. As you can see, our four locations brought in similar amounts of money. Campground fees are the major portion of our revenue at every campground. And, we exceeded last year by more than 4%.

Please bring your comments to our next manager's meeting on Nov. 1, 2014 at 10:00 a.m. at the Big Fox office. I will have a copy of our new promotional calendar to show you!

Sincerely,

Nate Hartford

Owner and General Manager

A+ Campgrounds					
Third Quarter Revenue					
	Big Fox	Middle Creek	Winding River	Crossroads	Total
Campground Fees	$152,918.24	$ 179,657.53	$ 178,634.80	$129,087.40	$640,297.97
Camp Store	69,975.23	39,444.60	58,456.33		167,876.16
Rentals	8,526.40			8,965.35	17,491.75
Other	5,567.54	5,834.00	3,982.85	6,141.00	21,525.39
Total	$236,987.41	$ 224,936.13	$ 241,073.98	$144,193.75	$847,191.27

(c)

Figure 6–1

Roadmap

In this chapter, you will learn how to create the publication shown in Figure 6–1. The following roadmap identifies general activities you will perform as you progress through this chapter:

1. EMPLOY REUSABLE PARTS such as business information sets, building blocks, and logos.
2. APPLY SHAPE EFFECTS such as glows, reflections, and 3-D effects.
3. INSERT and FORMAT TABLES.
4. CREATE a CALENDAR.
5. USE MASTER PAGES to insert objects that will appear on every page.
6. ADD BORDERART to help outline pages and tables.
7. EMBED or link a TABLE for advanced formatting.
8. USE EXCEL FUNCTIONALITY to add commands to publisher.

At the beginning of step instructions throughout the chapter, you will see an abbreviated form of this roadmap. The abbreviated roadmap uses colors to indicate chapter progress: gray means the chapter is beyond that activity, blue means the task being shown is covered in that activity, and black means that activity is yet to be covered. For example, the following abbreviated roadmap indicates the chapter would be showing a task in the Create Calendar activity.

1 EMPLOY REUSABLE PARTS | 2 APPLY SHAPE EFFECTS | 3 INSERT & FORMAT TABLES | **4 CREATE CALENDAR**

5 USE MASTER PAGES | 6 ADD BORDERART | 7 EMBED TABLE | 8 USE EXCEL FUNCTIONALITY

Use the abbreviated roadmap as a progress guide while you read or step through the instructions in this chapter.

To Run Publisher

If you are using a computer to step through the project in this chapter and you want your screens to match the figures in this book, you should change your screen's resolution to 1366 × 768. For information about how to change a computer's resolution, refer to the Office and Windows chapter at the beginning of this book.

The following steps run Publisher.

1 Scroll the Start screen and search for a Publisher 2013 tile. If your Start screen contains a Publisher 2013 tile, tap or click it to run Publisher and then proceed to Step 5. If the Start screen does not contain the Publisher 2013 tile, proceed to the next step to search for the Publisher app.

2 Swipe in from the right edge of the screen or point to the upper-right corner of the screen to display the Charms bar and then tap or click the Search charm on the Charms bar to display the Search menu.

3 Type **Publisher** as the search text in the Search box, and watch the search results appear in the Apps list.

4 Tap or click Publisher 2013 in the search results to run Publisher.

5 If the Publisher window is not maximized, tap or click the Maximize button on its title bar to maximize the window.

One of the few differences between Windows 7 and Windows 8 occurs in the steps to run Publisher. If you are using Windows 7, click the Start button, type **Publisher** in the 'Search programs and files' box, click Publisher 2013, and then, if necessary, maximize the Publisher window. For a summary of the steps to run Publisher in Windows 7, refer to the Quick Reference located at the back of this book.

Reusable Parts

The customer, A+ Campgrounds, wants several publications, including a list of campground amenities, a publicity calendar, and a letter to the managers. Certain objects will be repeated in all publications, including the color and font scheme you selected previously, the business information set, and the name of the company in a WordArt object to serve as a recognizable branding of the campground.

Why should I create reusable objects for branding?

Creating reusable components such as business sets, logos, and a stylistic company name helps create a positive perception of a company and creates identifiable branding. A brand identity should be communicated in multiple ways with frequency and consistency throughout the life of a business. Sometimes a brand is as simple as golden arches; other times it is a stylistic font that identifies a popular soda, no matter what the language. Developing and marketing a brand takes time and research. When desktop publishers are asked to help with brand recognition, they can suggest reusable colors, fonts, schemes, logos, business information sets, graphics, and other tools to assist the company in creating a customer-friendly, consistent brand.

To Select a Blank Publication and Adjust Settings

The following steps select an 8.5 × 11 blank print publication, adjust workspace settings, and choose schemes that will apply to the amenities table for A+ Campgrounds.

1 Tap or click the Blank 8.5 × 11" thumbnail in the New template gallery to create a blank publication in the Publisher window.

2 Collapse the Page Navigation pane.

3 If it is not selected already, tap or click the Special Characters button (HOME tab | Paragraph group) to display formatting marks.

4 Display the PAGE DESIGN tab.

5 Tap or click the Foundry color scheme (PAGE DESIGN tab | Schemes group) to choose a color scheme.

6 Tap or click the Scheme Fonts button (PAGE DESIGN tab | Schemes group) and then tap or click Flow to choose a font scheme.

To Change the Page Orientation

1 EMPLOY REUSABLE PARTS | 2 APPLY SHAPE EFFECTS | 3 INSERT & FORMAT TABLES | 4 CREATE CALENDAR
5 USE MASTER PAGES | 6 ADD BORDERART | 7 EMBED TABLE | 8 USE EXCEL FUNCTIONALITY

When a publication is in **portrait orientation**, the short edge of the paper is the top of the publication. You can instruct Publisher to lay out a publication in **landscape orientation**, so that the long edge of the paper is the top of the publication. The following steps change the page orientation of the publication from portrait to landscape. *Why? The table you will create is wider than it is tall, and will fit better on a page with landscape orientation.*

1

• Tap or click the 'Change Page Orientation' button (PAGE DESIGN tab | Page Setup group) to display the orientation options (Figure 6–2).

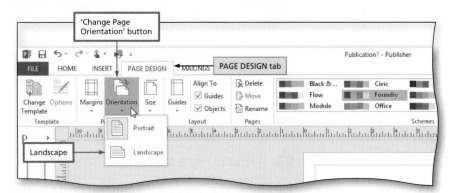

Figure 6–2

2

- Tap or click Landscape to change the orientation of the page (Figure 6–3).

Q&A

Could I have chosen a template with landscape orientation?

Yes, if you know in advance that you want landscape orientation, choose one of the landscape orientation templates. If you have already created objects, use the 'Change Page Orientation' button (PAGE DESIGN tab | Page Setup group).

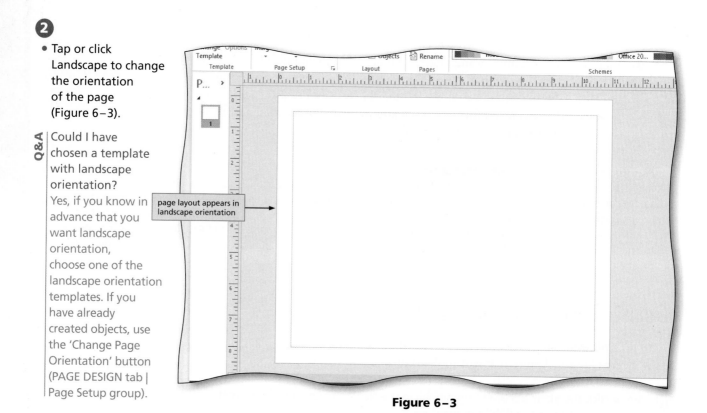

Figure 6–3

Creating a Business Information Set

Table 6–1 displays the data for each of the fields in the business information set that you will create in this project. Because you will be creating a graphical representation for the organization name, you will leave that field blank.

Table 6–1 Data for Business Information Fields	
Fields	**Data**
Individual name	Nate Hartford
Job position or title	Owner and General Manager
Organization name	
Address	632 Michigan Street Suite 501 Dugan, NH 03033
Phone, fax, and e-mail	Phone: 603-555-3123 Fax: 603-555-3125 E-mail: associates@walker.biz
Tagline or motto	Camping at its finest!
Logo	<none>
Business Information set name	A+ Campgrounds

© 2014 Cengage Learning

To Create a Business Information Set

The following steps create a business information set for A+ Campgrounds, which will be used in multiple publications.

1 Display the INSERT tab.

2 Tap or click the Business Information button (INSERT tab | Text group) to display the list of business information fields and commands.

③ Tap or click 'Edit Business Information' to display the Business Information dialog box. Tap or click the New button (Business Information dialog box).

④ Enter the data from Table 6–1, pressing the TAB key to advance from one field to the next (Figure 6–4).

⑤ Tap or click the Save button (Create New Business Information Set dialog box).

⑥ Tap or click the Update Publication button (Business Information dialog box).

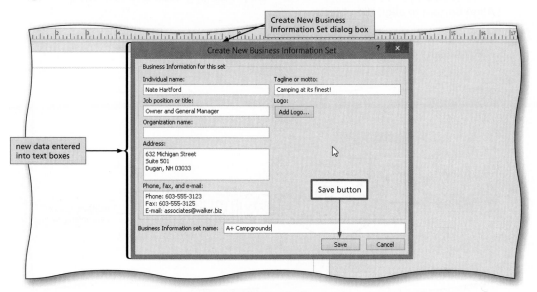

Figure 6–4

To Insert a WordArt Object

The following steps insert two WordArt objects and then group them to use as a brand.

① Zoom to 100% and, if necessary, display the INSERT tab.

② Tap or click the Insert WordArt button (INSERT tab | Text group) to display the WordArt gallery.

③ Tap or click the 'Fill - Cream, Outline - Blue' preview in the Plain WordArt Styles area of the WordArt gallery to select it.

④ Type **A+** in the Text text box (Edit WordArt Text dialog box) to enter the text.

⑤ If necessary, tap or click the Font arrow (Edit WordArt Text dialog box) and then tap or click Arial Black or a similar font.

⑥ If necessary, tap or click the Size arrow (Edit WordArt Text dialog box) and then tap or click 36 to choose a 36-point font size.

⑦ Tap or click the OK button (Edit WordArt Text dialog box) to close the dialog box and insert the WordArt object.

⑧ Tap or click the Shape Outline arrow (WORDART TOOLS FORMAT tab | WordArt Styles group), and then tap or click 'Accent 3 (RGB (114, 163, 118)), Darker 25%' in the color palette to outline the WordArt with a dark green color.

⑨ Tap or click the Shape Outline arrow (WORDART TOOLS FORMAT tab | WordArt Styles group), tap or click Weight in the Shape Outline gallery, and then tap or click the line size, 2¼ pt, to change the outline weight.

10 Drag the rotation handle of the WordArt object to the left, until the object is at an approximate 15-degree angle as shown in Figure 6–5.

11 Repeat Steps 1 through 9 to create a second WordArt object with the word, **Campgrounds**. Do not rotate it.

12 Drag to move the objects beside one another as shown in Figure 6–5. SHIFT+tap or SHIFT+click each of the two WordArt objects so that both are selected. Tap or click the Align button (WORDART TOOLS FORMAT tab | Arrange group), and then tap or click Align Bottom to align the objects.

13 With the two objects still selected, tap or click the Group button (WORDART TOOLS FORMAT tab | Arrange group) to group the two objects (Figure 6–5).

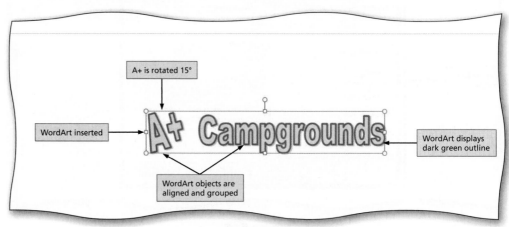

Figure 6–5

To Snap an Object to the Margin Guide

1 EMPLOY REUSABLE PARTS | 2 APPLY SHAPE EFFECTS | 3 INSERT & FORMAT TABLES | 4 CREATE CALENDAR
5 USE MASTER PAGES | 6 ADD BORDERART | 7 EMBED TABLE | 8 USE EXCEL FUNCTIONALITY

The following step moves the WordArt object to the top of the page and snaps it to the margin. *Why?* **Snapping** *is a magnet-like alignment that occurs between object borders and margin guides. Snapping is an easy way to align objects with the margin or with other objects, and snapping is better than dragging to an approximate location.*

1

- Display the PAGE DESIGN tab.

- Verify that both the Guides and Objects check boxes (PAGE DESIGN tab | Layout group) contain check marks.

- Drag the border of the object (in this case, the grouped WordArt) toward the top margin guide. When a blue snapping line appears even with the top of the object (Figure 6–6), lift your finger or release the mouse button to snap the object to the margin guide.

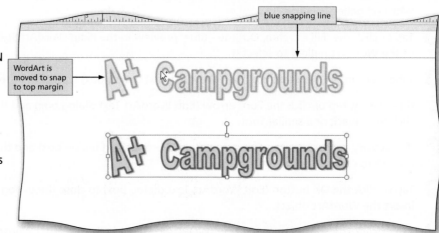

Figure 6–6

 Q&A How do I place the WordArt object more precisely?

Press and hold or right-click the WordArt object, and then tap or click Format Object on the shortcut menu. Tap or click the Layout tab (Format Object dialog box), and enter the precise measurements in the 'Position on page' text boxes.

To Align Items Relative to Margin Guides

Recall that in word processing applications, the right, center, and left alignment tools always refer to the current margins of the page. In desktop publication applications, the alignment tools refer to the text box in which you are working. You can align items relative to the margin of the page, however, by using the alignment options that exists on each of the formatting tabs (DRAWING TOOLS, WORDART TOOLS, and PICTURE TOOLS). The following steps align the WordArt object horizontally, relative to the margin guides.

1 Select the WordArt object and, if necessary, display the WORDART TOOLS FORMAT tab.

2 Tap or click the Align Objects button (WORDART TOOLS FORMAT tab | Arrange group) to display the alignment options.

3 Tap or click 'Relative to Margin Guides' to change how Publisher aligns the object.

4 Tap or click the Align Objects button (WORDART TOOLS FORMAT tab | Arrange group) again, to display the enabled alignment options.

5 Tap or click Align Center to center the WordArt object with respect to the margins (Figure 6–7).

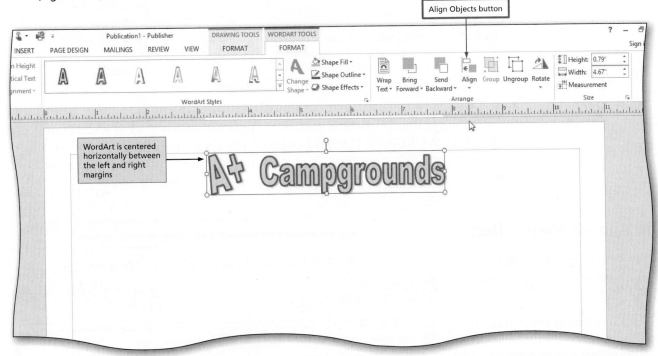

Figure 6–7

Shape Effects

Shape effects are a group of tools that change the design and style of a shape or WordArt. Recall that text effects were used in a previous chapter to fill and outline text. Shape effects are applied in a similar way. Many new shape effects are available in Publisher 2013, including advanced shadows, reflections, glow, soft edges, bevels, and 3-D rotations, as shown in Table 6–2 on the following page.

BTW

The Ribbon and Screen Resolution
Publisher may change how the groups and buttons within the groups appear on the ribbon, depending on the computer's screen resolution. Thus, your ribbon may look different from the ones in this book if you are using a screen resolution other than 1366 × 768.

Table 6–2 Shape Effects			
Effect	**Description**	**Gallery Options**	**Adjustable Settings**
Shadow	a semi-transparent shading is added to the shape to create the illusion of a shadow, giving the shape depth	outer inner perspective	transparency size blur angle distance
Reflection	a replicated shadow with matching borders is added to the shape to create the appearance of a reflection	variations	transparency size blur distance
Glow	color and shading is added around all sides of the shape so it seems to glow for decorative emphasis	variations	color size transparency
Soft Edges	blurs the edges of a shape inward a certain amount to make the border less harsh	point values	size
Bevel	shading and artificial shadows that emulate a three-dimensional beveled edge or chamfer, framing the shape	types	top bottom depth contour material lighting
3-D Rotation	rotates and angles, backfilling with a shadow effect to apply parallel, perspective, and oblique 3-D effects to a shape	parallel perspective	x rotation y rotation perspective

© 2014 Cengage Learning

A Shape Effects button is available on both the DRAWING TOOLS FORMAT tab and the WORDART TOOLS FORMAT tab. Each button displays a gallery, and when chosen, a dialog box with adjustable settings. You will use the 3-D Rotation tool in the next series of steps to create a 3-D version of the company name.

To Apply a Shape Effect

1 EMPLOY REUSABLE PARTS | 2 APPLY SHAPE EFFECTS | 3 INSERT & FORMAT TABLES | 4 CREATE CALENDAR
5 USE MASTER PAGES | 6 ADD BORDERART | 7 EMBED TABLE | 8 USE EXCEL FUNCTIONALITY

The following steps format the WordArt with the 3-D Rotation shape effect. *Why? The owner of the company wants a 3-D effect applied to the name of the business.*

1

- Scroll to the right so that objects on the screen will be visible when the gallery is open in the next step.

- If necessary, select the shape (in this case, the grouped WordArt) and then tap or click the Shape Effects button (WORDART TOOLS FORMAT tab | WordArt Styles group) to display the Shape Effects gallery (Figure 6–8).

 Experiment

- One at a time, tap or click each of the commands and view the choices in each gallery.

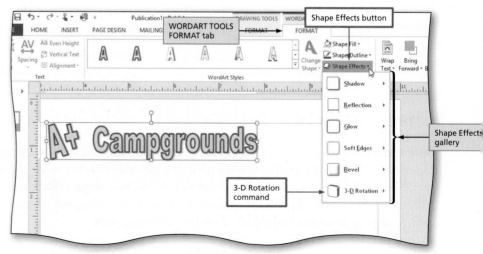

Figure 6–8

2

- Tap or click the desired shape effect (in this case, 3-D Rotation) to display the gallery (Figure 6–9).

 Experiment

- If you are using a mouse, point to various previews in the gallery and watch the WordArt change with live preview.

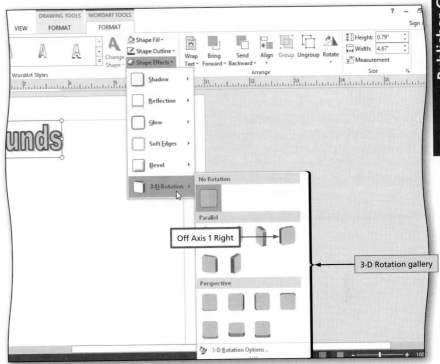

Figure 6–9

3

- Tap or click the desired 3-D Rotation shape effect (in this case, 'Off Axis 1 Right') to format the shape (Figure 6–10).

Q&A Is it OK if the WordArt extends above the margin?
Yes, the default margins are wide; your publication will print correctly.

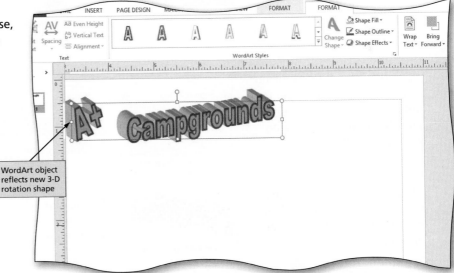

Figure 6–10

Other Ways

1. Tap or click Format WordArt Dialog Box Launcher (WORDART TOOLS FORMAT tab | WordArt Styles group), tap or click Shape Effects button (Colors and Lines tab), tap or click desired effect, tap or click Presets button (Format Shape dialog box), tap or click desired thumbnail, tap or click OK button (Format Shape dialog box), tap or click OK button (Format Object dialog box)

To Fine-Tune a Shape Effect

The following steps make changes to the shape effect by adjusting specific settings. *Why?* In this case, you have decided that the 3-D effect is too thick and you want to reduce its depth.

1

- With the shape still selected, tap or click the Shape Effects button (WORDART TOOLS FORMAT tab | WordArt Styles group) to display the Shape Effects gallery, and then tap or click the desired shape effect (in this case, 3-D Rotation) to open its gallery (Figure 6–11).

Q&A What is the difference between Parallel and Perspective rotations? Parallel rotations move the left or right side of the WordArt text to simulate a 3-D effect. Perspective rotations move the top or bottom of the WordArt text.

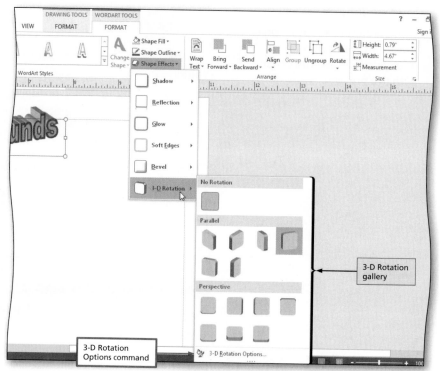

Figure 6–11

2

- Tap or click the Options command for the specific shape effect (3-D Rotation Options, in this case) to display the Format Shape dialog box (Figure 6–12).

Experiment

- Scroll through the choices in the Format Shape dialog box and tap or click various effects to look at their settings.

Q&A What does the Fill button do at the top of the Format Shape dialog box? The Fill button causes Fill settings to appear. The default value is a gray, solid fill for the 3-D effect. You can change the color and type of fill, or apply gradients.

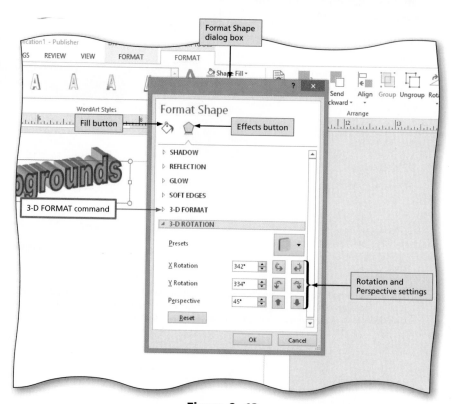

Figure 6–12

3

- Tap or click 3-D FORMAT in the list to display the settings.

- Select the text in the Depth Size text box, and then type 24 pt to enter a value smaller than the default setting (Figure 6–13).

 What does a smaller value do to the shape?
The smaller the value, the thinner the shadowing behind the object, creating the illusion of a more narrow 3-D depth.

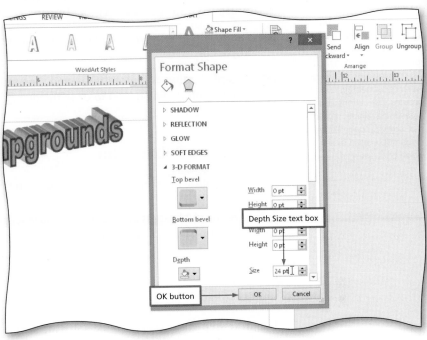

Figure 6–13

4

- Tap or click the OK button (Format Shape dialog box) to change the depth of the 3-D shape (Figure 6–14).

 What other options might I change when using a 3-D Rotation shape effect?
The X Rotation text box changes the width of the rotation; the Y Rotation text box changes the height of the rotation. The Perspective option only makes a change if you chose one of the perspective preset styles. It changes the width, height, and depth.

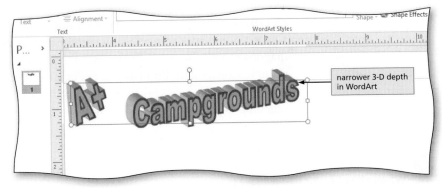

Figure 6–14

Other Ways

1. Tap or click Format WordArt Dialog Box Launcher (WORDART TOOLS FORMAT tab | WordArt Styles group), tap or click Shape Effects button (Colors and Lines tab), tap or click desired effect, choose desired settings (Format Shape dialog box), tap or click OK button (Format Shape dialog box), tap or click OK button (Format Object dialog box)

To Add an Object to the Building Block Library

The following steps add the formatted WordArt object to the Building Block library, so that you can use it in multiple publications.

1 Press and hold or right-click the WordArt object to display the shortcut menu and then tap or click 'Save as Building Block' to display the Create New Building Block dialog box.

2 Type `A+ Campgrounds Graphic` to replace the text in the Title text box.

BTW
WordArt
Design experts recommend using WordArt sparingly. As a rule, use WordArt as decoration rather than to convey information. Use only one WordArt object per publication.

BTW
BTWs
For a complete list of the BTWs found in the margins of this book, visit the BTW resource on the Student Companion Site located on www.cengagebrain.com. For detailed instructions about accessing available resources, visit www.cengage.com/ct/ studentdownload or see the inside back cover of this book.

3 Press the TAB key to move to the Description text box, and then type `WordArt name brand to use in all publications` to insert a description.

4 Tap or click the Keywords text box, and then type `logo, brand, a+` to enter keywords.

5 Accept all other default settings, and then tap or click the OK button (Create New Building Block dialog box) to close the dialog box.

To Save the Publication

The following step saves the publication with the changes made thus far.

1 Save the publication on your desired save location, using the file name, `A+ Campground Amenities Table`.

Using Tables

The next step is to create a table showing which campgrounds have which amenities (shown in Figure 6–1a on page PUB 315). A Publisher **table** is a collection of contiguous text boxes that are displayed in rows and columns. The intersection of a row and a column is called a **cell**, and cells are filled with text or graphical data. Within a table, you easily can rearrange rows and columns, change column widths and row heights, and insert diagonal lines. You can format the cells to give the table a professional appearance, using elements such as preset formats, shading, and cell diagonals. You also can edit the inner gridlines and outer border of a table. For these reasons, many Publisher users create tables rather than using large text boxes with tabbed columns. Tables allow you to enter data in columns as you would for a schedule, price list, resume, or table of contents.

CONSIDER THIS

When should you use a table?
Use tables to present numeric and tabular information in an easy-to-digest format. Work with the customer to design a table that is clear and concise. Make sure the overall heading and the row and column headings employ standard wording and measurements. Format the table for easy reading. Use recognizable labels for each row and column. Use standard scales and measures. Make sure the reader does not have to spend a lot of time to identify the purpose of the table and grasp the data they are seeking. Use borders, colors, fonts, and alignment to delineate each row and/or column.

The first step in creating a table is to insert an empty table in the publication. When inserting a table, you must specify the number of columns and rows you expect to use. The number of columns and rows is called the **dimension** of the table. In Publisher, the first number in a dimension is the number of columns, and the second is the number of rows. For example, in Publisher, a 2 × 1 table (pronounced "two by one") consists of two columns and one row.

To Insert an Empty Table

The following steps insert an empty table with 10 columns and four rows. **Why?** *The numbers are an estimate of how many you will need. If necessary, you can add more columns and insert more rows after creating the table.*

- Display the VIEW tab and then tap or click the Whole Page button (VIEW tab | Zoom group) to display the entire page.

- Display the INSERT tab.

- Tap or click the 'Add a Table' button (INSERT tab | Tables group) to display the Table gallery (Figure 6–15).

Q&A Where will the table be inserted?
Publisher inserts the table in the center of the workspace window.

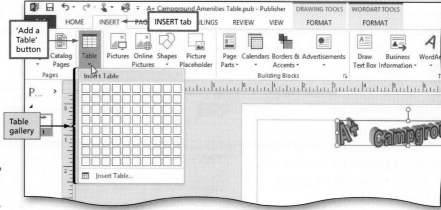

Figure 6–15

Experiment

- If using a mouse, point to various cells on the grid to see a preview of various table dimensions in the publication window.

- Tap or click the cell in the tenth column and fifth row of the grid to insert an empty 10 × 5 table (Figure 6–16).

Q&A What are the small circles in the table cells?
Each table cell has an **end-of-cell mark**, which is a formatting mark that assists you with selecting and formatting cells. Recall that formatting marks do not print on a hard copy. The end-of-cell marks currently are left-aligned, that is, positioned at the left edge of each cell.

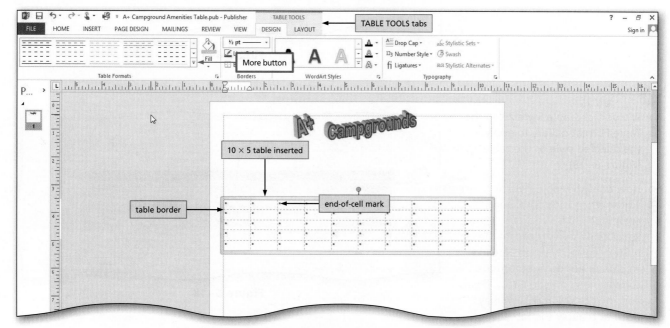

Figure 6–16

Other Ways

1. Tap or click 'Add a Table' button (INSERT tab | Tables group), tap or click Insert Table in Table gallery, enter number of columns and rows (Create Table dialog box), tap or click OK button

To Apply a Table Format

You may have noticed that the ribbon now displays two new tabs. *Why? When working with tables, the TABLE TOOLS LAYOUT tab offers buttons and commands that help you in inserting, deleting, merging, and aligning rows, columns, and cells; the TABLE TOOLS DESIGN tab provides formatting, borders, and alignment options.*

The Table Format gallery (TABLE TOOLS DESIGN tab | Table Formats group) allows you to format a table with a variety of colors and shading. The following steps apply a table format to the table in the publication. The format uses a dark background with white text for column and row headings, and a lighter background with black text for table data.

- If necessary, display the TABLE TOOLS DESIGN tab.

- Tap or click the More button in the Table Formats gallery (TABLE TOOLS DESIGN tab | Table Formats group) to expand the gallery (Figure 6–17).

Experiment

- If you are using a mouse, point to various table styles in the Table Formats gallery and watch the format of the table change in the publication window.

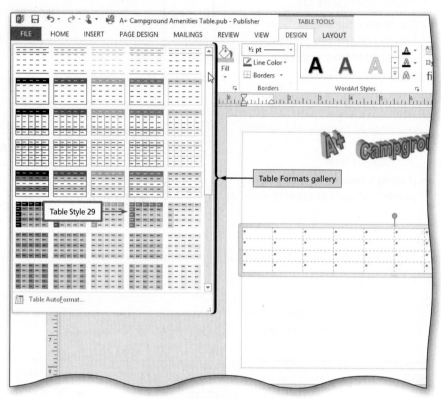

Figure 6–17

- Tap or click 'Table Style 29' in the Table Format gallery to apply the selected style to the table (Figure 6–18).

Q&A

How does the table style adjust when I add rows and columns?

Some table styles replicate the pattern correctly when you add a column, but do not alternate colors when you add a row. If you add rows or columns, you may need to reapply the table style.

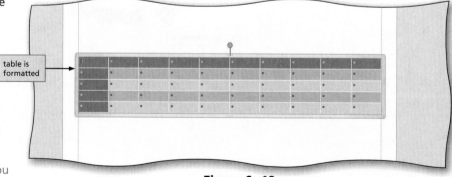

Figure 6–18

Other Ways

1. Tap or click More button (TABLE TOOLS DESIGN tab | Table Formats group), tap or click Table AutoFormat, select table format, tap or click OK button (Auto Format dialog box)

To Enter Data in a Table

The next step is to enter data in some of the cells of the empty table. To place data in a cell, you tap or click the cell and then type.

To advance rightward from one cell to the next, press the TAB key. When you are at the rightmost cell in a row, press the TAB key to move to the first cell in the next row. If you are at the end of the table, pressing the TAB key will add a new row to the table. You cannot add new rows or columns by using the ENTER key. *Why? The ENTER key is used to begin a new paragraph within a cell.* Pressing SHIFT+ENTER creates a new line within the cell without the extra spacing adding for a new paragraph. To move up or down within the table, use the arrow keys, or simply tap or click the desired cell.

The following steps enter data in the first row of the table, beginning with the second column.

1

- Zoom the table to 130% magnification.

- Tap or click the first row, second column cell to position the insertion point.

- Type **Full** and then press SHIFT+ENTER to create a soft return. Type **Hookups** to finish the column heading. Press the TAB key to advance the insertion point to the next cell.

- Type **Electricity** and then press the TAB key to advance the insertion point to the next cell (Figure 6–19).

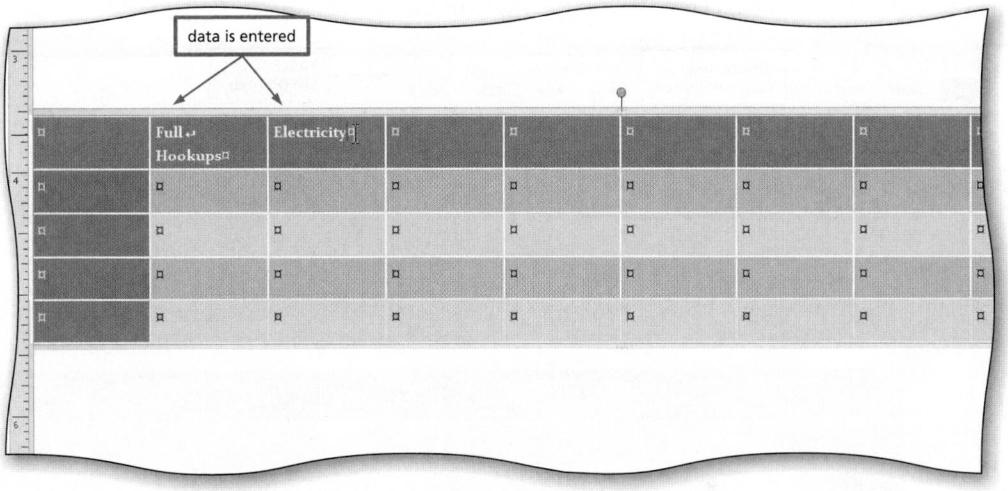

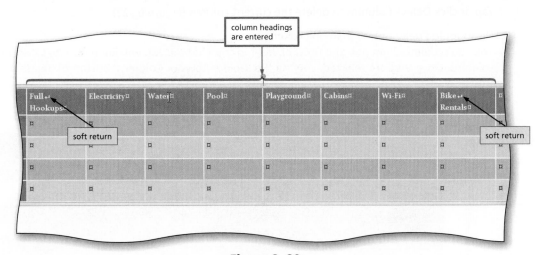

Figure 6–19

Q&A How do I edit cell contents if I make a mistake?
Tap or click in the cell and then correct the entry.

2

- Finish typing the columns headings as shown in Figure 6–20. Use the TAB key to advance the insertion point (Figure 6–20).

Q&A What if I have more data than will fit in a cell?
By default, the data you enter in a cell wraps just as text wraps between the margins of a text box. You can turn off that feature by tapping or clicking to remove the check mark in the 'Grow to Fit Text' check box (TABLE TOOLS LAYOUT tab | Size group).

Figure 6–20

To Delete a Column

The following steps delete column ten. *Why? You previously estimated how many columns you would need. You have one too many, so you will delete it.* Deleting a column also deletes any text or graphics in the column cells.

- If necessary, position the insertion point anywhere in the column that you wish to delete (in this case, column 10).
- Tap or click TABLE TOOLS LAYOUT on the ribbon to display the TABLE TOOLS LAYOUT tab.
- Tap or click the 'Delete Rows or Columns' button (TABLE TOOLS LAYOUT tab | Rows & Columns group) to display the gallery (Figure 6–21).

Q&A How would I delete just the data in the column?
Drag to select the cells in the column and then press the DELETE key. Or, press and hold or right-click the selection and then tap or click Delete Text on the shortcut menu.

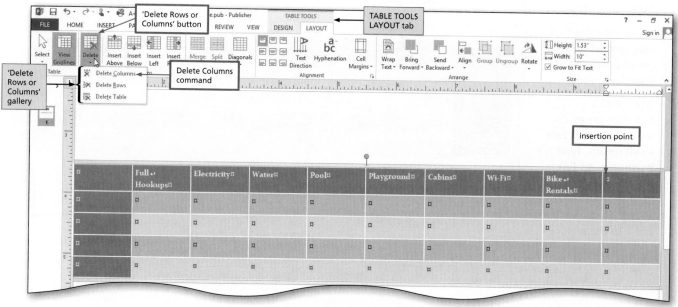

Figure 6–21

- Tap or click Delete Columns to delete the current column (Figure 6–22).

Q&A How would I delete more than one column?
You could delete them one at a time, or, later in this chapter, you will learn how to select multiple cells, rows, and columns. Once they are selected, you use the 'Delete Rows or Columns' button to delete them.

Figure 6–22

Other Ways

1. Press and hold or right-click cell, tap or click Delete on shortcut menu, tap or click Delete Columns

TO DELETE A ROW

If you wanted to delete a row in a table rather than a column, you would perform the following steps.

1. Position the insertion point in the row that you want to delete.
2. Tap or click the 'Delete Rows or Columns' button (TABLE TOOLS LAYOUT tab | Rows & Columns group), and then tap or click Delete Rows.

To Insert a Row

1 EMPLOY REUSABLE PARTS | **2** APPLY SHAPE EFFECTS | **3** INSERT & FORMAT TABLES | **4** CREATE CALENDAR
5 USE MASTER PAGES | **6** ADD BORDERART | **7** EMBED TABLE | **8** USE EXCEL FUNCTIONALITY

The next step is to insert a new row at the top of the table because you want to create a table heading on a row by itself at the top of the table. As discussed earlier, you can insert a row at the end of a table by positioning the insertion point in the bottom-right corner cell and then pressing the TAB key. You cannot use the TAB key to insert a row at the beginning or middle of a table. Instead, you use the 'Insert Rows Above' or 'Insert Rows Below' buttons. Where you place the insertion point is important before making a decision to insert above or below the current location. ***Why?*** *A new row takes on the formatting of the row that contains the insertion point.* For example, you might want to insert a new row in the A+ Campgrounds table between the first and second rows. If you place the insertion point in Row 1 and choose to insert below, the new row will be formatted as a header row (in this instance, with a dark green background and white text). If you place the insertion point in Row 2 and choose to insert above, the new row will be formatted to match the data cells (in this case, with a light green background and black text).

The following steps insert a row in a table using the ribbon.

- Position the mouse pointer somewhere in the first row of the table because you want to insert a row above this row.

- If necessary, display the TABLE TOOLS LAYOUT tab.

- Tap or click the 'Insert Rows Above' button (TABLE TOOLS LAYOUT tab | Rows & Columns group) to add a new row (Figure 6–23).

 **Experiment**

- On the TABLE TOOLS LAYOUT tab, point to each of the buttons in the Rows & Columns group to view the ScreenTips. In addition, look at the pictures on the buttons themselves, which will help you identify each function.

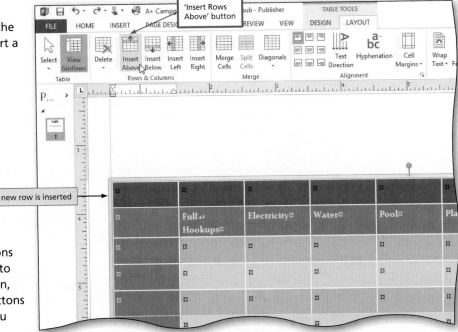

Figure 6–23

- Deselect by tapping or clicking outside the row.

Other Ways
1. Press and hold or right-click row, tap or click Insert on shortcut menu, tap or click appropriate Insert command

TO INSERT A COLUMN

If you wanted to insert a column in a table rather than a row, you would perform the following steps.

1. Position the insertion point in the column to the left or right of where you want to insert the column.

2. Tap or click the 'Insert Columns to the Left' button (TABLE TOOLS LAYOUT tab | Rows & Columns group) to insert a column to the left of the current column, or tap or click the 'Insert Columns to the Right' button (TABLE TOOLS LAYOUT tab | Rows & Columns group) to insert a column to the right of the current column. Or, you could press and hold or right-click the column, tap or point to Insert on the shortcut menu, and tap or click Insert Left or Insert Right on the Insert submenu.

Selecting Table Contents

When working with tables, you may need to select the contents of cells, rows, columns, or the entire table. Table 6–3 identifies ways to select various items in a table.

Table 6–3 Selecting Items in a Table	
Item to Select	**Action**
Cell	If you are using a mouse, point to the upper-left edge of the cell and click when the mouse pointer changes to a small solid upward-angled pointing arrow.
	Or, position the insertion point in the cell, tap or click the Select Table button (TABLE TOOLS LAYOUT tab | Table group), and then tap or click Select Cell on the Select Table gallery.
	Or, press and hold or right-click the cell, tap or point to Select on the shortcut menu, tap or click Select Cell.
Column	If you are using a mouse, point above the column and click when the mouse pointer changes to a small solid downward-pointing arrow.
	Or, position the insertion point in the column, tap or click the Select Table button (TABLE TOOLS LAYOUT tab | Table group), and then tap or click Select Column on the Select Table gallery.
	Or, press and hold or right-click the column, tap or click Select on the shortcut menu, tap or click Select Column.
Row	If you are using a mouse, point to the left of the row and tap or click when the mouse pointer changes to a right-pointing block arrow.
	Or, position the insertion point in the row, tap or click the Select Table button (TABLE TOOLS LAYOUT tab | Table group), and then tap or click Select Row on the Select Table gallery.
	Or, press and hold or right-click the row, tap or click Select on the shortcut menu, tap or click Select Row.
Multiple cells, rows, or columns adjacent to one another	Drag through cells, rows, or columns.
	Or, select first cell and then hold down the SHIFT key while selecting the next cell, row, or column.
Next cell	Press the TAB key.
Previous cell	Press SHIFT+TAB.
Table	Tap or click somewhere in the table, tap or click the Select Table button (TABLE TOOLS LAYOUT tab | Table group), and then tap or click Select Table on the Select Table gallery.
	Or, press and hold or right-click the table, tap or click Select on the shortcut menu, tap or click Select Table.

© 2014 Cengage Learning

To Select a Row

1 EMPLOY REUSABLE PARTS | 2 APPLY SHAPE EFFECTS | 3 INSERT & FORMAT TABLES | 4 CREATE CALENDAR
5 USE MASTER PAGES | 6 ADD BORDERART | 7 EMBED TABLE | 8 USE EXCEL FUNCTIONALITY

The following step selects the entire top row of the table. *Why? The cells must be selected in preparation for merging in subsequent steps.*

1

- If you are in touch mode, tap the left border of the table beside row one. If you are using a mouse, point to the left side of row one to display a right-pointing block arrow, and then tap or click to select the row (Figure 6–24).

Q&A

I do not see the arrow. What should I do?
Move the mouse pointer slightly to the left or right. The arrow appears when you are approximately 1/16-inch from the edge of the table.

How do I select multiple rows?
Point to the left side of the first row to display the right-pointing block arrow and then drag straight down until all desired rows are selected.

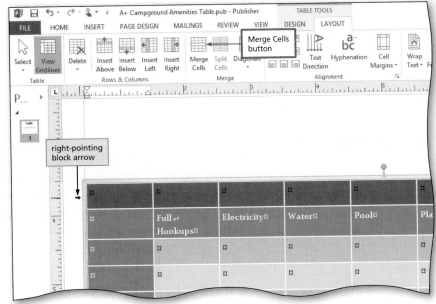

Figure 6–24

Other Ways

1. Tap or click in row, tap or click Select Table button (TABLE TOOLS LAYOUT tab | Table group), tap or click Select Row

2. Press and hold or right-click row, tap or click Select on shortcut menu, tap or click Select Row

1 EMPLOY REUSABLE PARTS | 2 APPLY SHAPE EFFECTS | 3 INSERT & FORMAT TABLES | 4 CREATE CALENDAR
5 USE MASTER PAGES | 6 ADD BORDERART | 7 EMBED TABLE | 8 USE EXCEL FUNCTIONALITY

To Merge Cells

The top row of the table is to contain the date of the week as a heading, which should be centered above the columns of the table. The row just selected has one cell for each column, in this case, nine cells. The heading of the table, however, should be in a single cell that spans all columns. Thus, the following step merges the nine cells into a single cell.

- If necessary, display the TABLE TOOLS LAYOUT tab.

- With the cells to merge selected (as shown in Figure 6–24), tap or click the Merge Cells button (TABLE TOOLS LAYOUT tab | Merge group) to merge the nine cells into one cell.

- Tap or click elsewhere in the table to view the merged cell (Figure 6–25).

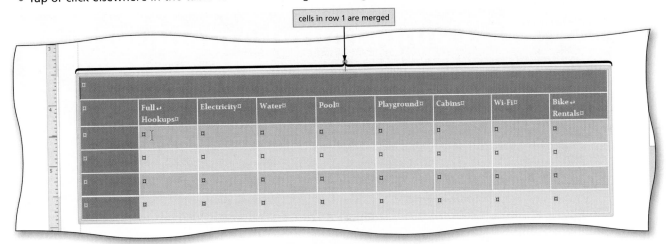

Figure 6–25

BTW
Touch Mode
The Touch/Mouse Mode button (Quick Access Toolbar) allows you to switch between touch mode and mouse mode. If you primarily use gestures, touch mode will add more space between commands in menus and on the ribbon.

TO SPLIT CELLS

Sometimes you want to split a merged cell back into multiple cells. If you wanted to split cells, you would perform the following steps.

1. Position the insertion point in the cell to split.
2. Tap or click the Split Cells button (TABLE TOOLS LAYOUT tab | Merge group).

1 EMPLOY REUSABLE PARTS | 2 APPLY SHAPE EFFECTS | 3 INSERT & FORMAT TABLES | **4 CREATE CALENDAR**
5 USE MASTER PAGES | 6 ADD BORDERART | 7 EMBED TABLE | 8 USE EXCEL FUNCTIONALITY

To Align Data in Cells

You can change the alignment and placement of text in table cells. In addition to aligning text horizontally in a cell (left, center, or right), you can align it vertically within a cell (top, center, bottom), change the text direction, adjust the cell margins, and even adjust the hyphenation. The following steps center data in cells both horizontally and vertically. *Why? Table headings typically are centered.*

- Position the insertion point in the first row of the table.
- Change the font size to 36 (HOME tab | Font group), and then type **Campground Amenities** as the heading.
- If necessary, display the TABLE TOOLS LAYOUT tab.
- Tap or click the Align Center button (TABLE TOOLS LAYOUT tab | Alignment group) to center the text both vertically and horizontally (Figure 6–26).

🔍 Experiment

- Tap or click other align buttons in the group to watch the text placement change. When you are finished, tap or click the Align Center button again.

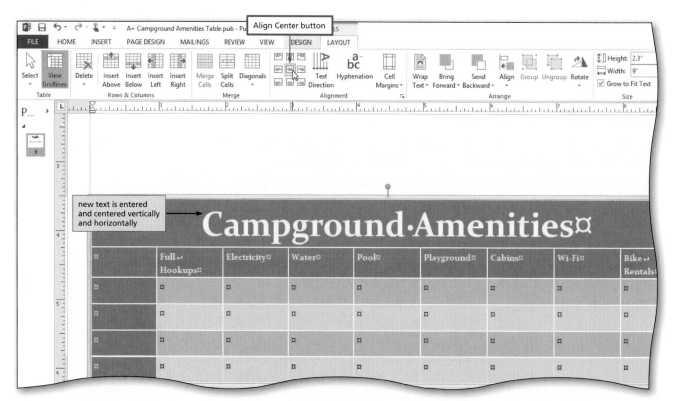

Figure 6–26

2

- Starting in the second cell of the second row, drag to select all of the cells in columns two through nine.
- Tap or click the Align Center button (TABLE TOOLS LAYOUT tab | Alignment group) to center the contents of the selected cells (Figure 6–27).

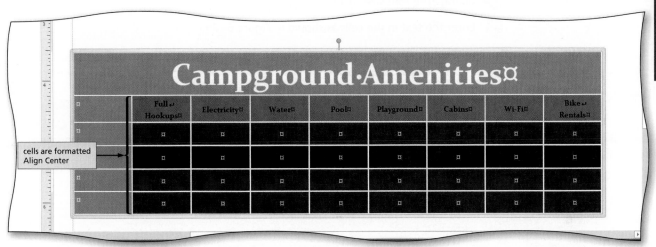

cells are formatted Align Center

Figure 6–27

To Align the First Column

The following steps align the first column of cell data to the left horizontally and centered vertically.

1 Drag through the cells in the first column to select them.

2 Tap or click the Align Center Left button (TABLE TOOLS LAYOUT tab | Alignment group) to align the contents of the first column (Figure 6–28).

BTW
Quick Reference
For a table that lists how to complete the tasks covered in this book using touch gestures, the mouse, ribbon, shortcut menu, and keyboard, see the Quick Reference Summary at the back of this book, or visit the Quick Reference resource on the Student Companion Site located on www.cengagebrain.com. For detailed instructions about accessing available resources, visit www.cengage.com/ct/studentdownload or see the inside back cover of this book.

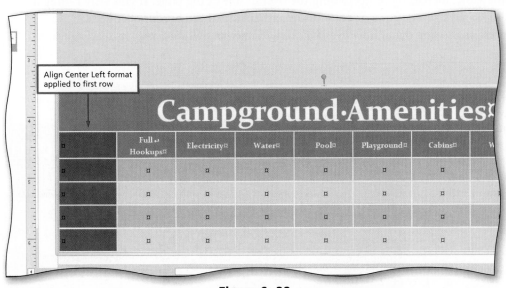

Align Center Left format applied to first row

Figure 6–28

To Change the Font Size and Enter Data

The following steps change the font size and enter data in the table.

1 Select all cells in rows two through six.

2 Change the font size to 12.

3 Enter the text in the cells as shown in Figure 6–29.

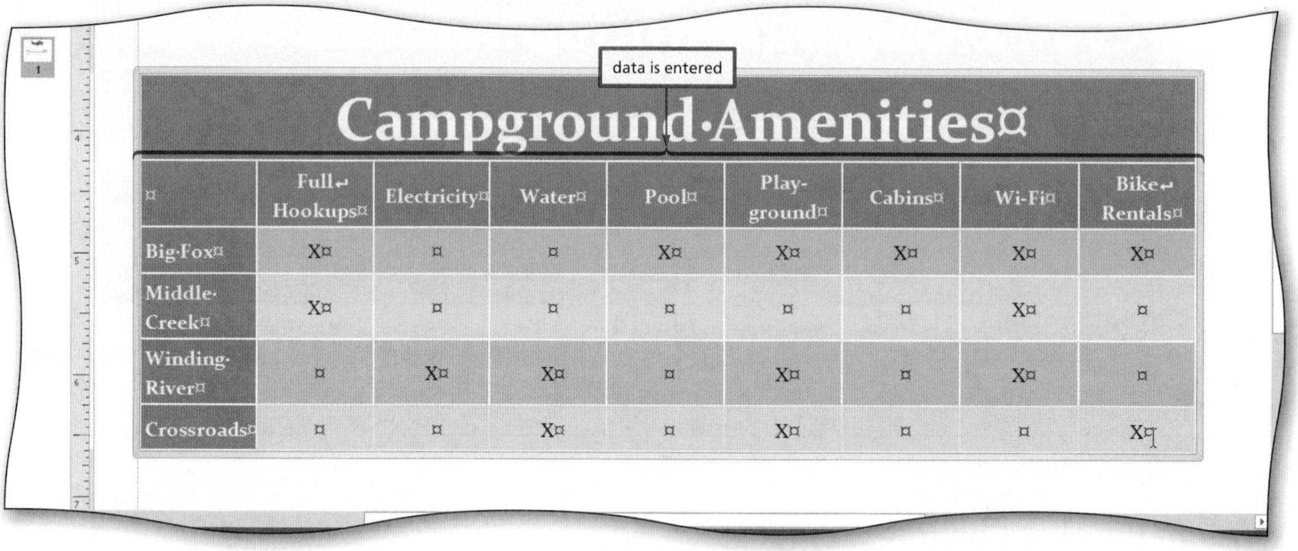

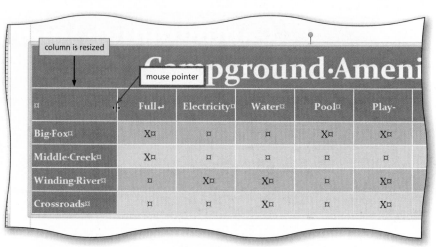

data is entered

Campground·Amenities¤

¤	Full⏎ Hookups¤	Electricity¤	Water¤	Pool¤	Play- ground¤	Cabins¤	Wi-Fi¤	Bike⏎ Rentals¤
Big·Fox¤	X¤	¤	¤	X¤	X¤	X¤	X¤	X¤
Middle· Creek¤	X¤	¤	¤	¤	¤	¤	X¤	¤
Winding· River¤	¤	X¤	X¤	¤	X¤	¤	X¤	¤
Crossroads¤	¤	¤	X¤	¤	X¤	¤	¤	X¤

Figure 6–29

To Change the Column Width

1 EMPLOY REUSABLE PARTS | 2 APPLY SHAPE EFFECTS | 3 INSERT & FORMAT TABLES | 4 CREATE CALENDAR
5 USE MASTER PAGES | 6 ADD BORDERART | 7 EMBED TABLE | 8 USE EXCEL FUNCTIONALITY

When you first create a table, all of the columns have the same width and all of the rows have the same height. To change the column width, drag the right border of the column. To change the row height, drag the bottom border of a row. When you drag a border, the current column or row changes size; all of the other columns or rows remain the same, increasing or decreasing the overall size of the table. If you SHIFT+drag a border, the table remains the same size; the rows or columns on either side of the border change size.

The following step resizes the first column. **Why?** *Widening the column will allow the row heading text to display on one line.*

1

- With no selection in the table, point to the border between the first two columns until the mouse pointer displays a double-headed arrow, and then drag to the right, approximately one-half inch, to increase the column width (Figure 6–30).

Figure 6–30

To Resize the Table

Just like the picture placeholder, the gray border or table placeholder that appears around the table can be dragged to reposition the table. In addition, if you have a mouse, you can drag the corners or sides to resize the table. The following steps resize the table to fit the lower portion of the publication. *Why? The table will be easier to read if it is enlarged.*

- Zoom to 70% and scroll to display the entire table.

- Using the mouse, point to the lower-right corner of the table border.

- When the mouse pointer changes to a double-headed arrow, drag down and to the right until the table border snaps to the lower-right corner margin guides (Figure 6–31).

Figure 6–31

Q&A What do I do if I have no mouse?
You can resize the table by using the Measurement toolbar. Tap the Object Size button on the status bar to display the Measurement toolbar and then enter 10" and 4.5" in the Width and Height text boxes, respectfully.

2

- Resize the table using the Measurement toolbar or use the mouse to drag the upper-left corner of the table border to a position that snaps to the left margin, just below the WordArt object (Figure 6–32).

Q&A Does the font size change?
No. Enlarging the table by dragging just creates more space around the text.

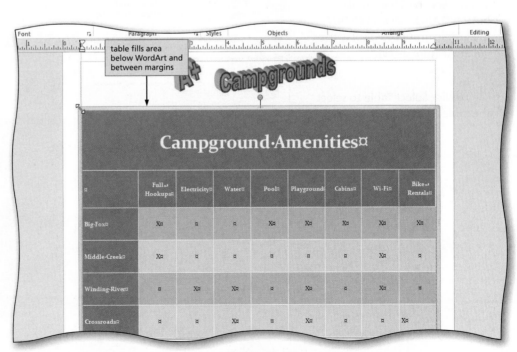

Figure 6–32

Other Ways

1. Press and hold or right-click table, tap or click Format Table on shortcut menu, enter size of table in Size and rotate area of Size tab (Format Table dialog box), tap or click OK button

Table Borders

In addition to applying a table style, you can create your own style of table by adding borders. A **border** is the line that displays along the edge of a cell, row, column, or table. It is good practice to format and create borders in the following order:

1. Make your selection. Publisher allows you to add borders to individual cells, rows, columns, or the entire table.

2. Set the weight of the border. The default value is 1/2 pt. but you can change the weight to various point values; the higher the point value, the thicker the border.

3. Set the color of the border. The shades of the color scheme colors display in a palette, but all colors are available.

4. Set the borders, choosing individual borders, inside or outside borders on multiple cells, cell diagonals, all borders, or no border at all. The default value is no borders for an unformatted table. When you choose the Border button (TABLE TOOLS DESIGN tab | Borders group), all weight and color settings are applied.

To Select a Table

1 EMPLOY REUSABLE PARTS | 2 APPLY SHAPE EFFECTS | 3 INSERT & FORMAT TABLES | 4 CREATE CALENDAR
5 USE MASTER PAGES | 6 ADD BORDERART | 7 EMBED TABLE | 8 USE EXCEL FUNCTIONALITY

The following steps select the table in preparation for adding borders to each cell. *Why?* *Border selections apply to the current cell or current selection.*

• Tap or click the table.

• If necessary, display the TABLE TOOLS LAYOUT tab.

• Tap or click the Select Table button (TABLE TOOLS LAYOUT tab | Table group) to display the gallery (Figure 6–33).

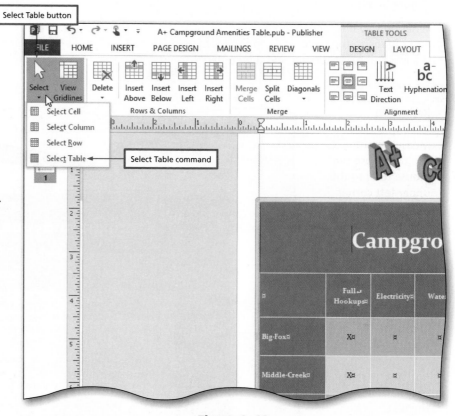

• Tap or click Select Table to select the table (shown in Figure 6–34).

Figure 6–33

Other Ways

1. Press and hold or right-click table, tap or click Select on shortcut menu, tap or click Select Table

To Change the Line Weight

The following steps change the weight of the border on all cells in the table. ***Why?*** *A thicker border will be more visible if the table is posted or put online.*

1

- Display the TABLE TOOLS DESIGN tab.

- With the desired portions of the table selected (in this case, the entire table), tap or click the Line Weight button (TABLE TOOLS DESIGN tab | Borders group) to display the Line Weight gallery (Figure 6–34).

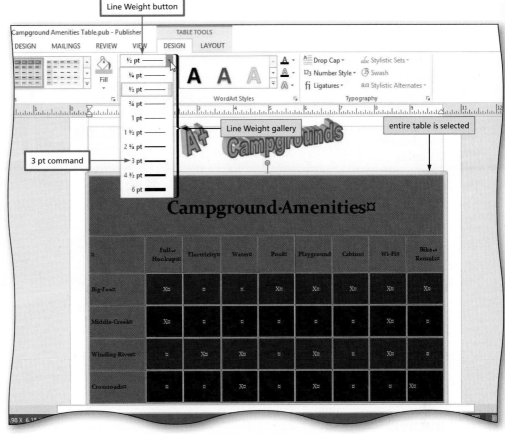

Figure 6–34

2

- Tap or click the 3 pt line weight to increase the size of the border (Figure 6–35).

Q&A Nothing seemed to happen. Did I do something wrong?
The default setting is No borders, so your weight setting will not be visible until you choose to add borders in subsequent steps.

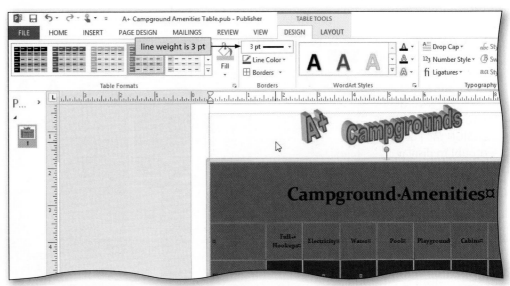

Figure 6–35

Other Ways

1. Press and hold or right-click table, tap or click Format Table on shortcut menu, tap or click Colors and Lines tab (Format Table dialog box), tap or click desired border preset, enter weight in Width text box, tap or click OK button

To Change the Border Color

The following steps change the border color. **Why?** *The default color is gray; black will make the borders stand out more.*

- With the desired portions of the table selected (in this case, the entire table), tap or click the Line Color button (TABLE TOOLS DESIGN tab | Borders group) to display the color gallery (Figure 6–36).

- Tap or click Main (Black) in the gallery to choose black as the color.

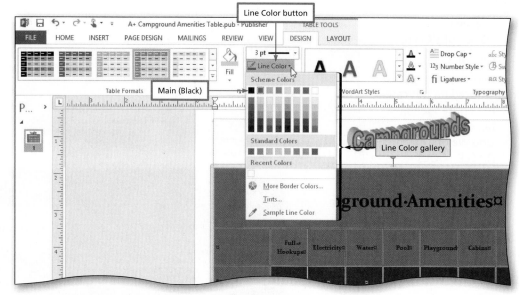

Figure 6–36

Other Ways

1. Press and hold or right-click table, tap or click Format Table on shortcut menu, tap or click Colors and Lines tab (Format Table dialog box), tap or click desired border preset, tap or click Color button, select color, tap or click OK button

To Add Borders

The following steps add a border to the cell edges. **Why?** *A border will make each cell stand out and make the columns and rows easier to read.*

- With the desired portions of the table selected (in this case, the entire table), tap or click the Borders arrow (TABLE TOOLS DESIGN tab | Borders group) to display the Borders gallery (Figure 6–37).

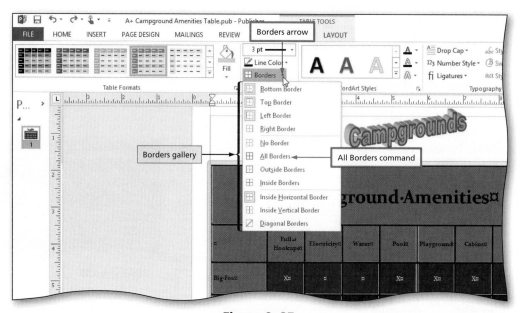

Figure 6–37

2

- Tap or click All Borders to add borders to the table.

- Tap or click outside the table to view the borders (Figure 6–38).

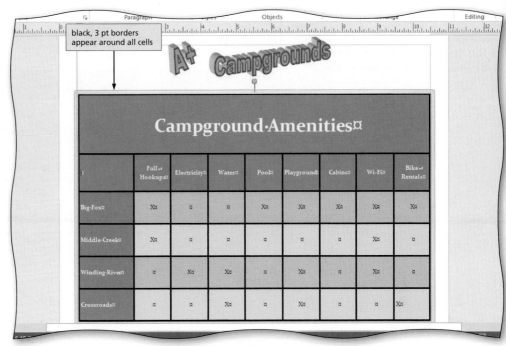

black, 3 pt borders appear around all cells

Figure 6–38

Other Ways

1. Press and hold or right-click table, tap or click Format Table on shortcut menu, tap or click Colors and Lines tab (Format Table dialog box), tap or click desired border preset, tap or click OK button

---

To Create a Cell Diagonal

1 EMPLOY REUSABLE PARTS | 2 APPLY SHAPE EFFECTS | 3 INSERT & FORMAT TABLES | 4 CREATE CALENDAR
5 USE MASTER PAGES | 6 ADD BORDERART | 7 EMBED TABLE | 8 USE EXCEL FUNCTIONALITY

The following steps create a cell diagonal. A **cell diagonal** is a line that splits the cell diagonally, creating two triangular text boxes. Commonly used for split headings or multiple entries per cell, the cell diagonal can be slanted from either corner. *Why? A cell diagonal will accommodate a heading for both the campground column and the amenities row — in the same cell.*

1

- Tap or click the empty cell in the first column, second row of the table.

- If necessary, display the TABLE TOOLS LAYOUT tab.

- Tap or click the Diagonals button (TABLE TOOLS LAYOUT tab | Merge group) to display the Diagonals gallery (Figure 6–39).

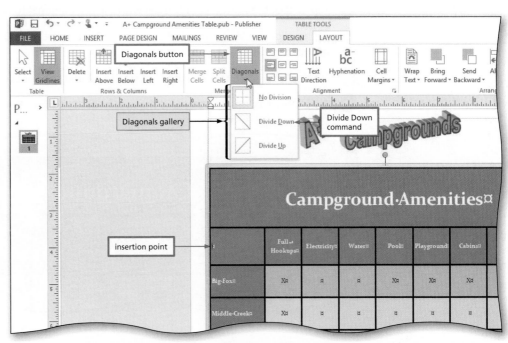

Diagonals button

Diagonals gallery

Divide Down command

insertion point

Figure 6–39

2

- Tap or click Divide Down to create a diagonal in the cell.

- Tap or click outside the table to deselect the cell (Figure 6–40).

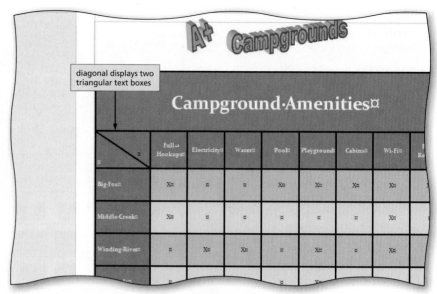

Figure 6–40

To Enter and Format Data in the Diagonal Cell

The following steps enter data into both halves of the diagonal cell.

1 Zoom to 100% magnification.

2 Tap or click the left half of the cell with the cell diagonal to position the insertion point.

3 Display the TABLE TOOLS LAYOUT tab.

4 Tap or click the 'Align Bottom Left' button (TABLE TOOLS LAYOUT tab | Alignment group) to select the alignment.

5 Type **Camp** to complete the column heading.

6 Tap or click the right half of the cell with the cell diagonal to position the insertion point.

7 Tap or click the 'Align Top Right' button (TABLE TOOLS LAYOUT tab | Alignment group) to set the alignment.

8 Display the HOME tab. Set the font size to 12 and the font color to white.

9 Type **Services** to complete the row heading (Figure 6–41).

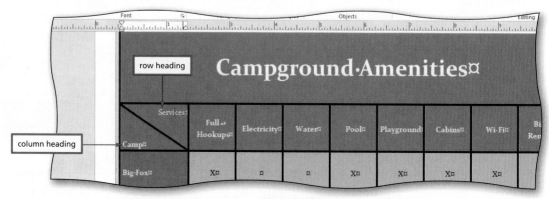

Figure 6–41

Deleting Table Data

To delete the contents of a cell, select the cell contents and then press the DELETE or BACKSPACE key. You also can drag and drop or cut and paste the contents of cells. To delete an entire table, select the table, tap or click the 'Delete Rows or Columns' button (TABLE TOOLS LAYOUT tab | Rows & Columns group), and then tap or click Delete Table on the Delete Rows or Columns gallery.

To Save the Publication Again

The following step saves the publication again.

1 Tap or click the Save button (Quick Access Toolbar) to save the publication in the same location with the same file name.

To Print the Amenities Table

If you wanted to print the publication, you would perform the following steps.

1. Tap or click the Print tab in the Backstage view to display the Print gallery.
2. Verify that the printer listed on the Printer Status button will print a hard copy of the publication. If necessary, tap or click the Printer Status button to display a list of available printer options and then tap or click the desired printer to change the currently selected printer.
3. Tap or click the Print button in the Print gallery to print the publication on the currently selected printer.
4. When the printer stops, retrieve the hard copy.

To Close a Publication without Quitting Publisher

The following step closes the publication without quitting Publisher.

1 Open Backstage view, and then tap or click the Close button to close the publication. If Publisher asks if you want to save the changes to the publication, tap or click the Don't Save button to return to the New template gallery.

Break Point: If you wish to take a break, this is a good place to do so. Exit Publisher. To resume at a later time, run Publisher and continue following the steps from this location forward.

Calendars

The next series of steps creates a calendar. A **calendar** is a specialized table or set of tables that Publisher can format with any combination of months and year. Calendar cells, like table cells, can be formatted with colors, borders, text, and styles. You can create calendars as independent, stand-alone publications, or insert them as building blocks into other publications. Calendars are used for many purposes other than just presenting the date. Information that changes from day to day can be presented as text in a calendar, such as school lunches, practice schedules, homework assignments, or appointments and meetings. Colors and graphics are used in calendars to display holidays, special events, reminders, and even phases of the moon.

BTW
Conserving Ink and Toner
If you want to conserve ink or toner, you can instruct Publisher to print draft quality documents by tapping or clicking FILE on the ribbon to open the Backstage view, and then tapping or clicking Print in the Backstage view to display the Print gallery. Tap or click the Printer Properties link, and then, depending on your printer, click the Print Quality button and choose Draft in the list. Close the Printer Properties dialog box and then tap or click the Print button as usual.

Why do companies create promotional pieces?

A **promotional piece,** or **promo,** is an inclusive term for a publication or article that includes advertising and marketing information for a product or service known to and purchased by customers and clients. Companies create promotional pieces that will increase company recognition. Make sure that promotional pieces are useful to customers and not just gimmicky. Remember that calendars date promotional material.

Including calendars in a publication dates the material, because the publication may not be useful after the calendar date has passed. Companies should consider carefully whether to include calendars in publications.

To Create a 12-Month Calendar

1 EMPLOY REUSABLE PARTS | 2 APPLY SHAPE EFFECTS | 3 INSERT & FORMAT TABLES | **4 CREATE CALENDAR**
5 USE MASTER PAGES | 6 ADD BORDERART | 7 EMBED TABLE | 8 USE EXCEL FUNCTIONALITY

The following steps create a 12-month calendar that A+ Campgrounds will use as a promotional piece.

- Tap or click BUILT-IN in the New template gallery (Backstage view) to display the built-in templates.
- Tap or click the Calendars thumbnail to display the calendar templates.
- Tap or click the Art Right calendar template to select it.
- Tap or click the Color scheme button in the Customize area, and then tap or click Foundry in the list to choose a color scheme.
- Tap or click the Font scheme button, and then tap or click Flow in the list to choose a font scheme.
- If necessary, tap or click the Business information button and then tap or click A+ Campgrounds to select it.
- If necessary, scroll to display the remaining settings (Figure 6–42).

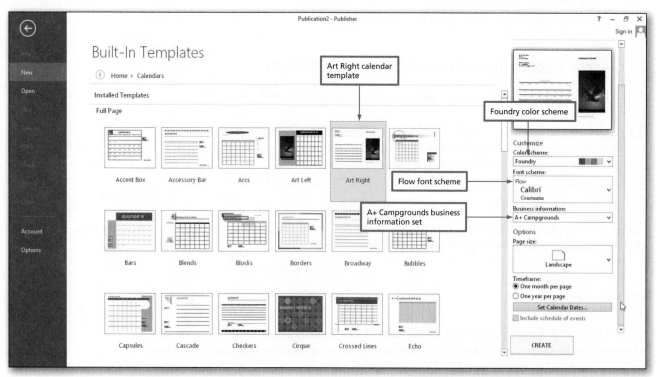

Figure 6–42

- If necessary, tap or click the Page size arrow in the Options area and then tap or click Landscape in the list to choose a landscape orientation.

- If necessary, tap or click 'One month per page' to select it.

- Tap or click the 'Set Calendar Dates' button to display the Set Calendar Dates dialog box (Figure 6–43).

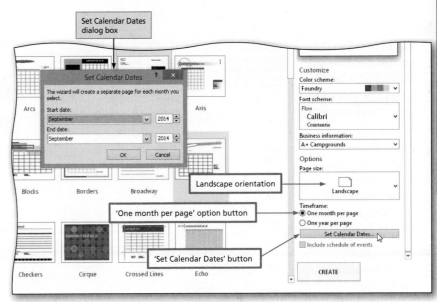

Figure 6–43

- Tap or click the Start date button (Set Calendar Dates dialog box) to display the list of months (Figure 6–44).

Q&A How can I create a one-month calendar?
To create just one month on one page, use the same month and date in both the Start date and End date boxes (Set Calendar Dates dialog box).

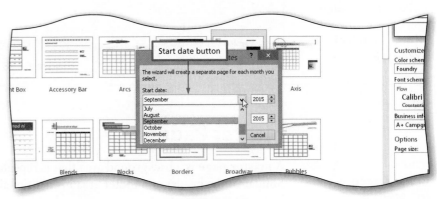

Figure 6–44

4

- Scroll as necessary and tap or click January to select the starting month.

- If necessary, tap or click the up or down arrow on the Start date year box (Set Calendar Dates dialog box) until 2015 is displayed.

- Tap or click the End date button, and then tap or click December to choose the ending month.

- If necessary, tap or click the up or down arrow on the End year box until 2015 is displayed (Figure 6–45).

Q&A What kind of object is the year box with the up and down arrows?
Microsoft refers to this as a numerical up and down box. It commonly is used for fixed data in a sequential list from which the user can choose. You also can type into a numerical up and down box.

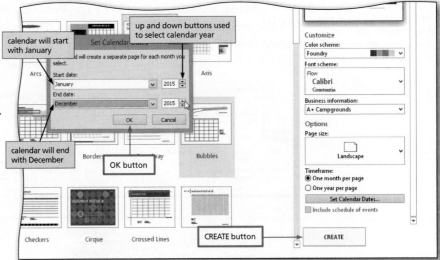

Figure 6–45

5

- Tap or click the OK button (Set Calendar Dates dialog box) to set the dates and close the dialog box.

- Tap or click the CREATE button (Backstage View | New template gallery) to create the calendar (Figure 6–46).

Q&A Why do so many thumbnails appear in the Page Navigation pane?
Because you selected a yearly calendar, Publisher created 12 pages, one for each month of the year.

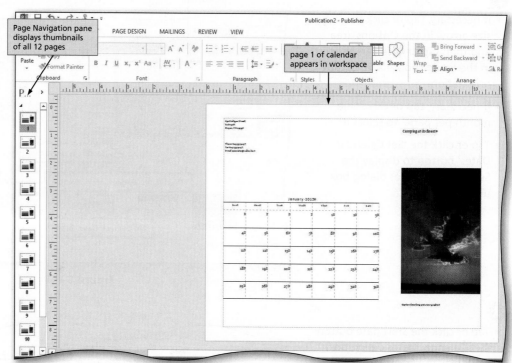

Figure 6–46

Master Pages

BTW
Touch Screen Differences
The Office and Windows interfaces may vary if you are using a touch screen. For this reason, you might notice that the function or appearance of your touch screen differs slightly from this chapter's presentation.

A **master page** is a background area that is repeated across all pages of a publication. Similar to the header and footer area in traditional word processing software, you only have to enter the information or insert the objects once to synchronize them across all pages. The master page is the ideal place for a watermark, a page border, or repeating text and graphics.

When accessing the master page, Publisher displays a new tab (Figure 6–47). While other tabs are available to help you manipulate objects on the master page, when finished, you should tap or click the 'Close Master Page' button (MASTER PAGE tab | Close group) to return to the main tabs on the ribbon.

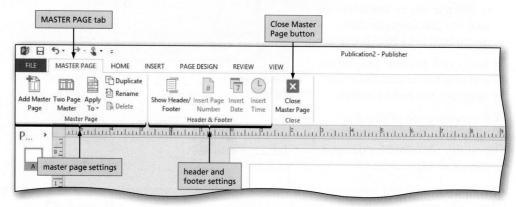

Figure 6–47

Each publication starts with one master page. If you have a multipage publication, you can choose to use two different master pages for cases such as facing pages in a book with different headers or graphics in the background of each page. If you want to display master page objects only on certain pages, the Apply To button (MASTER PAGE tab | Master Page group) provides several options. This is useful for cases such as background images on every page except the title page in a longer publication, or a watermark on the inside of a brochure but not on the front. In the calendar publication, you will create a background, page border and use the building block you created earlier in the chapter.

To View the Master Page

1 EMPLOY REUSABLE PARTS | 2 APPLY SHAPE EFFECTS | 3 INSERT & FORMAT TABLES | 4 CREATE CALENDAR

5 USE MASTER PAGES | 6 ADD BORDERART | 7 EMBED TABLE | 8 USE EXCEL FUNCTIONALITY

The following steps view the master page. *Why? The master page is a special page that cannot be accessed via the Page Navigation pane.*

1

- Tap or click VIEW on the ribbon to display the VIEW tab (Figure 6–48).

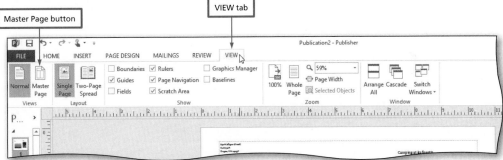

Figure 6–48

2

- Tap or click the Master Page button (VIEW tab | Views group) to access the master page (Figure 6–49).

Q&A Why is the scratch area a different color?
Publisher uses a different color to remind you that you are not in the regular publication window. It helps you to remember to close the master page before continuing with the other objects in the publication.

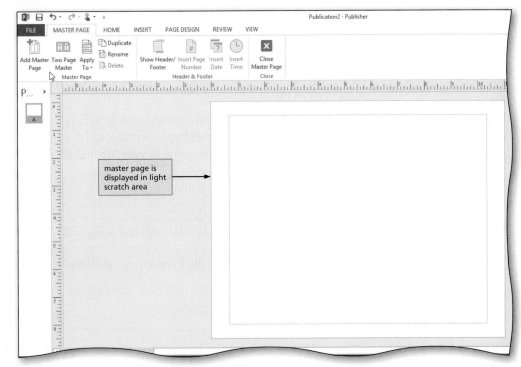

Figure 6–49

Other Ways

1. Tap or click the Master Pages button (PAGE DESIGN tab | Page Background group), tap or click 'Edit Master Pages'

2. Press CTRL+M

To Insert a Gradient Background

The following steps insert a gradient background on the master page.

1 Display the PAGE DESIGN tab.

2 Tap or click the Background button (PAGE DESIGN tab | Page Background group) to display the Background gallery.

3 Tap or click 'Accent 2 Horizontal Gradient' to apply a gradient to the master page (Figure 6–50).

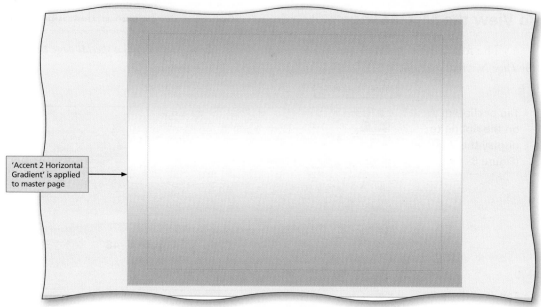

'Accent 2 Horizontal Gradient' is applied to master page

Figure 6–50

BorderArt

BorderArt is a group of customizable graphical borders, such as crosses, hearts, apples, balloons, or decorative shapes, which can be added as an edge or border to a shape, a text box, or the entire page. BorderArt makes the page margins stand out and adds interest to the page. Placing BorderArt on a master page causes the border to display on every page of the publication.

To Create BorderArt

1 EMPLOY REUSABLE PARTS | 2 APPLY SHAPE EFFECTS | 3 INSERT & FORMAT TABLES | 4 CREATE CALENDAR
5 USE MASTER PAGES | **6 ADD BORDERART** | **7 EMBED TABLE** | **8 USE EXCEL FUNCTIONALITY**

The following steps create a rectangle shape on the master page and apply BorderArt. *Why? BorderArt creates a page border for each page of the calendar.*

1

- Display the INSERT tab.

- Tap or click the Shapes button (INSERT tab | Illustrations group) and then tap or click the Rectangle shape.

- Drag to draw a rectangle that fills the entire page.

- Press and hold or right-click the shape to display the shortcut menu (Figure 6–51).

 Should I allow for a margin around the rectangle?

No. The company will send this publication out for professional printing and binding. Most professional printers can print right to the edge of the page.

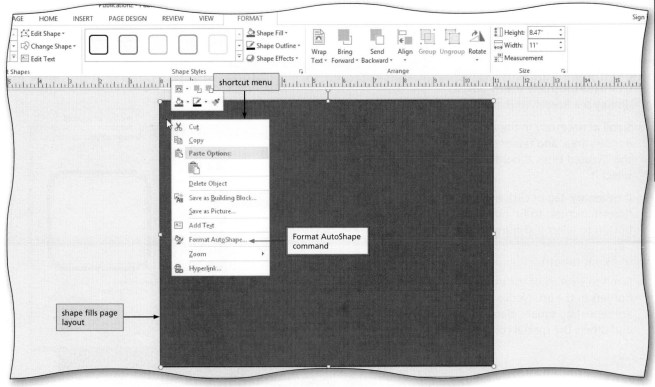

Figure 6–51

2

- Tap or click Format AutoShape on the shortcut menu to display the Format AutoShape dialog box.

- If necessary, tap or click the Colors and Lines tab. Tap or click the Fill Color button to display the Fill Color gallery (Figure 6–52).

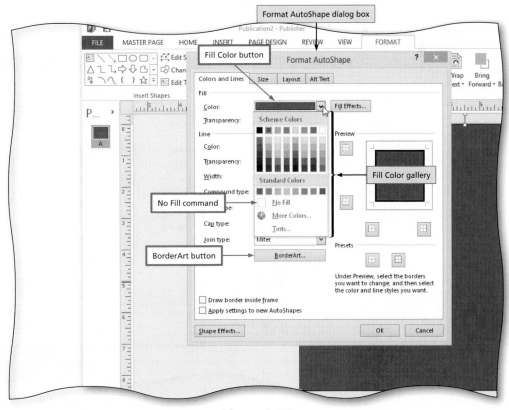

Figure 6–52

- Tap or click No Fill to create a shape without any fill color.

- Tap or click the BorderArt button (Format AutoShape dialog box) to display the BorderArt dialog box.

- Scroll as necessary in the Available Borders area, and tap or click the 'Twisted Lines 2' border to select it.

- If necessary, tap or click the 'Stretch pictures to fit' option button to select it (Figure 6–53).

Experiment

- Scroll to view all of the available borders in the list. Notice some are repeating square elements and others use special corners.

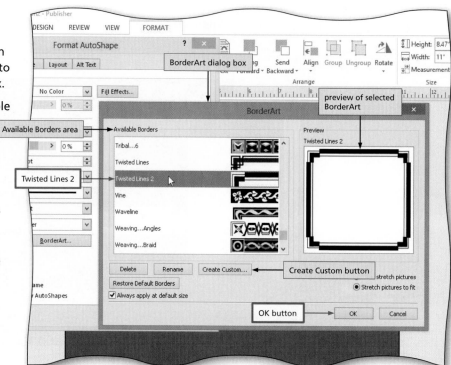

Figure 6–53

- Tap or click the OK button (BorderArt dialog box) to return to the Format AutoShape dialog box.

- Tap or click the Line Color button, and then choose the 'Accent 3 (RGB (114, 163, 118)), Darker 25%' color.

- Select the text in the Width text box, and then type 30 pt to enter the width (Figure 6–54).

Q&A Could I use one of my own pictures as a BorderArt?
Yes, you can tap or click the Create Custom button, shown in Figure 6–53, and then navigate to your storage location.

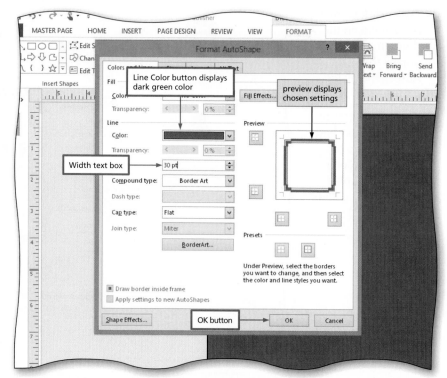

Figure 6–54

5

- Tap or click the OK button (Format AutoShape dialog box) to apply the border (Figure 6–55).

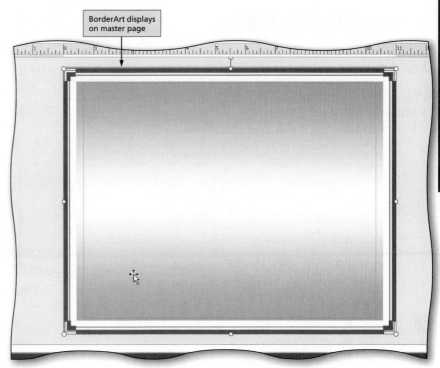

BorderArt displays on master page

Figure 6–55

Other Ways

1. Select shape, tap or click Format Shape Dialog Box Launcher (DRAWING TOOLS FORMAT tab | Shape Styles group), tap or click BorderArt button (Format AutoShape dialog box), select border, tap or click OK button (BorderArt dialog box), tap or click OK button (Format AutoShape dialog box)

To Insert a Building Block

The following steps insert a building block on the master page.

1 Display the INSERT tab.

2 Tap or click the Page Parts button (INSERT tab | Building Blocks group) to display the Page Parts gallery.

3 Tap or click A+ Campgrounds Graphic to insert the graphic on the master page.

4 Drag the graphic to a position approximately 2 inches from the top margin and 2 inches from the left margin on the master page (Figure 6–56).

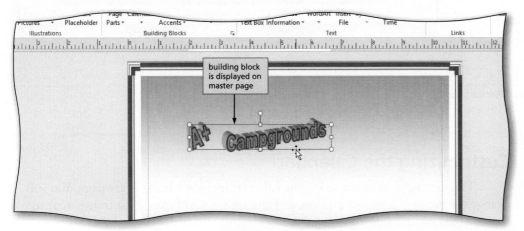

building block is displayed on master page

Figure 6–56

To Close the Master Page

The following steps close the master page and return to the regular page layout and Publisher workspace. *Why? You are finished with the background elements and need to work on the calendar pages themselves.*

1

• Display the MASTER PAGE tab (Figure 6–57).

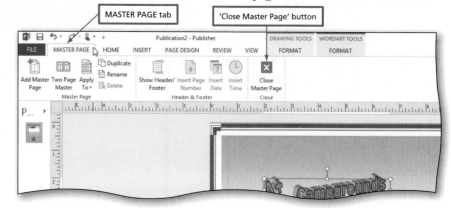

Figure 6–57

2

• Tap or click the 'Close Master Page' button (MASTER PAGE tab | Close group) to close the master page (Figure 6–58).

Q&A

What else could I add to the master page?

You could add a background effect, headers, footers, or any text or graphics that you want to appear on every page of the publication.

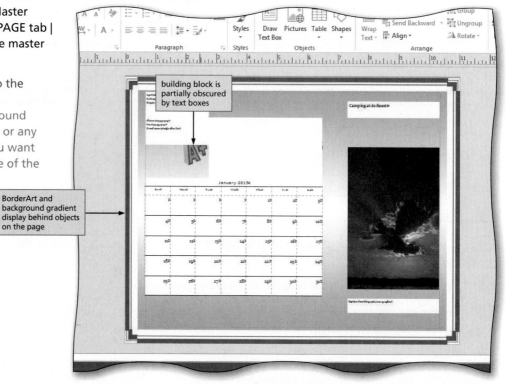

Figure 6–58

Other Ways

1. Tap or click Normal button (VIEW tab | Views group) 2. Press CTRL+M

Customizing the Calendar

The next steps in customizing the calendar include editing every page. You will change the picture, delete its caption, and change the text boxes to be transparent so that the background will show through.

To Select All

The following step selects all of the objects on the page. *Why? When you have a global change, such as setting the transparency, it is faster to change all of the objects at once, rather than one at a time.*

1

- If necessary, tap or click Page 1 in the Page Navigation pane.

- Press CTRL+A to select all of the objects on the page (Figure 6–59).

Q&A What is the blank object at the bottom of the page?

That is a placeholder for the logo from the Business Information set. Because you did not add a logo to the Business Information set, the placeholder is blank.

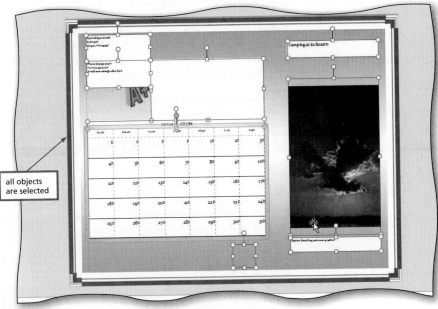

all objects are selected

Figure 6–59

Other Ways

1. Tap or click Select Button (HOME tab | Editing group), tap or click Select All

To Set the Transparency

The following steps make the objects on the page transparent. *Why? Making the objects transparent, especially the text boxes, will allow the background to show through.*

1

- With the desired object or objects selected, press CTRL+T to make the objects transparent (Figure 6–60).

Q&A Can you make objects nontransparent again?

Yes, the CTRL+T command is a toggle and turns transparency on and off.

2

- Tap or click the scratch area to deselect.

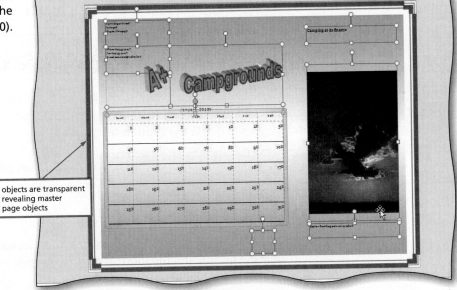

objects are transparent revealing master page objects

Figure 6–60

To Edit the Clip Art

The following steps edit the clip art image on page 1.

1 Tap or click the graphic on page 1 to select the picture placeholder. Tap or click again to select only the picture.

2 Press and hold or right-click the picture to display the shortcut menu. Tap or click Change Picture on the shortcut menu, and then tap or click Change Picture on the submenu. Using Office.com Clip Art, search for a picture related to winter or January. Select the picture and insert it.

3 Tap or click the border of the caption text box, and then press the DELETE key to delete the caption text box.

4 Delete the original picture that was swapped to the scratch area (Figure 6–61).

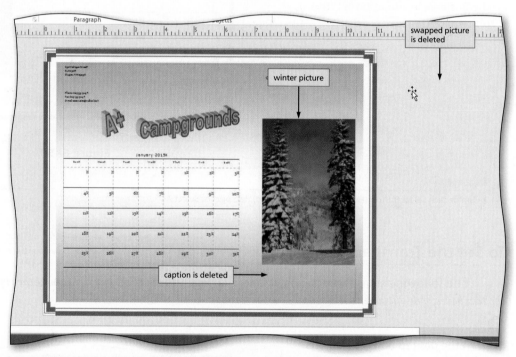

Figure 6–61

To Edit Other Pages in the Calendar

The following steps edit the rest of the pages in the calendar. On each page, you will select all of the objects and make them transparent. You will replace the graphic on each page, and delete the caption text box.

1 Tap or click the next page in the Page Navigation pane.

2 Press CTRL+A to select all of the objects.

3 Press CTRL+T to make the objects transparent.

4 Tap or click the graphic to select the picture placeholder. Tap or click again to select only the picture. Use the shortcut menu to change the picture. Search for a picture related to the month displayed on the page.

5 Repeat Steps 1 through 4 to change each page in the calendar.

To Save the Publication

The following step saves the calendar.

 Save the publication on your desired save location, using the file name,
`A+ Campground Calendar`.

To Print the Calendar

If you wanted to print the calendar, you would perform the following steps.

1. Tap or click the Print tab in the Backstage view to display the Print gallery.
2. Verify that the printer listed on the Printer Status button will print a hard copy of the publication. If necessary, tap or click the Printer Status button to display a list of available printer options and then tap or click the desired printer to change the currently selected printer.
3. Tap or click the Print button in the Print gallery to print the publication on the currently selected printer.
4. When the printer stops, retrieve the hard copy. The calendar will print on 12 pages of paper.

To Save the Calendar Pages as Images

If you wanted to send the calendar or other publication to a professional printer with each page as a separate image, you would perform the following steps.

1. Tap or click the FILE tab to open the Backstage view, and then tap or click the Export tab to display the Export gallery.
2. Tap or click the 'Save for Photo Printing' button to display the Save for Photo Printing gallery.
3. Tap or click the 'JPEG Images for Photo Printing' button, and then choose either the JPEG or the TIFF file format.
4. Tap or click the 'Save Image Set' button to display the Choose Location dialog box.
5. Tap or click the New folder button (Choose Location dialog box). Type the name of the new folder, such as Calendar Pages, and then press the ENTER key.
6. Tap or click the Select Folder button (Choose Location dialog box) to save the publication pages as images.

To Close the Calendar without Quitting Publisher

The following step closes the calendar without quitting Publisher.

 Open the Backstage view, and then tap or click the Close button to close the publication. If Publisher asks if you want to save the changes to the publication, tap or click the Don't Save button to return to the template gallery.

> **Break Point:** If you wish to take a break, this is a good place to do so. Exit Publisher. To resume at a later time, run Publisher and continue following the steps from this location forward.

Using Excel Tables

In Chapter 3, you learned how to edit a story using Microsoft Word from within Publisher. In this chapter, you will learn how to integrate Microsoft Excel when you create a Publisher table. An **Excel-enhanced table** is one that uses Excel tools to

BTW

Distributing a Document
Instead of printing and distributing a hard copy of a document, you can distribute the document electronically. Options include sending the document via email; posting it on cloud storage (such as SkyDrive) and sharing the file with others; posting it on a social networking site, blog, or other website; and sharing a link associated with an online location of the document. You also can create and share a PDF or XPS image of the document, so that users can view the file in Acrobat Reader or XPS Viewer instead of in Publisher.

enhance Publisher's table formatting capabilities, and one that adds table functionality to enhance your tables with items such as totals, averages, charts, and other financial functions. You can paste, create, or insert an Excel-enhanced table into your Publisher publication. Two types of Excel-enhanced tables are available: embedded and linked.

An **embedded** table uses Excel data and can be manipulated with some Excel functionality, but the data becomes part of the Publisher publication and must be edited with Publisher running. Publisher displays Excel tabs on the ribbon to help you edit an embedded table. Alternately, a **linked** table is connected permanently to an Excel worksheet; it is updated automatically from the Excel worksheet. When you edit a linked table, you actually are working in Excel, with full functionality. You can edit a linked table in Excel or Publisher. If you edit in Excel, the table is updated automatically the next time you open the Publisher publication. In either case, the data you use from the Excel file is called the **source** document. Publisher is the **destination** document.

CONSIDER THIS

How should you make the decision whether to embed a table or link a table?
The decision on which type of table to use depends on the data. You would embed a table when you want a static or unchanging table that you edit in Publisher. For example, a table from last year's sales probably is not going to change; thus, if you paste it into a Publisher brochure about the company's sales history, it will look the same each time you open the publication. You would link a table when the data is likely to change, and you want to make sure the publication reflects the current data in the Excel file. For example, suppose you link a portion or all of an Excel worksheet to a Publisher investment statement and update the worksheet quarterly in Excel. With a linked table, any time you open the investment statement in Publisher, the latest update of the worksheet will be displayed as part of the investment statement; in other words, the most current data will always appear in the statement.

The actual process of integrating an Excel table can be performed in one of three ways. You can create an embedded table from scratch, you can paste an embedded or linked table, or you can insert an embedded or linked table from a file.

In this project, you will create a letter and insert an embedded table. You then will format the Excel-enhanced table.

To Create the Letterhead

The following steps create a letterhead that A+ Campgrounds will use to send a letter and table to the managers.

1 Tap or click BUILT-IN in the New template gallery (Backstage view) to display the built-in templates.

2 Tap or click the Letterhead thumbnail to display the letterhead templates.

3 Tap or click the Arrows template to select it.

4 If necessary, tap or click the Color scheme button in the Customize area and then tap or click Foundry in the list to choose a color scheme.

5 If necessary, tap or click the Font scheme button and then tap or click Flow in the list to choose a font scheme.

6 If necessary, tap or click the Business information button and then tap or click A+ Campgrounds to select it.

7 If necessary, tap or click to remove the check mark in the Include logo check box.

8 Tap or click the CREATE button to create the letterhead (Figure 6–62).

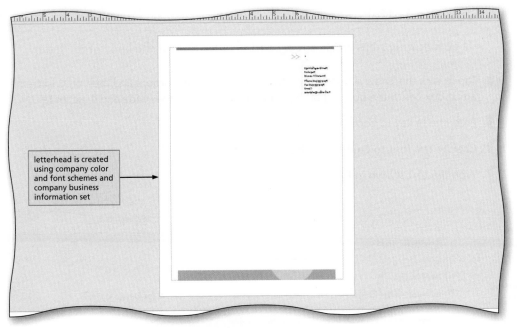

letterhead is created using company color and font schemes and company business information set

Figure 6–62

To Insert the Building Block

The following steps insert the A+ Campgrounds WordArt object into the publication.

1 Display the INSERT tab.

2 Tap or click the Page Parts button (INSERT tab | Building Blocks group), and then tap or click the A+ Campgrounds Graphic to insert it into the publication.

3 Drag the object to the upper portion of the page as shown in Figure 6–63.

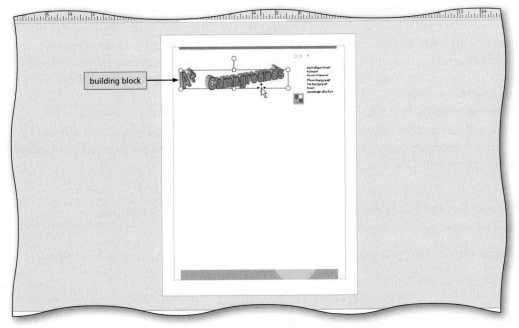

building block

Figure 6–63

To Type the Letter

The following steps create a text box and enter text for the body of the letter.

1 Tap or click the 'Draw a Text Box' button (INSERT tab | Text group) and then drag to create a text box below the building block, approximately 7.25 inches wide and 4 inches tall.

2 Press the F9 key to zoom to 100%.

3 Change the font to Calibri and the font size to 12 pt.

4 Type the text shown in Figure 6–64.

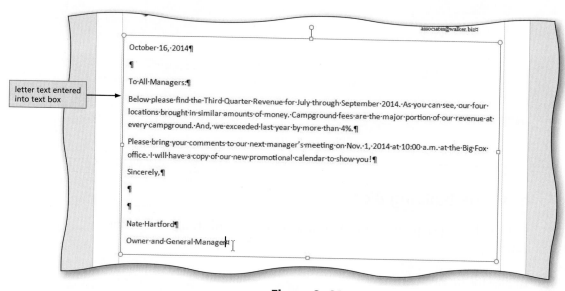

letter text entered into text box

October·16,·2014¶

¶

To·All·Managers:¶

Below·please·find·the·Third·Quarter·Revenue·for·July·through·September·2014.·As·you·can·see,·our·four· locations·brought·in·similar·amounts·of·money.·Campground·fees·are·the·major·portion·of·our·revenue·at· every·campground.·And,·we·exceeded·last·year·by·more·than·4%.¶

Please·bring·your·comments·to·our·next·manager's·meeting·on·Nov.·1,·2014·at·10:00·a.m.·at·the·Big·Fox· office.·I·will·have·a·copy·of·our·new·promotional·calendar·to·show·you!¶

Sincerely,¶

¶

¶

Nate·Hartford¶

Owner·and·General·Manager¶

Figure 6–64

To Create an Embedded Table

1 EMPLOY REUSABLE PARTS | 2 APPLY SHAPE EFFECTS | 3 INSERT & FORMAT TABLES | 4 CREATE CALENDAR
5 USE MASTER PAGES | 6 ADD BORDERART | **7 EMBED TABLE** | 8 USE EXCEL FUNCTIONALITY

Embedding means using a copy of a source document in a destination document without establishing a permanent link. Embedded objects can be edited; however, changes do not affect the source document. For example, if a business embedded an Excel worksheet into its Publisher electronic newsletter that contained updatable fields, users viewing the publication in Publisher could enter their personal data into the embedded table and recalculate the totals. Those users would not need access to the original Excel worksheet. *Why? Publisher embeds the necessary Excel commands.*

The following steps create an embedded table showing third quarter revenue for the four A+ Campgrounds locations. You will retrieve the values from an Excel file. To complete these steps, you will be required to use the Data Files for Students. Visit www.cengage.com/ct/studentdownload for detailed instructions or contact your instructor for information about accessing the required files.

1

● Scroll to the right of the page layout to display more of the scratch area in the Publisher workspace.

● Display the INSERT tab.

● Tap or click the Object button (INSERT tab | Text group) to display the Insert Object dialog box (Figure 6–65).

Q&A | Why should I insert the table in the scratch area?
| It is easier to work with tables outside of the publication and then move them onto the page layout after editing.

⊘ Experiment

● Scroll through the list of object types to view the different kinds of documents and graphics that you can embed. Tap or click the object types to read a description in the Result area.

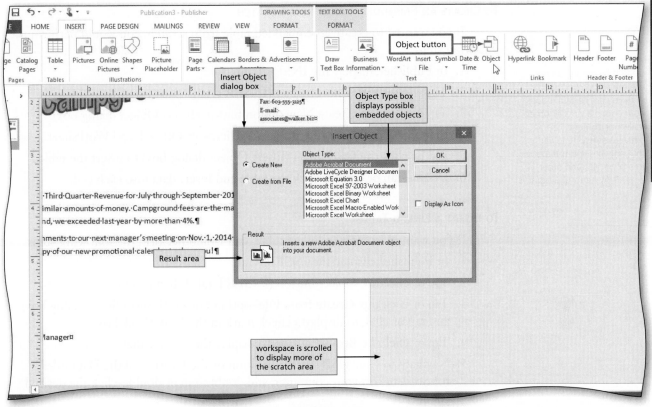

Figure 6–65

2

- Tap or click the 'Create from File' option button (Insert Object dialog box) (Figure 6–66).

What does the Create New option button do?
You would tap or click the Create New option button if you wanted to create an embedded table or other object from scratch.

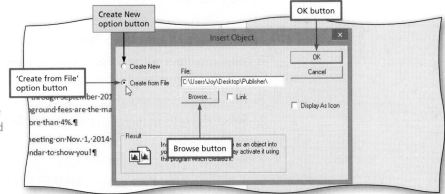

Figure 6–66

3

- Tap or click the Browse button to display the Browse dialog box.

- Navigate to the location of the Data Files for Students on your computer.

- Double-tap or double-click the Excel file named 'A+ Campground Third Quarter Revenue' (Browse dialog box) to select the file and return to the Insert Object dialog box.

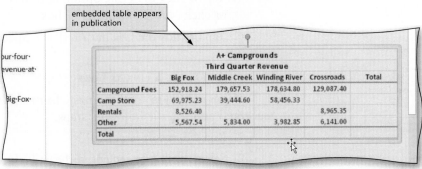

embedded table appears in publication

A+ Campgrounds Third Quarter Revenue					
	Big Fox	Middle Creek	Winding River	Crossroads	Total
Campground Fees	152,918.24	179,657.53	178,634.80	129,087.40	
Camp Store	69,975.23	39,444.60	58,456.33		
Rentals	8,526.40			8,965.35	
Other	5,567.54	5,834.00	3,982.85	6,141.00	
Total					

Figure 6–67

- Tap or click the OK button (Insert Object dialog box) to embed the data from the Excel file. If your system opens an Excel window, tap or click the Close button on the Excel title bar.

- If necessary, drag the border of the embedded table so it does not overlap the page layout (Figure 6–67).

BTW
External Files
When using files or objects created by others, do not use the source document until you are certain it does not contain a virus or other malicious content. Use an antivirus software to verify that any files you use are free of viruses and other potentially harmful programs.

To Create an Embedded Table from Scratch

If you wanted to create an embedded table from scratch, you would perform the following steps.

1. In Publisher, display the INSERT tab.
2. Tap or click the Object button (INSERT tab | Text group).
3. Tap or click the Create New option button (Insert Object dialog box).
4. In the Object Type box, tap or click Microsoft Office Excel Worksheet.
5. Tap or click the OK button (Insert Object dialog box) to insert the table.
6. Double-tap or double-click the table and insert data into each cell.

To Insert a Linked Table

If you wanted to create a linked table, you would perform the following steps.

1. In Publisher, display the INSERT tab.
2. Tap or click the Object button (INSERT tab | Text group).
3. Tap or click the 'Create from File' option button (Insert Object dialog box), and tap or click to display a check mark in the Link check box.
4. Tap or click the Browse button to display the Browse dialog box.
5. Navigate to your USB storage location or the location of the Data Files for Students on your computer, and double-tap or double-click the desired Excel file.
6. Tap or click the OK button (Insert Object dialog box) to link the data from the Excel file.

To Copy and Paste an Embedded Table

If you wanted to copy and paste from an Excel worksheet to create an embedded table, you would perform the following steps.

1. Run Microsoft Excel 2013.
2. Select the cells to include in the embedded table, and press CTRL+C to copy them.
3. Run Microsoft Publisher 2013.
4. Tap or click the Paste arrow (HOME tab | Clipboard group), and then tap or click Paste Special in the gallery.
5. Tap or click the Paste option button (Paste Special dialog box), and then tap or click New Table in the As box.
6. Tap or click the OK button (Paste Special dialog box) to embed the table.

To Copy and Paste a Linked Table

If you wanted to copy and paste from an Excel worksheet to create a linked table, you would perform the following steps.

1. Run Microsoft Excel 2013.
2. Select the cells to include in the embedded table, and press CTRL+C to copy them.
3. Run Microsoft Publisher 2013.

4. Tap or click the Paste arrow (HOME tab | Clipboard group), and then tap or click Paste Special in the gallery.

5. Tap or click the Paste Link option button (Paste Special dialog box).

6. Tap or click the OK button (Paste Special dialog box) to link the table.

To Format an Embedded Table

1 EMPLOY REUSABLE PARTS | 2 APPLY SHAPE EFFECTS | 3 INSERT & FORMAT TABLES | 4 CREATE CALENDAR
5 USE MASTER PAGES | 6 ADD BORDERART | 7 EMBED TABLE | **8 USE EXCEL FUNCTIONALITY**

When you double-tap or double-click an embedded object, most Microsoft apps activate a subset of the source application commands on a ribbon that appears in the destination application. *Why? The embedded features allow you to edit the object without opening the source app.*

The following steps format the first and last rows of numerical data in the embedded table. The Excel cell references in the following steps represent the intersection of the column (indicated by a capital letter) and the row (indicated by a number). For example, the first cell in column A is cell A1; the third cell in column B is cell B3, and so forth.

- Double-tap or double-click the table to display the Excel tabs on the Publisher ribbon.

- Drag through cells B4 through F4 to select them (Figure 6–68).

Q&A What happened to the FILE tab and the other Publisher tabs?
Publisher displays Excel functionality while you are working on an embedded table. When you tap or click outside the table, the Publisher tabs will reappear.

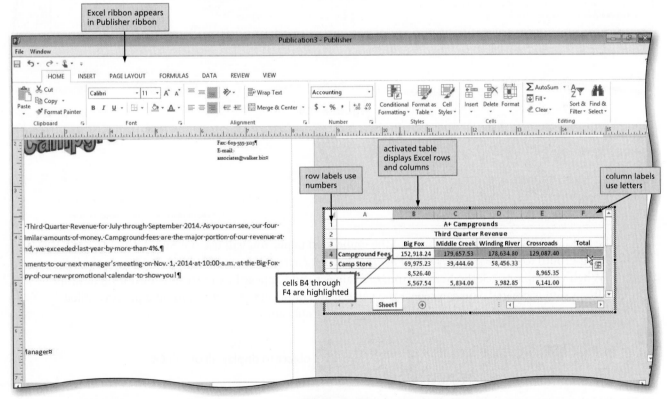

Figure 6–68

- Tap or click the 'Accounting Number Format' button (Excel HOME tab | Number group) to apply dollar signs to the cells (Figure 6–69).

Q&A The formatting is not showing up in cell F4. Did I do something wrong?

No. The formatting will show up as soon as you enter a value or sum in the cell in the next series of steps. Excel allows you to format empty cells.

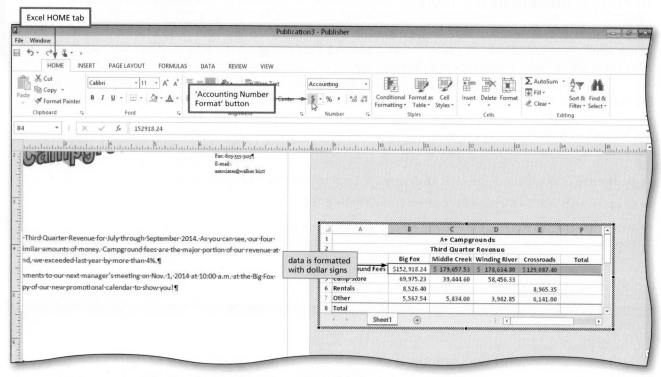

Figure 6–69

- Repeat Steps 1 and 2 for the range B8 through F8.

To Sum in an Embedded Table

1 EMPLOY REUSABLE PARTS | 2 APPLY SHAPE EFFECTS | 3 INSERT & FORMAT TABLES | 4 CREATE CALENDAR
5 USE MASTER PAGES | 6 ADD BORDERART | **7 EMBED TABLE** | 8 USE EXCEL FUNCTIONALITY

The following steps sum the columns of the embedded table. You will use the Sum button (Excel HOME tab | Editing group) to create a total. *Why? Publisher does not have a Sum command, so you must use the Excel function.* When you tap or click the Sum button, the values to add appear in a **marquee**, or dotted flashing border. After a sum is created, you can repeat the pattern and duplicate the procedure in a process called **replication**. Excel displays a special fill handle to help with replication.

- If necessary, drag the lower-center sizing handle of the Excel object to display all of cell B8.

- Tap or click cell B8 to position the insertion point.

- Tap or click the Sum button (Excel HOME tab | Editing group) to sum the cells, and then tap or click the Enter button on the formula bar to display the total (Figure 6–70).

Q&A What other math operations can I perform?

You can type any formula into the formula bar using real numbers or cell references. You also can tap or click the Microsoft Office Excel Help button on the ribbon to learn about many mathematical functions that will help you with formulas that are more complex.

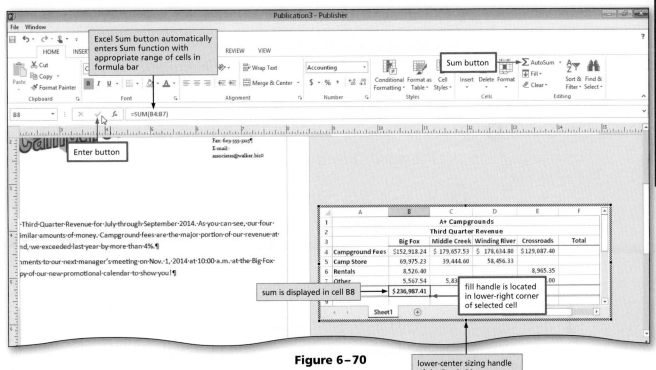

Figure 6–70

lower-center sizing handle of the Excel object

2

- Drag the fill handle in the lower-right corner of cell B8 across and through cells C8 through F8 to replicate the sum across the columns (Figure 6–71).

Q&A How does the fill handle replicate the sum?

When you drag to the right, the sum is adjusted to include the same number of cells above the total line in each column. When you drag down, the sum is adjusted to include cells to the left in each row.

What is the button that appears after replicating the function?

That is the Auto Fill Options button. If you tap or click the button, you have the choice of fill with or without formatting.

Figure 6–71

3

- If necessary, drag the right-center sizing handle of the Excel object to display all of cell F4.

- Tap or click cell F4 to position the insertion point.

- Tap or click the Sum button (Excel HOME tab | Editing group) to sum the cells and then tap or click the Enter button on the formula bar to display the total.

- Drag the fill handle in the lower-right corner of cell F4 down and through cells F5 through F7 to replicate the sum down the rows (Figure 6–72).

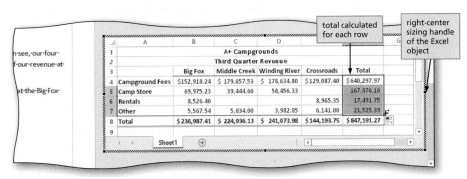

Figure 6–72

	Other Ways
1. To sum, press ALT+=	2. To replicate, tap or click Fill button (Excel HOME tab | Editing group), tap or click desired fill direction

To Move and Position the Table

The following steps move and reposition the embedded table.

1 Tap or click outside the table to display the table border.

2 Zoom to 80%. Scroll as necessary to view both the letter and the table.

3 Drag the border of the table to position the table in the lower portion of the letter as shown in Figure 6–73.

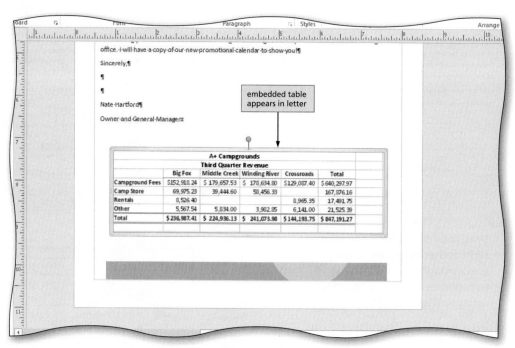

Figure 6–73

To Save the Letter

The following step saves the letter.

1 Save the publication on your desired save location, using the file name, `A+ Campground Manager Letter`.

To Print the Letter

If you wanted to print the letter, you would perform the following steps.

1. Tap or click the Print tab in the Backstage view to display the Print gallery.

2. Verify that the printer listed on the Printer Status button will print a hard copy of the publication. If necessary, tap or click the Printer Status button to display a list of available printer options and then tap or click the desired printer to change the currently selected printer.

3. Tap or click the Print button in the Print gallery to print the publication on the currently selected printer.

4. When the printer stops, retrieve the hard copy.

To Exit Publisher

This project is complete. The following steps exit Publisher. For a detailed example of the procedure summarized below, refer to the Office and Windows chapter at the beginning of this book.

1 To exit Publisher, tap or click the Close button on the right side of the title bar.

2 If a Microsoft Publisher dialog box is displayed, tap or click the Don't Save button so that any changes you have made are not saved.

Chapter Summary

In this chapter, you learned how to use tables to present data in efficient and meaningful ways. First, you formatted a WordArt object to assist in branding a company name. Next, you created and formatted tables and data, including the use of table styles, merging, and cell diagonals. Next, you created a calendar with a page border on the master page. Finally, you embedded data from Excel into a Publisher publication and used the Excel-enhanced tools to format the table and perform calculations. The items listed below include all the new Publisher skills you have learned in this chapter.

Creating and Formatting Tables
Add Borders (PUB 340)
Align Data in Cells (PUB 334)
Apply a Table Format (PUB 328)
Change Column Width (PUB 336)
Change the Border Color (PUB 340)
Change the Line Weight (PUB 339)
Change the Page Orientation
   (PUB 317)
Create a Cell Diagonal (PUB 341)
Delete a Column (PUB 330)
Delete a Row (PUB 331)
Enter Data in a Table (PUB 329)
Insert a Column (PUB 332)
Insert a Row (PUB 331)
Insert an Empty Table
   (PUB 327)
Merge Cells (PUB 333)
Resize the Table (PUB 337)
Select a Row (PUB 332)
Select a Table (PUB 338)
Split Cells (PUB 334)

Creating Calendars
Create a 12-Month Calendar
   (PUB 344)

Embedding and Linking Tables
Copy and Paste a Linked Table (PUB 360)
Copy and Paste an Embedded Table (PUB 360)
Create an Embedded Table (PUB 358)
Create an Embedded Table from Scratch (PUB 360)
Format an Embedded Table (PUB 361)
Insert a Linked Table (PUB 360)
Sum in an Embedded Table (PUB 362)

Enhancing with Shape Effects
Apply a Shape Effect (PUB 322)
Fine-Tune a Shape Effect (PUB 324)

Saving and Printing
Print the Amenities Table (PUB 343)
Print the Calendar (PUB 355)
Print the Letter (PUB 364)
Save the Calendar Pages as Images (PUB 355)

Selecting, Formatting, and Snapping
Create BorderArt (PUB 348)
Select All (PUB 353)
Set the Transparency (PUB 353)
Snap an Object to the Margin Guide (PUB 320)

Using Master Pages
Close the Master Page (PUB 352)
View the Master Page (PUB 347)

What decisions will you need to make when creating your next custom publication?
Use these guidelines as you complete the assignments in this chapter and create your own publications outside of this class.

   1. Choose reusable objects.
      a) Use business information sets.
      b) Use building blocks.
      c) Create new objects.
   2. Apply shape effects sparingly.

CONSIDER THIS

3. Create tables.

  a) Create and format a table.

  b) Enter data.

  c) Add table borders.

4. Create a calendar.

5. Use the master page for repeating items across pages.

6. Apply BorderArt to make pages or tables stand out.

7. If you need added functionality, embed an Excel table.

  a) Embed tables for static data edited in Publisher.

  b) Link tables when you want both Publisher and Excel to change and to use the full functionality of Excel.

How should you submit solutions to questions in the assignments identified with a ✹ symbol?
Every assignment in this book contains one or more questions identified with a ✹ symbol. These questions require you to think beyond the assigned publication. Present your solutions to the questions in the format required by your instructor. Possible formats may include one or more of these options: write the answer; create a document that contains the answer; present your answer to the class; discuss your answer in a group; record the answer as audio or video using a webcam, smartphone, or portable media player; or post answers on a blog, wiki, or website.

Apply Your Knowledge

Reinforce the skills and apply the concepts you learned in this chapter.

Formatting a Table

Note: To complete this assignment, you will be required to use the Data Files for Students. Visit www.cengage.com/ct/studentdownload for detailed instructions or contact your instructor for information about accessing the required files.

Instructions: Start Publisher. Open the publication, Apply 6–1 Monthly Expenses, from the Data Files for Students. The publication is a table of monthly expenses for state-wide meetings of the Alpha Omega Sorority. Figure 6–74 shows the formatted table.

Alpha Omega Sorority Monthly Meeting Expenses			
Expense　　　　　Month	January	February	March
Hall Rental	120.00	120.00	120.00
Postage	65.90	62.90	69.91
Computer and Wi-Fi	117.29	118.50	119.12
Paper Supplies	46.57	41.67	48.70
Food/Beverages	122.04	99.88	100.00
Awards	50.00	50.00	50.00
Total	521.80	492.95	507.73

Figure 6–74

Perform the following tasks:

1. Tap or click the table. Tap or click the More button (TABLE TOOLS DESIGN tab | Table Formats group). Tap or click 'Table Style 35' to apply the format to the table.

2. Tap or click the Select Table button (TABLE TOOLS LAYOUT tab | Table group), and then tap or click Select Table in the gallery to select the entire table. Display the HOME tab. Change the font size to 18.

3. Tap or click anywhere in the first row of the table. Tap or click the 'Insert Rows Above' button (TABLE TOOLS LAYOUT tab | Rows & Columns group) to insert a row above row 1.

4. With the new row still selected, tap or click the Merge Cells button (TABLE TOOLS LAYOUT tab | Merge group) to merge the cells in the new row. Enter the text, `Alpha Omega Sorority Monthly Meeting Expenses` to enter a title. Format the font size to be 22.

5. Center the title and the column headings. Right-align the numeric data.

6. Tap or click the first cell in the second row. Tap or click the Diagonals button (TABLE TOOLS LAYOUT tab | Merge group), and then tap or click Divide Down in the gallery to create a cell with a diagonal. Enter the text, `Expense`, in the left side of the split cell and tap or click the 'Align Bottom Left' button (TABLE TOOLS LAYOUT tab | Alignment group) to change the heading alignment. Enter the text, `Month`, in the right side of the split cell and tap or click the 'Align Top Right' button (TABLE TOOLS LAYOUT tab | Alignment group) to change the heading alignment. Change both headings to font size 14.

7. Select the entire table. Tap or click the Line Weight button (TABLE TOOLS DESIGN tab | Borders group) and choose a 2¼ pt line. Tap or click the Line color button (TABLE TOOLS DESIGN tab | Borders group) and choose the 'Accent 4 (Gold), Darker 25%' color. Tap or click the Borders arrow (TABLE TOOLS DESIGN tab | Borders group) and choose All Borders.

8. Tap or click the border of the table, and then align the table centered both horizontally and vertically, relative to the margins. (Hint: Tap or click the Align button (TABLE TOOLS LAYOUT tab | Arrange group) and make choices from there).

9. Draw a text box in the lower-right corner of the page and enter your name, and make other formatting decisions, if directed to do so by your instructor.

10. Open the Backstage view, and then tap or click Save As. Save the publication on your storage device, using the file name, Apply 6–1 Monthly Expenses Complete.

11. Print the publication with appropriate printer settings.

12. Submit the file as specified by your instructor.

13. ✹ Look at the totals in the table. Are you sure they are correct? How do you know? If the table were embedded or linked to Excel, what tools, commands, or functions would you have used to enhance or check the table?

Extend Your Knowledge

Extend the skills you learned in this chapter and experiment with new skills. You may need to use Help to complete the assignment.

Adding an Excel Chart to a Publication

Note: To complete this assignment, you will be required to use the Data Files for Students. Visit www.cengage.com/ct/studentdownload for detailed instructions or contact your instructor for information about accessing the required files.

Instructions: Open the publication, Extend 6-1 IT Majors Table from the Data Files for Students. You will add a 3-D Column chart to the publication so that it appears as shown in Figure 6–75 on the next page.

Continued >

Extend Your Knowledge *continued*

	Web Development	Networking	Database Management
Freshmen	24	18	20
Sophomores	19	21	24
Juniors	19	22	16
Seniors	15	20	16
Totals	77	81	76

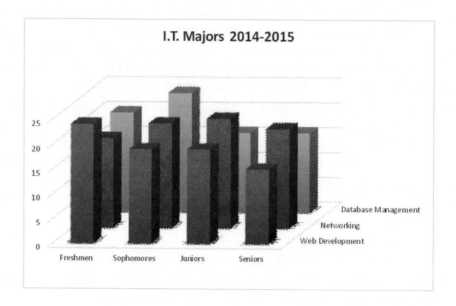

Figure 6–75

Perform the following tasks:

1. Use Help to learn more about adding an Excel chart to a Publisher publication.

2. Zoom to 40%. Double-tap or double-click the table so that the Excel tabs appear on the Publisher ribbon.

3. Drag the lower-center sizing handle of the table down, to fill the page.

4. If directed by your instructor to do so, change the major in cell B1 to your major and change the major in cell C1 to a friend's major.

5. Drag to select cells A1 through D5. Do not include the totals.

6. Display the Excel INSERT tab. Tap or click the 'Insert Column Chart' button (Excel INSERT tab | Charts group) to display the gallery, and then tap or click the 3-D Column preview to add the chart to the publication.

7. Tap or click the scratch area to return to Publisher. Zoom to 120% and, if necessary, scroll to center the chart in the workspace.

8. Double-tap or double-click the chart to enable the Excel tabs on the Publisher ribbon. Point to each part of the chart, labels, data columns, and legend to identify the various parts of the chart.

9. Display the Excel CHART TOOLS DESIGN tab. Tap or click the Style 5 thumbnail (CHART TOOLS DESIGN tab | Chart Styles group).

10. Tap or click to select the legend, and then press the DELETE key to delete the legend.

11. Select the text in the Chart Title, and then type `I.T. Majors 2014–2015` to replace the text.

12. Drag one of the top or bottom sizing handles on the chart to resize the chart to approximately 18 rows high. Drag a side sizing handle to increase the width of the chart to approximately six inches as measured on the horizontal ruler. Do not drag close to the edge of the workbook object.

13. Tap or click the table above the chart. Display the Excel VIEW tab. Tap or click to remove the check mark in the Gridlines check box (Excel VIEW tab | Show group).

14. Tap or click outside the table to display the Publisher tabs on the ribbon. Change the publication properties, as specified by your instructor. Save the revised publication with the file name, Extend 6-1 Majors Table Complete. Print the publication and then submit it in the format specified by your instructor.

15. Exit Publisher.

16. ✸ In reviewing the available types of charts and graphs, what other type of chart might make sense for the data in the table? Why would a pie chart be a poor choice?

Analyze, Correct, Improve

Analyze a publication, correct all errors, and improve the design.

Formatting a Table and Using WordArt

Note: To complete this assignment, you will be required to use the Data Files for Students. Visit www.cengage.com/ct/studentdownload for detailed instructions or contact your instructor for information about accessing the required files.

Instructions: Open the publication, Analyze 6-1 Music Table, from the Data Files for Students. You decide to improve the embedded table for a guitar store by changing the fonts, formatting it with dollar signs, providing row and column totals, and branding the name of the store with a WordArt object (Figure 6–76 on the next page).

Continued >

Analyze, Correct, Improve *continued*

Third Quarter Guitar Sales									
		North		East		West		South	Total
Classical	$	6,734	$	7,821	$	4,123	$	7,989	$	26,667
Steel String		5,423		2,134		6,574		3,401	17,532
Electric		3,495		6,291		7,345		7,098	24,229
Bass		5,462		2,923		8,034		5,135	21,554
Total	$	21,114	$	19,169	$	26,076	$	23,623	$	89,982

Figure 6–76

1. Correct The totals are missing for the rows and columns. Insert the Sum function in cell F3. Use the Fill handle to create totals for the other rows. Create totals for each column.

2. Improve Using the Excel tabs on the Publisher ribbon, format row 1 to increase the font size. Format the first row of numbers (row 3) and the last row of numbers (row 7) with dollar signs. If decimal places are displayed, tap or click the Decrease Decimal button (Excel HOME tab | Number group) until only whole dollar amounts are displayed. Add a formatted WordArt object above the table with the name of the company, Guitar Mania. Use the Master Page to insert a background gradient for the publication. Save the publication using the file name, Analyze 6-1 Music Table Complete. Submit the revised document in the format specified by your instructor.

3. ✹ What other kinds of formatting might you include in the table? Would you be able to do that if the table were only a Publisher table and not an embedded Excel table? When would you use one over the other?

In the Labs

Design, create, or modify a publication using the guidelines, concepts, and skills presented in this chapter. Labs 1 and 2, which increase in difficulty, require you to create a solution based on what you learned in the chapter; Lab 3 requires you to create a solution that uses cloud and web technologies, by learning and investigating on your own from general guidance.

Lab 1: Creating a Logo

Problem: The Town Diner would like to brand the name of the diner. The company has asked you to use your knowledge of shape effects to create a logo. Prepare the publication shown in Figure 6–77.

Figure 6–77

Perform the following tasks:

1. Run Publisher. In the template gallery, tap or click the Blank 11 × 8.5" thumbnail. Use the PAGE DESIGN tab to set the font scheme to Galley and the color scheme to Garnet.

2. Insert a WordArt object. Tap or click the 'Gradient Fill - Red, Outline -White' preview in the Plain WordArt Styles area of the WordArt gallery to select it. Type the word, `Town`, in the Edit WordArt Text dialog box. Tap or click the OK button (Edit WordArt Text dialog box) to insert the WordArt object on the page.

3. Tap or click the 'Change WordArt Shape' button, and then tap or click Can Up in the gallery to change the shape.

4. Tap or click the Shape Effects button (WORDART TOOLS FORMAT tab | WordArt Styles group), and then tap or click Shadow to display the Shadow Gallery. Tap or click the 'Perspective Diagonal Upper Right' preview to apply a shape effect.

5. Tap or click the Shape Effects button (WORDART TOOLS FORMAT tab | WordArt Styles group), and then tap or click Bevel to display the gallery. Tap or click the 3-D Options command to display the Format Shape dialog box. If necessary, tap or click 3-D Format to display the settings. Enter the values as shown in Table 6–4.

Table 6–4 3-D Format Settings

Setting	Value
Top bevel button	Angle
Top bevel Width text box	8
Top bevel Height text box	8
Bottom bevel Width text box	1.1
Bottom bevel Width text box	1.1
Depth Size text box	42
Contour Size text box	0
Material button	Matte
Lighting button	Bright Bottom

© 2014 Cengage Learning

6. Tap or click the Shape Outline button (WORDART TOOLS FORMAT tab | WordArt Styles) and then tap or click No Outline in the gallery.

7. Tap or click the Shape Fill button (WORDART TOOLS FORMAT tab | WordArt Styles), and then tap or click 'Hyperlink (RGB (153,0,0)), Lighter 80%' in the gallery.

8. Press and hold or right-click the WordArt object, and then tap or click Copy on the shortcut menu. Press and hold or right-click the page layout, away from the WordArt object, and then tap or click Paste on the shortcut menu to create a copy.

9. Tap or click the copy of the WordArt object. Tap or click the Edit Text button (WORDART TOOLS FORMAT tab | Text group), and change the text to Diner. Tap or click the OK button (Edit WordArt Text dialog box). Tap or click the 'Change WordArt Shape' button, and then tap or click Can Down in the gallery to change the shape.

10. Align both WordArt objects beside each other and group them. Resize the grouped object to approximately 5.5" × 2.25". Center align them horizontally and vertically, relative to the margin guides.

11. Save the publication with the name, `Lab 6-1 Town Diner Logo`.

12. Submit the file as directed by your instructor.

13. Exit Publisher.

14. ✹ Did the chosen color scheme affect the WordArt Styles? How do you know? What is the best way to change the color of WordArt? Why?

Lab 2: **Using BorderArt on a Calendar**

Problem: Your nephew's third grade teacher wants a calendar for next month. She will add events and assignments to the calendar, but she wants you to get it "set up." She reminds you to use a decorative border around the calendar (Figure 6–78).

Figure 6–78

Perform the following tasks:

1. Run Publisher. In the template gallery, choose the Pinstripes calendar from the BUILT-IN calendar templates. Choose the Citrus color scheme and the Casual font scheme. Choose a landscape orientation.

2. Choose a One month per page timeframe, and set the calendar dates to begin and end in October 2015 so that Publisher creates a single page with single month's calendar.

   If directed by your instructor to do so, choose the current month.

3. Create the publication. Change the picture to one that represents October, and delete the caption. Delete the picture in the scratch area.

4. Press and hold or right-click the colored rectangle in the background, and then tap or click Format AutoShape on the shortcut menu.

5. When Publisher displays the Format AutoShape dialog box, tap or click the BorderArt button to display the BorderArt dialog box. Choose the Candy Corn border art. Tap or click the OK button (BorderArt dialog box).

6. In the Format AutoShape dialog box, set the width to size 24 pt. Tap or click the OK button (Format AutoShape dialog box).

7. Drag a sizing handle to increase the size of the rectangle, slightly.

8. Change the publication properties, as specified by your instructor. Save the publication with the file name, Lab 6-2 Grade School Calendar.

9. Submit the publication in the format specified by your instructor.

10. Exit Publisher.

11. ✹ What kinds of things could you do to the cells in the calendar table to help the teacher enter data at a later date? Would you consider enlarging the table and reducing the size of the picture or omitting the picture? Why or why not?

Lab 3: Expand Your World: Cloud and Web Technologies
Uploading to Flickr

Problem: You would like to upload one of your publications to Flickr to show your friends, but Flickr does not accept the .pub format. You decide to investigate saving the publication as a TIF file.

Instructions:

1. Start Publisher and open a publication you have created. Tap or click FILE on the ribbon to open the Backstage view, and then tap or click Save As. Browse to your storage location.

2. Tap or click the 'Save as type' button (Save As dialog box), and then tap or click 'Tag Image File Format (*.tif)' in the list. Tap or click the Save button. Exit Publisher. If Publisher asks you to save the publication again, tap or click the Don't Save button.

3. Open a browser and go to http://flickr.com. Tap or click the Sign Up or Sign In command on the menu bar (Figure 6–79).

Figure 6–79

Continued >

In the Labs *continued*

4. Sign in with your Facebook, Google, or Yahoo! account. If you do not have any of those accounts, tap or click the 'Create New Account' button (Flickr window) and fill in the appropriate fields.

5. Once you are logged in, tap or click the Upload command on the menu bar. When the Upload window is displayed, tap or click the 'Choose photos and videos to upload' button. Navigate to the location of your TIF file, and double-tap or double-click the file to upload it. Add a short description.

6. Tap or click the 'Upload 1 Photo' button in the upper-right portion of the window, and then tap or click the 'Upload to Photostream' button when prompted to finish the upload process.

7. Press and hold or right-click the image in the Flickr window. Tap or click Copy shortcut on the shortcut menu to copy the web address to the clipboard.

8. Paste the image address in an email to your instructor.

9. Write a paragraph about your experience with the Flickr program. Include several advantages and disadvantages for collaborating in this manner.

10. Submit the assignment in the format specified by your instructor.

11. ✳ What other photo-sharing programs have you heard about or used? What are the advantages to a web-based, free service such as Flickr?

Consider This: Your Turn

Apply your creative thinking and problem solving skills to design and implement a solution.

1: Formatting a Book Order Table

Personal/Academic

Part 1: The office assistant for the Computer Technology department would like to have a publication that instructors could use to submit their book order information. She has asked you to create a publication in landscape orientation that includes a table with six columns and seven rows. Merge the cells in the first row, and then type **Bookstore Order Form** in the merged cells. The cells in the last row should be merged and provide a place for the instructor's name and the course number. The cell in the first column of the second row should display a Divide Down cell diagonal. Type **Course and Section Number** in the left side of the cell diagonal. Type **Book Information** in the right side of the cell diagonal. Across the other columns in row two, include headings for Author, Title, Edition or Date, Publisher, and ISBN. Format the table, cells, and borders appropriately.

Part 2: ✳ After creating this publication, what will be the best way to distribute it to faculty members? Is there a way that the data from the table could be automated to be sent directly to the bookstore? Could you save it as a web publication? Would that work? Why or why not?

2: Using a Master Page

Professional

Part 1: The Excelsior Springs Spa would like you to create a master page that they can use as a background for an upcoming brochure. Open a blank 11 × 8.5" publication. Go to the master page. Add a light blue gradient background. Create a WordArt object with a 3-D Rotation shape effect for the name of the spa. Return to the publication and save it.

Part 2: ✳ Do you think companies might use a master page as a letterhead template? What items from typical letterhead could be placed in the background? Which items would have to stay in the foreground? Why?

3: Collaborating on a Table of Contents
Research and Collaboration

Part 1: Microsoft maintains a blog site about Publisher at http://blogs.office.com/b/microsoft-publisher. Individually go to the Publisher blog and search for entries related to Publisher tables and tables of contents. Take notes about best practices and what other Publisher users have done. Then, collaborate with your classmates to create a table of contents for a fictitious textbook, using some of the ideas in the blog. Your table should contain at least 6 rows and 2 columns with appropriate headings. Format the table. See your instructor for ways to submit this assignment.

Part 2: ✳ Did you find some blog entries about using Word to create a table of contents? Which application seems better suited for a table of contents? Why?

Learn Online

Reinforce what you learned in this chapter with games, exercises, training, and many other online activities and resources.

Student Companion Site   Reinforce chapter terms and concepts using review questions, flash cards, practice tests, and interactive learning games, such as a crossword puzzle. These and other online activities and resources are available at no additional cost on www.cengagebrain.com. Visit www.cengage.com/ct/studentdownload for detailed instructions about accessing the resources available at the Student Companion Site.

7 | Advanced Formatting and Merging Publications with Data

Microsoft product screenshots used with permission from Microsoft Corporation.

Objectives

You will have mastered the material in this project when you can:

- Use the master page
- Recolor and compress a graphic to create a watermark
- Explain character spacing techniques
- Track and kern characters
- Use the Measurement toolbar to edit character spacing
- Set a tab stop and enter tabbed text
- Differentiate among tab styles

- Produce a form letter
- Use the Mail Merge Wizard to create form letters
- Create and edit a data source
- Use grouped field codes
- Select and filter records in a data source
- Insert field codes and preview results
- Print selected copies of merged publications

7 | Advanced Formatting and Merging Publications with Data

Introduction

Whether you want individual letters sent to everyone on a mailing list, personalized envelopes for a mass mailing, an invoice sent to all customers, or a printed set of mailing labels to apply to your brochures, you can use Publisher to maintain your data and make the task of mass mailing and merged document creation easier.

Merged publications, such as form letters, should be timely and professional looking yet, at the same time, personalized. Used regularly in both business and personal correspondence, a **form letter** has the same basic content no matter to whom it is sent; however, items such as name, address, city, state, and zip code change from one form letter to the next. Thus, form letters are personalized to the addressee. An individual is more likely to open and read a personalized letter or email than a standard Dear Sir or Dear Madam message. With word processing and database techniques, it is easy to generate individual, personalized documents for a large group and include features unique to desktop publishing. A **data source** or **data file** is a file that may contain only a list of names and addresses or also may include paths to pictures, product part numbers, postal bar codes, customer purchase history, accounts receivable, email addresses, and a variety of additional data that you may use in a merged publication.

Project — Merging Form Letters and Ticket Numbers

The project in this chapter creates a form letter and individual tickets with merged fields for each addressee from a Publisher mailing list, as shown in Figure 7–1. The letter, formatted with a graphic watermark (Figure 7–1a), thanks each person who bought tickets to a play. The ticket (Figure 7–1b) displays play and seating information.

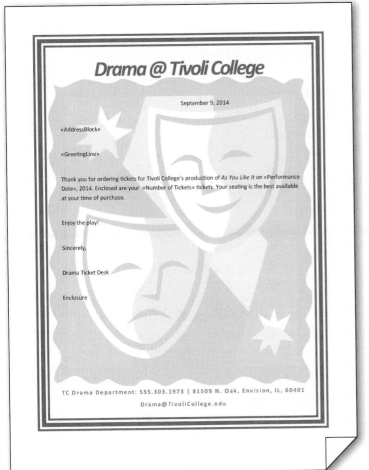

(a) Form Letter

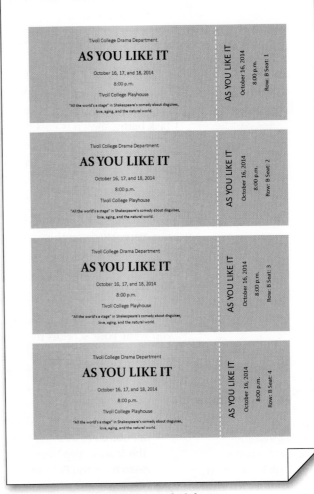

(b) Merged Tickets

Figure 7–1

The letter contains merged fields, including names, addresses, and the number of tickets. The ticket displays a unique ticket number, seat, and row.

Roadmap

In this chapter, you will learn how to create the publication shown in Figure 7–1. The following roadmap identifies general activities you will perform as you progress through this chapter:

1. USE the MASTER PAGE to place objects such as watermarks.
2. ADJUST GRAPHICS by editing the color brightness, contrast, and compression.
3. Change the SPACING BETWEEN CHARACTERS such as tracking, kerning, and scaling.
4. SET and use TABS.
5. USE the MAIL MERGE WIZARD to create a data source.
6. INSERT FIELD CODES in a form letter.
7. CREATE numbered TICKETS with ticket stubs.
8. USE the MAILINGS TAB to insert individual merge fields.

At the beginning of step instructions throughout the chapter, you will see an abbreviated form of this roadmap. The abbreviated roadmap uses colors to indicate chapter progress: gray means the chapter is beyond that activity, blue means the task being shown is covered in that activity, and black means that activity is yet to be covered. For example, the following abbreviated roadmap indicates the chapter would be showing a task in the Set Tabs activity.

1 USE MASTER PAGE | 2 ADJUST GRAPHICS | 3 SPACING BETWEEN CHARACTERS | **4 SET TABS**
5 USE MAIL MERGE WIZARD | 6 INSERT FIELD CODES | 7 CREATE TICKETS | 8 USE MAILINGS TAB

Use the abbreviated roadmap as a progress guide while you read or step through the instructions in this chapter.

To Run Publisher

If you are using a computer to step through the project in this chapter and you want your screens to match the figures in this book, you should change your screen's resolution to 1366 × 768. For information about how to change a computer's resolution, refer to the Office and Windows chapter at the beginning of this book.

The following steps run Publisher.

1 Scroll the Start screen and search for a Publisher 2013 tile. If your Start screen contains a Publisher 2013 tile, tap or click it to run Publisher and then proceed to Step 5. If the Start screen does not contain the Publisher 2013 tile, proceed to the next step to search for the Publisher app.

2 Swipe in from the right edge of the screen or point to the upper-right corner of the screen to display the Charms bar, and then tap or click the Search charm on the Charms bar to display the Search menu.

3 Type **Publisher** as the search text in the Search box, and watch the search results appear in the Apps list.

4 Tap or click Publisher 2013 in the search results to run Publisher.

5 If the Publisher window is not maximized, tap or click the Maximize button on its title bar to maximize the window.

One of the few differences between Windows 7 and Windows 8 occurs in the steps to run Publisher. If you are using Windows 7, click the Start button, type **Publisher** in the 'Search programs and files' box, click Publisher 2013, and then, if necessary, maximize the Publisher window. For a summary of the steps to run Publisher in Windows 7, refer to the Quick Reference located at the back of this book.

To Open a Publication

The following steps open the Drama Letterhead file from the Data Files for Students. See the inside back cover of this book for instructions on downloading the Data Files for Students, or contact your instructor for information about accessing the required files. For a detailed example of the procedure summarized below, refer to the Office and Windows chapter at the beginning of this book.

1 Tap or click 'Open Other Publications' in the left pane of the Publisher gallery, to display the Open gallery.

2 Navigate to the location of the file to be opened (in this case, the Chapter 07 folder in the Publisher folder).

3 Double-tap or double-click **Drama Letterhead** to open the selected publication in the Publisher window.

4 If necessary, collapse the Page Navigation pane and tap or click the Special Characters button (HOME tab | Paragraph group) to display special characters (Figure 7–2).

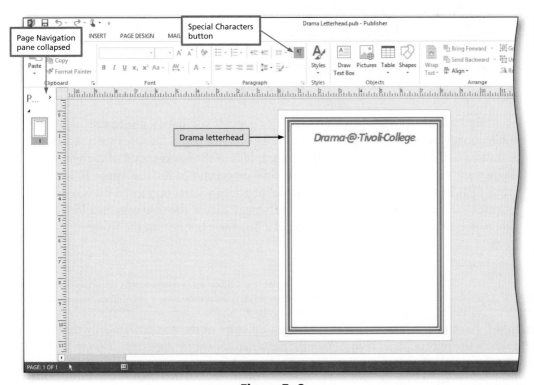

If you are using your finger on a touch screen and are having difficulty completing the steps in this chapter, consider using a stylus. Many people find it easier to be precise with a stylus than with a finger. In addition, with a stylus you see the pointer. If you still are having trouble completing the steps with a stylus, try using a mouse.

Figure 7–2

How do you use watermarks?

As a graphic visible in the background on some publications, watermarks may be translucent; others can be seen on the paper when held up to the light. Other times the paper itself has a watermark when it is manufactured. Watermarks are used as both decoration and identification, as well as to provide security solutions to prevent document fraud. Creating watermarks on the master page causes the watermark to repeat on each page of the publication. A master page can contain anything that you can put on a publication page, as well as headers, footers, page numbers, date and time, and layout guides that can be set up only on a master page.

CONSIDER THIS

Watermarks and Master Pages

A **watermark** is a semitransparent graphic that is visible in the background on a printed page. In Publisher, you create watermarks by placing text or graphics on a **master page**, which is a background area similar to the header and footer area in traditional word processing software. When accessing the master page, Publisher displays a new tool tab (Figure 7–3). While other tabs are available to help you manipulate objects on the master page, when finished, you should tap or click the 'Close Master Page' button (MASTER PAGE tab | Close group) to return to the main tabs on the ribbon.

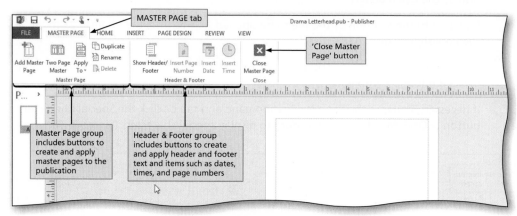

Figure 7–3

Each publication starts with one master page. If you have a multipage publication, you can choose to use two different master pages for cases such as facing pages in a book; you might want different graphics in the background of each page. If you want to display master page objects only on certain pages, the Apply To button (MASTER PAGE tab | Master Page group) provides several options. This is useful for cases such as background images on every page except the title page in a longer publication or a watermark on the inside of a brochure but not on the front.

To View the Master Page

1 USE MASTER PAGE | 2 ADJUST GRAPHICS | 3 SPACING BETWEEN CHARACTERS | 4 SET TABS
5 USE MAIL MERGE WIZARD | 6 INSERT FIELD CODES | 7 CREATE TICKETS | 8 USE MAILINGS TAB

In the Drama Letterhead, you will create a watermark that uses a picture of the comedy/tragedy theater masks. The following steps access the master page. *Why? Placing a picture on the master page keeps it out of the way, and prevents inadvertent editing.*

● Tap or click VIEW on the ribbon to display the VIEW tab (Figure 7–4).

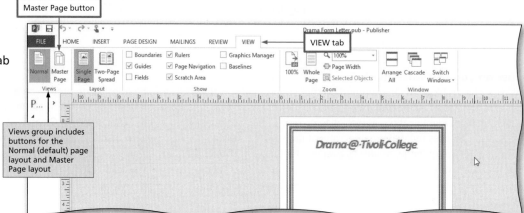

Figure 7–4

2

- Tap or click the Master Page button (VIEW tab | Views group) to access the master page (Figure 7–5).

Q&A Why is the scratch area a different color?

Publisher uses a different color to remind you that you are not in the regular publication window. It helps you to remember to close the master page before continuing with the other objects in the publication.

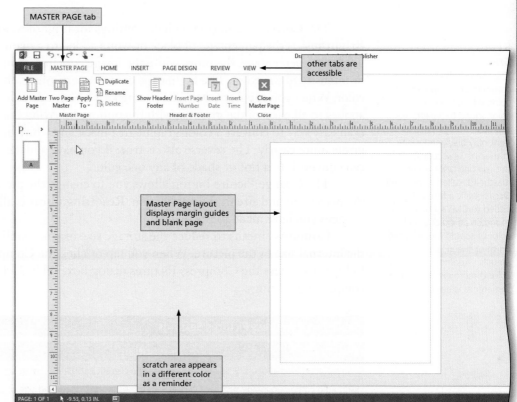

Figure 7–5

Other Ways

1. Tap or click Master Pages button (PAGE DESIGN tab | Page Background group), select appropriate master page

2. Press CTRL+M

Graphic Adjustments

Recall that you inserted graphics or pictures into publications by choosing them from your storage device and by importing them from Office.com Clip Art. In previous chapters, you added a picture style and created a formatted graphic shape. The Adjust group on the PICTURE TOOLS FORMAT tab provides ways to edit graphics other than by changing size, position, and style (Figure 7–6).

BTW
The Ribbon and Screen Resolution
Publisher may change how the groups and buttons within the groups appear on the ribbon, depending on the computer's screen resolution. Thus, your ribbon may look different from the ones in this book if you are using a screen resolution other than 1366 × 768.

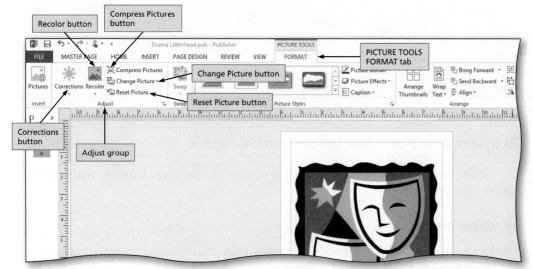

Figure 7–6

BTW
Spot Colors
You can use the Recolor command to create a spot color, which is an extra color added to a page. For example, many newspapers print only black and white in their news sections, but use one color for the masthead, called a spot color. Occasionally a fifth color is added to CMYK publications to match an exact brand color or to add a specialized finish or sheen, such as metallic. Adding a fifth spot color is more expensive, but sometimes is desirable.

The Corrections button includes settings for brightness and contrast. **Brightness** is the percentage of black or white added to a main color. The higher the brightness percentage, the more white the image contains. **Contrast** is the saturation or intensity of the color. The higher the contrast percentage, the more intense the color. When you **recolor** a graphic, you make a large-scale color change; the color applies to all parts of the graphic, with the option of leaving the black parts black. It is an easy way to convert a color graphic to a black and white line drawing so that it prints more clearly. The reverse also is true; if you have a black and white graphic, you can convert it to a tint or shade of any one color.

The Change Picture button allows you to change the picture while maintaining the placement and size in the publication. **Resetting** discards all of the formatting changes you have made to the picture.

Compress means to reduce the storage size of your publication by changing the internal size of the picture. When you tap or click the Compress Pictures button, Publisher displays the Compress Pictures dialog box. Table 7–1 describes the compression settings.

Table 7–1 Compress Pictures Settings

Setting	Description
Current combined image size	Displays the current combined size of all pictures in the publication
Estimated combined image size after compression	Displays the estimated combined size of all pictures in the publication after compression settings
'Delete cropped areas of pictures' check box	Deletes the pixel information that normally is stored for cropped areas of pictures
'Remove OLE data' check box	Removes the internal part of a graphic that is used when the graphic is linked or embedded. While the picture itself appears the same, you no longer are able to open that picture by using the software in which it was created originally.
Resample pictures check box	Makes a resized picture smaller by deleting the residual data from the picture's original size. You should avoid making the picture larger after resampling.
'Convert to JPEG where appropriate' check box	Converts the picture to a JPEG file
Commercial Printing option button	Compresses pictures to 300 pixels per inch (ppi). This option does not compress JPEG files.
Desktop Printing option button	Compresses pictures to 220 ppi and a 95 JPEG quality level
Web option button	Compresses pictures to 96 dots per inch (dpi) and a 75 JPEG quality level
'Apply to all pictures in the publication' option button	Applies the compression settings to all of the pictures in the publication
'Apply to selected pictures only' option button	Applies the compression settings to only the selected picture or pictures

To Insert and Place the Watermark Graphic

The following steps insert the graphic of comedy and tragedy masks that will be used for the watermark.

1 Display the INSERT tab.

2 Tap or click the Online Pictures button (INSERT tab | Illustrations group) to display the Insert Pictures dialog box.

3 Enter the term, `drama`, in the Office.com Clip Art search box, and then press the ENTER key. Choose a picture similar to the one in Figure 7–7.

4 Drag the corner sizing handles to resize the picture to fill the page, within the margin guides (Figure 7–7).

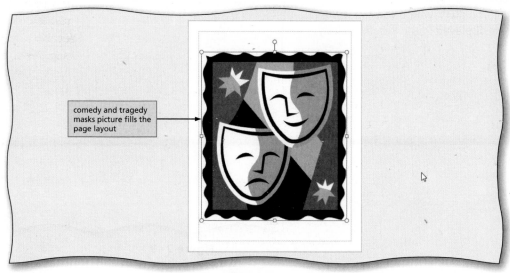

comedy and tragedy masks picture fills the page layout

Figure 7–7

To Recolor the Picture

1 USE MASTER PAGE | 2 ADJUST GRAPHICS | 3 SPACING BETWEEN CHARACTERS | 4 SET TABS
5 USE MAIL MERGE WIZARD | 6 INSERT FIELD CODES | 7 CREATE TICKETS | 8 USE MAILINGS TAB

The following steps recolor the picture. **Why?** *The downloaded graphic is too dark for a watermark; text inserted over the graphic would be difficult to read.*

1

• If necessary, with the picture selected, display the PICTURE TOOLS FORMAT tab.

• Tap or click the Recolor button (PICTURE TOOLS FORMAT tab | Adjust group) to display the Recolor gallery (Figure 7–8).

Experiment

• Point to each option in the Recolor gallery and watch the picture change on the master page.

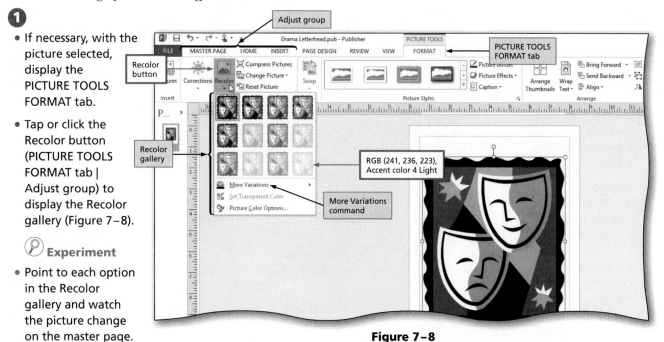

Adjust group

Recolor button

Recolor gallery

PICTURE TOOLS FORMAT tab

RGB (241, 236, 223), Accent color 4 Light

More Variations command

Figure 7–8

● Tap or click 'RGB (241, 236, 223), Accent color 4 Light' to change the picture to grayscale (Figure 7–9).

Q&A What does the More Variations command (Figure 7–8 on the previous page) in the Recolor gallery do?
It displays the Scheme Colors gallery, where you can choose different colors than those displayed in the Recolor gallery.

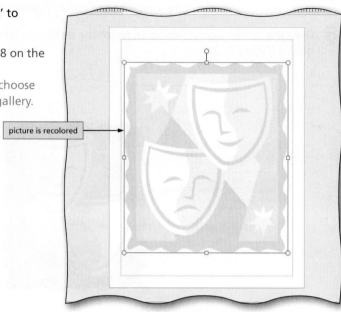

picture is recolored

Figure 7–9

Other Ways

1. Tap or click Recolor button (PICTURE TOOLS FORMAT tab | Adjust group), tap or click 'Picture Color Options' command, tap or click Color button (Format Picture dialog box | Picture tab), select color

To Edit the Brightness and Contrast

1 USE MASTER PAGE | 2 ADJUST GRAPHICS | 3 SPACING BETWEEN CHARACTERS | 4 SET TABS
5 USE MAIL MERGE WIZARD | 6 INSERT FIELD CODES | 7 CREATE TICKETS | 8 USE MAILINGS TAB

The following steps edit the brightness and contrast of the picture. *Why? Adjusting the brightness and contrast will make the features stand out, even as a watermark.*

● With the picture selected, tap or click the Corrections button (PICTURE TOOLS FORMAT tab | Adjust group) to display the Corrections gallery (Figure 7–10).

Q&A What does the 'Picture Corrections Options' command do?
If you tap or click the 'Picture Corrections Options' command, Publisher will display the Format Picture dialog box where you can edit exact settings for brightness, contrast, and transparency.

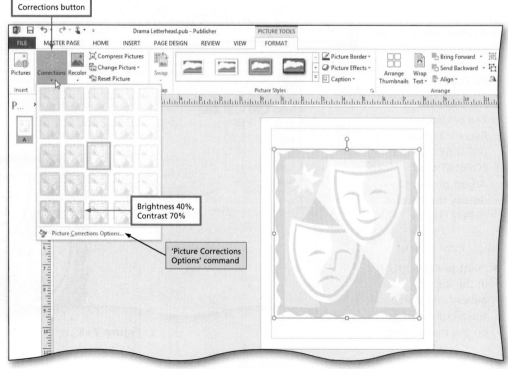

Corrections button

Brightness 40%, Contrast 70%

'Picture Corrections Options' command

Figure 7–10

- Tap or click 'Brightness: 40%, Contrast 70%' in the gallery to change the brightness and contrast (Figure 7–11).

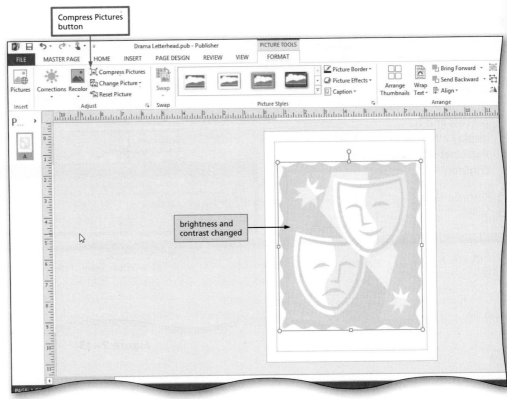

Figure 7–11

Other Ways

1. Tap or click Corrections button (PICTURE TOOLS FORMAT tab | Adjust group), tap or click 'Picture Corrections Options' command, drag Brightness or Contrast sliders (Format Picture dialog box | Picture tab)

1 USE MASTER PAGE | 2 ADJUST GRAPHICS | 3 SPACING BETWEEN CHARACTERS | 4 SET TABS
5 USE MAIL MERGE WIZARD | 6 INSERT FIELD CODES | 7 CREATE TICKETS | 8 USE MAILINGS TAB

To Compress the Picture

The following steps compress the picture. *Why? A compressed picture will reduce the size of the file when it is saved.*

- With the picture selected, tap or click the Compress Pictures button (PICTURE TOOLS FORMAT tab | Adjust group) to display the Compress Pictures dialog box.

- Tap or click the Desktop Printing option button to compress the picture for desktop printing.

- If necessary, tap or click the 'Apply to all pictures in the publication' option button to compress only the masks picture (Figure 7–12).

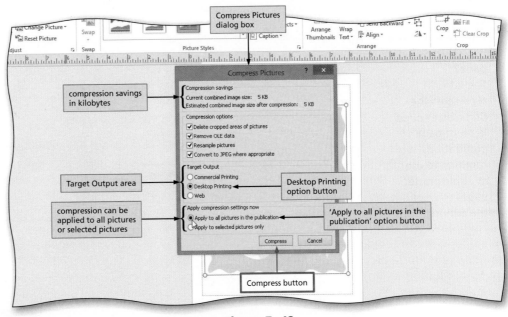

Figure 7–12

- Tap or click the
  Compress button
  (Compress Pictures
  dialog box) to begin
  the compressing
  process and to
  display a Microsoft
  Publisher dialog box
  (Figure 7–13).

Q&A How much storage
space will I save?
The size of the
saved file will vary,
but you should
save approximately
100 kilobytes.

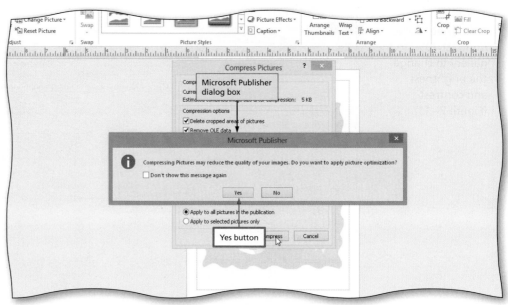

Figure 7–13

- Tap or click the Yes button (Microsoft Publisher dialog box) to confirm the compression.

To Close the Master Page

1 USE MASTER PAGE | 2 ADJUST GRAPHICS | 3 SPACING BETWEEN CHARACTERS | 4 SET TABS
5 USE MAIL MERGE WIZARD | 6 INSERT FIELD CODES | 7 CREATE TICKETS | 8 USE MAILINGS TAB

The following steps close the master page and returns to the regular page layout and Publisher workspace.
Why? You can close the master page because you have finished creating the watermark.

- Display the
  MASTER PAGE tab
  (Figure 7–14).

Q&A What does the letter
A represent in the
Page Navigation
pane?
The letter A
represents the
first master page.
In multi-page
publications, it is
common to use
multiple master
pages throughout
the publication.

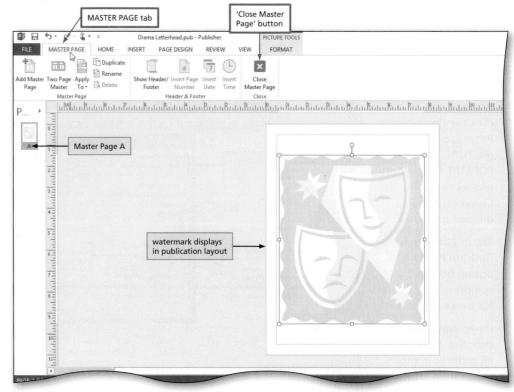

Figure 7–14

2

- Tap or click the 'Close Master Page' button (MASTER PAGE tab | Close group) to close the master page (Figure 7–15).

Q&A What else could I add to the master page? You could add a background effect, headers, footers, or any text or graphics that you want to appear on every page of the publication.

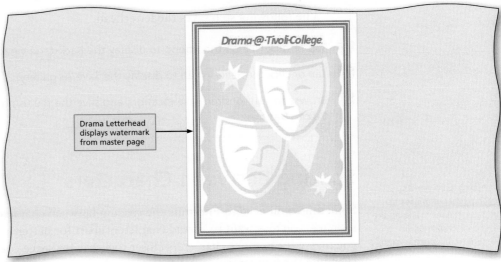

Drama Letterhead displays watermark from master page

Figure 7–15

Other Ways

1. Press CTRL+M

To Insert Letterhead Information

The following steps create a text box at the bottom of the page and enter text for the contact information.

1 Zoom to 130% and then scroll to the lower portion of the page layout.

2 Tap or click the 'Draw a Text Box' button (HOME tab | Objects group) and then drag to draw a text box that fills the area between the graphic and the border.

3 Type `TC Drama Department: 555.303.1973 | 81509 N. Oak, Envision, IL, 60401` and then press the ENTER key.

4 Type `Drama@TivoliCollege.edu` to enter the email address.

5 Select both lines and then press CTRL+E to center the text.

6 With the text still selected, tap or click the Font Color arrow (TEXT BOX TOOLS FORMAT tab | Font group) and then tap or click 'Accent 3 (RGB (56, 145, 167))' to choose a color in the color scheme.

7 With the text still selected, tap or click the Font Size box and enter 12 to change the font size.

8 Tap or click anywhere in the text box to deselect (Figure 7–16).

BTW
BTWs
For a complete list of the BTWs found in the margins of this book, visit the BTW resource on the Student Companion Site located on www.cengagebrain.com. For detailed instructions about accessing available resources, visit www.cengage.com/ct/ studentdownload or see the inside back cover of this book.

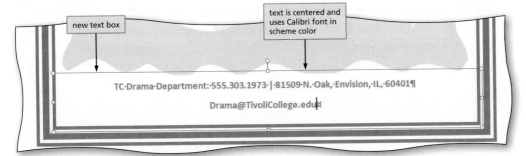

new text box

text is centered and uses Calibri font in scheme color

TC·Drama·Department:·555.303.1973·|·81509·N.·Oak,·Envision,·IL,·60401¶

Drama@TivoliCollege.edu

Figure 7–16

To Save the Letterhead

The following step saves the letterhead.

1 Tap or click FILE on the ribbon to display the Backstage view.

2 Tap or click the Save As tab to display the Save As gallery.

3 Browse to your desired save location, and save the file using the file name, `Drama Form Letter`.

BTW

Scaling Graphics

Scaling, when it applies to graphics, means changing the vertical or horizontal size of the graphic by a percentage. Scaling can create interesting graphic effects. For example, a square graphic could become a long thin graphic suitable for use as a single border if the scale height were increased to 200% and the scale width were reduced to 50%. Caricature drawings and intentionally distorted photographs routinely use scaling. When used for resizing, scaling is appropriate to make a graphic fit in tight places.

BTW

Kerning

The term kerning comes from the printing industry where typesetters would shave off portions of the rectangular letter blocks so that letters could fit closer together. The kern is the part of a metal typeface that projects beyond its body.

BTW

Leading

Leading is similar to tracking, except that it applies formatting to the line spacing instead of character spacing. Leading measures the vertical distance between lines of text — ignoring any letters that descend below the line.

Spacing Between Characters

Sometimes you need to fine-tune the spacing between characters on the page. For instance, you may want to spread characters apart for better legibility. Other times, you may want to move characters closer together for space considerations, without changing the font or font size. Or, you may be using a font that employs **proportional spacing**, or different widths for different characters. For example, in a proportionally spaced font, the letter i is narrower than the letter m. This book uses a proportionally spaced font, as do most books, newspapers, and magazines.

The opposite of proportional spacing is **monospacing**, in which every letter is the same width. Older printers and monitors were limited to monospaced fonts because of the dot matrix used to create the characters. Now, almost all printers, with the exception of line printers, are capable of printing with either proportionally spaced or monospaced fonts. Because most fonts use proportional spacing, the scaling, tracking, and kerning features in Publisher allow you many ways to make very precise character spacing adjustments.

Scaling, the process of shrinking or stretching text, changes the width of individual characters in text boxes. Recall that the WordArt toolbar has a button for scaling; however, scaling also can be applied to any text box by using the Measurement toolbar.

Tracking, or **character spacing**, refers to the adjustment of the general spacing between all selected characters. Tracking text compensates for the spacing irregularities caused when you make text much bigger or much smaller. For example, smaller type is easier to read when it has been tracked loosely. Tracking maintains the original height of the font and overrides adjustments made by justification of the margins. Tracking is available only if you are working on a print publication. It is not available with web publications.

Kerning, or **track kerning**, is a special form of tracking related to pairs of characters that can appear too close together or too far apart, even with standard tracking. Kerning can create the appearance of even spacing and is used to fit text into a given space or adjust line breaks. For instance, certain uppercase letters such as T, V, W, and Y often are kerned when they are preceded or followed by a lowercase a, e, i, o, or u. With manual kerning, Publisher lets you choose from normal, expanded, and condensed kerning for special effects. Text in smaller point sizes usually does not need to be kerned, unless the font contains many serifs.

You can adjust the spacing between characters using the lower three boxes on the Measurement toolbar boxes as explained in Table 7–2. Some spacing techniques also can be performed using the ribbon or in dialog boxes.

Box Name	Specifies	Preset Unit of Measurement
Table 7–2 Character Spacing Tools on the Measurement Toolbar		
Tracking	General space between characters	Percent
Text Scaling	Width of the text	Percent
Kerning	Subtle space between paired characters	Point size

© 2014 Cengage Learning

1 USE MASTER PAGE | 2 ADJUST GRAPHICS | 3 SPACING BETWEEN CHARACTERS | 4 SET TABS
5 USE MAIL MERGE WIZARD | 6 INSERT FIELD CODES | 7 CREATE TICKETS | 8 USE MAILINGS TAB

To Track Characters

The following steps track the small text at the bottom of the page more loosely. *Why? Small text is harder to read when the letters are very close together.*

- If necessary, tap or click the text in the text box to position the insertion point.
- Press CTRL+A to select all of the text.
- Tap or click the Character Spacing button (TEXT BOX TOOLS FORMAT tab | Font group) to display the Character Spacing gallery (Figure 7–17).

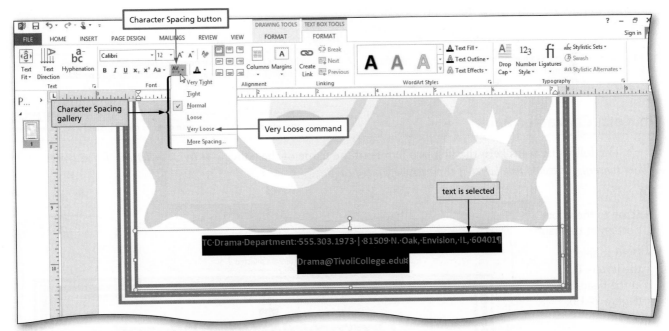

Figure 7–17

Experiment

- Point to each of the choices in the Character Spacing gallery, and watch how the text changes.

Q&A What is the difference between tracking, scaling, and autofitting?

Tracking increases or decreases the spaces between the characters. Scaling changes the width of the characters themselves. Autofitting changes the font size, which is both the width and height of the characters.

2

- Tap or click Very Loose to track the text more loosely (Figure 7–18).

How can I tell if the text changed?
You can tap or click the Undo button (Quick Access Toolbar) and then tap or click the Redo Button (Quick Access Toolbar) to see the before and after effects of tracking.

How is tracking measured?
Tracking is a percentage of how much space is inserted between characters. Tight tracking reduces the percentage. Loose tracking increases the percentage. When you choose Very Loose, the text is tracked 125%.

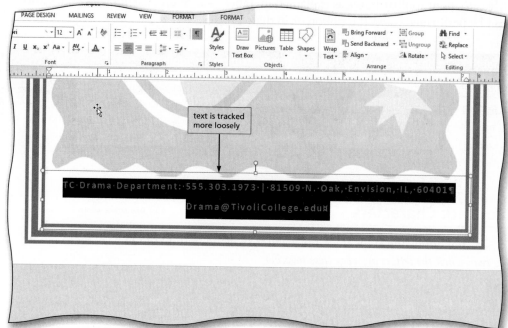

Figure 7–18

Other Ways

1. Tap or click Object Size button on status bar, enter tracking setting in Tracking box on Measurement toolbar

2. Press and hold or right-click text, point to Change Text, tap or click Character Spacing, enter tracking settings (Character Spacing dialog box)

To Kern Character Pairs

1 USE MASTER PAGE | 2 ADJUST GRAPHICS | 3 SPACING BETWEEN CHARACTERS | 4 SET TABS
5 USE MAIL MERGE WIZARD | 6 INSERT FIELD CODES | 7 CREATE TICKETS | 8 USE MAILINGS TAB

The following steps kern the first two letters of the name of the college. *Why? The letters, T and i, are almost touching. It would look better if they were separated slightly.*

1

- Scroll to the upper portion of the page.

- Drag to select the letters Ti in the heading (Figure 7–19).

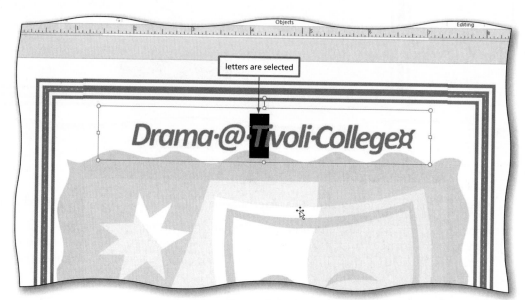

Figure 7–19

2

- Tap or click the Object Size button on the status bar to display the Measurement toolbar.
- Drag through the text in the Kerning box to select it (Figure 7–20).

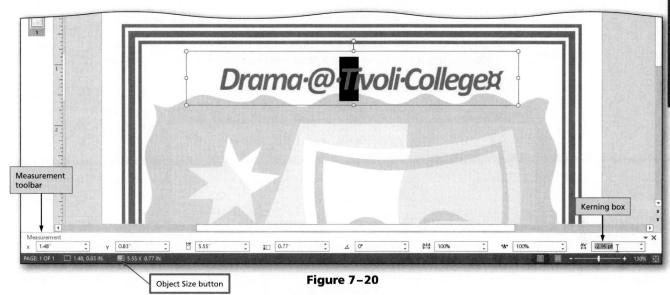

Figure 7–20

3

- Type -2 and then press the ENTER key to move the letter 'i' slightly further away from the letter 'T'.

- Tap or click outside the selection to deselect the text (Figure 7–21).

Q&A How is kerning measured?

When you enter a value in the Kerning box (Measurement toolbar), it changes the points between characters. Recall that a point is approximately equal to 1/72nd of an inch. The higher the number, the further apart the characters will appear.

Figure 7–21

Other Ways

1. Press and hold or right-click selected text, point to Change Text on shortcut menu, tap or click Character Spacing, enter kerning settings (Character Spacing dialog box), tap or click OK button

2. Tap or click Character Spacing button (HOME tab | Font group), tap or click More Spacing, enter kerning settings (Character spacing dialog box), tap or click OK button

3. Press CTRL+SHIFT+RIGHT BRACKET (]) to increase space, press CTRL+SHIFT+LEFT BRACKET ([) to decrease space

BTW
Touch Mode
The Touch/Mouse Mode button (Quick Access Toolbar) allows you to switch between touch mode and mouse mode. If you primarily use gestures, touch mode will add more space between commands in menus and on the ribbon.

To Create a Text Box

The following steps create a text box that will contain the body text of the letter itself.

1 Tap or click the 'Show Whole Page' button on the status bar to display the whole page.

2 Display the HOME tab and then tap or click the 'Draw a Text Box' button (HOME tab | Objects group). Drag to draw a large text box in the middle of the page.

3 Set the Font Size to 12.

4 Use the Measurement toolbar to enter the following settings: Horizontal Position 1", Vertical Position 2", Width 6.5", and Height 7.25" (Figure 7–22).

5 Close the Measurement toolbar.

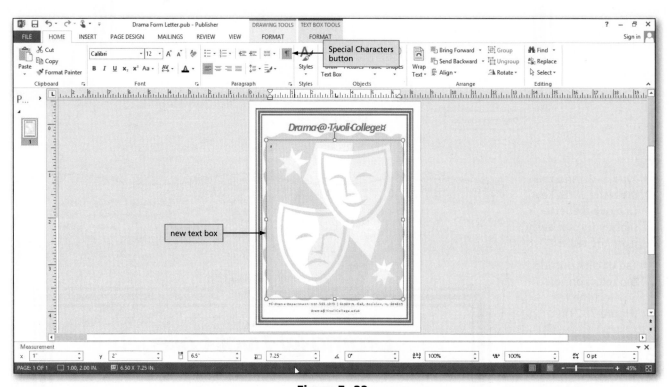

Figure 7–22

BTW
Displaying Rulers
To turn the rulers on or off, press CTRL+R or click the Rulers check box (VIEW tab | Show group).

Working with Tabs and the Ruler

The **ruler** appears above the Publisher workspace and contains buttons, markers, margins, and measurements to help you place text, and objects. Publisher uses tabs and markers to help position tab stops, margins, and indentures within text boxes. A **tab**, or **tab stop**, is a horizontal location inside a text box designated by a tab stop marker on the Publisher ruler. A **tab stop marker** appears darkened on the ruler as either a straight line, L-shaped marker or T-shaped marker. A **margin marker** appears as either a gray pentagon or gray rectangle on the ruler. Margin markers set and indicate margins on the left and right of a text box. A special **first-line indent marker** allows you to change the left margin for the first line only in a paragraph. The typing area within the text box boundaries appears in light gray on the ruler; the rest of the ruler is a darker gray. Numbers on the ruler represent inches, but inches can be changed to centimeters, picas, pixels, or points. The **tab selector** is located at the left end of the ruler. It displays an icon representing the alignment of the text at the tab stop (Figure 7–23).

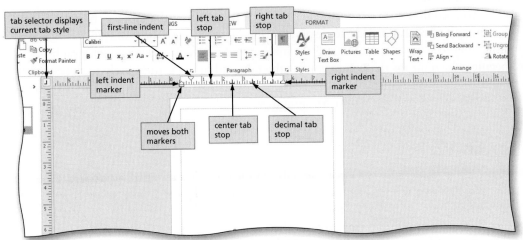

Figure 7–23

Table 7–3 explains the functions of the markers and buttons on the ruler, as well as how to modify them.

Table 7–3 Ruler Tools			
Tool Name	**Description**	**How to Change**	**Other Ways**
First-line indent marker	A downward-pointing pentagon that indicates the position at which paragraphs begin	Drag to desired location	Double-tap or double-click margin marker, enter location in First line box (Paragraph dialog box)
Left indent marker	An upward-pointing pentagon that indicates the left position at which text wraps	Drag to desired location	Double-tap or double-click margin marker, enter location in Left box (Paragraph dialog box)
Move both markers	A small rectangle used to move both the left indent marker and the first-line indent marker at the same time	Drag to desired location	Press and hold or right-click text box, tap or click 'Format Text Box', tap or click Text Box tab (Format Text box dialog box), enter text box margins
Object margins	Gray indicates the area outside the object margin; white indicates the area inside the object margin	Resize object	Press and hold or right-click text box, tap or click 'Format Text Box', tap or click Size tab (Format Text box dialog box), enter height and width
Right indent marker	An upward-pointing pentagon that indicates the rightmost position at which text wraps to the next line	Drag to desired location	Double-tap or double-click margin marker, enter location in Right box (Paragraph dialog box)
Tab selector	Displays the current alignment setting: left, right, center, or leader	Tap or click to toggle choice	Double-tap or double-click tab stop marker, select alignment (Paragraph dialog box)
Tab stop marker	Displays the location of a tab stop	Tap or click to create; drag to move	Double-tap or double-click ruler, set tab stop location (Paragraph dialog box)

BTW
Zero Point
You also can CTRL+drag or CTRL+tap or CTRL+click the tab selector to change the publication's **zero point** or **ruler origin**. The zero point is the position of 0 inches on the ruler. It is useful for measuring the width and height of objects on the page without having to add or subtract from a number other than zero. To change the ruler back, double-tap or double-click the tab selector.

BTW
Leader Tabs
A **leader tab** is a special type of right tab in which the blank space to the left of the text is filled with a specific character. Customized via the Tabs dialog box, a leader repeats the character from the previous text or tab stop to fill in the tabbed gap. For example, a printed musical program might contain the name of the composition on the left and the composer on the right. Using a leader tab, that space in between could be filled by dots or periods to help the viewer's eye follow across to the corresponding composer.

BTW
Leader Tab Characters
Available leader tab character styles include None, Dot, Dash, Line, and Bullet.

© 2014 Cengage Learning

BTW
Units of Measurement
If you want to change the unit of measurement on the ruler, display the Backstage view, and then tap or click Options. Tap or click Advanced, and then tap or click the 'Show measurements in units of' arrow. Choose the preferred unit of measurement, and then tap or click the OK button (Publisher Options dialog box).

BTW
Tab Stop Alignment
The tab stop alignment can be changed by tapping or clicking the Paragraph Setting Dialog Box Launcher (HOME tab | Paragraph group), by double-tapping or double-clicking an existing marker, or by tapping or clicking the tab selector until it displays the type of tab that you want.

BTW
Default Tabs
Default tabs are set every .5 inches in a text box; default tabs do not display markers.

BTW
Tabs vs. Indents
Sometimes it is difficult to determine whether to use tab stops or indents. Use tab stops when you want to indent paragraphs as you go, or when you want a simple column. When the tab stop is positioned for a long passage of text, using the TAB key to indent the first line of each paragraph is inefficient, because you must press it each time you begin a new paragraph. In these cases, it is better to use an indent because it automatically carries forward when you press the ENTER key.

Recall that the Special Characters button (HOME tab | Paragraph group) shown in Figure 7–22 makes special nonprinting characters visible to help you format text passages, including tab characters (→), end-of-paragraph marks (¶), and end-of-frame marks (¤).

You can drag markers to any place on the ruler within the text box boundaries. You can tap or click a marker to display a dotted line through the publication, which allows you to see in advance where the marker will be set. Markers are paragraph-specific, which means that when you set the tabs and indents, they apply to the current paragraph. Once the tabs and indents are set, however, pressing the ENTER key carries forward the markers to the next paragraph.

Setting Tabs

Publisher offers two ways to set tabs. With a text box selected, you can choose the type of tab you want by tapping or clicking the tab selector button until the appropriate icon is displayed. You then can tap or click at the desired tab location in the ruler. The icon will appear on the ruler.

A second way to set tabs in a text box is by using the Tabs tab in the Paragraph dialog box (Figure 7–24). You can access the Paragraph dialog box, by double-tapping or double-clicking the ruler, or by tapping or clicking the Paragraph Settings Dialog Box Launcher (HOME tab | Paragraph group).

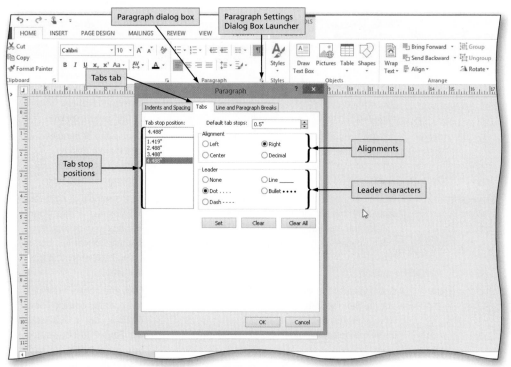

Figure 7–24

With tab stops, you can align text to the left, right, center, or at a decimal character. Publisher also can insert special leading characters before a tab, such as dashes, dots, or lines. Table 7–4 lists the types of tab alignments and their common uses.

Table 7–4 Types of Tab Alignments

Name	Icon	Action	Purpose
Left tab		Text begins at tab stop and is inserted to the right	Used for most tabbing
Right tab		Text begins at tab stop and is inserted to the left	Used for indexes, programs, and lists
Center tab		Text is centered at the tab stop as it is typed	Used to center a list within a column
Decimal tab		Aligns numbers only, based on a decimal point, independent of the number of digits	Used for aligning currency amounts in a list
Leader tab		Text begins at tab stop and is inserted to the left; space preceding the tab is filled with chosen character	Used for table of contents, printed programs, church bulletins, etc.

© 2014 Cengage Learning

The tab stop alignment can be changed by tapping or clicking the Paragraph Settings Dialog Box Launcher (HOME tab | Paragraph group), by double-tapping or double-clicking an existing marker, or by tapping or clicking the tab selector until it displays the type of tab that you want. The Leader character only can be changed using the Paragraph dialog box.

1 USE MASTER PAGE | 2 ADJUST GRAPHICS | 3 SPACING BETWEEN CHARACTERS | 4 SET TABS
5 USE MAIL MERGE WIZARD | 6 INSERT FIELD CODES | 7 CREATE TICKETS | 8 USE MAILINGS TAB

To Set a Tab Stop

The following step uses the horizontal ruler to set, or insert, a tab stop at the 3.25" position in the form letter text box. **Why?** *The standard Modified Block format of letter writing displays the date at the center of the letter, horizontally.*

1

- With the insertion point located in the main text box of the form letter, press the F9 key to zoom to 100%.

- Tap or click the horizontal ruler at the 3.25" mark to create a left tab stop. Move the mouse pointer to view the tab stop marker (Figure 7–25).

left tab stop

Figure 7–25

Q&A Is the tab always a left-aligned tab?
Left-aligned is the default tab setting. If you want to change the tab type, tap or click the tab selector until you see the tab type you want and then tap or click the ruler at the tab stop location.

 Experiment

- Tap or click the Paragraph Settings Dialog Box Launcher (HOME tab | Paragraph group), and then tap or click the Tabs tab to view the tab setting. Tap or click the Close button (Paragraph dialog box).

Other Ways

1. Tap or click Paragraph Settings Dialog Box Launcher button (HOME tab | Paragraph group), tap or click Tabs tab (Paragraph dialog box), set tab stop, tap or click OK button

To Enter Tabbed Text

The following steps enter tabbed text. *Why? Pressing the* TAB *key will move the insertion point to the center of the letter, ready for the date to be entered.*

1

- Press the TAB key to move the insertion point to the tab stop (Figure 7–26).

Q&A How do I delete a tab?

To delete a tab, drag the tab marker from its location in the ruler to the tab selector and drop it there. Or, you can tap or click the Paragraph Settings Dialog Box Launcher (HOME tab | Paragraph group) and then tap or click the Tabs tab (Paragraph dialog box). Select the tab stop location, and tap or click the Clear button.

Figure 7–26

2

- Display the INSERT tab on the ribbon.

- Tap or click the 'Date & Time' button (INSERT tab | Text group) to display the Date and Time dialog box.

- Tap or click the third available format, and tap or click the Update automatically check box (Figure 7–27).

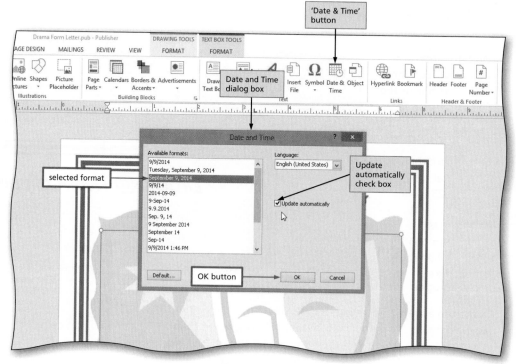

Figure 7–27

- Tap or click the OK button (Date and Time Dialog box) to insert the current date at the tab stop.

- Press the ENTER key twice to insert a blank line (Figure 7–28).

Why is my date different?
Publisher inserts the current date; your display should reflect the current date (the date you create this publication).

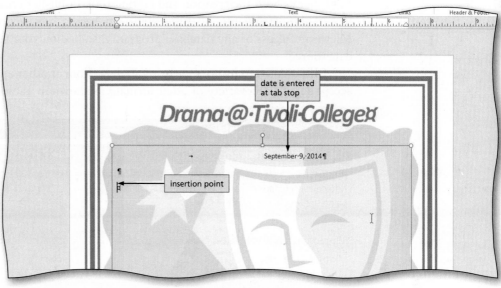

Figure 7–28

To Save an Existing Publication with the Same File Name

You have made several modifications to the publication since you last saved it. Thus, you should save it again.

1 Tap or click the Save button on the Quick Access Toolbar to overwrite the previously saved file.

Break Point: If you wish to take a break, this is a good place to do so. Exit Publisher. To resume at a later time, run Publisher, open the file named, Drama Form Letter, and then continue following the steps from this location forward.

Merging Data Into Publications

The process of generating an individualized publication for mass mailing involves creating a main publication and a data source. The main publication contains the constant or unchanging text, punctuation, space, and graphics, embedded with variables or changing values from the data source. A data source or database is a file where you store all addresses or other personal information for customers, friends and family, or merchants with whom you do business. The term **database** generically describes a collection of data, organized in a manner that allows easy access, retrieval, and use of that data. **Merging** is the process of combining the contents of a data source with a main publication.

Personalized contact with your customers can result in increased revenue. Addressing customers by name and remembering their preferences is the kind of personal attention that builds customer loyalty. When retail establishments keep close track of customers' interests, customers usually respond by returning and spending more time and money there. When you include content in a mailing that addresses your customers' specific interests, the customers are more likely to pay attention and respond.

BTW
Main Publications
When you open a main publication, Publisher attempts to open the associated data source file, too. If the data source is not in exactly the same location (i.e., drive and folder) as when it originally was merged and saved, Publisher displays a dialog box indicating that it cannot find the data source. When this occurs, tap or click the 'Find Data Source' button to display the Open Data Source dialog box, and locate the data source file yourself.

Publisher allows users to create data sources internally, which means using Publisher as both the creation and editing tool. Publisher creates a database that can be edited independently by using Microsoft Access; however, you do not need to have Microsoft Access or any database program installed on your system to use a Publisher data source.

If you plan to **import**, or bring in data, from another application, Publisher can accept data from a variety of other formats, as shown in Table 7–5.

Table 7–5 Data Formats	
Data-Creation Program	**File Extension**
Any text files, such as those generated with WordPad or Notepad where tabs or commas separate the columns, and paragraph marks separate the rows	.txt, .prn, .csv, .tab, and .asc
dBase	.dbf
Microsoft Access (database tables and projects)	.ade, .adp, .mdb .mde, .accdb, and .accde
Microsoft Data links	.udl
Microsoft Excel	.xls and .xlsx
Microsoft FoxPro	.fxd
Microsoft List Builder	.bcm
Microsoft Office Address Lists	.mdb
Microsoft Office List Shortcuts	.ols
Microsoft Outlook (Contacts list)	.pst
Microsoft Word (tables or merge data documents)	.doc, .docx, and .docm
ODBC File DSNs	.dsn
SQL Server and Office Database Connections	.odc
Webpages	.htm, .html, .asp, .mht, .mhtml

© 2014 Cengage Learning

Creating a Data Source

A data source is a file that contains the data that changes from one merged publication to the next. As shown in Figure 7–29, a data source often is shown as a table that consists of a series of rows and columns. Each row is called a **record**. The first row of a data source is called the **header record** because it identifies the name of each column. Each row below the header row is called a **data record**. Data records contain the text that varies in each copy of the merged publication. The data source for this project contains five data records. In this project, each data record identifies a different person who has purchased tickets for a play. Thus, the five form letters will be generated from this data source.

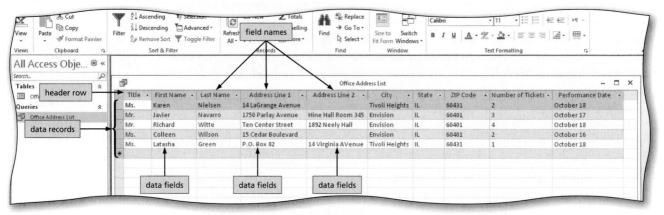

Figure 7–29

Each column in the data sources is called a **data field**. A data field represents a group of similar data. Each data field must be identified uniquely with a name, called a **field name**. For example, First Name is the name of the data field (column) that contains the first names of those who purchased tickets. In this project, the data source contains ten data fields with the following field names. Title, First Name, Last Name, Company Name, Address Line 1, Address Line 2, City, State, ZIP Code, and Number of Tickets.

In Publisher, data sources sometimes are called **recipient lists** or **address lists**. Publisher allows you to create as many data sources as you like, providing a customizable interface in which to enter the data.

How do you know what to include as a data source?

When you create a data source, you will need to determine the fields it should contain. That is, you will need to identify the data that will vary from one merged document to the next. Following are a few important points about fields:

- For each field, you may be required to create a field name. Because data sources often contain the same fields, some programs create a list of commonly used field names that you may use.

- Field names must be unique; that is, no two field names may be the same.

- Fields may be listed in any order in the data source. That is, the order of fields has no effect on the order in which they will print in the main document.

- Organize fields so that they are flexible. For example, break the name into separate fields: title, first name, and last name. This arrangement allows you to customize fields.

---

1 USE MASTER PAGE | 2 ADJUST GRAPHICS | 3 SPACING BETWEEN CHARACTERS | 4 SET TABS
5 USE MAIL MERGE WIZARD | 6 INSERT FIELD CODES | 7 CREATE TICKETS | 8 USE MAILINGS TAB

To Use the Mail Merge Wizard

A **wizard** is a tool that guides you through the steps of a process or task by asking a series of questions or presenting options. The following steps begin the process of creating a data source by using the Mail Merge Wizard. **Why?** *The Mail Merge Wizard displays a task pane with steps to create the data source and the form letter.*

- Tap or click MAILINGS on the ribbon to display the MAILINGS tab.

- Tap or click the Mail Merge arrow (MAILINGS tab | Start group) to display the list (Figure 7–30).

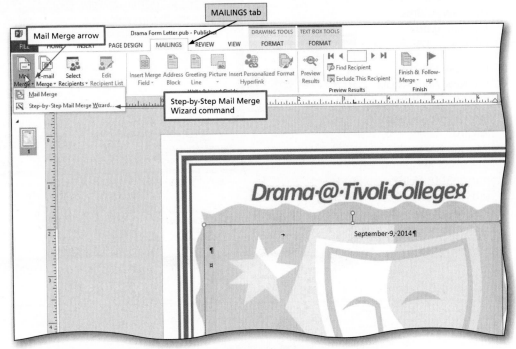

Figure 7–30

2

- Tap or click 'Step-by-Step Mail Merge Wizard' to display the Mail Merge task pane.

- Tap or click the 'Type a new list' option button (Mail Merge task pane) to select it (Figure 7–31).

Q&A Can I use other tabs and ribbon commands while the Mail Merge task pane is open?
Yes, the task pane will remain open in the workspace while you edit the form letter.

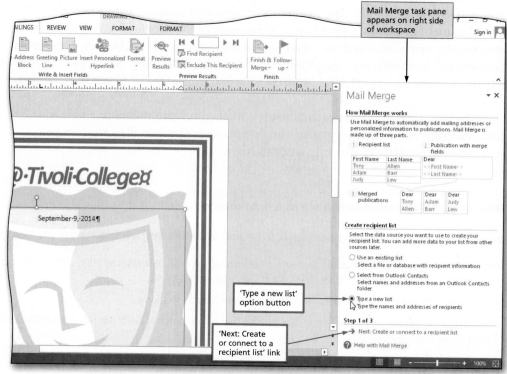

Figure 7–31

3

- Tap or click the 'Next: Create or connect to a recipient list' link at the bottom of the task pane to display the New Address List dialog box (Figure 7–32).

Q&A How can I display the New Address List dialog box without going through the wizard?
You can tap or click the Select Recipients button (MAILINGS tab | Start group), and then tap or click Type a New List.

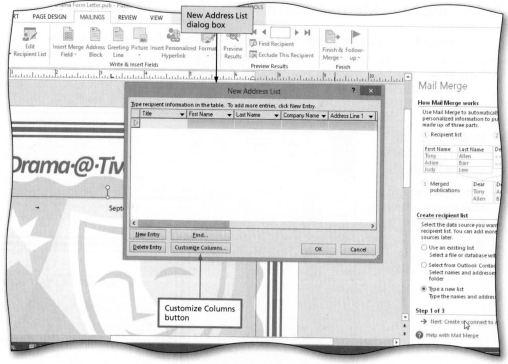

Figure 7–32

To Customize Data Source Columns

Publisher provides a list of 13 commonly used field names. This project uses 8 of the 13 field names supplied by Publisher: Title, First Name, Last Name, Address Line 1, Address Line 2, City, State, ZIP Code. This project does not use the other five field names supplied by Publisher: Company Name, Country or Region, Home Phone, Work Phone, and E-mail Address. Thus, you will delete those field names and create two new fields, Number of Tickets and Performance Date. *Why? As you create the letter, you will need to reference the number of tickets and performance date for each customer.*

The following steps customize the columns in the New Address List dialog box.

1

- With the New Address List dialog box displayed, tap or click the Customize Columns button (New Address List dialog box) to display the Customize Address List dialog box.

- Tap or click Company Name in the Field Names area to select it (Figure 7–33).

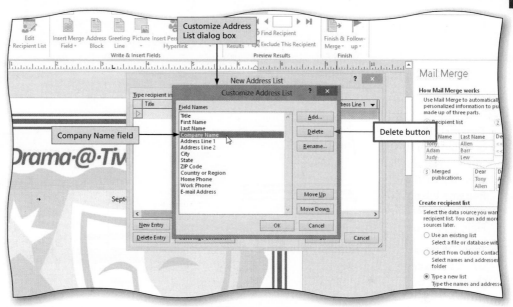

Figure 7–33

2

- Tap or click the Delete button (Customize Address List dialog box) to delete the field. When Publisher displays a dialog box asking if you are sure you want to delete the field, tap or click the Yes button (Microsoft Publisher dialog box) (Figure 7–34).

Q&A What other options do I have for customization? You can add a new column, rename a column to better describe its contents, or move columns up and down to place the fields in the desired order.

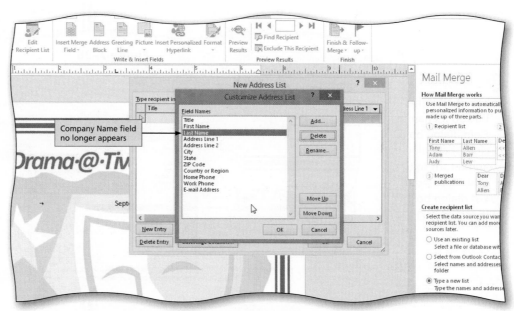

Figure 7–34

3

- Select, delete, and confirm the deletion of the Work Phone and E-mail Address fields (Figure 7–35).

Q&A Can I delete multiple columns at one time?

No, you must select them and delete them individually.

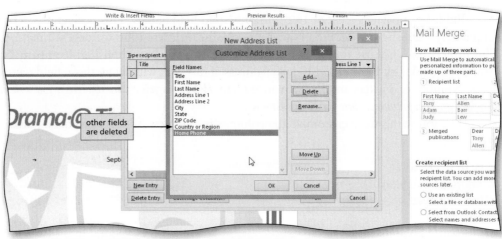

Figure 7–35

4

- Tap or click 'Country or Region' in the list of Field Names, and then tap or click the Rename button to display the Rename Field dialog box.

- Type **Number of Tickets** in the To text box (Figure 7–36).

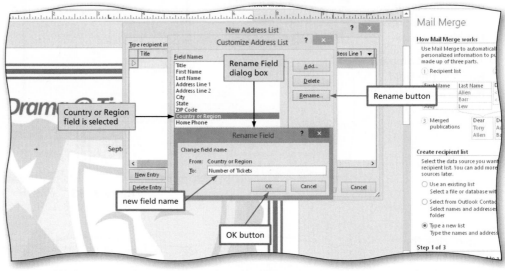

Figure 7–36

5

- Tap or click the OK button (Rename Field dialog box) to close the dialog box and return to the Customize Address List dialog box (Figure 7–37).

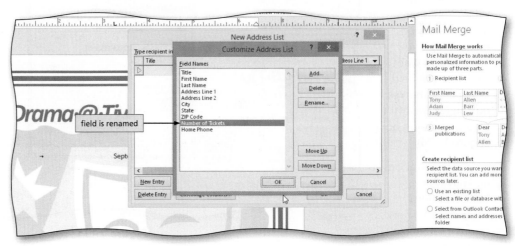

Figure 7–37

6

- Repeat Steps 4 and 5 to rename the Home Phone field to **Performance Date**.

- If the fields are not in the same order as shown in Figure 7–38, select a field and then tap or click the Move Up button or the Move Down button to correct the order.

 **Experiment**

Figure 7–38

- Experiment with moving the fields to different locations by selecting individual fields and then tapping or clicking the Move Up button or the Move Down button.

7

- Tap or click the OK button (Customize Address List dialog box) to close the dialog box and return to the New Address List dialog box.

- Scroll to the right to see the new fields (Figure 7–39).

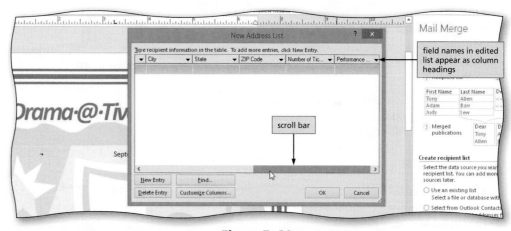

Figure 7–39

Entering Data in the Data Source

Table 7–6 displays the customer data for five people who bought tickets to the play.

Table 7–6 Customer Data									
Title	First Name	Last Name	Address1	Address2	City	State	ZIP Code	Number of Tickets	Performance Date
Ms.	Karen	Nielsen	14 LaGrange Avenue		Tivoli Heights	IL	60431	2	October 18
Mr.	Javier	Navarro	1750 Parlay Avenue	Hine Hall Room 345	Envision	IL	60401	3	October 17
Mr.	Richard	Witte	Ten Center Street	1492 Neely Hall	Envision	IL	60401	4	October 18
Ms.	Colleen	Wilson	15 Cedar Boulevard		Envision	IL	60401	2	October 16
Ms.	Latasha	Green	P.O. Box 82	14 Virginia Avenue	Tivoli Heights	IL	60431	1	October 18

© 2014 Cengage Learning

Notice that some customers have no Address Line 2. For those customers, you will leave that field blank. As you enter data, do not press the SPACEBAR at the end of the field. Extra spaces can interfere with the display of the merged fields.

To Enter Data in the Data Source File

The following steps enter the first record into the data source file, using the information from Table 7–6. You will use the tab key to move from field to field. **Why?** *As in a Publisher table, the tab key automatically moves to the next cell for data entry.*

1

- With the New Address List dialog box displayed, scroll as necessary to tap or click the box in the first row, below the Title heading.

- Type **Ms.** in the Title box, and then press the TAB key.

- Type **Karen** in the First Name box, and then press the TAB key.

- Type **Nielsen** in the Last Name box, and then press the TAB key (Figure 7–40).

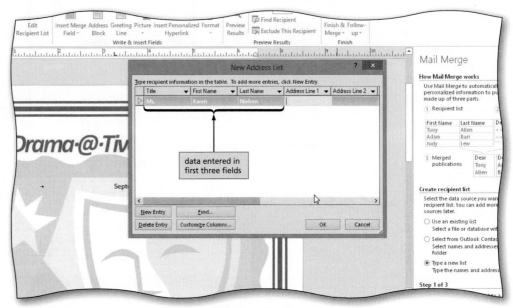

Figure 7–40

What if the data is wider than the entry field?
Publisher will allow up to 256 characters in each entry field and move the text to the left, out of sight, as you type. The text that is not displayed will be saved with the rest of the data.

2

- Continue to enter data from the first row in Table 7–6. Press the TAB key to advance to each new entry field. Press the TAB key twice to leave a field empty. Do not press the TAB key at the end of the row (Figure 7–41).

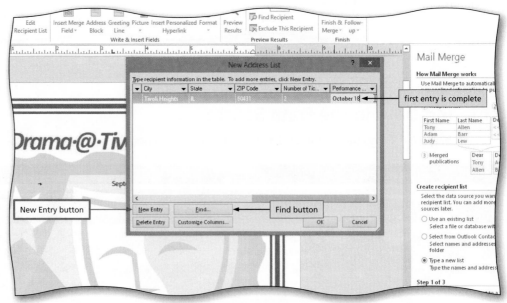

Figure 7–41

What does the Find button do?
When you tap or click the Find button, Publisher displays the Find Entry dialog box. In this dialog box, you can look for specific pieces of data that have been typed so far in the data source. The Find Entry dialog box lets you search the entire list or specific fields.

To Create New Entries in the Data Source

The next step creates new entries or rows in the data source. *Why? Each new record (or customer in this case) must be on a row by itself.*

- Tap or click the New Entry button (New Address List dialog box) to create a new row in the list, and then enter the data from the second row of Table 7–6.

- Continue to add data from Table 7–6, tapping or clicking the New Entry button (New Address List dialog box) after each row of information in the table is complete.
Press the TAB key to move from field to field. Press the TAB key twice to skip an empty field.

- When you complete the last entry, do not tap or click the New Entry button (New Address List dialog box) (Figure 7–42).

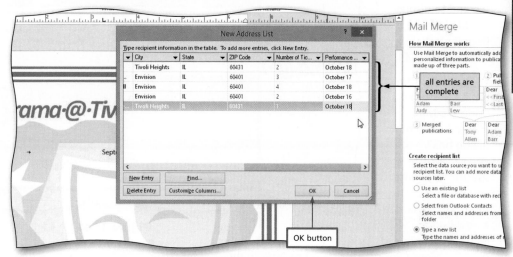

Figure 7–42

To Save the Data Source

The following steps save the data source file with the name Ticket Orders. *Why? You must save the data source in order to merge it with the form letter.* It is best to save the form letter and the data source in the same directory.

- Tap or click the OK button (New Address List dialog box) to display the Save Address List dialog box.

- Type **Ticket Orders** in the File name box. Do not press the ENTER key

- Navigate to the same save location in which you saved the Drama Form Letter file (Figure 7–43).

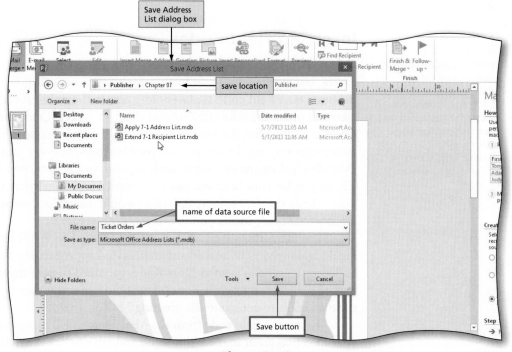

Figure 7–43

2

- Tap or click the Save button (Save Address List dialog box) to save the file and to display the Mail Merge Recipients dialog box (Figure 7–44).

Q&A What kinds of tasks can be performed using the Mail Merge Recipients dialog box?
You can select specific recipients, add new recipients, filter, sort, or create a new list. You will learn more about the Mail Merge Recipients dialog box later in the chapter.

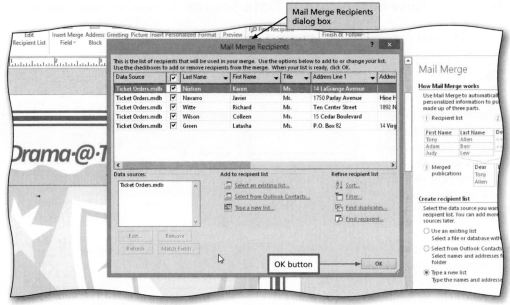

Figure 7–44

3

- Tap or click the OK button (Mail Merge Recipients dialog box) to close the dialog box.

What is included in the main document for the form letter?
A main document contains both the constant, or unchanging, text, as well as field codes for merged fields. Be sure the main document for the form letter includes all essential business letter elements. All business letters should contain a date line, inside address, message, and signature block. Many business letters contain additional items such as a special mailing notation(s), an attention line, a salutation, a subject line, a complimentary close, reference initials, and an enclosure notation. It should use proper grammar, correct spelling, logically constructed sentences, flowing paragraphs, and sound ideas. Be sure to proofread it carefully.

BTW
Empty Fields
If your data source contains empty or blank fields, Publisher will omit the field when the publication is merged. For instance, if no second address line exists, Publisher will move up the other fields during the print process in order to fill the gap.

Inserting Field Codes

A publication designed for merging not only must be connected to its data source, but also must contain form fields, sometimes called field codes, in the publication. A **field code** is placeholder text in the publication that shows Publisher where to insert the information from the data source. Once the publication is merged with the address list, the field codes are replaced by unique information. For example, a form letter may say, Thank you for your business, to every customer, but follow it with the individual customer's name, such as John. In this case, you would type the words, Thank you for your business, insert a comma, and then insert the field code, First Name, from the data source. Publisher would insert the customer's name so that the letter would read, Thank you for your business, John.

You can format, copy, move, or delete a field code just as you would regular text. Field codes need to be spaced and punctuated appropriately. For instance, if you want to display a greeting such as Dear Katie, you need to type the word, Dear, followed by a space before inserting the First Name field code. You then would type a comma after the field code, to complete the greeting.

To insert a field code from the Mail Merge task pane, you either can position your insertion point in the publication and tap or click the field code, or drag the field code from the task pane to the publication, dropping it at the appropriate location.

Publisher allows you to insert field codes from the address list into the main publication one field at a time or in predefined groups. For example, if you wanted to display the amount due from an address list, you would choose that one field from the task pane. To use predefined groups, you would use a **grouped field code**, which is a set of standard fields, such as typical address fields or salutation fields, preformatted and spaced with appropriate words and punctuation. For example, instead of entering the field codes for Title, First Name, Last Name, Company Name, Address Line 1, and so on, you can choose the grouped field, Address Block, that includes all the fields displayed correctly.

To Insert Grouped Field Codes

1 USE MASTER PAGE | 2 ADJUST GRAPHICS | 3 SPACING BETWEEN CHARACTERS | 4 SET TABS
5 USE MAIL MERGE WIZARD | 6 INSERT FIELD CODES | **7 CREATE TICKETS** | **8 USE MAILINGS TAB**

The following steps insert grouped field codes for the address block and greeting line in the form letter. *Why? The grouped field codes contain the correct fields, spaced and formatted appropriately.*

- Tap or click in the text box to ensure that the insertion point is positioned two lines below the date in the publication.

- Zoom to 130%.

- Tap or click the Address block link (Mail Merge task pane) to display the Insert Address Block dialog box.

- If necessary, tap or click each of the enabled check boxes so that they contain check marks.

- If necessary, tap or click the format, Mr. Joshua Randall Jr., in the 'Insert recipient's name in this format' list. If necessary, tap or click the Previous button in the Preview area until the first recipient in your data source is displayed (Figure 7–45).

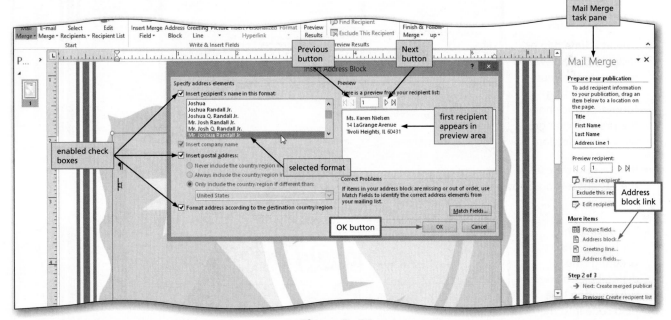

Figure 7–45

Q&A What is the difference between an Address block and Address fields?

The Address block link will include fields in the current data source. If you choose Address fields, Publisher displays a list of typical address fields that could be matched with different data sources. That way, if you choose to send a form letter to two different address lists, Publisher will try to match the fields consistently. For example, one address source might include a middle initial or company name, while another one might not.

Experiment

- One at a time, tap or click the formats in the 'Insert recipient's name in this format' list. View the changes in the preview. Tap or click the Next button to view other entries from the address list.

2

- Tap or click the OK button to insert the address block into the form letter.

- Tap or click at the end of the inserted address block to reveal the field code (Figure 7–46).

What do the chevron symbols represent? Each field code displays chevrons to let you know that it is not actual text.

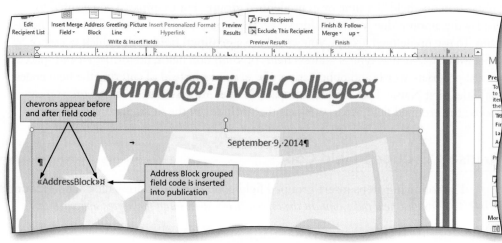

Figure 7–46

3

- Press the ENTER key twice, and then tap or click the Greeting line link (Mail Merge task pane) to display the Insert Greeting Line dialog box.

🔍 **Experiment**

- One at a time, tap or click the box arrows to view the various kinds of greeting formats. Notice how the preview changes with each selection.

- If necessary, choose the various settings shown in Figure 7–47.

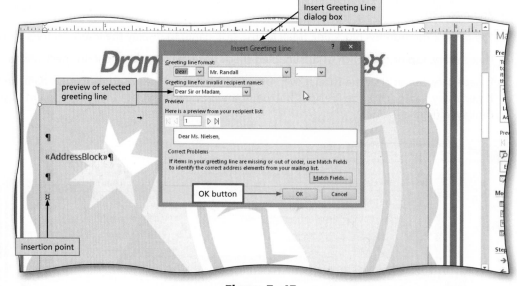

Figure 7–47

4

- Tap or click the OK button (Insert Greeting Line dialog box) to insert the Greeting Line field code into the publication.

- Tap or click after the Greeting Line field code, and then press the ENTER key twice to move the insertion point in the publication (Figure 7–48).

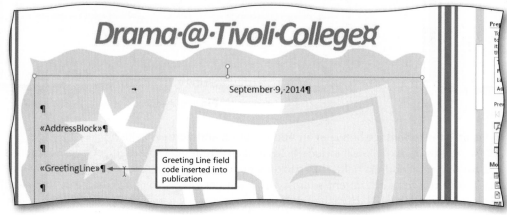

Figure 7–48

Other Ways

1. Tap or click Address Block or Greeting Line button (MAILINGS tab | Write & Insert Fields group), select format, tap or click OK button

To Insert Individual Field Codes

The following steps insert individual field codes as you type the body of the form letter. *Why? Using individualized data in the body of the letter helps personalize the form letter.* You will finish the merge process later in this chapter.

1

- Zoom to 100%.

- With the insertion point positioned two lines below the greeting line, type **Thank you for ordering tickets for Tivoli College's production of As You Like It on** and then press the SPACEBAR key.

- Select the words **As You Like It** and then press CTRL+I to italicize the name of the play.

- Position the insertion point at the end of the line (Figure 7–49).

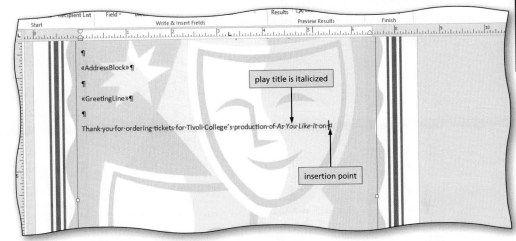

Figure 7–49

2

- In the task pane, scroll in the list of recipient information to display the Performance Date field code.

- Tap or click Performance Date to insert the field code into the publication.

- Type **, 2014.** to complete the sentence.

- Press the SPACEBAR key to insert a space (Figure 7–50).

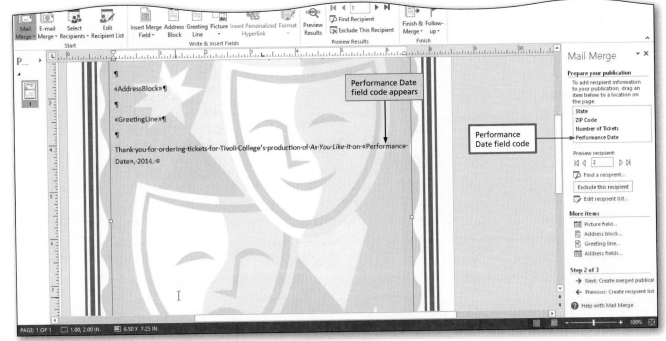

Figure 7–50

③

- Type **Enclosed are your** and then press the SPACEBAR key again.
- In the Mail Merge task pane, tap or click 'Number of Tickets' to enter the field code, press the SPACEBAR key, and then type **tickets.** to complete the sentence.
- Press the SPACEBAR key and then type **Your seating is the best available at your time of purchase.** to complete the sentence.
- Press the ENTER key twice to insert a blank line (Figure 7–51).

Q&A Why did my line wrap differently?
Subtle differences in the width of the text box can create a big difference in where wordwrap occurs. Your line may wrap at a different location.

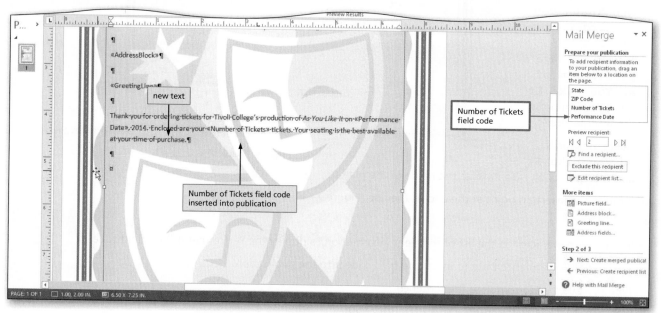

Figure 7–51

④

- Type **Enjoy the play!** and then press the ENTER key twice.

- Type **Sincerely,** and then press the ENTER key twice.

- Type **Drama Ticket Desk** and then press the ENTER key twice.

  If directed by your instructor to do so, enter your name instead of Drama Ticket Desk.

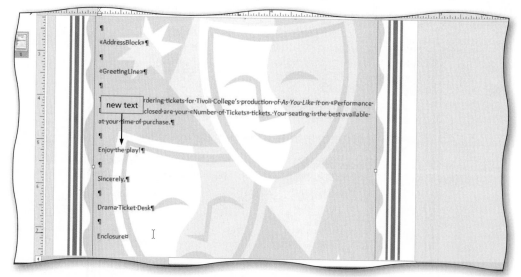

Figure 7–52

- Type **Enclosure** to finish the letter.

- Zoom and scroll as necessary to display all of the field codes (Figure 7–52).

Other Ways

1. Drag field from Mail Merge task pane into publication

2. Tap or click 'Insert Merge Field' button (MAILINGS tab | Write & Insert Fields group), tap or click field

How do you merge the data source to create the form letters?

Merging is the process of combining the contents of a data source with a main document. You can print the merged letters on the printer or place them in a new document, which you later can edit. You also have the options of merging all data in a data source or merging just a portion of it from a filter or sort.

---

1 USE MASTER PAGE | 2 ADJUST GRAPHICS | 3 SPACING BETWEEN CHARACTERS | 4 SET TABS
5 USE MAIL MERGE WIZARD | 6 INSERT FIELD CODES | **7 CREATE TICKETS** | 8 USE MAILINGS TAB

To Create the Merged Publication

The following step creates the merged publication. ***Why?*** *You need to create an individualized letter to each recipient.*

- Tap or click the 'Next: Create merged publications' link at the bottom of the Mail Merge task pane (Figure 7–53).

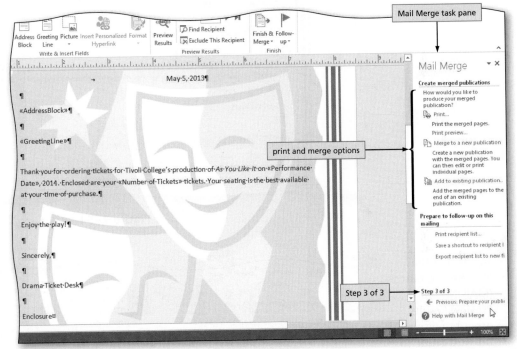

Figure 7–53

Managing Merged Publications

You have several choices in previewing, saving, printing, and exporting merged publications. Table 7–7 describes the merged publication options.

Table 7–7 Merged Publication Options

Option	Description
Print	Print all pages with merged data, one at a time.
Print Preview	Preview each page of the merged pages.
Merge to a new publication	Create a new publication with the merged pages, which you can edit further or print.
Add to existing publication	Add the merged pages to the end of the existing publication.
Print recipient list	Create a hard copy of the recipient list of the current merge for your records, including filters or sorts.
Save a shortcut to recipient list	Create a shortcut to the address list used in the current merge.
Export recipient list to new file	Create a new file based on the filtered or sorted address list used in the current merge.
Preview Results group on MAILINGS tab	Traverse each page of the merged pages. Find and exclude data.

To Preview the Form Letters

The following steps preview the form letters. ***Why?*** *It is always a good idea to preview the result of the merge before printing the letters.*

1

- Tap or click the Preview Results button (MAILINGS tab | Preview Results group) to display the first record (Figure 7–54).

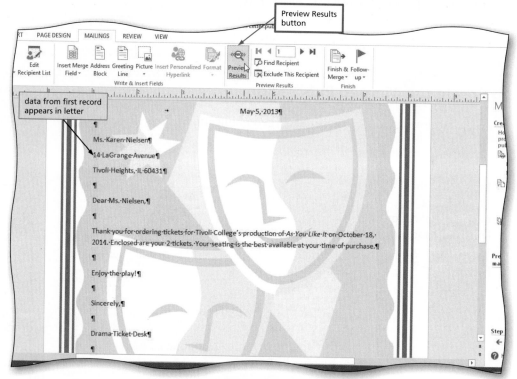

Figure 7–54

2

- Tap or click the Next Record button (MAILINGS tab | Preview Results group) to display the next letter (Figure 7–55).

 Experiment

- Tap or click the Next Record and Previous Record buttons to move through the various merged letters.

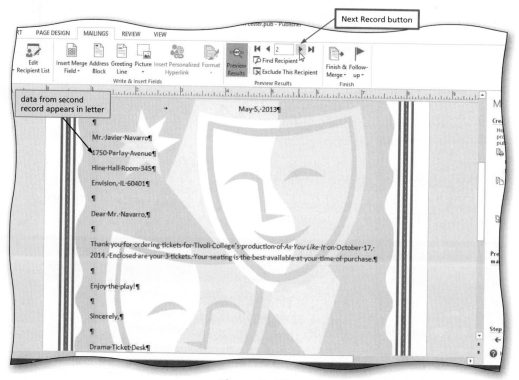

Figure 7–55

Other Ways

1. Tap or click Print preview link (Mail Merge task pane, Step 3 of 3), tap or click the Next Sheet button

TO PRINT MERGED PAGES

If you wanted to print the merged publication, you would perform the following steps.

1. Ready the printer. Tap or click the Print link (Mail Merge task pane).
2. When Publisher displays the Backstage view, verify the printer name that appears on the Printer Status button will print a hard copy of the publication. If necessary, tap or click the Printer Status button to display a list of available printer options, and then tap or click the desired printer to change the currently selected printer.
3. Tap or click the Print button to print the merged pages.
4. Retrieve the printouts.

To Close the Mail Merge Task Pane

The following step closes the Mail Merge task pane.

1 Tap or click the Close button on the Mail Merge task pane title bar to close the task pane.

To Save Again

The publication is complete. The following step saves the document again.

1 Tap or click the Save button on the Quick Access Toolbar to overwrite the previously saved file.

To Close the Publication

The next step closes the publication without quitting Publisher.

1 Display the Backstage view and then tap or click the Close command to close the publication without exiting Publisher.

BTW
Conserving Ink and Toner
If you want to conserve ink or toner, you can instruct Publisher to print draft quality documents by tapping or clicking FILE on the ribbon to open the Backstage view, and then tapping or clicking Print in the Backstage view to display the Print gallery. Tap or click the Printer Properties link, and then, depending on your printer, click the Print Quality button and choose Draft in the list. Close the Printer Properties dialog box and then tap or click the Print button as usual.

Break Point: If you wish to take a break, this is a good place to do so. Exit Publisher. To resume at a later time, run Publisher and continue following the steps from this location forward.

TO OPEN A FILE WITH A CONNECTED DATA SOURCE

When you open a file with a connected data source, Publisher may ask you to reconnect to the database, especially if the form file or the data source file has been moved. If you need to reconnect, you would perform the following steps.

1. Run Publisher and open a form file.
2. If Publisher displays a Microsoft Publisher dialog box reminding you of the data connection, tap or click the Yes button.
3. If Publisher cannot find the connection, Publisher will display a second dialog box, asking if you would like to work without the connection or try to reconnect. Tap or click the 'Try to reconnect to the data source' option button (Microsoft Publisher dialog box), and then tap or click the Continue button.
4. Publisher will display a Select Data Source dialog box. Navigate to the location of your data source. Double-tap or double-click the data source file to connect the database.
5. If Publisher displays a Select Table dialog box, select the appropriate table, and then tap or click the OK button to merge the data source with the form letter.

BTW
Quick Reference
For a table that lists how to complete the tasks covered in this book using touch gestures, the mouse, ribbon, shortcut menu, and keyboard, see the Quick Reference Summary at the back of this book, or visit the Quick Reference resource on the Student Companion Site located on www.cengagebrain.com. For detailed instructions about accessing available resources, visit www.cengage.com/ct/ studentdownload or see the inside back cover of this book.

Creating Tickets

A **ticket** is a paper document or voucher that proves a person has paid for admission or is entitled to a service. Tickets come in all sizes and are used for events, establishments, raffles, exchanges, or even as proof of receipt. Tickets may be numbered and may identify certain seating, dates, times, and charges. Tickets sometimes have a tear-off or ticket stub that is detached once the service is rendered.

The people who purchased tickets will receive the tickets along with the form letter. The theater venue has a database of rows and seat numbers that you will merge with the ticket publication to produce a ticket for each seat in the theater, which is stored in a Microsoft Excel worksheet. This time, you will merge and insert field codes manually rather than through the wizard.

To Copy the Data Source File

Publisher recommends that the publication and its data source reside in the same folder location; therefore, the following steps copy the Microsoft Excel worksheet file from the Data Files for Students to your save location. To complete these steps, you will be required to use the Data Files for Students. Visit www.cengage.com/ct/studentdownload for detailed instructions or contact your instructor for information about accessing the required files. If you already have downloaded the Data Files for Students to the same location that you are using to create files in this chapter, you can skip these steps.

1 Tap or click the File Explorer App button on the Windows taskbar to open a File Explorer window.

2 Navigate to the location of the Data Files for Students.

3 In the Chapter 07 folder, press and hold or right-click the 'Ticket Number and Seating List' file to display its shortcut menu, and then tap or click Copy on the shortcut menu to copy the file.

4 Navigate to the location in which you saved the downloaded template.

5 Press and hold or right-click a blank part of the right pane in the folder to display the folder's shortcut menu, and then tap or click Paste on the shortcut menu to paste the file.

6 Close the File Explorer window.

To Open the Drama Ticket File

The following steps open the Drama Ticket file from the Data Files for Students. Visit www.cengage.com/ct/studentdownload for detailed instructions or contact your instructor for information about accessing the required files.

1 In the Publisher window, tap or click Open in the Backstage view to display the Open gallery.

2 Navigate to the location of the file to be opened in the Data Files for Students (in this case, the Chapter 07 folder in the Publisher folder).

3 Double-tap or double-click Drama Ticket to open the selected file and display the opened publication in the Publisher window. If necessary, zoom to whole page.

4 If necessary save the file in the same location as the 'Ticket Number and Seating List' file (Figure 7–56).

BTW
Touch Screen Differences
The Office and Windows interfaces may vary if you are using a touch screen. For this reason, you might notice that the function or appearance of your touch screen differs slightly from this chapter's presentation.

BTW
Distributing a Document
Instead of printing and distributing a hard copy of a document, you can distribute the document electronically. Options include sending the document via email; posting it on cloud storage (such as SkyDrive) and sharing the file with others; posting it on a social networking site, blog, or other website; and sharing a link associated with an online location of the document. You also can create and share a PDF or XPS image of the document, so that users can view the file in Acrobat Reader or XPS Viewer instead of in Publisher.

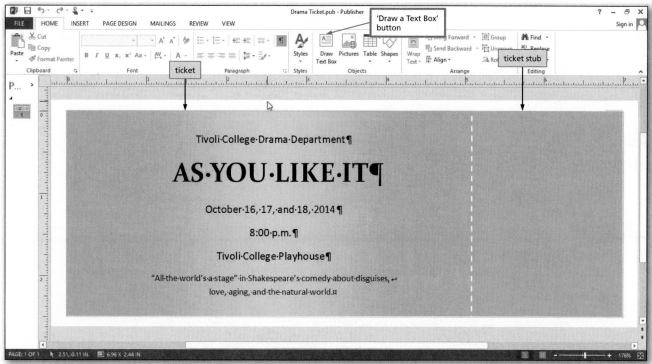

Figure 7–56

To Change the Text Direction

The following steps create a text box and change the text direction so the ticket stub reads the bottom of the stub to the top of the stub. *Why? It is common for tickets stubs to be printed sideways on the ticket for easy tear-off and reading by those who seat the attendees.*

1

- Tap or click the 'Draw a Text Box' button (HOME tab | Objects group), and then drag to draw a text box that fills the area to the side of the dotted line (Figure 7–57).

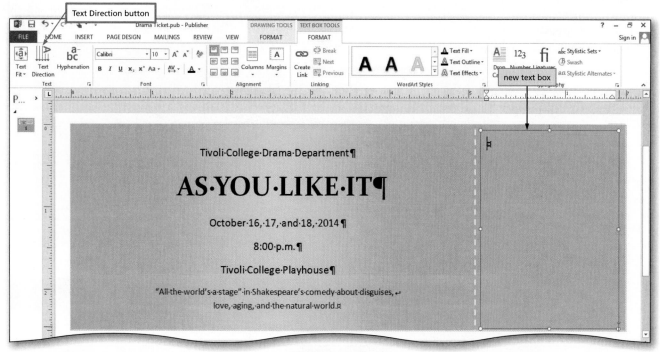

Figure 7–57

2

- Tap or click the Text Direction button (TEXT BOX TOOLS FORMAT tab | Text group), to change the direction of the text (Figure 7–58).

Q&A Which direction did Publisher rotate the text?
The text box rotated 90-degrees clockwise.

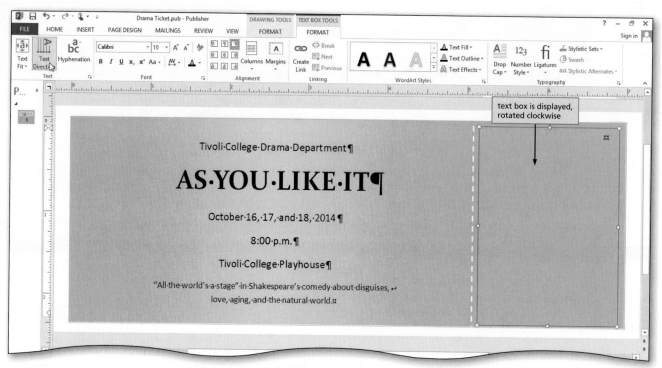

Figure 7–58

3

- Drag the rotation handle of the text box straight down to invert the box 180-degrees (Figure 7–59).

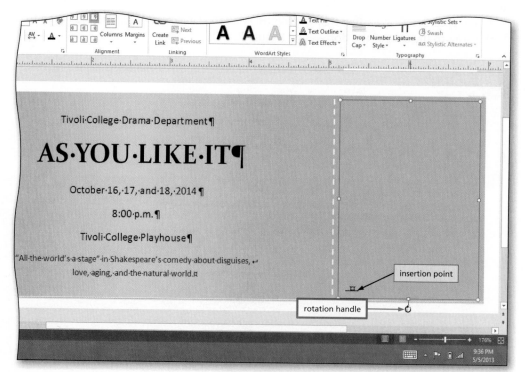

Figure 7–59

To Edit the Ticket Stub Further

The following steps edit the description area of the ticket.

1 With the insertion point in the ticket stub text box, change the font to size 18 pt, and then press CTRL+E to center the text.

2 Type **AS YOU LIKE IT** and then press the ENTER key to enter the first line of the ticket stub.

3 Press the ENTER key to start a new line, and then change the font size to 12 pt (Figure 7–60).

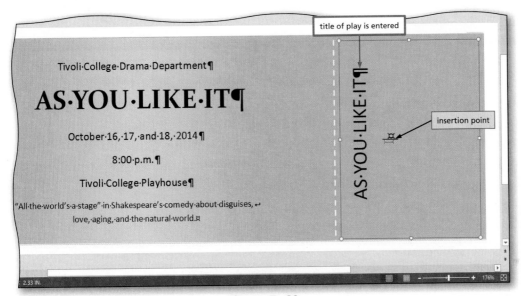

Figure 7–60

The MAILINGS Tab

The MAILINGS tab (Figure 7–61) contains buttons and boxes to help you merge publications and data sources manually rather than through the wizard. The Start group connects you with your data source and provides access to creating, editing, and filtering lists. The Write & Insert Fields group allows you to place field codes in your publication. Using the Preview Results group, you can preview the merged publication in the publication window rather than in the Print gallery. Finally, the Finish group provides access to the same merge management tasks that are contained in the Mail Merge task pane.

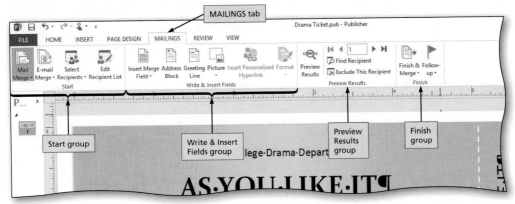

Figure 7–61

To Select Recipients

The following steps select recipients from the Microsoft Excel worksheet that you copied to your save location earlier. *Why? The file contains the ticket numbers, seats, and rows for the play.*

- If necessary, tap or click MAILINGS on the ribbon to display the MAILINGS tab.

- Tap or click the Select Recipients button (MAILINGS tab | Start group) to display its list (Figure 7–62).

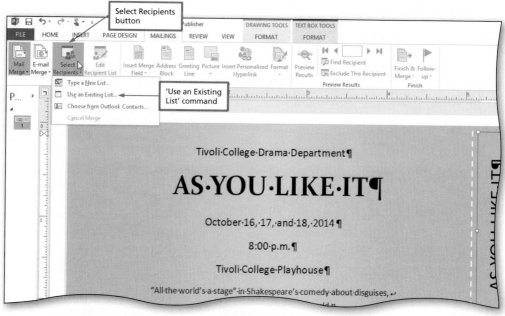

Figure 7–62

- Tap or click 'Use an Existing List' to open the Select Data Source Dialog box.

- Navigate to the location of the file to be opened (in this case, the Chapter 07 folder in the Publisher folder) (Figure 7–63).

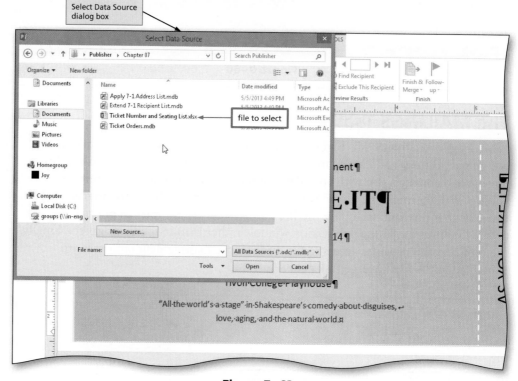

Figure 7–63

- Double-tap or double-click 'Ticket Number and Seating List' to open the Select Table dialog box.

- If necessary, tap or click the appropriate table in the list (in this case, 'As You Like It$').

- If necessary, tap or click to display a check mark in the 'First row of data contains column headers' check box (Figure 7–64).

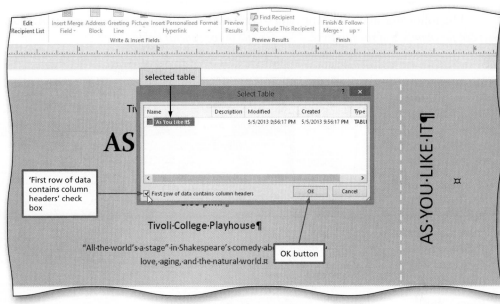

Figure 7–64

What if my Microsoft Excel worksheet contains multiple tables?
The Select Table dialog box allows you to choose different sheets in the Excel file, should they contain any data.

- Tap or click the OK button (Select Table dialog box) to select the table and display the Mail Merge Recipients dialog box (Figure 7–65).

What does the Data sources box do?
When you select the database in the data sources box, the buttons below the box become enabled. You then can edit, remove, refresh or match fields in the database.

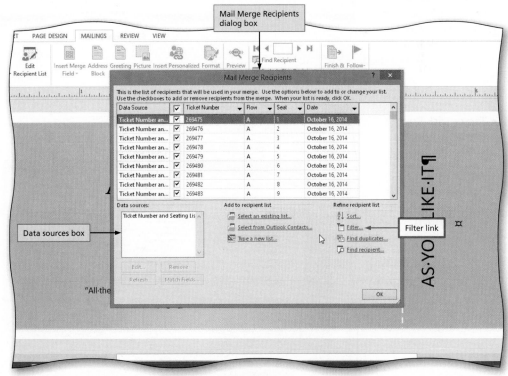

Figure 7–65

To Filter Data

The following steps filter the data so that no tickets will be issued for row A. **Why?** *Row A tickets are reserved for members of the faculty and not for sale to the general public.*

1

- Tap or click the Filter link (Mail Merge Recipients dialog box) to display the Filter and Sort dialog box.

- If necessary, tap or click the Filter Records tab and then tap or click the Field arrow to display its list (Figure 7–66).

Q&A

What is the difference between filter and sort?
Filtering examines all records, and displays only those that meet specific criteria that you specify. Sorting merely rearranges the records in a specific order, but displays them all.

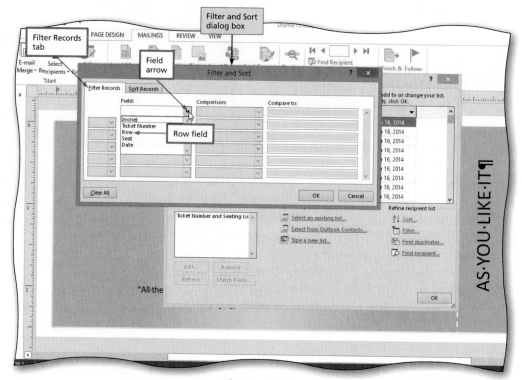

Figure 7–66

2

- Tap or click Row in the list to filter by row.

- Tap or click the Comparison arrow to display its list (Figure 7–67).

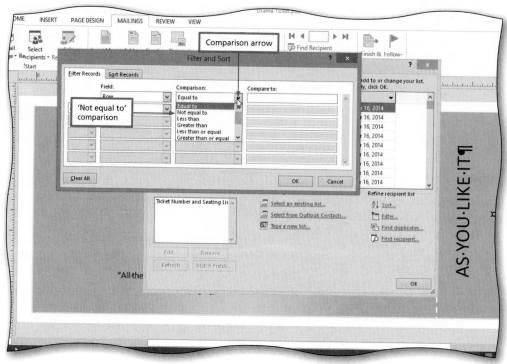

Figure 7–67

3

- Tap or click 'Not equal to' in the Comparison list to filter rows that are not equal to A.

- Press the TAB key to advance to the Compare to box, and then type **A** to insert the Compare to value (Figure 7–68).

Q&A Will the filter delete all the tickets in row A?
No. It changes only which tickets will be used in the merge. The filter and sort links do not change your data source or mail merge permanently.

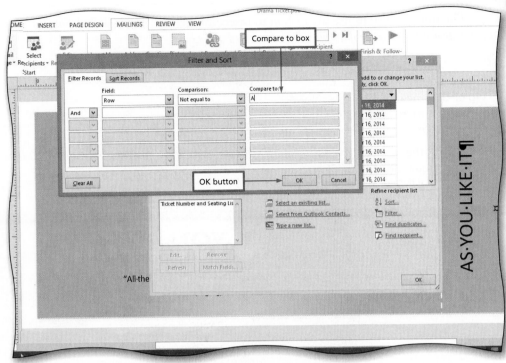

Figure 7–68

4

- Tap or click the OK button (Filter and Sort dialog box) to accept the filter and return to the Mail Merge Recipients dialog box (Figure 7–69).

Q&A How did the recipient list change?
Compare Figure 7–65 to Figure 7–69. Notice the ticket rows now start with row B. Row A has been filtered out.

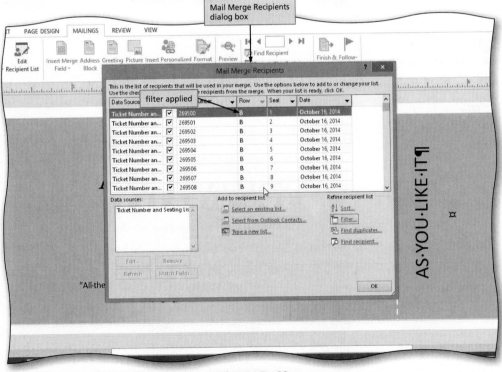

Figure 7–69

5

- Tap or click the OK button (Mail Merge Recipients dialog box) to close the dialog box.

To Insert Merge Field Codes

The following steps use the ribbon to insert merge field codes. **Why?** *Sometimes using the MAILINGS tab on the ribbon is easier if the data file has been created already.*

1
- In the publication, tap or click the blank line in the ticket stub text box.
- Tap or click the 'Insert Merge Field' button (MAILINGS tab | Write & Insert Fields group) to display the list of fields (Figure 7–70).

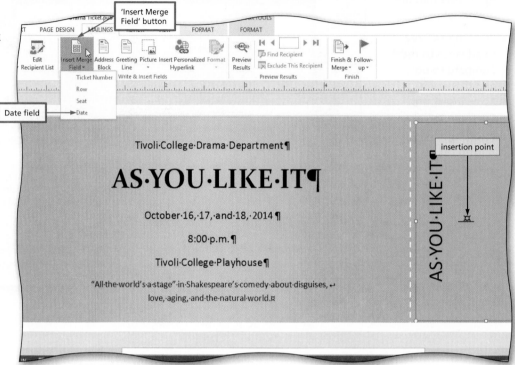

Figure 7–70

2
- Tap or click Date in the list to insert the field code (Figure 7–71).

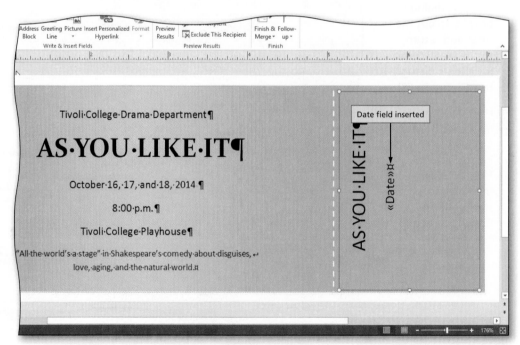

Figure 7–71

3

- Press the ENTER key to move to the next line, and then type **8:00 p.m.**
- Press the ENTER key again, type **Row:,** and press the SPACEBAR key to begin the next line.
- Repeat Steps 1 and 2 to insert the field code for Row.
- Press the SPACEBAR key, type **Seat:,** press the SPACEBAR key, and then enter the field code for Seat (Figure 7–72).

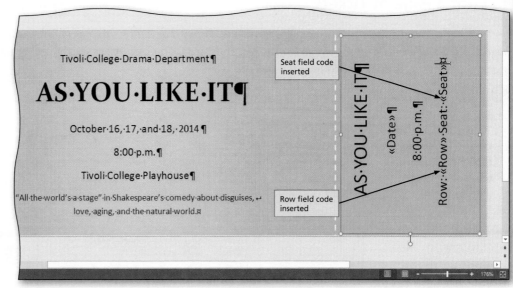

Figure 7–72

How do I format the data in the field codes?

You can format field codes in the same way you format text in other parts of your publication. If the field is an Address Block or Greeting Line, you can edit the text using the Format button (MAILINGS tab | Write & Insert Fields group).

Other Ways

1. Tap or click 'Insert Merge Field' button (MAILINGS tab | Write & Insert Fields group), tap or click desired field

To Preview Results

The following step uses the ribbon to preview the merged publication in the Publisher workspace.

1 Tap or click the Preview Results button (MAILINGS tab | Preview Results group) to display the data in the publication, rather than the field codes (Figure 7–73).

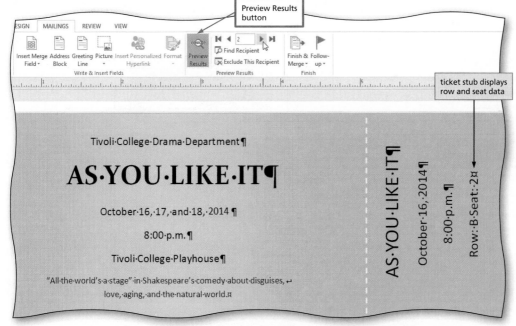

Figure 7–73

To Print a Page of Tickets

The following steps print one page of tickets. *Why? The data source has many numbered tickets. Printing one page as a test will ensure that the merge has worked.* If desired, you can insert special ticket paper or a heavy card stock paper in the printer to produce the tickets.

1

- Tap or click the 'Finish & Merge' button (MAILINGS tab | Finish group) to display its list (Figure 7–74).

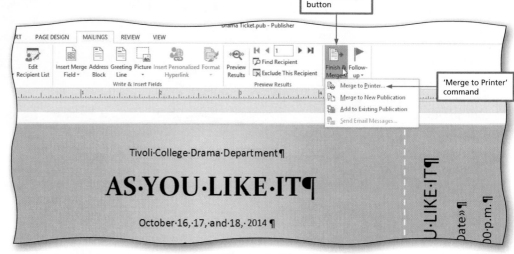

Figure 7–74

2

- Tap or click 'Merge to Printer' to open the Print gallery in the Backstage view.

- Verify the printer name that appears on the Printer Status button will print a hard copy of the publication. If necessary, tap or click the Printer Status button to display a list of available printer options, and then tap or click the desired printer to change the currently selected printer.

- In the Settings area, tap or click the 'Print All Records' button to display its list (Figure 7–75).

Q&A Why do all of the tickets display the same number?
The 'Merge to Printer' command creates one record per page. You will change that setting in the next step.

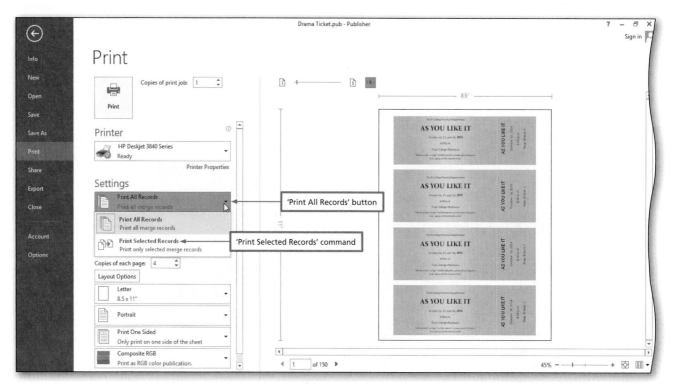

Figure 7–75

3

- Tap or click 'Print Selected Records' to specify which tickets to print.
- Tap or click the Records text box, and then type 1-4 to print the first four tickets (Figure 7–76).

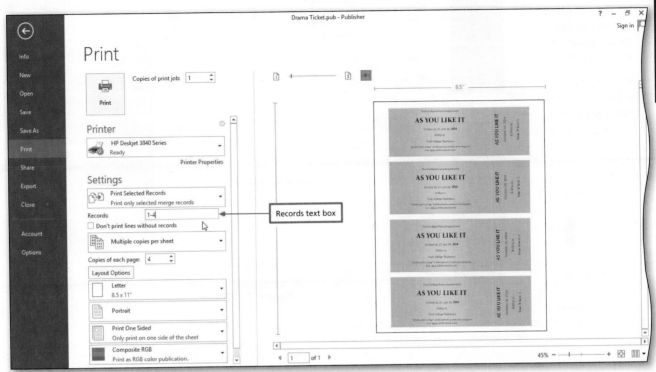

Figure 7–76

- Tap or click the 'Multiple copies per sheet' button to display its list (Figure 7–77).

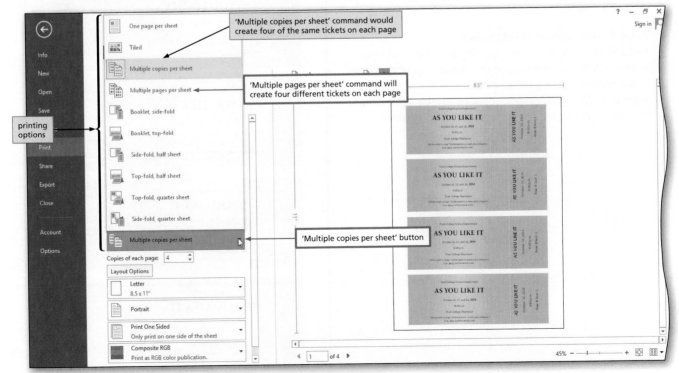

Figure 7–77

4

- Tap or click 'Multiple pages per sheet' to choose the option.

- Verify that other settings match those shown in Figure 7–78.

Q&A

What is the difference between 'Multiple copies per sheet' and 'Multiple pages per sheet'? When you print more than one copy per page, the 'Multiple copies per sheet' command repeats the record data on all the copies on your printed page. The 'Multiple pages per sheet' command does not repeat the data; each ticket on the printed page has a different row, seat, and ticket number.

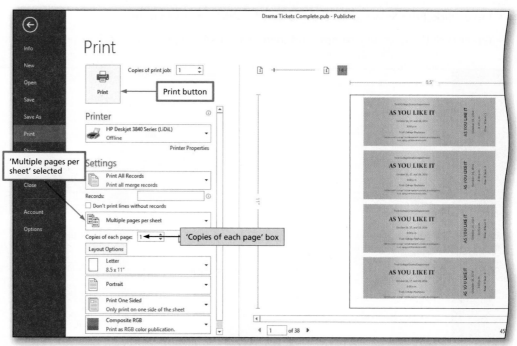

Figure 7–78

5

- Tap or click the Print button in the Print gallery to print the publication on the currently selected printer.

- When the printer stops, retrieve the hard copy (Figure 7–79).

Q&A

What if I have special ticket paper? You will need to determine the size and shape of the tickets and the dimensions of the paper. Tap or click the Letter button (Print gallery) and choose the appropriate page size. When using special paper, print a draft sample on regular paper before printing your entire database.

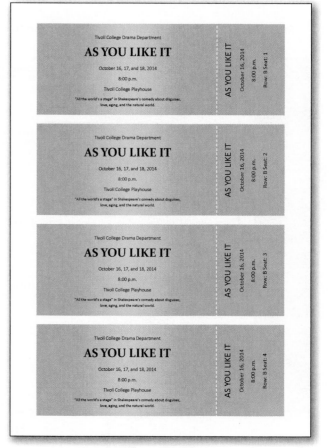

Figure 7–79

To Save the Publication with a New File Name

The tickets are complete. You should save the file with a new file name.

1 Save the file on your storage location with the name **Drama Tickets Complete**. Save the file in the same folder as the data source.

To Exit Publisher

This project is complete. The following steps exit Publisher.

1 To exit Publisher, tap or click the Close button on the right side of the title bar.

2 If a Microsoft Publisher dialog box is displayed, tap or click the Don't Save button so that any editing changes you have made are not saved.

Chapter Summary

In this chapter, you have learned how to merge data files with publications. First, you created a form letter with a watermark and special character and tab formatting in the letterhead. Then, you created a Publisher data source, customizing the fields. Next, you merged the form letter with the data source, inserting field codes. Finally, you created a ticket and used a Microsoft Excel data file to merge fields manually using the ribbon. You printed one page of tickets. The items listed below include all the new Publisher skills you have learned in this chapter.

Editing Graphics
Compress the Picture (PUB 387)
Edit the Brightness and Contrast (PUB 386)
Recolor the Picture (PUB 385)

Editing Master Pages
Close the Master Page (PUB 388)
View the Master Page (PUB 382)

Printing
Print Merged Pages (PUB 415)
Print a Page of Tickets (PUB 426)

Tabbing
Change the Text Direction (PUB 417)
Enter Tabbed Text (PUB 398)
Set a Tab Stop (PUB 397)

Tracking and Kerning
Kern Character Pairs (PUB 392)
Track Characters (PUB 391)

Using Mail Merge
Create the Merged Publication (PUB 413)
Create New Entries in the Data
Source (PUB 407)
Customize Data Source Columns (PUB 403)
Enter Data in the Data Source File (PUB 406)
Filter Data (PUB 422)
Insert Grouped Field Codes (PUB 409)
Insert Individual Field Codes (PUB 411)
Insert Merge Field Codes (PUB 424)
Preview the Form Letters (PUB 414)
Open a File with a Connected Data
Source (PUB 415)
Save the Data Source (PUB 407)
Select Recipients (PUB 420)
Use the Mail Merge Wizard (PUB 401)

CONSIDER THIS

What decisions will you need to make when creating your next business publication?
Use these guidelines as you complete the assignments in this chapter and create your own publications outside of this class.

1. Use a master page to place repeating objects.

2. Create a watermark.

    a) Use recoloring, brightness, and contrast techniques to fade necessary graphics while retaining detail.

3. To make text easier to read, use character spacing, tracking, and kerning techniques.

4. Set necessary tab stops.

    a) Use leader tabs to fill tabbed areas, if necessary.

    b) Use decimal tabs for dollars and cents.

5. Determine the data source.

    a) Use Access, Excel, or other files as data sources

    b) Create necessary data sources

    c) Set publication properties.

6. Create the form letter.

    a) Use field codes and grouped field codes to insert changing parts of the letter.

    b) Filter and sort the data as necessary.

7. Merge the form letter and the data source.

    a) Proofread and check a merged copy of the publication.

CONSIDER THIS

How should you submit solutions to questions in the assignments identified with a **symbol?**
Every assignment in this book contains one or more questions identified with a ✸ symbol. These questions require you to think beyond the assigned publication. Present your solutions to the questions in the format required by your instructor. Possible formats may include one or more of these options: write the answer; create a document that contains the answer; present your answer to the class; discuss your answer in a group; record the answer as audio or video using a webcam, smartphone, or portable media player; or post answers on a blog, wiki, or website.

Apply Your Knowledge

Reinforce the skills and apply the concepts you learned in this chapter.

Creating Merged Invoices

Note: To complete this assignment, you will be required to use the Data Files for Students. Visit www.cengage.com/ct/studentdownload for detailed instructions or contact your instructor for information about accessing the required files.

Instructions: Start Publisher. If necessary, copy the data source file, Apply 7-1 Address List, from the Data Files for Students to your storage location and appropriate folder. See page PUB 416 for instructions on copying and pasting the file from one folder to another. The data will be merged with an invoice to produce billing information for a fitness club. You are to kern characters, set tabs, edit the address list, and then merge and print. The first merged invoice is shown in Figure 7–80.

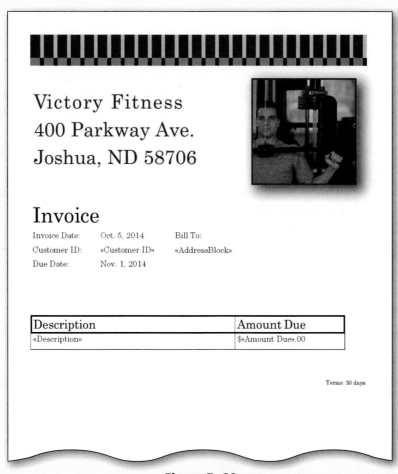

Figure 7–80

Perform the following tasks:

1. Open the publication, Apply 7-1 Victory Fitness Invoice from the Data Files for Students. Save the publication on your storage device, in the same folder as the Apply 7-1 Address list, with the new name Apply 7-1 Victory Fitness Invoice Complete.

2. Drag to select the letters Vi in the company name. Press the F9 key to zoom to 100%. Tap or click the Object Size button on the Publisher status bar to display the Measurement toolbar. In the Kerning box, type -3 to move the two letters closer together. Close the Measurement toolbar.

3. Tap or click the text box for Invoice Date, Customer ID, and Due Date. Press CTRL+A to select all of the text. Tap or click the 1.5" mark on the horizontal ruler to set a left tab. In the text box, tap or click after the words, Invoice Date:, and then press the TAB key. Type Oct. 5, 2014 at the tab stop to enter the Invoice Date. Repeat the process for the Due Date and type Nov. 1, 2014 at the tab stop.

4. Display the MAILINGS tab. Tap or click the Mail Merge arrow (MAILINGS tab | Start group), and then tap or click 'Step-by-Step Mail Merge Wizard'.

5. In the Mail Merge task pane, if necessary, tap or click the 'Use an existing list' option button and then tap or click the 'Next: Create or connect to a recipient list' link. When Publisher displays the Select Data Source dialog box, navigate to your storage device and then double-tap or double-click the file, Apply 7-1 Address List.

6. In the Mail Merge Recipients dialog box, select the file name, Apply 7-1 Address List.mdb, in the Data sources box and then tap or click the Edit button (Mail Merge Recipients dialog box) to display the Edit Data Source dialog box.

Continued >

Apply Your Knowledge *continued*

7. Tap or click the New Entry button (Edit Data Source dialog box), and enter your name and address as new data. Create a fictitious description and dollar amount. Tap or click the OK button. When Publisher asks if you want to update and save the list, tap or click the Yes button. When the Mail Merge Recipients dialog box again is displayed, tap or click the OK button.

8. In the publication, select the three lines of placeholder text in the Bill To text box. In the Mail Merge task pane, tap or click the Address block link, and choose an appropriate address style in the Insert Address Block dialog box. Tap or click the OK button (Insert Address Block dialog box) to close the dialog box.

9. In the publication, in the Invoice information text box, tap or click to the right of the words, Customer ID. Press the TAB key to move the insertion point to the tab stop. Insert the Customer ID field from the Mail Merge task pane.

10. Tap or click in the table cell below the word, Description. Insert the Description field from the Mail Merge task pane.

11. Tap or click the table cell below the words, Amount Due. Type $ to begin the entry. Insert the Amount Due field from the Mail Merge task pane. Type .00 to finish the entry.

12. Save the publication again, using the same file name, on your storage device.

13. If you wish to print hard copies of the merged publication, do the following:

    a. Proceed to the next wizard step. (Mail Merge task pane). Tap or click the Print link (Mail Merge task pane) to display the Print gallery in the Backstage view.

    b. Verify the printer name that appears on the Printer Status button will print a hard copy of the publication. If necessary, tap or click the Printer Status button to display a list of available printer options, and then tap or click the desired printer to change the currently selected printer.

    c. Change any other settings. If you wish to print only one page, type 1 in the Records box.

    d. Tap or click the Print button in the Backstage view to print the merged pages.

    e. Retrieve the printouts.

14. Submit the files as specified by your instructor.

15. ✸ What kind of data source files would you expect to find with invoice generation? Do you think most small businesses use Access or Excel to store their invoice data? If you were asked about database options, what would you recommend for use with Publisher?

Extend Your Knowledge

Extend the skills you learned in this chapter and experiment with new skills. You may need to use Help to complete the assignment.

Filtering and Sorting a Recipient List

Note: To complete this assignment, you will be required to use the Data Files for Students. Visit www.cengage.com/ct/studentdownload for detailed instructions or contact your instructor for information about accessing the required files.

Instructions: If necessary, copy the data source file, Extend 7-1 Recipient List, from the Data Files for Students to your storage location and appropriate folder. See page PUB 416 for instructions on copying and pasting the file from one folder to another. Open the publication, Extend 7-1 First America Bank Envelope, from the Data Files for Students.

In this assignment, you will filter an address list for recipients living in two specific cities. Next, you will sort the list by last name and then by first name to create an alphabetical listing. Finally, you will apply the merged address block to an envelope publication.

Perform the following tasks:

1. Use Help to learn more about printing, exporting, filtering, and sorting recipient lists.

2. Save the publication with the name, Extend 7-1 First America Bank Envelope Complete.

3. To prevent any changes to the return address and logo, move them to the master page as follows: select all (CTRL+A), and then cut (CTRL+X). Go to the master page and paste (CTRL+V) all objects to the master page. Close the master page.

4. Access the Mail Merge task pane. Use the list named Extend 7-1 Recipient List from your storage location.

5. In the Mail Merge Recipients List dialog box, tap or click the Filter link. Choose to filter the list with City equal to Eden. Tap or click the And box arrow (Filter and Sort dialog box), then tap or click OR to add a second filter with City equal to Gladstone.

6. In the Mail Merge Recipients dialog box, tap or click the Sort link. Sort the list alphabetically first by last name and then by first name, in ascending order (Figure 7–81).

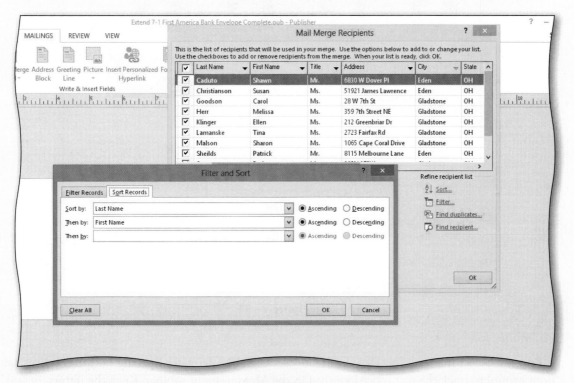

Figure 7–81

7. In the Mail Merge task pane, if necessary, tap or click the 'Next: Create or connect to a recipient list' link. Select the grouped field named Address block. Choose an appropriate address style. When Publisher displays the text box, autofit, resize, and reposition the text box so that it creates an appropriate envelope address.

8. Return to the Mail Merge task pane and proceed to the next wizard step. Tap or click the 'Export recipient list to a new file' link (Mail Merge task pane), and save the filtered list with the file name, Extend 7-1 Eden and Gladstone Residents.

9. Tap or click the 'Print recipient list' link (Mail Merge task pane) and include only the First Name, Last Name, Address, City, State, and Zip Code fields. Submit the copies to your instructor.

10. ✴ List two other ways you could generate envelopes if you do not have access to a printer with an envelope feed.

Analyze, Correct, Improve

Analyze a publication, correct all errors, and improve the design.

Correcting Character and Field Spacing

Note: To complete this assignment, you will be required to use the Data Files for Students. Visit www.cengage.com/ct/studentdownload for detailed instructions or contact your instructor for information about accessing the required files.

Instructions: Open the publication, Analyze 7-1 Golf Course Label, from the Data Files for Students. The publication is a large mailing label with tracking and spacing errors, as well as errors in the formatting of the field codes. The banner at the top also needs to be recolored as shown in Figure 7–82. You are to correct the errors and compress the pictures.

Figure 7–82

Perform the following tasks:

1. Correct Select the text, Tee Time Golf Course. Use the Character Spacing button (HOME tab | Font group) to track the text more loosely. On the Measurement toolbar, Kern the letters Te and Ti in Tee Time to -2. In the address field codes, insert spaces between each field code. Insert a comma after the field code, City.

2. Improve Select the banner graphic at the top of the label. Use the PICTURE TOOLS FORMAT tab and the Adjust group to recolor the graphic. Use a darker variation of the green coloring. Adjust the brightness and contrast to bring out the details. Compress all pictures in the publication to reduce the file size. Save the publication with the file name, Analyze 7-1 Golf Course Label Complete. Submit the revised document in the format specified by your instructor.

3. ✺ Would this publication be effective as a post card? If so, what changes would you have to make to the publication?

In the Labs

Design, create, or modify a publication using the guidelines, concepts, and skills presented in this chapter. Labs 1 and 2, which increase in difficulty, require you to create a solution based on what you learned in the chapter; Lab 3 requires you to create a solution that uses cloud and web technologies, by learning and investigating on your own from general guidance.

Lab 1: **Creating an Address List**

Problem: Your company had a booth at the Home Show last month. Many visitors to the show stopped by and filled out cards of interest in your products. Your boss has asked you to enter them into an address list for future mailings.

Perform the following tasks:

1. Run Publisher and create a blank 8.5 × 11" page.

2. Access the Step-by-Step Mail Merge Wizard and tap or click the 'Type a new list' option button.

3. Tap or click the 'Next: Create or connect to a recipient list' link at the bottom of the Mail Merge task pane. When the New Address List dialog box is displayed, tap or click the Customize Columns button (New Address List dialog box) and then delete all columns that do not appear in Table 7–8. When you are finished, tap or click the OK button (Customize Address List dialog box) to return to the New Address List dialog box.

Table 7–8 Home Show Interest List

Title	First Name	Last Name	Address	City	State	Zip Code
Mr.	Dang	Chou	764 Clay Street	Antioch	NE	68504
Ms.	Michelle	Knight	267 Green Way	Antioch	NE	68504
Mr.	Raphael	Garcia	345 Norton Ave.	Antioch	NE	68504
Mr.	Patrick	See	1422 88th St.	Antioch	NE	68504

© 2014 Cengage Learning

4. Enter the data from Table 7–8. If requested by your instructor, enter your name and address as a fifth record to the address list. When Publisher asks you to name the address list, navigate to your storage device and save the file with the name, Lab 7-1 Home Show Interest Cards.

5. Sort the list by last name.

6. Tap or click the OK button (Mail Merge Recipients Dialog box). If Publisher asks to update the data, tap or click the Yes button.

7. Tap or click the 'Next: Create merged publications' link at the bottom of the Mail Merge task pane. Tap or click the link, 'Print recipient list' to display the Print List dialog box (Figure 7–83 on the next page).

Continued >

In the Labs continued

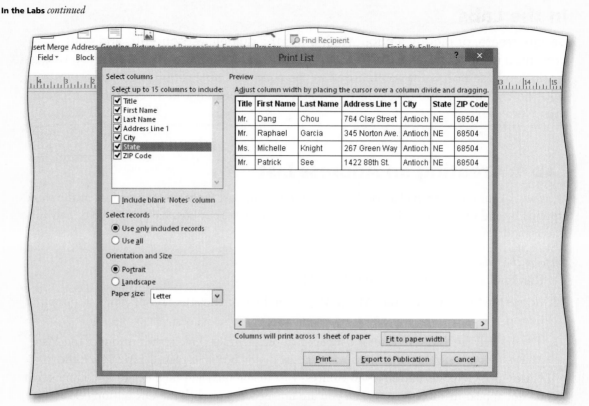

Figure 7–83

8. Select all of the check boxes so they are included in the list. Tap or click the Use all option button. Tap or click the Landscape button. Adjust the columns as necessary in the Preview area.

9. Tap or click the Print button and then print the list. Exit Publisher without saving the publication. Submit the data source file, Lab 7-1 Home Show Interest Cards, as directed by your instructor.

10. ✱ What other fields of data might a company include on interest cards? How could Publisher make use of that data?

Lab 2: **Merging with an Excel File**

Note: To complete this assignment, you will be required to use the Data Files for Students. Visit www.cengage.com/ct/studentdownload for detailed instructions or contact your instructor for information about accessing the required files.

Problem: A club on your campus is sponsoring a lecture on the Baader-Meinhof phenomenon. Baader-Meinhof is the phenomenon where a person hears about some obscure piece of information — often an unfamiliar word or name — and soon afterwards encounters the same topic again, sometimes repeatedly. The club has a ticket template. The college also has given you an Excel spreadsheet that contains the seat numbers; however due to construction, only the center section is available for the lecture. The ticket template and spreadsheet are located in the Data Files for Students. If necessary, copy and paste both files to your storage location, in the same folder. The merged ticket is shown in Figure 7–84.

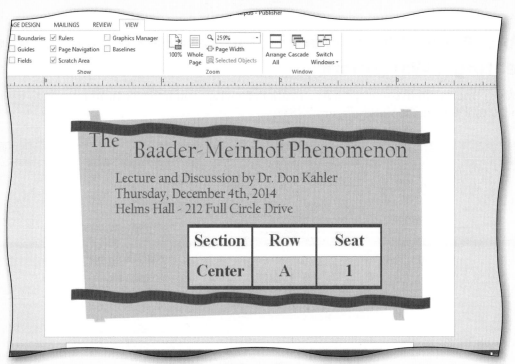

Figure 7–84

Perform the following tasks:

1. From a File Explorer window, open the file Lab 7-2 Tickets template.

2. Enter the text into the template text boxes as shown in Figure 7–84. Enter the headings, but do not enter the section, row or column data.

3. Use the MAILINGS tab to choose to use an existing list. When Publisher displays the Select Data Source dialog box, navigate to your storage device and choose the Lab 7-2 Ticket Seat Numbers file. Choose the only table listed in the file.

4. In the Mail Merge Recipients dialog box, tap or click the Filter command, and then filter the numbers so that the only tickets that will print are those in the center section.

5. In the publication, Use the MAILINGS tab to insert the field codes into the appropriate locations in the small table. Format the field codes to match the column headings in the table. Center-align the field codes.

6. Save the file as a regular publication on your storage device with the name, Lab 7-2 Tickets Complete.

7. ☀ How can you be sure that the tickets will print correctly? What are the advantages and disadvantages to buying prescored paper to create tickets? What are the advantages and disadvantages of sending the tickets out for publication?

Continued >

In the Labs *continued*

Lab 3: Expand Your World: Cloud and Web Technologies
Creating a Watermark

Problem: You would like to insert a watermark in a picture you have taken. You decide to try a Web 2.0 tool named, PicMarkr (Figure 7–85).

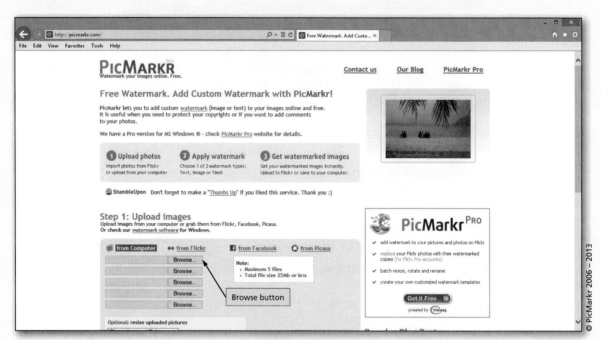

Figure 7–85

Instructions: Perform the following tasks:

Part 1: Open a browser and go to PicMarkr.com. Tap or click the Browse or Choose File buttons in the Step 1: Upload images section and navigate to a picture that you have taken. When you are finished uploading, scroll down and tap or click the 'OK! Go to Step2' button. When PicMarkr displays Step 2, enter your name in the Text to display box in the Text watermark section, and then choose a placement in the Watermark align area. Tap or click the Continue button. When PicMarkr is finished, download the pictures and then insert them into a publication. Submit the assignment in the format specified by your instructor.

Part 2: ✺ How does PicMarkr compare to creating a watermark in Publisher? What steps would you have to take in Publisher to create the same effect? How does the transparency of the picture and the master page affect your decision? Could you put the picture on the master page and the watermark in the main publication and then save the file as a Tiff?

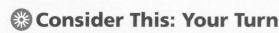 Consider This: Your Turn

Apply your creative thinking and problem solving skills to design and implement a solution.

1: Create a Movie Logo

Personal/Academic

Create a one-page flyer from scratch, advertising your favorite movie. Design a text-based logo for the title of the movie. Use a font that goes with the theme of the movie. For example, a comedy movie might use the Joker, Jokewood, or Comic Sans fonts; a classic movie might use a serif font; or a horror movie might use the Showcard Gothic or the Chiller font. Use the Measurement toolbar to edit the character spacing. Use a font size of at least 48 pt. Adjust the text scaling of the first letter of each word to give your text logo its own special character. Kern at least one character pair to improve the logo. Change the tracking on all of the characters. If your logo is two lines of text, experiment with the line spacing to add more visual contrast to the logo.

2: Using Leader Tabs

Professional

The Lunch and a Song series would like a one-page program about its upcoming event. Create a publication that is 5.5 inches wide and 8.5 inches tall. Use WordArt to create a decorative title with the words **Lunch and a Song**. Draw a large text box to fill the area below the WordArt from margin to margin. Set a left tab at .5 inches. Double-tap or double-click the ruler to display the Paragraph dialog box and the Tabs tab. Set a right tab at 4 inches and use the Dot Leader setting. Enter several songs with the title at the first tab and the composer or artist at the second tab.

3: Looking at Watermarks

Research and Collaboration

Part 1: Have each member of your group collect copies of documents with watermarks. Sources might include the school library, offices, publications, books, and mailings. As a group look at the watermarks and make a list of of the five best ones. Write down several characteristics about each watermark, such as color, placement, text, pictures, contrast, brightness. Include your group's opinion about the purpose of the watermark. See your instructor for ways to submit this assignment.

Part 2: ✳ Why were some watermarks better than others? Why do you think the documents need a watermark? What do you think the legal implications might be?

Learn Online

Reinforce what you learned in this chapter with games, exercises, training, and many other online activities and resources.

Student Companion Site Reinforce chapter terms and concepts using review questions, flash cards, practice tests, and interactive learning games, such as a crossword puzzle. These and other online activities and resources are available at no additional cost on www.cengagebrain.com. Visit www.cengage.com/ct/studentdownload for detailed instructions about accessing the resources available at the Student Companion Site.

Index

Quick Reference Summary

Microsoft Publisher 2013 Complete Quick Reference

Task	Page Number	Ribbon	Other On-Screen Areas	Shortcut Menu	Keyboard Shortcut
Align Data in Cells	PUB 334	Align buttons (TABLE TOOLS LAYOUT tab | Alignment group)			
Arrange Thumbnails	PUB 85	Arrange Thumbnails button (PICTURE TOOLS FORMAT tab | Arrange group)		Arrange Thumbnails	
Autofit Text	PUB 28	Text Fit button (TEXT BOX TOOLS FORMAT tab | Text group), Best Fit or Format Text Box Dialog Box Launcher (TEXT BOX TOOLS FORMAT tab | Text group), Text Box tab (Text Box dialog box), Best fit button		Best Fit	
Automatic Date, Insert	PUB 275	'Date & Time' button (INSERT tab | Text group), Update automatically check box (Date and Time dialog box)			
Background	PUB 50	Background button (PAGE DESIGN tab | Page Background group)		'Apply to Background', Fill	
Blank Publication, Select	PUB 197	Blank thumbnails (FILE tab | New tab)			
Bold	PUB 27	Bold button (HOME tab | Font group) or Font Dialog Box Launcher (HOME tab | Font group), Font style arrow (Font dialog box), Bold	Bold button on mini toolbar	Change Text, Font, Font style arrow (Font dialog box), Bold	CTRL+B
BorderArt, Create'	PUB 348	Format Shape Dialog Box Launcher (DRAWING TOOLS FORMAT tab | Shape Styles group), Colors and Lines tab (Format AutoShape dialog box), BorderArt button		Format AutoShape, Colors and Lines tab (Format AutoShape dialog box), BorderArt button	
Boundaries	PUB 12	Boundaries check box (VIEW tab | Show group)			CTRL+SHIFT+O
Break Link	PUB 147	Break button (TEXT BOX TOOLS FORMAT tab | Linking group)			

Microsoft Publisher 2013 Complete Quick Reference (continued)

Task	Page Number	Ribbon	Other On-Screen Areas	Shortcut Menu	Keyboard Shortcut
Building Block, Delete	PUB 241	Show Building Block Library Dialog Box Launcher (INSERT tab | Building Blocks group), Page Parts folder (Building Block Library dialog box), press and hold or right-click object, Delete			
Building Block, Save	PUB 213	Page Parts button (INSERT tab | Building Blocks group), 'Add Selection to Page Parts Gallery' (Create New Building Block dialog box)		Save as Building Block (Create New Building Block dialog box)	
Bullet, Create Custom	PUB 228	Bullets button (HOME tab | Paragraph group), Bullets and Numbering, Character button (Bullets and Numbering dialog box)			
Business Card, Create	PUB 294		BUILT-IN (Publisher template gallery), Business Cards thumbnail		
Business Card, Print	PUB 297		FILE tab | Print tab, Pages button, 'Multiple copies per sheet'		CTRL+P
Business Information Set, Create	PUB 263	Business Information button (INSERT tab | Text group), Edit Business Information, New button (Business Information dialog box)	Smart tag button, 'Edit Business Information', New button (Business Information dialog box) or 'Edit Business Information' button (Publisher template gallery), New button, Save button (Create New Business Information Set dialog box)		
Business Information Set, Delete	PUB 303	Business Information button (INSERT tab | Text group), 'Edit Business Information', Delete button (Business Information dialog box)			
Calendar, Create	PUB 344	Calendars thumbnails (FILE tab | New tab) or Calendars button (INSERT tab | Building Blocks group)			
Captions Gallery	PUB 107	Caption button (PICTURE TOOLS FORMAT tab | Picture Styles group)			
Cell Diagonal, Create	PUB 341	Diagonals button (TABLE TOOLS LAYOUT tab | Merge group)			
Check Spelling as You Type	PUB 21			Choose correct word	
Check Spelling of Entire Publication	PUB 109	Spelling button (REVIEW tab | Spelling group)			F7

Microsoft Publisher 2013 Complete Quick Reference *(continued)*

Task	Page Number	Ribbon	Other On-Screen Areas	Shortcut Menu	Keyboard Shortcut
Color Scheme, Change	PUB 202	More button (PAGE DESIGN tab | Schemes group), 'Create New Color Scheme'			
Color Scheme, Create New	PUB 200	More button (PAGE DESIGN tab | Schemes group), 'Create New Color Scheme'	Color scheme button (template information pane), Create new		
Color Scheme, Delete	PUB 242	More button (PAGE DESIGN tab | Schemes group), press and hold or right-click scheme, Delete Scheme			
Column Width, Change	PUB 336		Drag column border		
Column, Delete	PUB 330	'Delete Rows or Columns' button (TABLE TOOLS LAYOUT tab | Rows & Columns group)		Delete, Delete Columns	
Column, Insert	PUB 332	'Insert Columns to the Left' button or 'Insert Columns to the Right' (TABLE TOOLS LAYOUT tab | Rows & Columns group)		Insert, Insert Left or Insert Right	
Continue a Story across Pages	PUB 144		Yes or No button (Microsoft Publisher dialog box) until desired location is reached		
Continue a Story across Pages, Manually	PUB 147	Create Link button (TEXT BOX TOOLS FORMAT tab | Linking group), navigate to desired text box, tap or click text box	Text in Overflow button on selected text box	'Create Text Box Link'	
Continued Notice, Insert	PUB 148	Format Text Box Dialog Box Launcher (TEXT BOX TOOLS FORMAT tab | Text group), Text Box tab (Format Text Box dialog box), 'Include "Continued on page . . ."' check box		Format Text Box, Text Box tab (Format Text Box dialog box), 'Include "Continued on page . . ."' check box	
Copy Text	PUB 79	Copy button (HOME tab | Clipboard group)		Copy	CTRL+C
Coupon, Insert	PUB 169	Advertisements button (INSERT tab | Building Blocks group) or Show Building Blocks Library Dialog Box Launcher (INSERT tab | Building Blocks group), Advertisements folder (Building Block Library dialog box)			
Custom Margins	PUB 200	Adjust Margins button (PAGE DESIGN tab | Page Setup group), Custom Margins, Margin Guides tab (Layout Guides dialog box)			
Custom Page Size	PUB 198	'Choose Page Size' button (PAGE DESIGN tab | Page Setup group), 'Create New Page Size'	'More Blank Page Sizes' thumbnail (Publisher template gallery), 'Create new page size' thumbnail		
Custom Page, Delete	PUB 243	'Choose Page Size' button (PAGE DESIGN tab | Page Setup group), press and hold or right-click custom page, Delete	Press and hold or right-click custom template (Publisher template gallery), Delete		

Microsoft Publisher 2013 Complete Quick Reference (continued)

Task	Page Number	Ribbon	Other On-Screen Areas	Shortcut Menu	Keyboard Shortcut
Customize Ribbon	PUB 153	Customize Ribbon button (FILE tab | Options), Customize Ribbon		Customize the Ribbon	
Customize Ribbon, Remove	PUB 183	Customize Ribbon button (FILE tab | Options), Customize Ribbon, Reset button (Publisher Options dialog box)		Customize the Ribbon, Reset button (Publisher Options dialog box)	
Cut Text	PUB 78	Cut button (HOME tab | Clipboard group)		Cut	CTRL+X
Data Source, Create New Entries	PUB 403		New Entry button (New Address List dialog box)		
Data Source, Customize Columns	PUB 403		Customize Columns button (New Address List dialog box)		
Data Source, Save	PUB 407		Save button (Save Address List dialog box)		
Design Checker, Run	PUB 110	Run Design Checker button (FILE tab | Info tab)			
Drag-and-Drop Text	PUB 177		Drag selected text to new location, then lift finger or release mouse button		
Drop Cap	PUB 103	Drop Cap button (TEXT BOX TOOLS FORMAT tab | Typography group)			
Embedded Table, Copy and Paste	PUB 360	Paste arrow (HOME tab | Clipboard group), Paste Special, Paste option button (Paste Special dialog box)			
Embedded Table, Create	PUB 358	Object button (INSERT tab | Text group), 'Create from File' option button (Insert Object dialog box)			
Embedded Table, Format	PUB 361	Use ribbon in active program to select and apply various formats			
Embedded Table, Sum	PUB 362	Sum button (Excel HOME tab | Editing group)			ALT+=
Envelope, Create	PUB 290		BUILT-IN (Publisher template gallery), Envelopes thumbnails		
Envelope, Print	PUB 292	FILE tab | Print tab, Tiled button, Envelope			CTRL+P
Exit	PUB 47		Close button on title bar		ALT+F4
Field Codes, Insert Grouped	PUB 409	Address Block button or Greeting Line button (MAILINGS tab | Write & Insert Fields group)	Tap or click field code link (Mail Merge task pane)		
Field Codes, Insert Individual	PUB 411		Select field from Mail Merge task pane or drag field from Mail Merge task pane into publication		

Microsoft Publisher 2013 Complete Quick Reference *(continued)*

Task	Page Number	Ribbon	Other On-Screen Areas	Shortcut Menu	Keyboard Shortcut
Filter Data	PUB 422		Filter link (Mail Merge Recipients dialog box), Filter Records tab (Filter and Sort dialog box)		
Font Color, Sample	PUB 270	Font Color arrow (TEXT BOX TOOLS FORMAT tab | Font group), 'Sample Font Color', sample color in workspace			
Font Scheme, Create New	PUB 203	Scheme Fonts button (PAGE DESIGN tab | Schemes group), 'Create New Font Scheme'	'Font scheme button (template information pane), Create new		
Font Scheme, Delete	PUB 242	Scheme Fonts button (PAGE DESIGN tab | Schemes group), press and hold or right-click scheme, Delete Scheme			
Font Size, Decrease	PUB 31	Font Size arrow (HOME tab | Font group) or Decrease Font Size button (HOME tab | Font group)	Font Size arrow on mini toolbar or Decrease Font Size button on mini toolbar	Change Text, Font, Font size arrow (Font dialog box)	CTRL+SHIFT+<
Font Size, Increase	PUB 31	Font Size arrow (HOME tab | Font group) or Increase Font Size button (HOME tab | Font group)	Font Size arrow on mini toolbar or Increase Font Size button on mini toolbar	Change Text, Font, Font size arrow (Font dialog box)	CTRL+SHIFT+>
Font, Change	PUB 98	Font arrow (HOME tab | Font group)	Font arrow on mini toolbar	Change Text, Font, Font text box	CTRL+SHIFT+F
Fonts, Embed	PUB 302	'Manage Embedded Fonts' button (FILE tab | Info tab)			
Format Painter	PUB 88	Format Painter button (HOME tab | Clipboard group)	Format Painter button on mini toolbar		CTRL+SHIFT+C, then CTRL+SHIFT+V
Formatting Marks, Display	PUB 77	Special Characters button (HOME tab | Paragraph group)			CTRL+SHIFT+Y
Gradient, Apply to Text	PUB 219	Font Color arrow (HOME tab | Font group), Fill Effects, Gradient fill button (Format Shape dialog box) or Format Shape Dialog Box Launcher (DRAWING TOOLS FORMAT tab | Shape Styles group), Colors and Lines tab (Format Text Box dialog box), Fill Effects button		Format Text Box, Colors and Lines tab (Format Text Box dialog box), Fill Effects button	
Graphic, Group	PUB 210	Group button (DRAWING TOOLS FORMAT tab | Arrange group)		Group	SHIFT+CTRL+G
Graphic, Recolor	PUB 234	Recolor button (PICTURE TOOLS FORMAT tab | Adjust group)		Format Picture, Picture tab (Format Picture dialog box), Color button	
Graphic, Rotate	PUB 210	Rotate Objects button (DRAWING TOOLS FORMAT tab | Arrange group) or Rotate Objects button (DRAWING TOOLS FORMAT tab | Arrange group), Free Rotate	Rotation text box (Measurement toolbar) or drag rotation handle	Format Object, Size tab, Size and Rotate area (Format Object dialog box)	

Microsoft Publisher 2013 Complete Quick Reference *(continued)*

Task	Page Number	Ribbon	Other On-Screen Areas	Shortcut Menu	Keyboard Shortcut
Graphic, Ungroup	PUB 207	Ungroup button (DRAWING TOOLS FORMAT tab | Arrange group)		Ungroup	SHIFT+CTRL+G
Hyperlink, Insert	PUB 48	Add a Hyperlink button (INSERT tab | Links group)		Hyperlink	CTRL+K
Hyphenation, Check	PUB 180	Hyphenation button (TEXT BOX TOOLS FORMAT tab | Text group), Manual button (Hyphenation dialog box)			CTRL+SHIFT+H
Import a File	PUB 142	Insert File button (INSERT tab | Text group)		Change Text, Text File	
Italicize	PUB 28	Italic button (HOME tab | Font group) or Font Dialog Box Launcher (HOME tab | Font group), Font style arrow (Font Dialog box), Italic	Italic button on mini toolbar	Change Text, Font, Font style arrow (Font dialog box), Italic	CTRL+I
Kern Character Pairs	PUB 392	Character Spacing button (TEXT BOX TOOLS FORMAT tab | Font group)	Kerning text box (Measurement toolbar)	Change Text, Character Spacing	
Ligatures, Enable	PUB 100	Ligatures button (TEXT BOX TOOLS FORMAT tab | Typography group) or Symbol button (INSERT tab | Text group)			
Line Spacing, Change	PUB 216	Line Spacing button (HOME tab | Paragraph group) or Paragraph Settings Dialog Box Launcher (HOME tab | Paragraph group)		Change Text, Paragraph, Indents and Spacing tab, Line spacing area (Paragraph dialog box)	
Link Text Boxes	PUB 147	Create Link button (TEXT BOX TOOLS FORMAT tab | Linking group)	Text in Overflow button on selected text box	'Create Text Box Link'	
Linked Table, Copy and Paste	PUB 360	Paste arrow (HOME tab | Clipboard group), Paste Special, Paste Link option button (Paste Special dialog box)			
Linked Table, Create	PUB 360	Object button (INSERT tab | Text group), 'Create from File' option button, Link check box (Insert Object dialog box)			
Mail Merge Wizard	PUB 401	Mail Merge arrow (MAILINGS tab | Start group), 'Step-By-Step Mail Merge Wizard'			
Master Page, Close	PUB 352	'Close Master Page' button (MASTER PAGE tab | Close group) or Normal button (VIEW tab | Views group)			CTRL+M
Master Page, View	PUB 347	Master Page button (VIEW tab | Views group) or Master Pages button (PAGE DESIGN tab | Page Background group)			CTRL+M

Microsoft Publisher 2013 Complete Quick Reference *(continued)*

Task	Page Number	Ribbon	Other On-Screen Areas	Shortcut Menu	Keyboard Shortcut
Maximize	PUB 4		Maximize button on Publisher title bar or double-tap or double-click title bar	Maximize button on Publisher title bar	
Measurement Toolbar, Display	PUB 268	Measurement button (DRAWING TOOLS FORMAT tab | Size group)	Object Position button or Object Size button on status bar		
Measurement Toolbar, Position Objects	PUB 269		Position text boxes on Measurement toolbar	Format	
Merge Cells	PUB 333	Merge Cells button (TABLE TOOLS LAYOUT tab | Merge group)			
Merge Field Codes, Insert	PUB 424	'Insert Merge Field' button (MAILINGS tab | Write & Insert Fields group)	field link (Mail Merge task pane)		
Merged Publication, Create	PUB 413		'Next: Create merged publication' link (Mail Merge task pane)		
Object, Align	PUB 42	Align button (DRAWING TOOLS FORMAT tab | Arrange group) or Align button (PICTURE TOOLS FORMAT tab | Arrange group) or specific alignment button (TEXT BOX TOOLS tab | Alignment group)	Drag object until visual layout guides appear		
Object, Align Relative to Margin Guides	PUB 221	Align button (DRAWING TOOLS FORMAT tab | Arrange group), 'Relative to Margin Guides', Align button (DRAWING TOOLS FORMAT tab | Arrange group), choose alignment			
Object, Bring to Front	PUB 168	Bring Forward arrow (DRAWING TOOLS FORMAT tab | Arrange group), 'Bring to Front' or Bring Forward arrow (PICTURE TOOLS FORMAT tab | Arrange group), Bring Forward	Bring Forward button on mini toolbar		
Object, Delete	PUB 24	Cut button (HOME tab | Clipboard group)		Delete Object	DELETE or BACKSPACE or CTRL+X
Object, Move	PUB 41		Drag boundary or Object Position button on status bar, x and y text boxes on Measurement toolbar		
Object, Resize	PUB 42		Drag corner sizing handle or Object Size button on status bar, Width and Height text boxes on Measurement toolbar	Format Object, Size tab (Format Object dialog box), Size and rotate area or Format Picture, Size tab (Format Picture dialog box), Size and rotate area or Format Text Box, Size tab (Format Text Box dialog box), Size and rotate area	

Microsoft Publisher 2013 Complete Quick Reference *(continued)*

Task	Page Number	Ribbon	Other On-Screen Areas	Shortcut Menu	Keyboard Shortcut
Object, Send to Back	PUB 168	Send Backward arrow (DRAWING TOOLS FORMAT tab | Arrange group), 'Send to Back' or Send Backward arrow (PICTURE TOOLS FORMAT tab | Arrange group), Send Backward	Send Backward button on mini toolbar		
Online Pictures, Insert	PUB 83	Online Pictures button (INSERT tab | Illustrations group)			
Pack and Go Wizard	PUB 116	'Save for a Commercial Printer' link (FILE tab | Export tab), Pack and Go Wizard button			
Page Navigation Pane, Collapse	PUB 14		'Collapse Page Navigation Pane' button in Page Navigation pane		
Page Navigation Pane, Expand	PUB 14		'Expand Page Navigation Pane' button in Page Navigation pane		
Page Navigation Pane, Hide	PUB 13	Page Navigation check box (VIEW tab | Show group)	'Current page in publication' button on status bar		
Page Navigation Pane, Open	PUB 11	Page Navigation check box (VIEW tab | Show group)	'Current page in publication' button on status bar		
Page Options, Set	PUB 135	Options button (PAGE DESIGN tab | Template group)			
Page Orientation, Change	PUB 317	'Change Page Orientation' button (PAGE DESIGN tab | Page Setup group)			
Pages, Add	PUB 138	Insert Blank Page button (INSERT tab | Pages group)	Page thumbnail (Page Navigation pane), Insert Page		SHIFT+CTRL+N
Pages, Change	PUB 91		Page thumbnail (Page Navigation pane)		CTRL+PAGE DOWN or CTRL+PAGE DOWN or F12
Pages, Delete	PUB 138		Page thumbnail (Page Navigation pane), Delete		
Paste Text	PUB 79	Paste button (HOME tab | Clipboard group)		Paste	CTRL+V
Picture Fill, Create	PUB 233	Shape Fill arrow (DRAWING TOOLS FORMAT tab | Shape Styles group), Picture, search for picture, Insert button (Office.com Clip Art dialog box)	Shape Fill arrow on mini toolbar, Picture, search for picture, Insert button, (Office.com Clip Art dialog box)	Format AutoShape, Colors and Lines tab (Format AutoShape dialog box), Fill Effects button, 'Picture or texture fill' button (Format Shape dialog box)	
Picture Style, Apply	PUB 36	More button (PICTURE TOOLS FORMAT tab | Picture Styles group)			
Picture, Change Border Style	PUB 37	Picture Border button (PICTURE TOOLS FORMAT tab | Picture Styles group) or Format Shape Dialog Box Launcher (PICTURE TOOLS FORMAT tab | Picture Styles group), Colors and Lines tab (Format Picture dialog box)		Format Picture, Colors and Lines tab (Format Picture dialog box)	

Microsoft Publisher 2013 Complete Quick Reference *(continued)*

Task	Page Number	Ribbon	Other On-Screen Areas	Shortcut Menu	Keyboard Shortcut
Picture, Compress	PUB 387	Compress Pictures button (PICTURE TOOLS FORMAT tab | Adjust group)			
Picture, Insert from a File	PUB 39	Pictures button (INSERT tab | Illustrations group)	Placeholder icon, Browse (Insert Pictures dialog box)		
Picture, Use as Background	PUB 87	Background button (PAGE DESIGN tab | Page Background group), More Backgrounds		Apply to Background, Fill	
Placeholder Text, Replace	PUB 17		Select text, type new text		
Portable Format, Publish	PUB 299	'Create PDF/XPS' button (FILE tab | Export tab), 'Save as type' button (Publish as PDF or XPS) or Save As button (FILE tab | Save As tab), 'Save as type' button (Save As dialog box)			
Preview Form Letters	PUB 414	Preview Results button (MAILINGS tab | Preview Results group)	Print preview link (Mail Merge task pane)		
Preview Multiple Pages	PUB 112	'View Multiple Sheets' button (FILE tab | Print tab)			
Print	PUB 44	Print button (FILE tab | Print tab)			CTRL+P
Print Merged Pages	PUB 415	'Finish & Merge' button (MAILINGS tab | Finish group), Merge to Printer	Print link (Mail Merge task pane)		
Print, On Both Sides	PUB 114	'Print One Sided' button (FILE tab | Print tab) or Printer Properties link (FILE tab | Print tab), Page Setup tab			CTRL+P
Print, On Special Paper	PUB 113	Letter button (FILE tab | Print tab) or Printer Properties link (FILE tab | Print tab), Page Setup tab			CTRL+P
Publication Options, Choose	PUB 8	Template thumbnail (FILE tab | New tab), Color scheme or Font scheme button			
Publication Properties, Change	PUB 182	Publication Properties button (FILE tab | Info tab)			
Pull Quote, Insert	PUB 164	Page Parts button (INSERT tab | Building Blocks group) or Show Building Blocks Library Dialog Box Launcher (INSERT tab | Building Blocks group), Page Parts folder (Building Block Library dialog box)			
Read-Only Attribute, Set	PUB 286			Press and hold or right-click file in File Explorer, Properties, General tab (Properties dialog box), Read-only check box	
Row, Delete	PUB 331	'Delete Rows or Columns' button (TABLE TOOLS LAYOUT tab | Rows & Columns group)		Delete, Delete Rows	

Microsoft Publisher 2013 Complete Quick Reference *(continued)*

Task	Page Number	Ribbon	Other On-Screen Areas	Shortcut Menu	Keyboard Shortcut
Row, Insert	PUB 331	'Insert Rows Above' button or 'Insert Rows Below' button (TABLE TOOLS LAYOUT tab | Rows & Columns group)		Insert, Insert Above or Insert Below	
Run Publisher	PUB 4		Publisher 2013 tile on Windows 8 Start screen or Publisher 2013 in Charms bar search results		
Save as Web Publication	PUB 51	Publish HTML link (FILE tab | Export tab), Publish HTML button, 'Save as type' button (Publish to the Web dialog box) or Save As button (FILE tab), 'Save as type' button (Save As dialog box)			
Save New Publication	PUB 25	Save tab (FILE tab)	Save button (Quick Access Toolbar)		CTRL+S or F12 or CTRL+F12
Save Publication, New File Name	PUB 25	Save As tab (FILE tab)			F12 or CTRL+F12
Save Publication, Same File Name	PUB 33	Save tab (FILE tab)	Save button (Quick Access Toolbar)		CTRL+S
Select All Objects	PUB 353	Select button (HOME tab | Editing group)			CTRL+A
Select All Text	PUB 16		Drag through text		CTRL+A
Select Cell	PUB 332	Select button (TABLE TOOLS LAYOUT tab | Table group), Select Cell	Triple-tap or triple-click cell	Select, Select Cell	CTRL+A
Select Column	PUB 332	Select button (TABLE TOOLS LAYOUT tab | Table group), Select Column	If using a mouse, point to top border of column and click	Select, Select Column	
Select Next Cell	PUB 332				TAB
Select Previous Cell	PUB 332				SHIFT+TAB
Select Recipients	PUB 420	Select Recipients button (MAILINGS tab | Start group)	'Use an existing list' link (Mail Merge task pane)		
Select Row	PUB 332	Select button (TABLE TOOLS LAYOUT tab | Table group), Select Row	If using a mouse, point to left border of row and click	Select, Select Row	
Select Table	PUB 338	Select Table button (TABLE TOOLS LAYOUT tab | Table group), Select Table		Select, Select Table	
Set Transparency	PUB 353	Shape Fill arrow (DRAWING TOOLS FORMAT tab | Shape Styles group), 'More Fill Colors', Transparency slider (Colors dialog box)			CTRL+T
Shape Style, Choose	PUB 232	More button (DRAWING TOOLS FORMAT tab | Shape Styles group)			
Shape, Crop to	PUB 236	Crop button (PICTURE TOOLS FORMAT tab | Crop group), 'Crop to Shape'		Format AutoShape, Colors and Lines tab (Format AutoShape dialog box), Color button	

Microsoft Publisher 2013 Complete Quick Reference *(continued)*

Task	Page Number	Ribbon	Other On-Screen Areas	Shortcut Menu	Keyboard Shortcut
Shape, Insert	PUB 231	Shapes button (INSERT tab | Illustrations group) or More button (DRAWING TOOLS FORMAT tab | Insert Shapes group)			
Snap Object to Margin Guide	PUB 320		Drag object until blue snapping line is displayed		
Split Cells	PUB 334	Split Cells button (TABLE TOOLS LAYOUT tab | Merge group)			
Story, Follow Across Pages	PUB 145	Previous or Next button (TEXT BOX TOOLS FORMAT tab | Linking group)	Previous or Next button on selected text box		CTRL+TAB
Style, Apply New	PUB 272	Styles button (HOME tab | Styles group)			
Style, Create New	PUB 271	Styles button (HOME tab | Styles group), New Style			
Stylistic Set	PUB 100	Stylistic Sets button (TEXT BOX TOOLS FORMAT tab | Typography group)			
Swap Picture	PUB 82	Swap button (PICTURE TOOLS FORMAT tab | Swap group)	Swap icon, drag swap icon to new location	Swap button on mini toolbar	
Tab Stop, Set	PUB 397	Paragraph Settings Dialog Box Launcher (HOME tab | Paragraph group), Tabs tab (Paragraph dialog box)	Tap or click horizontal ruler		
Tabbed Text, Enter	PUB 398				TAB
Table Borders, Add	PUB 340	Borders arrow (TABLE TOOLS DESIGN tab | Borders group)		Format Table, Colors and Lines tab (Format Table dialog box)	
Table Borders, Change Color	PUB 340	Line Color button (TABLE TOOLS DESIGN tab | Borders group)		Format Table, Colors and Lines tab (Format Table dialog box)	
Table Format, Apply	PUB 328	More button (TABLE TOOLS DESIGN tab | Table Formats group) or More button (TABLE TOOLS DESIGN tab | Table Formats group), Table AutoFormat			
Table, Insert	PUB 327	'Add a Table' button (INSERT tab | Tables group) or 'Add a Table' button (INSERT tab | Tables group), Insert Table			
Table, Resize	PUB 337		Drag corner table border	Format Table, Size tab, enter table size (Format Table dialog box)	
Tear-Offs, Edit	PUB 23		Select tear-off text, type new text		
Template, Create	PUB 182	Save As tab (FILE tab), 'Save As type' button (Save As dialog box)			
Template, Select	PUB 6	Template thumbnail (FILE tab | New tab)	Template thumbnail on Publisher start screen		

Microsoft Publisher 2013 Complete Quick Reference *(continued)*

Task	Page Number	Ribbon	Other On-Screen Areas	Shortcut Menu	Keyboard Shortcut
Text Box, Draw	PUB 16	'Draw Text Box' button (INSERT tab | Text group) or Draw Text Box button (HOME tab | Objects group)			
Text Direction, Change	PUB 32	Text Direction button (TEXT BOX TOOLS FORMAT tab | Text group)			
Text Direction, Change	PUB 417	Text Direction button (TEXT BOX TOOLS FORMAT tab | Text group)			
Track Characters	PUB 391	Character Spacing button (TEXT BOX TOOLS FORMAT tab | Font group)	Tracking text box on Measurement toolbar	Change Text, Character Spacing	
Underline	PUB 31	Underline button (HOME tab | Font group) or Font Dialog Box Launcher (HOME tab | Font group), Font style arrow (Font Dialog box), Underline	Underline button on mini toolbar	Change Text, Font, Font style arrow (Font dialog box), Underline	CTRL+U
Undo	PUB 16		Undo button on Quick Access Toolbar	Undo	CTRL+Z
Word Art Object, Change Shape	PUB 224	'Change WordArt Shape' button (WORDART TOOLS FORMAT tab | WordArt Styles group)	'Change WordArt Shape' button on mini toolbar		
WordArt Object, Change Shape Effect	PUB 322	Shape Effects button (WORDART TOOLS FORMAT tab | WordArt Styles group) or Format WordArt Dialog Box Launcher (WORDART TOOLS FORMAT tab | WordArt Styles group), Shape Effects button (Colors and Lines tab)			
WordArt Object, Insert	PUB 223	WordArt button (INSERT tab | Text group)			
Wrap Text	PUB 227	Wrap Text button (DRAWING TOOLS FORMAT tab | Arrange group) or Format Text Box Dialog Box Launcher (TEXT BOX TOOLS FORMAT tab | Text group), Layout tab, Wrapping Style area (Format Text Box)	Wrap Text button on mini toolbar	Format Text Box, Layout tab, Wrapping Style area (Format Text Box)	
Zoom	PUB 15	Zoom text box (VIEW tab | Zoom group) or Zoom arrow (VIEW tab | Zoom group)	Zoom slider or Zoom In or Zoom Out button on status bar or Touch Mode: Stretch or pinch as necessary	Zoom	F9
Zoom Objects	PUB 15	Selected Objects button (VIEW tab | Zoom group)	Touch Mode: Stretch or pinch as necessary	Zoom, Selected Objects	F9
Zoom Page Width	PUB 15	Page Width button (VIEW tab | Zoom group)	Touch Mode: Stretch or pinch as necessary	Zoom, Page Width	
Zoom Whole Page	PUB 15	Whole Page button (VIEW tab | Zoom group)	Show Whole Page button on status bar or Touch Mode: Stretch or pinch as necessary	Zoom, Whole Page	CTRL+SHIFT+L

Important Notes for Windows 7 Users

The screen shots in this book show Microsoft Office 2013 running in Windows 8. If you are using Microsoft Windows 7, however, you still can use this book because Office 2013 runs virtually the same way on both platforms. You will encounter only minor differences if you are using Windows 7. Read this section to understand the differences.

Dialog Boxes

If you are a Windows 7 user, the dialog boxes shown in this book will look slightly different than what you see on your screen. Dialog boxes for Windows 8 have a title bar with a solid color, and the dialog box name is centered on the title bar. Beyond these superficial differences in appearance, however, the options in the dialog boxes across both platforms are the same. For instance, Figures 1 and 2 show the Font dialog box in Windows 7 and the Font dialog box in Windows 8.

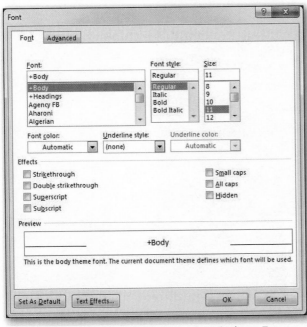

Figure 1   Font Dialog Box in Windows 7

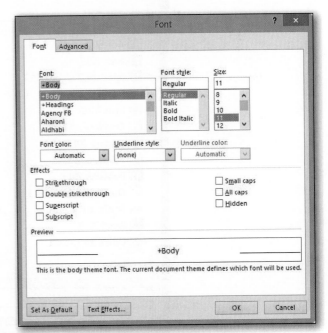

Figure 2   Font Dialog Box in Windows 8

Alternate Steps for Running an App in Windows 7

Nearly all of the steps in this book work exactly the same way for Windows 7 users; however, running an app (or program/application) requires different steps for Windows 7. The following steps show how to run an app in Windows 7.

Running an App (or Program/Application) Using Windows 7

1. Click the Start button on the taskbar to display the Start menu.
2. Click All Programs and then click the Microsoft Office 2013 folder (Figure 3).
3. If necessary, click the name of the folder containing the app you want to run.
4. Click the name of the app you want to run (such as Excel 2013).

Figure 3   Running an App Using the Windows 7 Start Menu